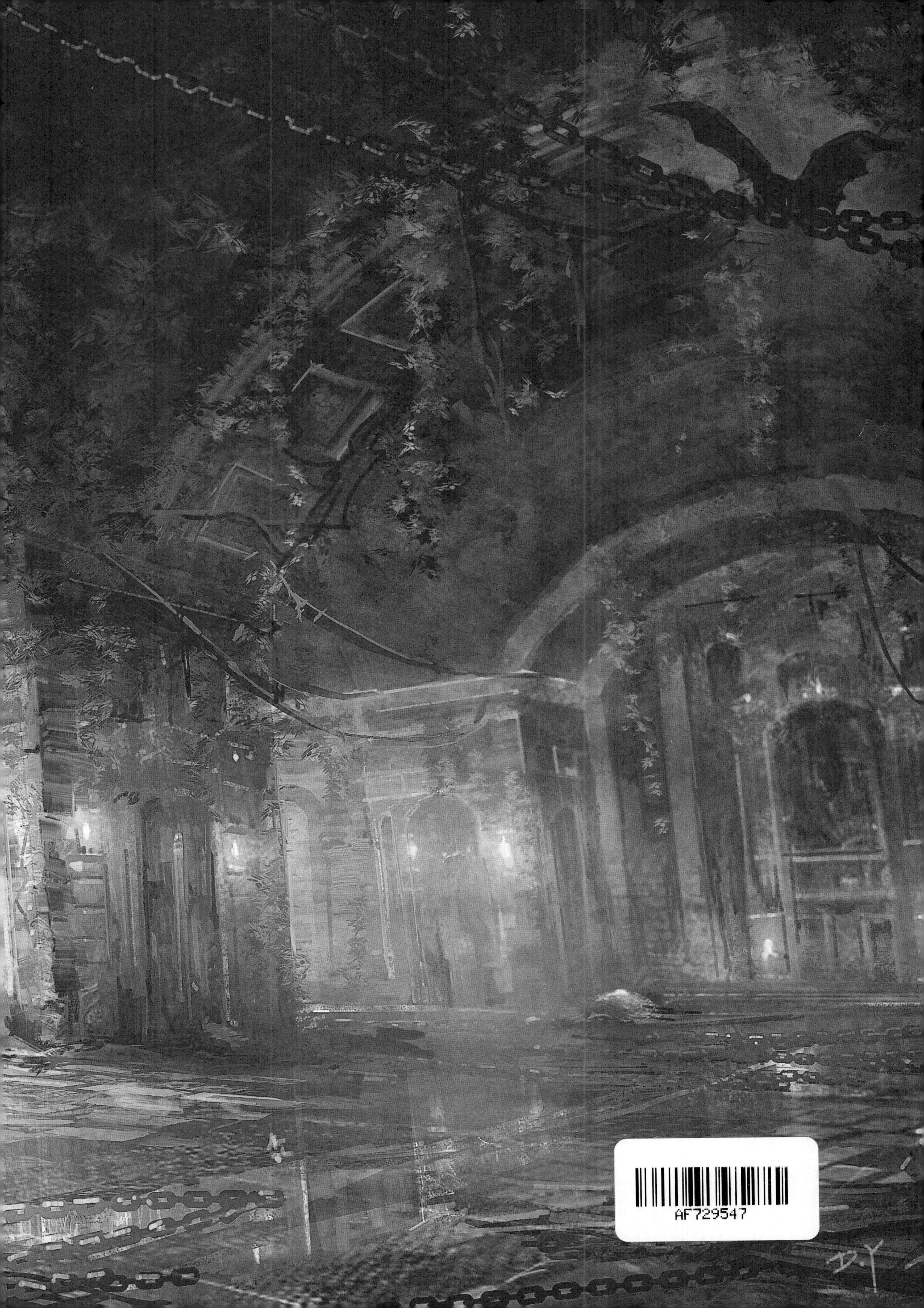

ASSASSIN'S CREED

THE COMPLETE VISUAL HISTORY

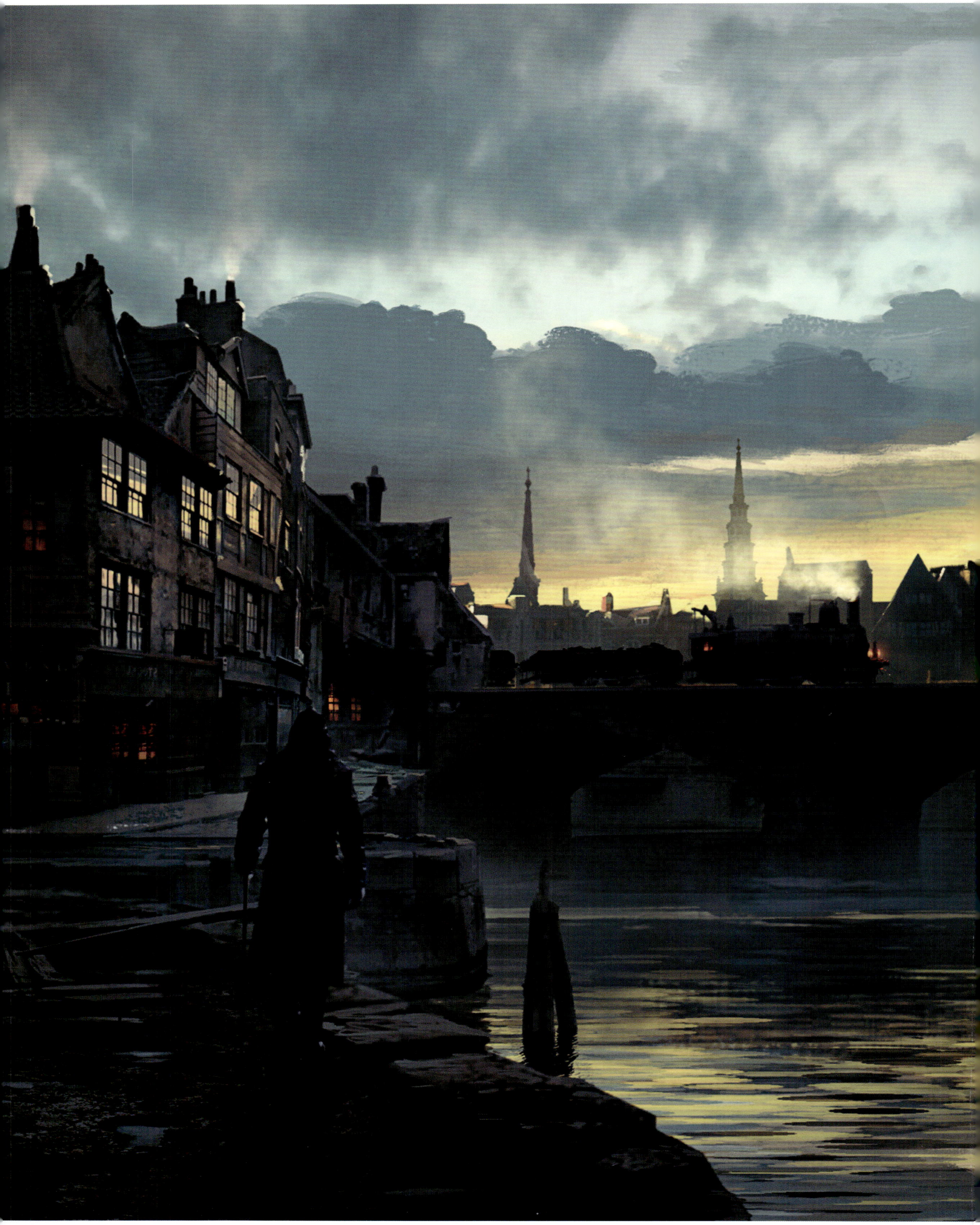

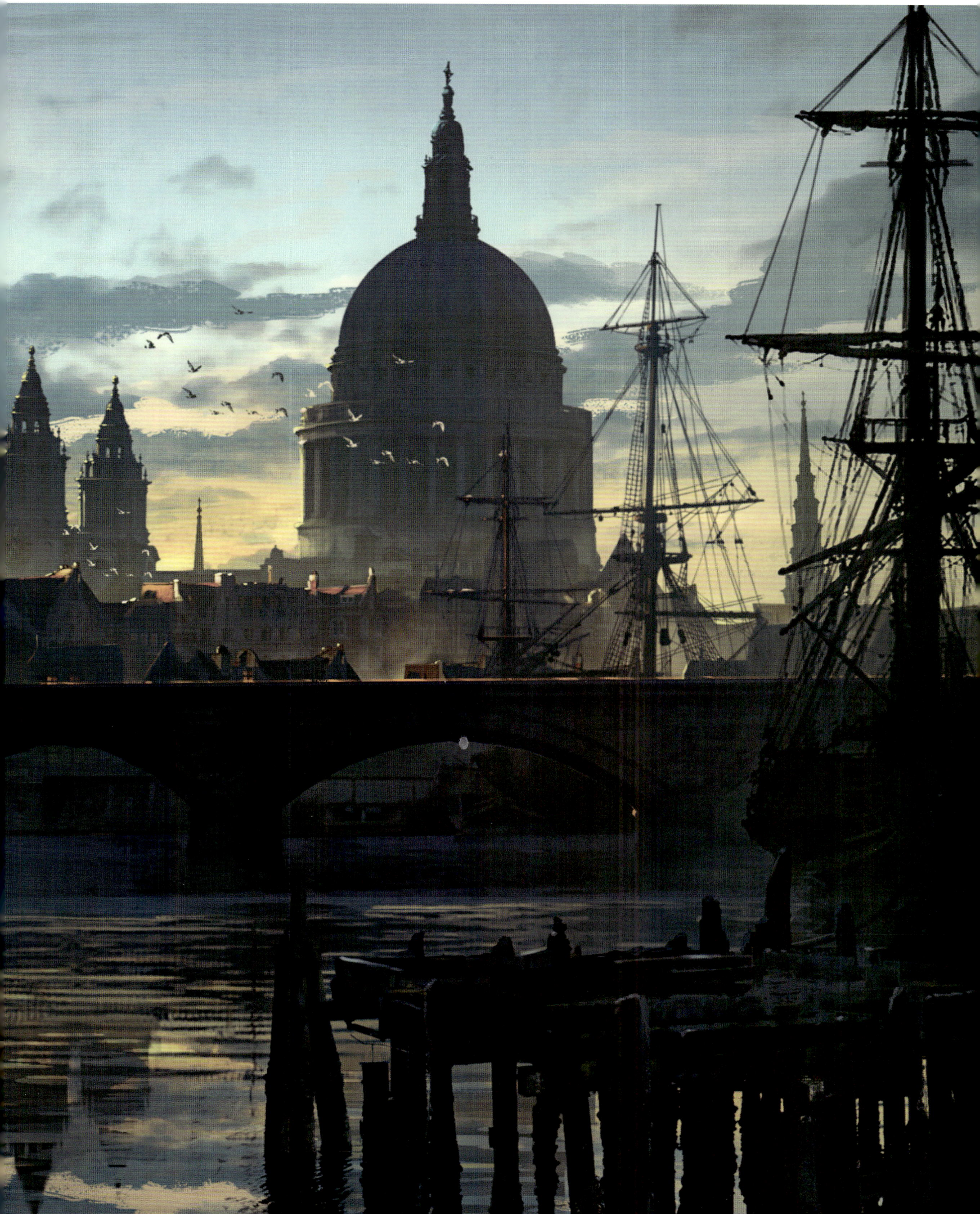

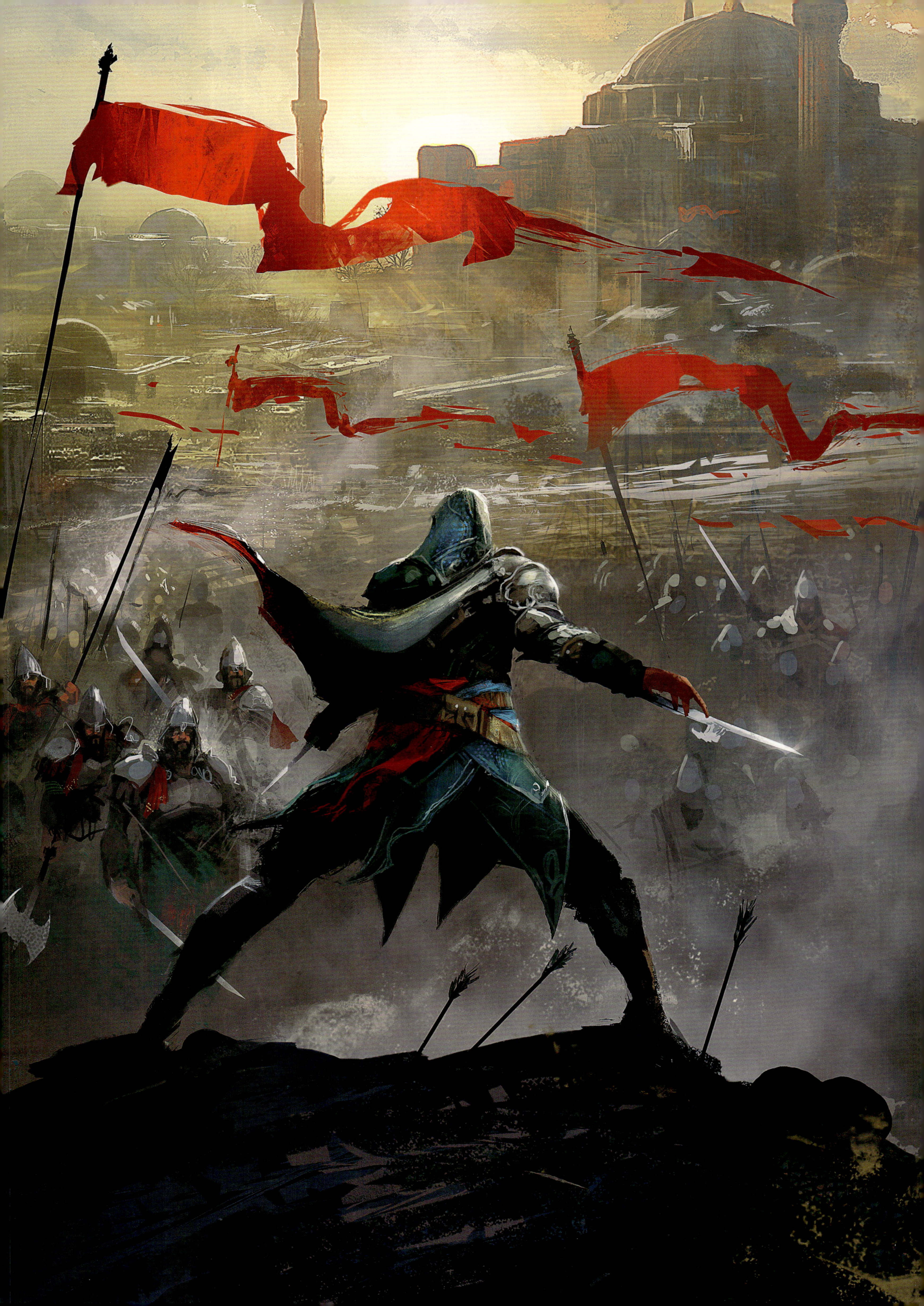

ASSASSIN'S CREED®

THE COMPLETE VISUAL HISTORY

Written by Matthew Miller

Foreword by Raphaël Lacoste

TITAN BOOKS

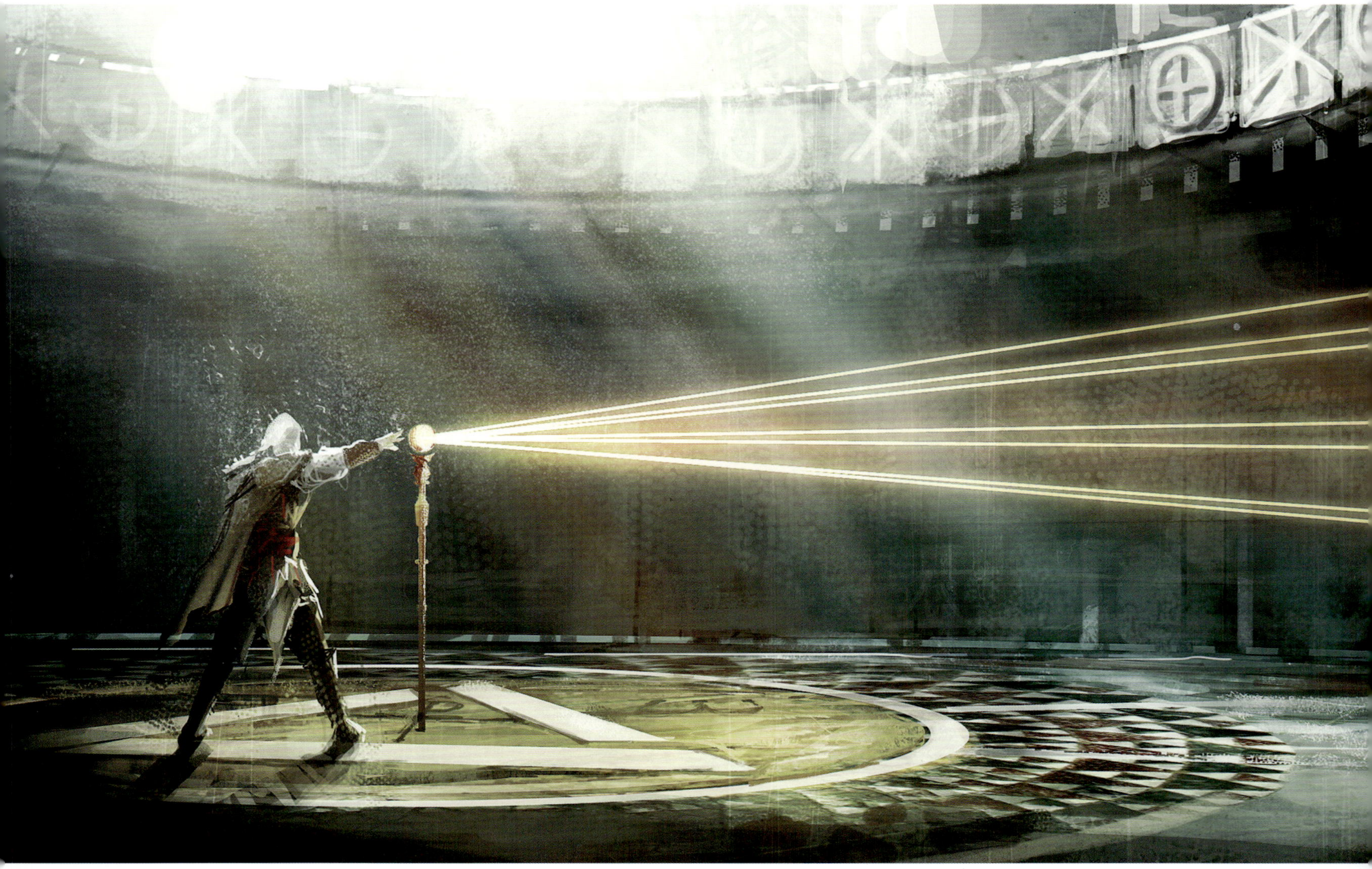

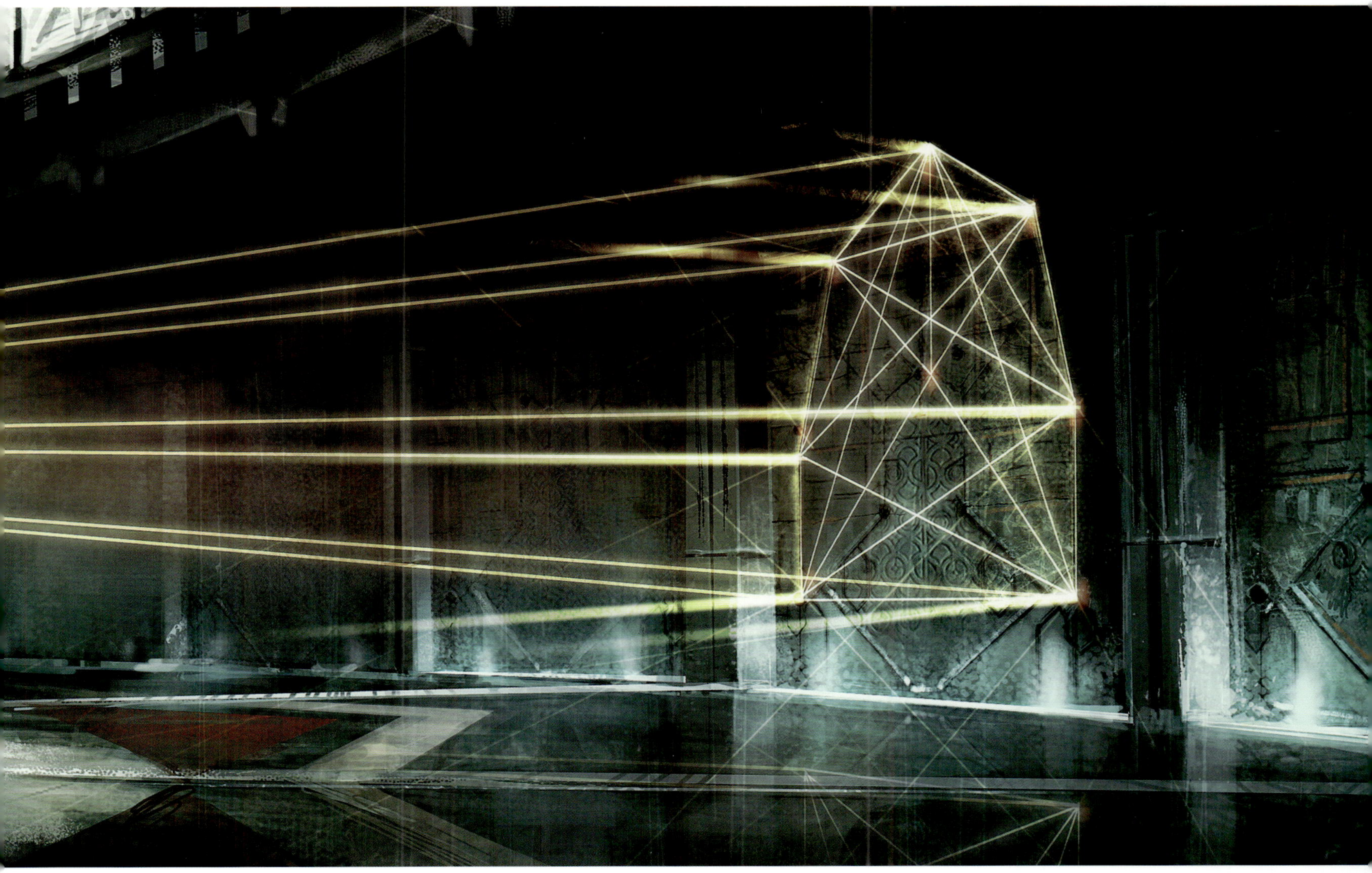

CONTENTS

	Foreword, by Raphaël Lacoste	10
	Introduction	12
1	THE MIDDLE AGES	16
2	THE RENAISSANCE	50
3	THE AMERICAN REVOLUTION	92
4	THE SEVEN YEARS' WAR—PART 1	128
5	THE GOLDEN AGE OF PIRACY	146
6	THE SEVEN YEARS' WAR—PART 2	178
7	THE FRENCH REVOLUTION	196
8	THE INDUSTRIAL REVOLUTION	228
9	CHRONICLES	258
10	THE WORLD BEFORE	276
11	BEYOND GAMES	298
	Conclusion	314
	Artist Credits	316

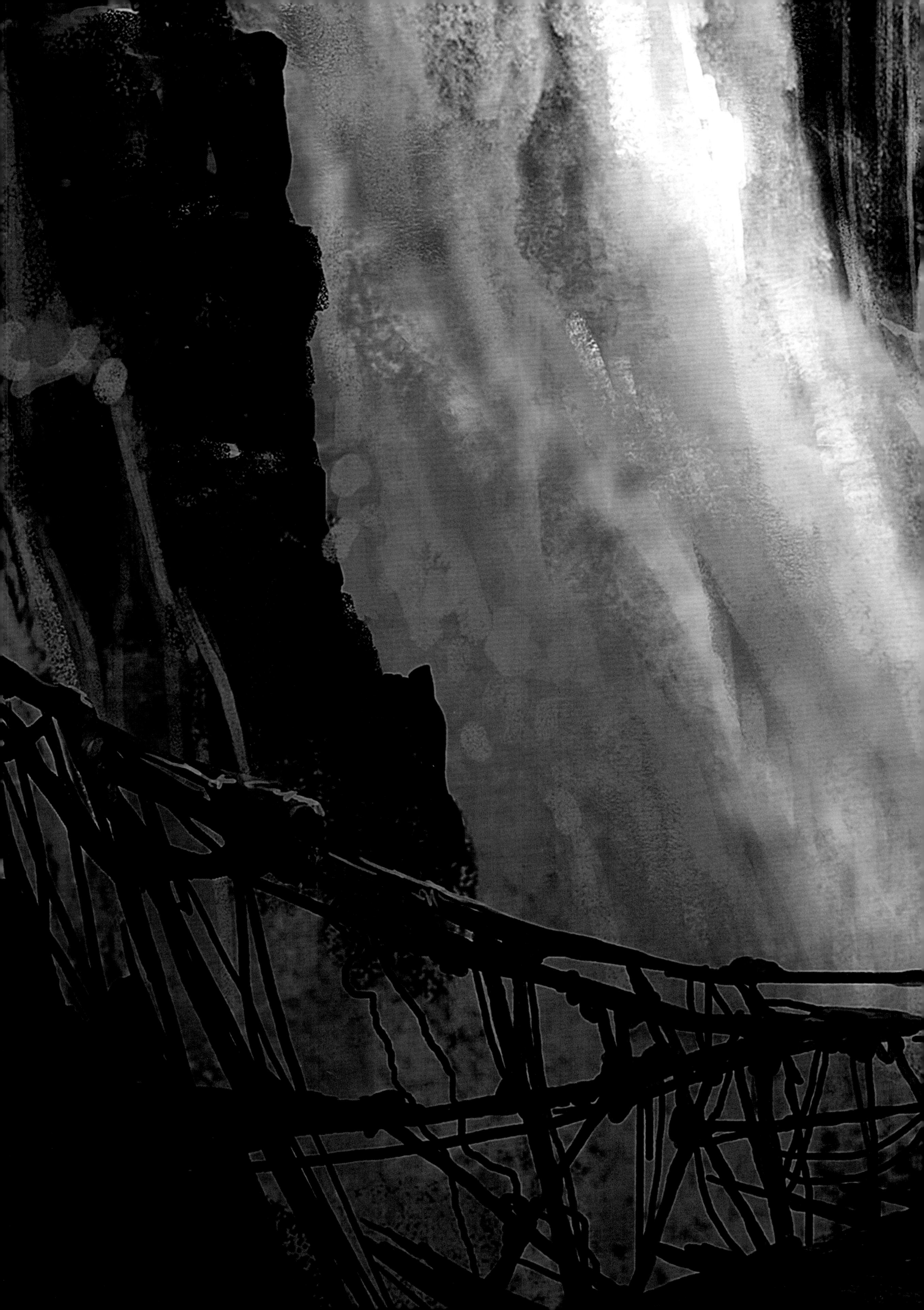

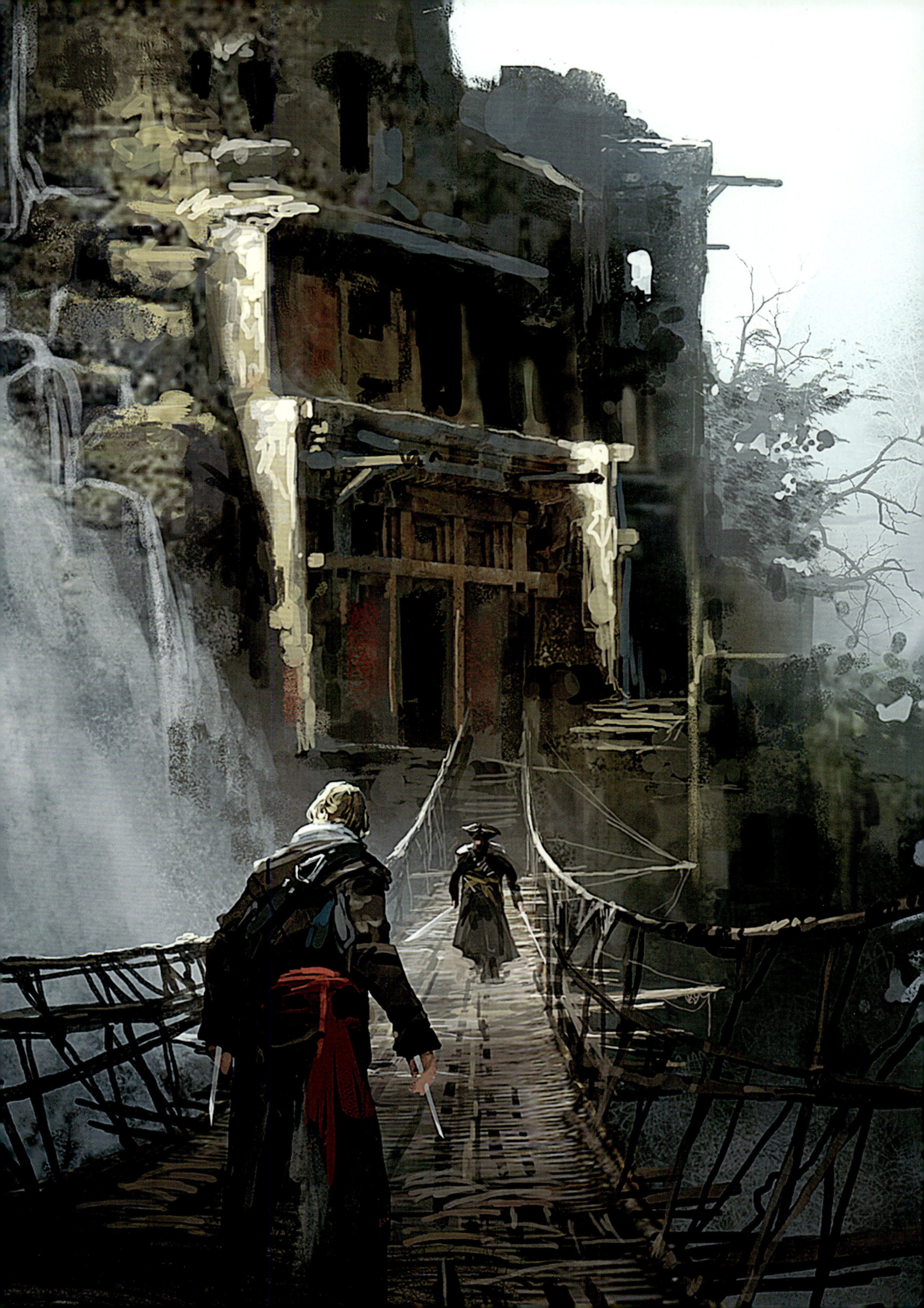

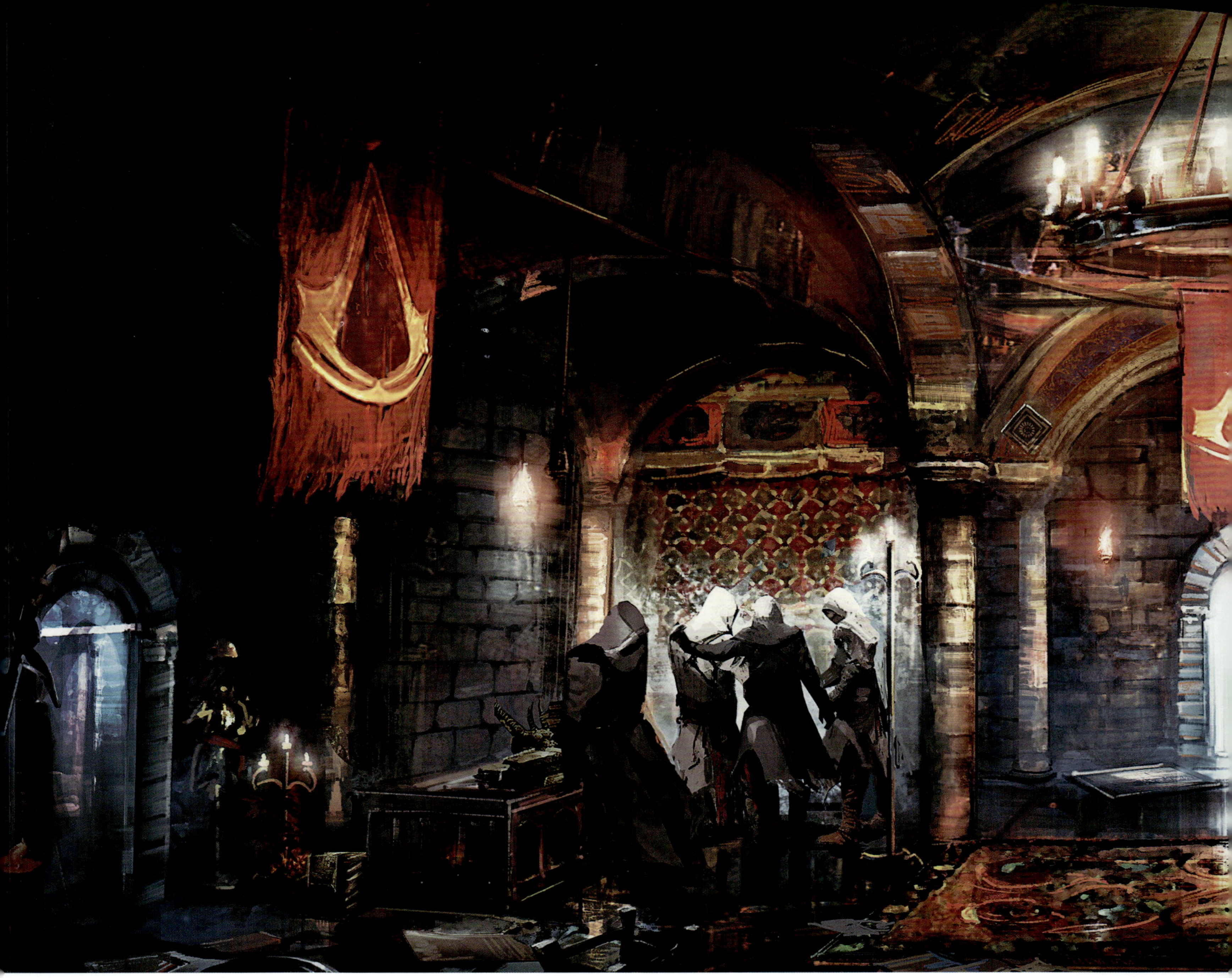

FOREWORD

Assassin's Creed is about reimagining and reliving history, and with every installment we aim to create plausible worlds and credible immersion for our fans. Through consistent evolution of our art direction, we have created a distinct, unique style for our universe. But for me, art direction is also about constructing meaningful moments that give rise to a wide range of emotions. That is why I feel it's important to stylize and emphasize elements of real landscapes, iconic architecture, and historical characters.

The world of Assassin's Creed was created to stir the imagination, to travel in time in order to discover epic locations and witness some of the world's most pivotal moments in history. I hope this book will bring you back to your best memories of Assassin's Creed and take you on a new journey of discovery of our art.

—RAPHAËL LACOSTE

Brand Art Director, Assassin's Creed

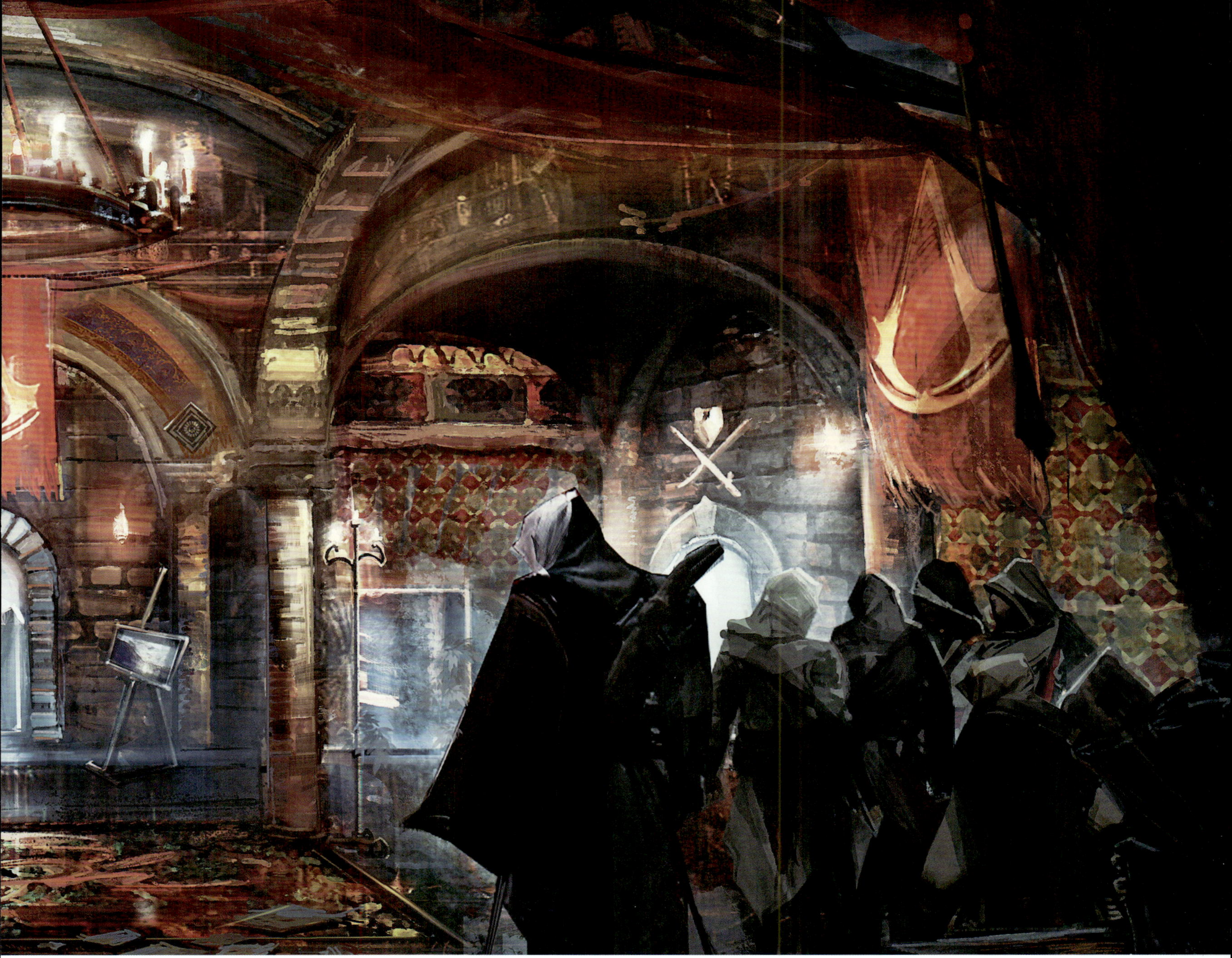

THESE PAGES: Concept of Ezio's hideout from *Assassin's Creed: Brotherhood* (Donglu Yu).

INTRODUCTION

The Brotherhood at the center of Assassin's Creed works within a system of irony and paradox. Here is a group of women and men bound together to promote peace and freedom, and yet they kill as a means to an end. They wage war against those who would control mankind and impose rules, yet they cling to tradit on.

Like the Brotherhood whose fiction they've so carefully crafted, the developers at Ubisoft have a complicated and seemingly paradox cal relationship with their own work. The franchise has repeatedly established its own rules about style and setting, only to break them in order to push boundaries. No single character, gameplay mechanic, art style, or concept is accepted as an absolute without question. Again and again, the teams steering Assassin's Creed into the future balance the traditions, ideas, and mechanics that have come before against the need for innovation. With each passing year, Assassin's Creed continues to defy expectations, steering into historical settings and experimenting with characters in a perpetual cycle of reinvention.

New ideas are permitted and encouraged, from combat and traversal mechanics to new mini-games and upgrade systems. If the series is all about freerunning through the city, what happens if the game moves to the wilderness or the open seas? If one character is the glue connecting all the installments together, can the franchise continue without him? Through experimentation, Assassin's Creed has hit upon a huge number of successes but remains willing to take risks and try something different.

A great deal of credit goes to the brilliant fictional framework of Assassin's Creed, where, in the distant past, an ancient race of precursor beings created humanity only to perish following a devastating catastrophe. Mankind is left to fend for itself, and among the best and brightest of humanity, two opposing factions form: the Assassins and the Templars. The Assassins believe in freedom for everyone and a brighter future where all share in knowledge and power. The Templars, on the other hand, believe that true peace and order can only be achieved if mankind is led by an enlightened few.

The final piece of the puzzle grounds the series in the present day. Powerful technology gives modern-day Assassins and Templars the ability to peer back through the genetic memories of their own ancestors, reliving the past as if they were there. The endless conflict continues, informed by the past and shaping the world we live in today.

The philosophical divide between Assassins and Templars echoes throughout every age of history, and that's exactly where Assassin's Creed finds its success: the playground of history. From the religion-fueled Crusades of the Middle Ages to the dawn of democracy in the Western world and beyond, the series leaps between time periods, telling and retelling the conflict between Assassins and Templars with different heroes, villains, and backdrops. The conflict remains the same; the details are endlessly mutable.

At first glance, it's a wildly ambitious and complicated setup for an action-focused video game. And yet it's that very complexity that has provided Assassin's Creed the framework it needed to expand its universe with each passing year.

The elaborate narrative holds together in large part thanks to a consistent but evolving vision that governs the artistic presentation of one game after the next. Each new entry catapults the player into a different moment in history, each re-created with an eye toward both accuracy and wish fulfillment. What might it be like to meet Leonardo da Vinci or climb the towering walls of Notre Dame Cathedral? How does it feel to stand atop Bunker Hill as the first shots are fired or to walk the gas-lit streets of London at the height of the Industrial Revolution? Ubisoft's artists have gone to the well of history time and again and drawn out visions that cleverly meld fact with fiction.

In the pages ahead, we dive into that well of history with the artists who have conceived Assassin's Creed each and every step along the way. Their beautiful visualizations inspired the thousands of game developers who have contributed to the series over the years, but crafted as they are by artists at the top of their field, many of these pieces transcend their utility and tell a story all their own.

OPPOSITE: Concept of the Chartres Cathedral, which was not included in *Assassin's Creed: Unity* (Ludovic Ribardière).

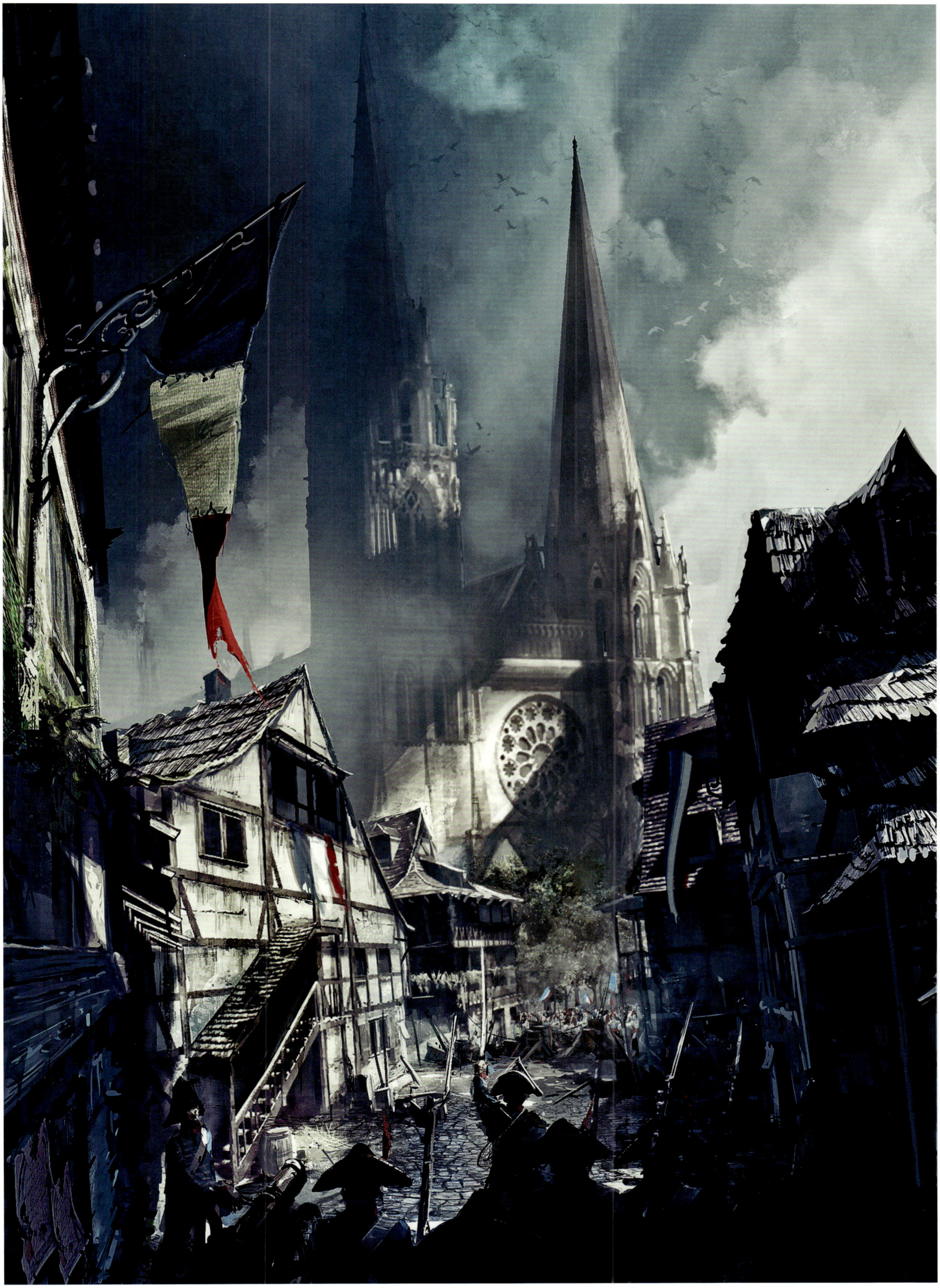

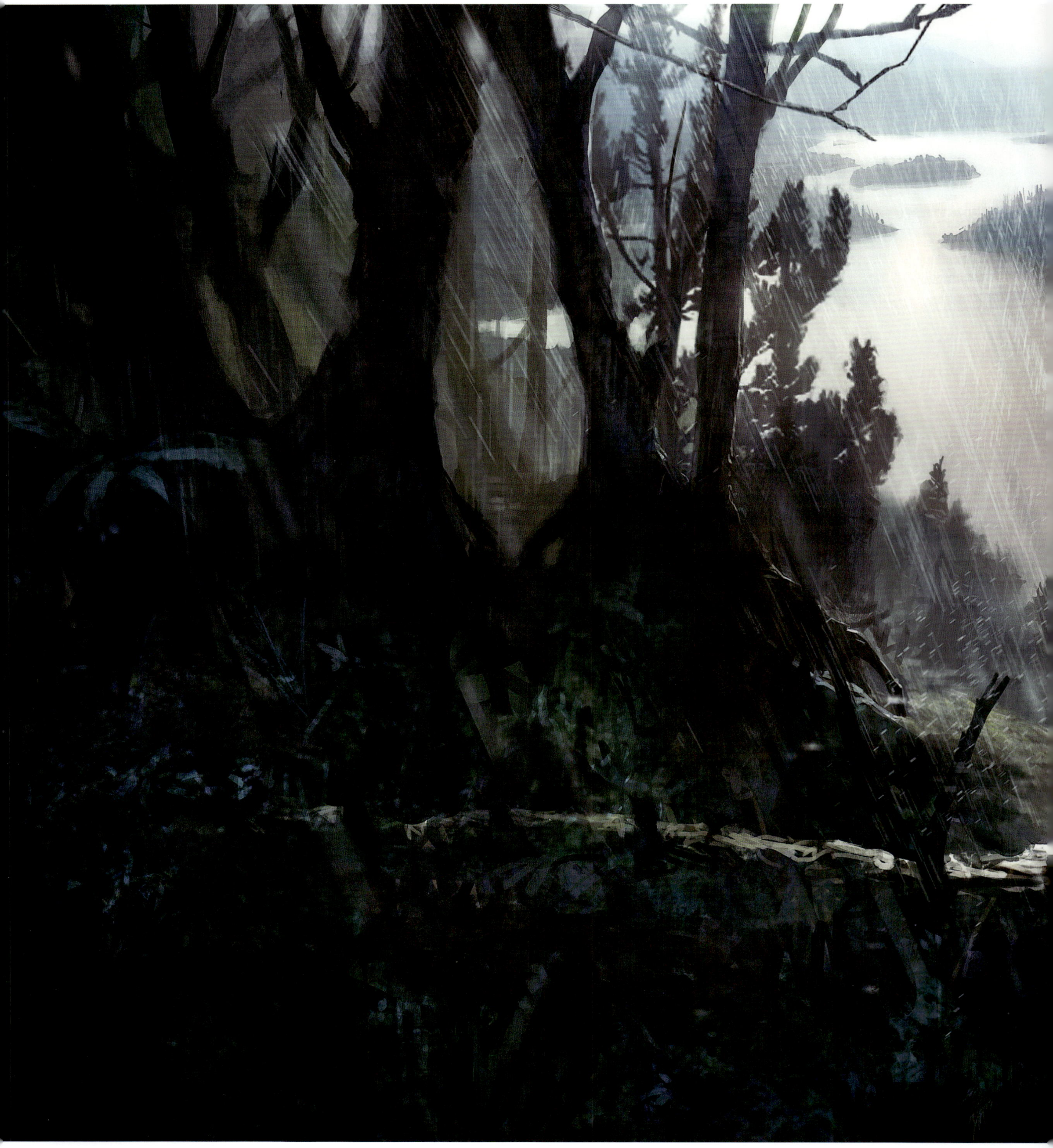

ABOVE: Artwork for *Assassin's Creed III* contrasting the denseness of the trees with the grand scale of the River Valley (Gilles Beloeil).
FOLLOWING PAGES: The plains of Arsuf from *Assassin's Creed I* (David Levy).

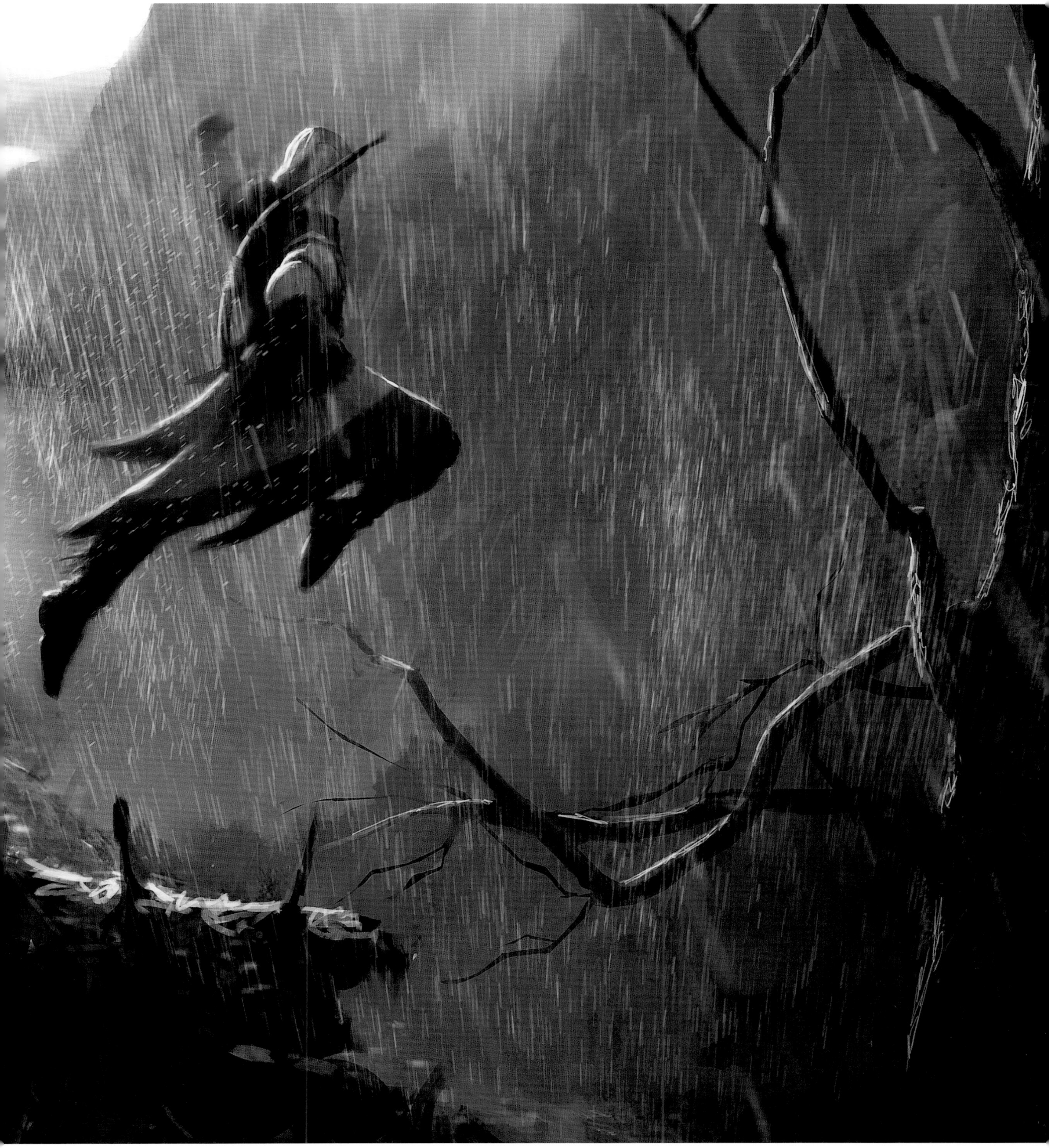

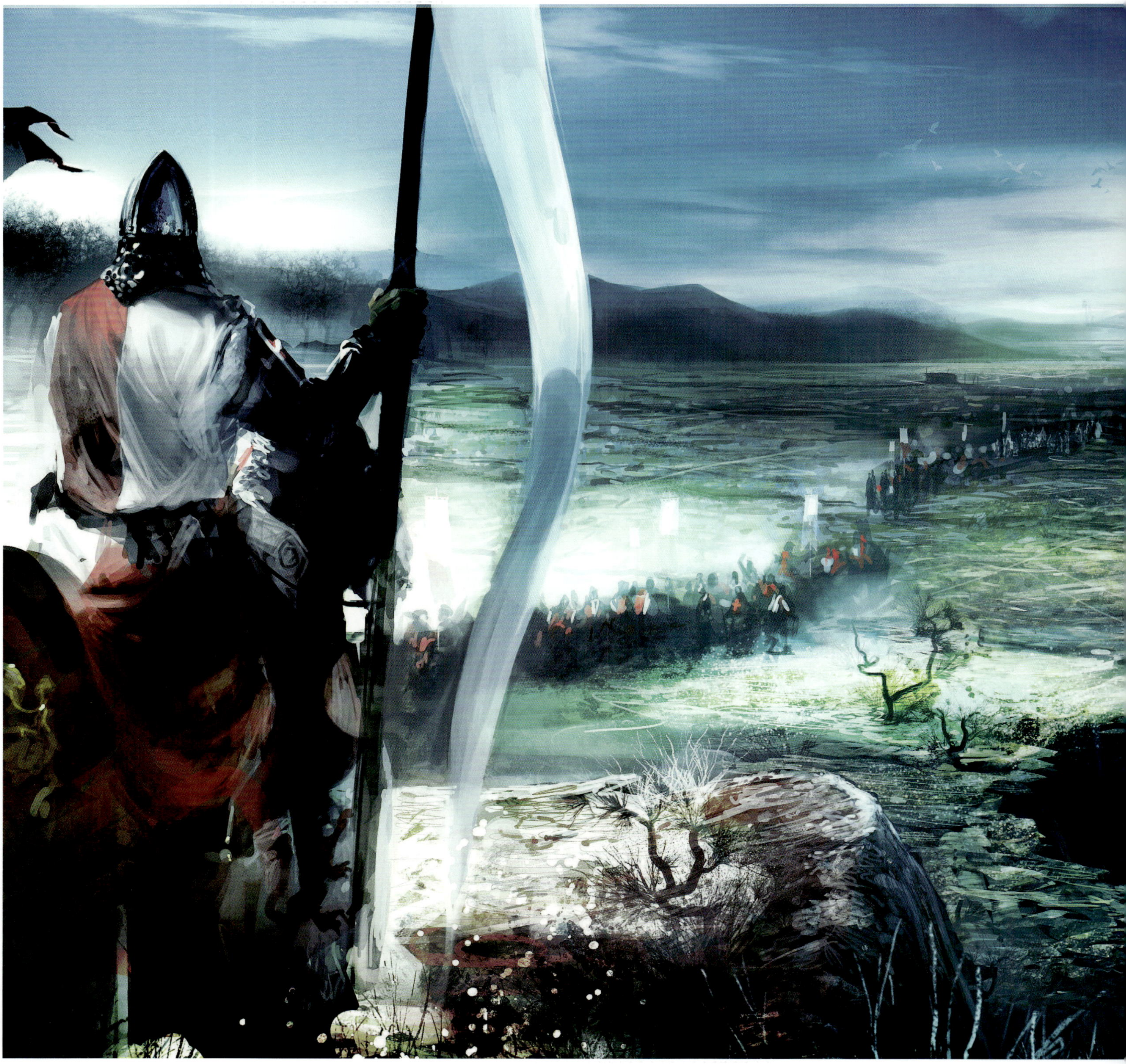

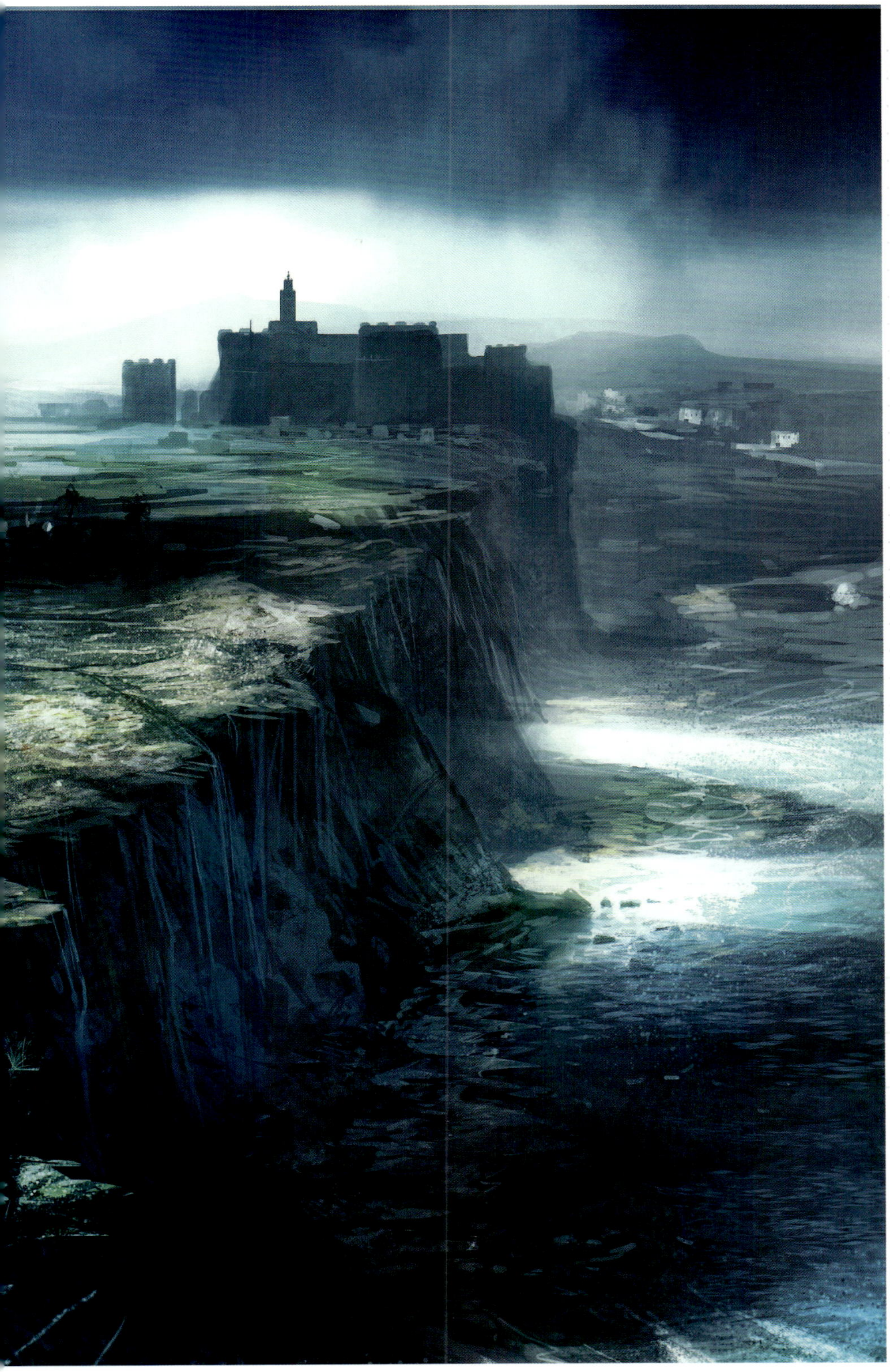

1 THE MIDDLE AGES

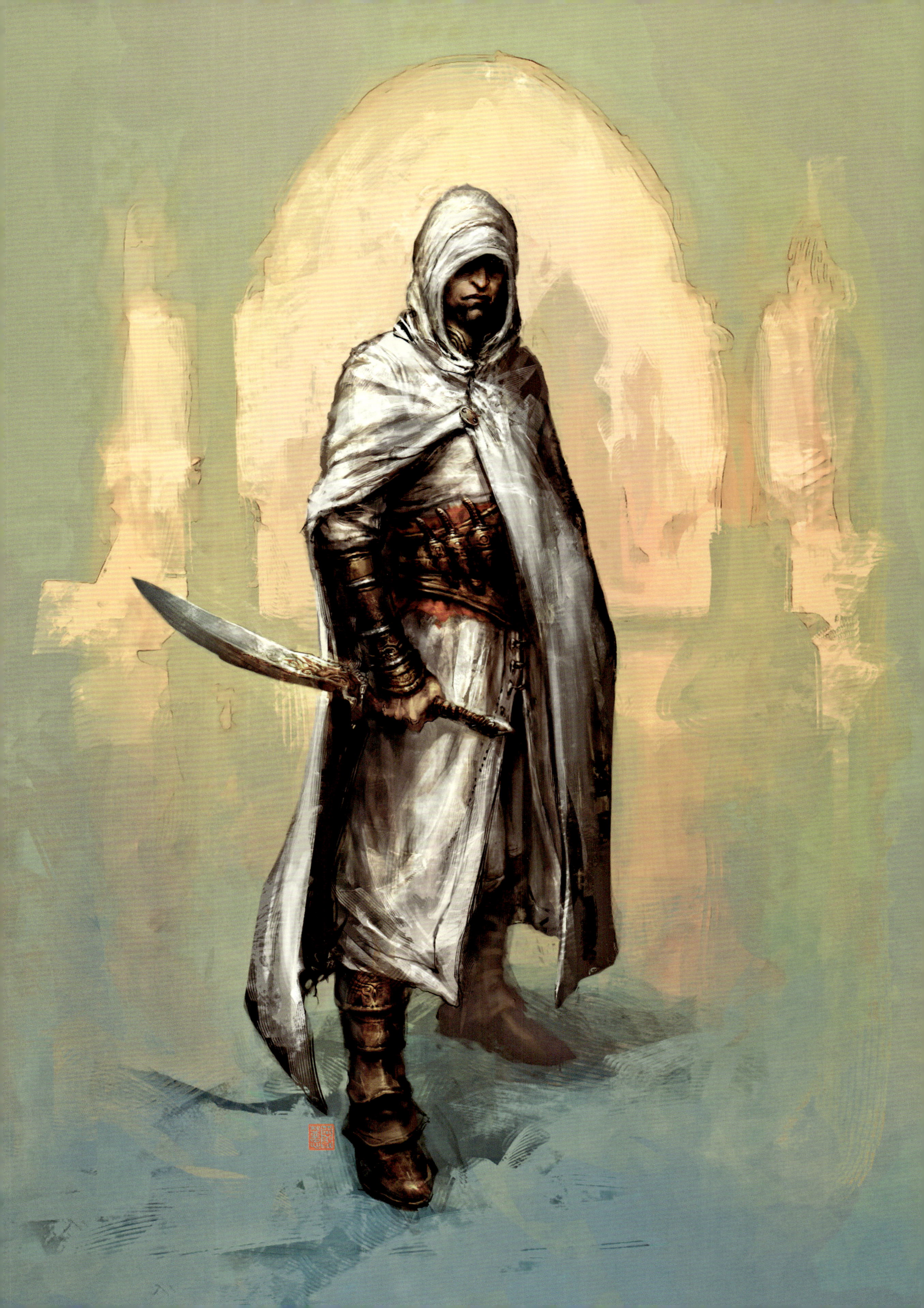

ONE ICON BIRTHS ANOTHER

Nearly a decade after Assassin's Creed first came to the attention of gamers around the world, it's hard to imagine that the series as we know it might never have come to exist. Millions of players all around the world, more than a dozen distinct games, an array of novels, multiple comics, a number of toy lines, and even animation and film treatments have made the franchise a heavyweight in the modern-day game world and a clear flagship property for Ubisoft.

However, in the beginning, Assassin's Creed wasn't a new series at all. Instead, the earliest inklings of what Assassin's Creed would one day become emerged from the small team that had split off after the completion of *Prince of Persia: Sands of Time* with a mandate to craft a novel direction for the Prince as a new generation of game consoles hit the market. "It was intended to be the next *Prince of Persia*," says Jean Guesdon, brand creative director for Assassin's Creed. "The main difference at the time was the shift from fantasy to realism in terms of setting."

Artist Khai Nguyen was one of the first to try his hand at visualizing the Assassin. Creative director Patrice Désilets would come to Nguyen with ideas inspired by historical manuscripts and ask for those ideas to be translated into art. Those earliest imaginings drew upon nineteenth-century Orientalist paintings as a starting point.

The first concept-art pieces maintained some of the same vibrant and whimsical qualities that had previously defined the adventures of the acrobatic Prince. As time passed, the creative team saw the potential for something more grounded that wouldn't lose the excitement of an agile and dangerous lead at the center of the action.

"We were going for a more realistic direction, but we also wanted to keep the more spectacular elements that are critical to action-adventure games," says brand art director Raphaël Lacoste. "It was this enhanced treatment of real history, characters, and environments that changed the premise of the game compared to its predecessor." Ambition was high in the earliest days of concept development, and everything from including multiple Assassins and cooperative gameplay was considered. "Patrice talked about co-op gameplay a lot," Khai remembers. "I attempted to visualize these ideas in my artwork, at one point showing a dagger-wielding Assassin hiding in the shadows on one side and a female Assassin holding a little crossbow on the other. We pretty much knew that co-op was too ambitious for our project at the time, but we wanted to dream big before we had to concern ourselves with time and production constraints."

But even as the team adjusted to more realistic expectations for a first game, it was clear that they were onto something special. Increasingly, the concept art established a world and character that felt too far from *Prince of Persia* to maintain the same moniker. This white-robed protagonist had a fantastical edge but felt like he could be part of the real world. "We chose a direction that invited a well-grounded, mature visual treatment," Raphaël says. "In every aspect of the game—from the animation to the way we rendered the environments—we were striving to be meticulous and thorough in how we presented the world and its characters." Successive concept art and story development made it clear that this new idea was headed somewhere different and unexpected, away from the brilliant colors and magical viziers of the Prince of Persia series and into the territory of world history. But if history was to be the backdrop, what moment in time was the right one in which to plant this new seed?

OPPOSITE: An early concept of the Assassin who would become known as Altaïr. Inspired by Orientalist paintings, the hood added a sense of mystery to the Assassin aesthetic and would become iconic for the franchise (Thierry Doizon).

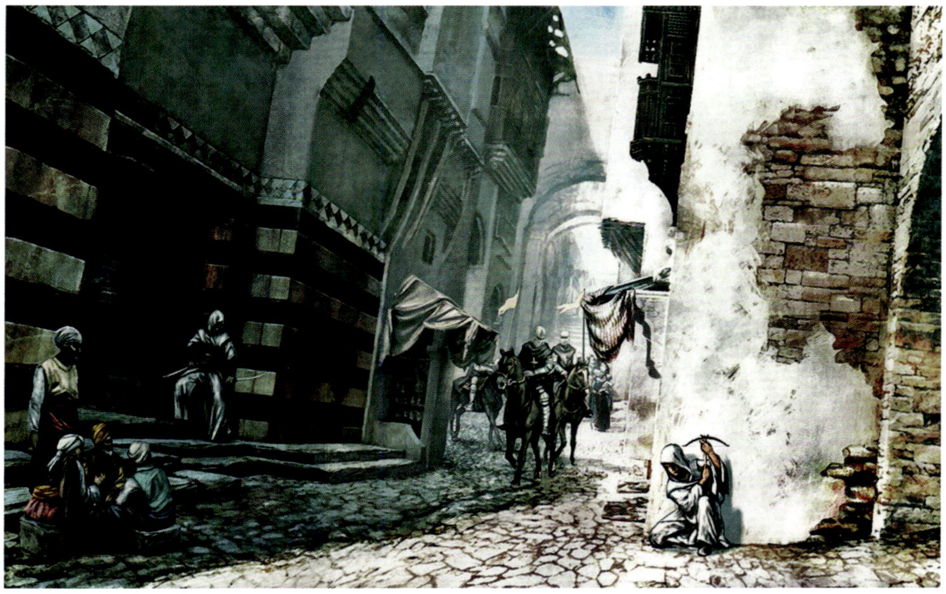

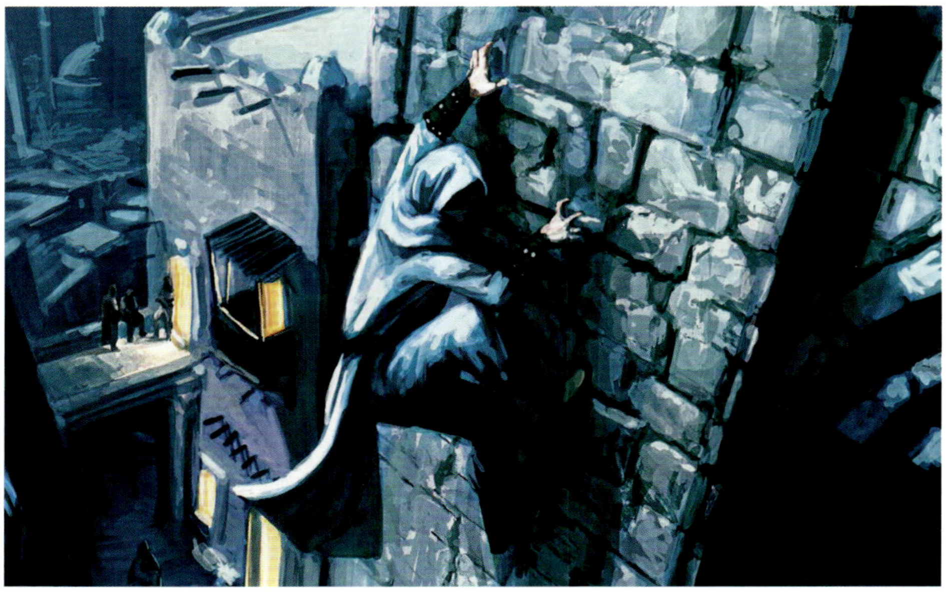

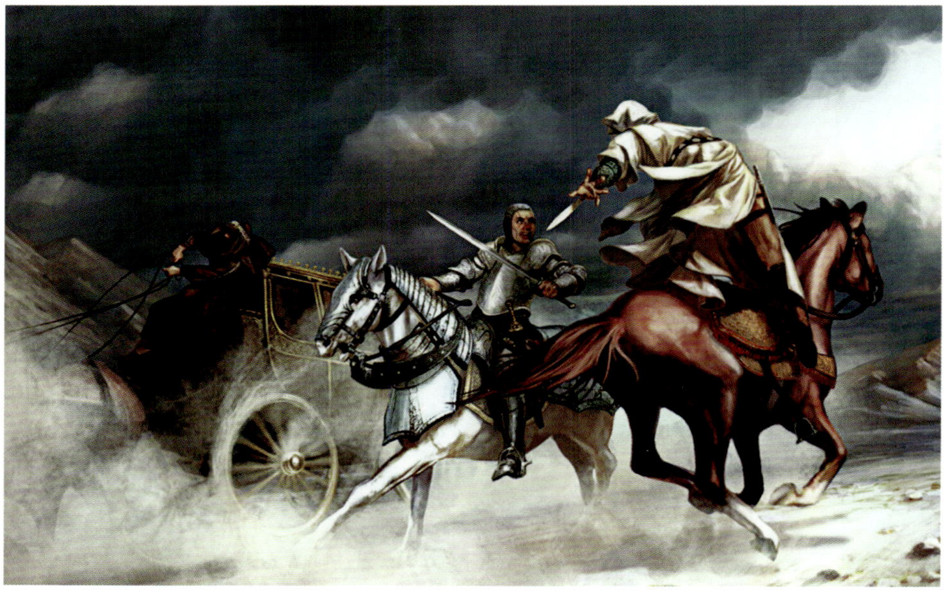

THIS PAGE: Early narrative illustrations (Khai Nguyen).
OPPOSITE: Another early Assassin concept featuring the symbolic eagle in the background (Khai Nguyen).

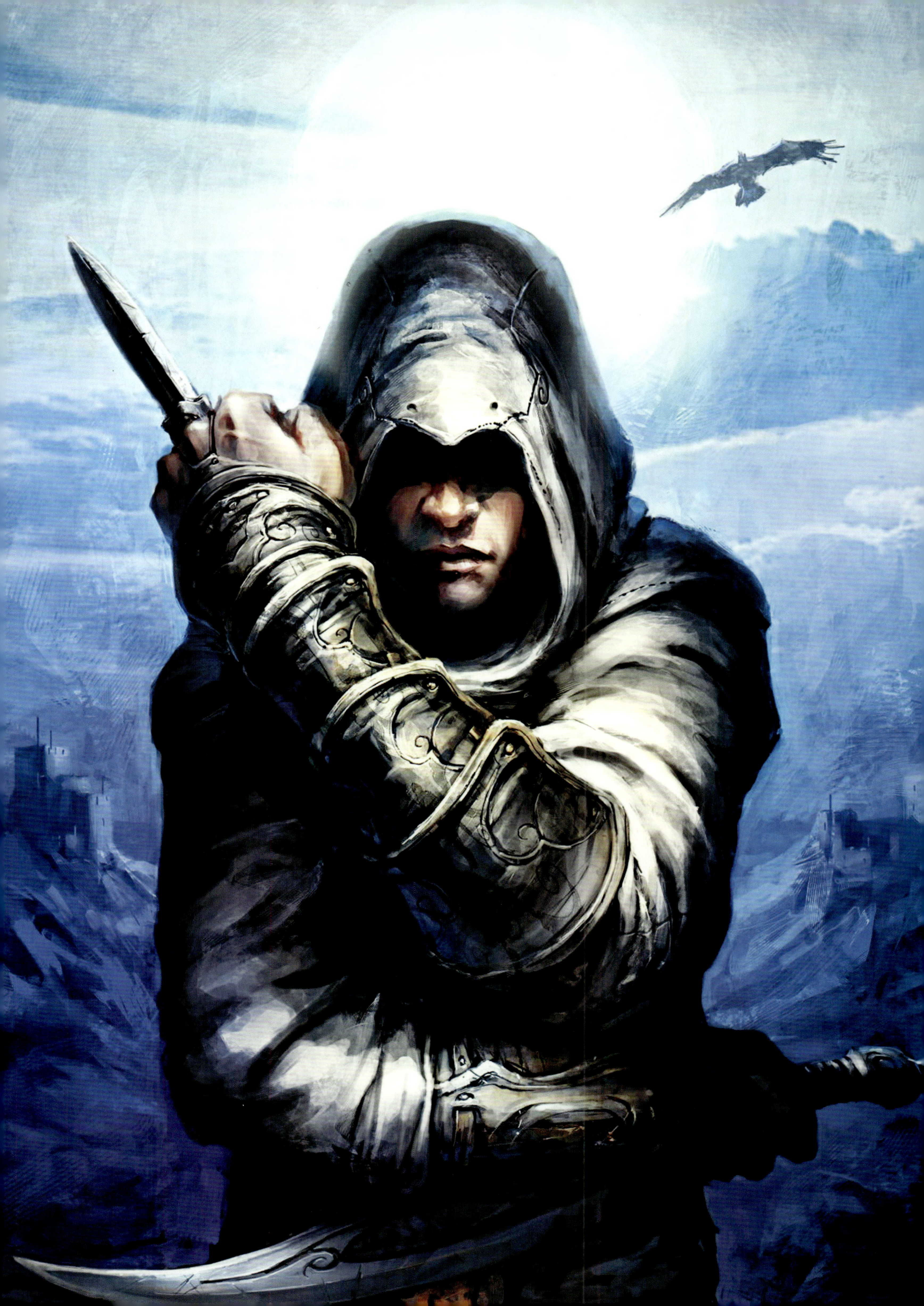

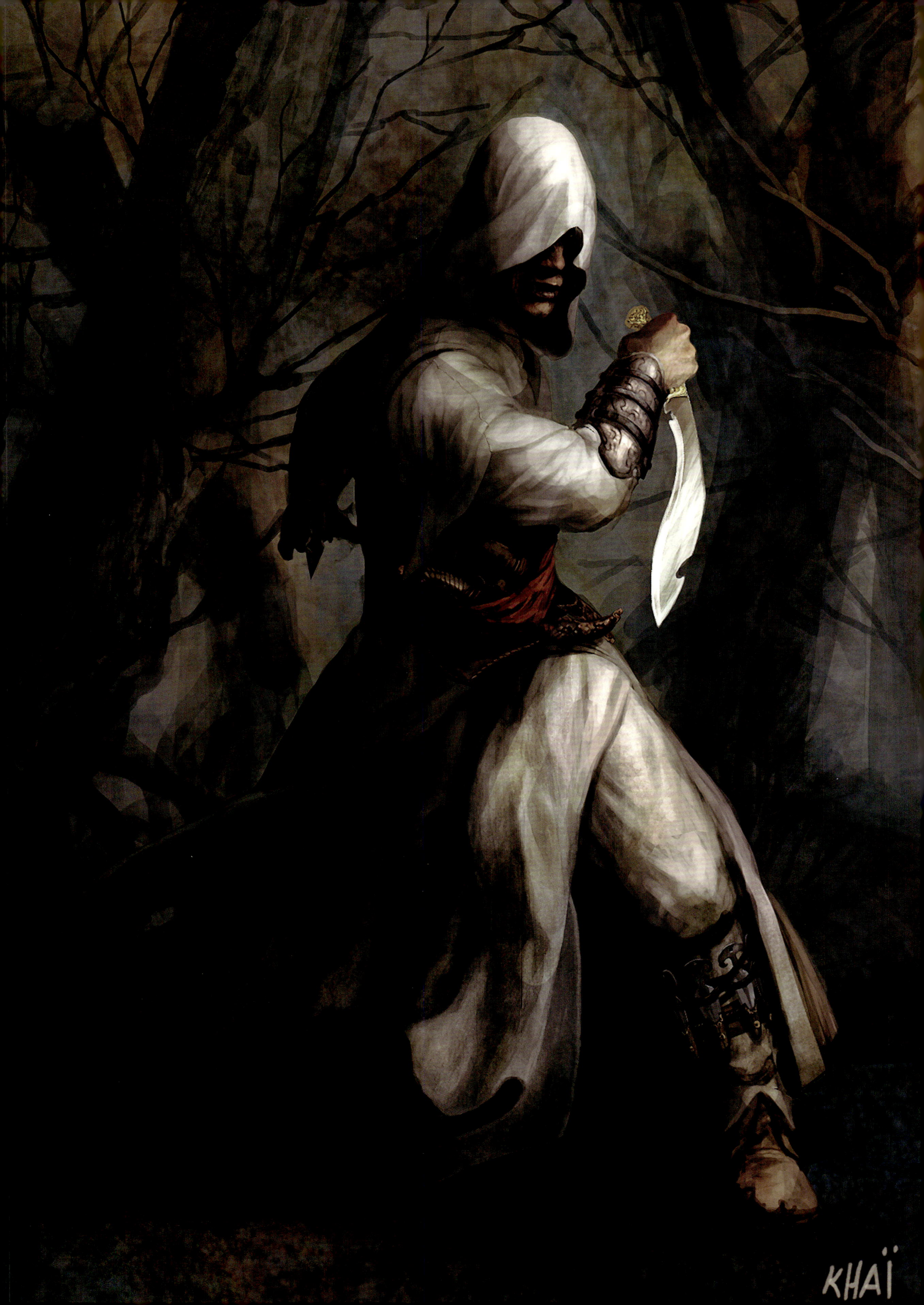
KHAÏ

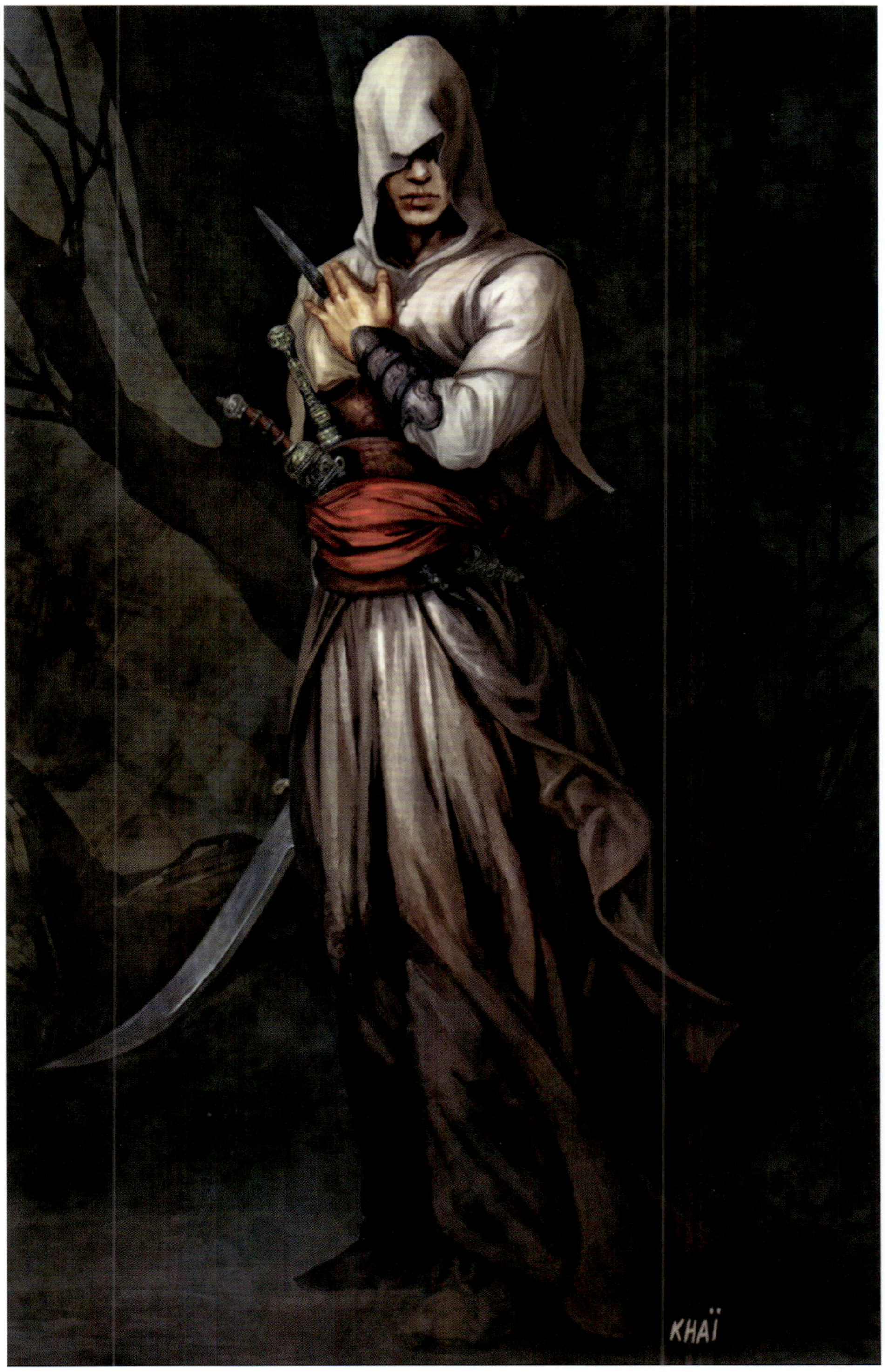

THESE PAGES: Some of the very first concepts of Assassin's Creed's first Assassin. The long robes created a dramatic and statuesque profile but showed dynamic movement in action (Khai Nguyen).
FOLLOWING PAGES: Early artwork of the South Kingdom (Raphaël Lacoste).

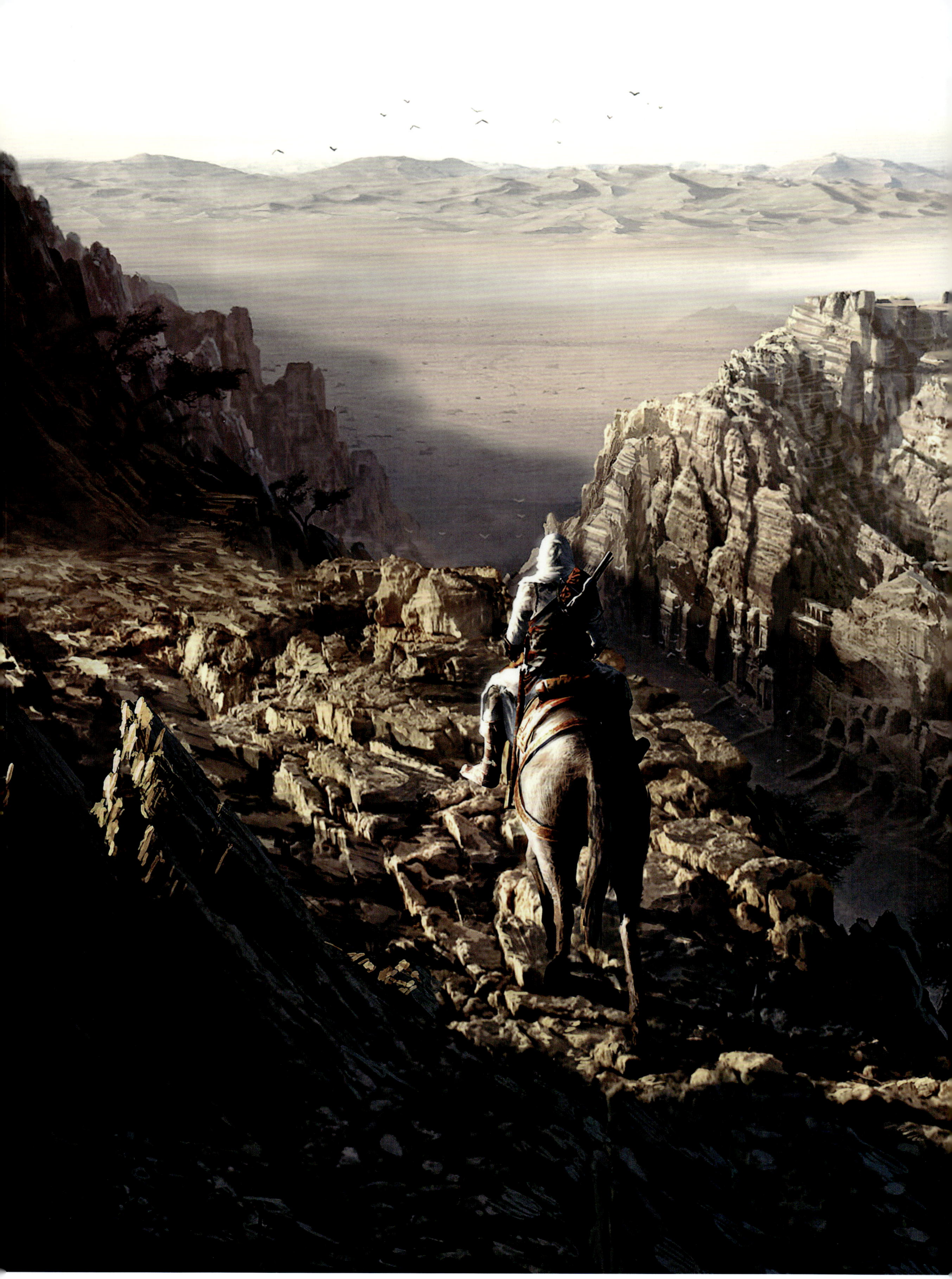

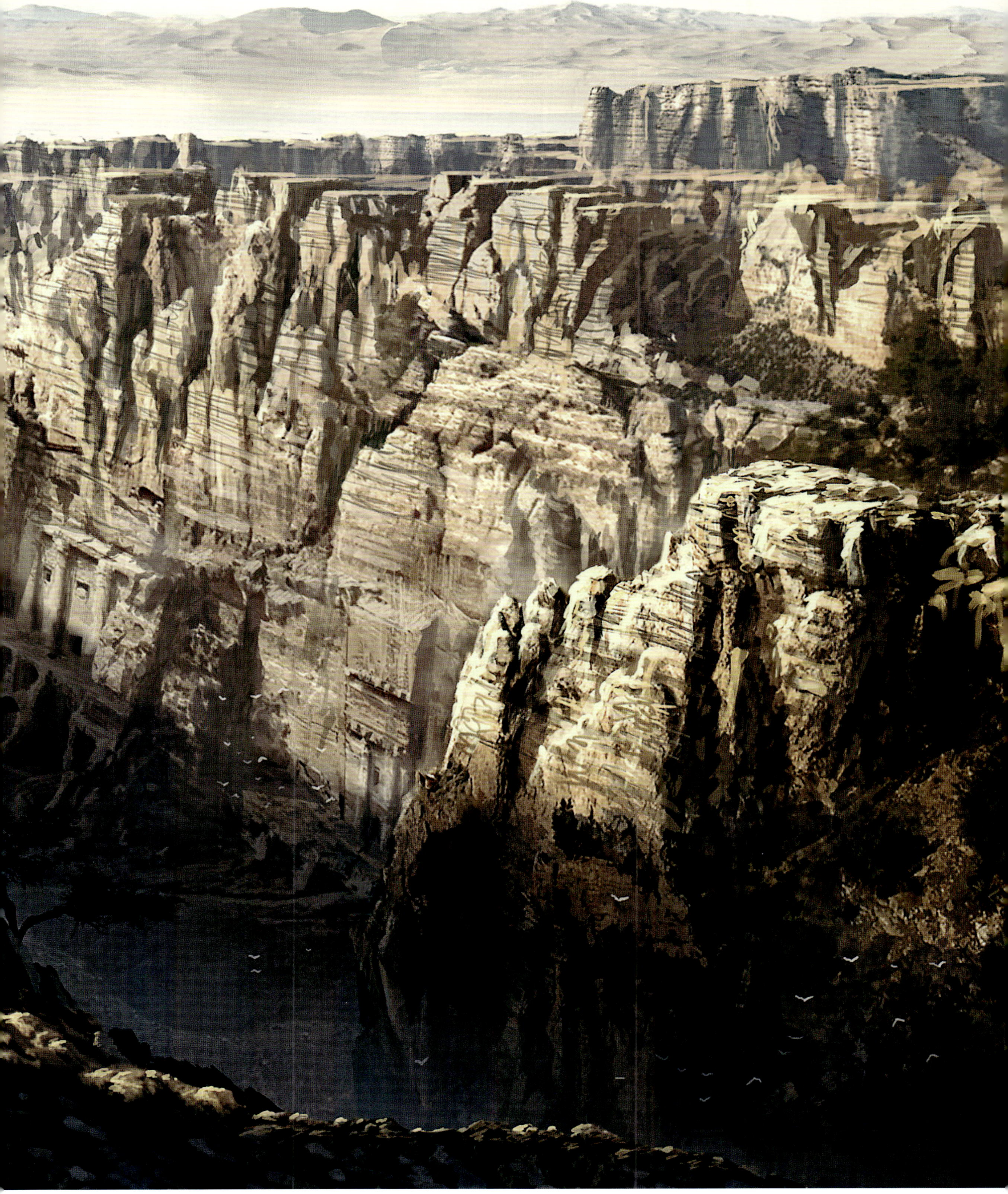

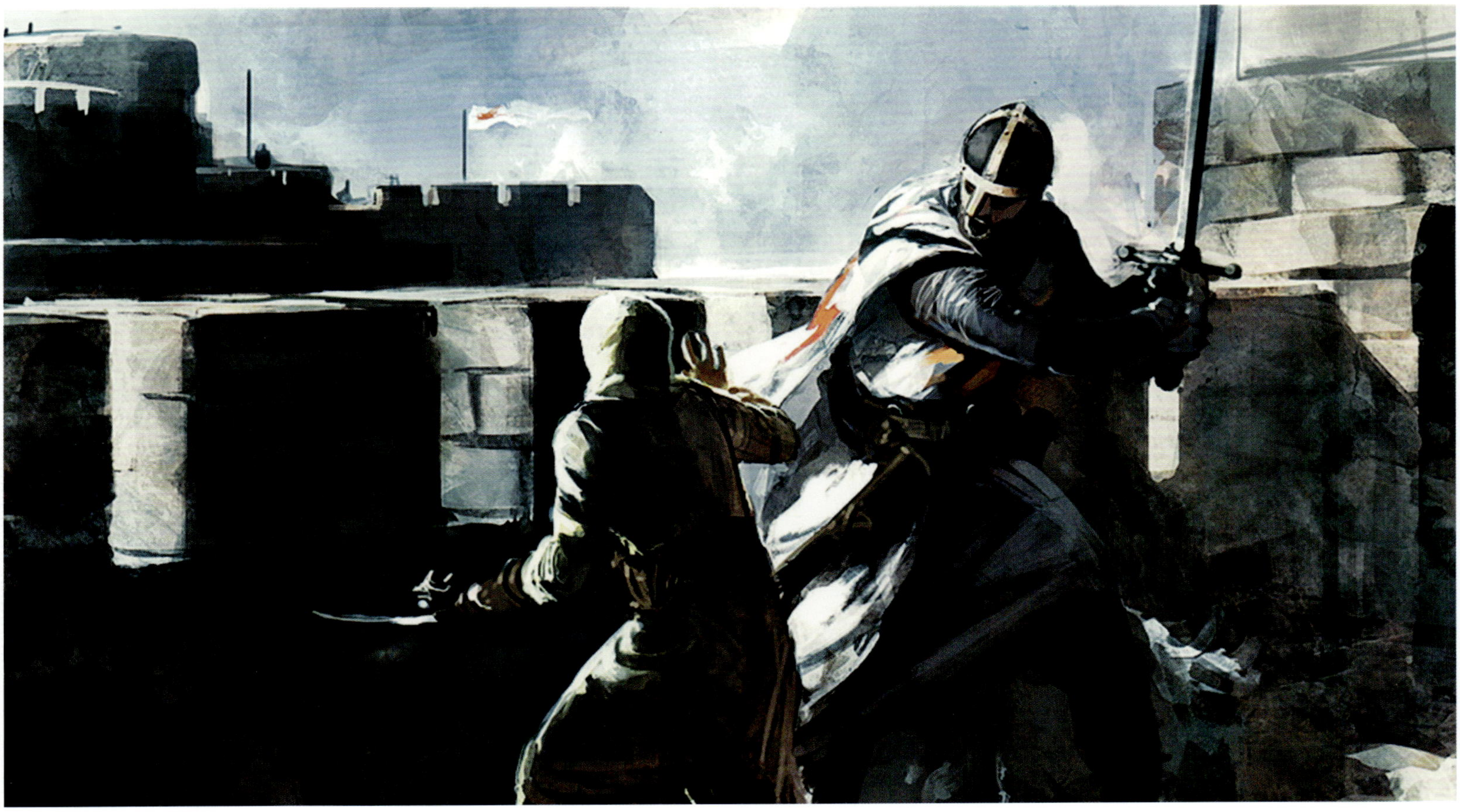

THE THIRD CRUSADE

The Holy Land in 1191 was a hotbed of conflict. Multiple Christian monarchs, including Richard the Lion-Heart, had led their armies into lands considered holy ground to three of the world's great religions. The Muslim sultan, Saladin, stubbornly held back the European invaders from their most prized goal, the city of Jerusalem.

History describes two orders that did indeed wind their way through the time period. The Knights Templar were elite soldiers of the Crusades bedecked in immaculate white uniforms that bore a distinctive red cross. Meanwhile, a secretive sect referred to as the Assassins was feared far and wide through the region for their tactics of targeted political killings.

Assassin's Creed took this setup and ran with it. The Templars and Assassins weren't just players in the devastating Crusades, they were ancient enemies that had secretly competed for hundreds of years. The stakes were higher than control of the Holy Land; the Assassins and Templars fought over the fate of mankind's freedom. Assassins envisioned a world where everything was permitted and people were free to shape their own destinies. The Templars thought they knew better—to them, mankind was meant to be ruled.

Rather than paint the two central conflicting orders in stark contrast, the Assassins and Templars share a number of visual traits, including matching color schemes that allude to their shared origins. Nonetheless, the flowing lines of the Assassins and the blocky, straight lines of the Templar uniform provide a visual distinction that would maintain significance as the series continued. "The visual style of the Assassins is quite organic, whereas for the Templars we aim to use stricter, cleaner lines," Raphaël explains. "The factions distinguish themselves visually in terms of shape and composition, with the Assassins being inspired by the sleek lines of a bird of prey and the Templars by the rigid, straight, and symmetrical lines of their old castles and fortresses."

Of the two historical orders, Ubisoft took far more liberties with the design of the secretive Assassins than their cross-emblazoned enemies. The Templars were more of a known and researched force during the Third Crusade, and as such, their appearance in that first game was strongly rooted in historical data. The sharp edges, lines, and clear cross-shape would come to define the visual language of the Templars for the games to come, even as subsequent teams would experiment with visual designs that took the Order further afield.

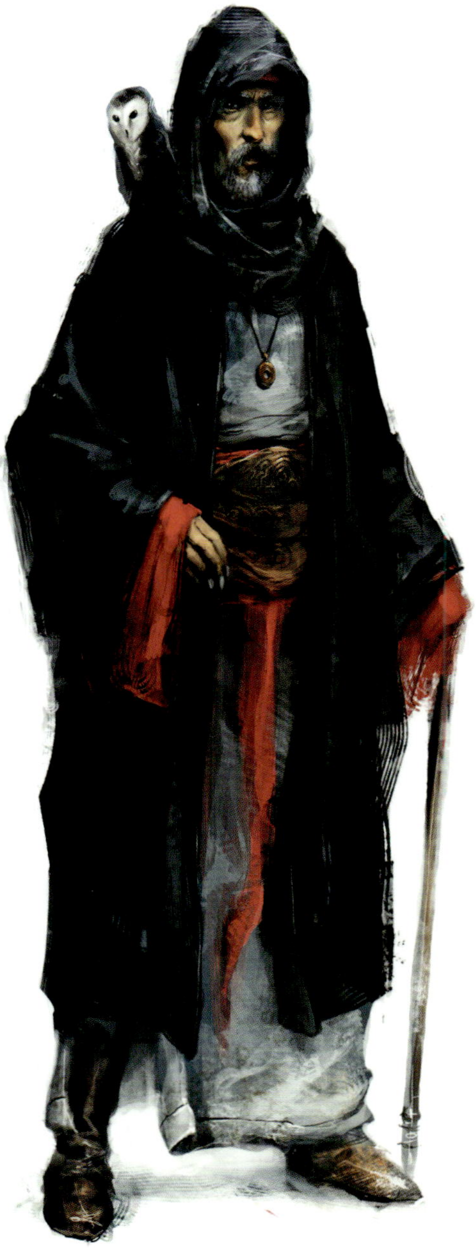

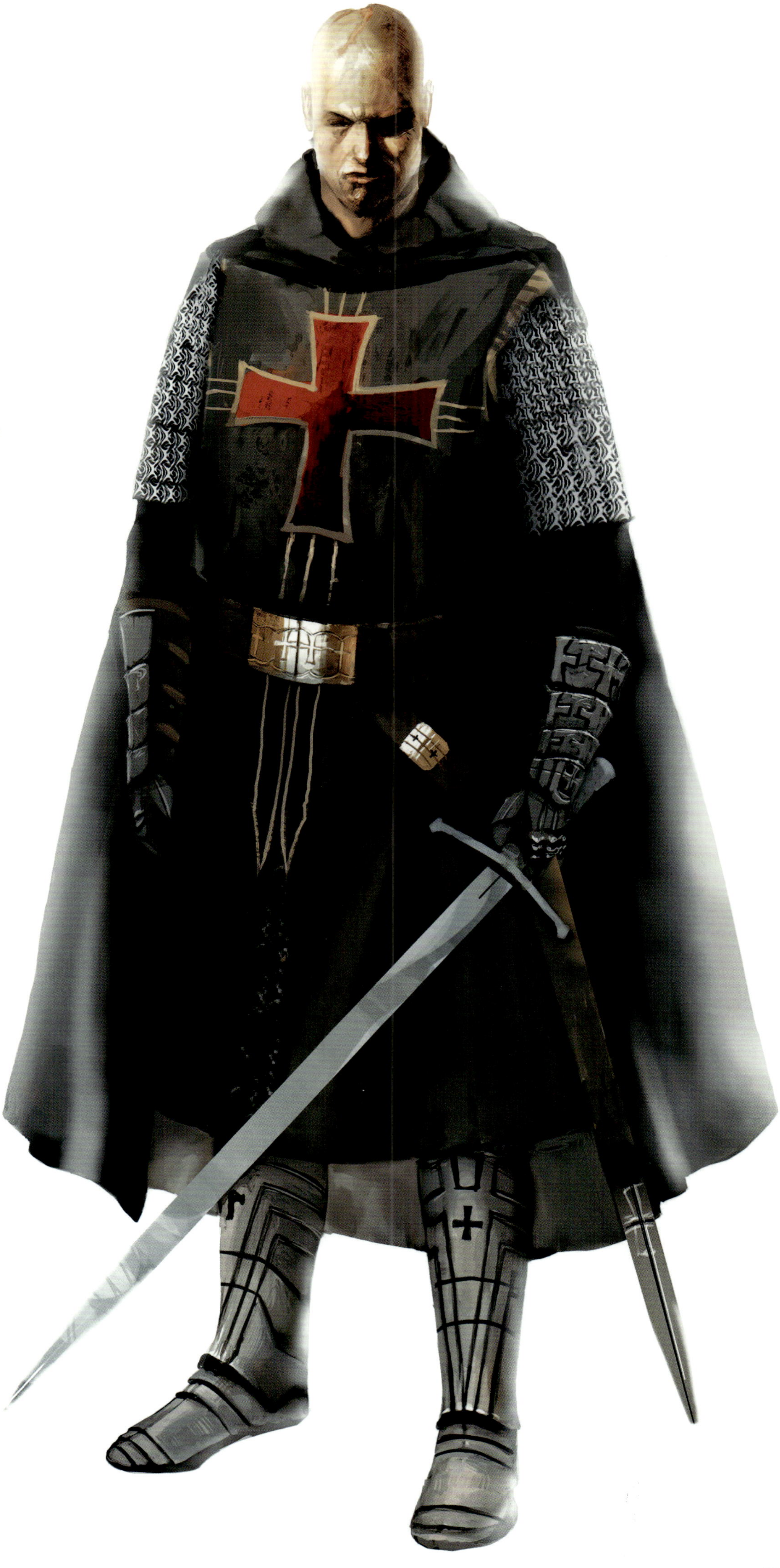

OPPOSITE: Narrative illustration showcasing the imposing stature of a Templar soldier (David Levy).
ABOVE LEFT: Early concept of Altaïr's Mentor, Al Mualim (Patrick Desgreniers).
ABOVE RIGHT: Robert de Sable's design features subtle iterations of the Templar symbol on his bracers, belt, and sword (Patrick Desgreniers).

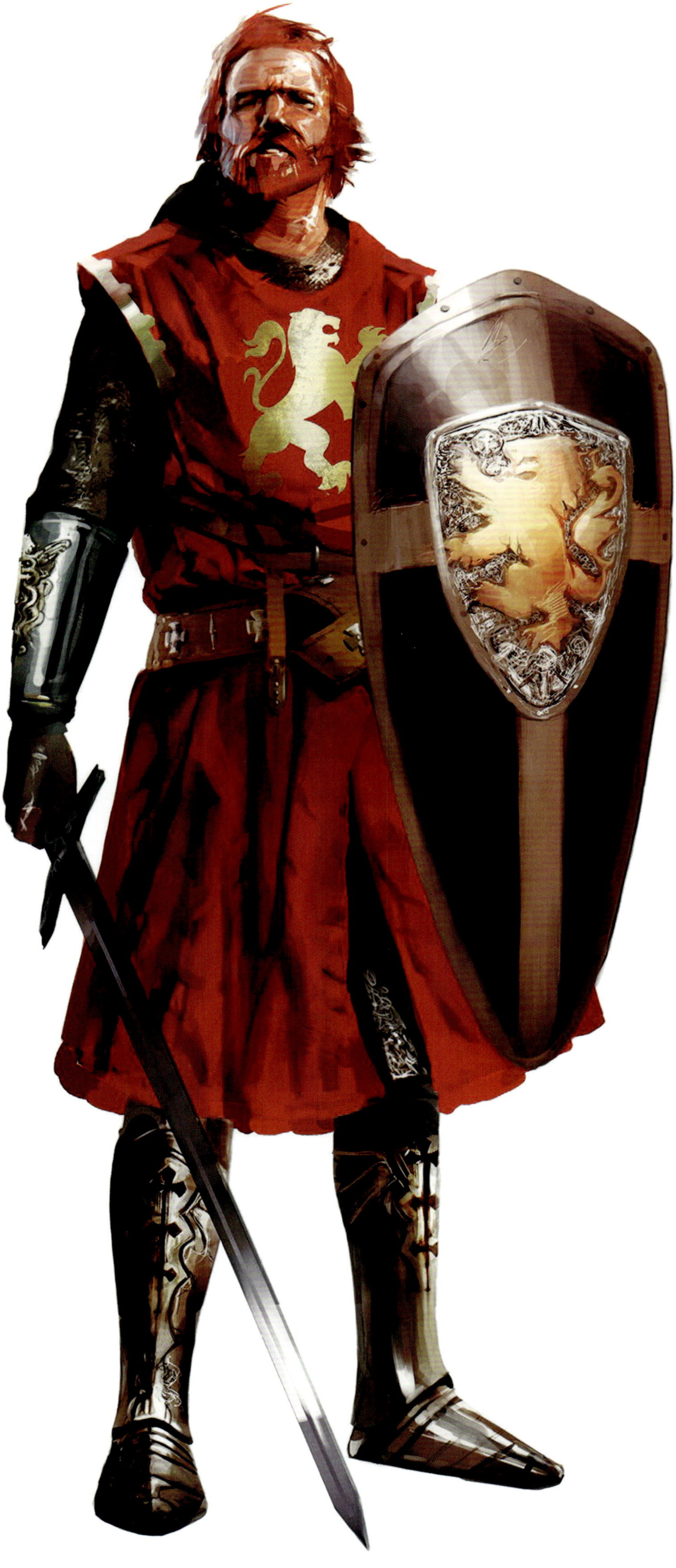

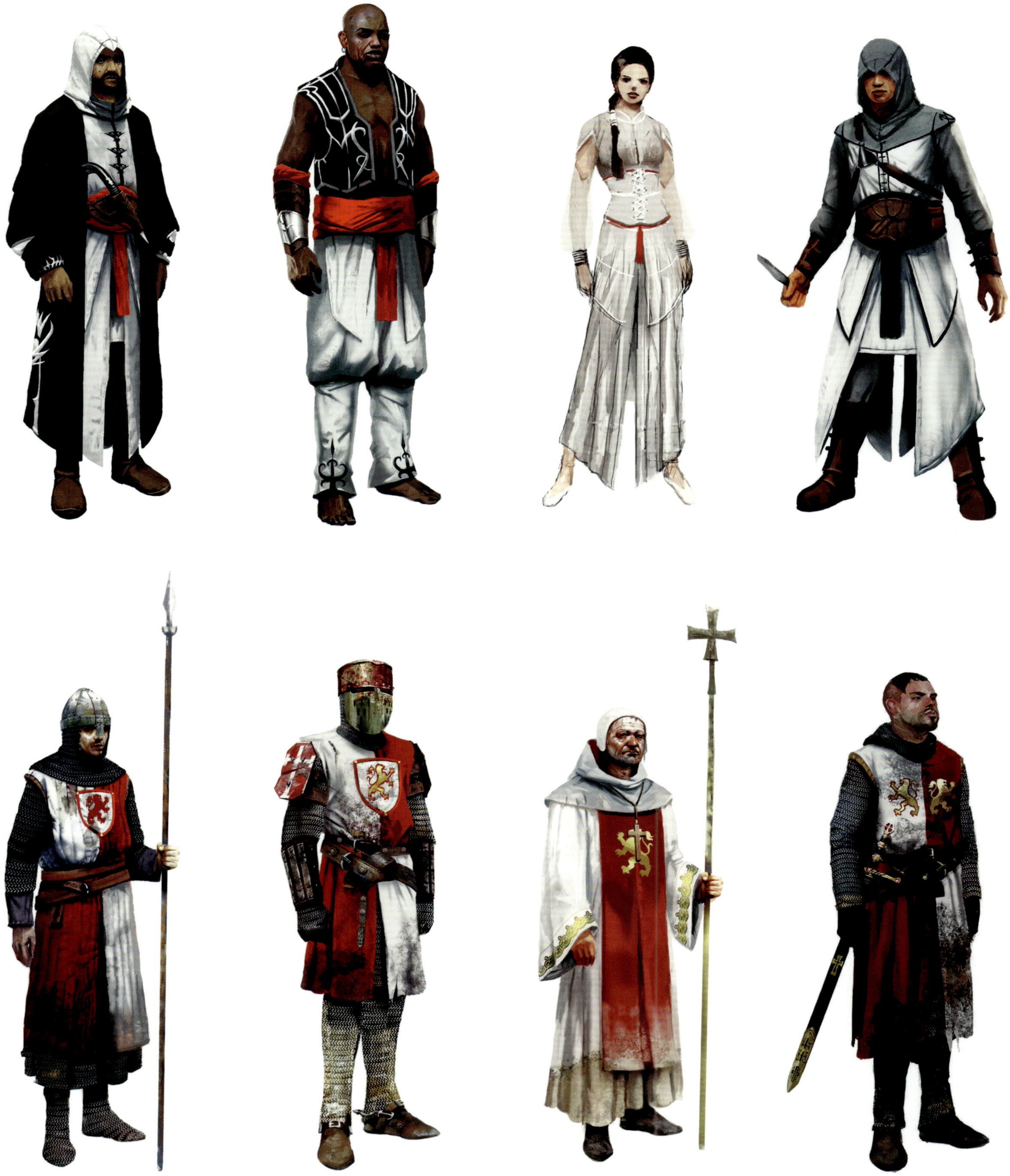

OPPOSITE: Inspired by medieval paintings, Richard the Lion-Heart's noble pose and iconic armor allow players to easily identify him (Patrick Desgreniers).
THIS PAGE: A selection of Christian and Assassin character concepts (Patrick Desgreniers).

A DIFFERENT KIND OF HERO

Altaïr Ibn-La'Ahad may have begun his life as a new variation on an old character, but his final appearance in the first *Assassin's Creed* indelibly established the intrigue of the Assassin Brotherhood—a new hero for a new kind of game. His throwing knives and bristling weaponry recalled classical imaginings of the stealth warrior, but his layered robes, reminiscent of the wings of a bird, added mystic overtones. An obscuring hood hid his face, yet the bright whites and reds seemed to defy the apparent attempt at stealth. His appearance was a collision of conflicting ideas and seemingly contrary goals.

The clashing visual cues echoed the character's conflicted personality. As he first appears, Altaïr isn't especially likeable, bound up in his own narcissism and pride and unable to see past his own mistakes. After being disciplined by his Mentor, Altaïr's trials force him to reconcile a new vision of both who he is and what the Brotherhood is meant to be. That increased discipline and self-knowledge was reflected in his apparel as a slow buildup of weaponry and armor, which shaped the character's appearance at the same pace as his internal evolution.

Beyond supporting his developing persona, Altaïr's accoutrements were also undeniably cool. "In the beginning, the design we had for Altaïr was maybe too romantic," Raphaël says. "His robes and silhouette were too extravagant. We had to refine that to get something more appropriate and efficient for an Assassin. Altaïr is very focused, and you see that reflected in his final design. The shape of his hood, for instance, which was very open in the beginning, became narrower to cast a shadow on his face and add to his mysterious personality." Here was a video game hero who looked different from any that had come before—a superhero from eight hundred years ago, dispatching villains like a bird of prey.

The allusions to a raptor in flight were by no means coincidental. From frozen silhouette to attacker dropping down from above, Altaïr and his outfit were meant to recall the eagle: "It's an animal that inspires, and you cannot demean it. It really is the king of the air," says Jean. "The eagle gives the impression of being unstoppable. He is above you, able to observe everything. He is a predator, very carefully picking his targets. He is strong, but agile; fast, but patient." Indeed, this juxtaposition of stillness and movement served as a major point of inspiration. "It was important to show the specific gameplay aspects of being in high profile and low profile, and how these two states change the character not just in terms of look, but also personality," says Khai. "I made the character wear long flowing robes that were sleek and statuesque when perfectly still but become dynamic in action." As Altaïr leaps, his robes fold back like wings in descent. The hidden blade extends like a talon. The dipped head and tight hood curve down to a point, like a beak. Even the name Altaïr was taken from an Arabic translation of "flying eagle."

The bright white color added to the eagle imagery, but it also served notice that Altaïr was a different sort of stealth hero. Rather than sneak through shadows, Altaïr could blend with the crowd and slip amongst groups of passing priests. Meanwhile, the red sash contrasted a white purity of purpose against the bloody work this soldier personified. "Red and white are the iconic colors of Assassin's Creed," Raphaël explains. "The symbolism and brightness of these colors were qualities that distinguished us from other games, which often used darker color schemes." Unlike many of the later heroes, Altaïr was a stoic soldier, driven by duty and, later, by a search for the knowledge needed to maintain the Brotherhood he would eventually mentor. As such, his uniform maintained a simplicity of design and lack of extravagance that helped define the character. Moreover, by fortunate happenstance, that simplicity made it the ideal template for every hero that would follow.

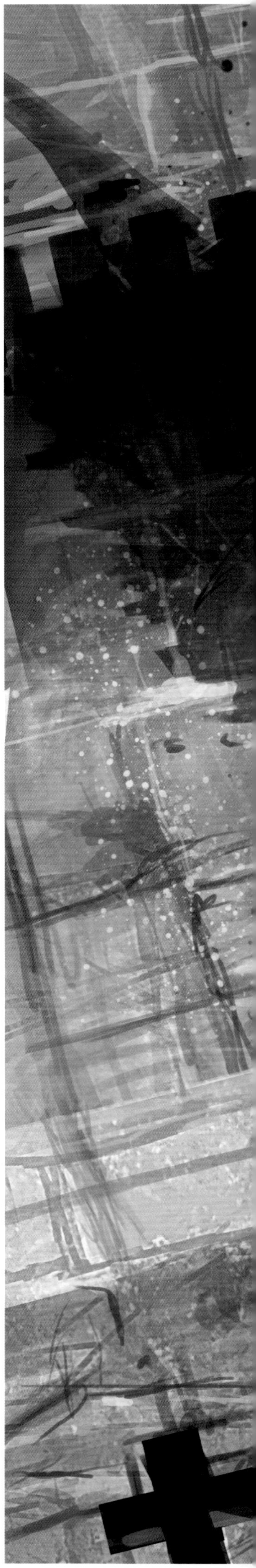

OPPOSITE: When Altaïr performs aerial moves such as the "Leap of Faith," his robes open like the wings of an eagle, giving him the appearance of weightlessness (Patrick Desgreniers).

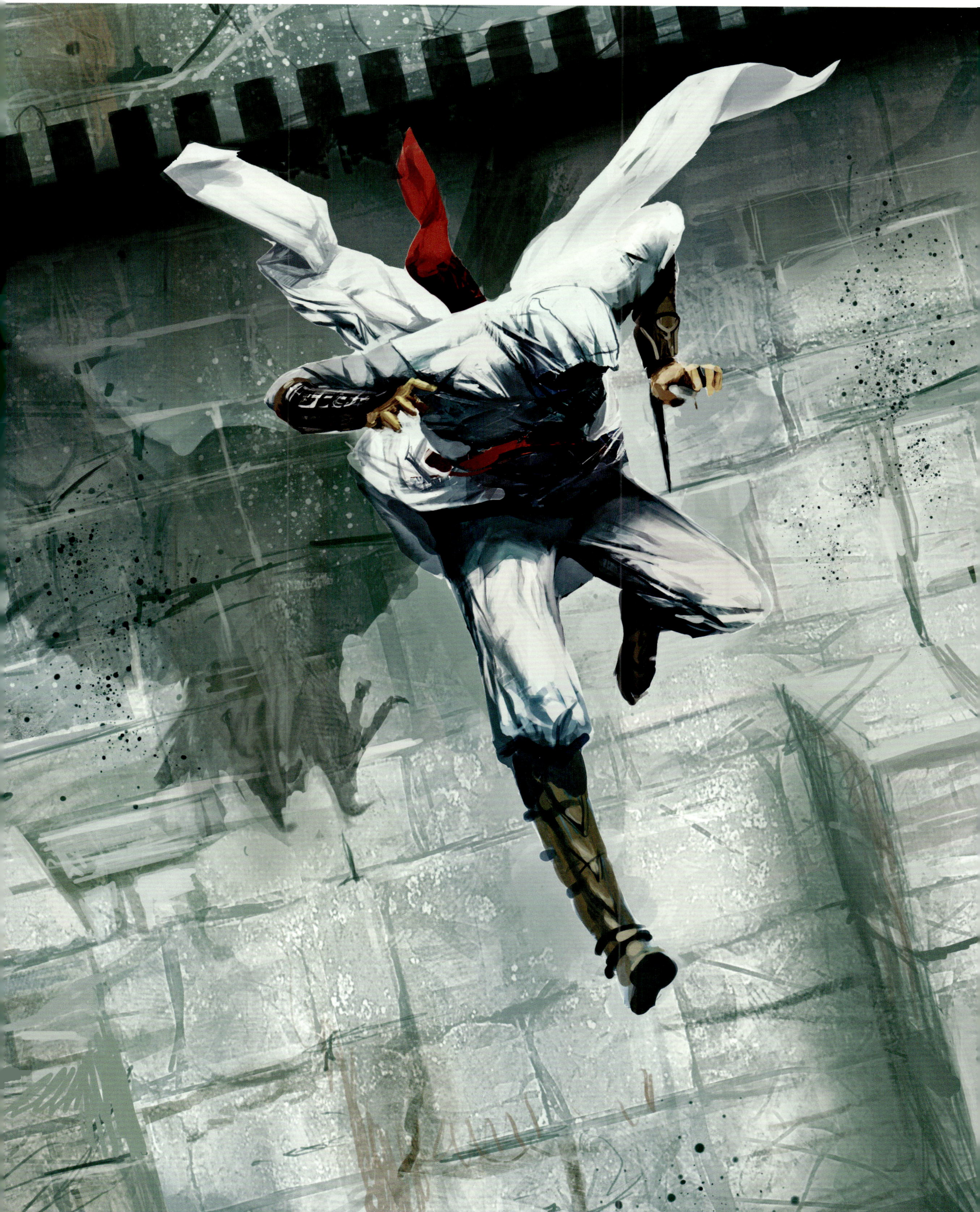

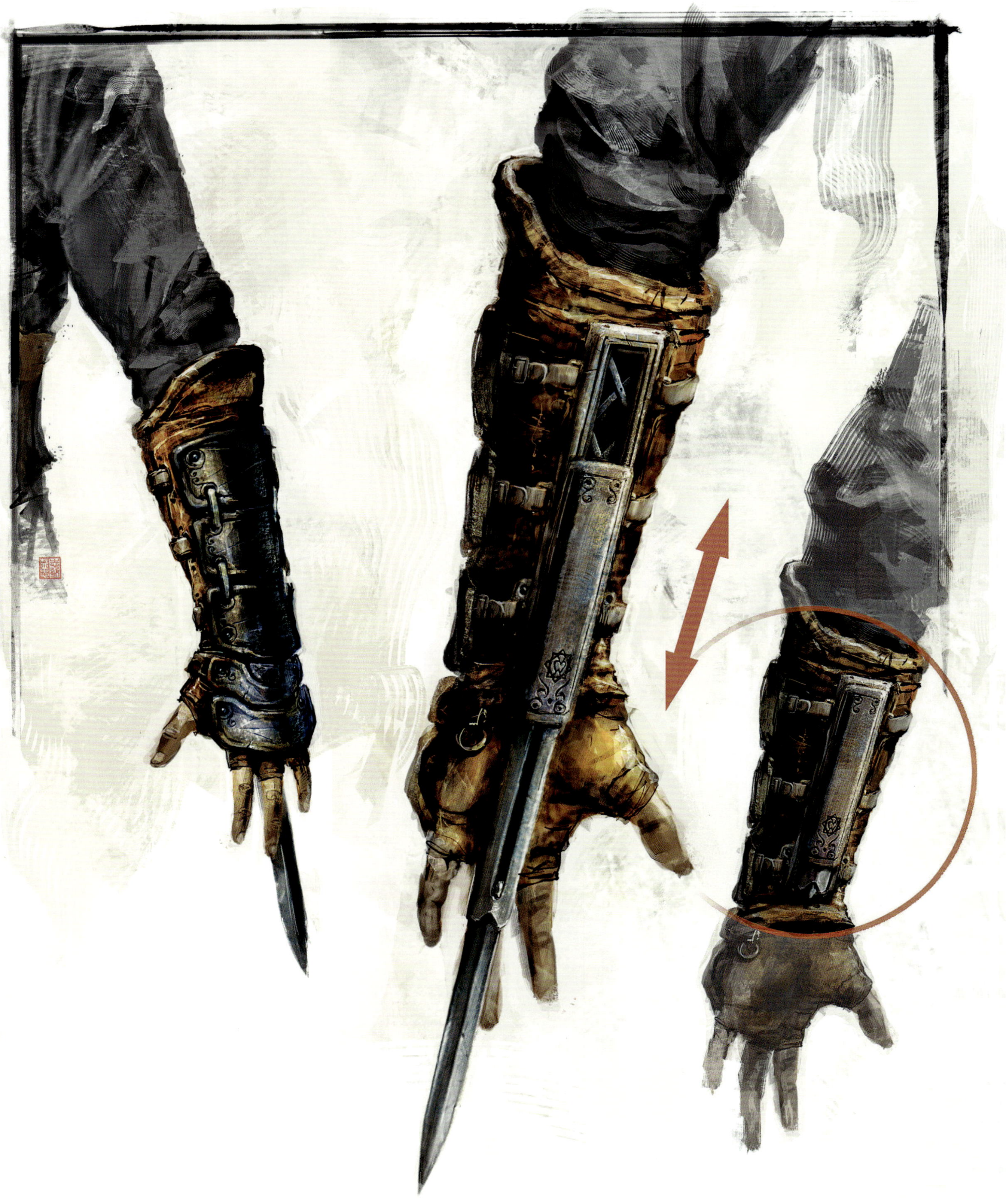

AN ICONIC WEAPON

The hidden blade has a special charm within the sphere of video game weapons. Its thoroughly improbable historical accuracy is forgiven in the same way we accept a hay bale as a perfectly reasonable landing pad for a jump from hundreds of feet above: because it's fun. The original blade was wrapped up in a brutal ceremony that included the loss of a finger, symbolizing its bearer's sacrifice to his or her duty. Not only did the hidden blade offer the final piece of Altaïr's ensemble, but in that first game, it doubled as the most powerful weapon—if you could nail the precise timing required.

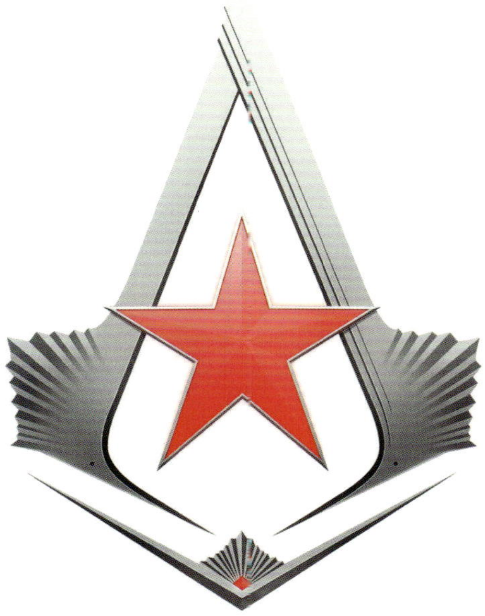

THE EVER-CHANGING CREST

Like Altaïr's iconic visual treatment, the now unmistakable Assassin's Creed logo is rooted in allusions to the eagle. The hooks on the bottom recall exposed claws. The raised tip suggests the beak. Within this framework, subsequent installments played with the concept, adding a skull to reflect a pirate flag, referencing the sharp cut of a French Revolution guillotine, and, most recently, the metalwork of the Industrial Revolution. Each version of the crest remains visually consistent but communicates the setting and the passage of time.

OPPOSITE: Early Assassins removed their ring fingers because they would be in the way of the blade. The practice was abandoned with the improved functionality of later iterations (Thierry Doizon).
THIS PAGE: Crests for *Assassin's Creed: The Fall*, *Assassin's Creed: Unity*, *Assassin's Creed III*, *Assassin's Creed IV: Black Flag*, and *Assassin's Creed: Syndicate*.

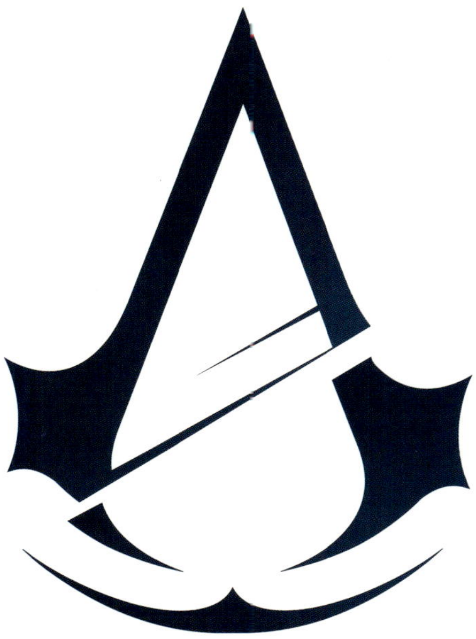

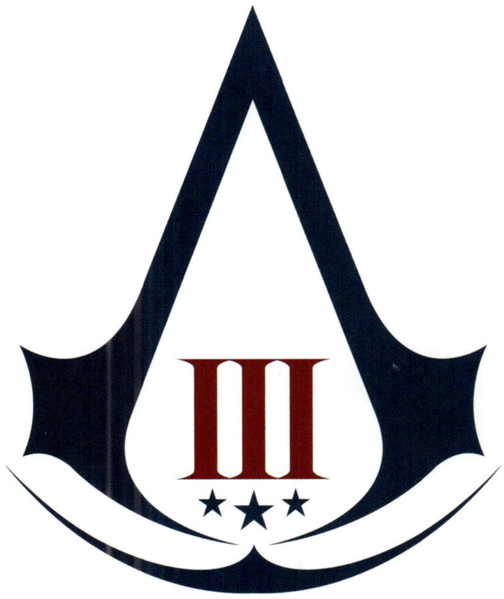

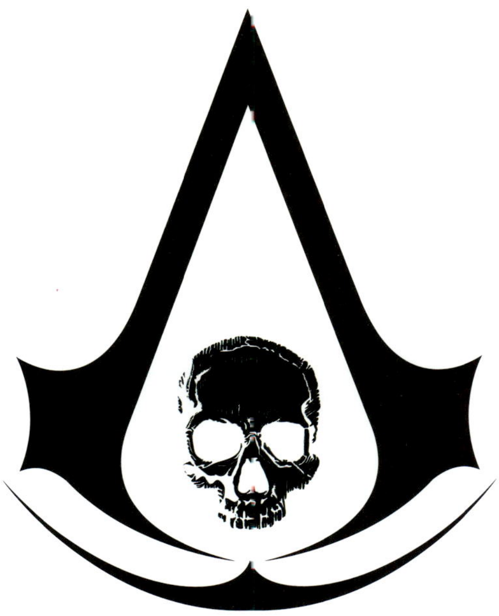

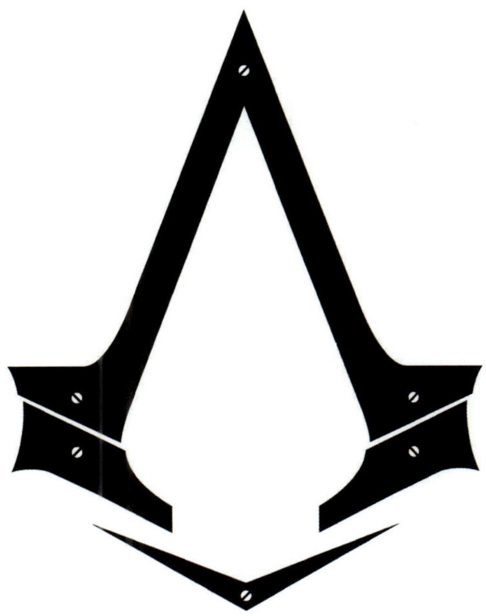

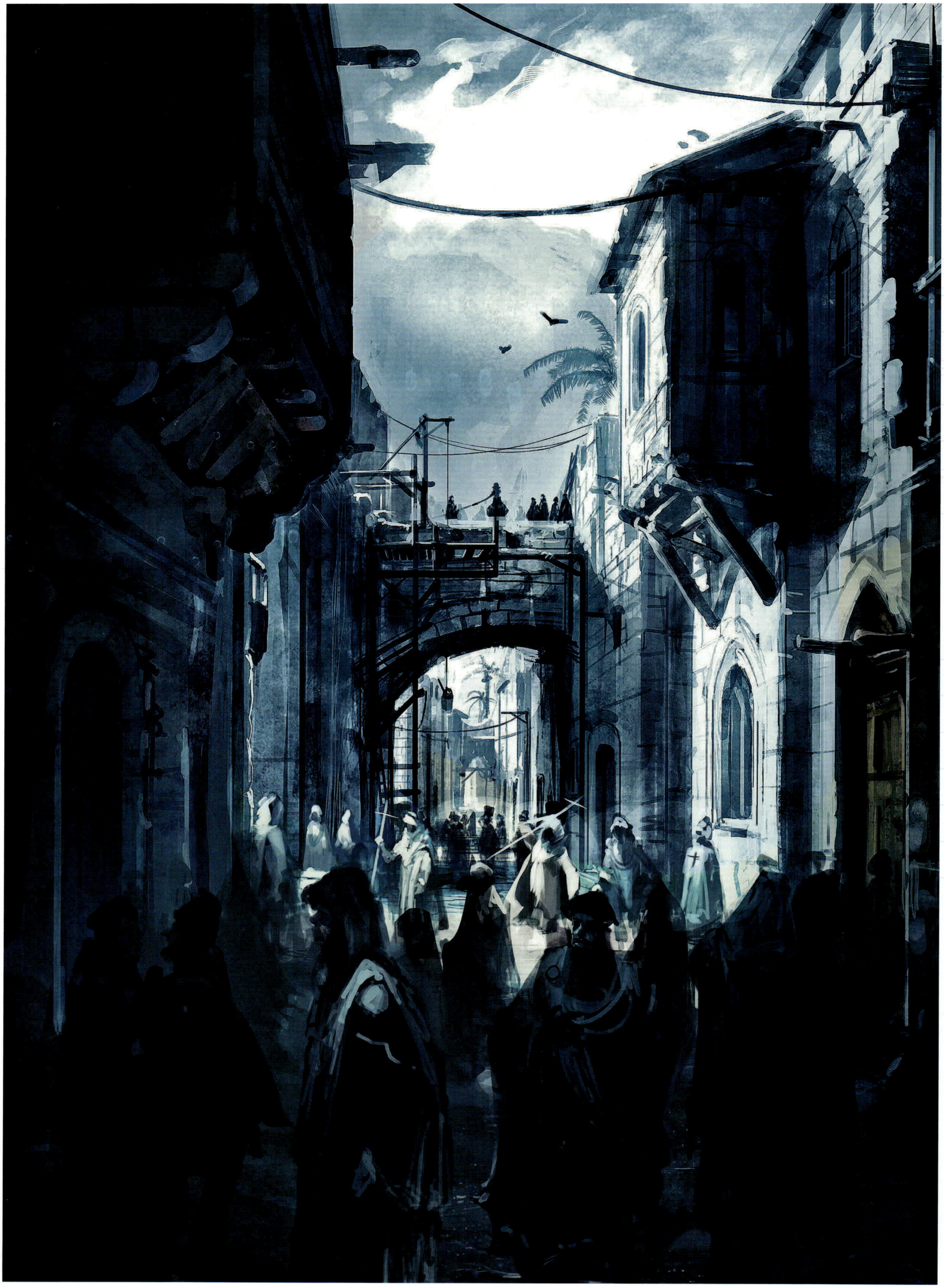

THREE PERSPECTIVES

While the tension of conflicting ideologies was a fundamental feature of *Assassin's Creed* from the outset, Ubisoft was careful not to paint the conflict in black and white or tie either the Assassins or Templars too closely to the religious paths that had defined each within recorded history. Altaïr's targets weren't chosen because of their worldly alliances, but because of their ties to the shadow conflict between these two ancient orders. But how do you reinforce that sentiment for players just entering this new world?

Ubisoft's novel solution came through a setting that demanded that its hero infiltrate every side of the Crusade across a vast open world. "You had to fight the Templars, but you could find them on different sides, or outside, of the historical conflicts of the time. After all, the Templars have always had their own agenda," Jean says. "In order to represent the wide variety of historical perspectives and cultures you would encounter, we decided that the cities that were featured needed to be visually clearly defined." A world took shape defined by three interconnected but distinct cities tied together by the open sprawl of a medieval rural kingdom. Each city would have a clear-cut and bold artistic direction and a defined purpose for communicating that singular moment in history during the summer of 1191. The cities also needed to reinforce the move away from *Prince of Persia* and help establish *Assassin's Creed* with its own visual identity. "We were very bold in the direction that we took," says Raphaël. "For each city, we chose a specific color palette and a stylized, almost monochromatic, treatment. At this point, the very beginning of *Assassin's Creed*, we wanted to establish a clear visual contrast between the franchises."

Individual cities were defined by their place in culture and history. Acre had borne the brunt of the Crusaders' assault, and its ruined buildings and bleak gray and blue color palette expressed the ravages it had faced. New construction brought Christian churches into the landscape while simultaneously offering exciting high points from which to observe a target. "Acre was a city that had just been through a big war and was almost destroyed," Raphaël says. "So the mood of the city is relatively dark with a lot of deep gray and blue tones. The feeling when you enter Acre is that of a war-torn place, heavy and grim." Damascus was crafted in sharp contrast to Acre's ruined visage. The city was richly draped in the splendor of Arabic art and tradition. Rich, golden mosques dominated the horizon. Huge sprawling markets depicted merchants hawking their silken wares. The bright yellows were a striking contrast to Acre's bleak blues. "Damascus has a more Arabic style," Raphaël says. "The city was rich and opulent, and featured magnificent architecture, like the incredible Mosque of Umayyad. Damascus was designed to evoke a very distinct feeling. It's a city of huge markets with beautiful riads and an impressive skyline filled with domes and minarets." Jerusalem stood in contrast to both Acre and Damascus. Its streets embraced lively colors and the grand colliding of cultures. "The visual treatment of Jerusalem featured gradients of orange, yellow, and green," says Raphaël. "The city had an atmosphere that was lush, and very spiritual, reflecting its religious importance." Holy sites devoted to various faiths abounded across the city, including Solomon's famed temple, which housed one of the Apples of Eden that would spur so much of the conflict to follow throughout the subsequent stories. Multiple forces vied for the city, and Altaïr would need to bring down targets on all sides.

The color and architecture distinctions between the cities did more than create visual variety. Each city provided a different perspective on the cultural climate of the Third Crusade, even as Altaïr's own adventure intersected with historical events. Players bore witness to multiple perspectives on the war, but the battle between Assassin and Templar transcended that conflict. "We purposely never touched religion or politics, and we centered the narrative of the game on the underlying conflict between the Assassins and Templars," Jean says. "Because of that, we could include characters that may have had differing personal convictions, but it wouldn't affect the core of our story."

OPPOSITE: The cold blue coloring of Acre gave the city a modern and war-torn atmosphere (Nicolas Bouvier).

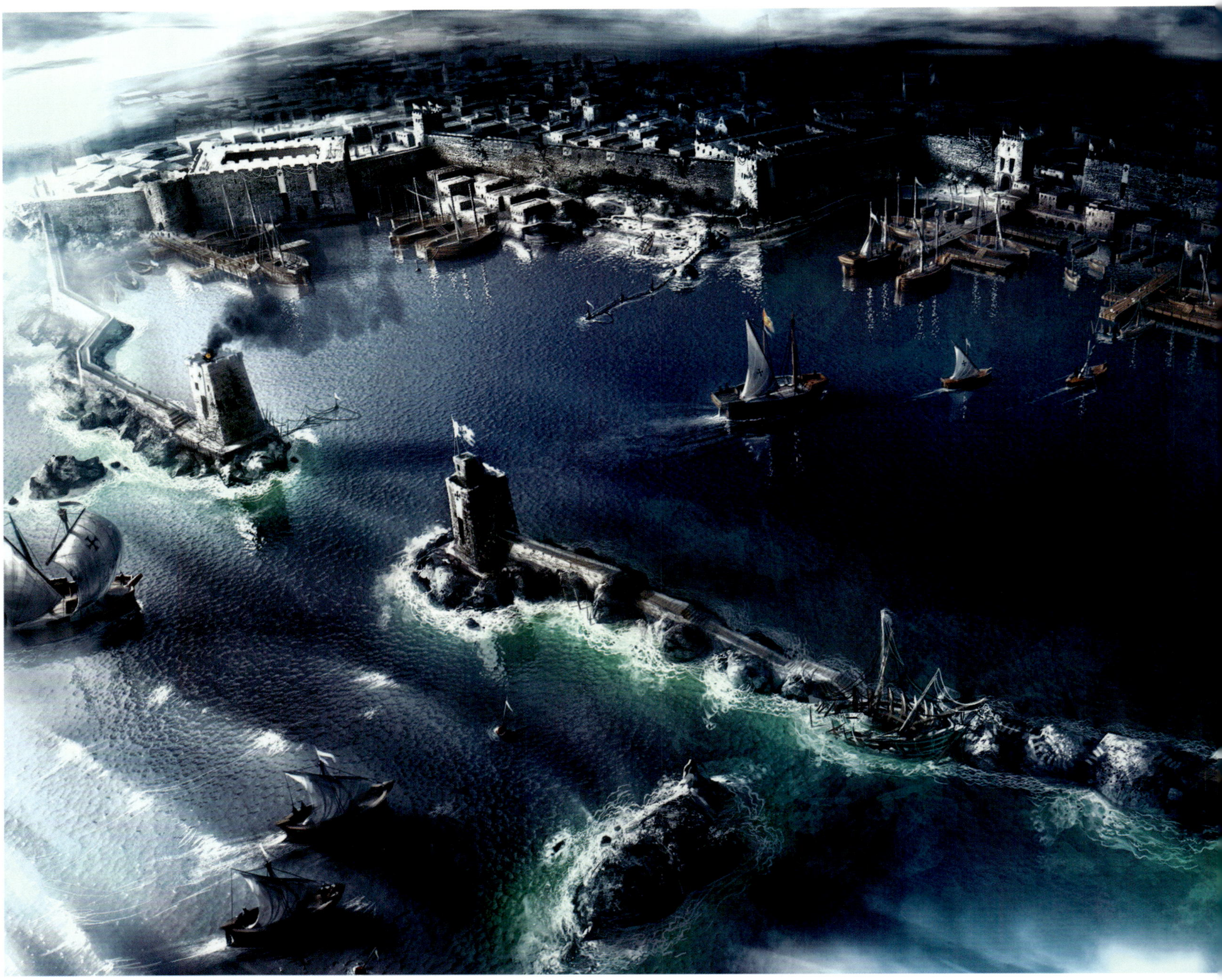

THIS PAGE: Acre presented a diverse mixture of Christian and Muslim architecture and designs (David Levy, Nicolas Bouvier, Patrick Desgreniers).
FOLLOWING PAGES: Award-winning artwork of the Damascus bazaar (Nicolas Bouvier and Patrick Desgreniers).

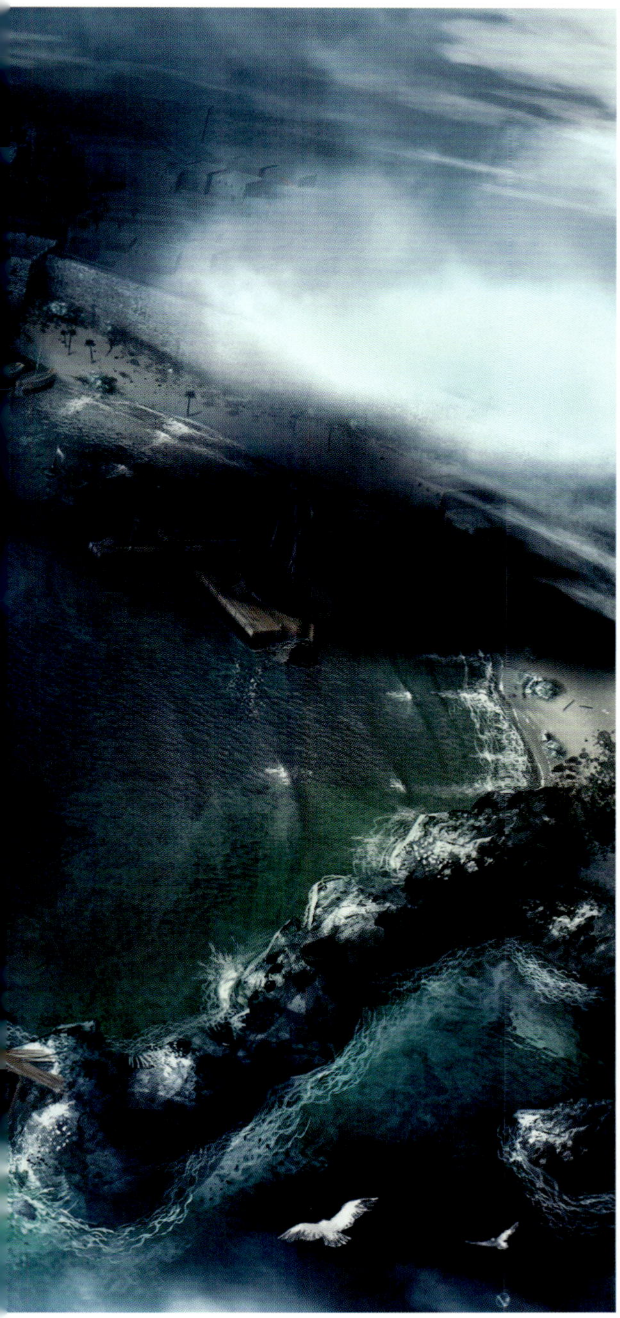

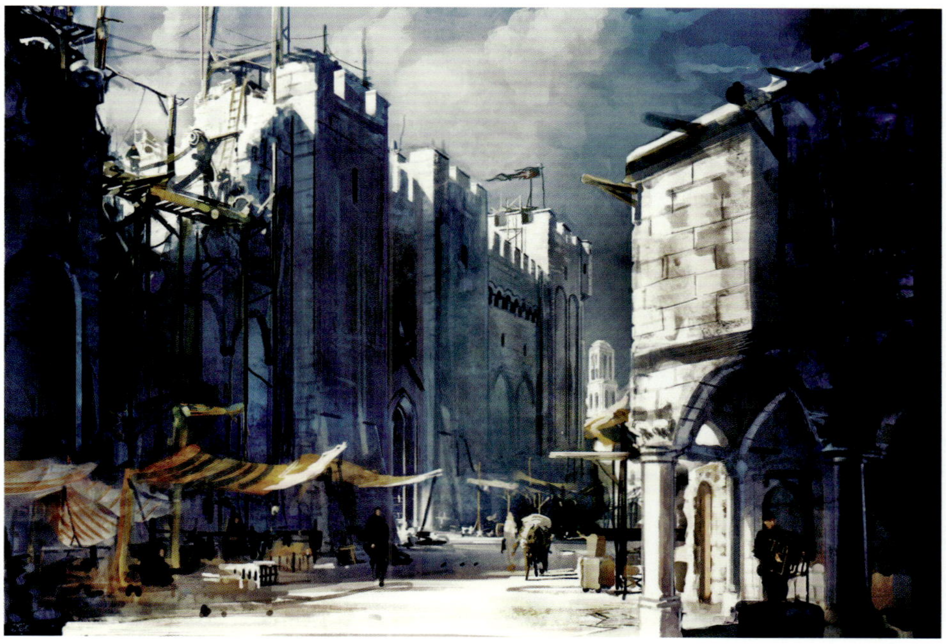

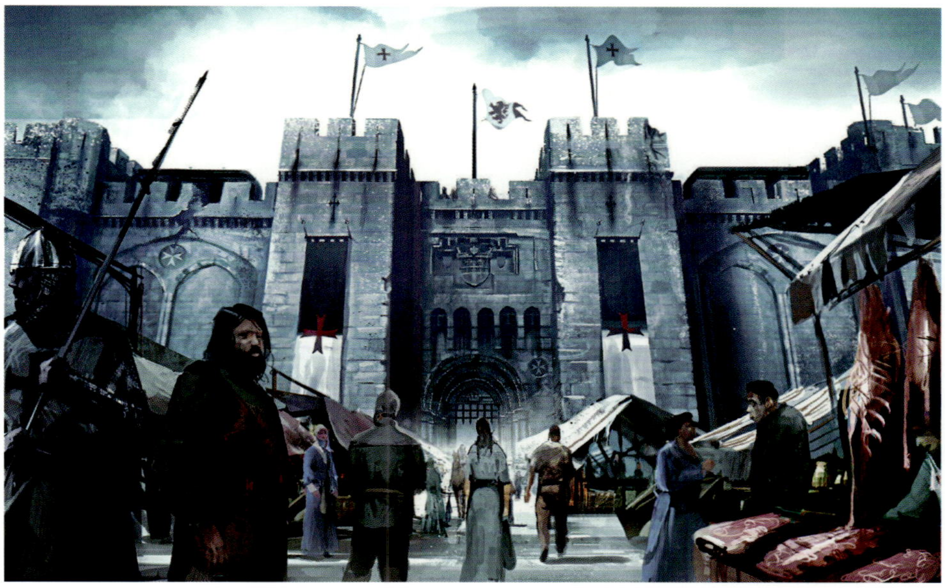

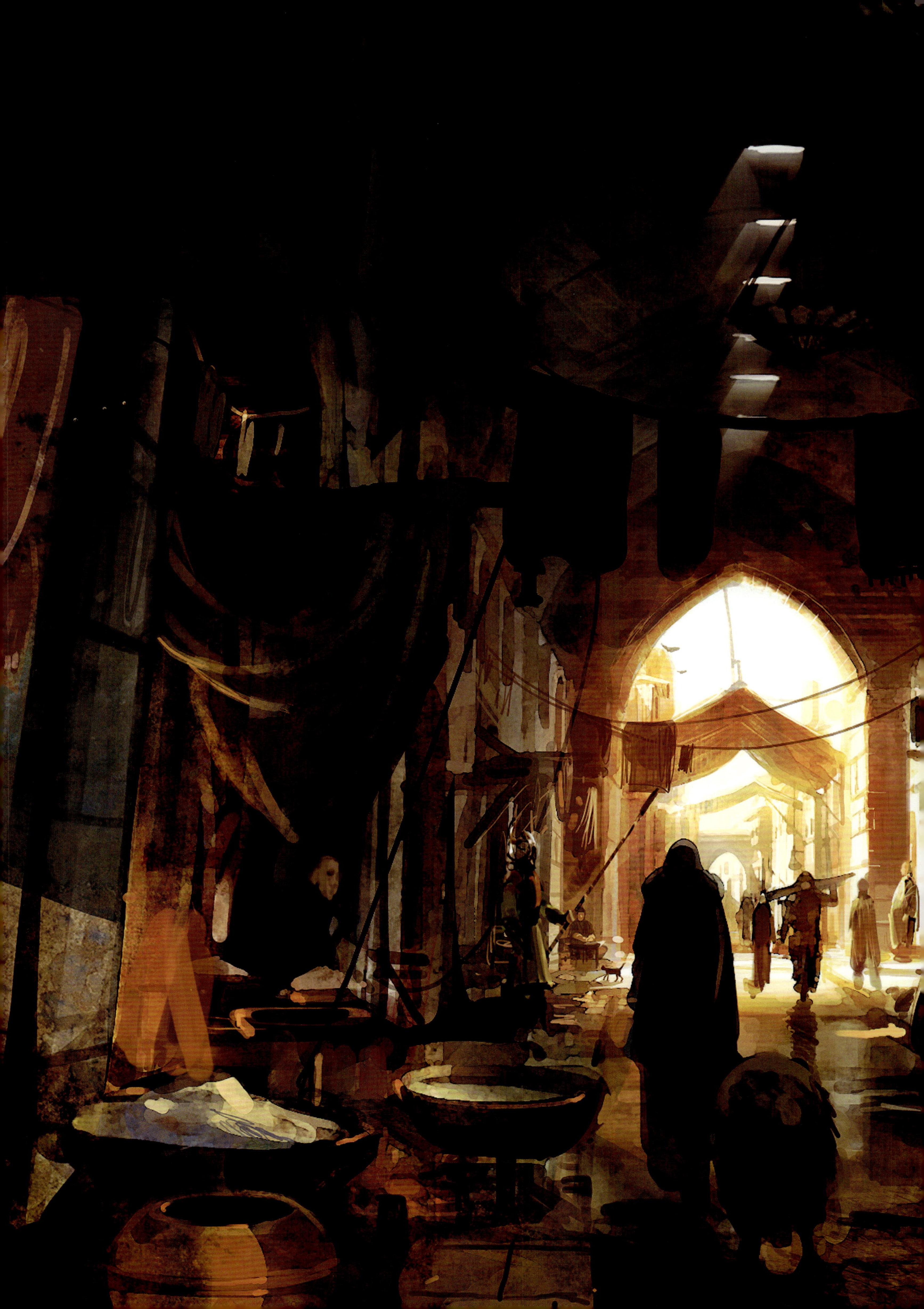

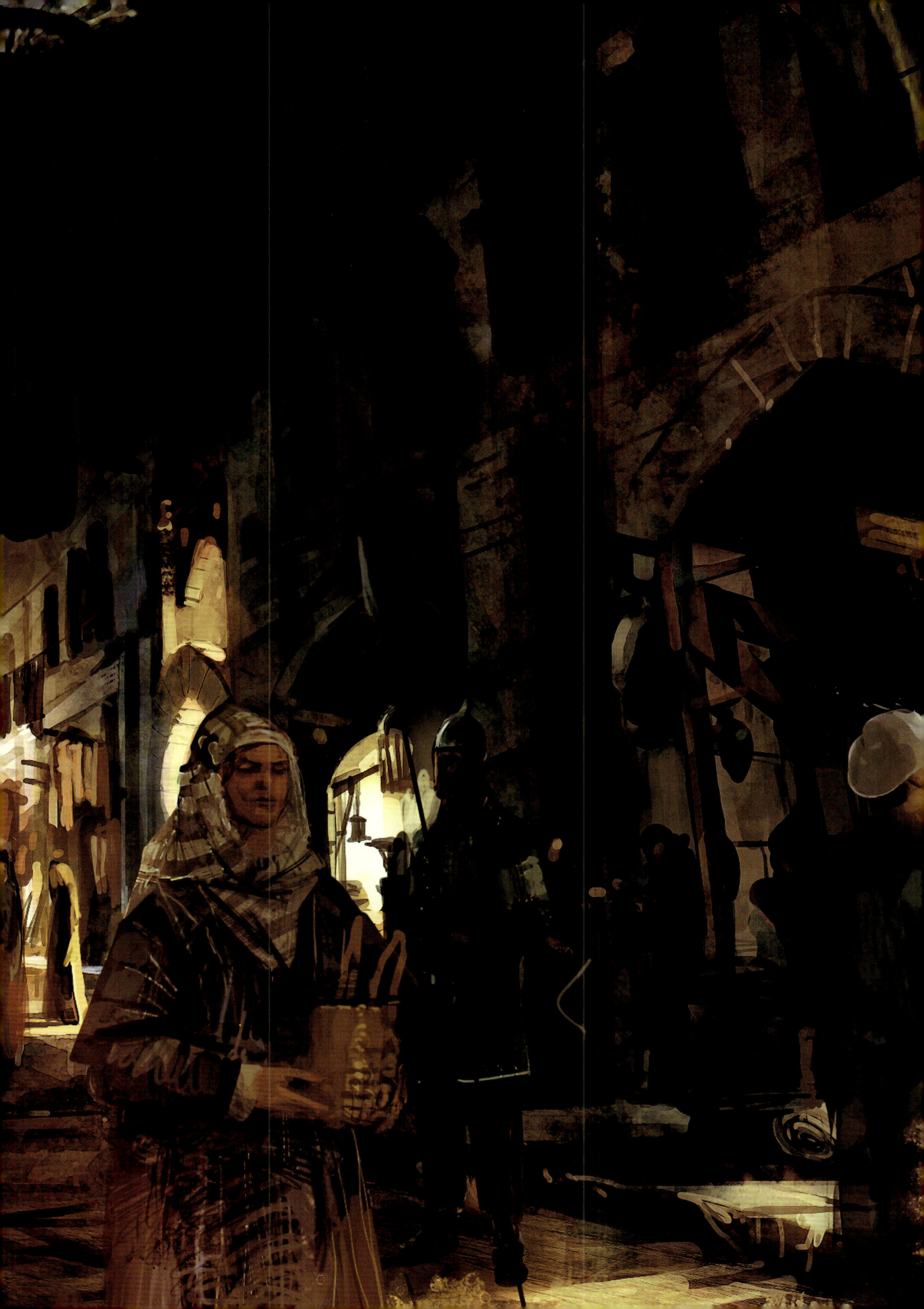

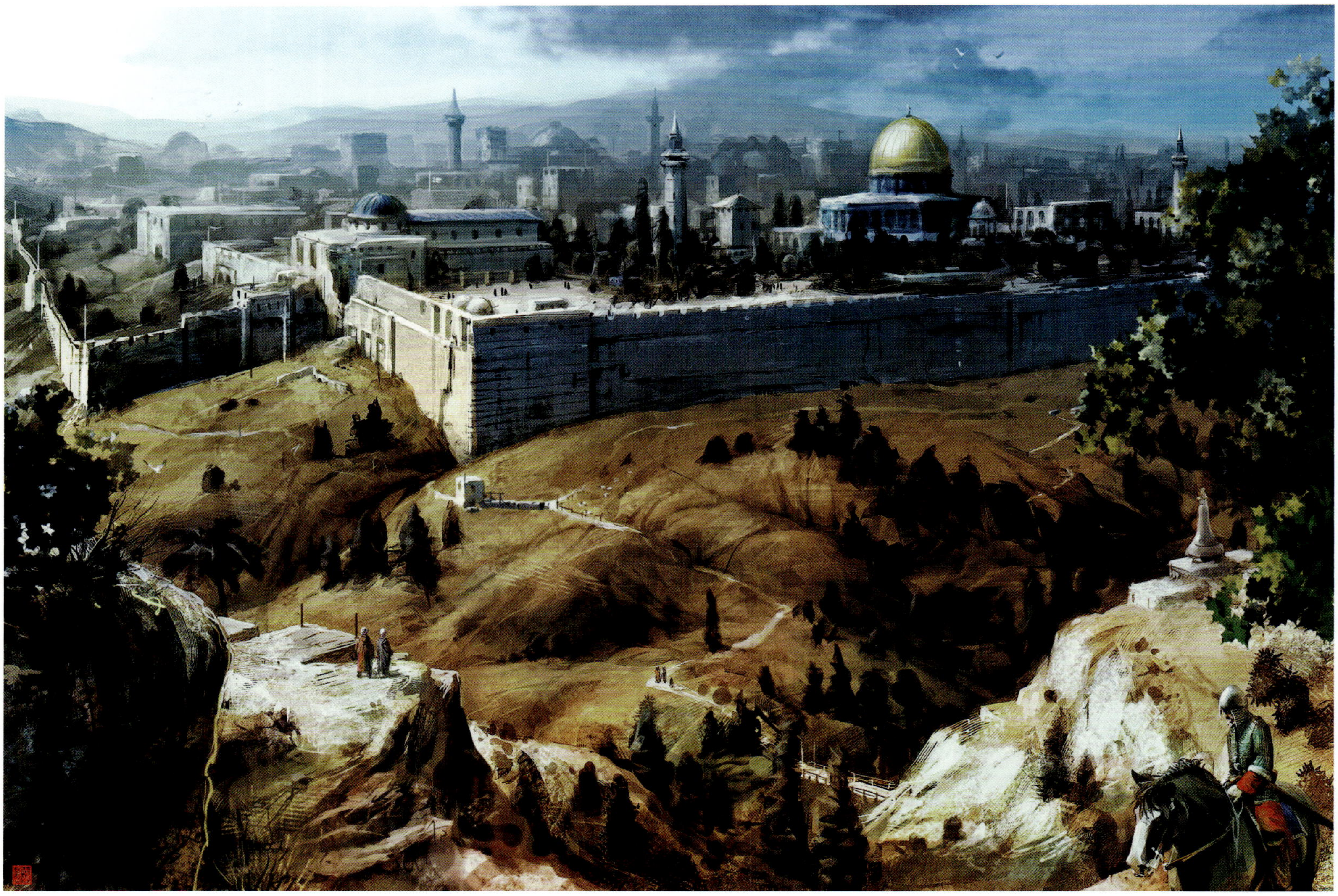

THIS PAGE: Ubisoft artists designed the city of Jerusalem to be as accurate as possible to the actual city's layout in the third century (Thierry Doizon).

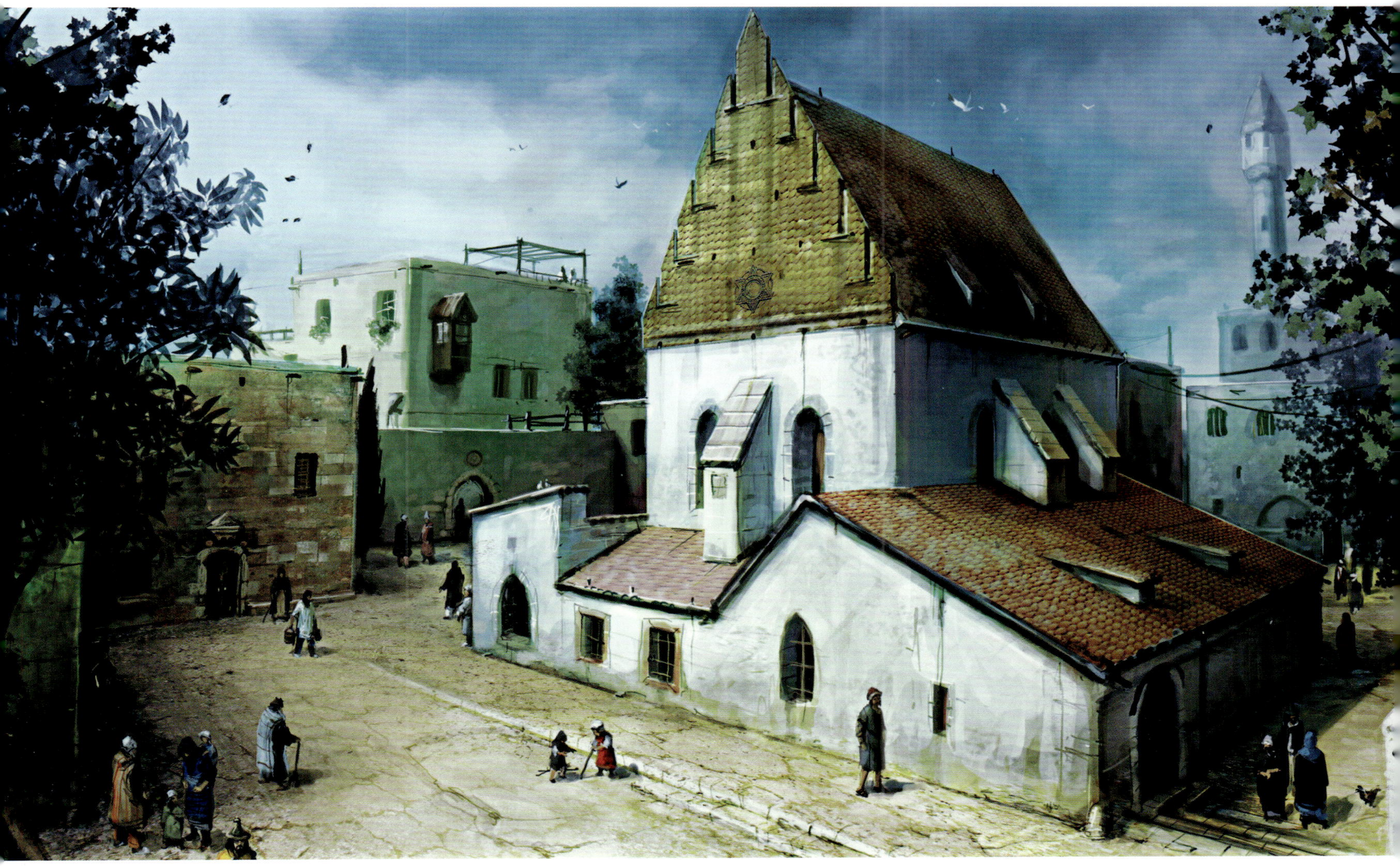

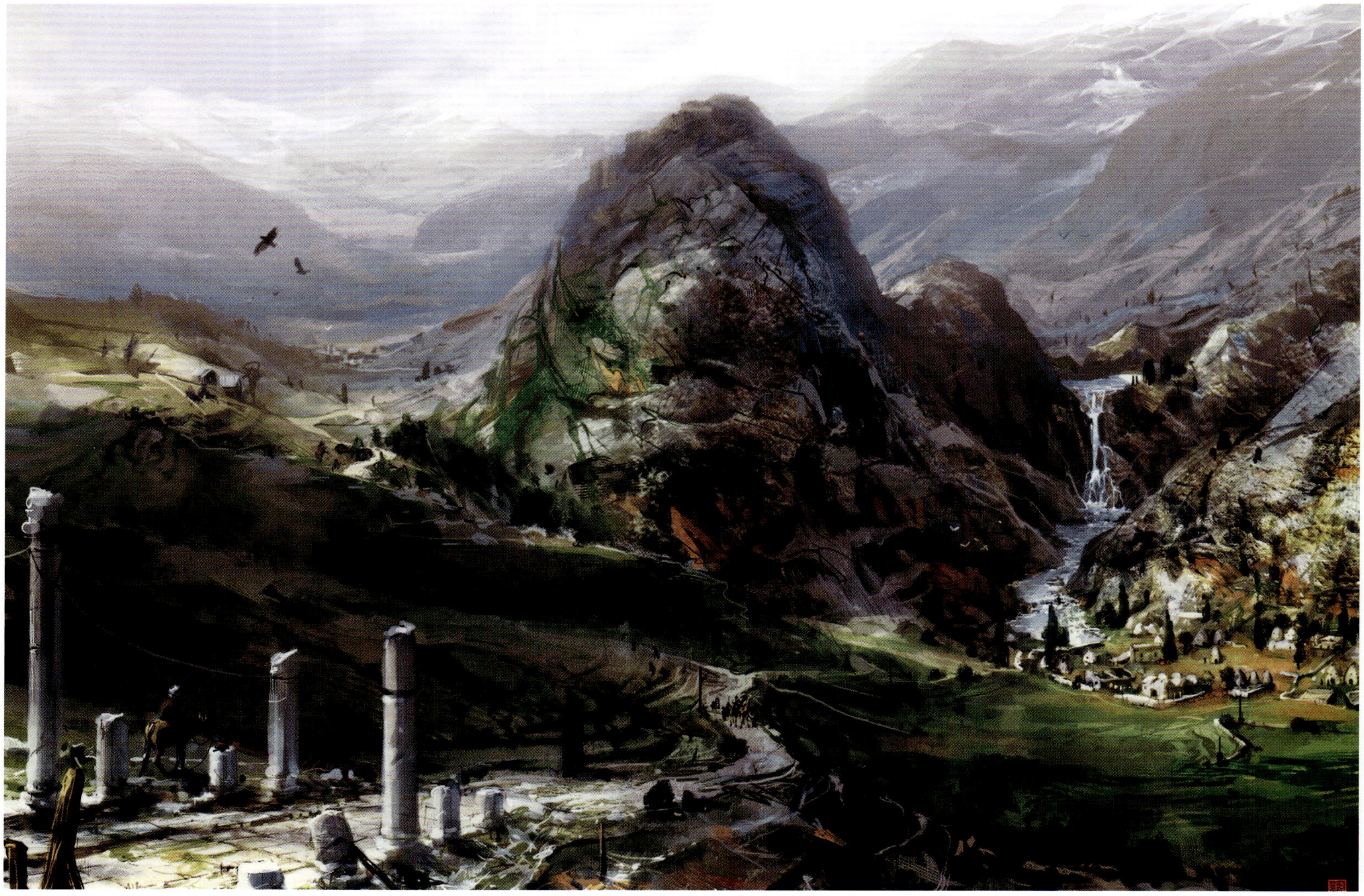

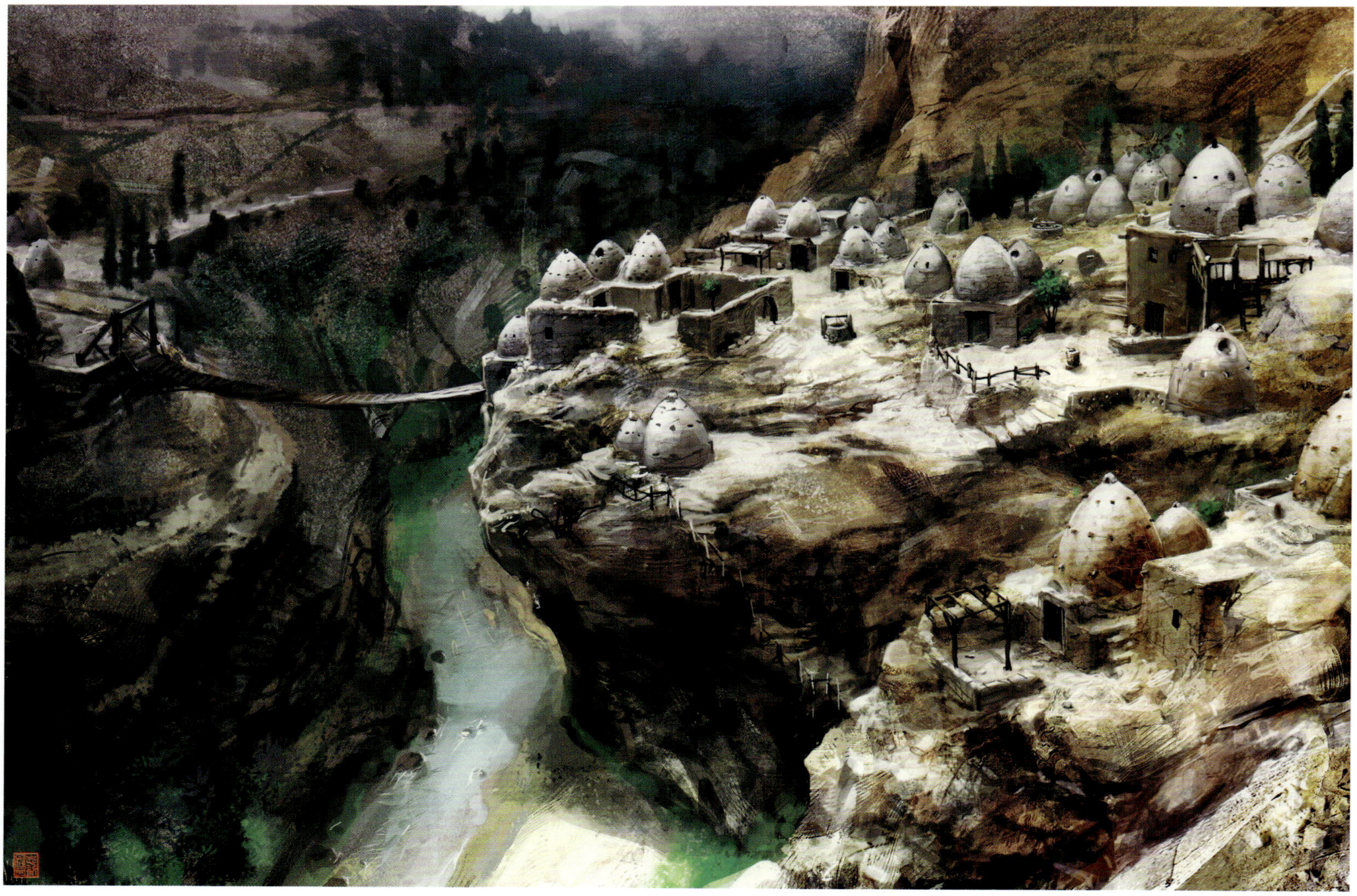

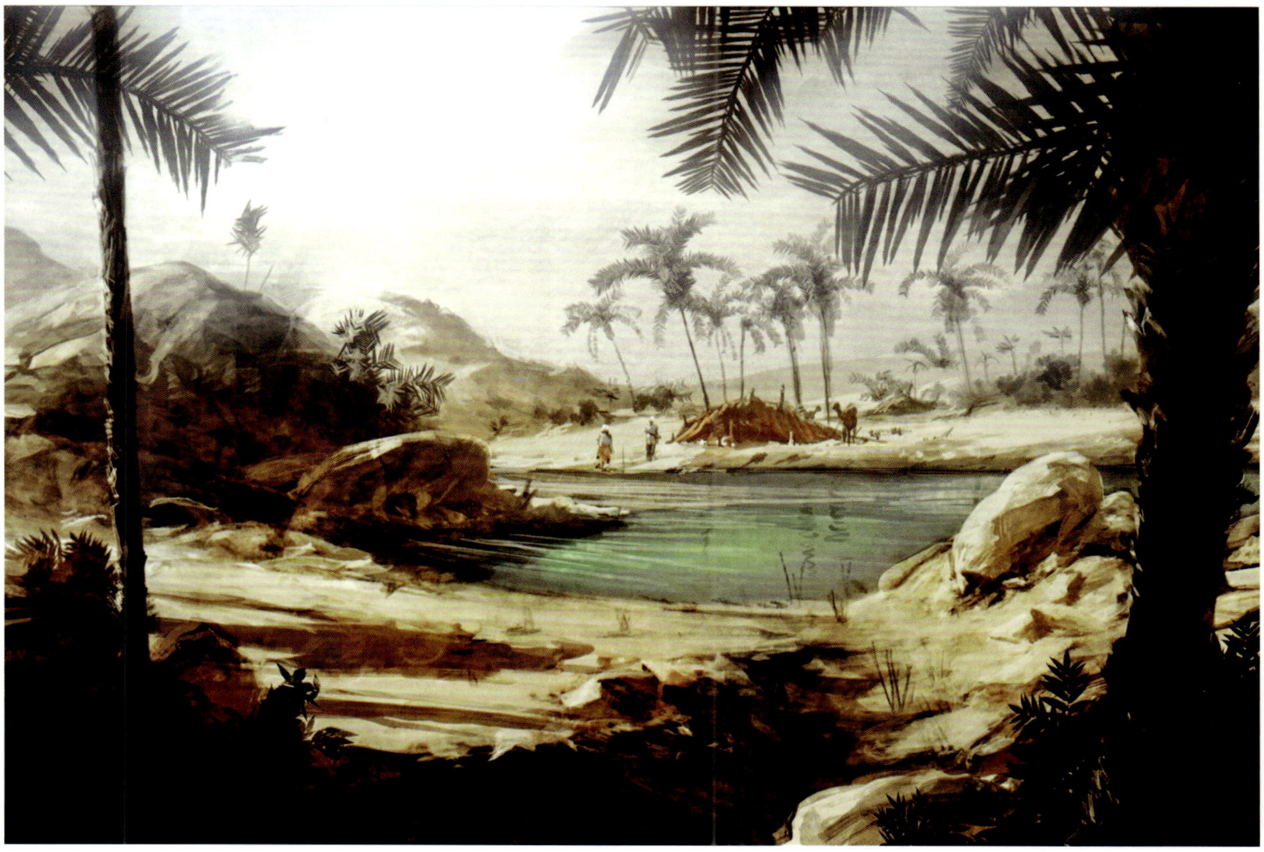

CONNECTING CONFLICTS

OPPOSITE TOP: The Kingdom represents both a physical and a spiritual journey between cities (Thierry Doizon).
OPPOSITE BOTTOM: Concept art of a village in the North Kingdom (Thierry Doizon).
ABOVE: An oasis in the North Kingdom stands in sharp contrast to the war-torn and heavily populated cities (Thierry Doizon).

The three distinct urban locales provided the bulk of *Assassin's Creed*'s action, but a sense of authenticity and immersion would have been absent if the player simply loaded back and forth between chosen cities without ever seeing how they were interconnected or why our hero needed to travel between them.

The Kingdom provided a large part of the solution. Here was a vast landscape of hills and plains and a low-lying lake that led into tortuous mountain paths. Ancient ruins alluded to the cultures that had come before. Small villages dotted the landscape, ensuring a sense of life outside the cities. "I love the way we re-created certain areas of ancient Syria and the Middle East," Raphaël says. "We included many elements and details, like small villages, oases, and ruins in the mountains, to give the area the unique flavor of a journey." From an artistic perspective, the Kingdom also allowed the team to make a more gradual transition between the stark colors and emotional vibe of each of the major cities. "The landscape was a hub between the cities," Raphaël says. "Not many fights occur there—it's a very nice, spiritual passage between all the cities." The Kingdom included fewer opportunities for gameplay than the cities. But as a first pass at integrating a wild environment, it provided a sense of epic scale that the original *Assassin's Creed* would have otherwise lacked. The series would not return to such a large-scale treatment of open wilderness until the American Frontier of *Assassin's Creed III*.

If the Kingdom explained how Altaïr traversed between the major cities, Masyaf answered the question of why. Modeled after one of the authentic bases of the historical Assassins in Syria, the castle of Masyaf as it appears in *Assassin's Creed* is a striking edifice. "The road to Masyaf was something extraordinary; it offered visually interesting moments," Raphaël says. "The player would pass through the Arch of Palmyra, a famous landmark in Syria, and though it might not be set in the right geographical location, it would create a very memorable transition." Towering over the small village it protects, the Assassins' hideout could only be reached by a dangerous series of switchbacks and narrow canyons that led to a small gatehouse and into an open courtyard filled with Assassins learning their trade.

The Assassins' retreat has an air of strength and unyielding fortitude, and its high mountain seat echoed the Assassins' preferred perch high above their prey. Masyaf also introduced one of the rarely broken rules of the franchise: Every Assassin needs a remarkable place to call home.

SETTING A TONE

In later years, the Ubisoft development teams behind subsequent Assassin's Creed games have followed "history is our playground" as a guiding mantra, but in the beginning, history was instead a blank slate ripe for interpretation. How closely did Assassin's Creed need to stick to the historical timeline? Where did the history end and the fiction begin? And from an art direction standpoint, what sacrifices could be made in the balance between accuracy and grandeur?

The first *Assassin's Creed* established a benchmark. Whenever possible, history needed to be respected, with major moments acknowledged rather than ignored. As the historical data became less concrete, so too did the team's devotion to rigid presentation. By the second game in the franchise, the developers would codify it as the "Rule of Thirty Seconds." "Everything in terms of location, people, and events that we wanted to put in the game was determined by the Rule of Thirty Seconds—everything would need to be easily found within that timeframe in a basic Google search. We needed to be precise," Jean explains. If the date of a target's death is hard to ignore, then it was important to the team to get it right. But if the circumstances around that death are less known or are open to interpretation, the team is offered room to play.

The castle at Masyaf proves the concept. Quick Internet investigations reveal its historical existence and show off its imposing walls, but the details are nebulous. What of the quaint village at the castle's base? Or the surrounding landscape? In many cases, bending the rules to produce that awe-inspiring moment as you gallop headlong toward the castle was worth the blurring of historical veracity. "With Masyaf, we amplified the size of the castle, and we exaggerated the mountain behind the village, because we wanted to create an epic stage that would inspire emotion and awe," Raphaël says.

As *Assassin's Creed* took shape, one of the defining voices behind that vision was Patrice Désilets. As creative director in the early days of the franchise, his contributions helped shape what would come later. "For Patrice, *Assassin's Creed* was not just a video game," says Jean. "He was always pushing us to think about it as an entertainment experience." Patrice insisted on the importance of authenticity in the Animus experience. Game mechanics and visual presentation needed to be explainable within the constraints of the DNA-reading computer and not pull players out into perceiving the game elements any more than was necessary. "He was not afraid to try things that seemed radical, even if in the end they didn't make it," Jean says.

While many fans were disappointed when Patrice left Ubisoft in 2010, it's clear that by that point the team and franchise had become far more than any one individual and had started a locomotive that wasn't halting any time soon. "When I first joined *Assassin's Creed*, it already had a certain aura," Jean says. "This was the big one. What really struck me at that time was the humility of the people. They were not actually conscious of the beast they were creating. The team was doing something that was bigger than the sum of all of us. It was sad when Patrice left, but people come and go, and it's the team spirit that makes us feel like we are part of something bigger."

Working together, the artists on the first *Assassin's Creed* established a firm visual framework rife with possibility, and players recognized that potential for the franchise to grow into something more. With Altaïr now at the height of his power, the Third Crusade made for a compelling setting and left many eager to spend more time in the Middle Ages. But Ubisoft had other plans.

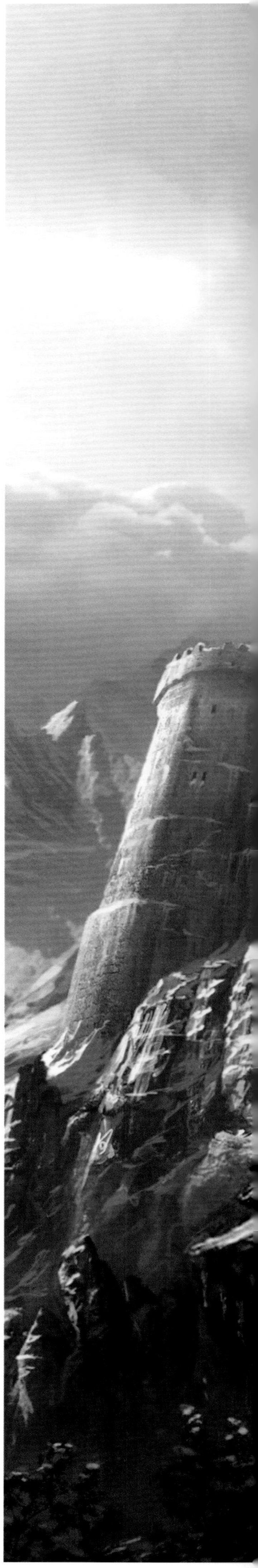

OPPOSITE: Arrival at Masyaf (Raphaël Lacoste).

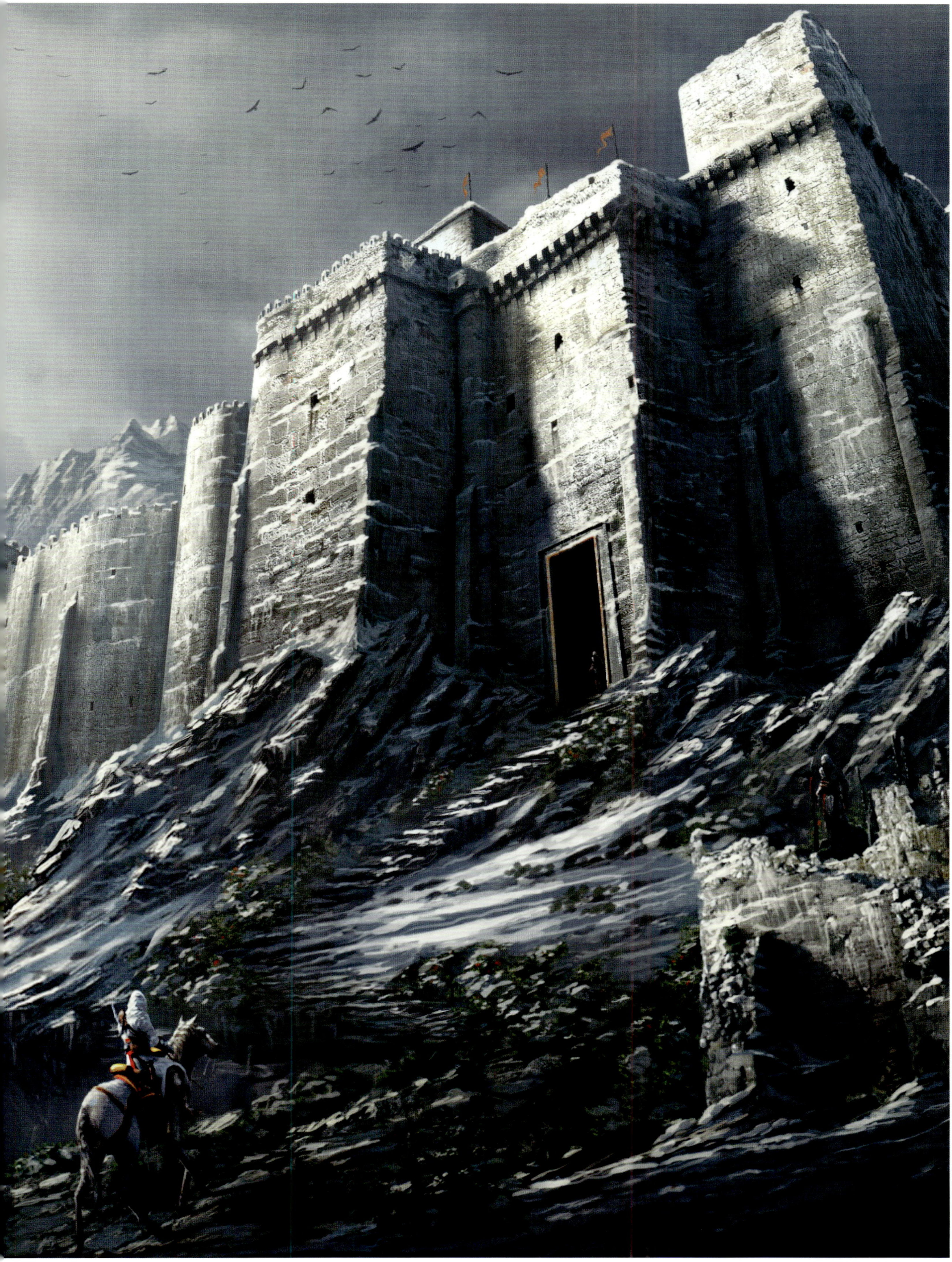

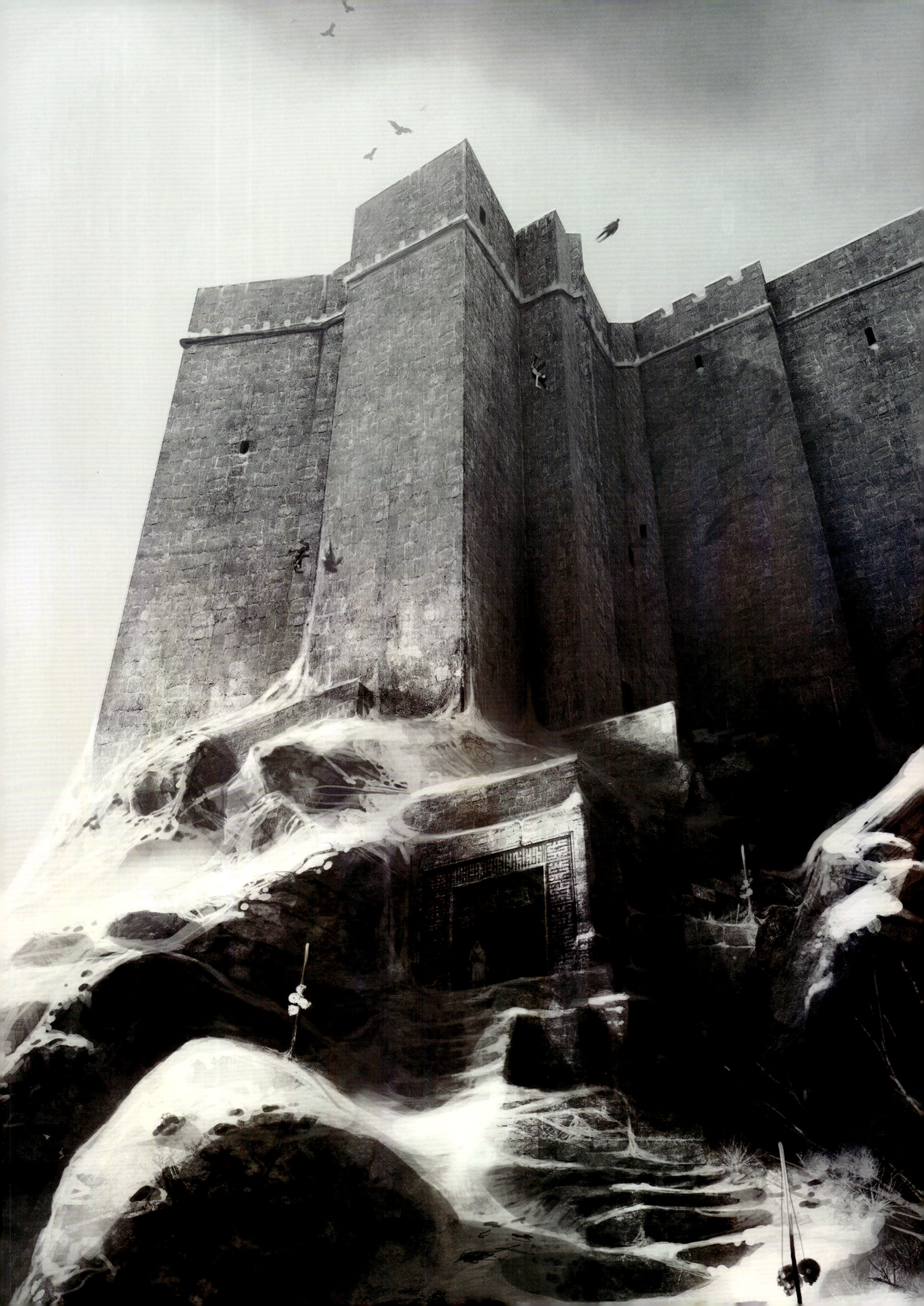

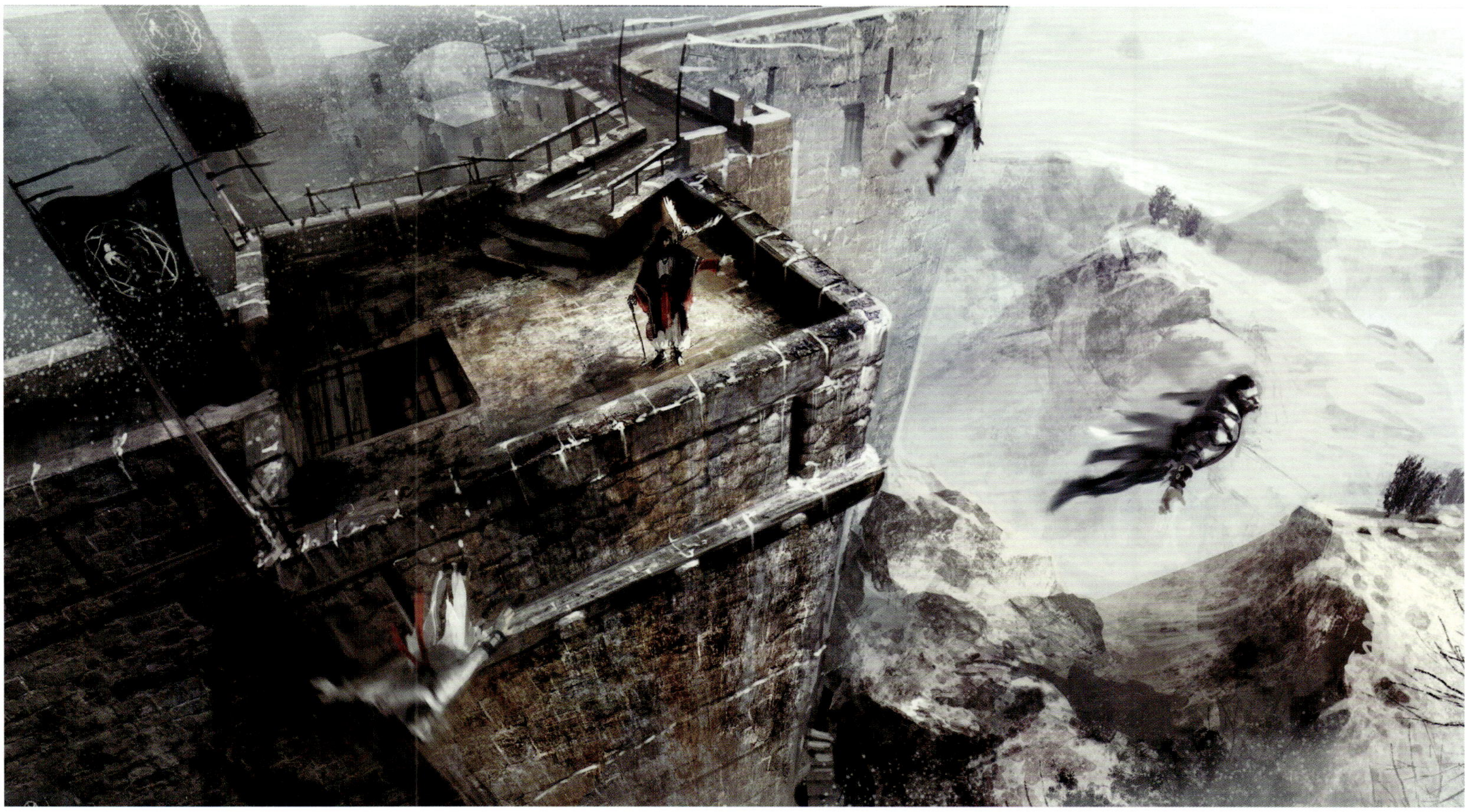

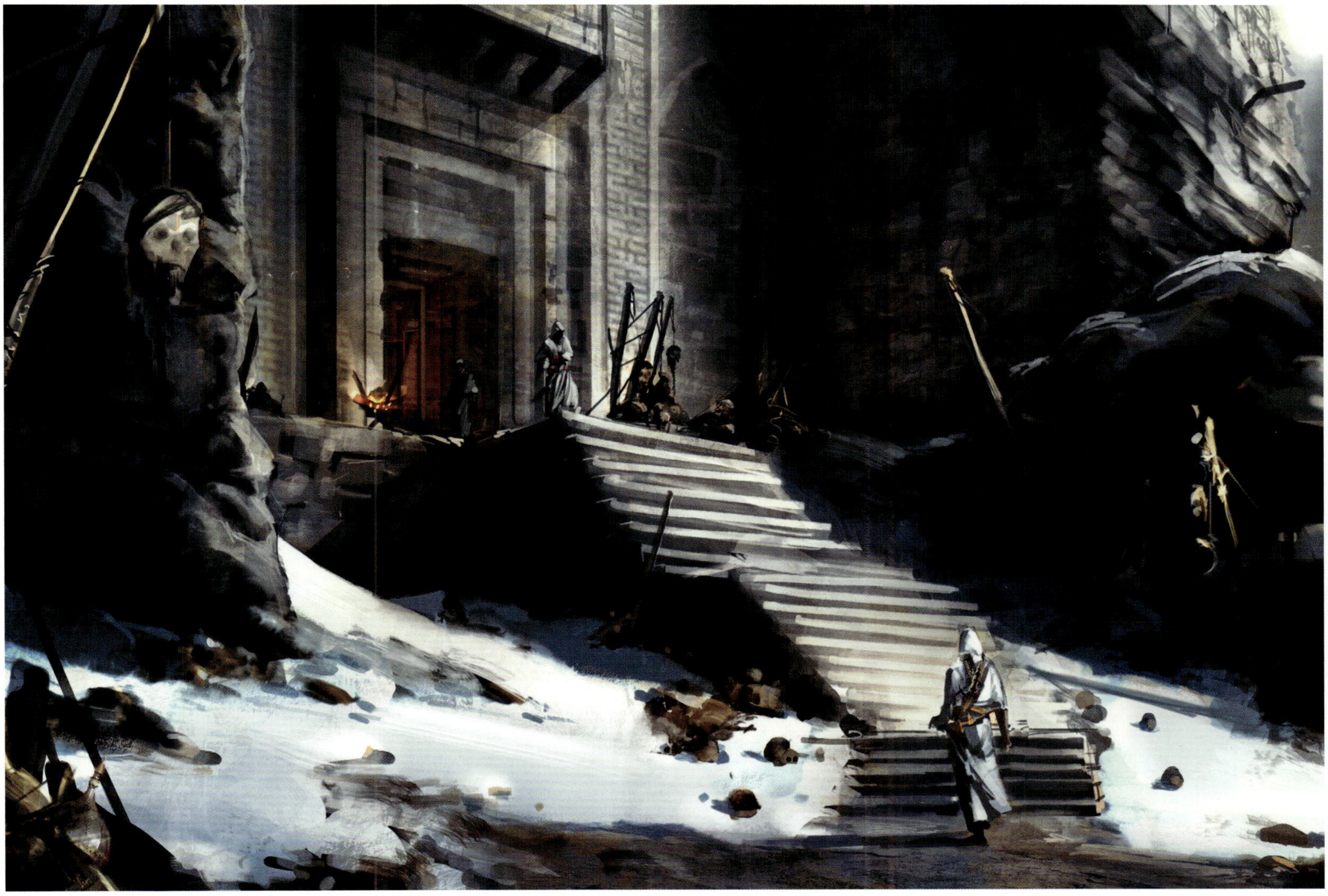

THESE PAGES: A dramatic structure in the mountains, Masyaf made for a powerful and mysterious base for the Assassin Brotherhood (David Levy, Artist Unknown).
FOLLOWING PAGES: Altaïr rides through the Arch of Palmyra in the North Kingdom (Raphaël Lacoste).

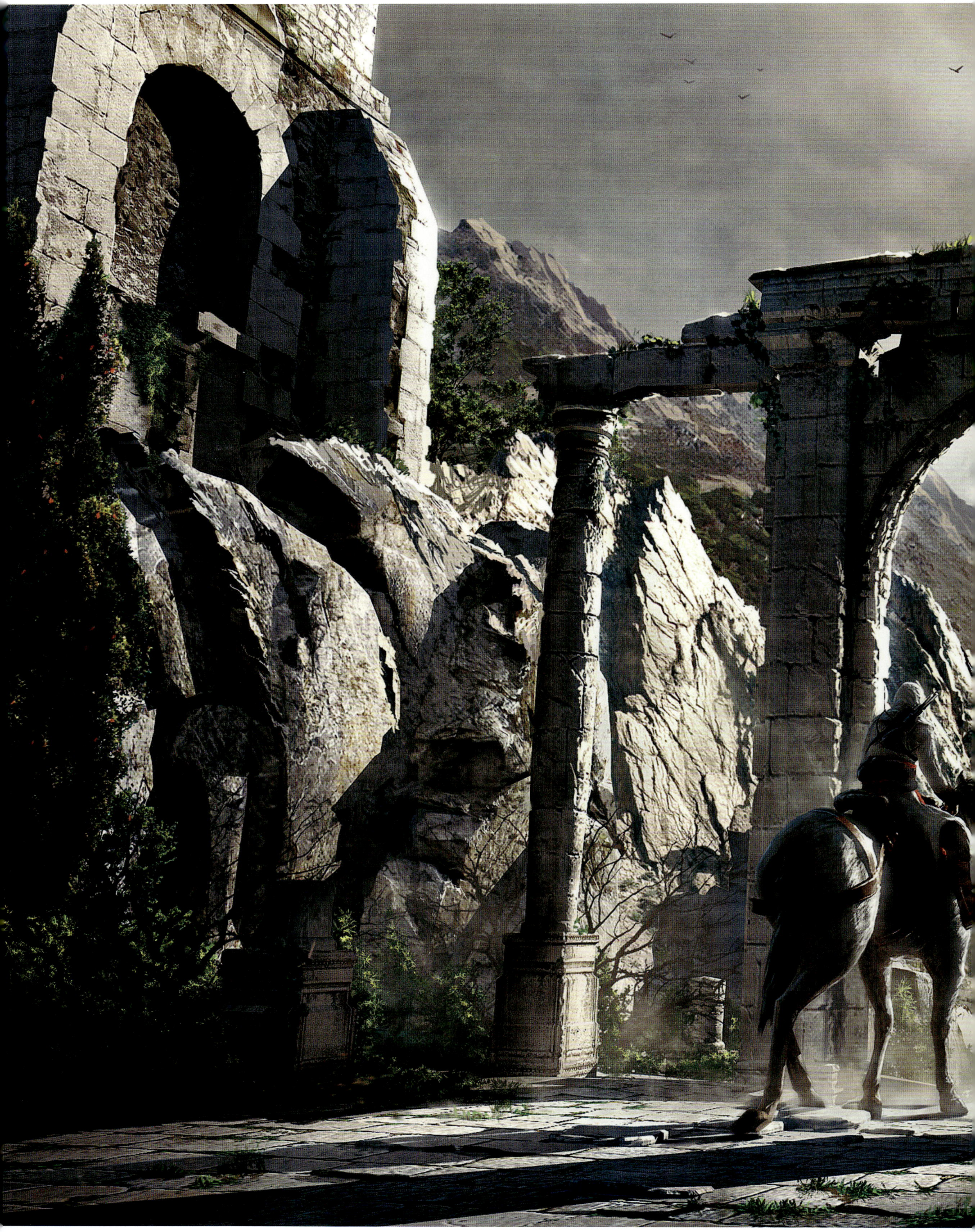

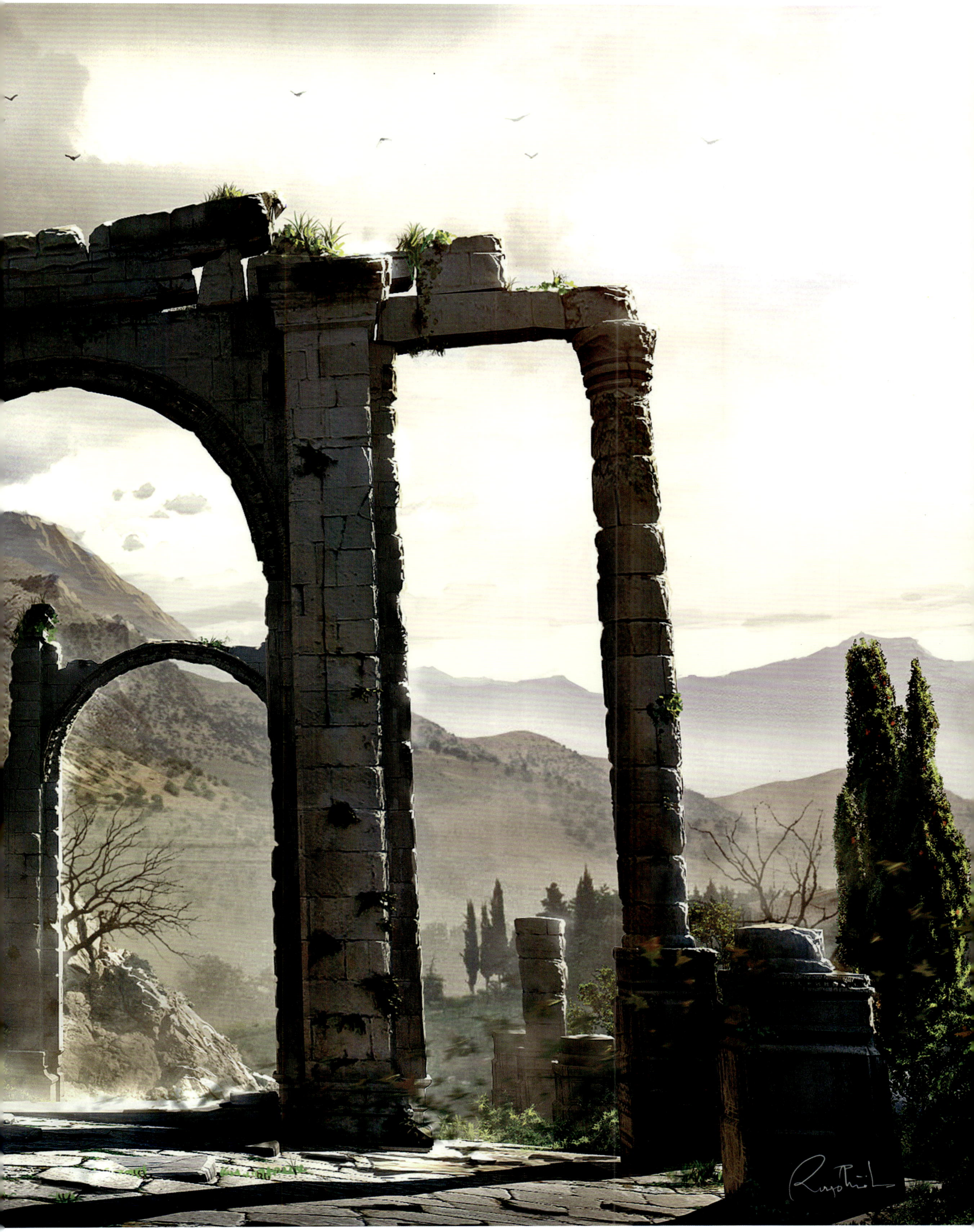

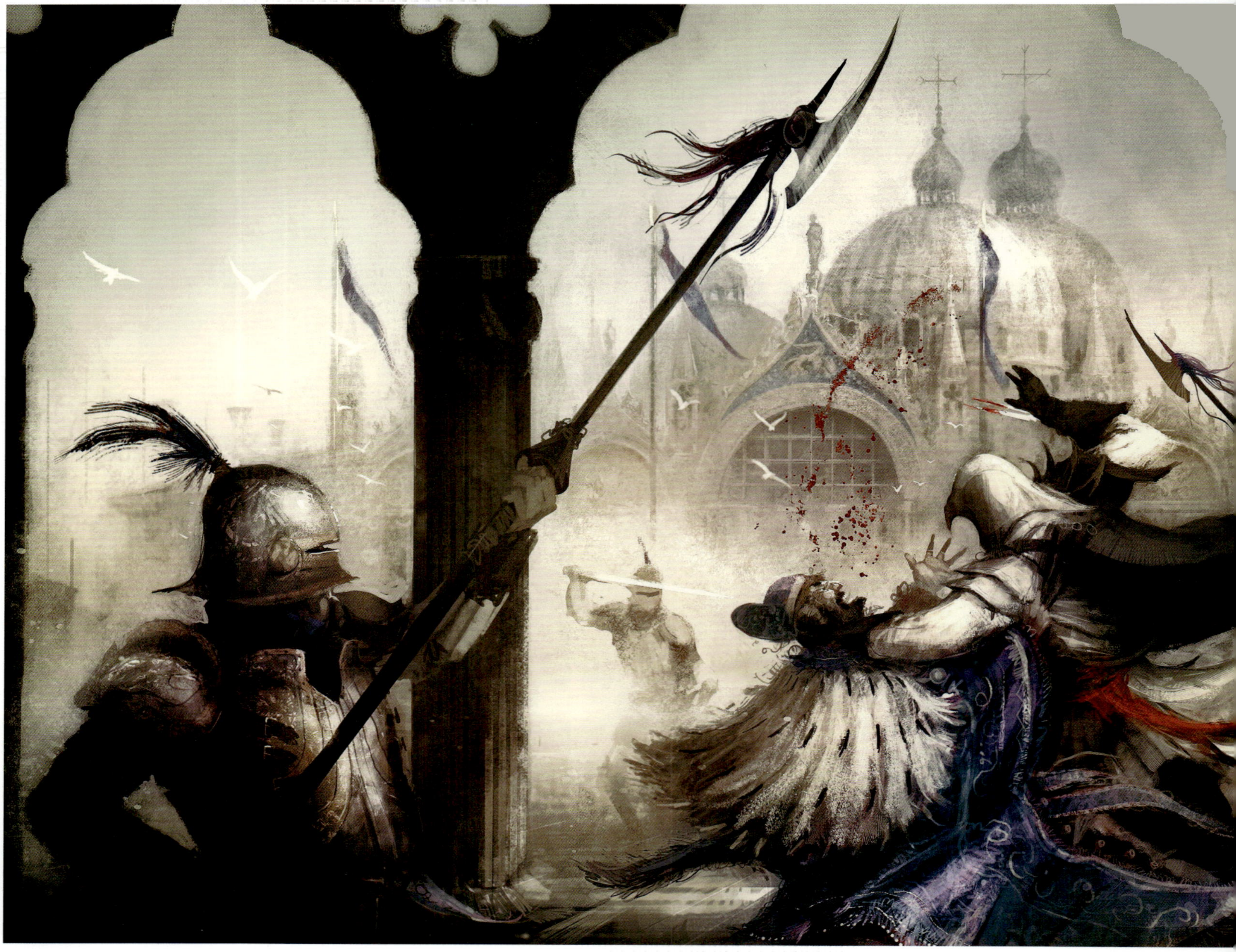

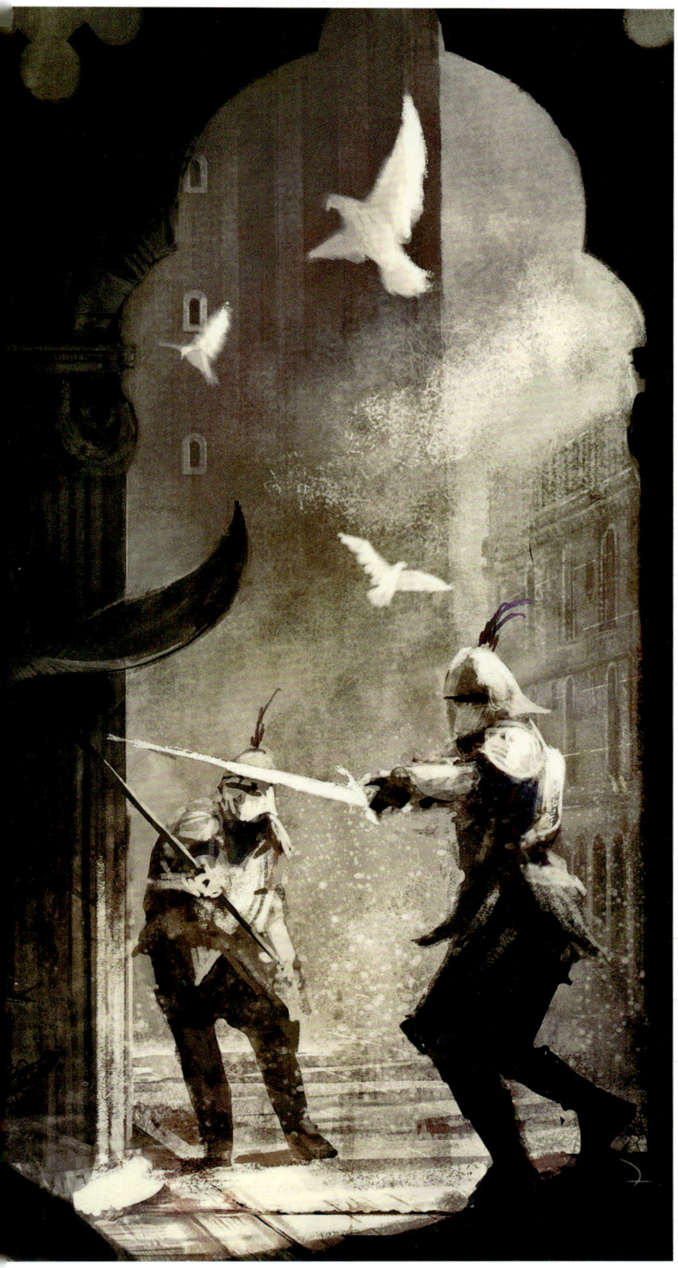

2 THE RENAISSANCE

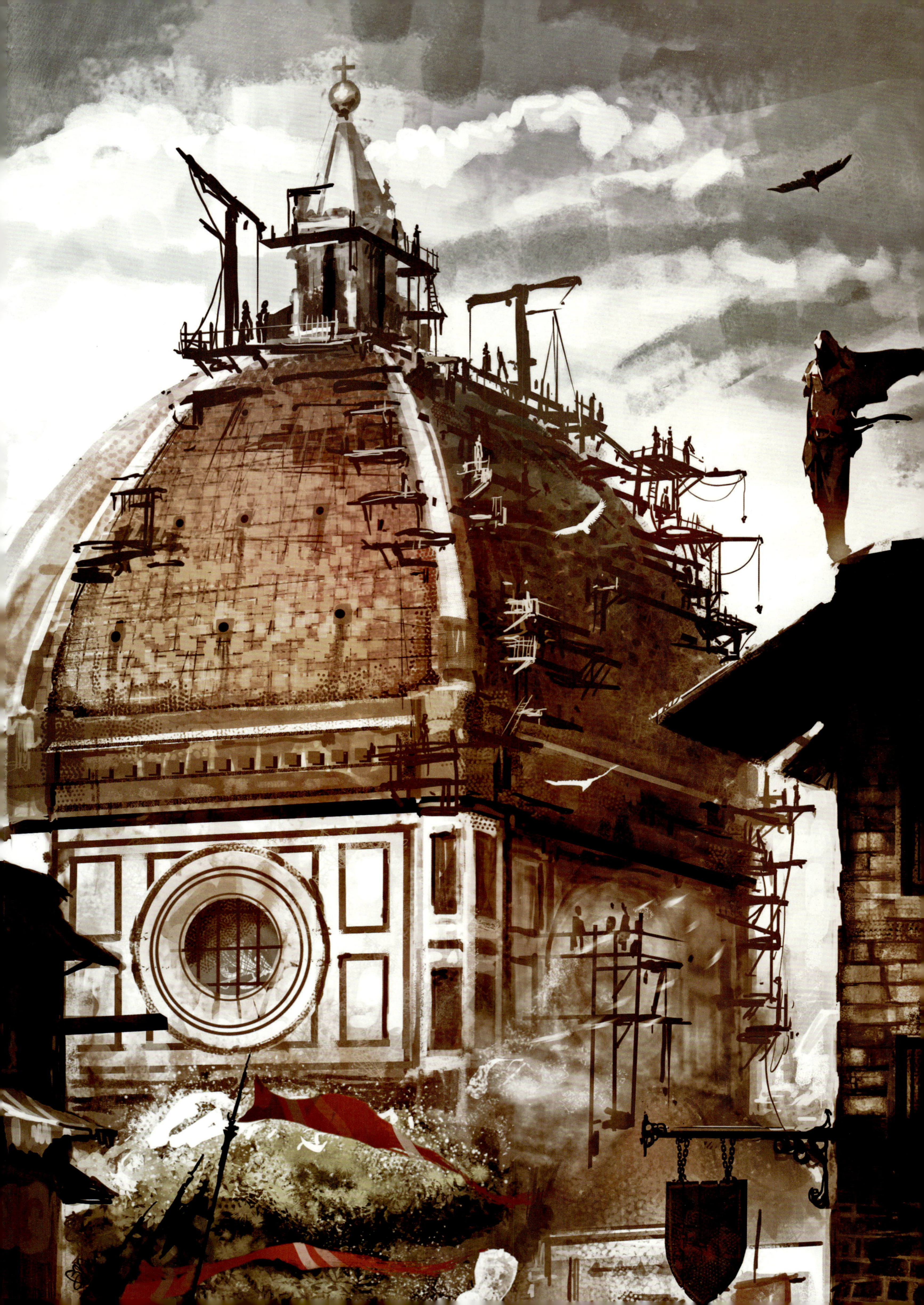

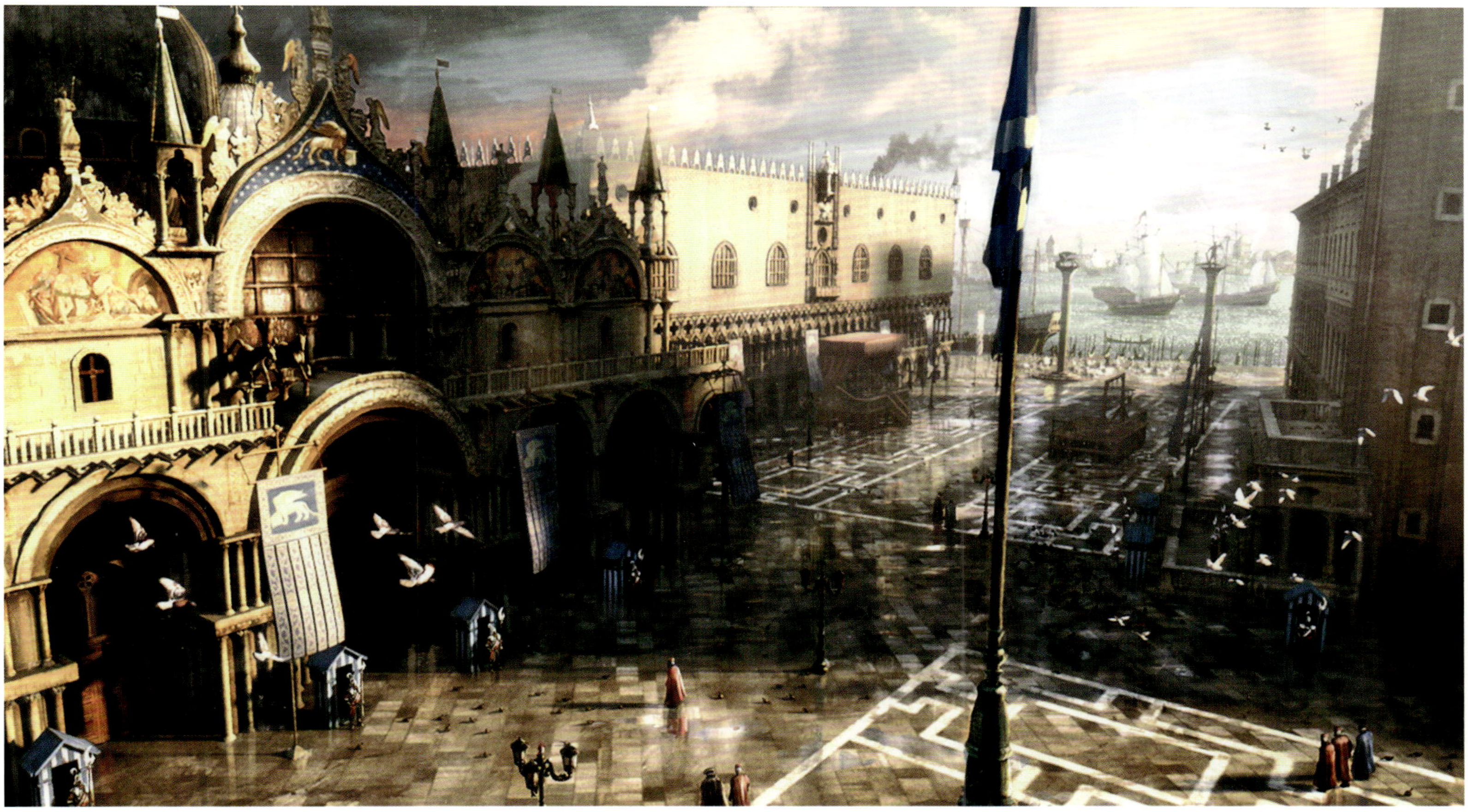

STARTING FRESH

The first *Assassin's Creed* had garnered success beyond expectations. Altaïr's adventures during the Third Crusade struck a chord, thanks to an amalgam of historical fiction, taut action gameplay, open world exploration, and a twist of science fiction. The heady combination was a breath of fresh air in a market dominated by more familiar video game fare.

The question remained of whether lightning could strike twice. Unbeknownst to its fans, *Assassin's Creed II* was heading in a surprising new direction, abandoning its first hero to history and charging forward into the Italian Renaissance. A new protagonist was set to come onstage, and against the backdrop of the most important historical events and people of the Renaissance, we would see his life unfold in its entirety.

An ambitious initial plan proposed that a single game would tell the story of Ezio Auditore, and we would witness his passage from childhood to old age over the course of *Assassin's Creed II*. The extensive biographical plans for this character would indeed come to pass, and through the adventures of this charismatic new lead, the series would reach incredible heights of popularity. However, it would take three games to fully unpack Ezio's story and ensure his place for many fans as one of the most beloved and memorable characters in the Assassin's Creed universe.

PREVIOUS PAGES: A vivid assassination scene in the Piazza San Marco (Martin Deschambault).
OPPOSITE: Iconic concept of the Basilica Santa Maria del Fiore under construction (Martin Deschambault).
ABOVE: For well-known cities like Venice, Ubisoft artists focused on creating historically accurate landmarks and distinctive color palettes (Gilles Beloeil).

BIRTH OF A HERO

Ezio Auditore da Firenze was born in Florence at the height of the Italian Renaissance, and thanks to Animus technology, players were present to witness his birth. However, the man who would one day become Mentor of the Italian Brotherhood remained oblivious to his heritage until he was a teenager. His father, an active member of the Assassins, was hanged, as were Ezio's brothers, due to the machinations of the Templars, and Ezio was forced to flee with his mother and sister to the family's country estate. There, with the help of his uncle, Ezio began to train as an Assassin and set out to confront his father's killers. His path of vengeance would lead to Rodrigo Borgia, a man better known to history as Pope Alexander VI.

Ezio's narrative arc demanded a new artistic vision that felt fresh and inventive but that didn't stray so far from the template established by Altaïr as to be unrecognizable. The character artist team spent months exploring ideas for this new hero, each one a test case to see how the character might fit within the growing mythology. "When we're in the concept phase, we have a lot of liberty as artists," Raphaël says. "We can't have the full script yet. We don't have all the gameplay and level designs, so we have a lot of freedom to build a universe. You can create a character with different tools and weapons, add some symbolic elements, and that can give a lot of inspiration to the game designers. When you see part of your creations in the game, it's very satisfying, as it was just an idea, an illustration at first."

Ezio's development process was not an easy one. Anything new might feel too singular and dissolve the clear identity *Assassin's Creed* had established with its first game. Move too far in the other direction and simply replicate Altaïr, and the shift to a new character would be without purpose. A second main character would also go a long way toward establishing what was the standard for an Assassin and what elements were open to interpretation moving forward. It was essential that Ezio look and feel just right. "It might seem obvious to many now, but we put a lot of effort into identifying the key iconic design elements of a central assassin. The white color, the touch of red, the hood—we tried many different things before determining the final look. Ezio needed to be recognizable as an Assassin, yet stand apart from Altair," explains senior concept artist Vincent Gaigneux.

The earliest conceptions for the Italian Assassin were exciting and dramatic but felt too far away from that invisible sense of what fit within the franchise. Additional explorations abandoned the clean bright white of an eagle and instead used the crow as a much bleaker animal totem. "One of the first mistakes I made in the beginning was going for something very dark," Mohamed says. "We talked about changing the symbol of the eagle to something different, like a crow, but we found that it went too far in the other direction, with the crow representing death and poison. So we threw away that idea." The art team even actively tried to move away from the hood—an idea that would gain ground in later installments—but this early in the life of the franchise, it was clear that the hood still needed to be an indelible part of the Assassin's identity.

The final design for Ezio was a romantic and debonair hero who felt at home within the high culture and art of the period. Mohamed cites Shakespeare's *Merchant of Venice* and the carefree Bassanio as an early inspiration for Ezio's pre-Assassin personality. Rather than have his family's tragic fate steal away his nobility, Ezio's style was impeccable and elaborate. The entire artistic team began to embrace the allure of this Casanova Assassin. Complex filigree lined his armor and buckles, and a flared collar added to his dashing charm. "He was more flamboyant, a playboy, and he had a sense of humor," Mohamed explains. Even his weapons felt less utilitarian than those worn by his ancestor—the hidden blade was decorative and elaborate but maintained its deadly sting.

Ezio's struggles over the course of *Assassin's Creed II* painted him as a bundle of contradictions. He was a ladies' man, but he rarely deviated from his mission and seldom engaged in romance. He was driven by revenge, yet in his conversations he came across as amiable and friendly. His charm and charisma put him in stark contrast to stoic Altaïr, and he was just what the series needed to prove its potential to reinvent itself. Even so, Ezio's debut in *Assassin's Creed II* was only a beginning; the character had new layers to uncover as the story continued.

OPPOSITE: The minute details of Ezio's early costume reflect Renaissance patterns and color schemes (Martin Deschambault).

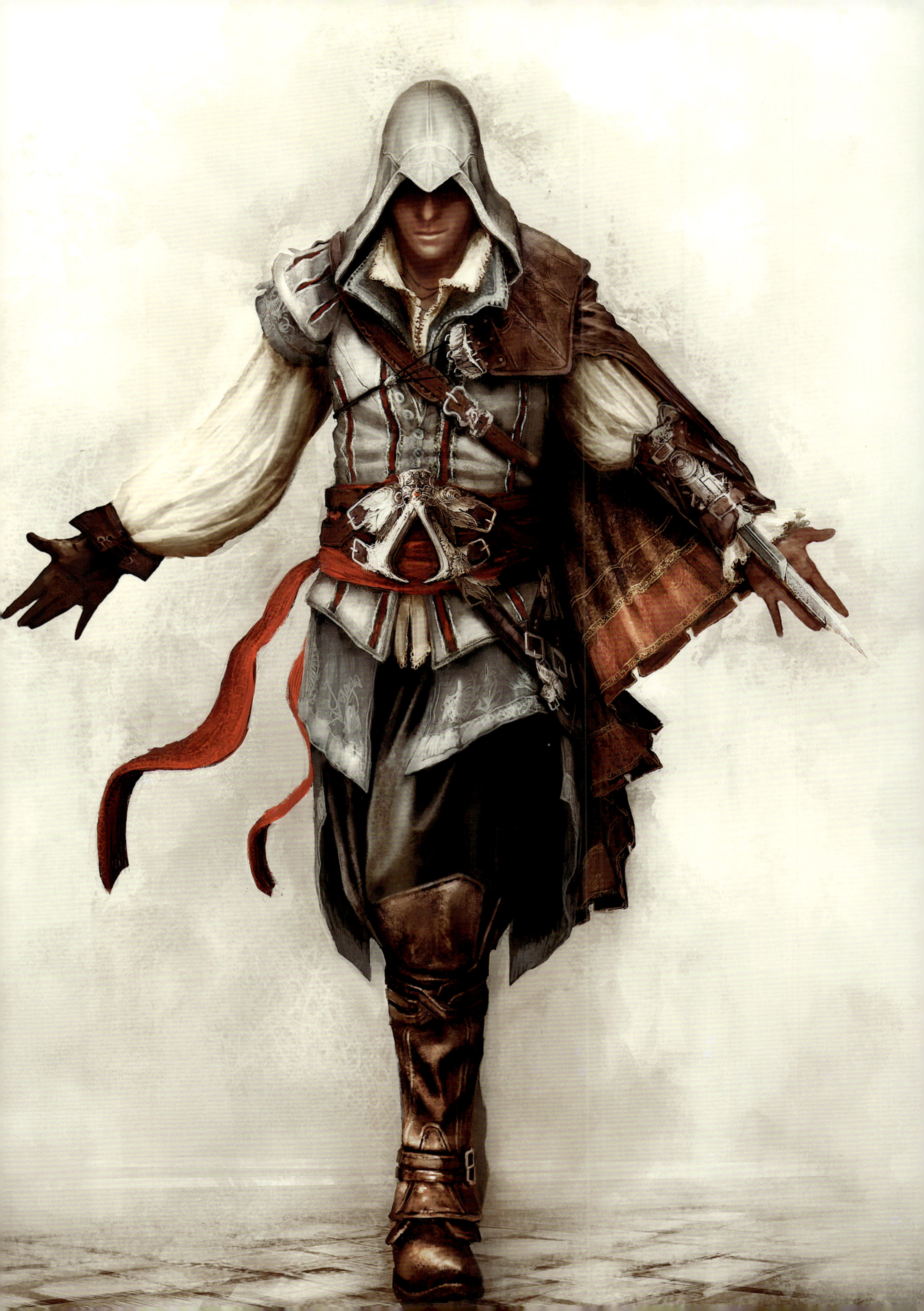

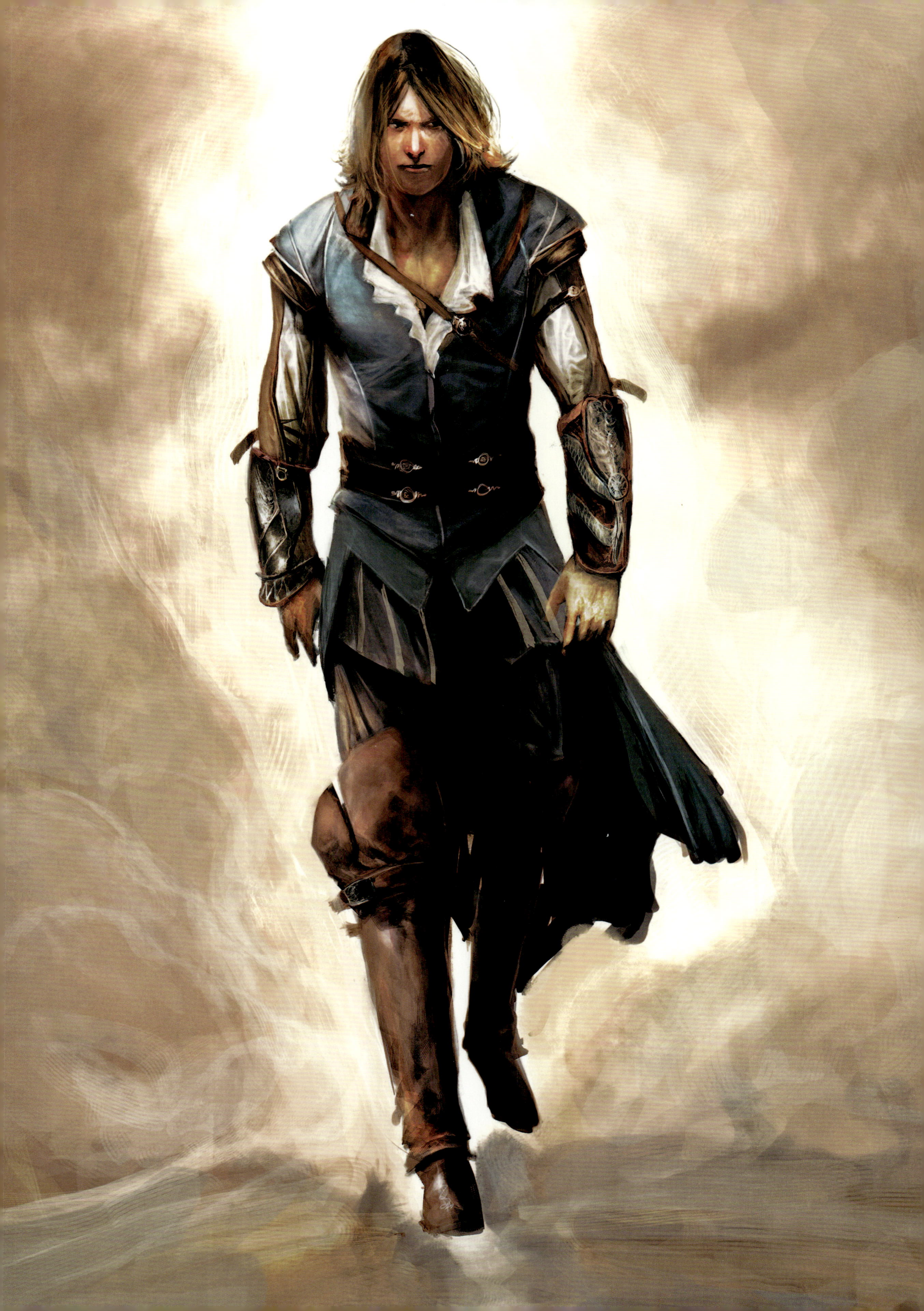

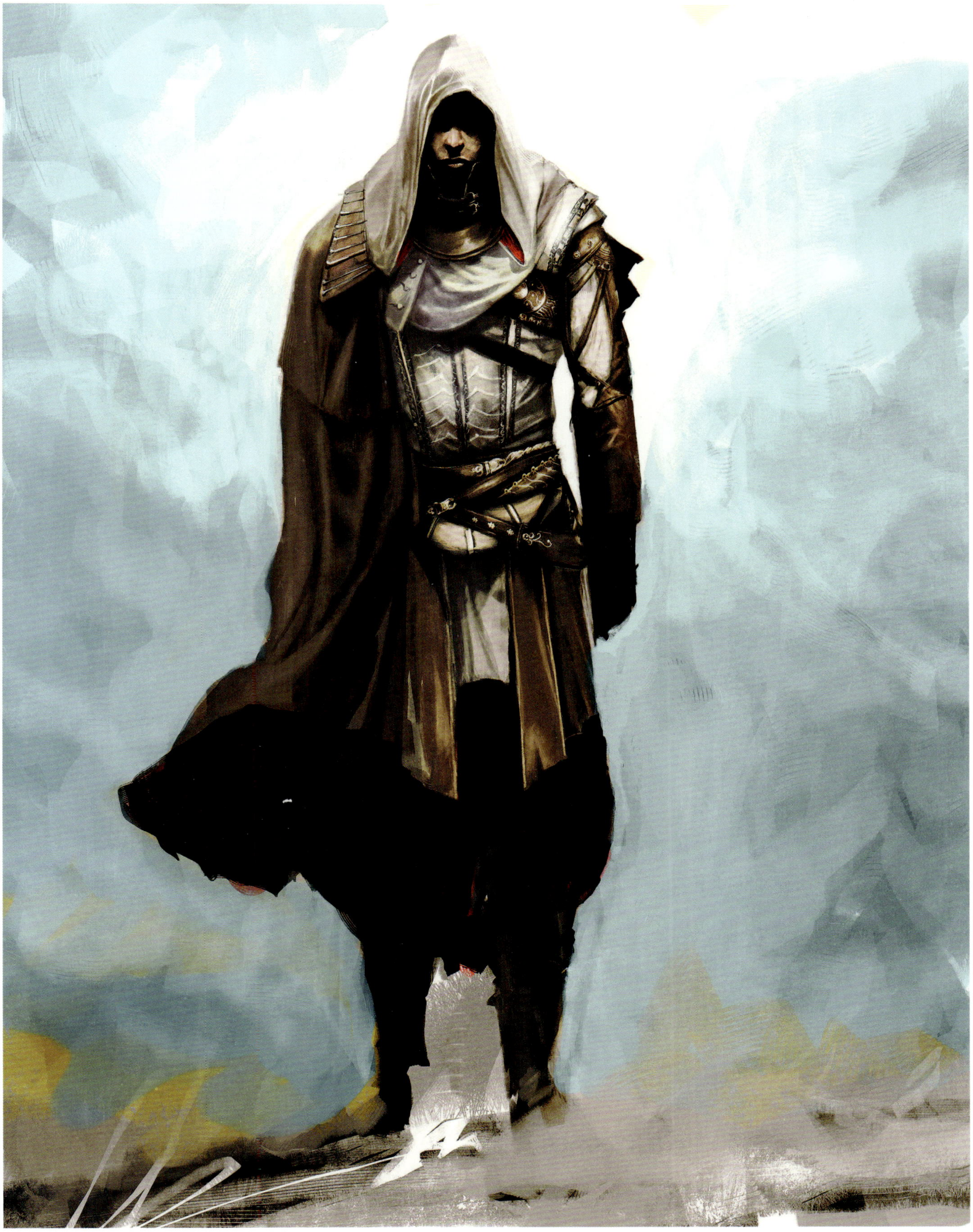

OPPOSITE: Early Ezio concepts were influenced by the symbol of a crow rather than an eagle (Vincent Gaigneux).
ABOVE: This early Ezio exploration reflects the evolution from Altaïr's design (Vincent Gaigneux).

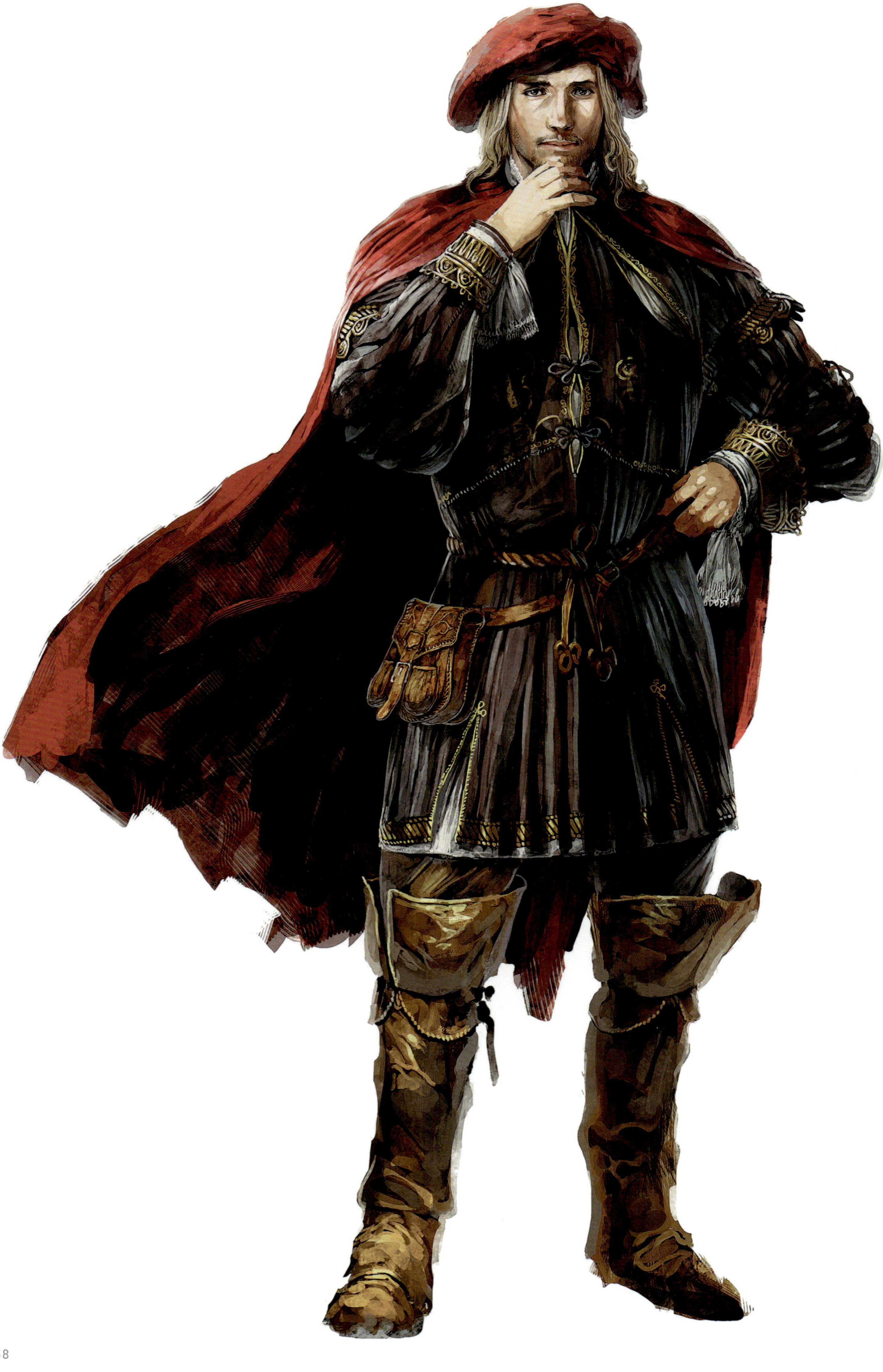

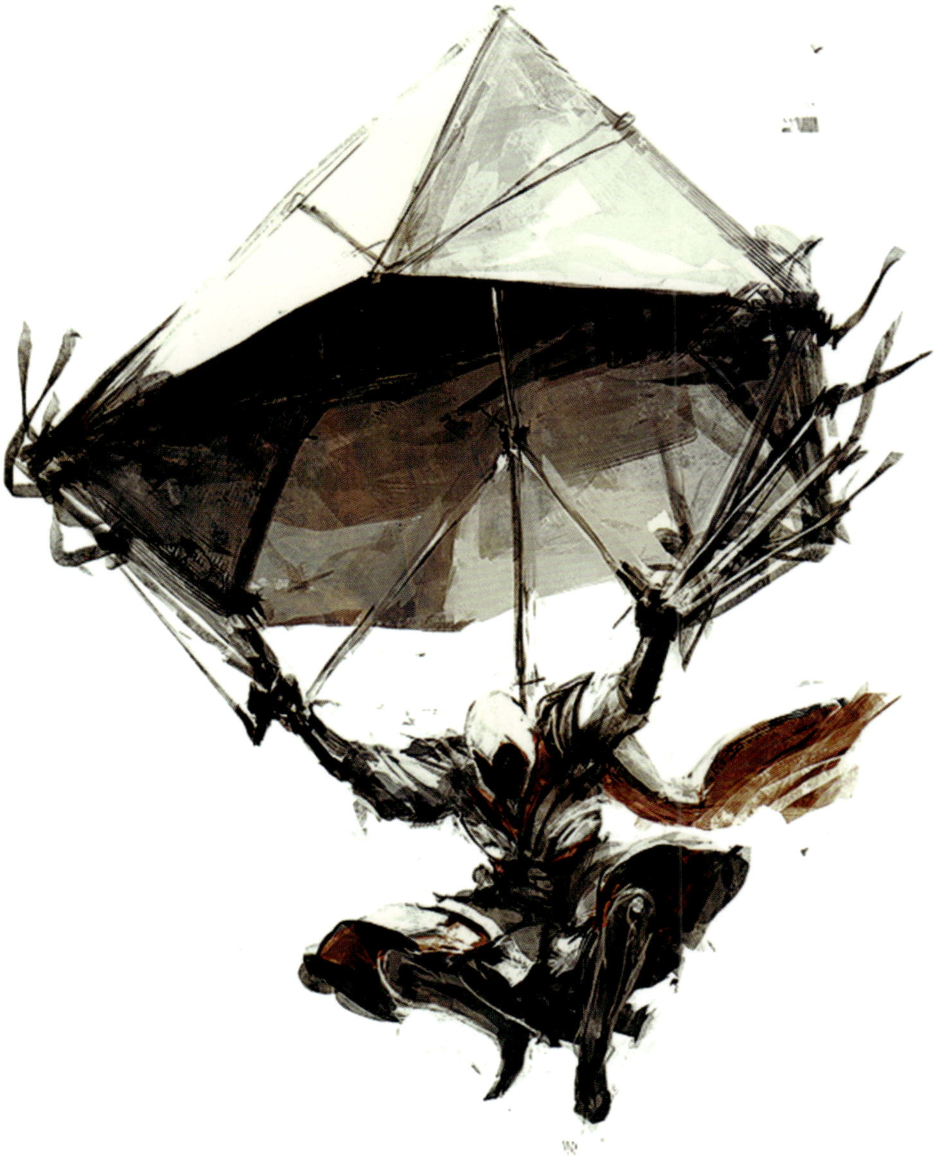

ARCHITECTS OF THE RENAISSANCE

Italy in the 1500s was home to some of the greatest artists and minds of the Western world—people whose ideas would shape civilization for generations. For Ubisoft's writers and artists, it was a chance to draw some of these figures into the ongoing story of the Assassin/Templar conflict and put a new twist on history's understanding of such renowned individuals.

Chief among these notable individuals was Leonardo da Vinci. History tells us of the man's achievements in engineering, sculpture, mathematics, painting, and more. Rather than embrace the picture of the older man depicted in da Vinci's famous self-portrait, the Leonardo we meet in the games is a young man still doubting his abilities and talent. His carefree attitude and studious capabilities made him a perfect friend to Ezio, and many of the Assassin's exploits wouldn't have come to pass without Leonardo's involvement. The inventor helps repair and improve the hidden blade and even creates the flying machine that Ezio uses in a couple of his most harrowing encounters.

Other renowned figures also found their way into the Assassin's Creed lore during this period. The political philosopher Niccolò Machiavelli turned out to be a leading member of the Assassins. The brazen Countess of Forli, Caterina Sforza, proved her mettle in various conflicts against the Templars and would at one point spend an amorous night with Ezio. Rodrigo Borgia was also a vivid presence as the Templar villain at the heart of the game's conspiracy. As one of the most controversial popes in the history of the Catholic Church, he was a man of tremendous power and a suitably dangerous foe for Ezio's first adventure.

OPPOSITE: Character art of Leonardo da Vinci (Patrick Lambert).
ABOVE: Leonardo da Vinci's parachute sketch (Patrick Lambert).

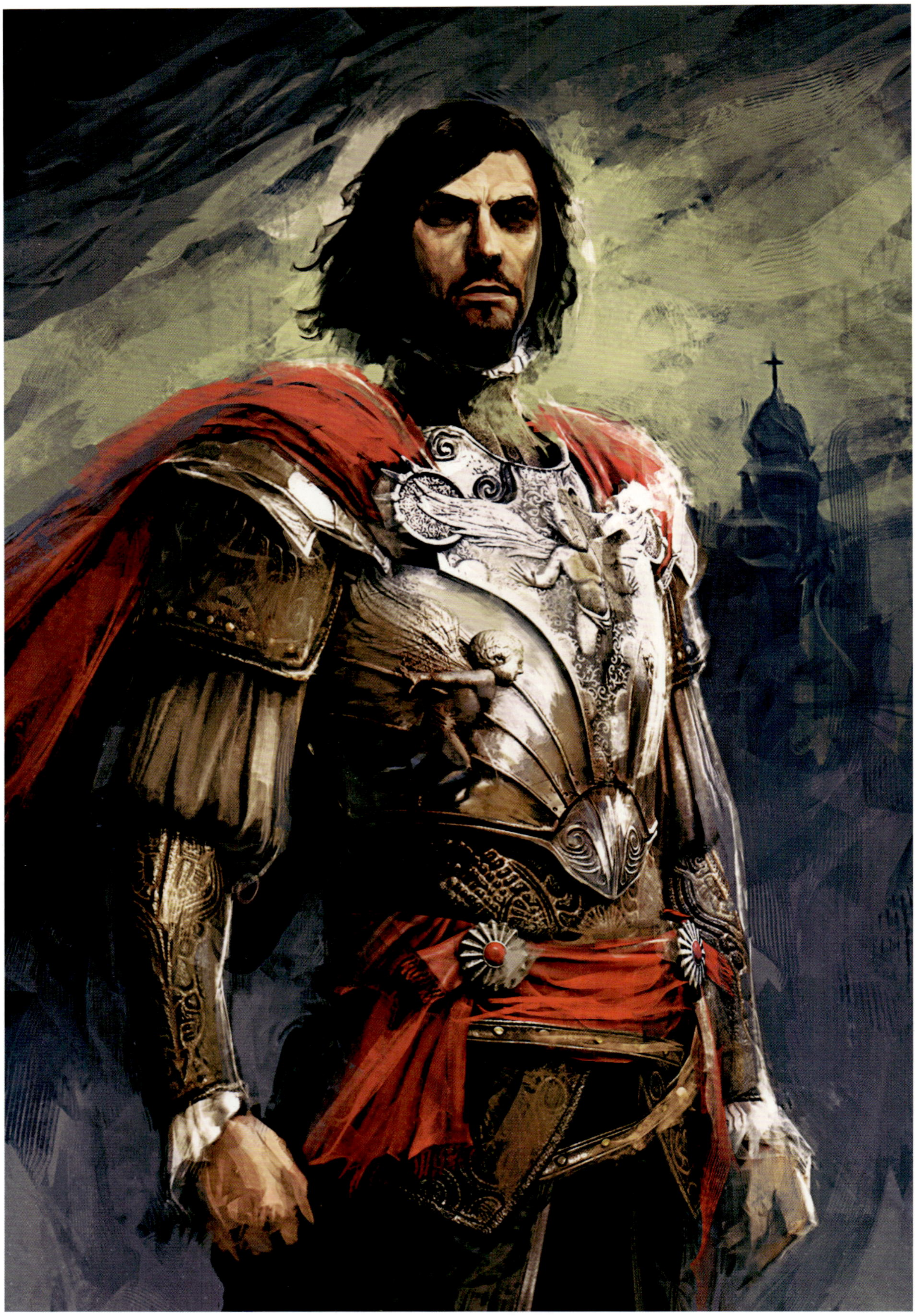

ABOVE: Cesare Borgia's design was inspired by Julius Caesar, as evidenced by his red cape and detailed armor (Patrick Lambert).

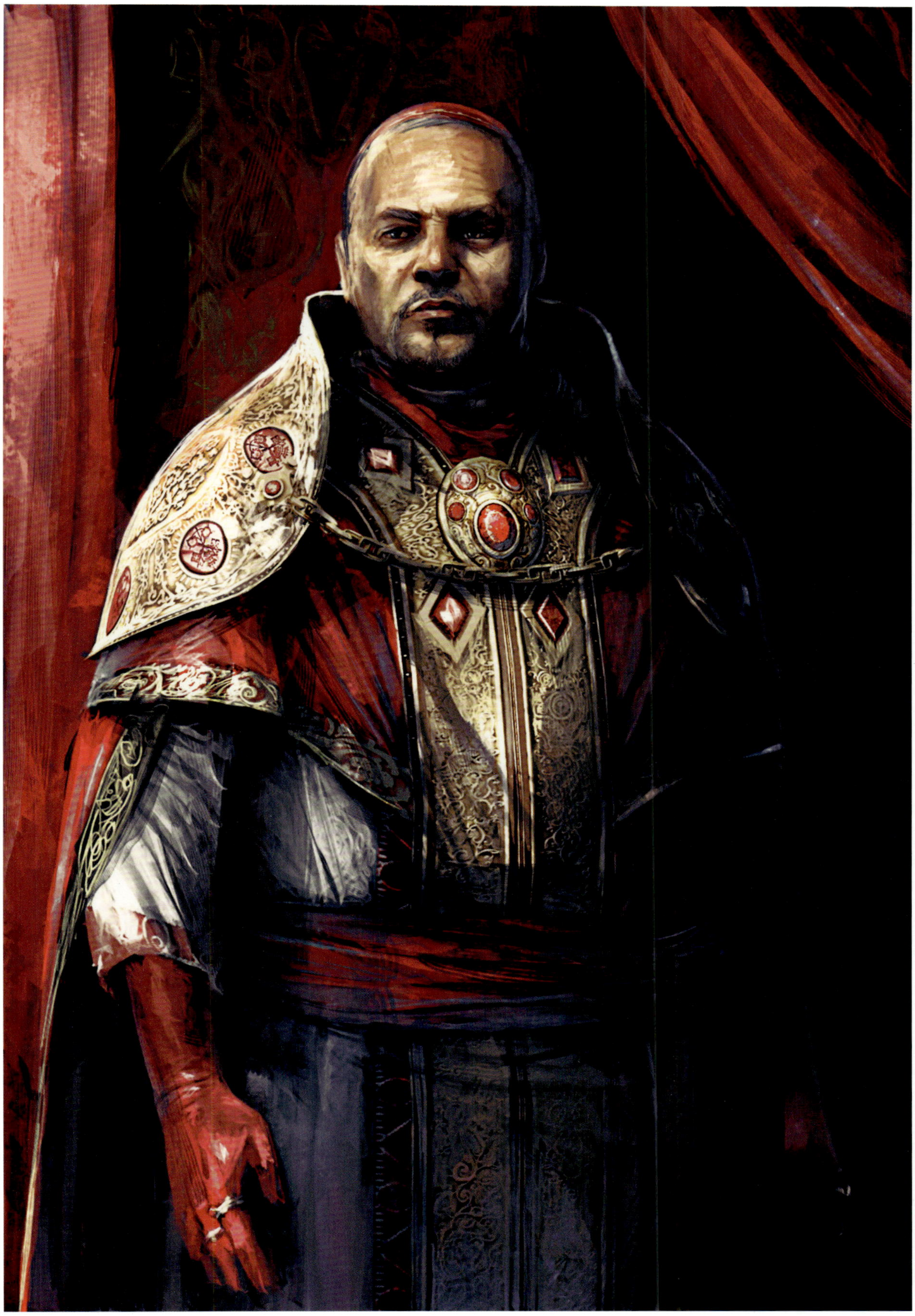

ABOVE: Portrait of Rodrigo Borgia in traditional papal regalia (character design by Vincent Gaigneux, artworks Patrick Lambert).

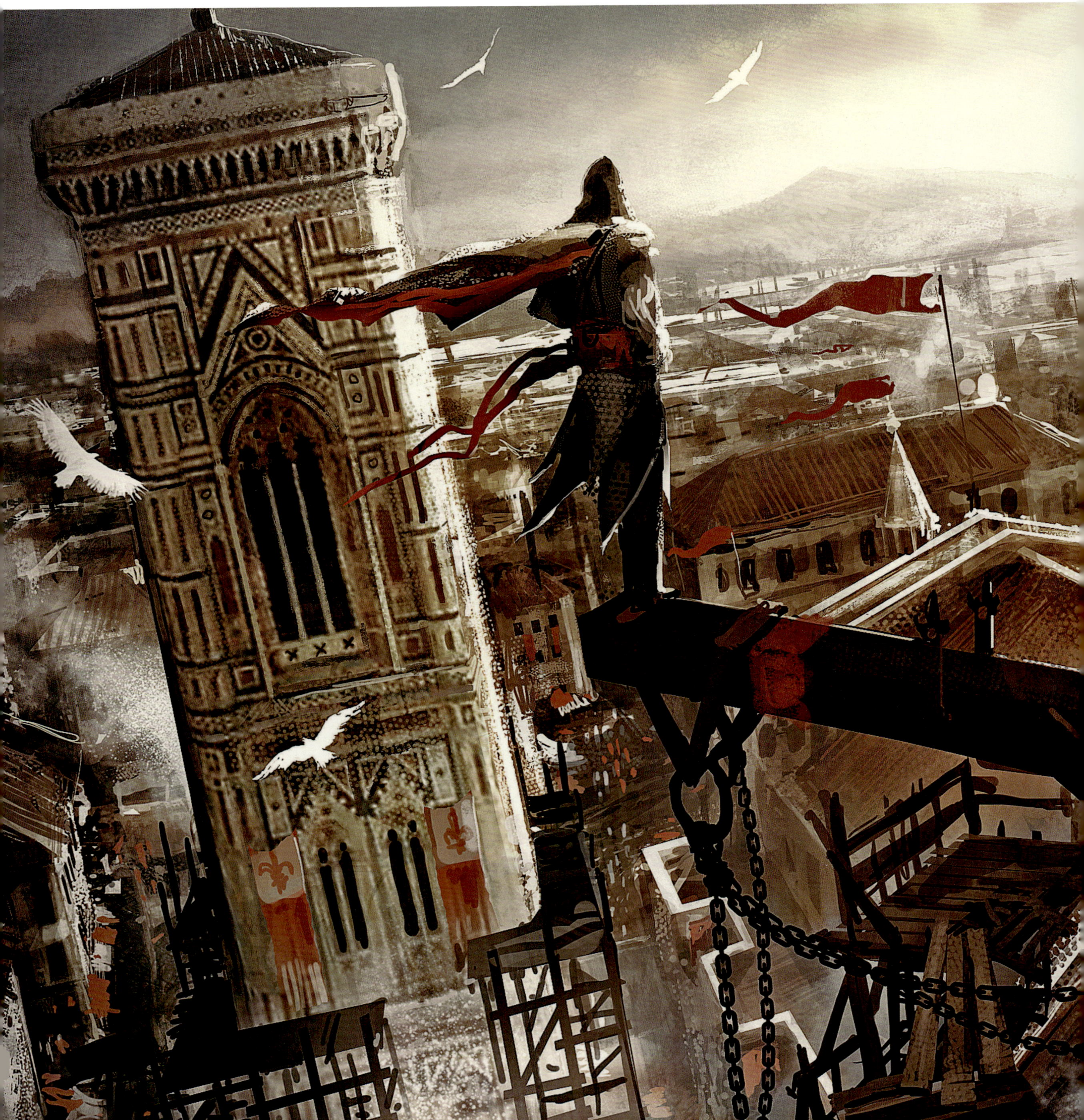

ABOVE: Concepts for the Florence cathedral, parts of which were under construction during the time the game took place, included the scaffolding to reinforce the sense of scale and to provide the level designers with climbable objects (Martin Deschambault).

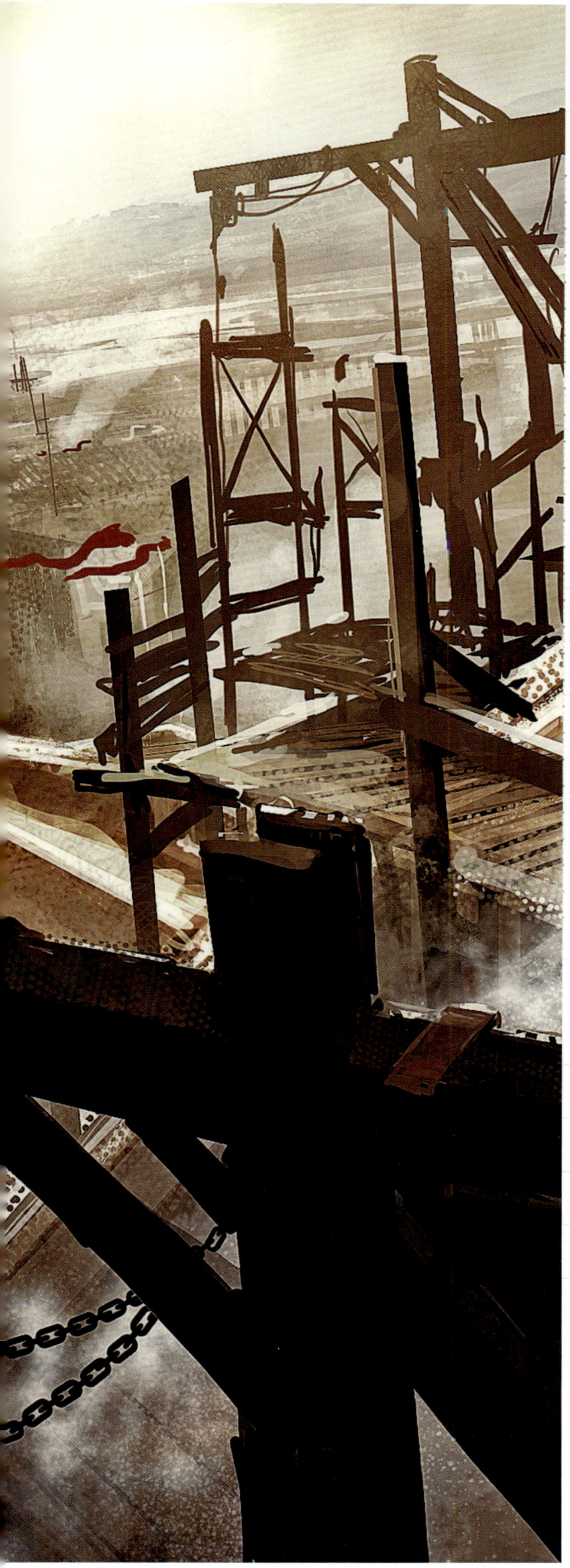

A LAND IN TRANSITION

Contrary to some popular perception of the period, the days of Leonardo da Vinci and Machiavelli were not peaceful and simple. While art, science, banking, and architecture were taking profound steps forward, the many competing families of the period transformed the idyllic cities and countryside into one minor war zone after another.

The artists behind *Assassin's Creed II* faced the challenge of presenting two ends of the spectrum. Elegant buildings in Venice and Florence offered a testament to man's ingenuity, but the scenes that would unfold near those landmarks were often bloody affairs involving conspiracy and murder. The juxtaposition of great beauty and lethal violence would increasingly become a visual touchstone for the franchise.

Each city had to meet dual goals: present a thrilling tour around some of history's most notable architecture but also act as a meaningful and exciting gameplay space. Florence was a city of high culture and riches. The advent of modern banking had been kind to the city, and Ezio's hometown shone with the marvels of classical architecture. The stalwart Ponte Vecchio bridge would serve as the arena for one of Ezio's first battles, establishing his enmity with the villainous Pazzi family. And the magnificent Cattedrale di Santa Maria del Fiore offered a stunning view of the city and acted as the highest climbable point in the game. "It was one of the biggest monuments featured in an Assassin's Creed game up to that point," Mohamed says. "We spent a lot of time making sure we could build the cathedral without hindering the performance of the game. Another major challenge was finding the right scale, because it was important that the building was memorable and didn't lose that sense of gravity that it has in real life."

Just as the preceding cities of Acre, Damascus, and Jerusalem were defined by bold color palettes, the cities of *Assassin's Creed II* had similar identifiers, if slightly more subtle in expression. Florence was dominated by ochres and browns—warm colors that felt like home—and the air had orange overtones, speaking to the implied heat of summer. Venice was dominated by saturated colors lined with white frames, lending a classical, artistic quality. The blues of the water were accentuated in postproduction, always keeping the canals in the back of a player's mind. Those world-famous canals offered another path for Ezio's explorations, with small boats acting as escape paths for the Assassin as he fled dangerous encounters. The Piazza San Marco was an impressive backdrop, but the ability to climb up the walls of the famous square offered an even more awe-inducing perspective. The famous bridge, the Ponte di Rialto, already graced the crossing of the Grand Canal, but historians revealed that the stone structure would not be constructed until decades later; the in-game crossing would be made of wood. "These historians make the past a dynamic reality for us," Jean says. "This is why I think people love Assassin's Creed, because history can be incredibly fascinating and fun. History is so much more than just learning dates from a book. When you understand the logic of the world in a specific period of time, a lot of details that might have been ignored previously start to make sense. The Rialto Bridge is a typical example. The bridge is made of wide stones today, but originally it was wooden with a moveable central part that could be raised in order to let tall ships go through." In between these larger metropolises, smaller cities like Forli offered a glimpse of city life melded with rural. Marshy lowlands led up to the small but impressive city headed by Caterina Sforza. The city felt dirty with its gray walls and muddy brown roads. And San Gimignano provided a sharp contrast to the wide avenues of Florence; the fortress town's high walls and tight passages made for an exciting navigational challenge. In between the cities, the Italian countryside was beautiful, with rolling hills and scattered trees. While the open area between cities was smaller than the large Kingdom space in the previous game, players were still provided the sense of a vast and interconnected world.

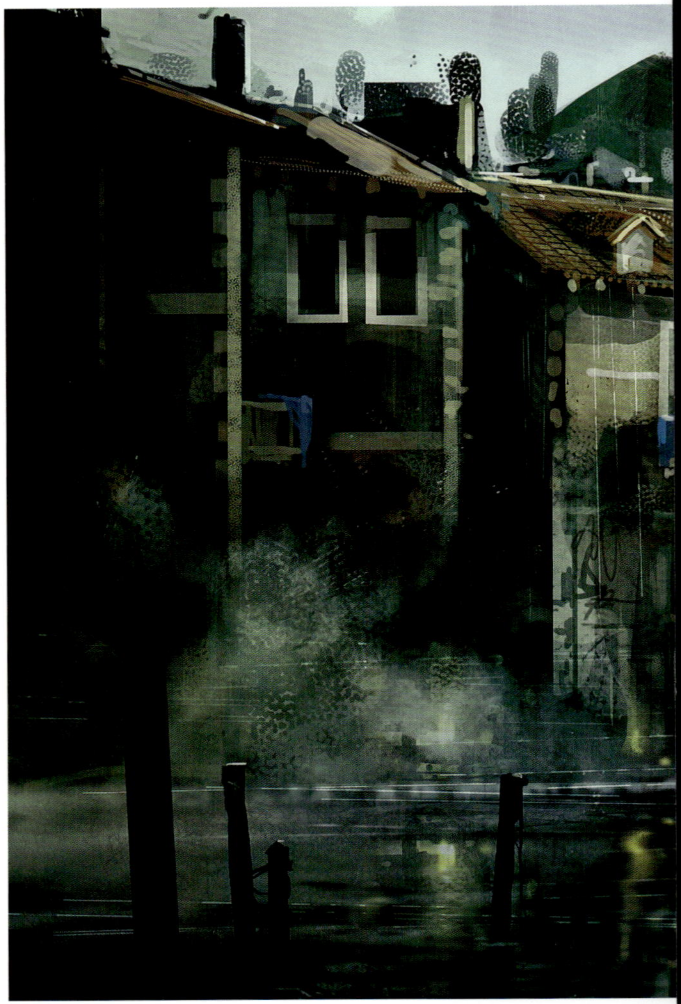

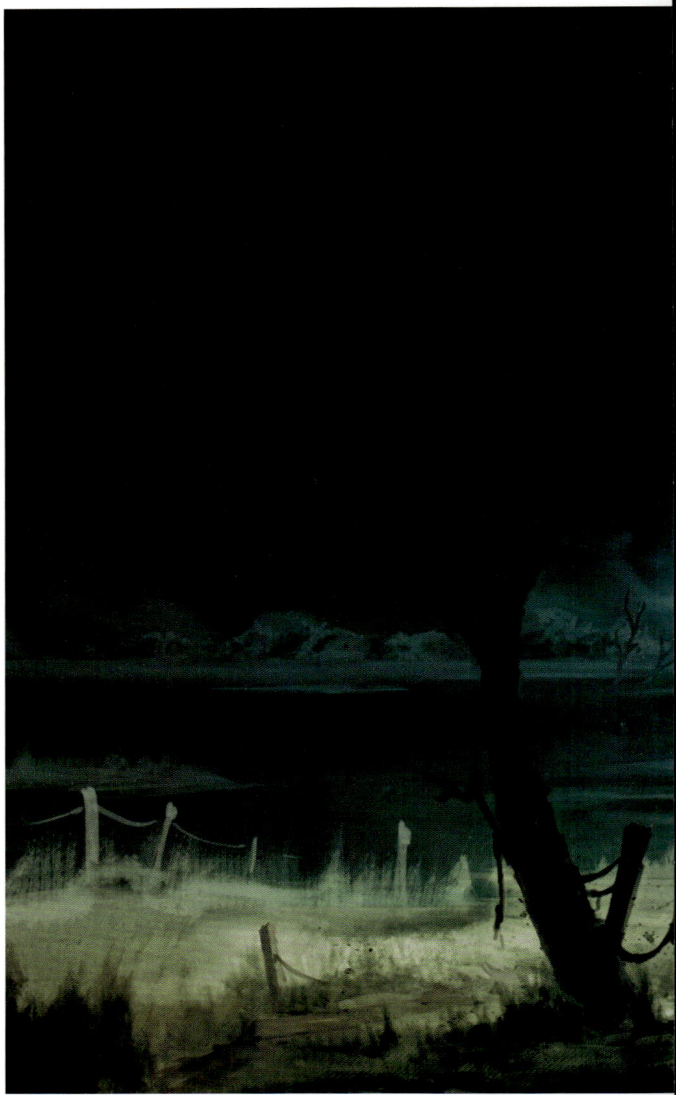

TOP RIGHT: Concepts of Venice featured saturated colors and white frames around doors and windows (Martin Deschambault).
BOTTOM RIGHT: Forli's gray and bluish tones produced a hazy, smoggy atmosphere (Maxime Desmettre).

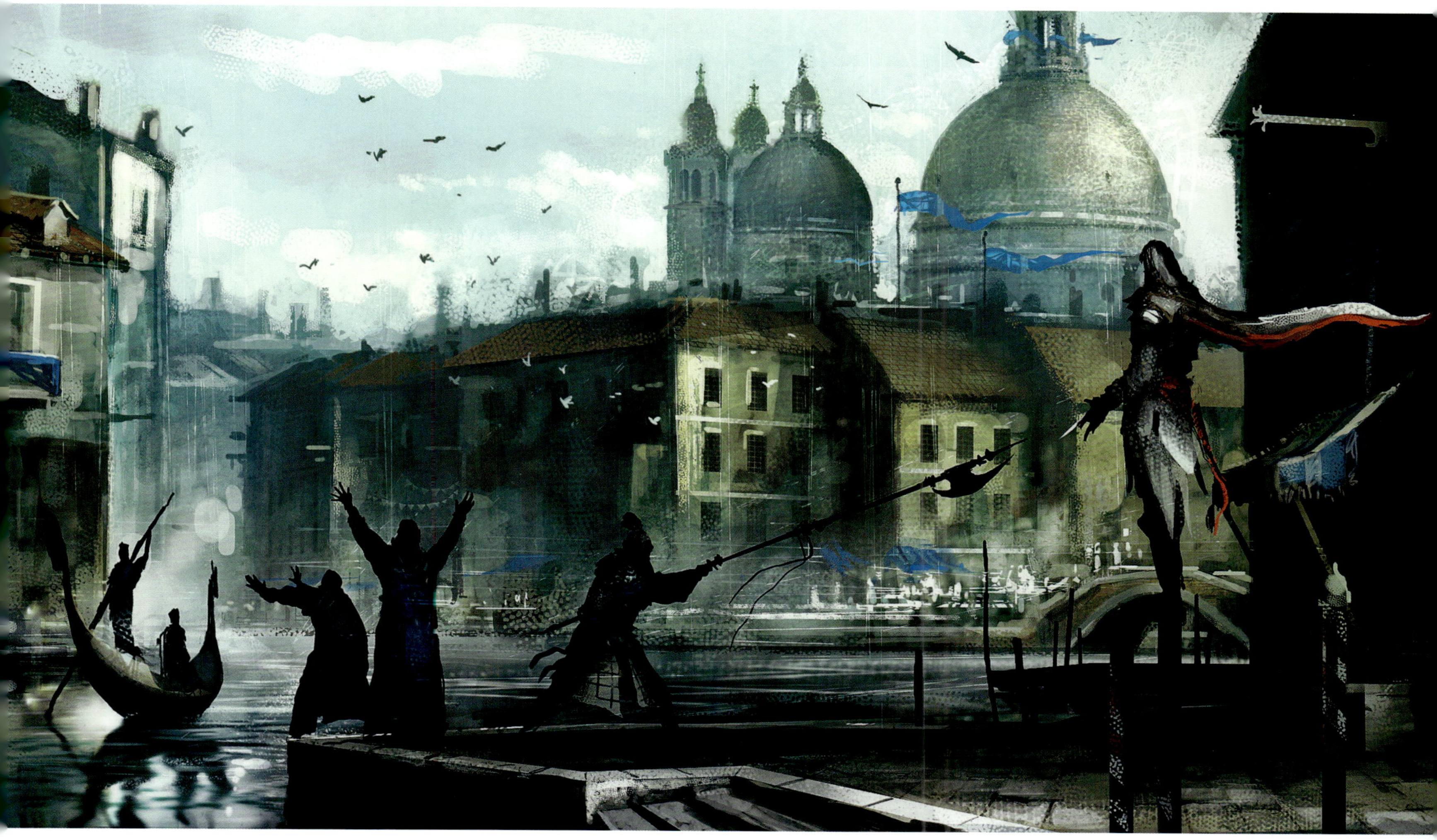

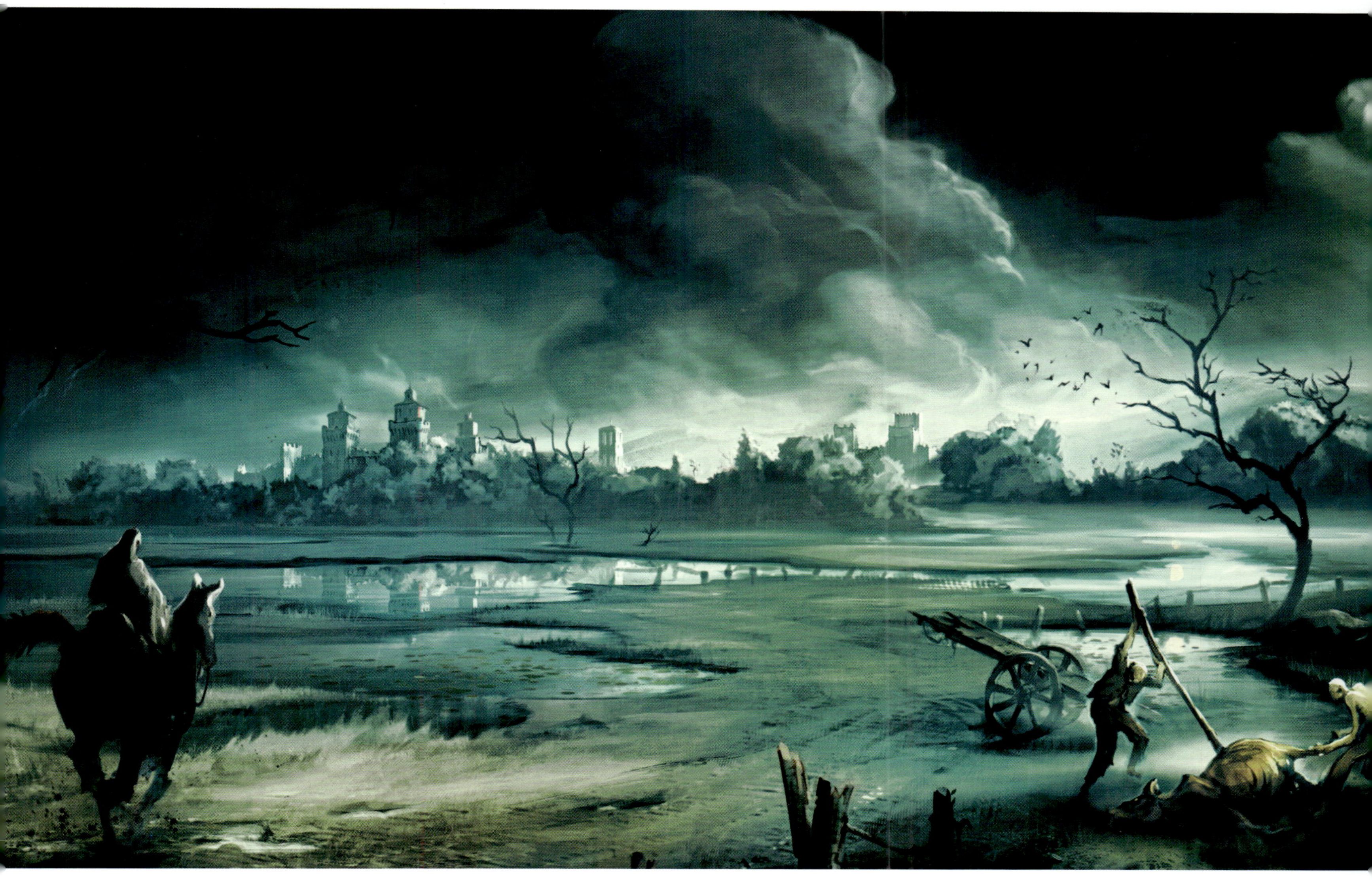

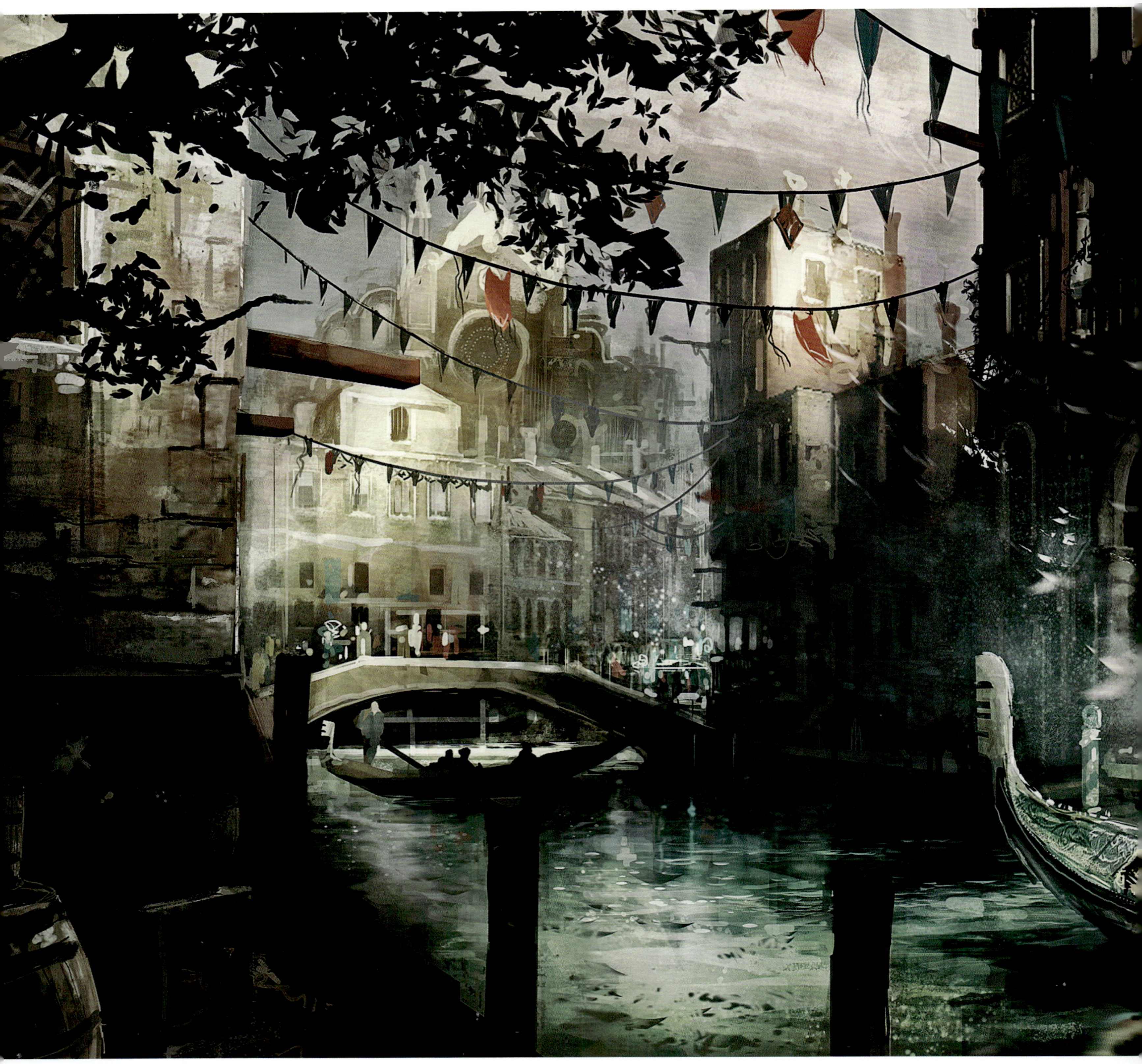

THESE PAGES: Venice's color palette was inspired by the city's famous waterways (Martin Deschambault).

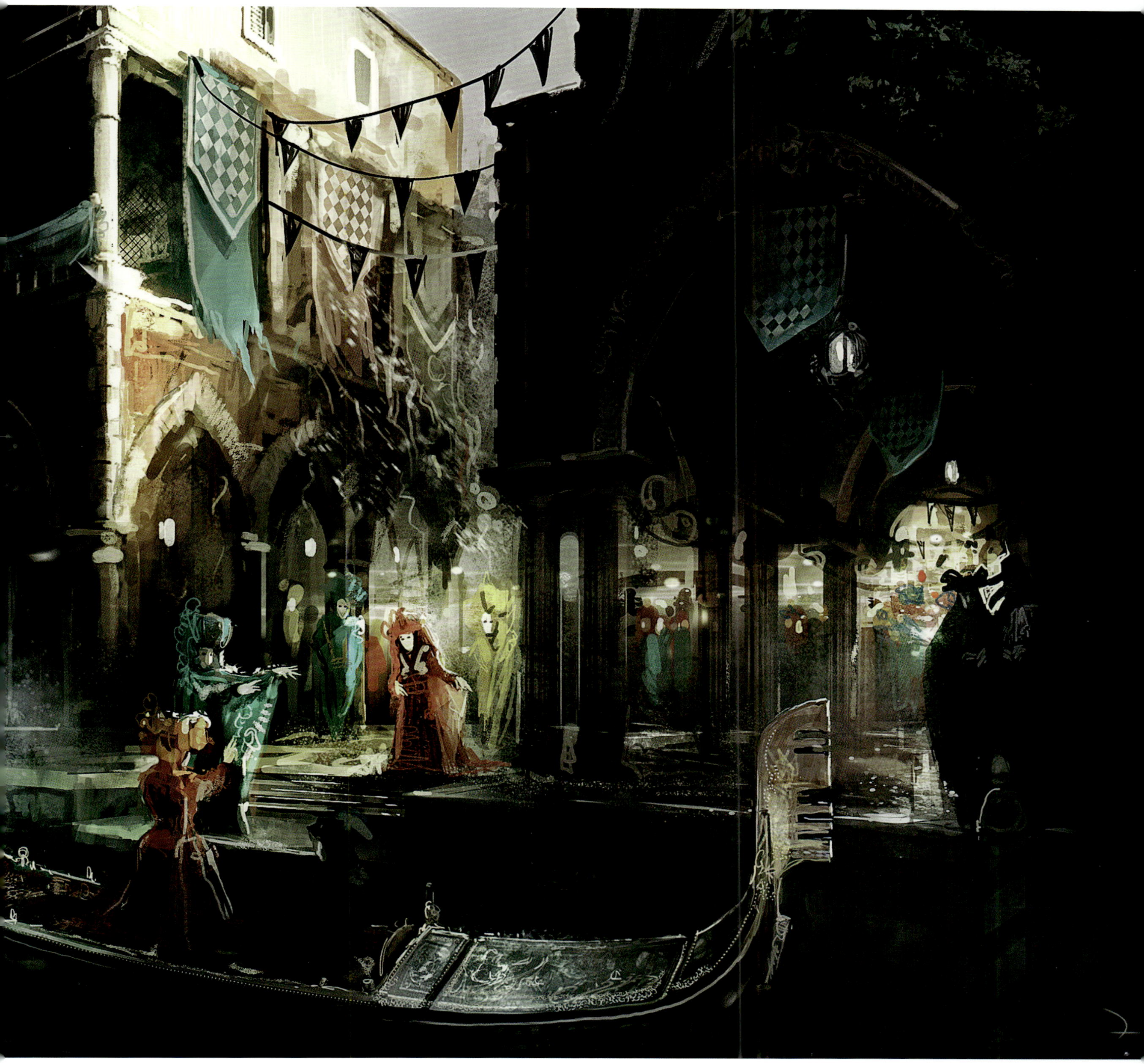

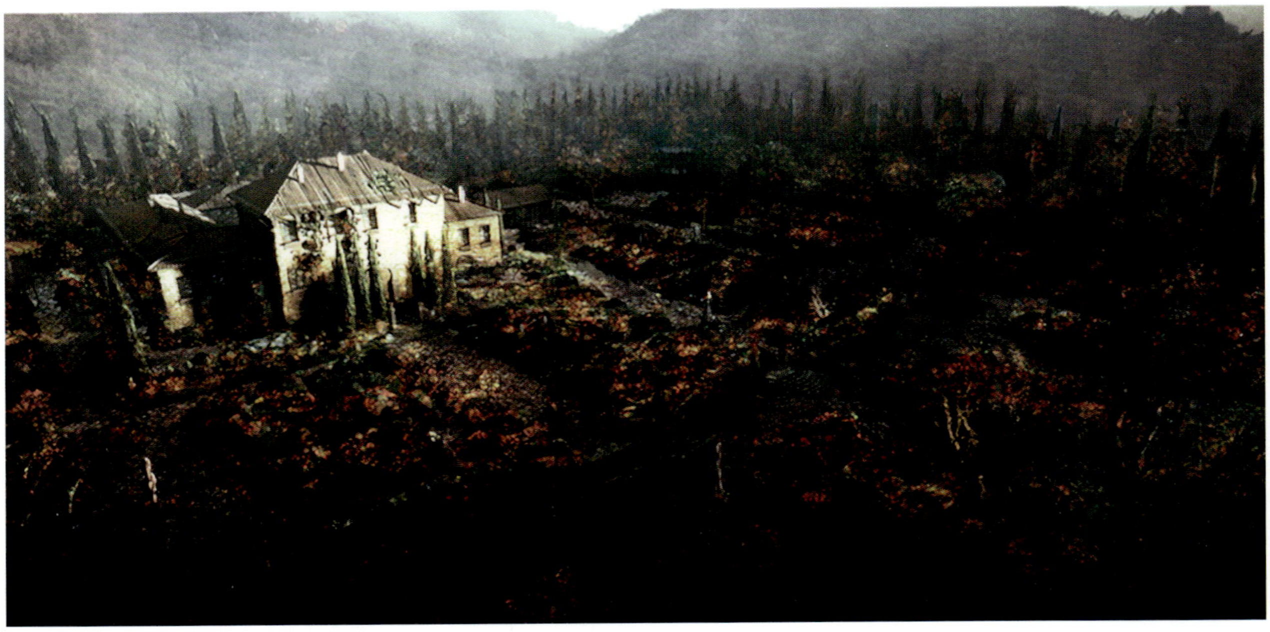

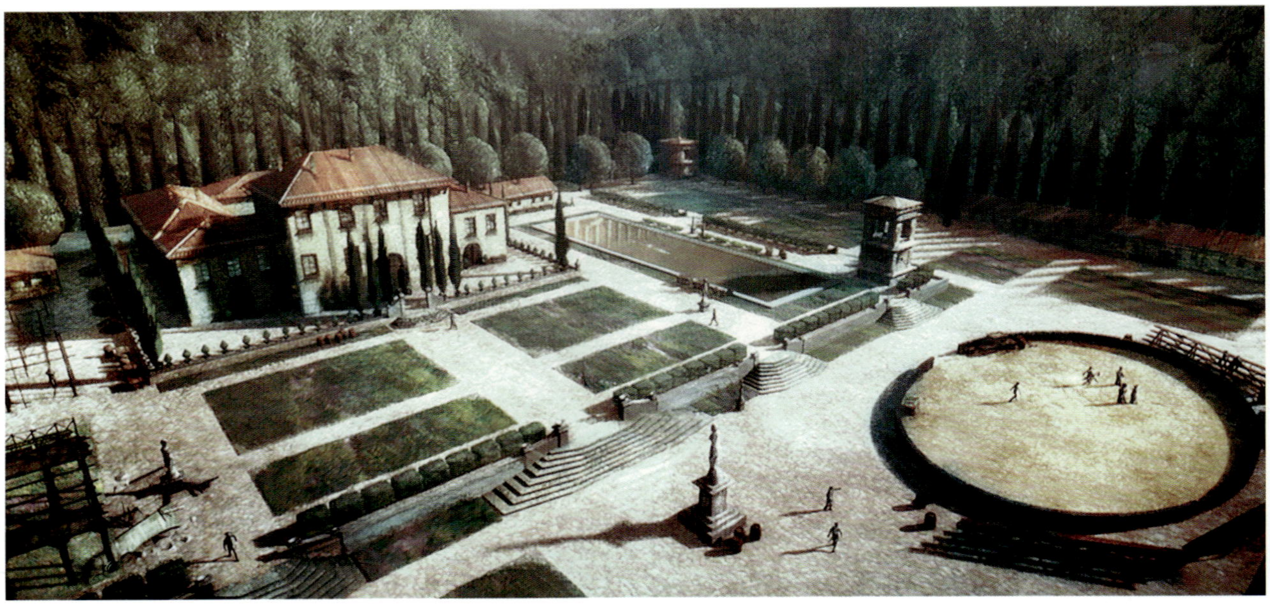

A CIVILIZED RETREAT

Altaïr had Masyaf as a base, but Ezio's noble background lent itself to something more refined. The quiet town of Monteriggioni was a retreat and home to Ezio throughout his first game, and it provided something new to the series: the chance to create a home that grew and changed as the game progressed.

Even before being enriched through investments by Ezio, Monteriggioni was an impressive and beautiful settlement. The quaint Italian village was dominated by old yellowed stone and green vegetation, lending a lived-in, peaceful air to the locale. The town wrapped itself around a low hill atop which sat the Villa Auditore. Inside, stylish interiors and expensive furniture were reminders of the noble background of the Auditore family. Hiding behind the expensive trappings, the villa held secret passages and artfully crafted statues of Assassins from ages past.

With time and money, Monteriggioni transformed. Shops reopened, along with a barracks for the town guard and even a brothel and thieves' guild. With the help of additional investments, the church, well, and mines could be unlocked as new areas of exploration. At the villa, Ezio could build up an impressive collection of actual paintings from famous Renaissance painters and then stroll through the gallery to peruse the finest works of the age.

Unfortunately for Ezio, all his hard work would eventually be undone. In a narrative twist that made it clear that *Assassin's Creed: Brotherhood* was moving in a new direction, the opening scenes of that next installment in the franchise saw the devastation of the pastoral hideaway.

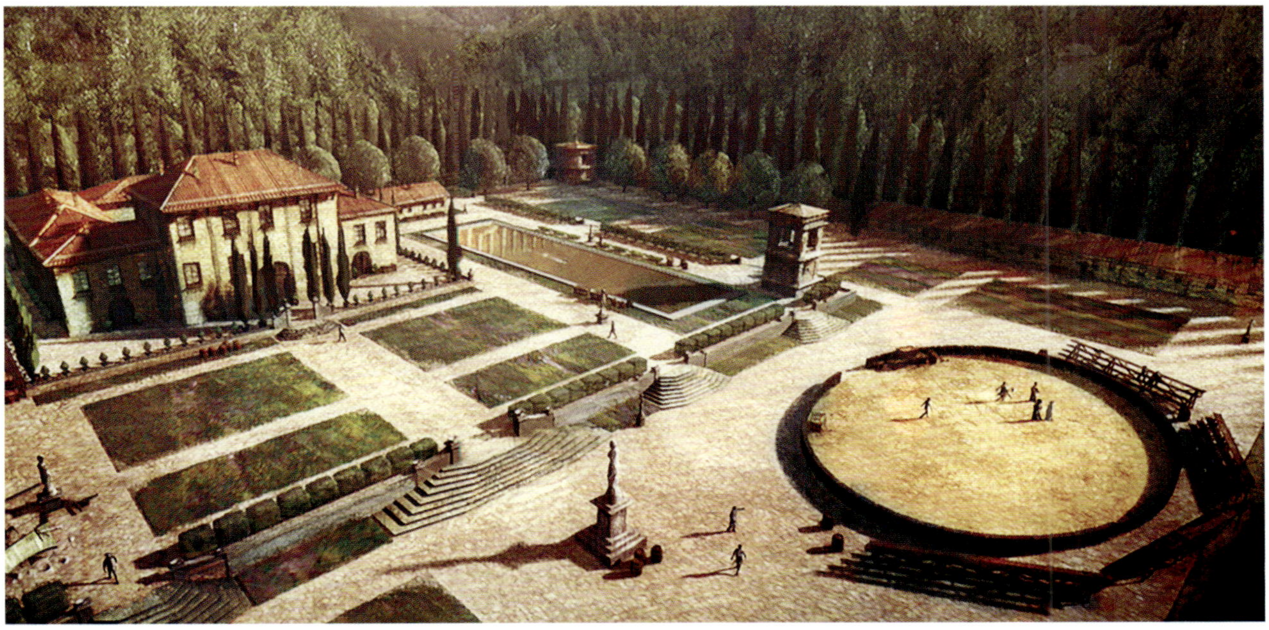

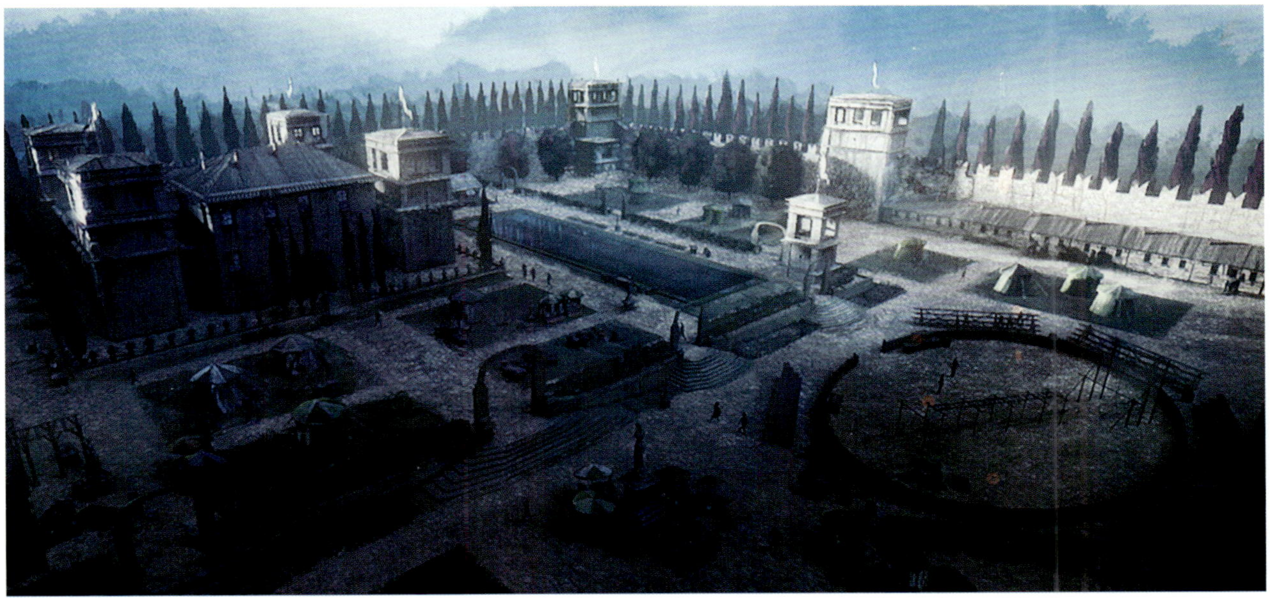

PASSING TIME

The introduction of shifting times of day presented new challenges to the team. "In the first *Assassin's Creed*, the lighting changes between levels because the time of day is fixed. In *Assassin's Creed II* the time was changing, so the colors changed as well," Mohamed recalls. "So I needed to find a cycle of colors where, even if the light changes, they would remain almost identical. That was the way that we managed to create a unique flavor for each city." Whether early in the game in the streets of Florence or as Ezio's adventures took him on to other cities, each place needed a color identity that would shine through, no matter the time of day. The artists forged ahead with plans to give each city its own clear tone and historical panache, while maintaining a broader visual style that helped *Assassin's Creed II* establish its own identity independent of the franchise's first entry.

THESE PAGES: Artwork showing the contrast in times of day at the villa (Gilles Beloeil).

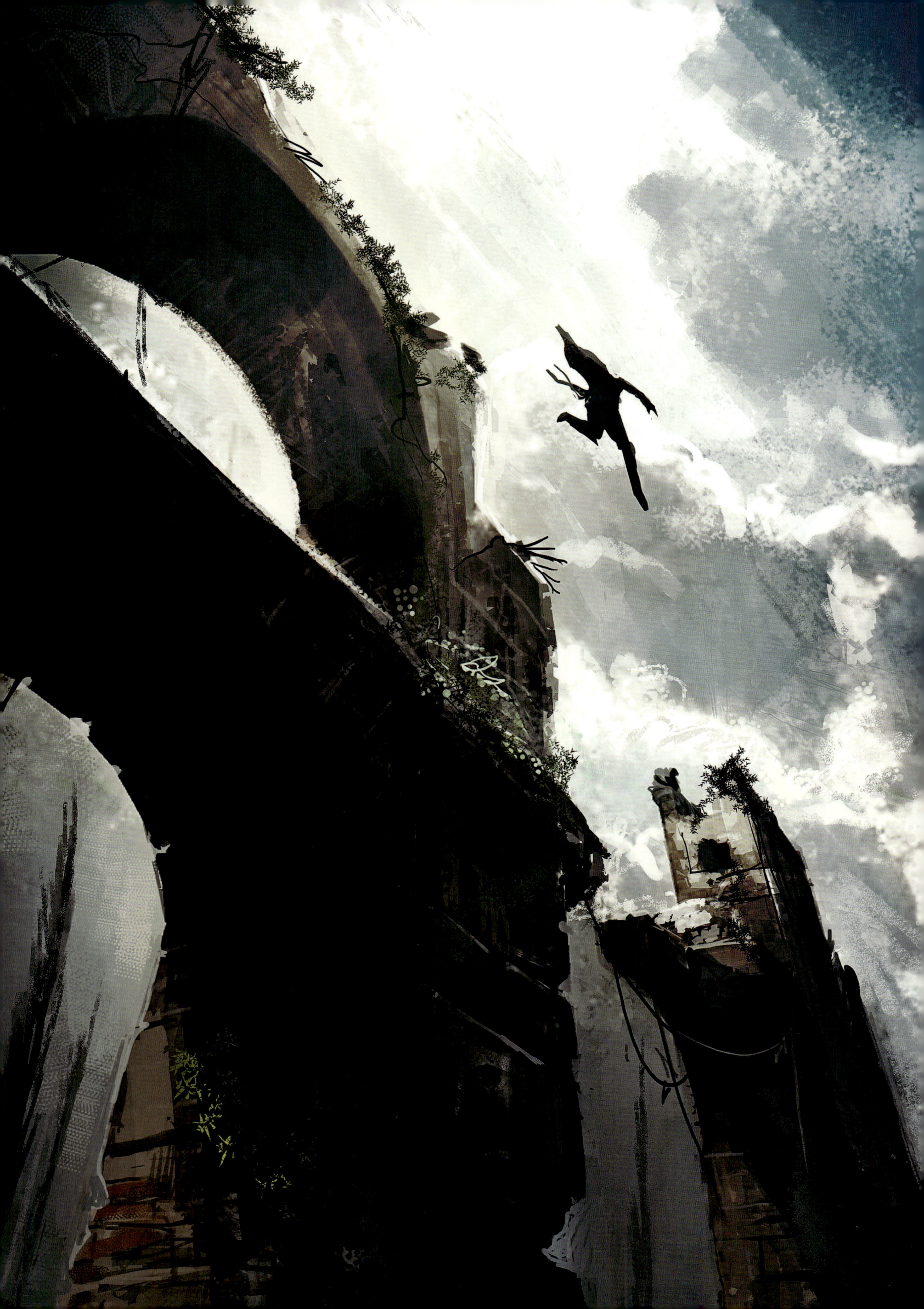

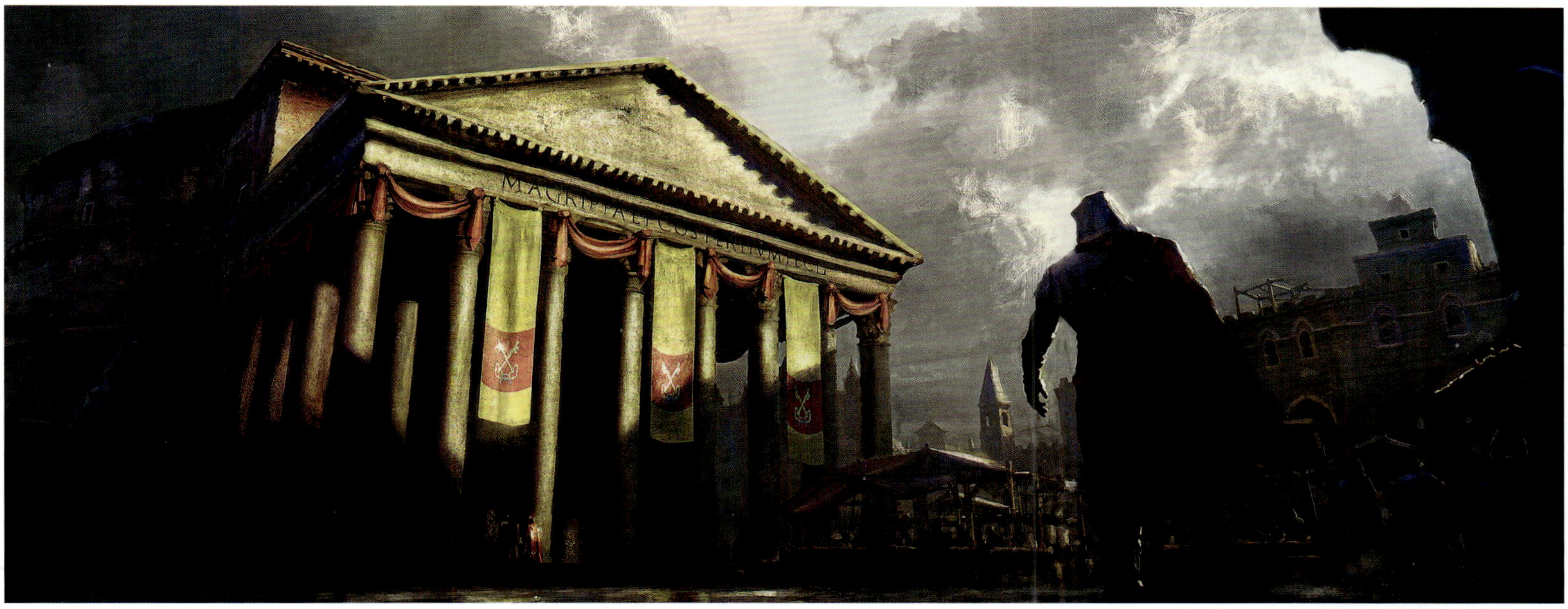

WHERE ALL ROADS LEAD

The final confrontation in *Assassin's Creed II* offered a glimpse of Italy's most renowned city and the innermost sanctum of the Catholic Church. However, it wasn't until *Assassin's Creed: Brotherhood* that Rome would get the full spotlight. After Rodrigo's illegitimate son, Cesare Borgia, assaulted and besieged Monteriggioni, Ezio was forced to relocate to Rome, where he would spearhead the revitalization of the Assassin Brotherhood.

Rome proved to be an artistic tour de force for the development team: a single, massive urban environment instead of several smaller ones. Eliminating the need to focus on multiple cities and wilderness locations, the artists were able to focus on the details and complexity of the Eternal City. Ancient ruins dotted the cityscape from the massive Colosseum to the Pantheon. Remains of aqueducts lined the streets, offering alluring avenues for challenging climbs and runs. The Castel Sant'Angelo was rendered as a seemingly impenetrable fortress of the papacy. Perhaps most impressive, the iconic Basilica di San Pietro dominated a good portion of the skyline and served as a suitable venue for some of *Brotherhood*'s most powerful and dramatic moments. The art and design team had specific goals in mind for Rome, and they were willing to bend the historical record to achieve them. The Rome of history is an amalgam of the many cultures, empires, and religions that have called it home, often coexisting side by side. In *Brotherhood*, specific parts of the city were set aside to communicate the scope of the city's grand timeline. The southernmost reaches recalled ancient Rome, with its fluted colonnades and tumbled ruins; red and brown touches communicated great age. Farther north, the middle of the city spoke to medieval expansion; there, brown and white buildings felt more utilitarian than their older forebears. Finally, the northern reaches of the city were dominated by churches and castles; the yellow and white tones accentuated the Baroque architecture and style.

While Rome was the most detailed and massive city yet crafted for the Assassin's Creed fiction, the biggest accomplishment came in visualizing and realizing its slow revitalization. By steadily confronting and overtaking the towers held by the allies of the Borgia family, Ezio opened up entire sections of the city for renovation. Like a macrocosm of Monteriggioni rebuilding efforts in the previous game, Rome grew and improved as players poured time and money in. Previously decrepit streets were suddenly lined with blacksmith and tailor shops. Empty stalls became populated with stabled horses. Ruined landmarks received suitable repairs. Not only was Rome one of the largest single maps in franchise history but it was one that responded dynamically to player interaction, going through a metamorphosis over the course of the *Brotherhood* adventure.

OPPOSITE: The art direction for Rome emphasized the historical layers of the city, as demonstrated by this concept of the aqueducts (Martin Deschambault).
ABOVE: Ezio approaches the Pantheon (Gilles Beloeil).

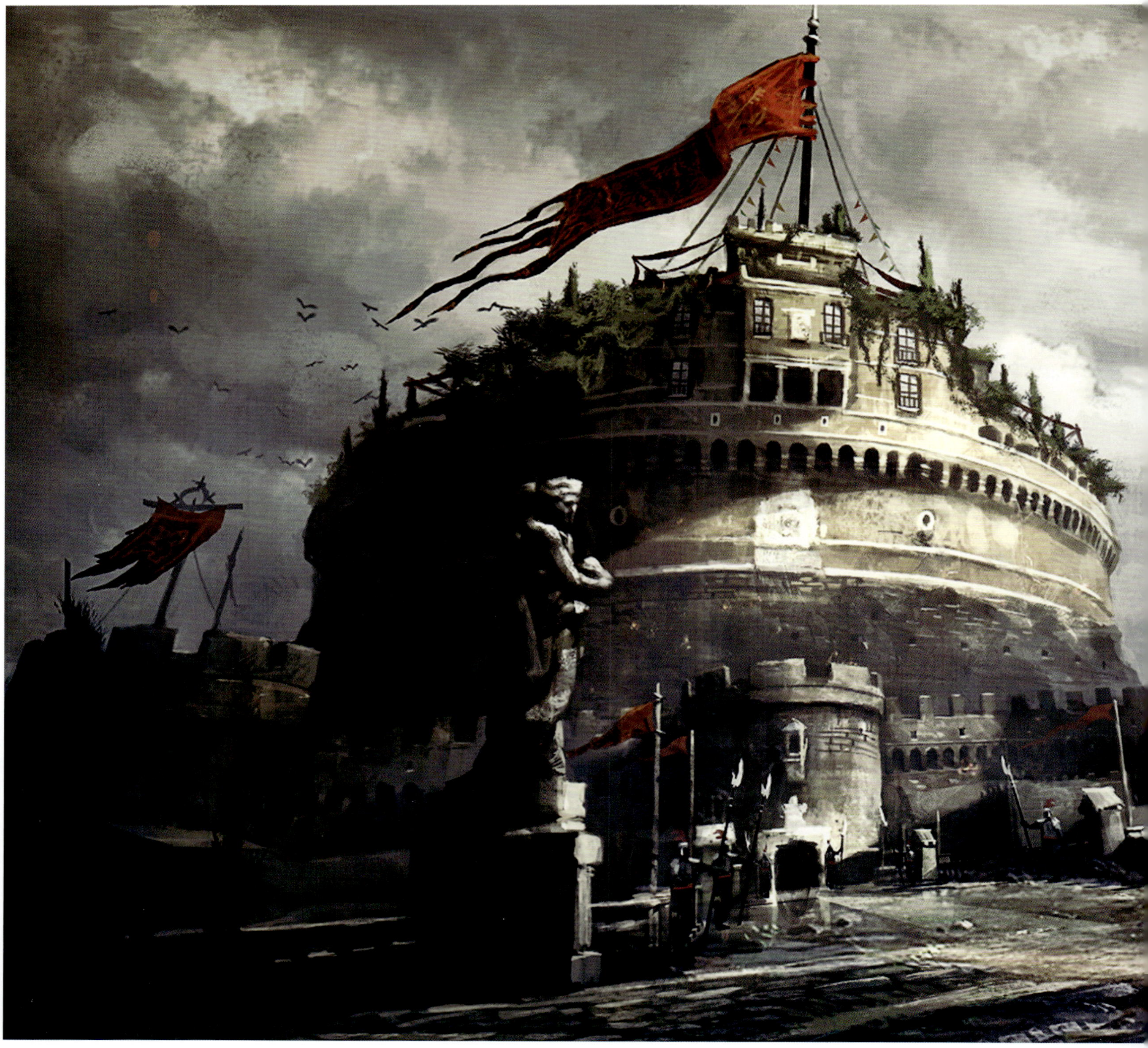

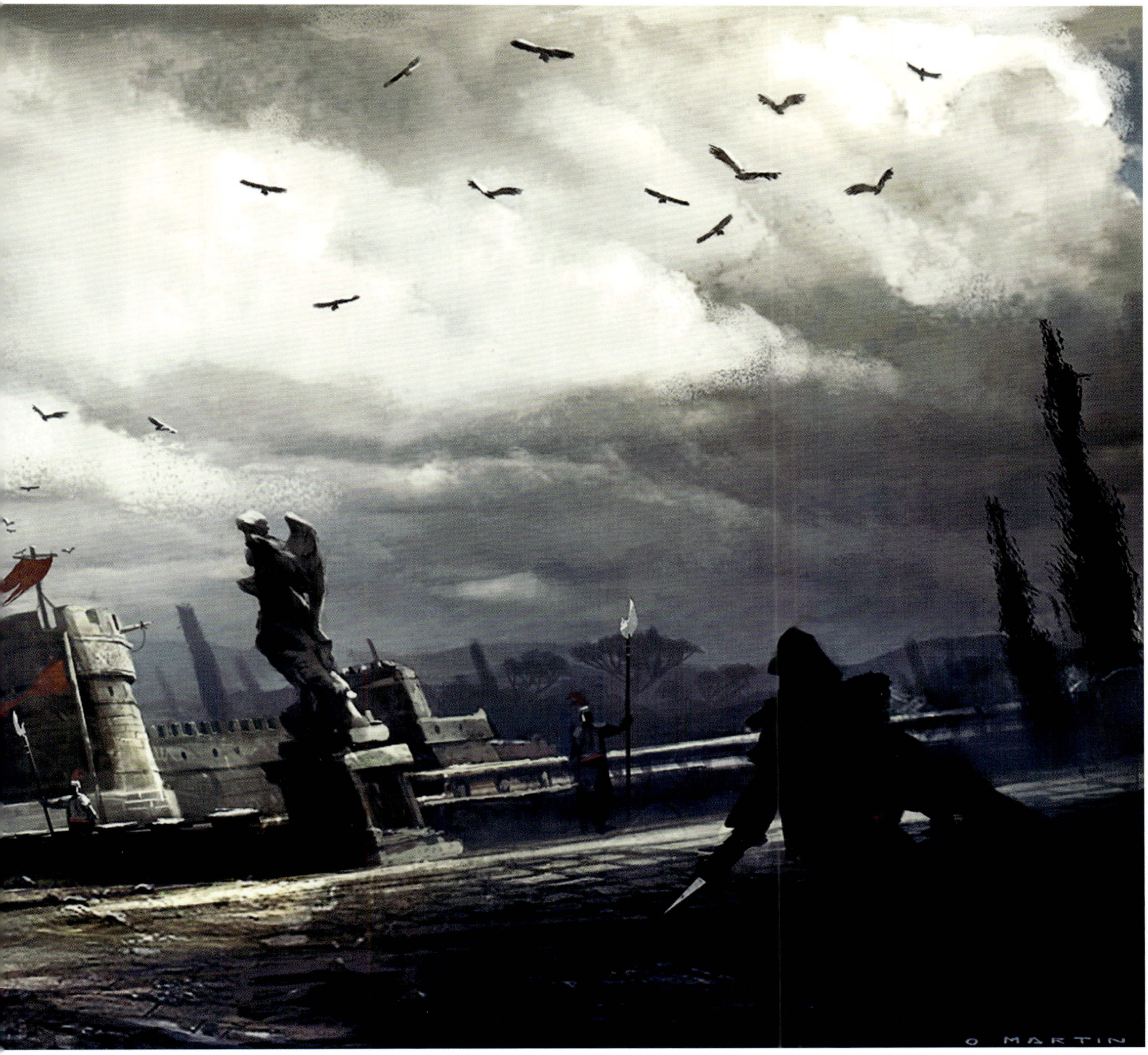

THESE PAGES: Digital painting of the Castel Sant'Angelo (Olivier Martin).

THE BORGIAS

The first two games in Ezio's trilogy set him squarely against one of Italy's most wealthy and politically connected families. Ubisoft chose to paint the Borgias in an uncompromising light; it was hard to marshal much sympathy for their incestuous relationships and murderous ways.

The family patriarch, Rodrigo, exuded a brooding menace throughout *Assassin's Creed II*. His machinations not only led to the death of many in Ezio's family, but his broader ambitions led to his questionable ascension to the papacy. His long, squared-off robes lent a sense of authority and menace, while remaining rooted in the style of the Templar Order he helped lead.

By the time *Brotherhood* began, Rodrigo's power had been rendered largely ineffectual after a final climactic confrontation with Ezio, in which he was defeated and humiliated. Instead, it was his illegitimate son, Cesare Borgia, who would become a true nemesis to our hero. Art director Mohamed Gambouz recalls early inspirations for the character, looking to the lavish costumes of recent historical filmmaking and mixing in classic Shakespearean overtones. "At that time, I had just seen the movie *Elizabeth: The Golden Age*, and I thought the lead character played by Spanish actor Jordi Mollà would perfectly fit Cesare Borgia," Mohamed says. "So I started working from there, trying to find a compelling visual look for him, and we mixed it with iconic elements from *Julius Caesar*, such as a red robe, cape, and antique armor. This is one of the characters that I liked working on the most."

Lucrezia Borgia, Cesare's younger sister, had the smallest role but was perhaps the most nuanced of the Borgias. For Lucrezia, the art team started from a strange inspiration. The Tarantino film *Kill Bill* presented a striking and dangerous figure with Uma Thurman's interpretation of The Bride, and early art for Lucrezia latched onto the dangerous feminine mystique. "She was the first one I had in mind once I read the story of Lucrezia Borgia," Mohamed says. Ultimately, Lucrezia would take on a strangely tragic quality, even if it was hard to ever mount much affection for the calculating character.

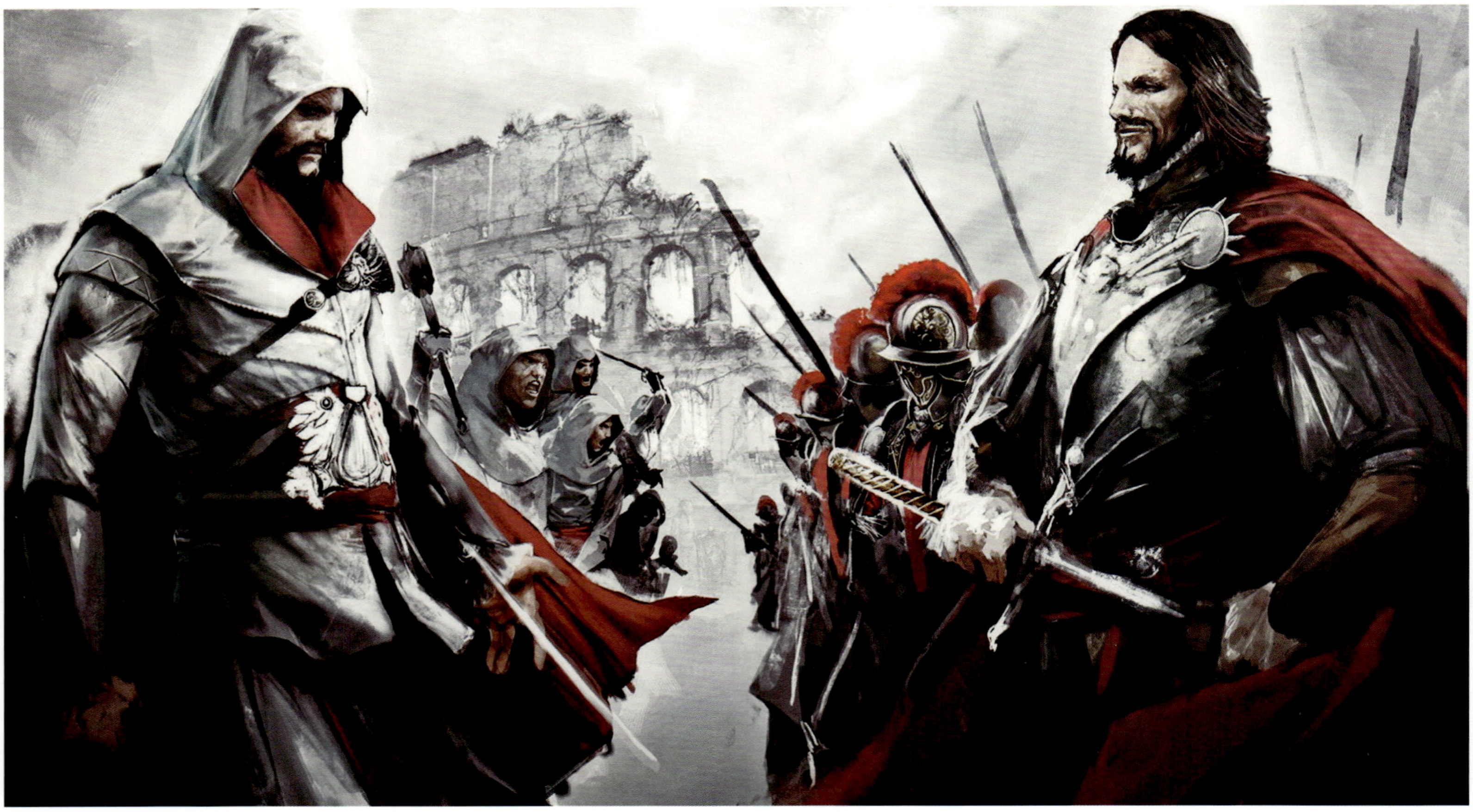

OPPOSITE: Character art for Lucrezia Borgia (Vincent Gaigneux).
ABOVE: Ezio's Brotherhood stands off against Cesare Borgia and his soldiers (Vincent Gaigneux).

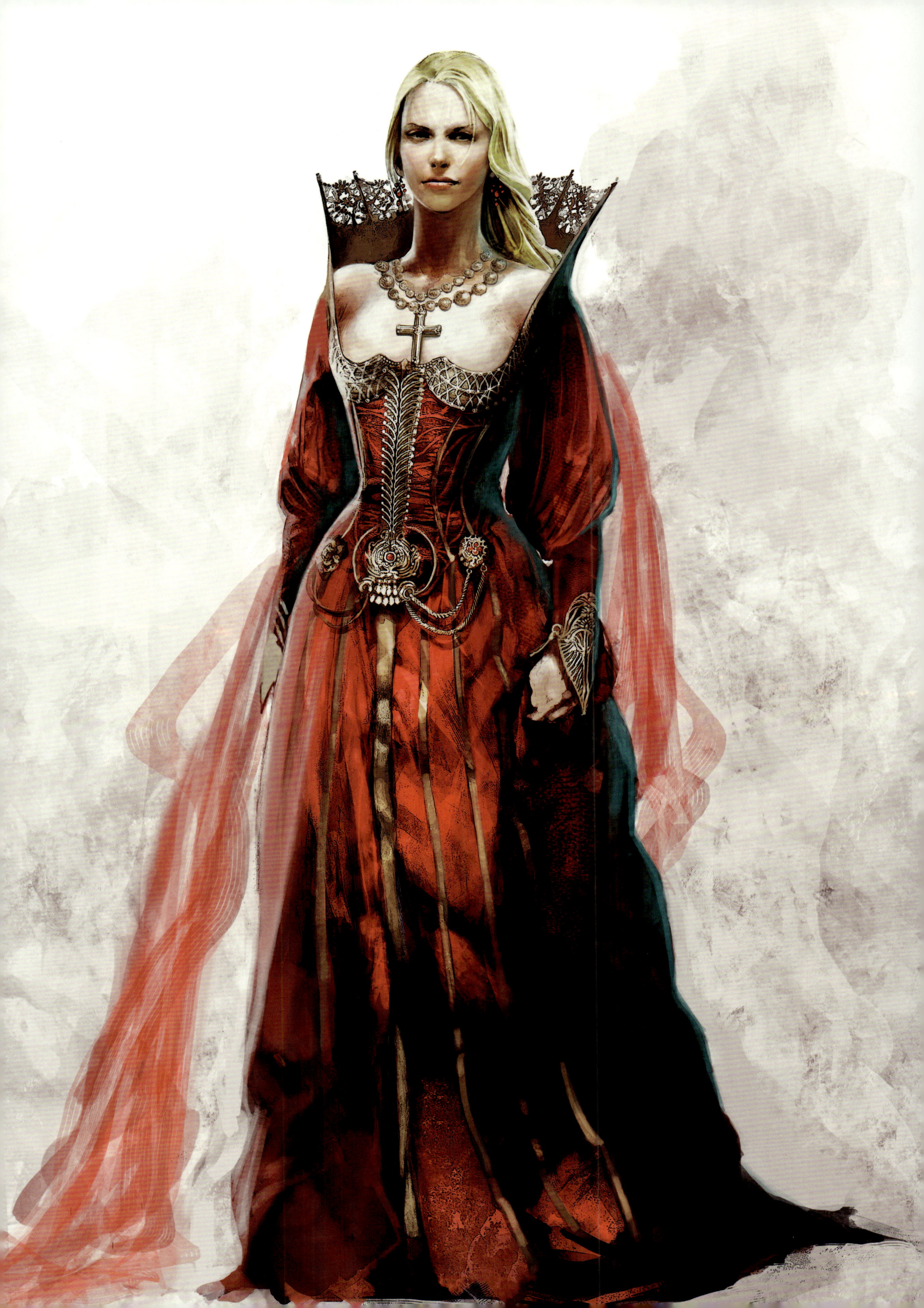

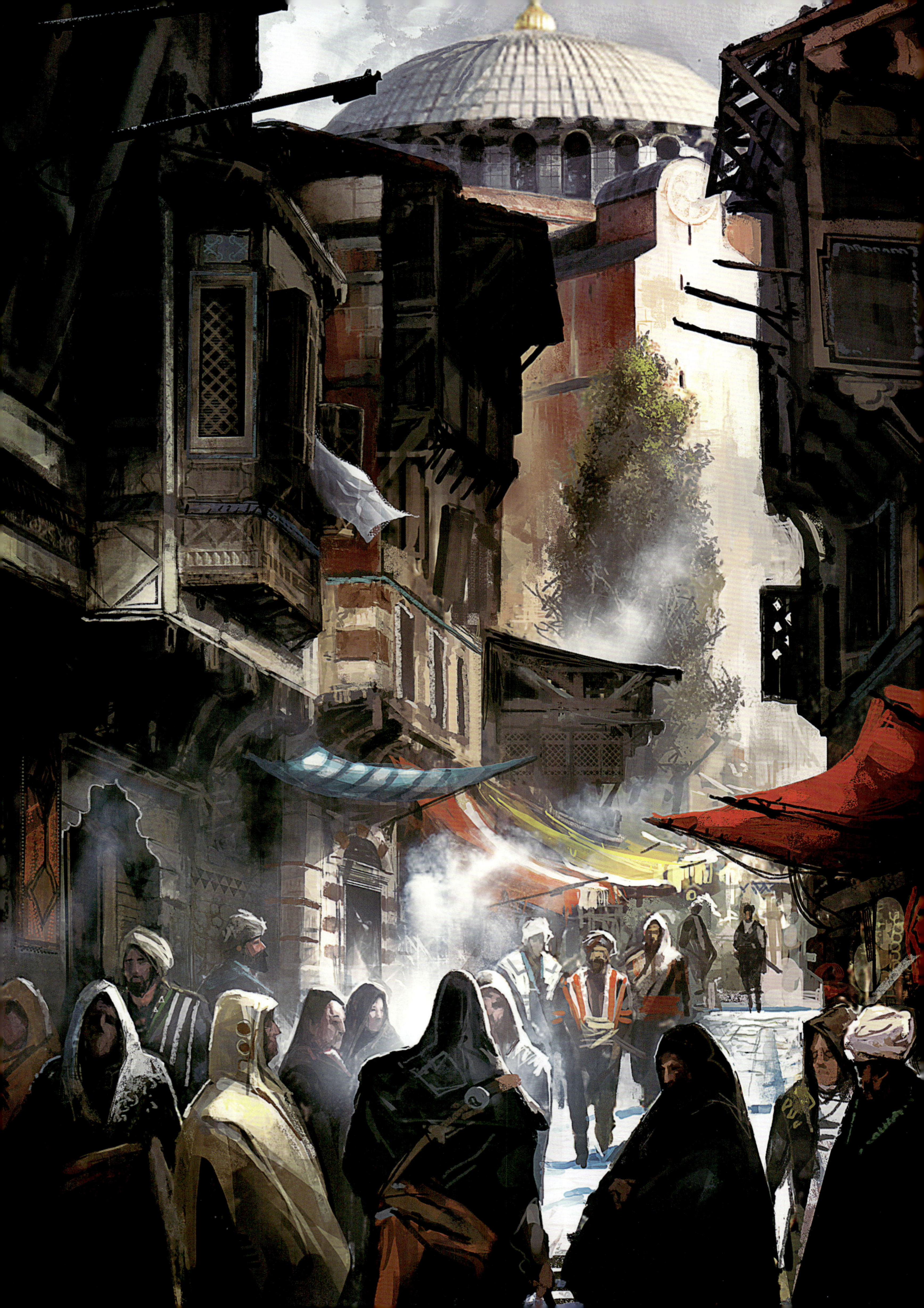

STRANGER IN A STRANGE LAND

The third act of Ezio's grand adventure played out in *Assassin's Creed: Revelations*, and it would take him east, far from the comforts of home in Italy, to the cosmopolitan and exotic city of Constantinople. After a lifetime of death and revenge, an older Ezio searched for some sense of meaning behind the violence and a semblance of wisdom amid the chaos. His trip to Constantinople would eventually provide some of the answers he sought but would not mitigate the conflict that had followed him all his life. Ezio's arrival coincided with the final days of the reign of Bayezid II, and the Assassin's presence was pivotal in settling the balance of power in the region.

Straddling the line between East and West, Constantinople had already been shaken by decades of fierce conflict. The Ottomans were still consolidating their rule after taking the city from the Byzantines, who had previously held the city for centuries. The remnants of the Byzantines offered a fierce resistance against the Ottoman Janissaries, and Ezio's arrival and restoration of the Assassins only complicated matters.

The convoluted political and cultural conflicts made for a fascinating artistic backdrop, and the team found their greatest inspiration through a visit to the modern-day site. "We went to Istanbul to get visual references, but the city looks very different now," Raphaël says. "We had to do a lot of additional research, but at the same time, it offered us a lot of freedom in our interpretation. The historical elements and the major landmarks have to be very authentic in order to immerse the player in history. But to enhance the vibrant and exotic mood of Constantinople, we let ourselves be inspired by classical engravers and painters like Ivan Aivazovsky."

The research trip to Istanbul was extensive and invaluable for capturing the tone of the ancient city. From a close look at landmarks to getting a feel for the quality of the lighting, in-person photography made a huge difference. "We went in two groups, and each spent one week there and took more than two thousand photos," Raphaël recalls. "The weather was really, really bad, but because of that, we didn't have any shadows in the textures. The textures were just perfect because of the diffused, overcast lighting. We took photos of all the textures of the Topkapi Palace and the mosaics, and we used that to make the textures of the world."

Constantinople felt different from the western European sites of *Assassin's Creed II* and *Brotherhood*. The city was split into distinct districts that showed the spread of wealth and poverty across the city, from the hovels of Constantine to the varied cultures of the Galata District, the commerce of the Bayezid District, and on through the opulent mosques and palaces of the Imperial section of the city. "We tried to create bold differences between all the districts," Raphaël says. "The city is full of interesting visual contrasts. When you are in the poor district, you might see a crooked wooden house with people looking down from dark windows above. It has a rough, gritty atmosphere. In the rich district, the marble structures have clean vertical lines. With majestic landmarks and colorful decorations, it's an almost mystical area."

Constantinople had no shortage of fascinating sites to visit. The Grand Bazaar, for example, was a maze of colorful stalls and shouting merchants. "The original idea was to do the Grand Bazaar as it is, but it's very, very big," Jean says. "When the team went there, they realized that its mazelike quality was crucial. So we rendered the corridors with the shops, but we didn't need to replicate the exact, full bazaar. We were able to reduce its scale without losing the sense of it."

Beyond the markets of the city, memories of classical Greece were on display in the ruins of the Hippodrome. The Arsenal district was home to every culture imaginable as spices, textiles, and ships from across the world commingled in the port. And the majestic Hagia Sophia was one of the largest and most awe-inspiring structures to yet appear in the series; the climb through its interior was memorable and vertigo-inducing.

While Constantinople served as the chief locale for Ezio's adventures in *Assassin's Creed: Revelations*, the most unusual and exotic location was reserved for late in the game. A short ship ride found Ezio entering the Templar stronghold of Cappadocia. Loosely based on a real historical city built almost entirely underground, Ezio's infiltration of the massive cavern saw him climbing up stalagmites and ducking into buildings carved from solid rock. "Cappadocia provided us with an opportunity to do something very different from Constantinople," Raphaël says. "The underground city in Cappadocia is inspired by Derinkuyu, Turkey, which has an ancient underground city spread out over multiple levels. This location really spoke to the imagination of the artists and level designers, as it was so very different from the traditional cities we had created before for Assassin's Creed." The visual effect of the settlement was powerful, especially during a climactic escape from the subterranean town as smoke slowly overwhelmed its inhabitants.

OPPOSITE: Constantinople's corridors and shops were designed to create the sense of a maze (Martin Deschambault).

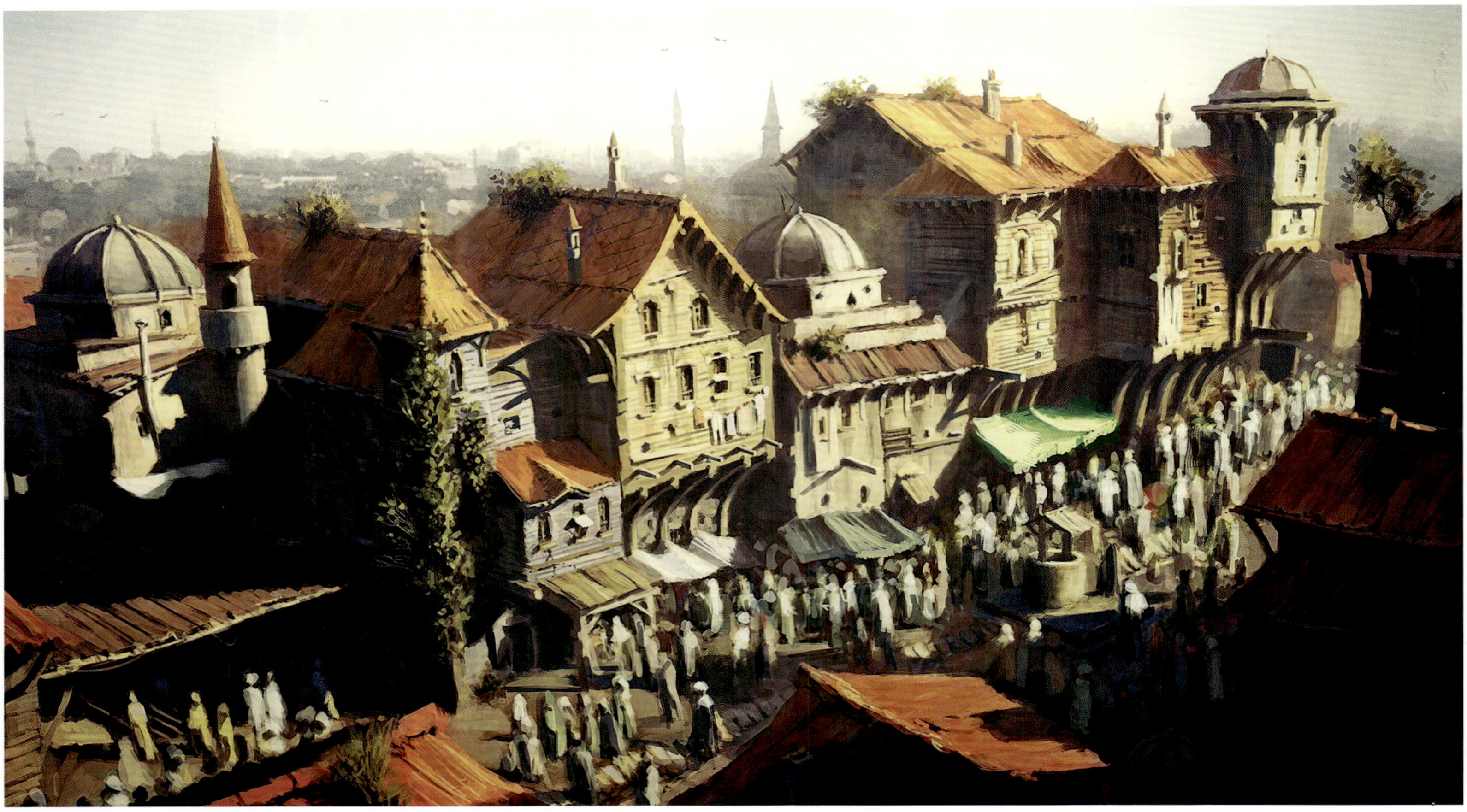

ABOVE: Concept of a Constantinople poor district (Gilles Beloeil).
OPPOSITE: *Assassin's Creed: Revelations* featured exotic architecture and a darker color palette than previous games (Martin Deschambault).

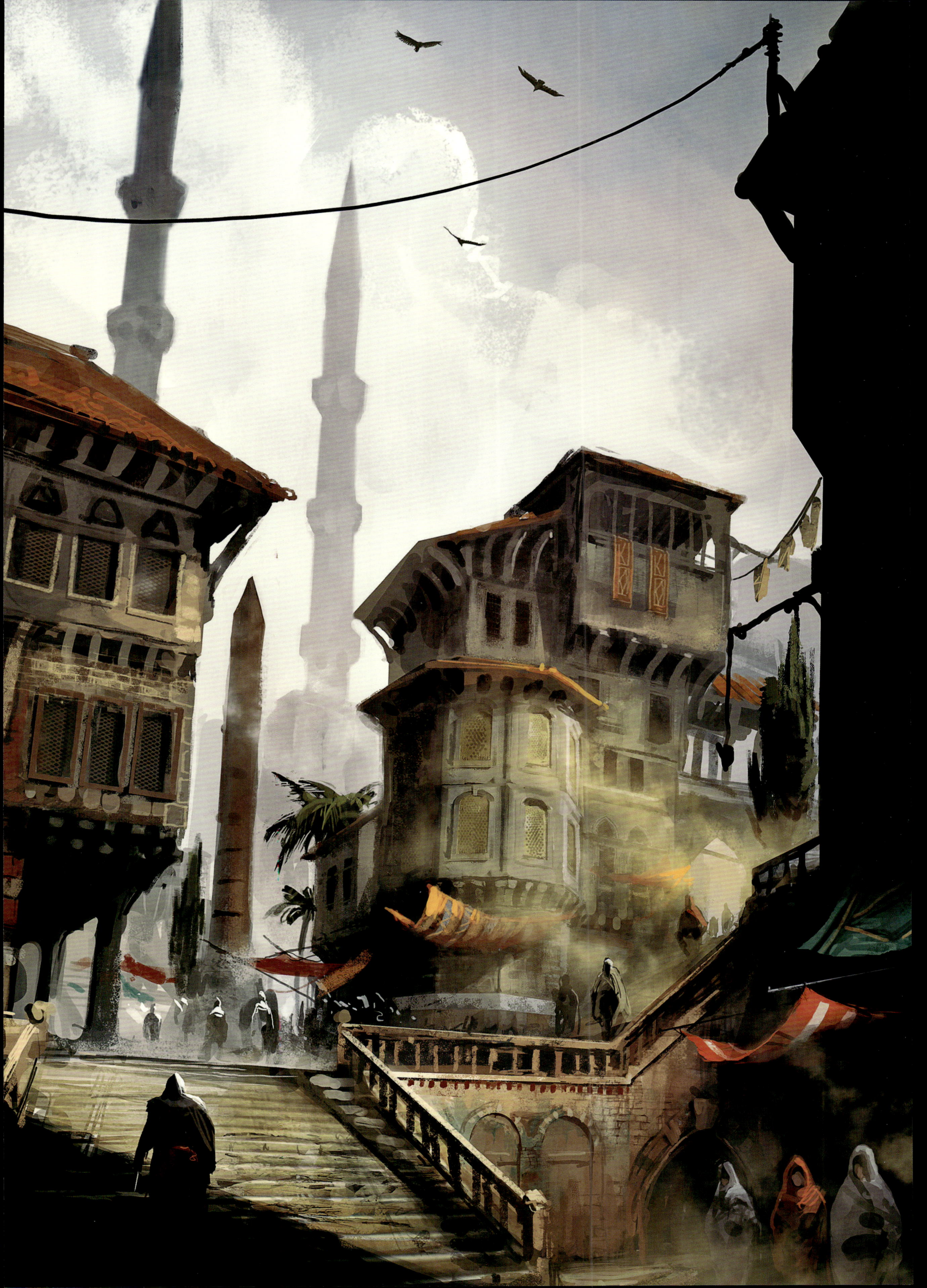

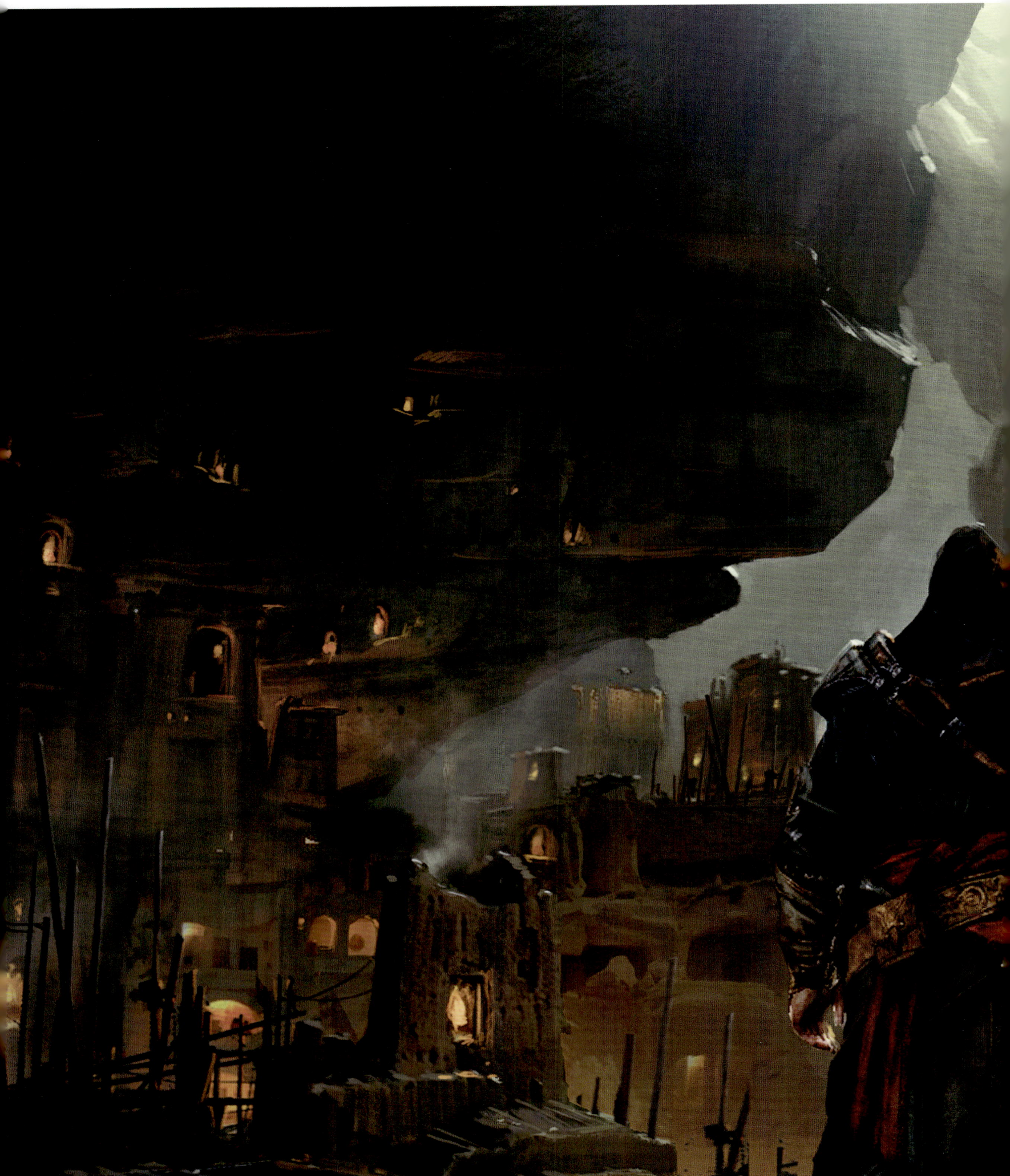

THESE PAGES: Digital painting of the underground city of Cappadocia (Raphaël Lacoste).

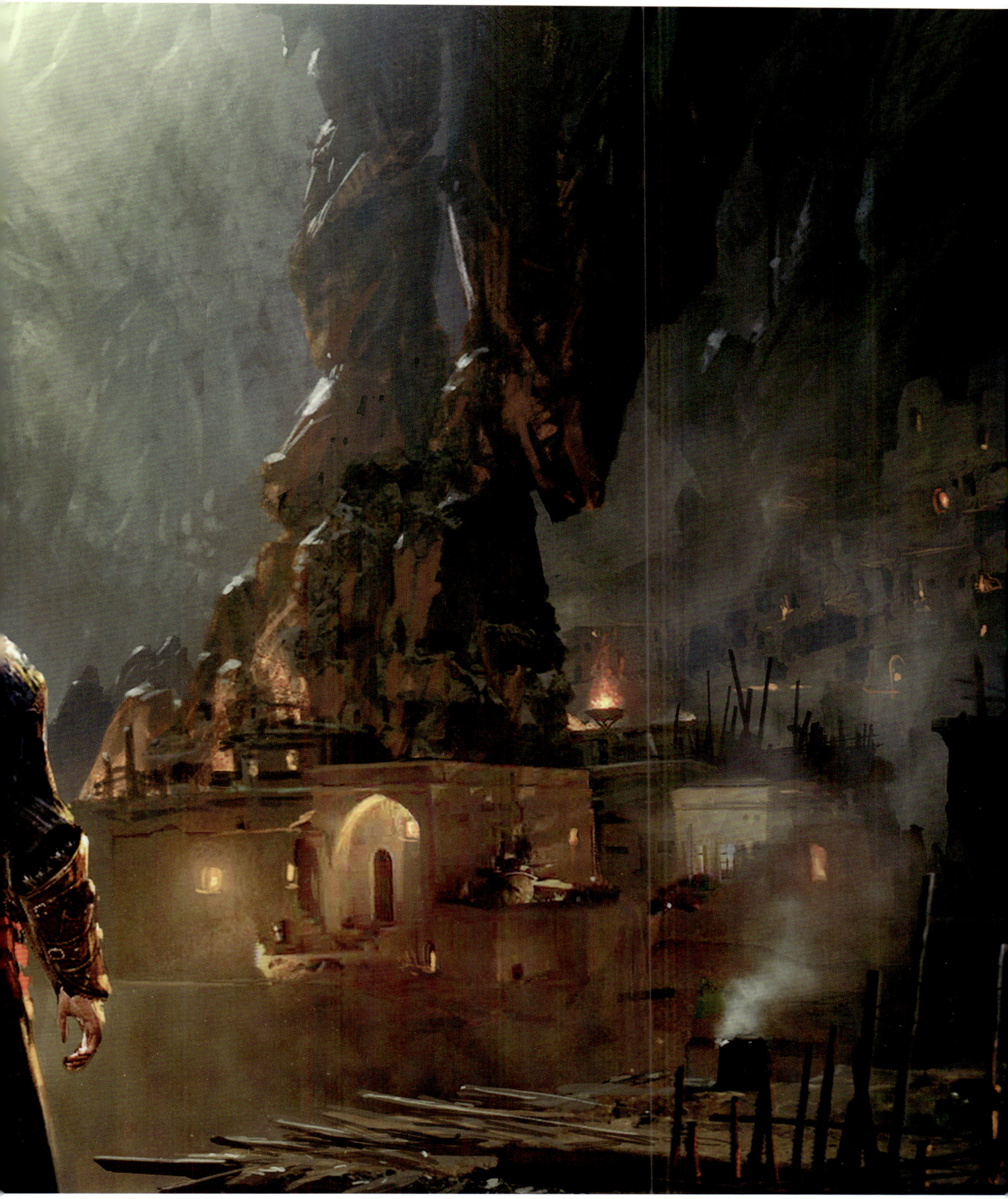

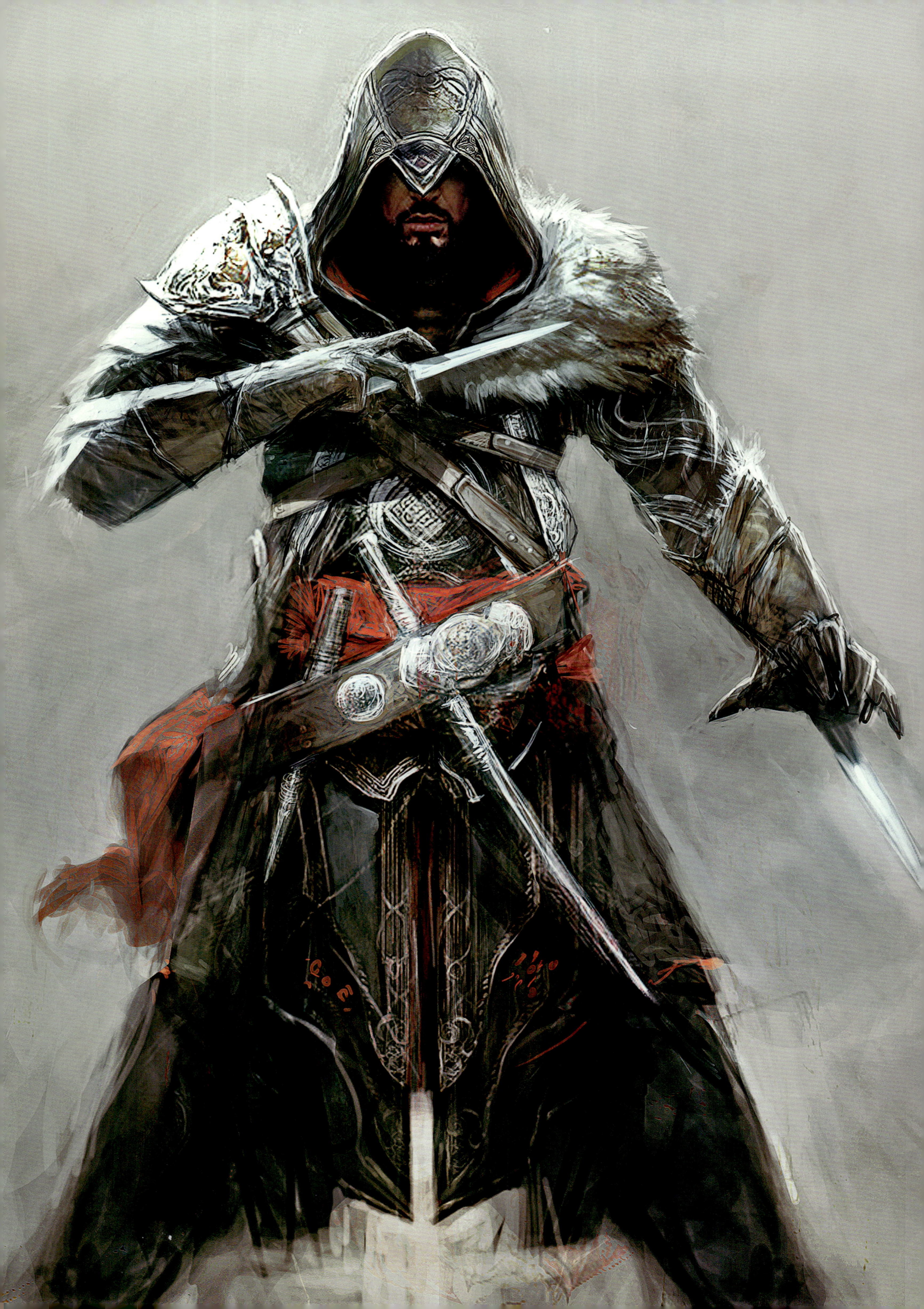

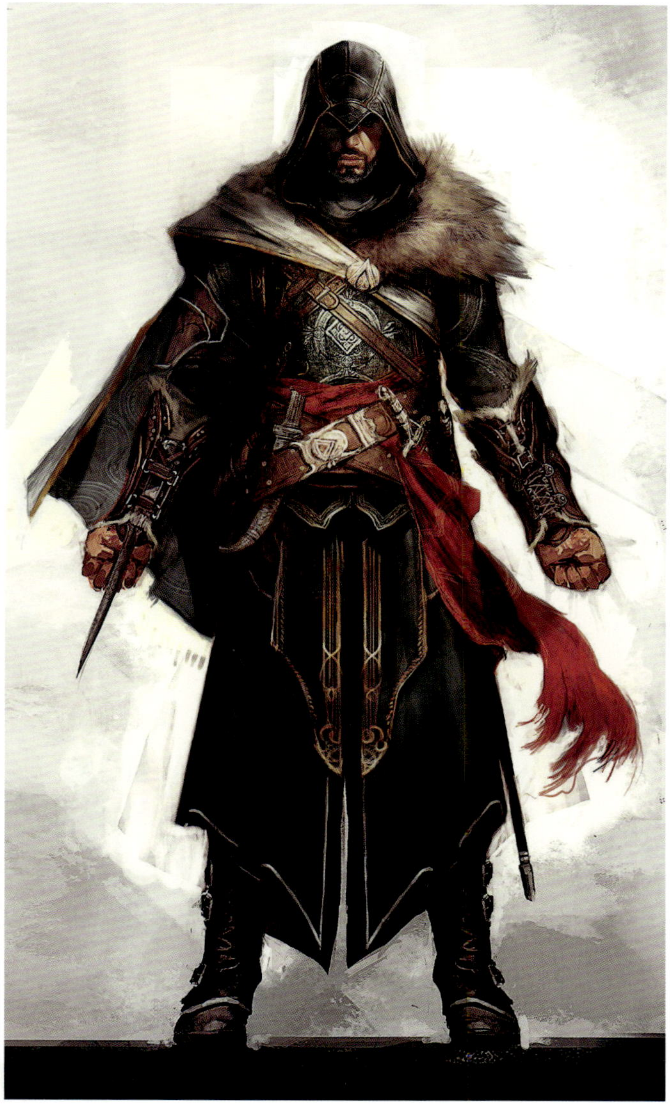

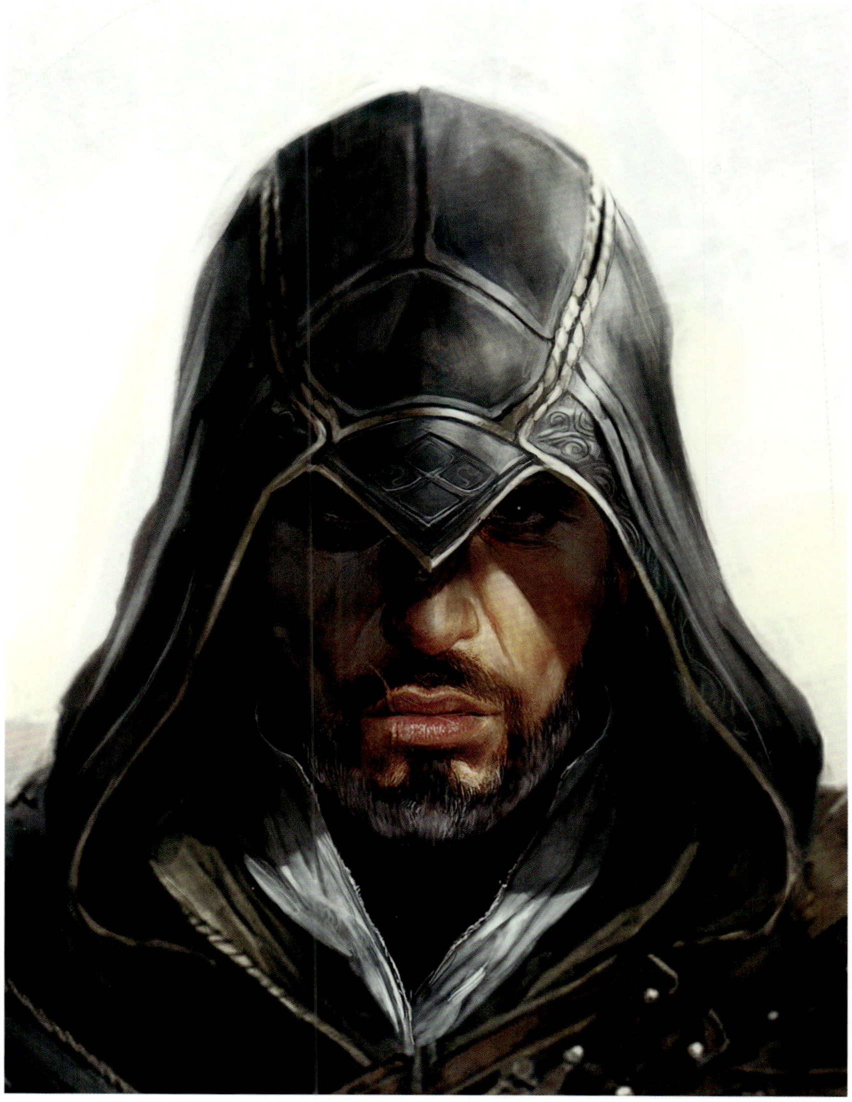

DESIGNING THE CENTERPIECE

Few elements of a game's make up are more crucial than the main character. As the center of the player's experience, the protagonist shapes the fantasy and vicarious thrills on offer. Character artists for Assassin's Creed have faced unusual challenges as they aim to shape new heroes for each installment. For one, each new Assassin must walk the line between historical authenticity and excitement. In addition, each character needs to feel true to the heritage of previous heroes but simultaneously distinct. "Main characters are tough because they take a long time, and they change often over the course of the design process. The essence is invariably there, but you can go in many directions and make several tweaks. There are always many iterations of the same character," says character artist Jeff Simpson. "You're taking something that exists either historically or in the imagination of people and trying to represent it as something that feels fresh and yet authentic at the same time."

OPPOSITE: Ezio's *Revelations* costume features detailed Ottoman embroidery (Jeff Simpson).
THIS PAGE: With its heavier fabrics and darker colors, Ezio's robes are those of a traveler (Jeff Simpson).

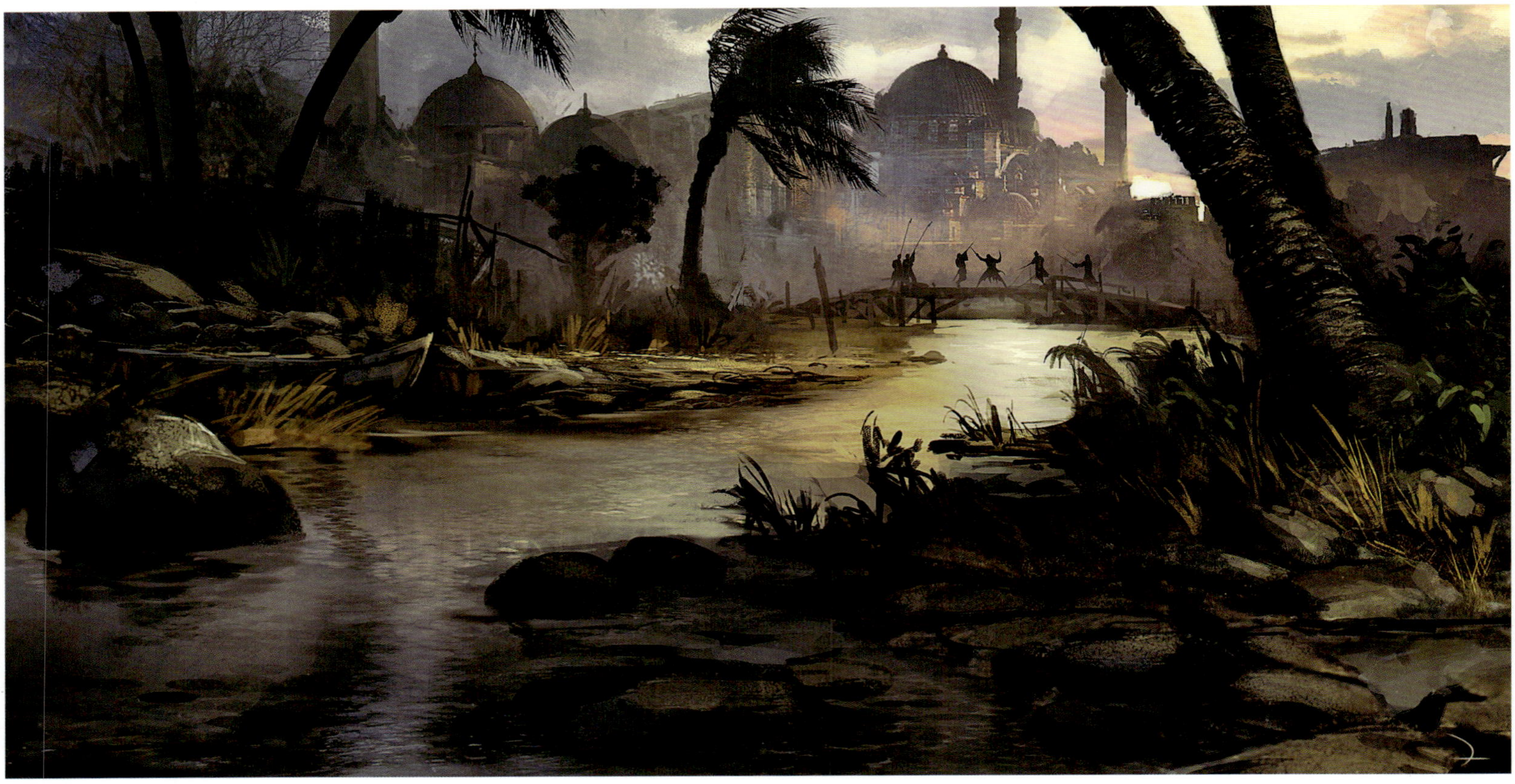

EMPIRE MOVERS

Revelations found Constantinople at a pivotal moment in its history when several forces competed for power. The two sons of the reigning sultan, Ahmet and Selim, conspired against one another in pursuit of the throne. Of greater interest, the game also introduced seventeen-year-old Suleiman. Destined to one day become one of the most powerful kings in the world, this untested teenager found a friend in Ezio and admired the man's leadership and determination. Meanwhile, Manuel Palaiologos plied his power as a leading force in the Templar Order to try and reinstate his family's control and take what he saw as his rightful place as head of a reborn Byzantine Empire.

ABOVE: Artwork of Constantinople (Martin Deschambault).
OPPOSITE: Character art of Selim, the younger son of the reigning sultan (Jeff Simpson).

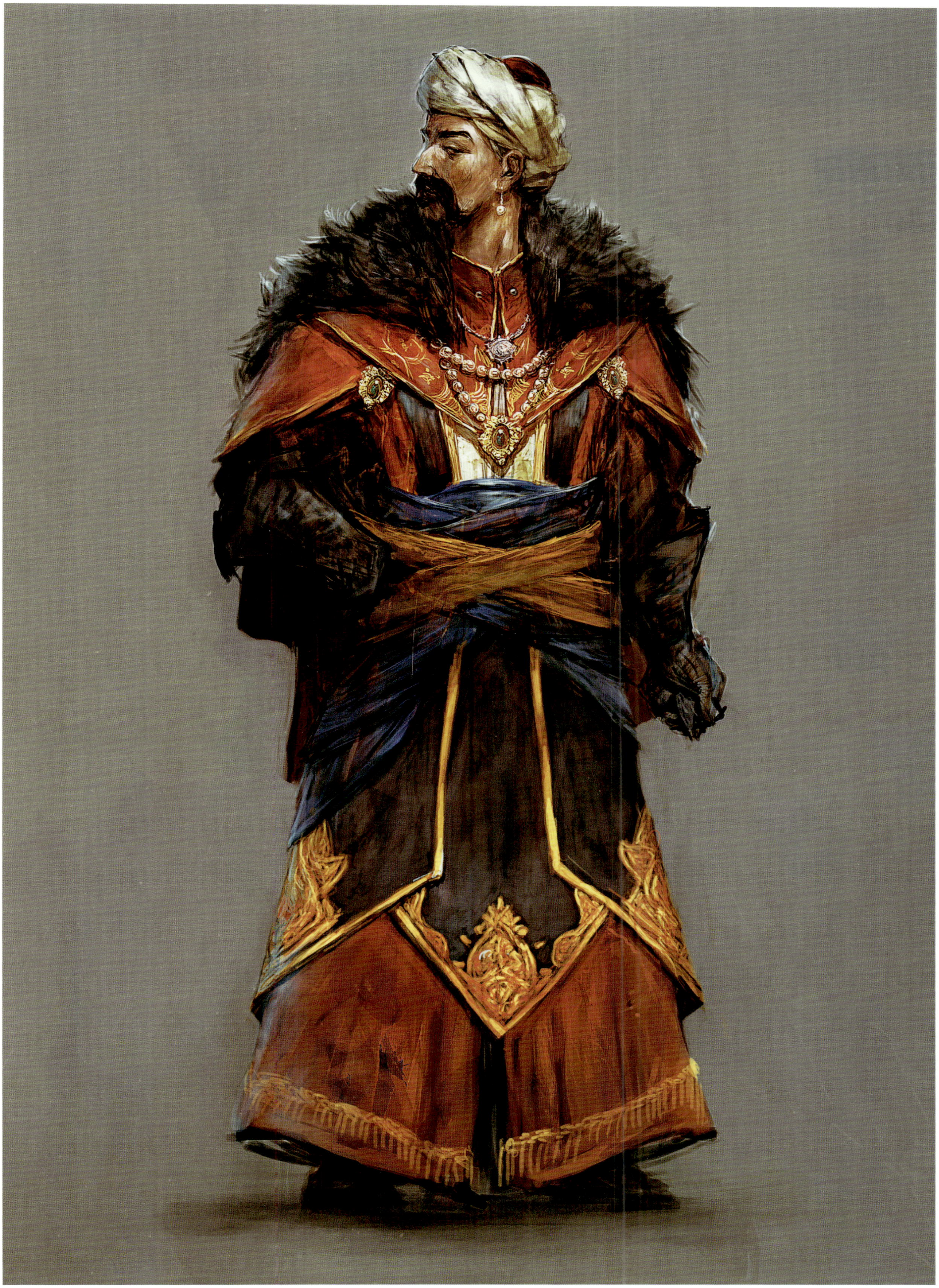

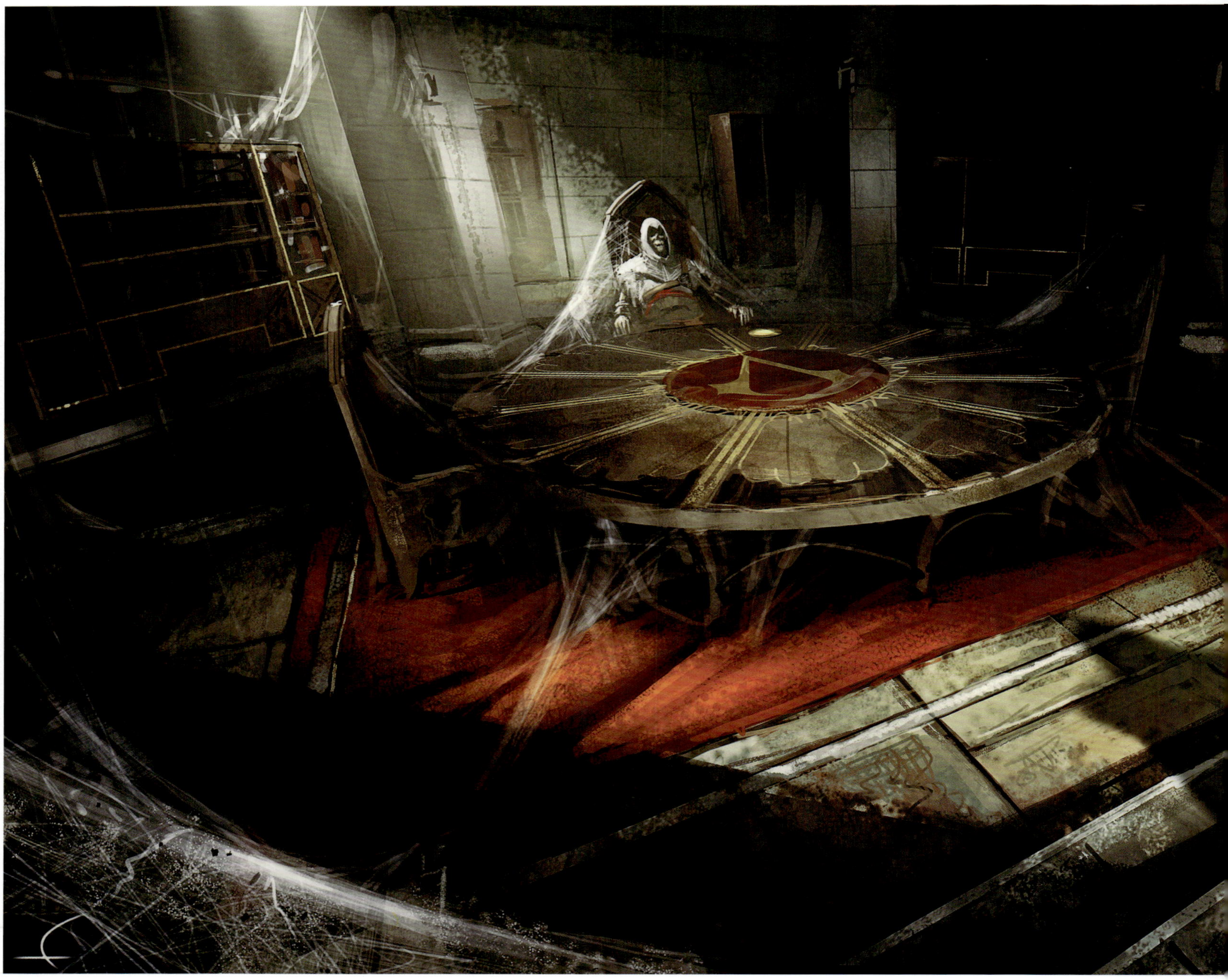

FINAL DAYS

Assassin's Creed: Revelations was a chance to wrap up a lot of loose ends before moving on to new stories in the third numbered installment. While the Constantinople adventure provided glimpses of Ezio coming to terms with his life, *Revelations* also allowed the artists and writers to return to their old friend, Altaïr, and finally close the book on the original franchise hero.

Through the power of the mystical discs Ezio discovered throughout the game, we returned once again to Masyaf to witness critical moments in Altaïr's life after he became Mentor of the Levantine Assassins. The most striking depiction was the last memory, when we see a seemingly decrepit Altaïr still driven by duty and a quest for knowledge as he commits one final task in the name of the Brotherhood.

It was also time to bid farewell to Ezio, whose momentous existence had changed him in important ways. "We see the three acts of his life," Jean says. "His early adventures throughout *Assassin's Creed II* are about revenge and being forced into the life of an Assassin, ending with him embracing his path with the black robes. Ezio becomes this very solid, very focused, and dedicated Mentor in *Brotherhood*," Jean says. "His much simpler costume reflects this transition." By Ezio's last outing in *Revelations*, he was searching for meaning. "It's a man on a path toward himself and, in the end, realizing who he wants to be," Jean suggests. "His costume already reflects the fact that he's a traveler. All he cares for now is personal answers; he doesn't care so much about what others think of him."

Ezio's discoveries during *Revelations* finally allowed him to leave the Assassins behind to begin a family.

ABOVE: Even in death, Altaïr shows unwavering dedication to the Brotherhood (Martin Deschambault).
OPPOSITE: Narrative artwork for *Assassin's Creed: Project Legacy* (Ludovic Ribardière).

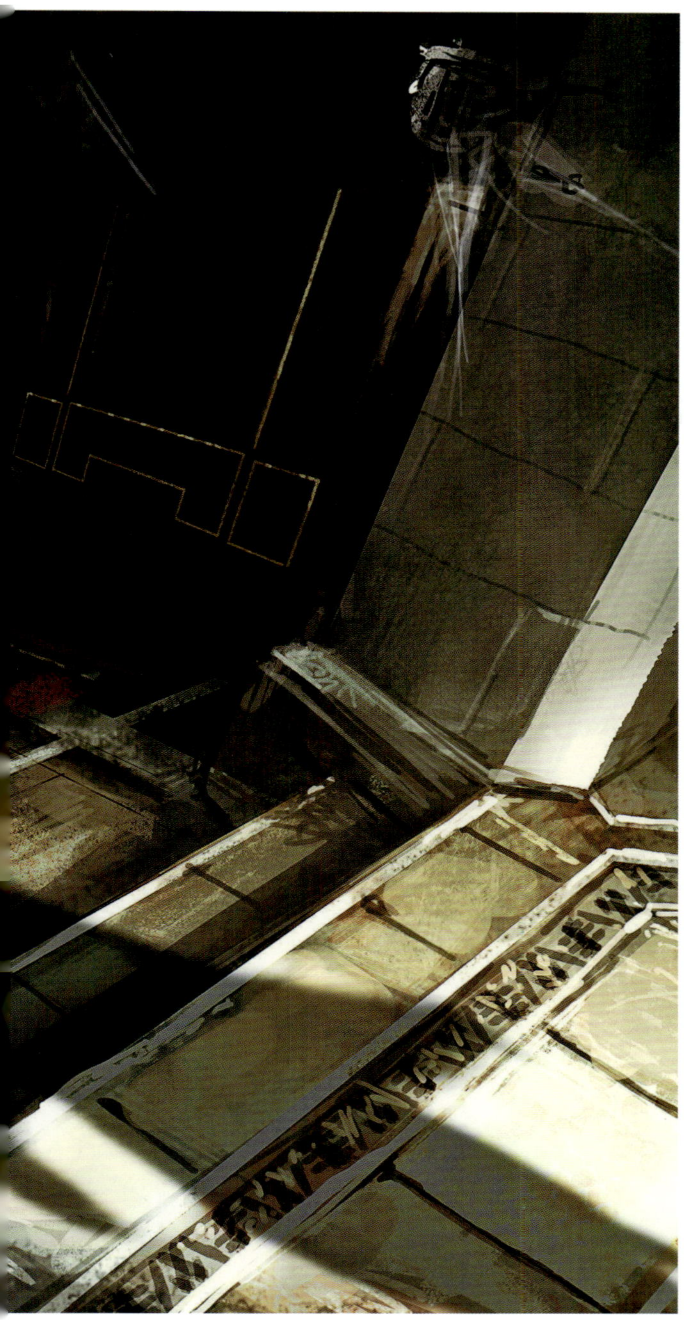

A LASTING LEGACY

While development of major releases continued unabated, the Altaïr and Ezio storylines continued to spawn related projects that slowly expanded upon the Assassin's Creed canon. One of the most unusual and visually distinct was the Facebook game entitled *Project Legacy*. As recruits at Abstergo, players were asked to delve into memories that initially fleshed out the storyline of the Assassin and Templar conflict during the Renaissance. However, with the interjection of the mysterious Erudito hacking collective, *Project Legacy* also offered glimpses into historical moments as long ago as ancient Greece and as recent as 1800s London. "*Legacy* had a lot of lore, a lot of stories, without breaking the rules of the universe," Jean shares. "For me, it was a workshop where we tried different things, and when we started working on *Black Flag*, I often referred to *Project Legacy*."

The offshoot game offered ample opportunity for artists to experiment with ideas, fleshing out characters and settings that might never have otherwise entered the fiction. It also provided an opportunity to further explore the first version of the Animus, since the game was meant to be an Abstergo product. "We took the visual identity of the Animus from the first Assassin's Creed game and made it the key artistic framework of *Project Legacy*," Jean says. "Because the game is set in-universe, it had to be consistent with the tones, the colors, and the shapes of the Assassin's Creed menus."

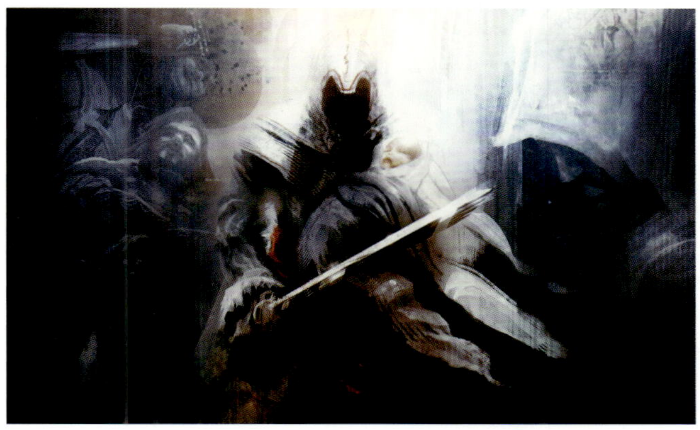

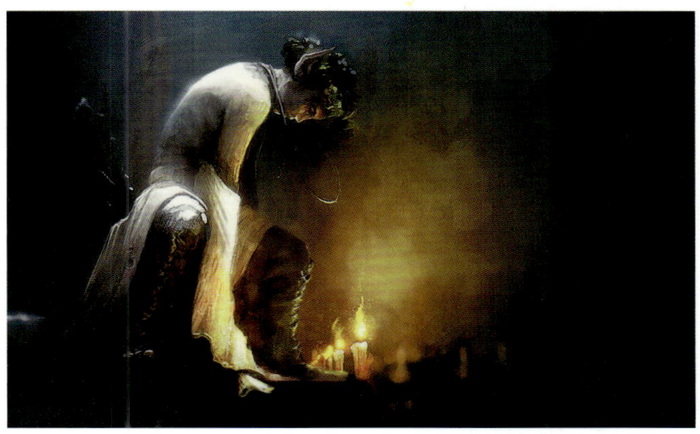

However, the animated short entitled *Assassin's Creed: Embers* offered fans one last chance to see the great Assassin in action. Now an old man living contentedly in the country near Florence, Ezio passes on his knowledge to one more Assassin, the Chinese woman named Shao Jun. She has brought trouble with her from home, and a confrontation with her would-be killers ends in a hard-fought victory. Ezio finds some semblance of peace at last and finally comes to terms with the measure of time, liberty, and love that has been given to him.

With the completion of *Revelations* and the release of *Embers*, at long last we had a conclusive end to the story of the central heroes that had driven the franchise for its first five years. The next major chapter would take fans across the sea to a new world and give the creators at Ubisoft a new canvas on which to paint.

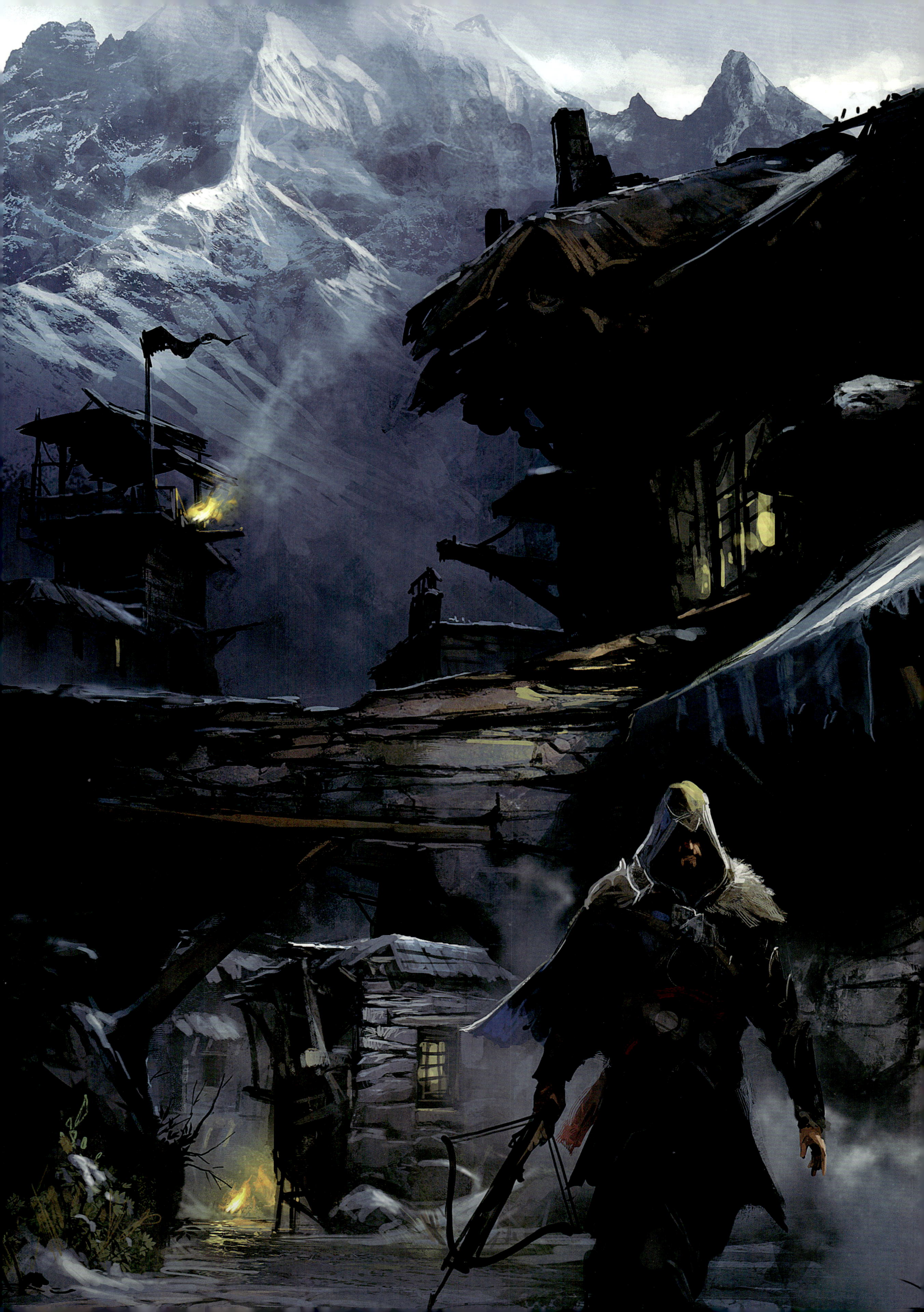

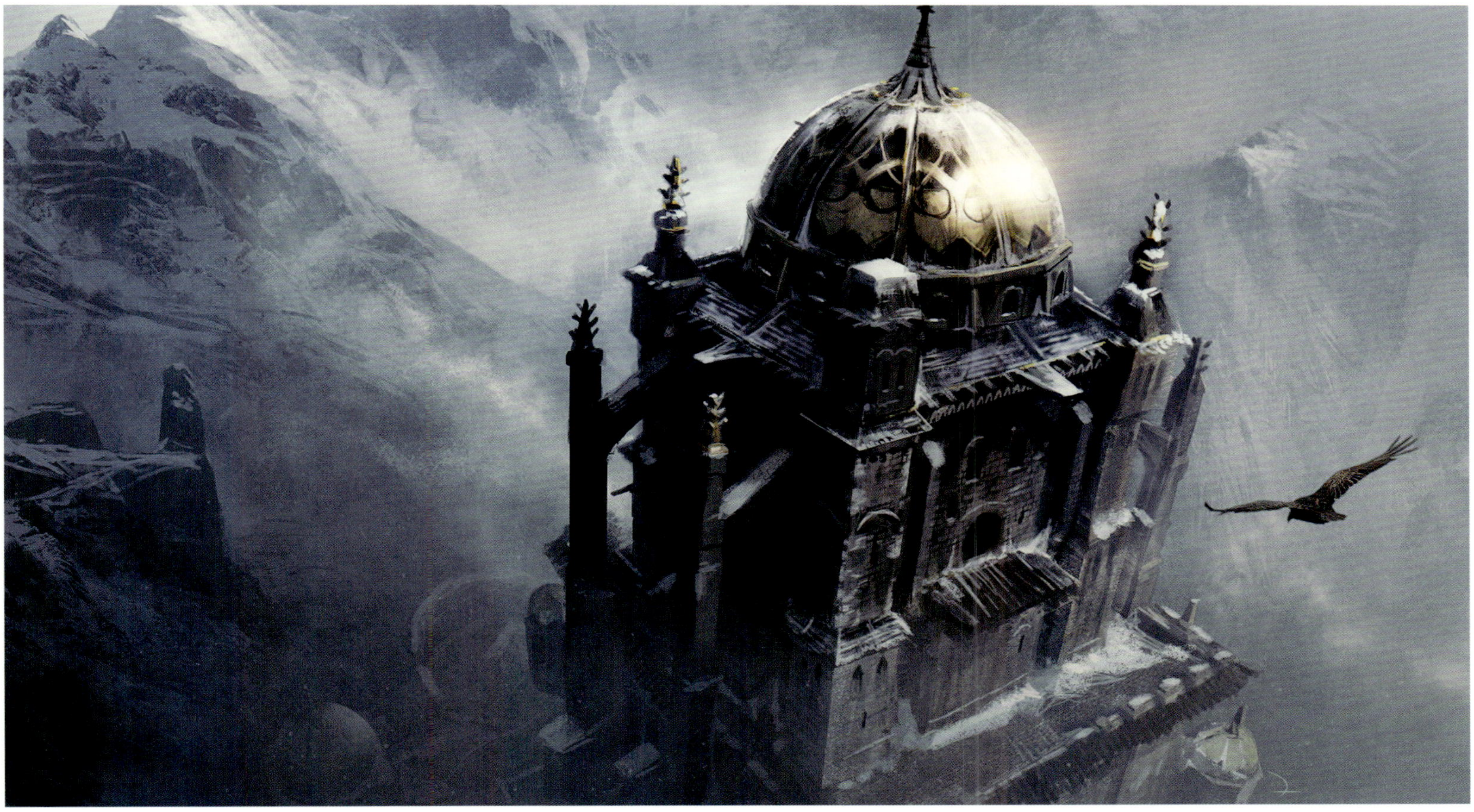

OPPOSITE: Ezio's return to Masyaf (Martin Deschambault).
ABOVE: The architecture of Masyaf's dome matched the flowing, curved lines of the Assassin aesthetic (Martin Deschambault).

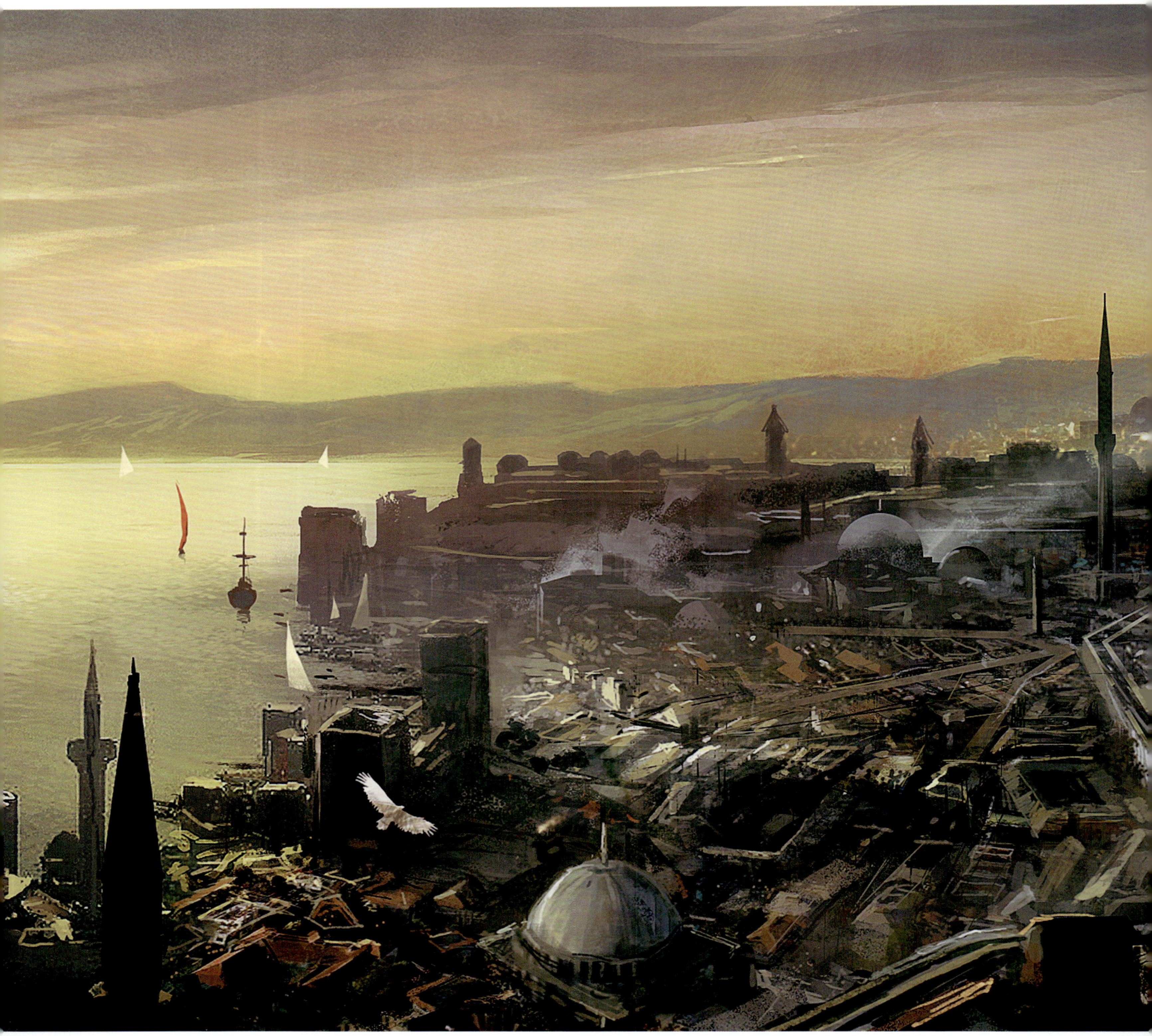

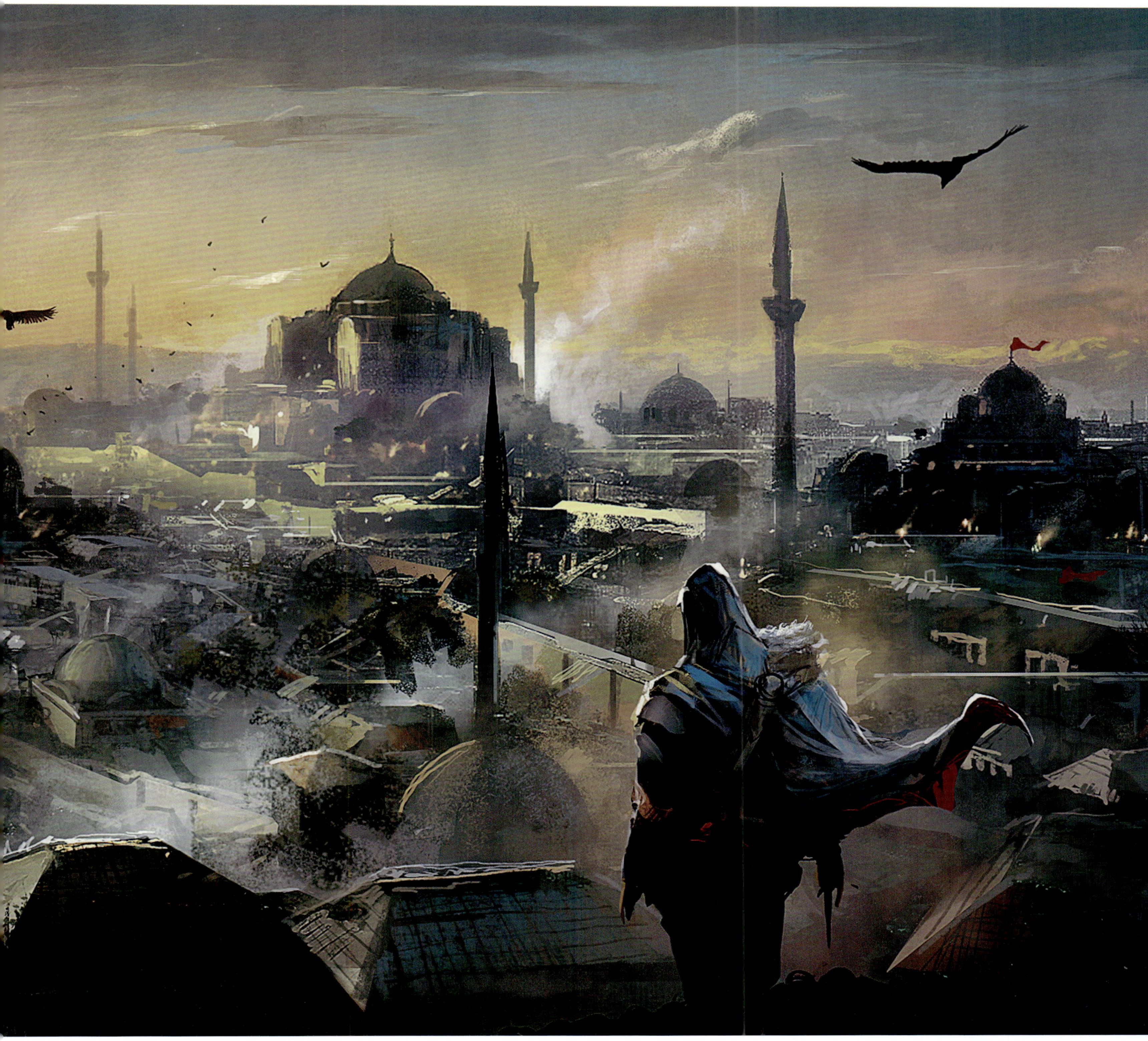

THESE PAGES: Stunning vista of Constantinople (Martin Deschambault).

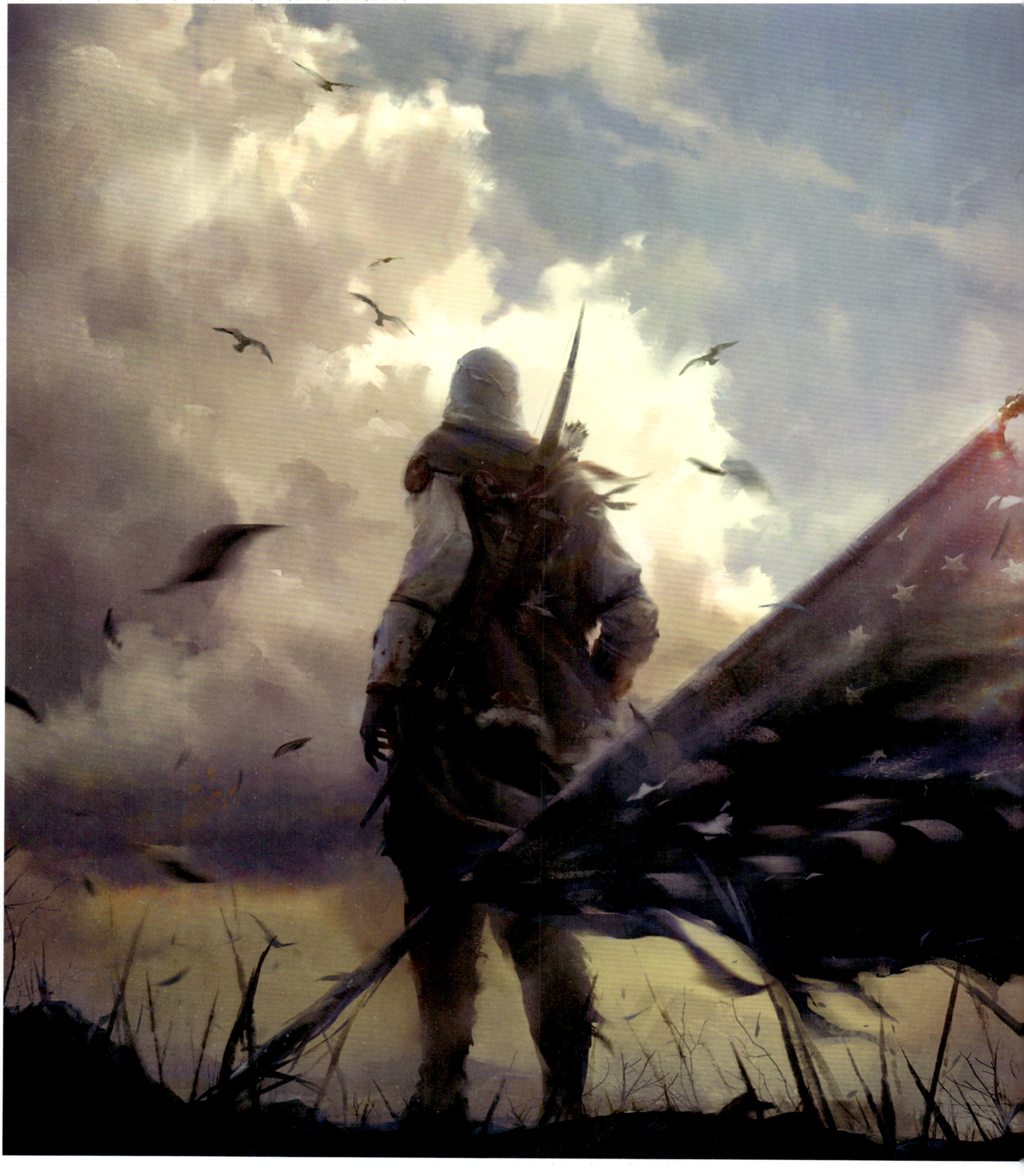

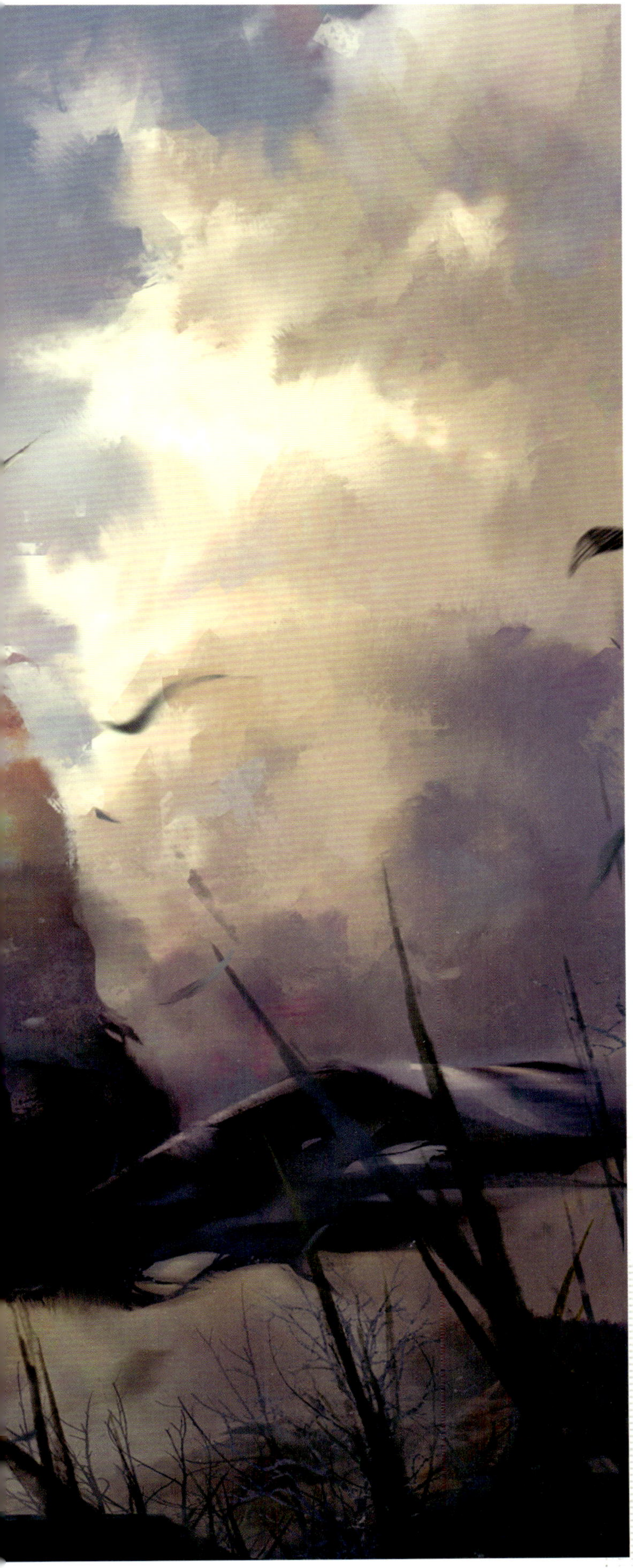

3 THE AMERICAN REVOLUTION

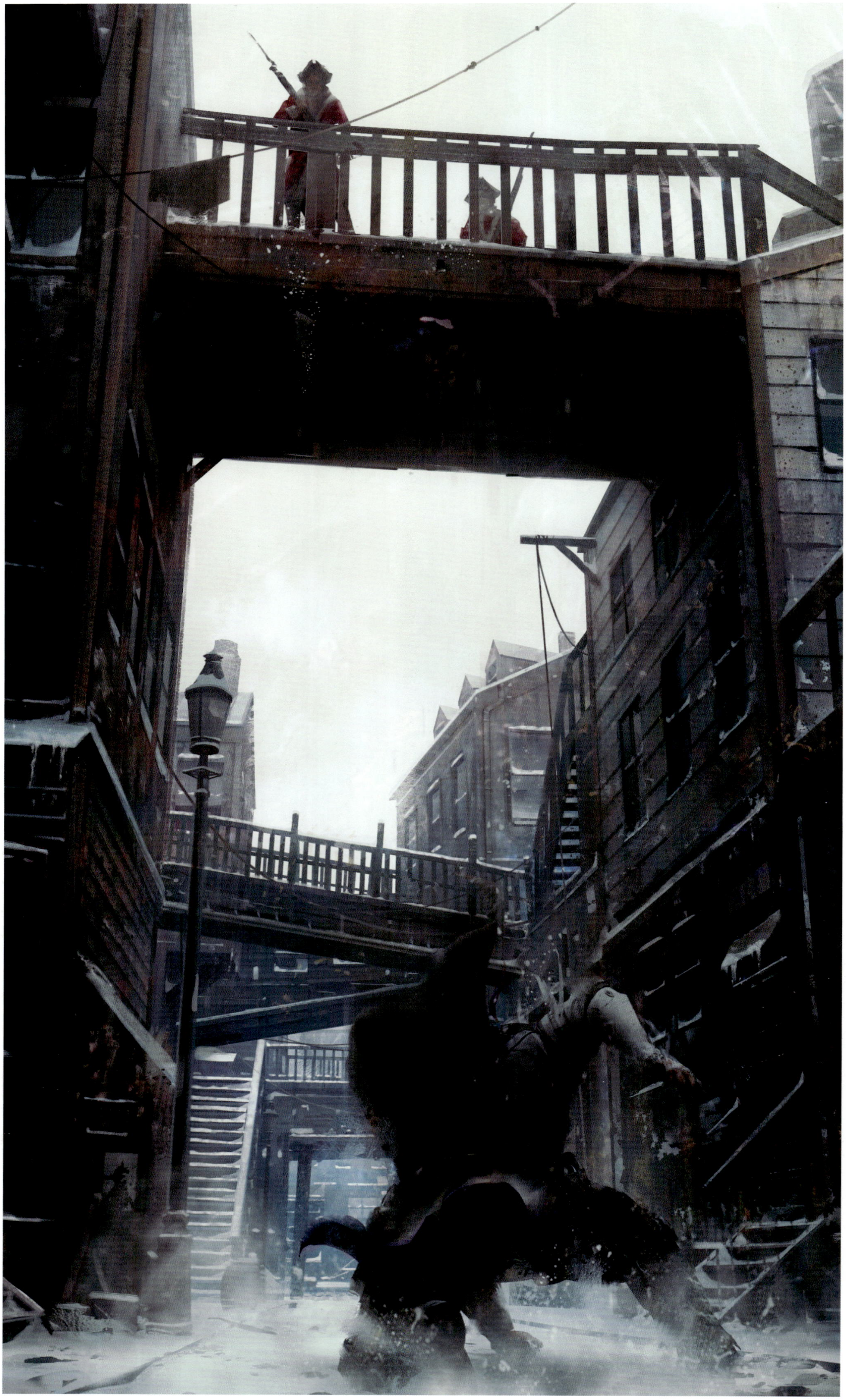

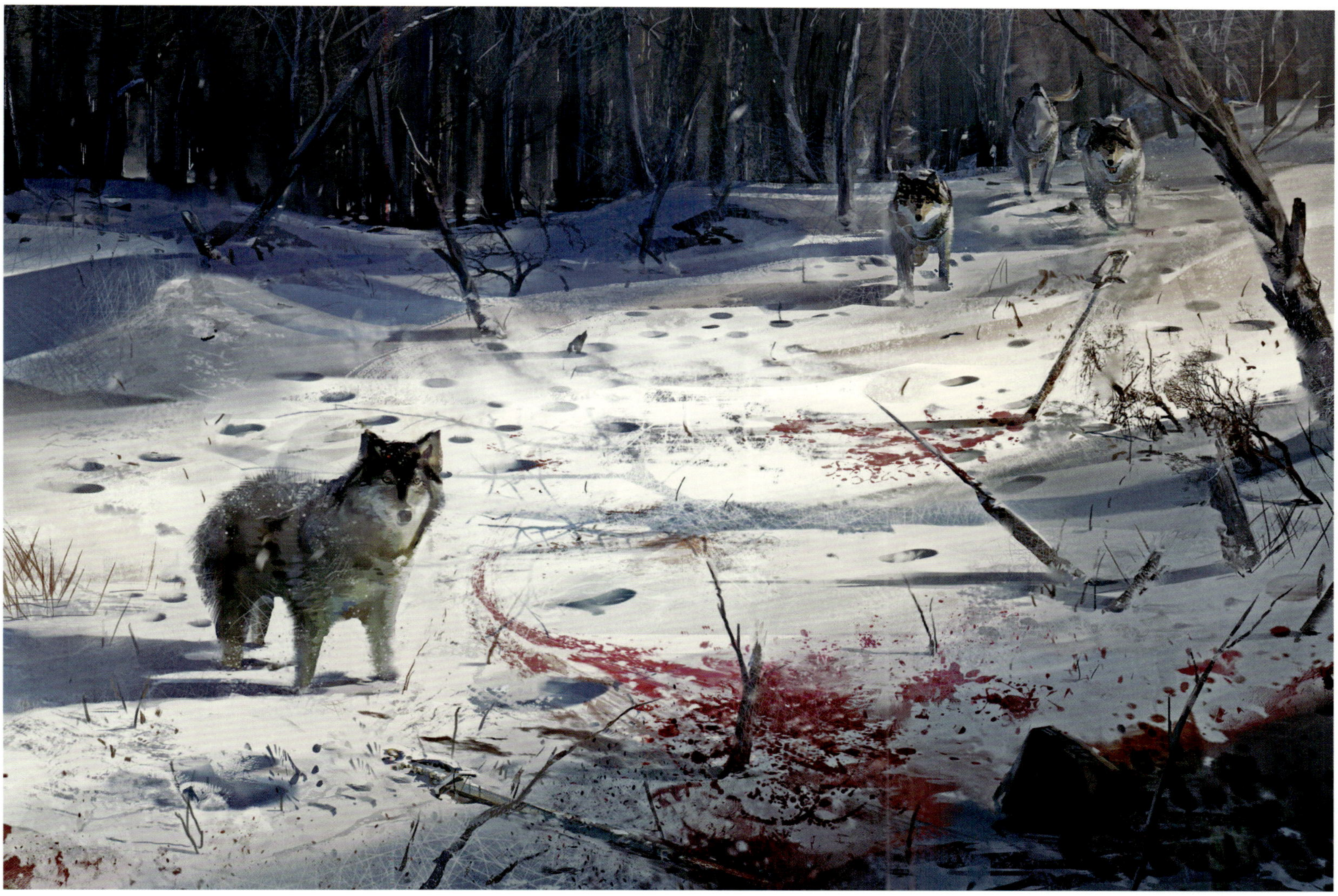

A NEW WORLD

Assassin's Creed III opened the door on North America. A fresh continent and time period called for a fresh vision. After three games focused on a single hero, the next numbered entry in the Assassin's Creed chronology proved unafraid to veer from expectations and explore new territory. By choosing the American colonies as a backdrop, *Assassin's Creed III* did more than jump continents. The young cities of New York and Boston didn't have ancient historical edifices like the Colosseum or the Hagia Sophia, but this new land had no shortage of grandeur as the game stepped outside into the unspoiled splendor of the American wilderness and its coastlines. The forested Frontier was a new sandbox where granite cliffs replaced cathedral walls and gnarled trees could stand in for castle towers. Meanwhile, the first glimpses of the naval experience emerged, providing yet another twist on expectations and an opportunity for the series' artists to confront new challenges on the high seas.

Character artists also faced a potent challenge. Ezio had been a richly realized and beloved symbol of the franchise, defined by an elaborate style and disarming charisma. The new protagonist, Connor Kenway, had big shoes to fill; his reserved personality and the mixed heritage of his culture and apparel spoke to a different sort of hero. He was everything but a copy of Ezio and once again proved the franchise's ability to continually redefine itself.

PREVIOUS PAGES: Artwork symbolizing Connor's dedication to freedom (William Wu).
OPPOSITE: Concept art showcasing Connor's dynamic movement (William Wu).
ABOVE: Early Frontier artwork of wolves tracking the blood of a fallen soldier (William Wu).

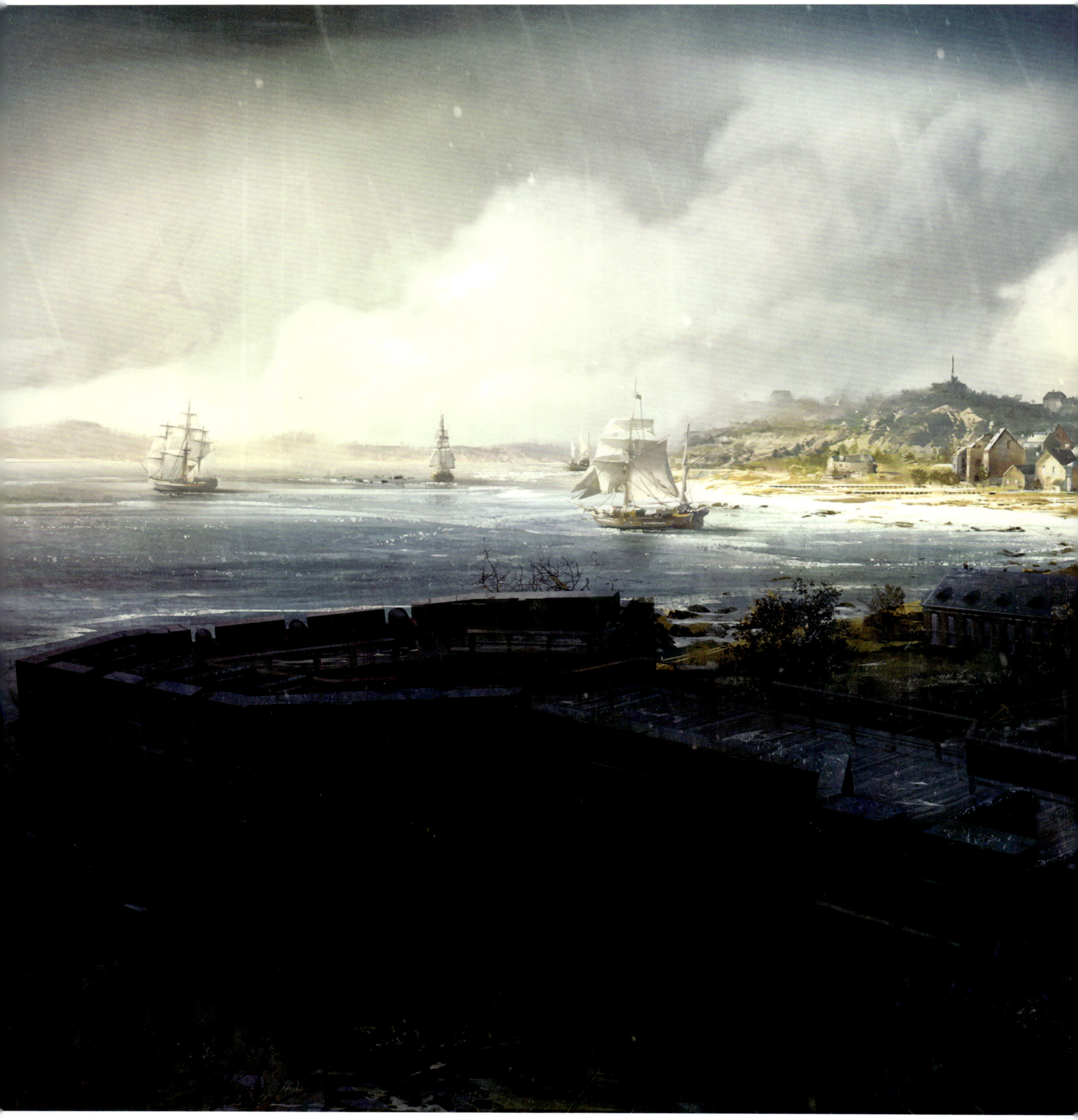

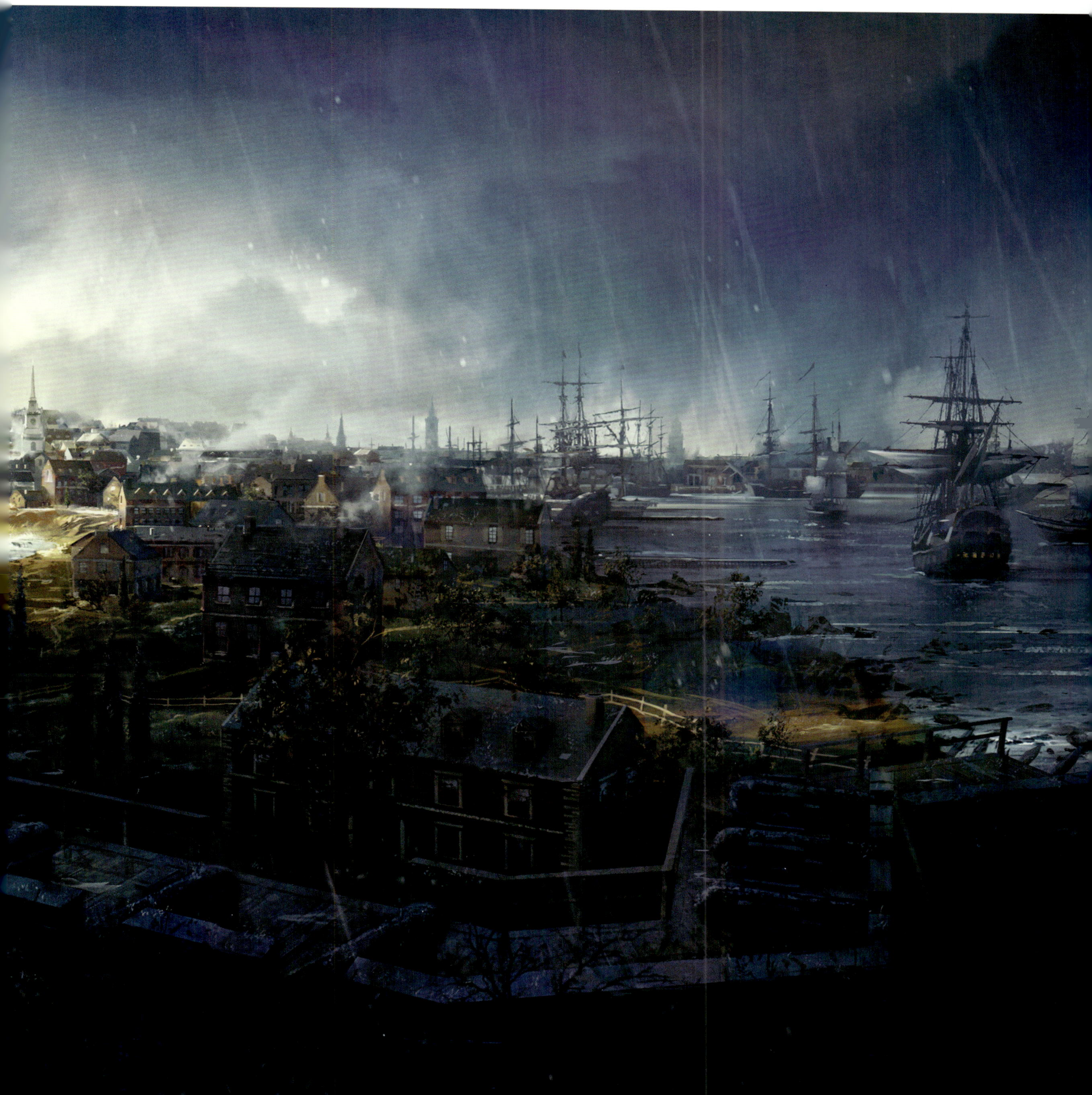

THESE PAGES: Early concept of Boston showcasing the fort and changing weather patterns (William Wu).

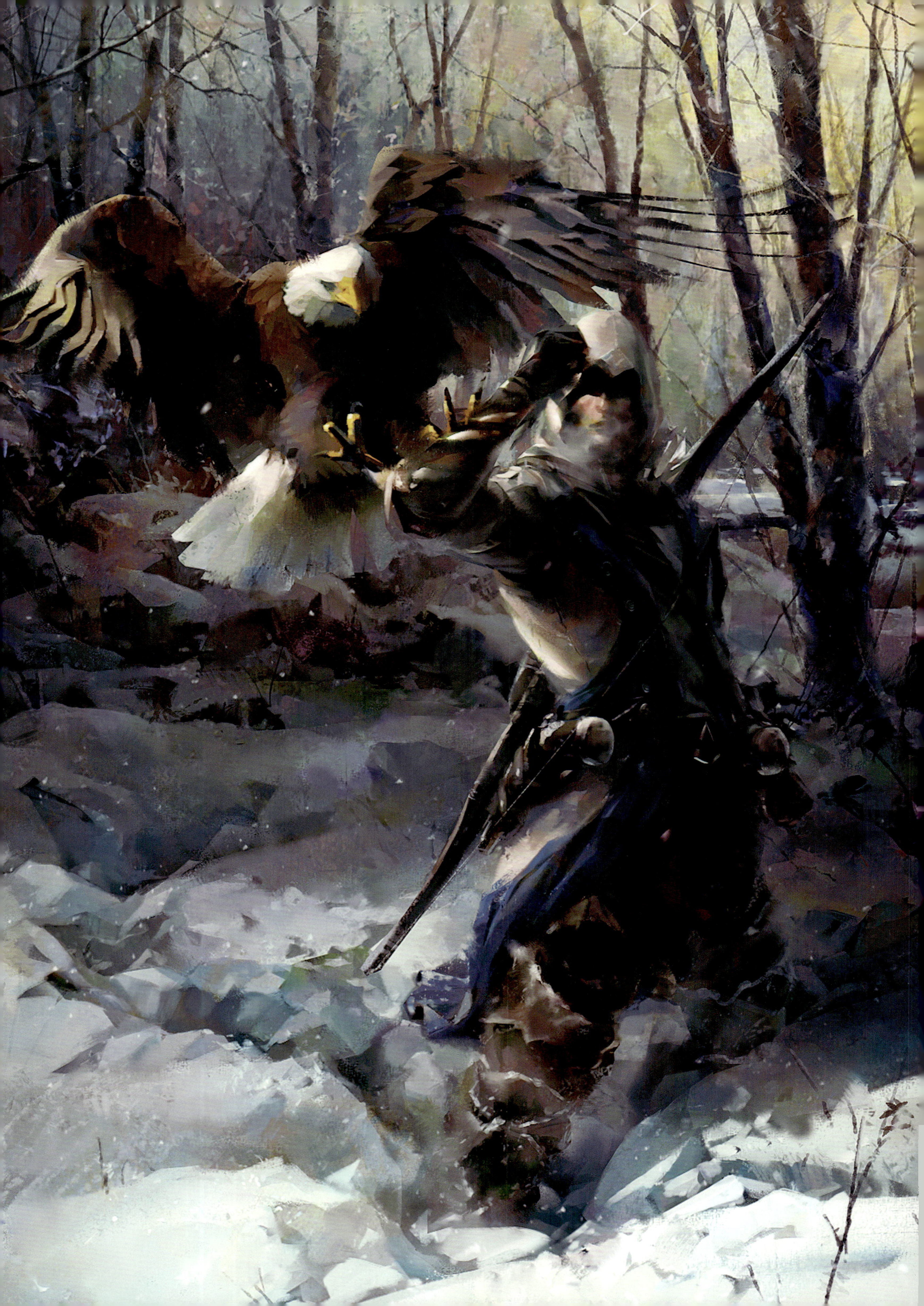

A MAN OF TWO WORLDS

Connor Kenway was born Ratonhnhaké:ton, a member of a Native American tribe long ago entrusted with the protection of an ancient site of the First Civilization. After seeing his tribe face near-extinction at the hands of the Templars, Connor was driven to join the Assassins and confront those who devastated his people. Tragically, his father was the head of the very organization that perpetrated the attack, leaving Connor a man trapped between the two branches of his own ancestry. Senior concept artist Remko Troost explains, "He's torn between these two worlds, and this had to be expressed in his design. In fact, he doesn't really know to which world he belongs."

Visually, everything about Connor spoke to the struggle to meld these two competing aspects of self. Early designs of the character strongly embraced the Native American aspects of his personality, suggesting an Assassin that felt only marginally informed by either his European paternity or his inherited path as an Assassin. Next, the pendulum swung far in the other direction, with a look that almost abandoned any native iconography. The final take on Connor offered a subtler interpretation.

"Two different cultures exist within the same guy. You have to show both of them, but he also has to pass easily inside a town like New York or Boston," says Remko. "So we finally settled on key details here and there, like the arrows on his back. The boots were also quite traditional, but you can hide them with the jacket." As Connor wandered the Colonial streets, his jacket, silver buttons and buckles, and tailored belts wouldn't feel out of place amongst the fur traders and Frontiersmen with whom he would mingle. More importantly, those European accoutrements were a natural fit for the iconic Assassin hood that still defined the character. His native loyalties only made themselves apparent upon closer inspection, but they established who Connor was in his heart. Thigh-high moccasin boots and half-hidden native jewelry spoke to how he had grown up. In combat, his slashing tomahawk and brutal finesse added wolf overtones to the long-established eagle metaphors inherent to the Assassin style. Connor's native bow completed the ensemble and added both an unmistakable new slant to the character silhouette and a quintessential ranged weapon to join the long-established melee powers of the hidden blade.

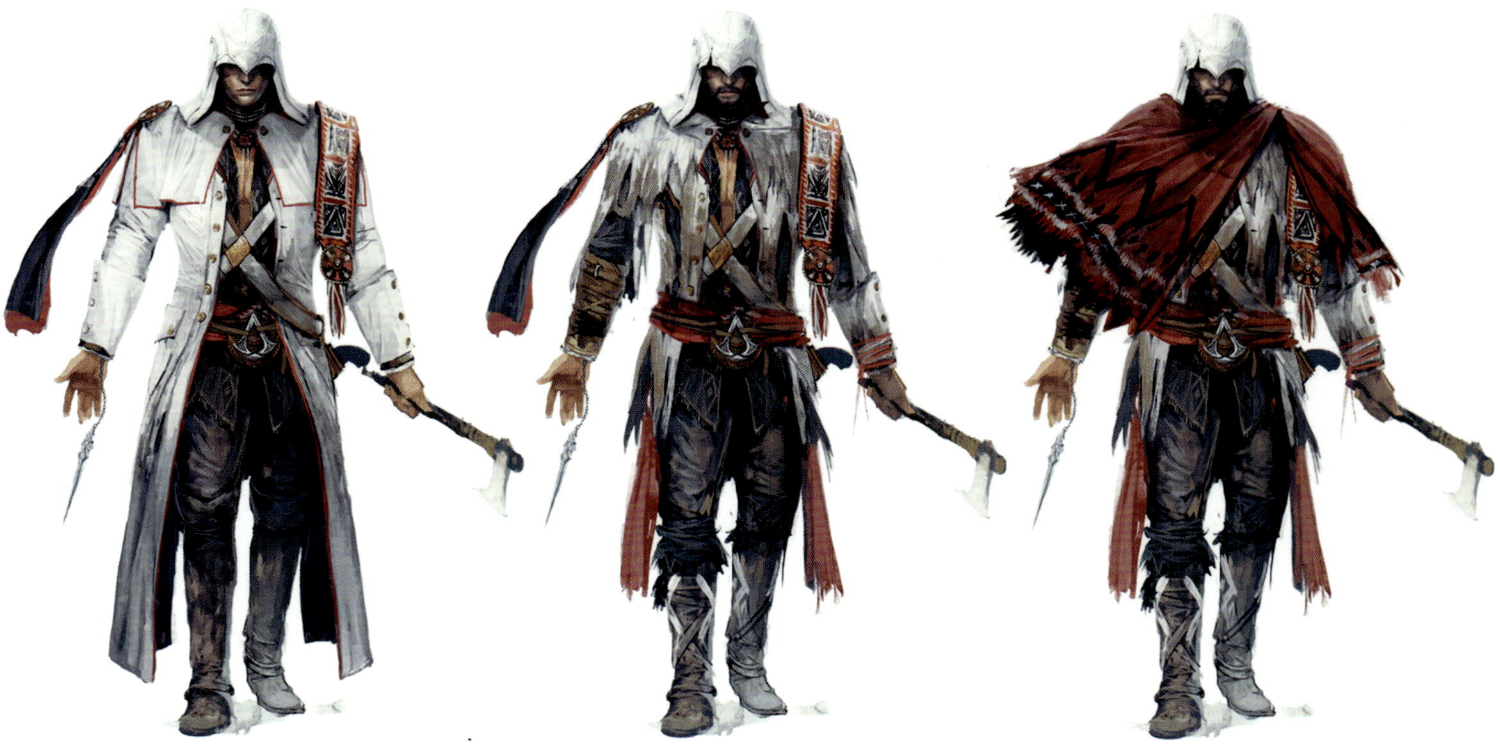

OPPOSITE: Artwork demonstrating Connor's bond with the natural world (William Wu).
ABOVE: Very early concepts of Connor's outfit used Native American elements to emphasize his heritage (Patrick Lambert).

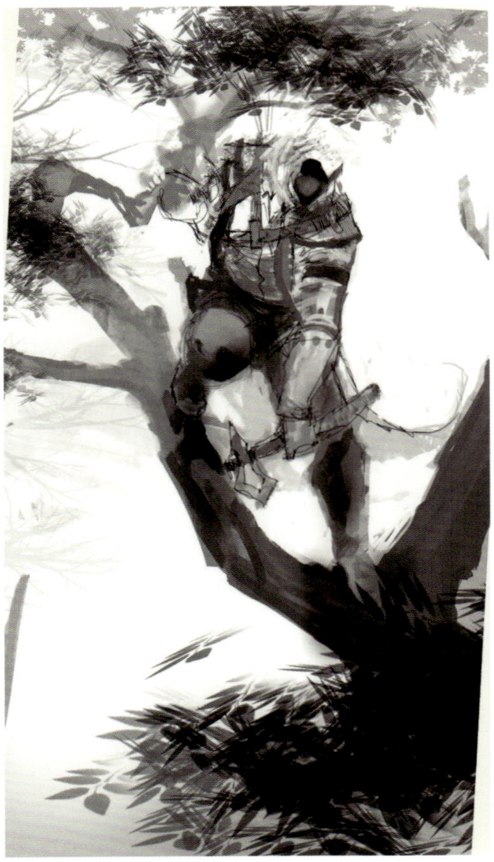

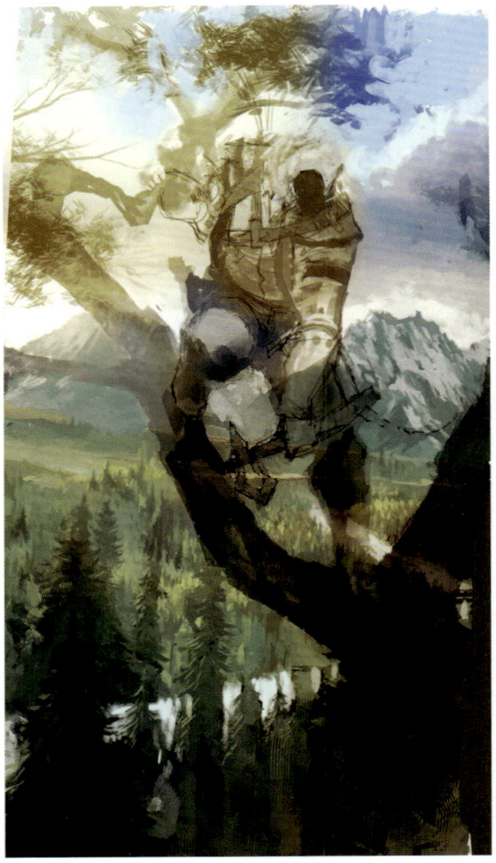

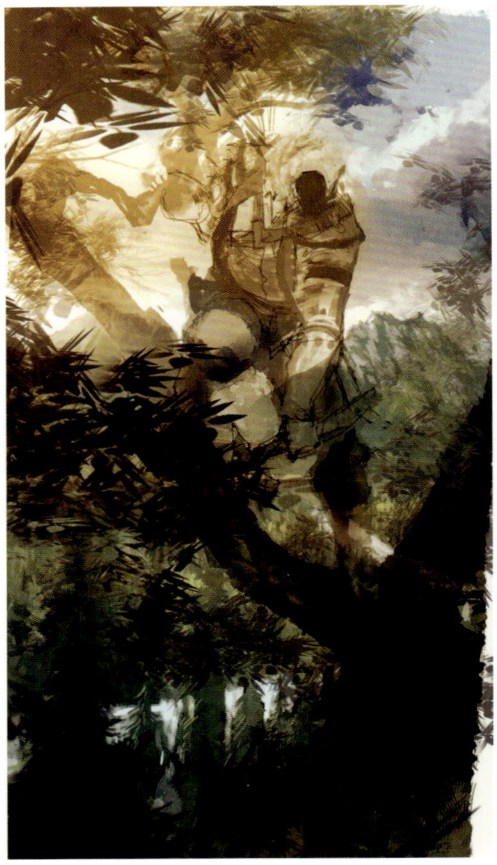

THESE PAGES: The stages of a Connor concept from initial black-and-white drawing to final artwork (Remko Troost).

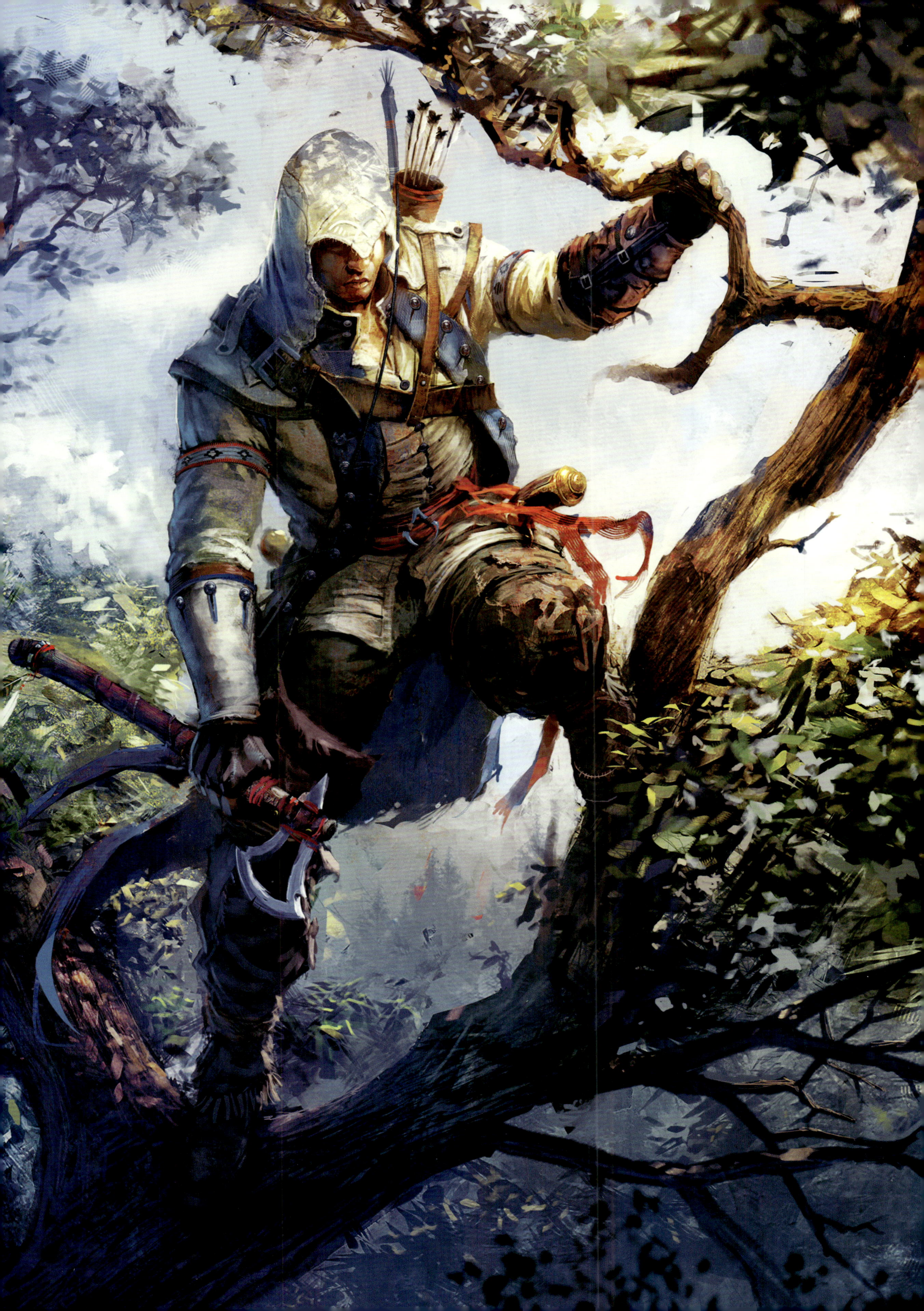

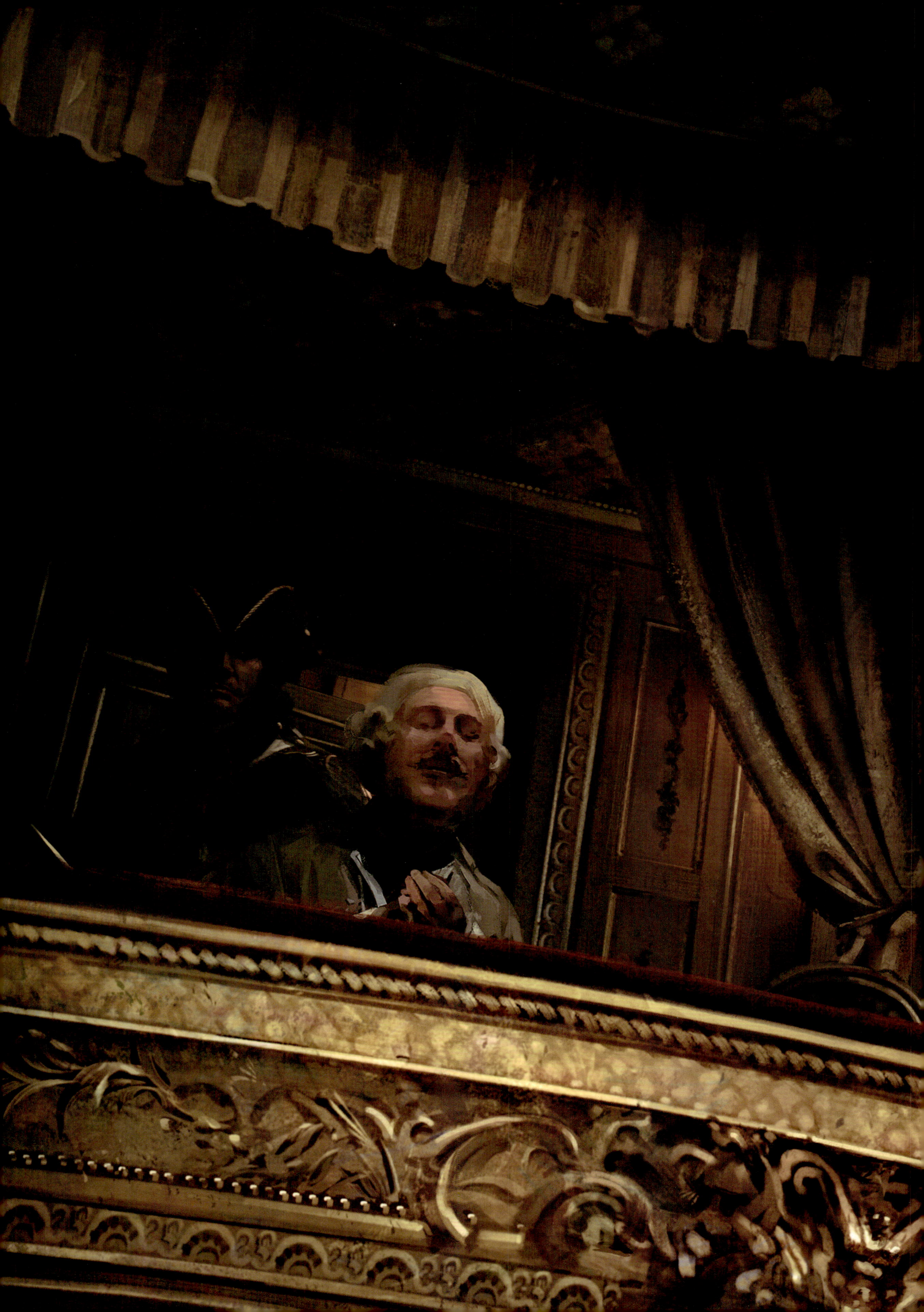

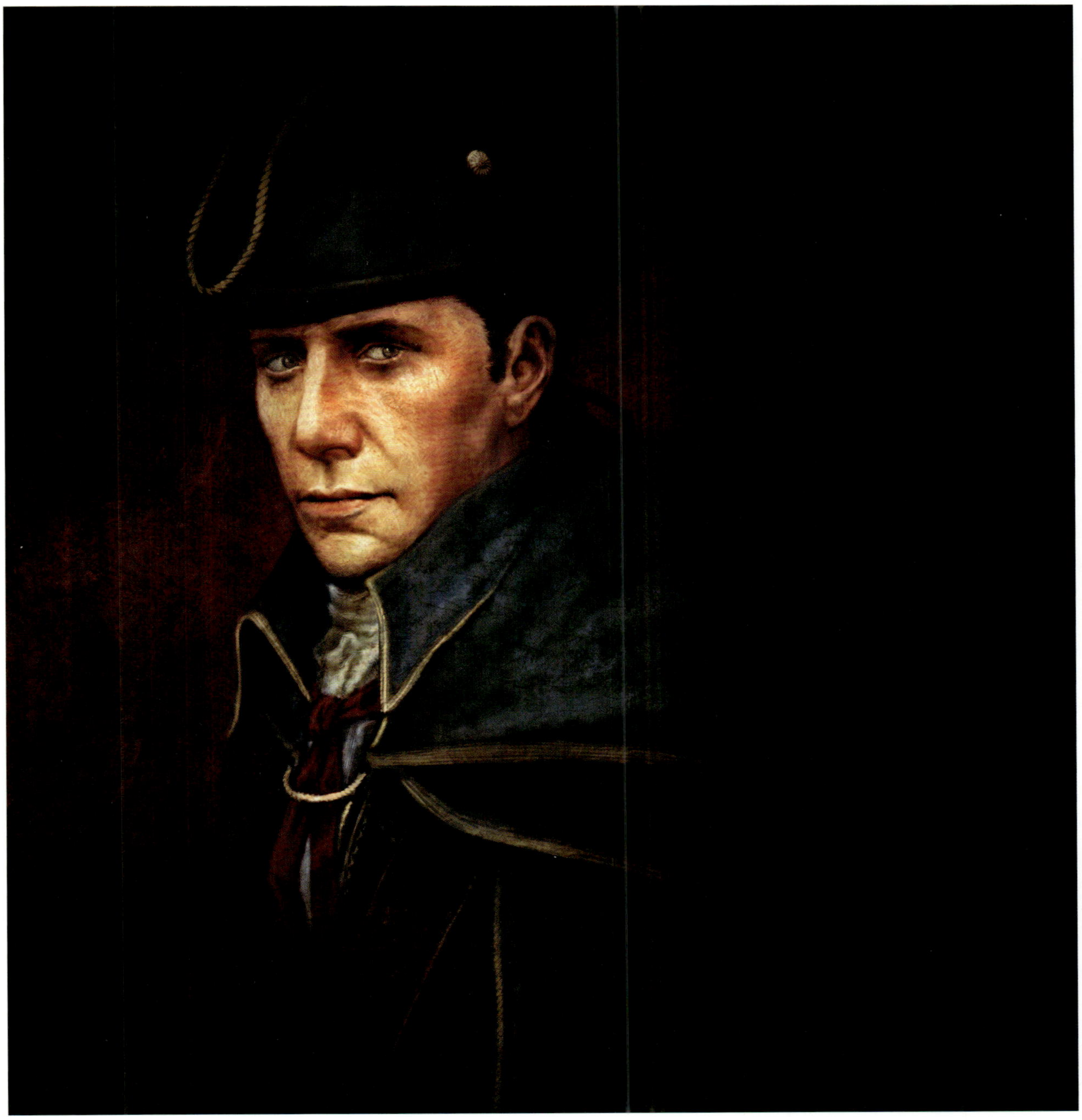

ONLY AS GOOD AS ITS VILLAINS

The opening of *Assassin's Creed III* was a surprising departure from the form that invested the player into hours of playtime not as the story's hero but as its antagonist. The daring approach translated to a slower path into the game's main gameplay loops, but the technique allowed for a fascinating twist on the established series formula. Players were forced to experience life in the shoes of the very assassination targets that would arise later in the game.

The novel opening made the cast of Templars in *Assassin's Creed III* the most fleshed out and understandable villains in the series up to that point. The Templars of *Assassin's Creed III* were each visually distinct, but little hints helped give away their true allegiances. As the playable character for the early hours of the game, the disciplined Haytham Kenway emerged as a particularly nuanced and intriguing opponent in latter sequences. "As we were coming to better understand the story of Haytham, we gave him almost a general's outfit," says art director The Chihn Ngo. "The structure of his coat is very, very rigid. It's what we wanted to showcase about him."

OPPOSITE: Haytham prepares to assassinate a patron in the Royal Opera House (William Wu).
ABOVE: Haytham was designed as a "dark James Bond," a character who has a darker edge but also a quick wit and strong convictions (Stéphane Turgeon).

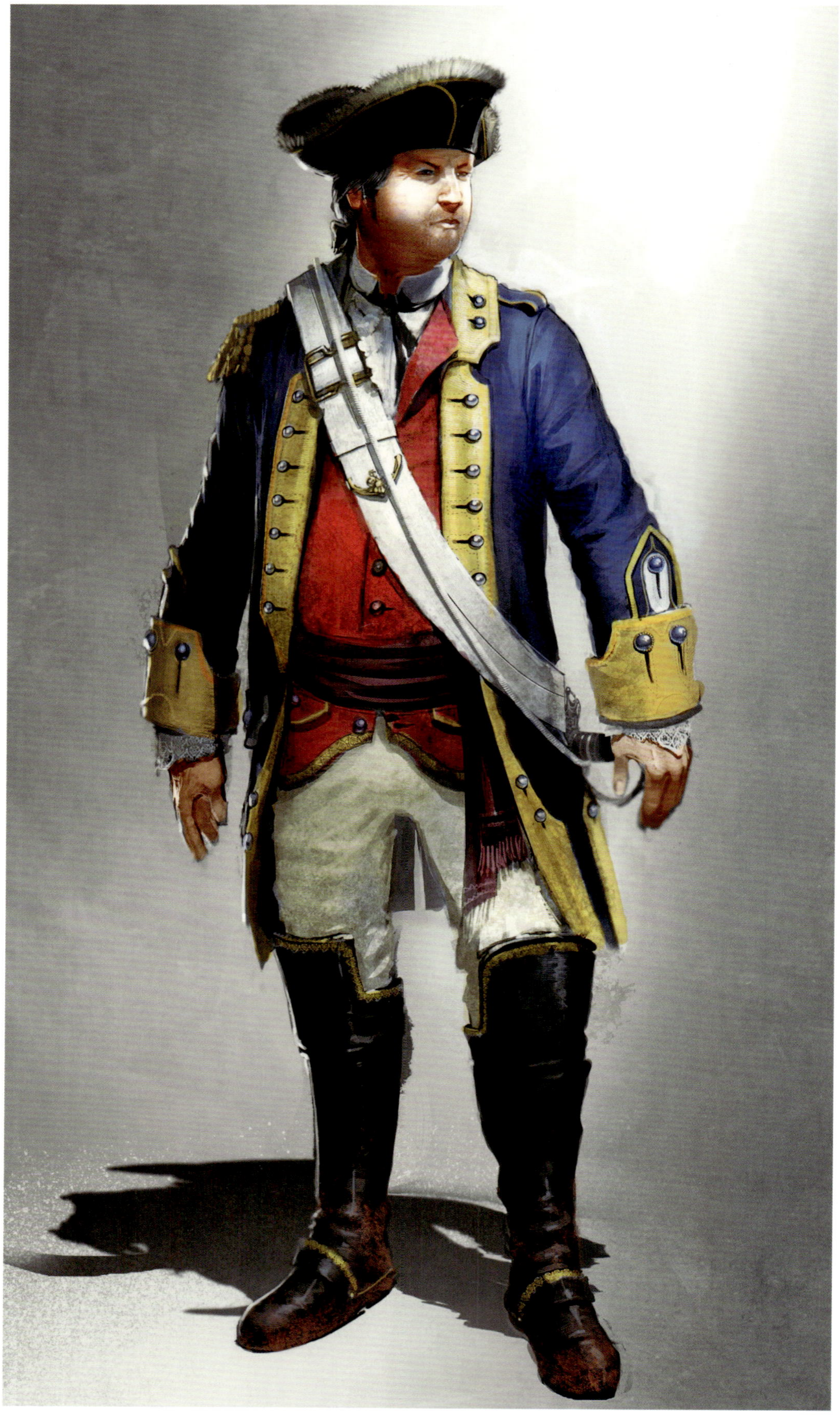

ABOVE: Early concept of Thomas Hickey (Remko Troost).
OPPOSITE: Portrait of Charles Lee with his small dog, Spado, representing his nervous and impulsive behavior. Lee's Pomeranian would never make it into the game (Remko Troost).

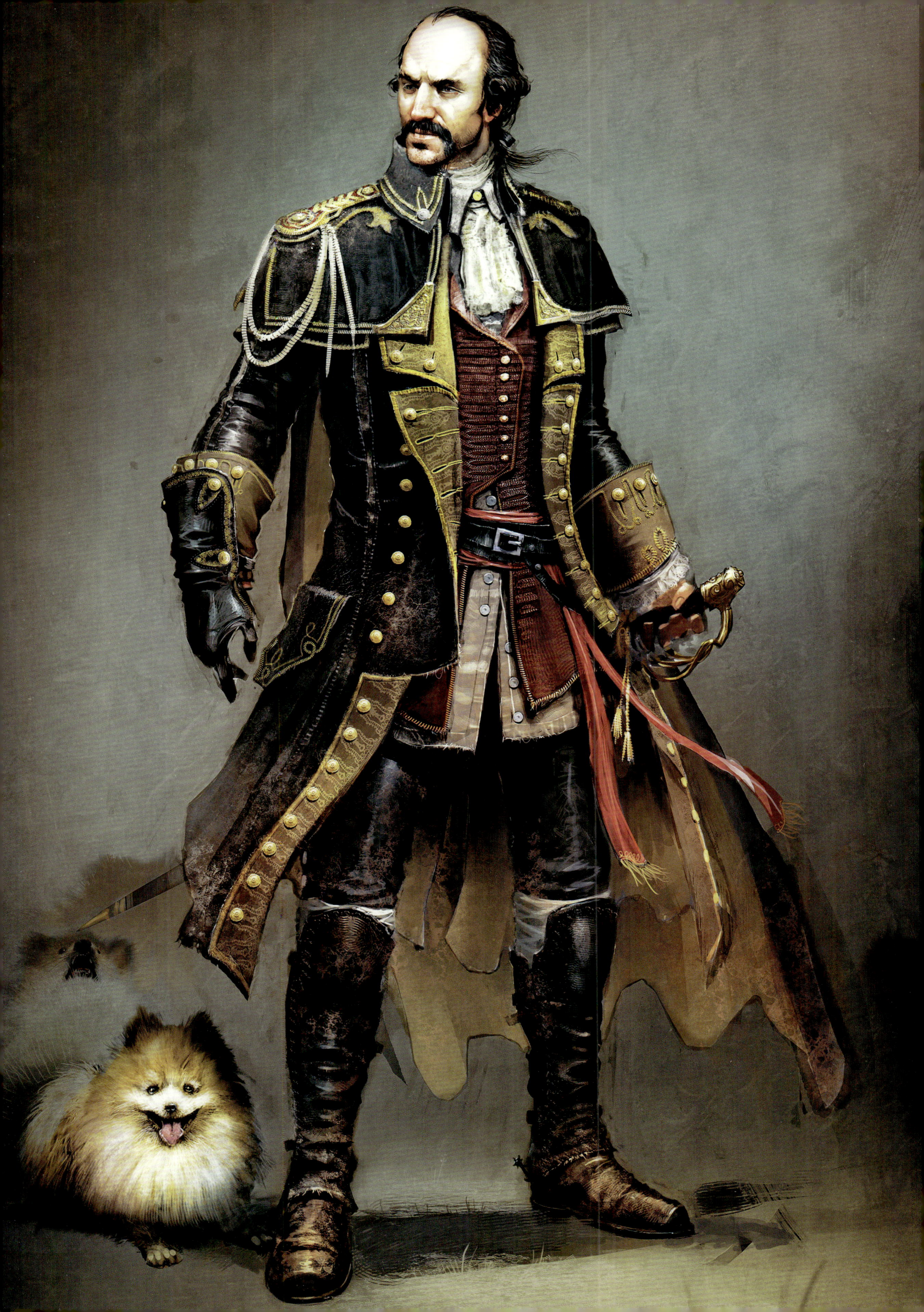

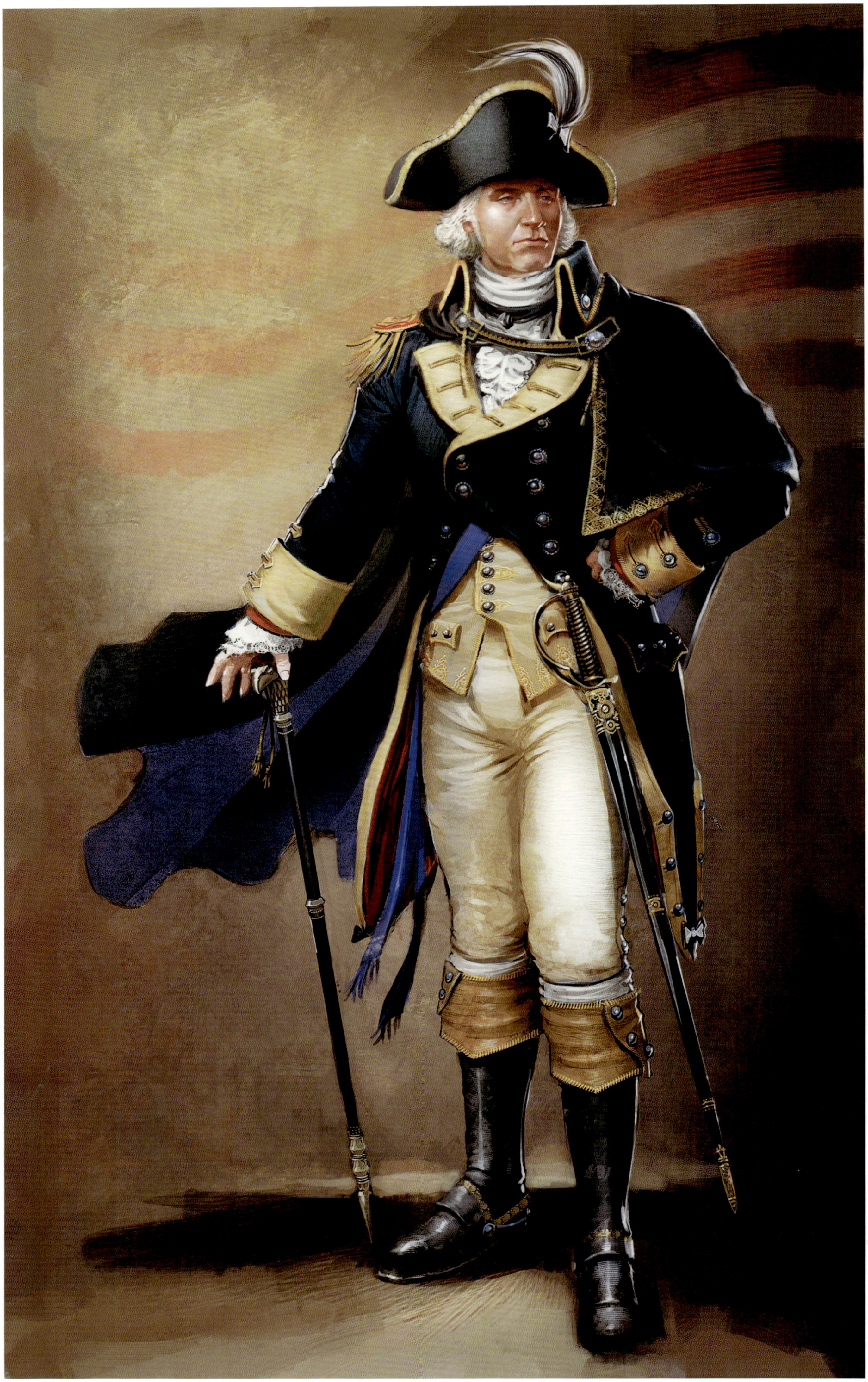

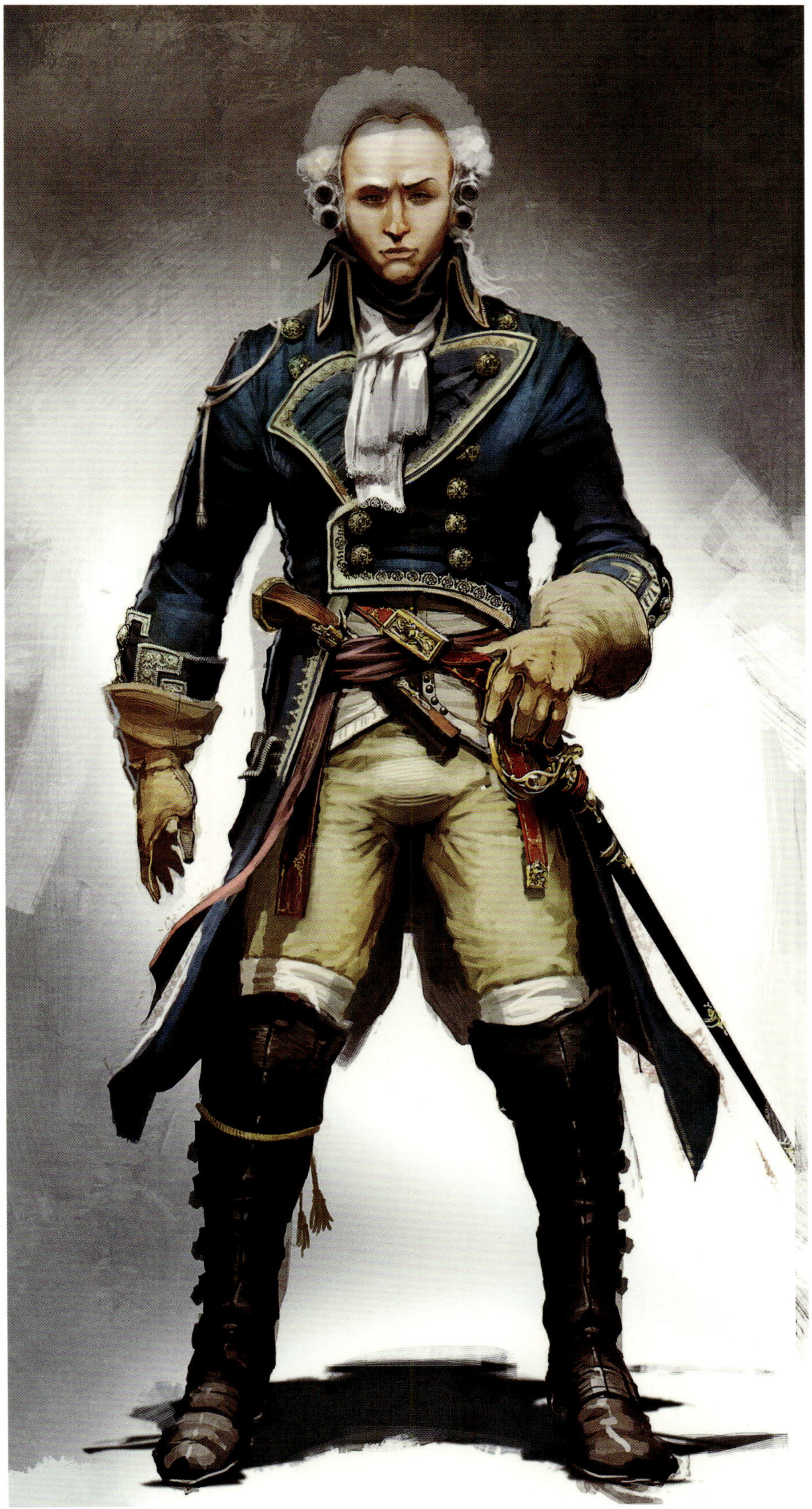

OUR FOREFATHERS BROUGHT FORTH

Previous installments had always played with real life figures, including historical mainstays like Richard the Lion-Heart and Leonardo da Vinci. *Assassin's Creed III* allowed the team to tackle more recent historical personages and offer their own interpretations of America's founding leaders. Benjamin Franklin, George Washington, Paul Revere, and Marquis de Lafayette were only some of the legendary heroes and statesmen depicted during Connor's adventures. By painting each as a compelling character first and historical icon a distant second, these individuals who figured so prominently in the nation's birth felt genuine within the story.

OPPOSITE: Illustrations for George Washington depicted an imposing, trust-inspiring man of standing and presence (Remko Troost).
ABOVE: Marquis de Lafayette's structured coat and straight posture illustrate his sense of pride and strength of will (Remko Troost).

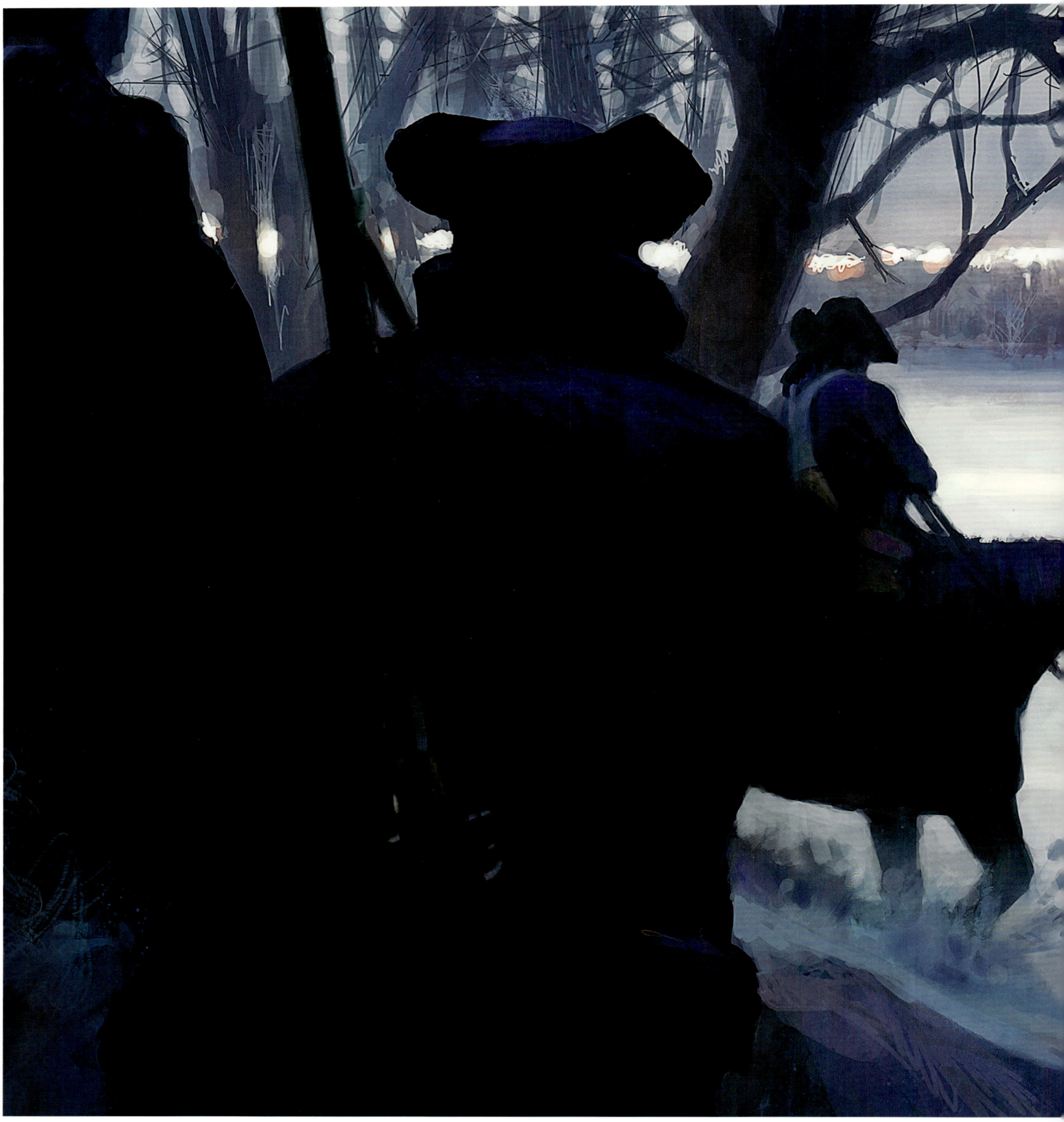

THESE PAGES: Soldiers crossing the vast open space of a frozen lake (Gilles Beloeil).

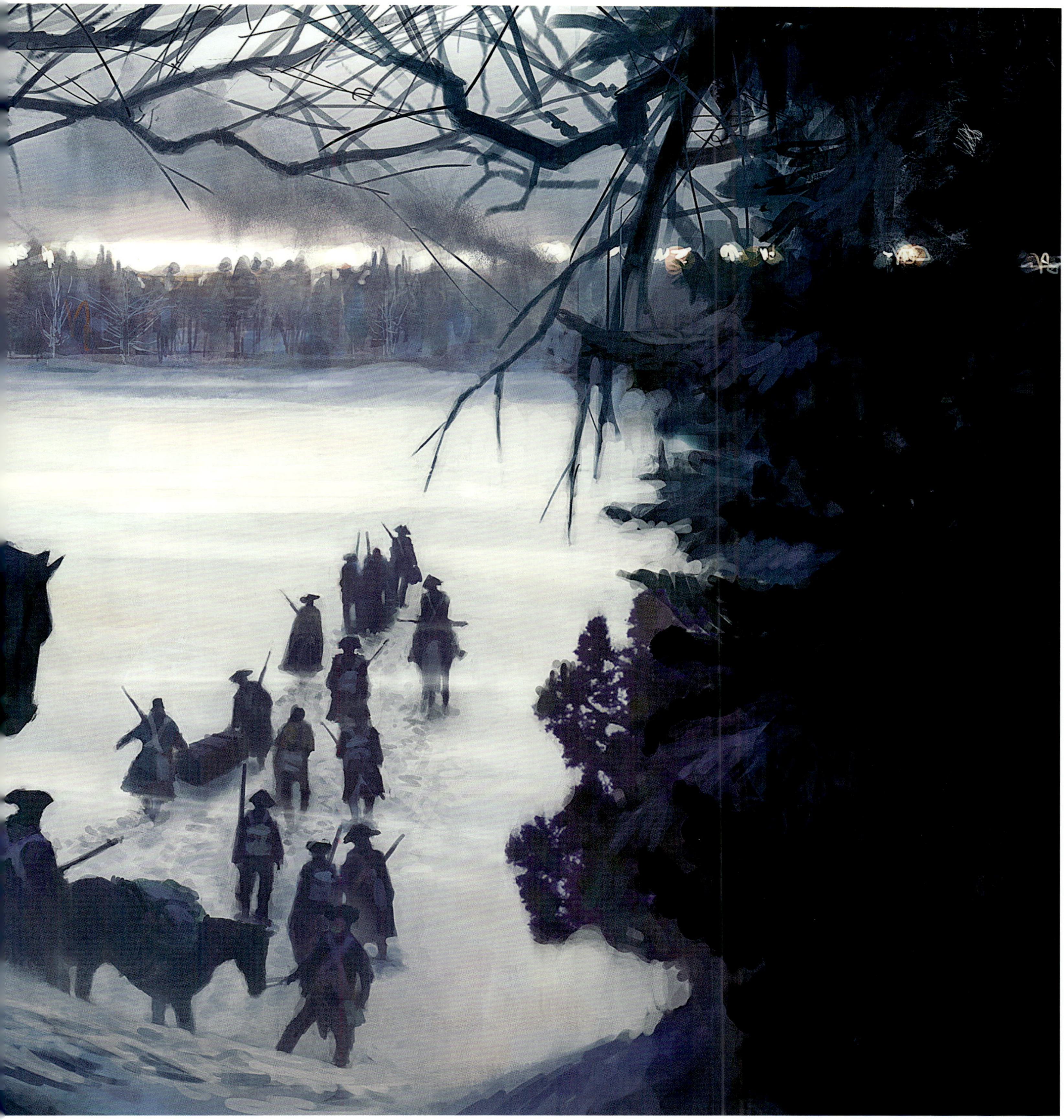

ALL IN THE DETAILS

Assassin's Creed III reflected some major changes in the franchise, not just in moving on from the Ezio storyline but in a shift to a new continent and the addition of extensive, traversable wildernesses and a dynamically shifting weather system. Ngo guided the team to a focus on detail and scene composition, especially in the game's many outdoor locales. Without identifiable landmarks in the forests and fields, the art direction focused on making individual trees, hills, rocks, and other features feel distinct rather than look like a repeated tileset you might see in other open-world games. Ngo also cited inspiration from the chiaroscuro style of painting, which emphasizes dramatic contrasts between light and dark—a quality that is evident in many of *Assassin's Creed III*'s most striking concept pieces.

THE NEAR FRONTIER

In 1776, one didn't need to travel far from the coast to reach the untamed Frontier. The forests and cliffsides of the American Northwest presented a new tapestry of colors, shapes, and lighting to catch the eye, not to mention a brand new play space that felt worlds away from the urban-centered exploration of earlier games. "All of a sudden, the franchise had everything," Jean says. "The tree climbing was a huge technical development that had to be done."

The Frontier was a sprawling environment, larger all by itself than *Brotherhood*'s entire depiction of Rome. Another game could afford to have trees and rocks as mere obstacles to mark the boundaries of the playable space, but the freerunning and climbing of Assassin's Creed meant that nearly every branch, trunk, or boulder needed to be both beautiful and functional within the level design. "In an open world, the experience of immersion is crucial, and the art direction has a huge role in creating a very engaging video game," Raphaël says. "So we aim to create something that not only feels realistic, but that also sparks the player's imagination."

High hills dipped into low valleys, and interspersed cave structures added an additional interior dynamic that made the Frontier feel as deep as it was broad. "How can you tell a story about the Colonies and the foundation of a country without talking about this wilderness?" Jean says. "I remember Alex Hutchinson, the creative director, saying that we know the Frontier as the far West, but at the time, the Frontier was right there. And it was hard because the country was nature. So we just couldn't ignore nature; it had to be in the game. And this spilled over into the personality of Connor. He was a part of this land, at least half. You cannot tell the story of a half-Mohawk person if you do not take the wilderness into account." Connor's childhood in the woods made his agility on trees and mountainsides feel natural and unforced. As an open world ripe for exploration, the Frontier validated the nature of the Connor character and vice versa.

Assassin's Creed had always prided itself on making its play spaces feel alive, so instead of crowds of merchants and pedestrians, the Frontier was filled with deer, wolves, and all manner of fauna. Whether it was rabbits hiding in the brush or a cougar leaping to attack from the shadows, the constant movement and activity delivered a sense of authenticity unmatched in outdoor video game environments of the time.

The addition of a wilderness setting added new colors to the gameplay and artistic palette of the franchise, and it's hard to overstate the area's importance for where the series would go next. "We chose blue accents because it differentiated Connor from Ezio, and it's a natural, fresh color," explains Ngo. "It is organic and reminds you of the wilderness; the sky, water, and the cold of winter." By opening up the Frontier as part of the traversal path, subsequent franchise entries were free to break entirely from the urban mold whenever required. Equally important, the Frontier provided us some of the most breathtaking vistas and scenes of the series.

OPPOSITE: Hunting in the dense forests of old North America (William Wu).

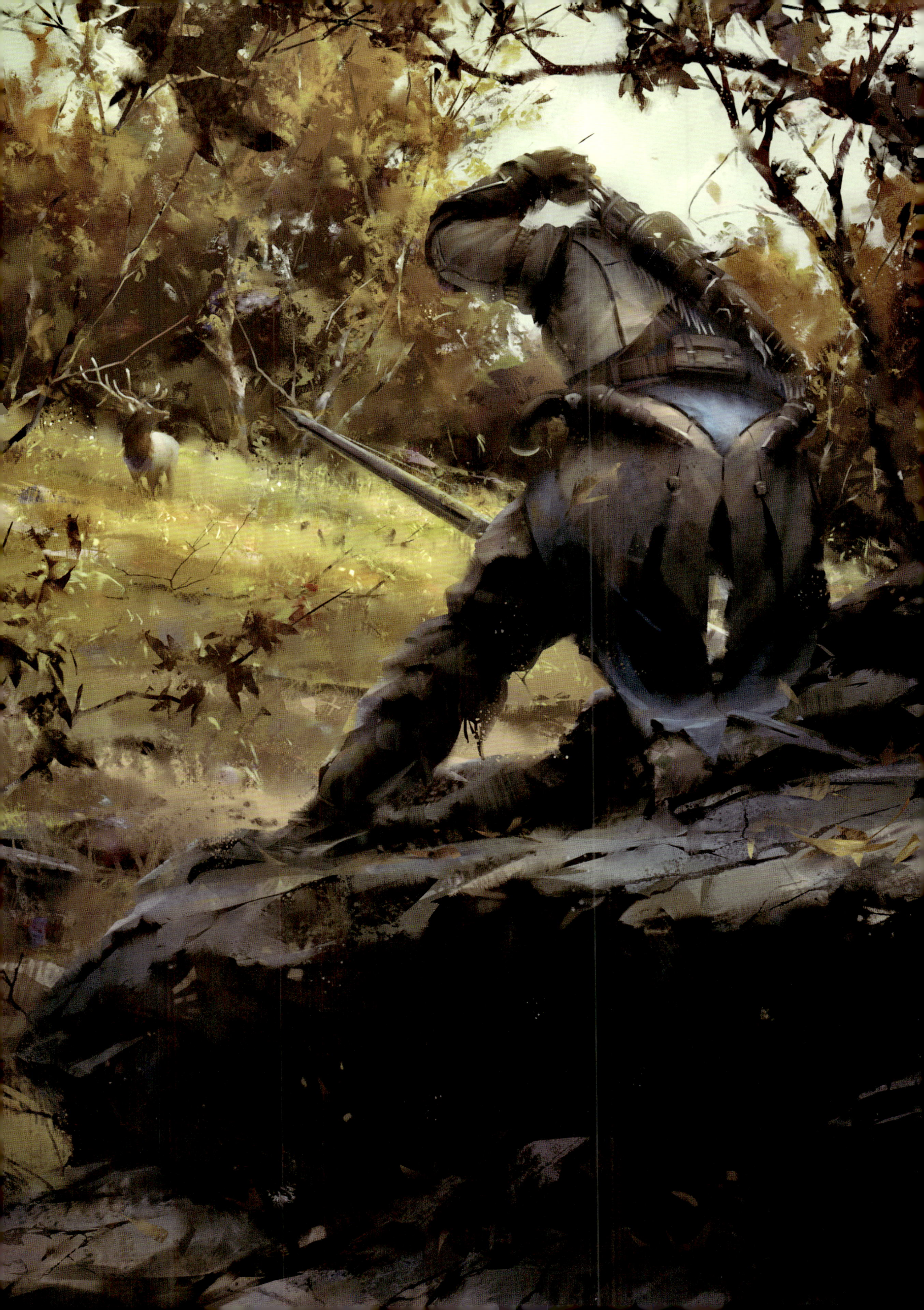

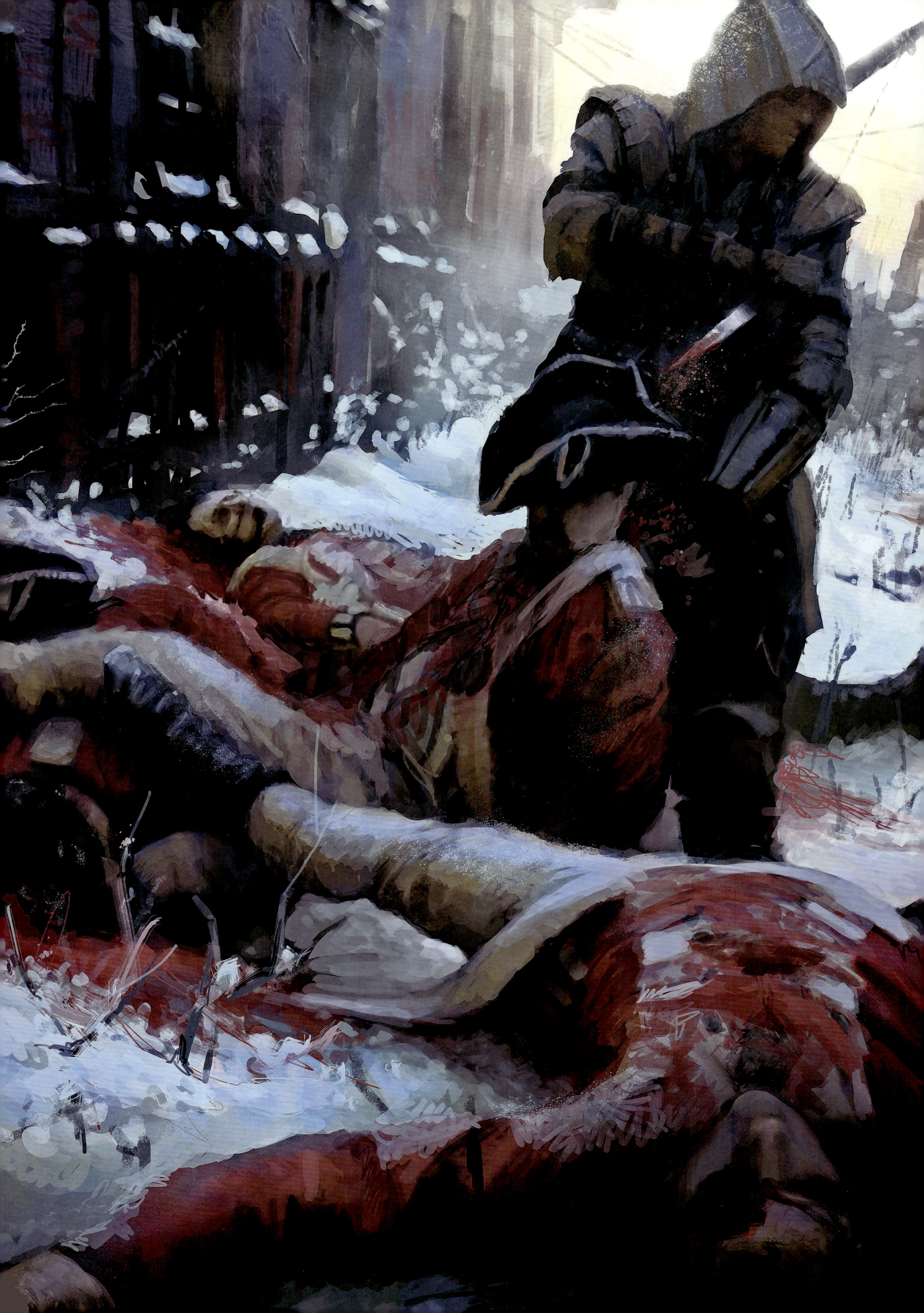

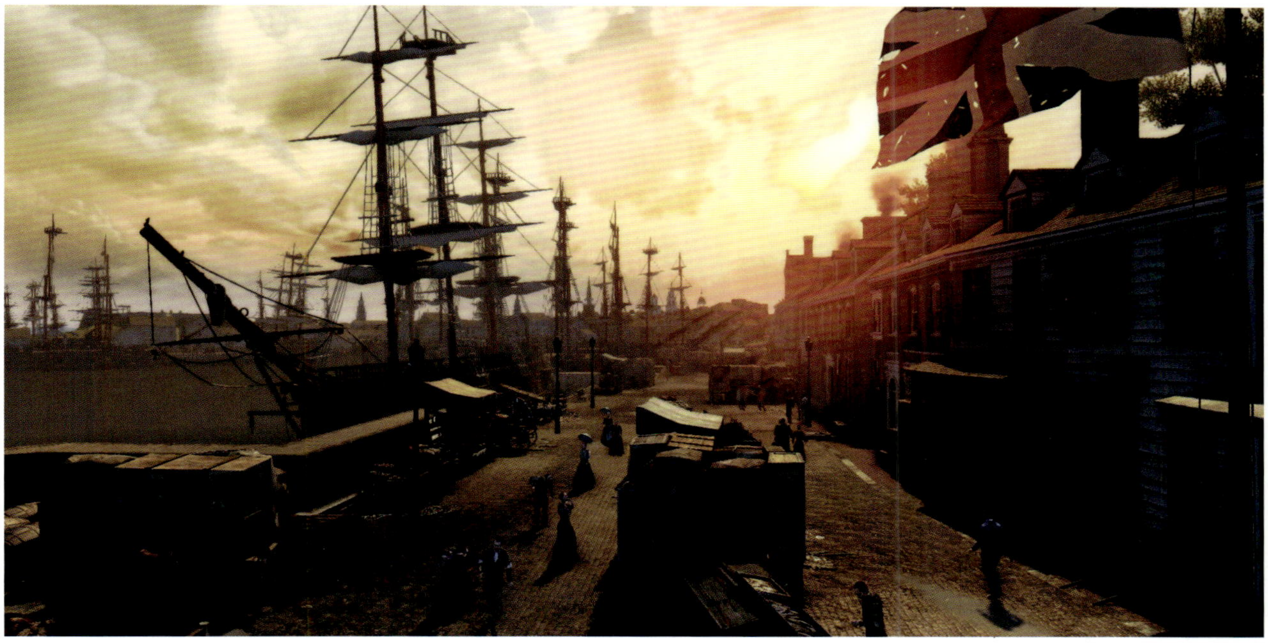

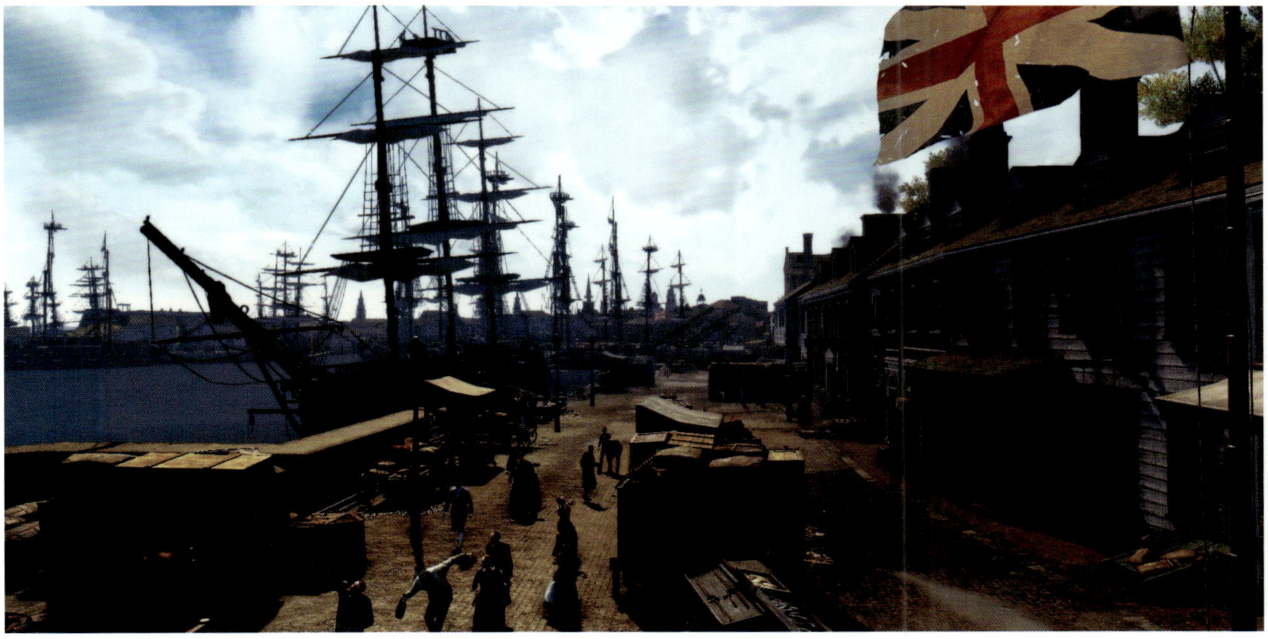

THE SEASON TURNS

The passage of time in *Assassin's Creed III* would have felt lacking if not for another major innovation: the passing of seasons, which offered both visual and gameplay variety. The green hues of summer provided ample opportunities for open exploration and varied encounters. Add in a thick layer of brilliant white snow with the onset of winter and the entire environment changed. Paths through the treetops took on increasing importance as an alternative to slow trudging through the drifts. Dark-furred animals (or darkly clothed assassination targets) became easier to see.

For the artists, the addition of distinct seasons meant a significant additional layer of work. Every major area needed to look beautiful and authentic, no matter the time of year. "One of the first things I remember thinking was, 'We need to have weather,'" recalls Ngo. "Weather is something that fills the spaces—the snow, the fog, the rain. These are very atmospheric elements, and this was something new in *Assassin's Creed III*." The resulting effort paid off, with natural vistas and cities that provided a profound sense of change as the years progressed.

OPPOSITE: Artwork contrasting the purity of the snow with the darkness of battle (Gilles Beloeil).
ABOVE: Renders showing time of day comparisons.

A FIRST GLIMPSE OF THE SEA

Few additions to the Assassin's Creed formula had so important a long-term effect as the introduction of the naval experience, thanks in large part to the innovative work completed by Ubisoft Singapore. While limited in scope for *Assassin's Creed III*, the beauty of sailing the high seas, combined with the potential for a whole new gameplay twist, ensured that more than one subsequent game would make sailing a centerpiece. "It was incredible," Jean says. "During the development of *Assassin's Creed III*, everybody internally knew that this section of the game would be something very, very fresh. I mean, the feeling, the mass of these ships plunging into the waves with the wind—it was a very powerful experience."

Connor's missions away from dry land were self-contained affairs rather than full open-world zones, but the ship-to-ship encounters were exciting, and the beauty of Ubisoft's water-rendering technology was breathtaking. While more development would be required to capitalize on the experience, Ubisoft realized it had found a special new angle on the franchise.

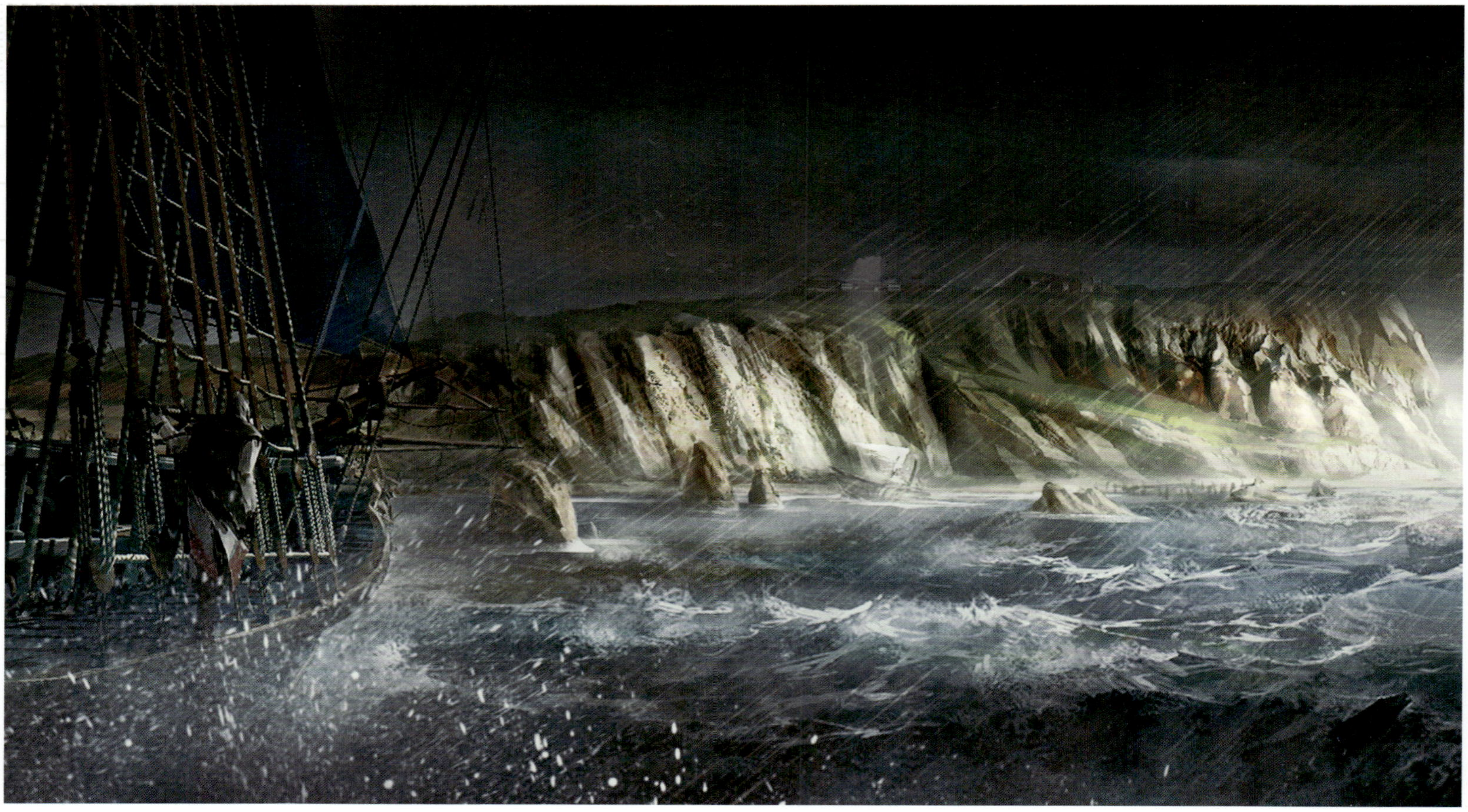

ABOVE: Concept art of the ocean's sudden changes in weather (Max Qin).
OPPOSITE: Dynamic concept of the naval version of the high-profile assassination (Nick Tan Chee Eng).

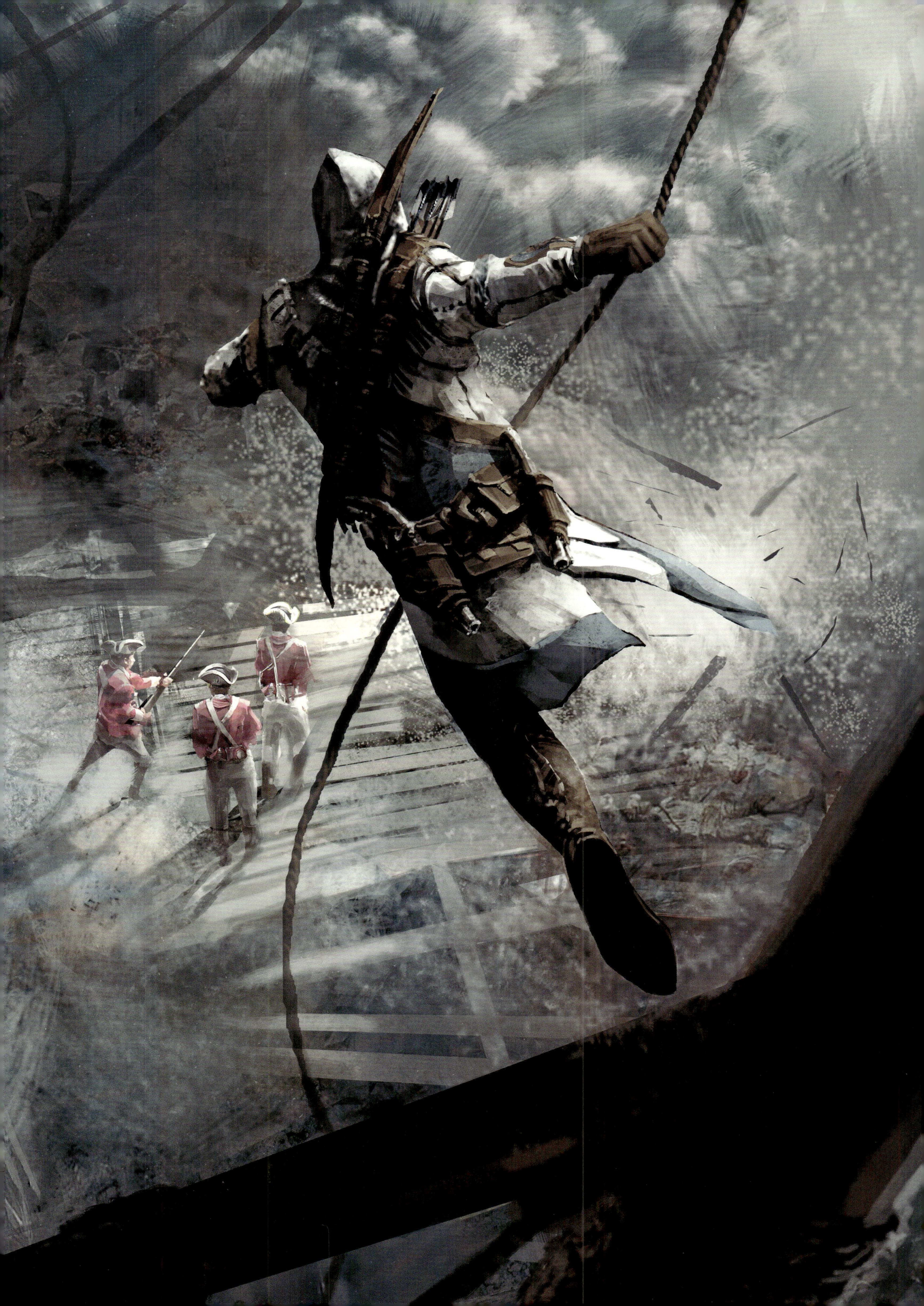

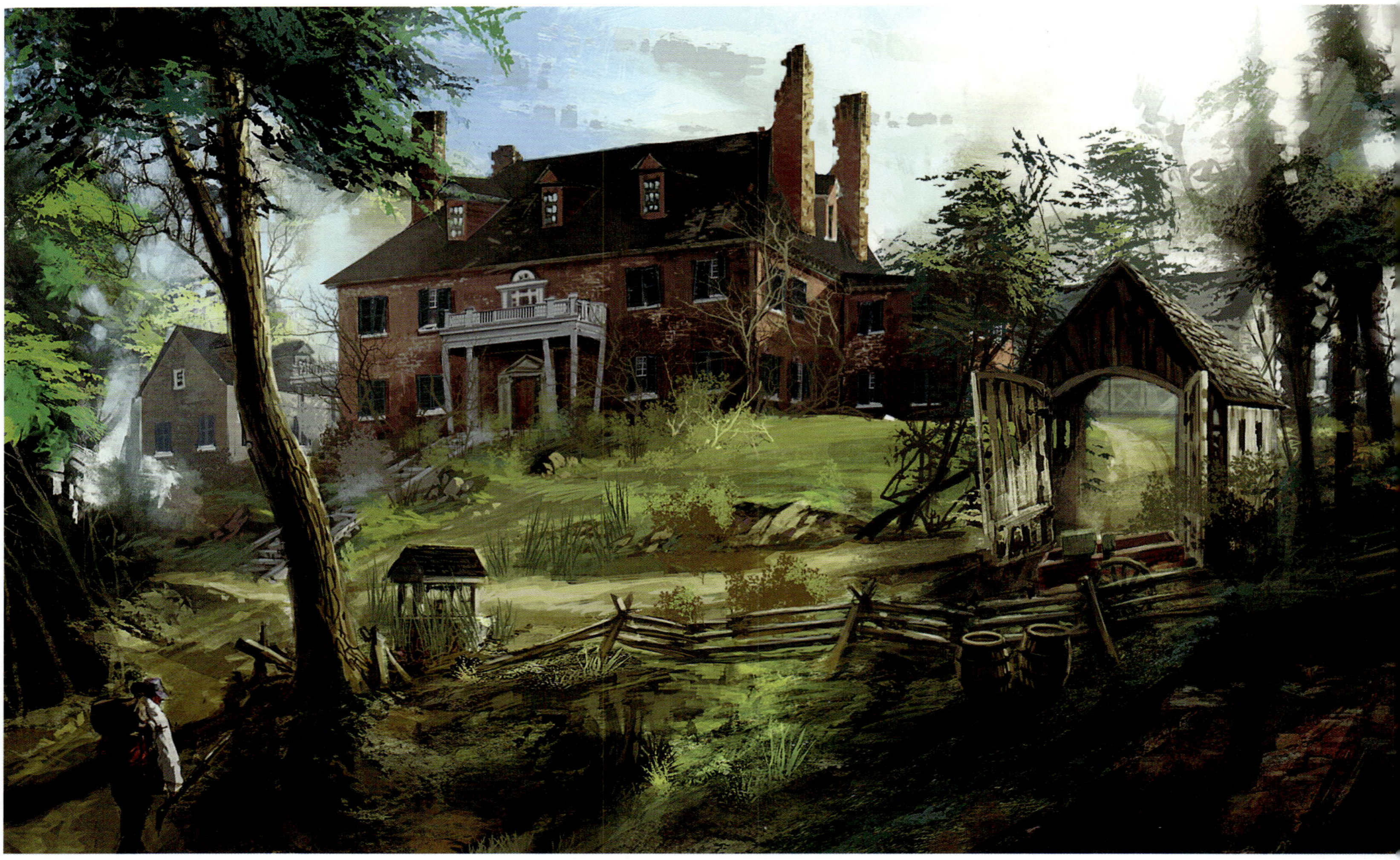

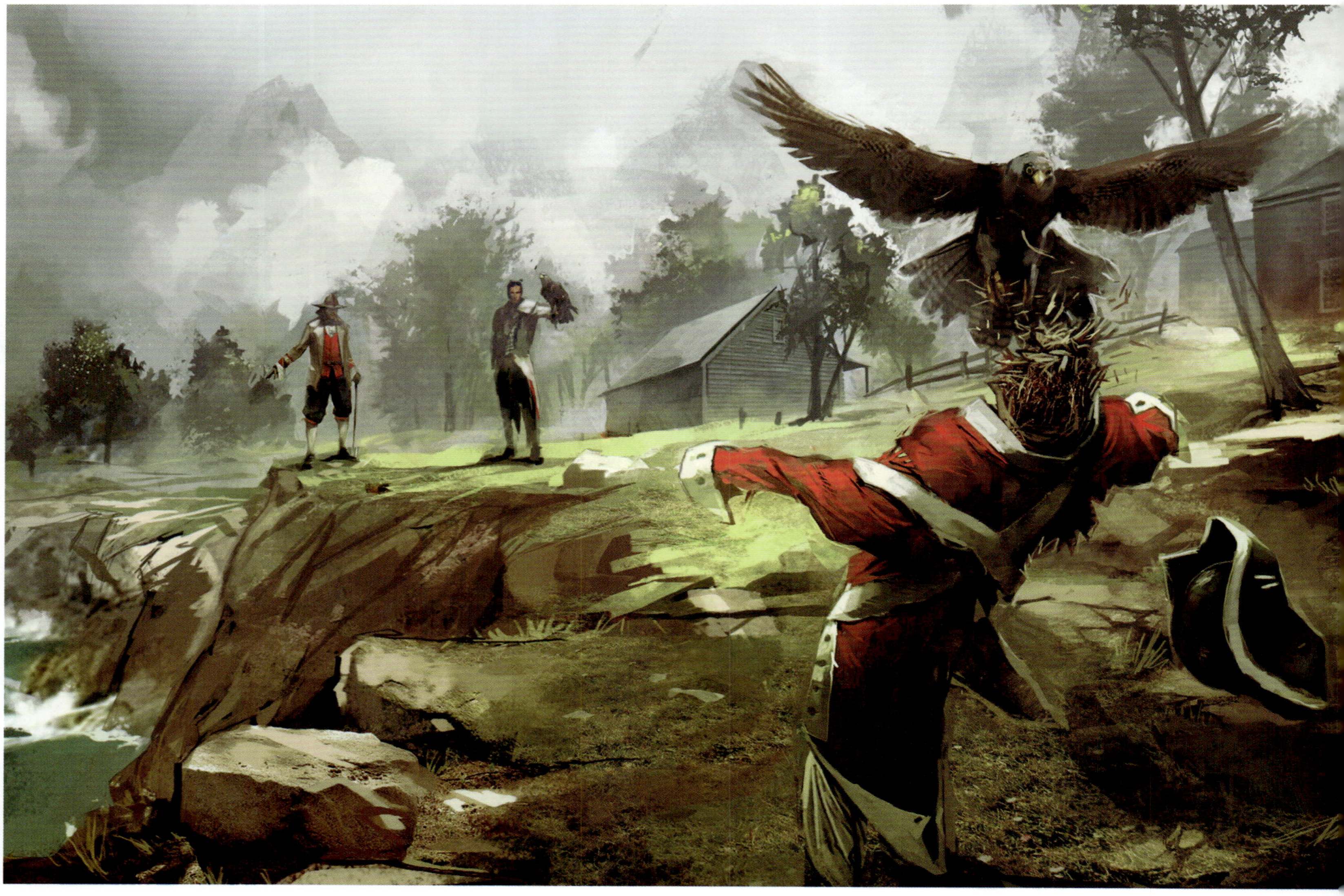

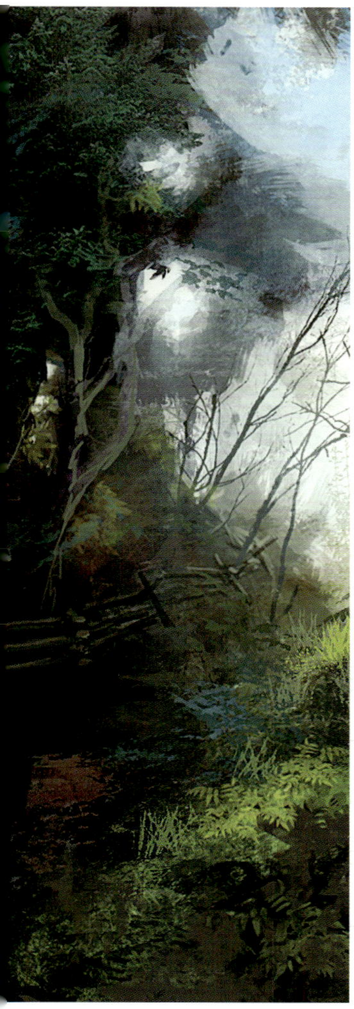

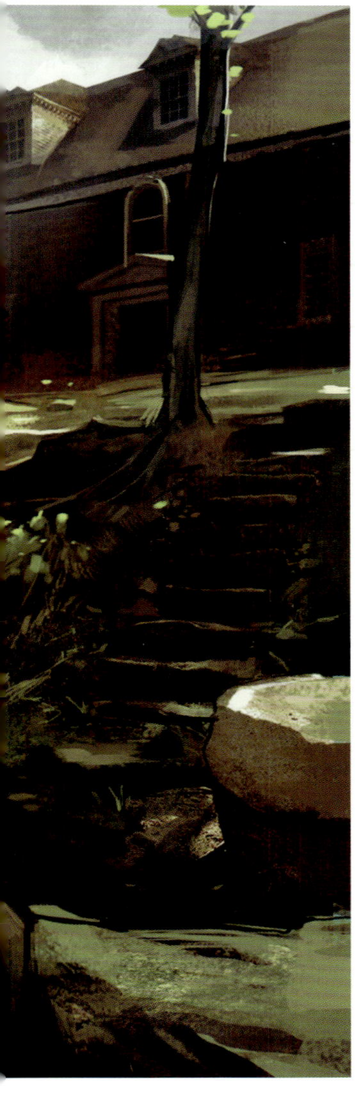

A PLACE TO CALL HOME

Like all the Assassins that came before, Connor needed a launchpad for his adventures and a place to return to that felt like a reasonable retreat from death and danger. However, no home base before or since has felt as large, involved, or interwoven into the narrative as the Homestead.

The mansion that overlooked a port bay was only the beginning of a much larger and more involved locale that grew and changed as players took the time to get involved with village life. The promise of a new, safe home on the Frontier drew distinct characters to the burgeoning hamlet, and what was once an empty forest began to see the planting of farms, the building of a church, and even the establishment of relationships and marriages. Like so many aspects of *Assassin's Creed III*, the Homestead excelled at communicating time's march. The narrative roots of endearing village characters and the artistic challenge of a location that was always changing made this base feel more like a home than any previous location in the series.

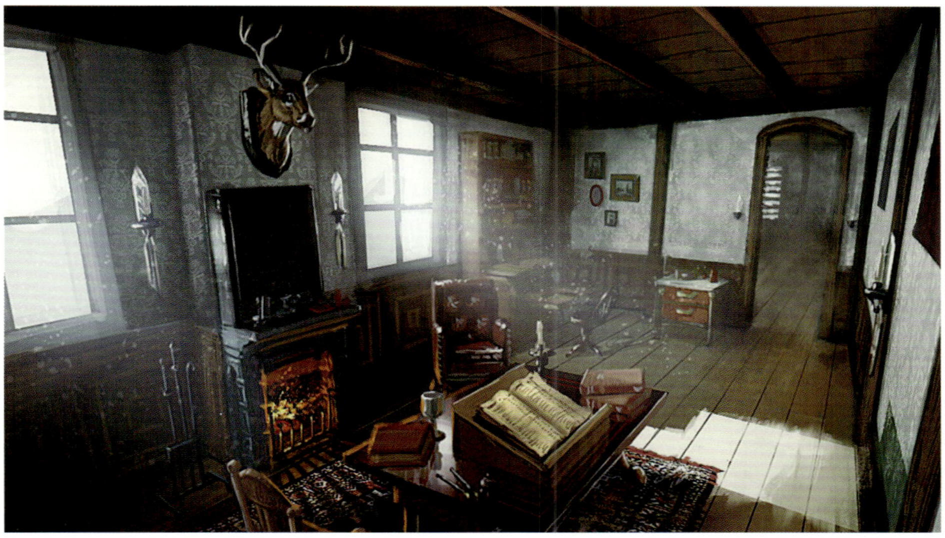

TOP LEFT: Exterior view of the Homestead manor contrasting the natural with man-made structures (Grant Hillier).
BOTTOM LEFT: Artwork of the back of the manor (Guillaume Menuel).
ABOVE: The warm tones and intricate details of the study encourage exploration (Grant Hillier).

EARLY METROPOLIS

The two great cities of Boston and New York were still in their infancy during the days of the American Revolution, but both were already abuzz with life and change. Each of the cities was created using extant city plans from the period wherever possible, and when history allowed, a few of the memorable landmarks that had already been built, like Boston's Old State House. As always, the focus remained on balancing historical veracity with artistic license. "It's always an interesting challenge, because if we stick too much to realism, sometimes it's just not visually striking enough," explains senior concept artist Martin Deschambault. "But on the other hand, if we take too much liberty, we risk falling into the fantasy category. The line is very thin, but I really like the challenge. The key is the artistic reinterpretation of reality."

Boston felt like a city still deeply rooted in the organic—trees, dirt roads, free-roaming domesticated animals, and rolling hills. The city had an active trade and port scene, and the brick houses and churches were anchors of civilization.

New York's defining features were the remnants of the great fire of 1776—a whole swath of the city devastated by flame and smoke. The ruins were filled with broken doorways and half-standing chimneys, and the city's poorest had no choice but to call the area home. Elsewhere, the city teemed with activity, and British Redcoats made their occupation known through constant patrols.

Throughout the process of recreating these early American cities, historical advisors helped to keep the visualization on track. "It's very inspiring when you talk with the historians, because they've got some fascinating anecdotes," Raphaël says. "They will say something very simple, but that could have an effect on the art direction, on the storyline, on the game mechanics." Even so, the art team reserved the right to let artistic concerns override minor inconsistencies. "In *Assassin's Creed III*, certain details in the houses were removed because the historians pointed out they shouldn't be there," Raphaël continues. "But sometimes it's more important to get the right feeling than to be completely historically accurate. Of course, if a house was made of wood, it shouldn't be made of stone. But if one type of wood paneling fits the mood better than another, we would pick the one that sets the right tone, as those details can sometimes make the difference when it comes to creating a specific atmosphere. Image composition and level design are also very important when it comes to balancing the creation of buildings."

OPPOSITE: Painting of a New York street (William Wu).

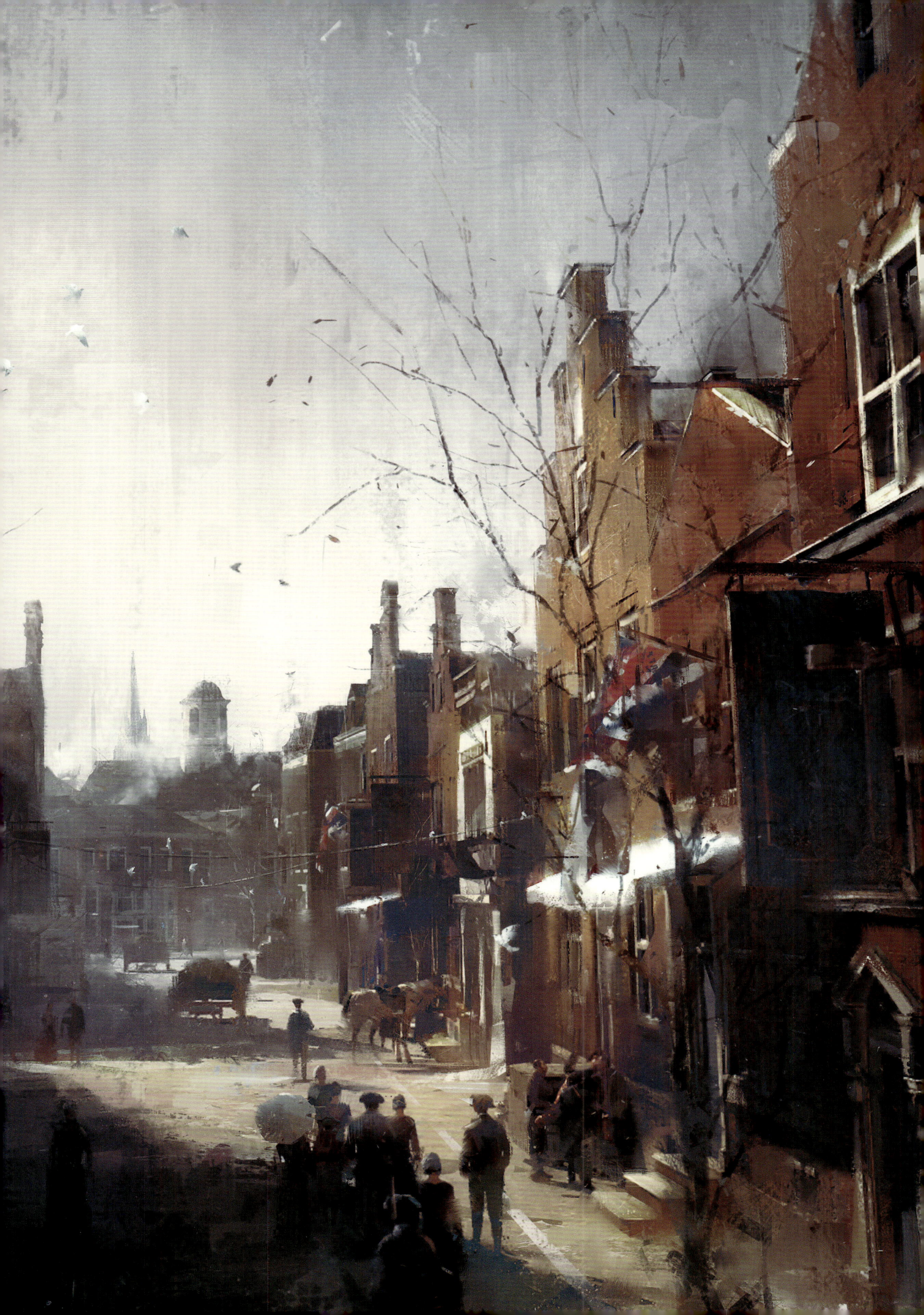

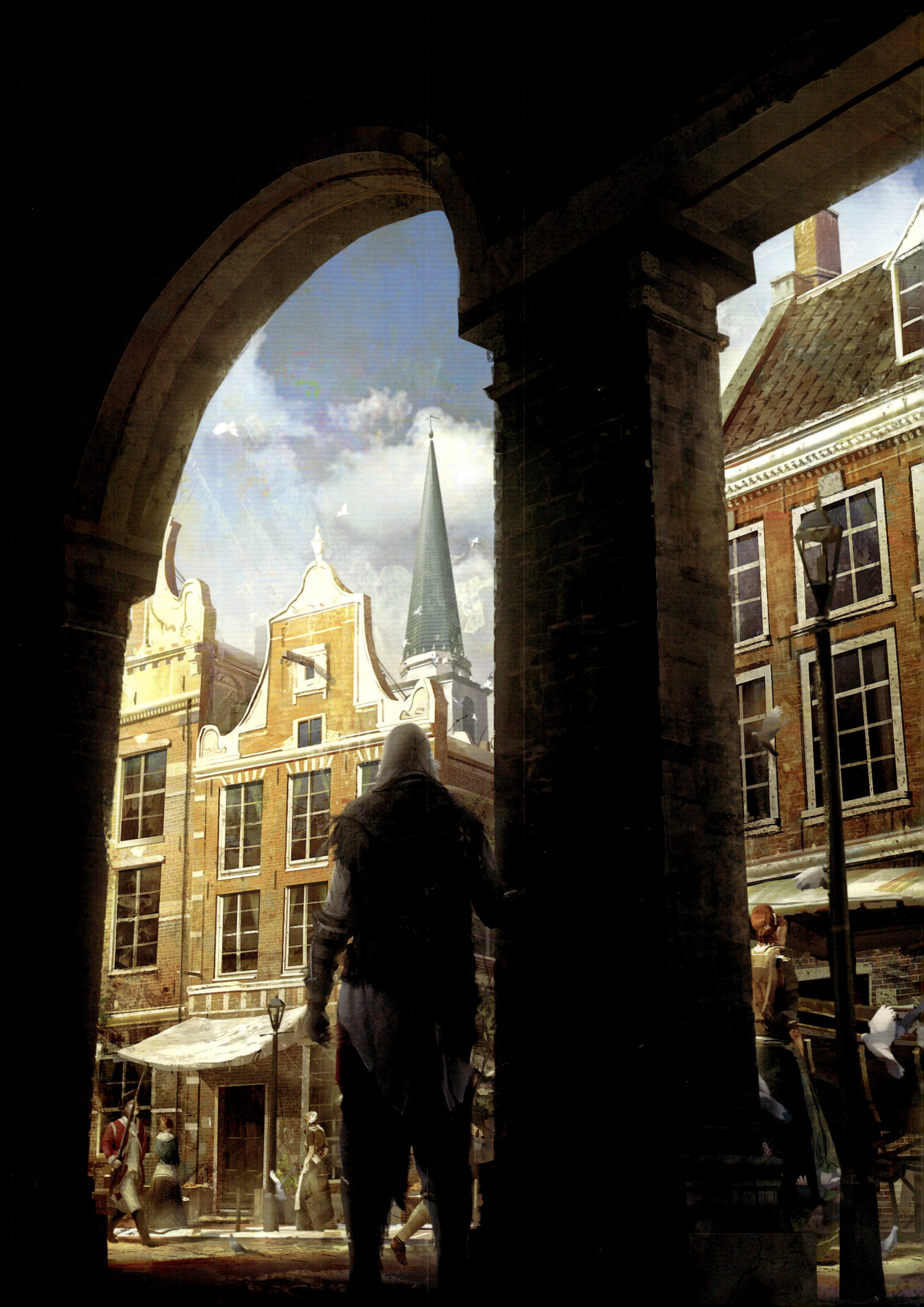

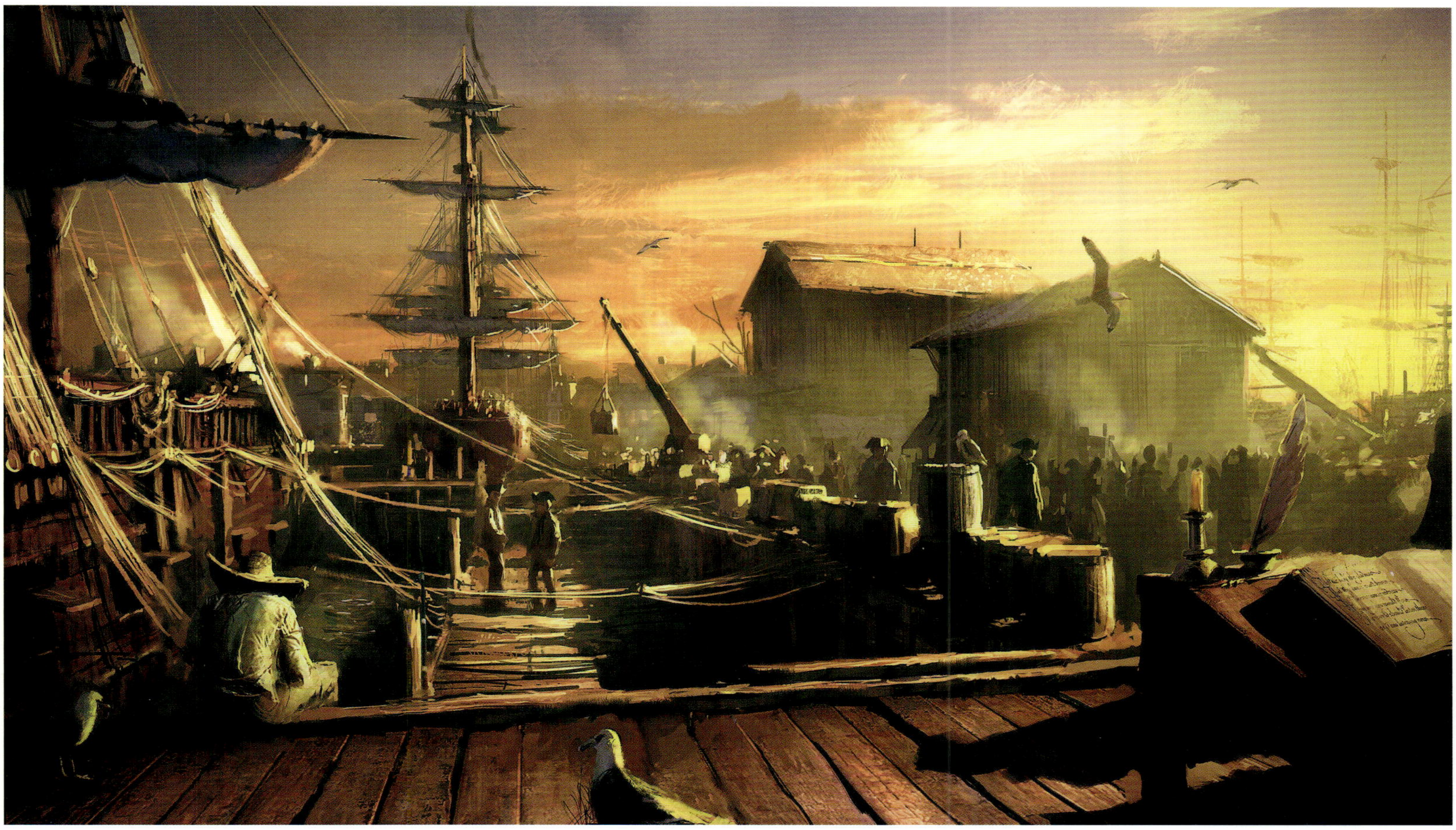

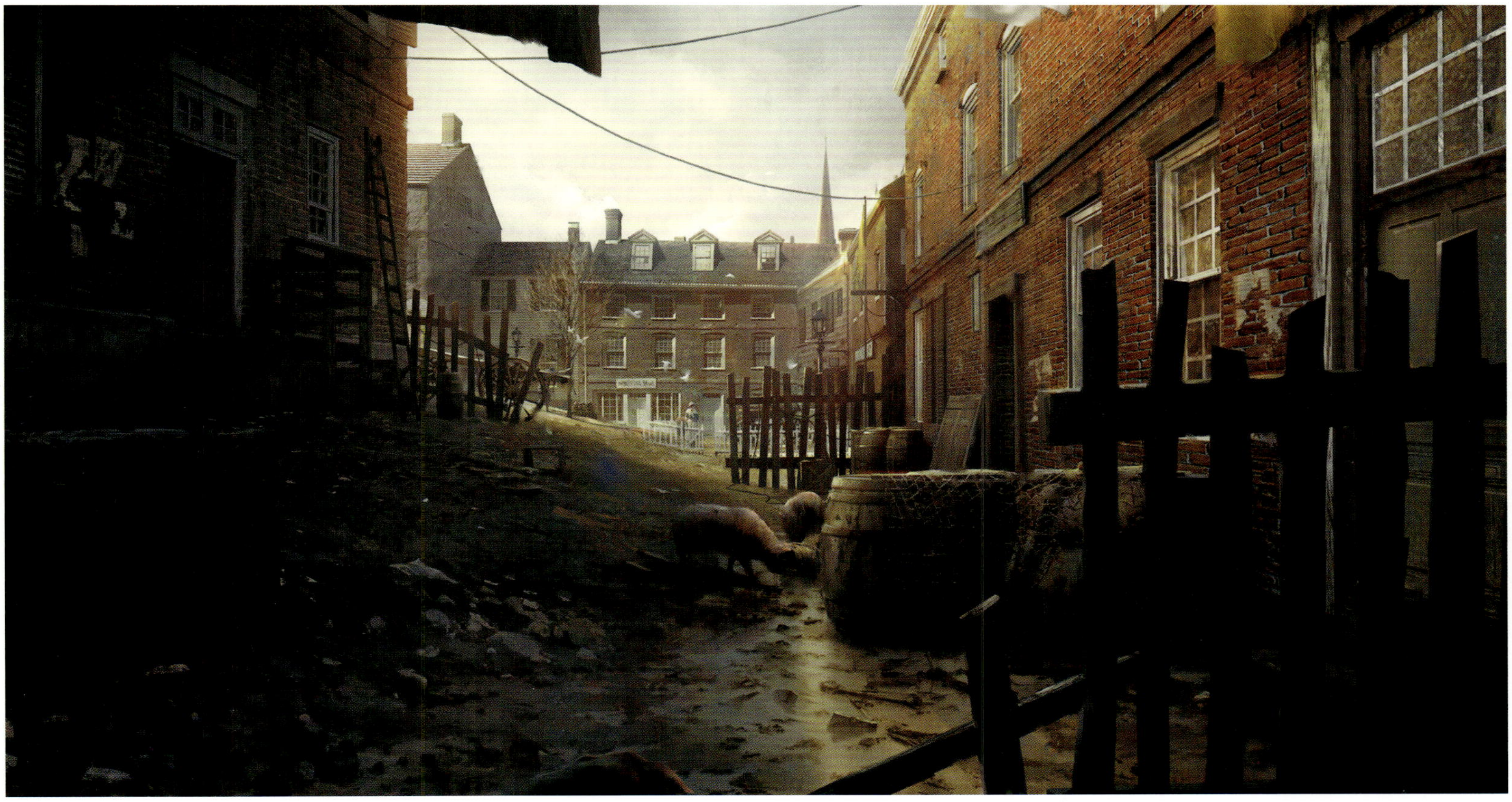

OPPOSITE: Connor's design had to reflect his heritage yet allow him to blend in with civilians in cities like New York (William Wu).
TOP: Artwork of a Boston dock at sunset (Gilles Beloeil).
BOTTOM: Illustration of a Boston alley (William Wu).

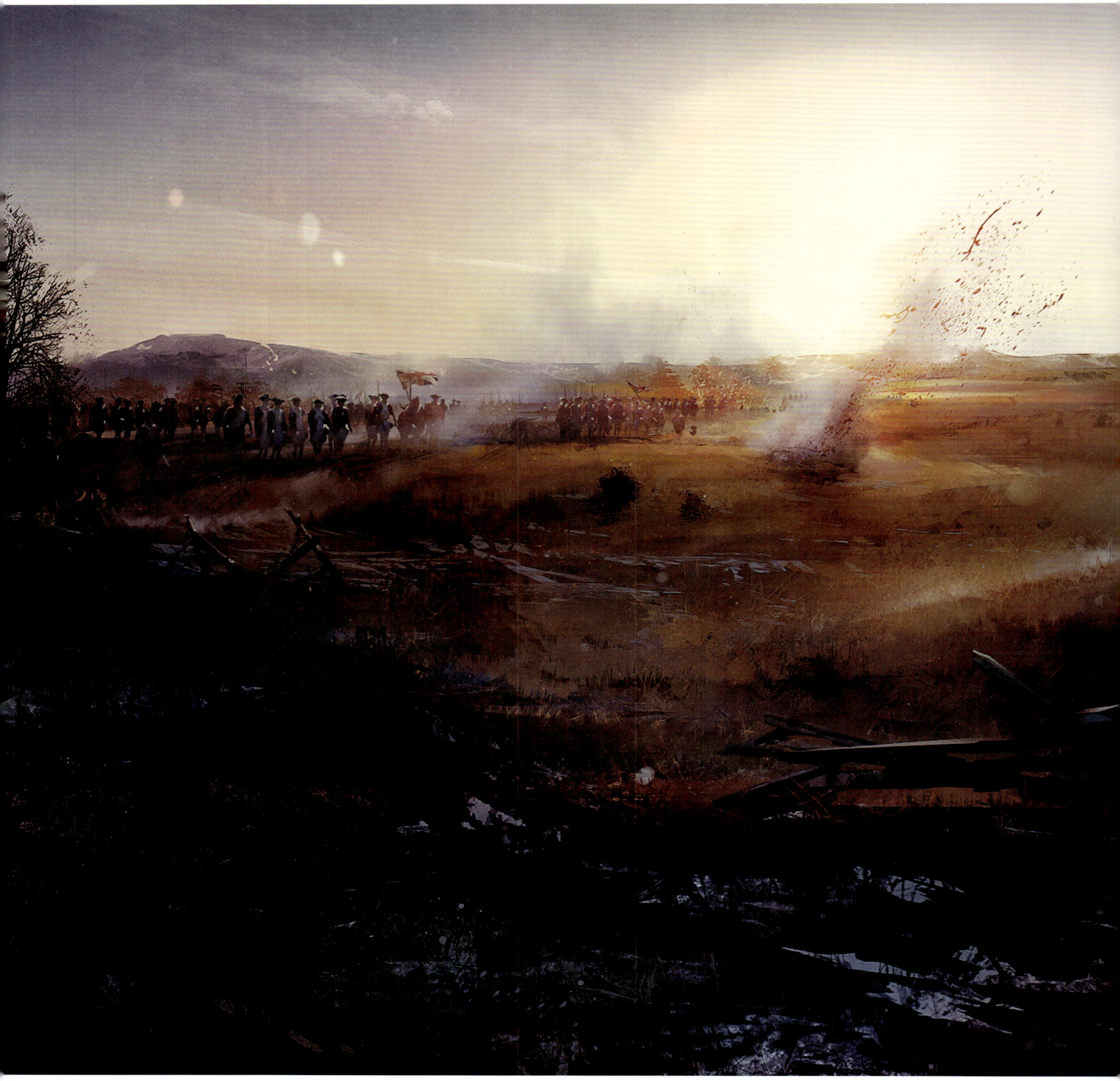

THESE PAGES: Illustration of the Battle of Monmouth with sunset lighting (William Wu).

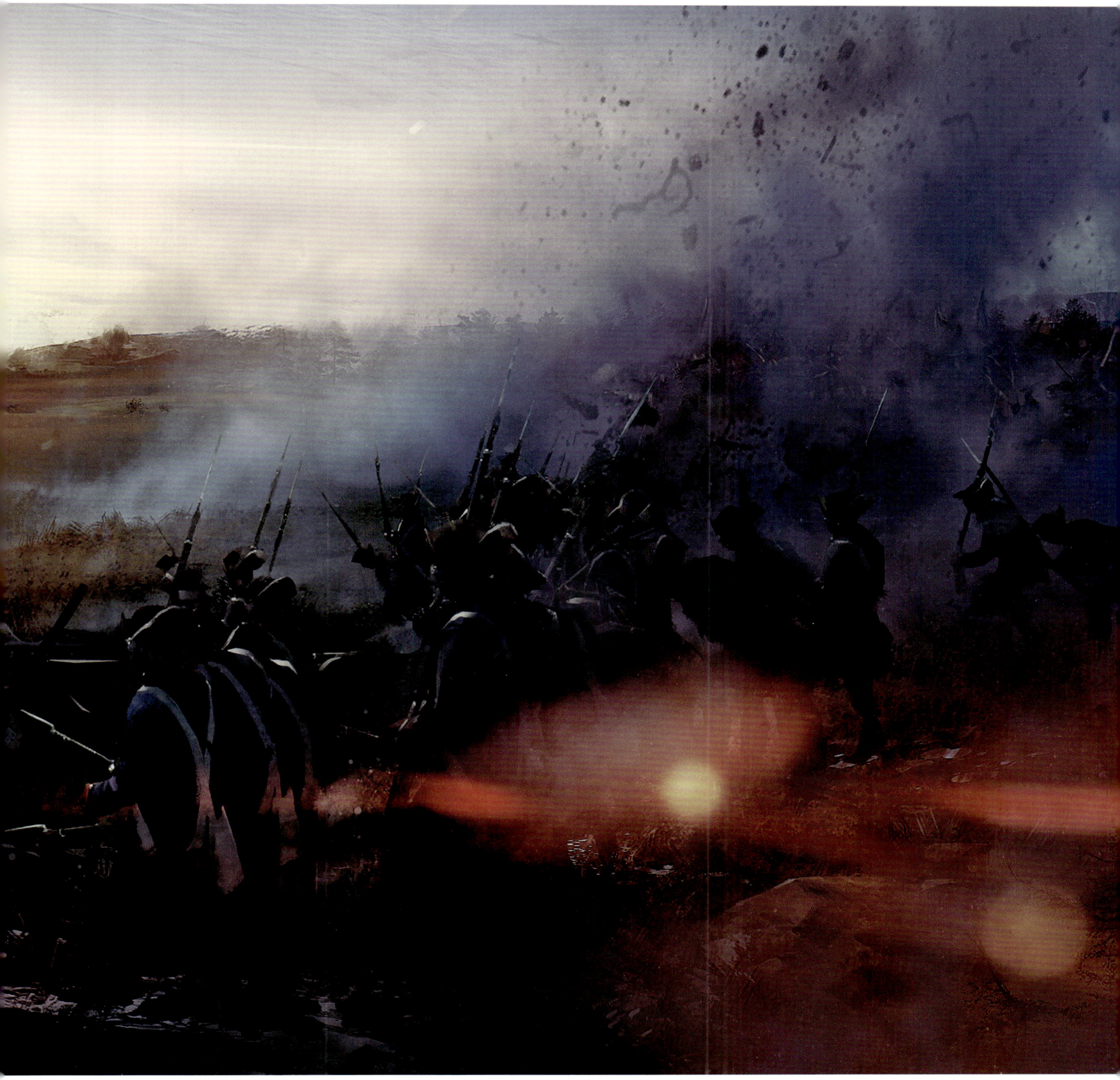

BATTLEFIELDS

Whether in Bunker Hill or Lexington and Concord, some of the revolution's greatest combat was intertwined with Connor's story. Using these military sites ensured that Connor's personal missions always unraveled alongside the larger struggle of the revolution. Huge numbers of enemy soldiers and clever use of perspective and distance helped the actual battle scenes feel epic and devastating.

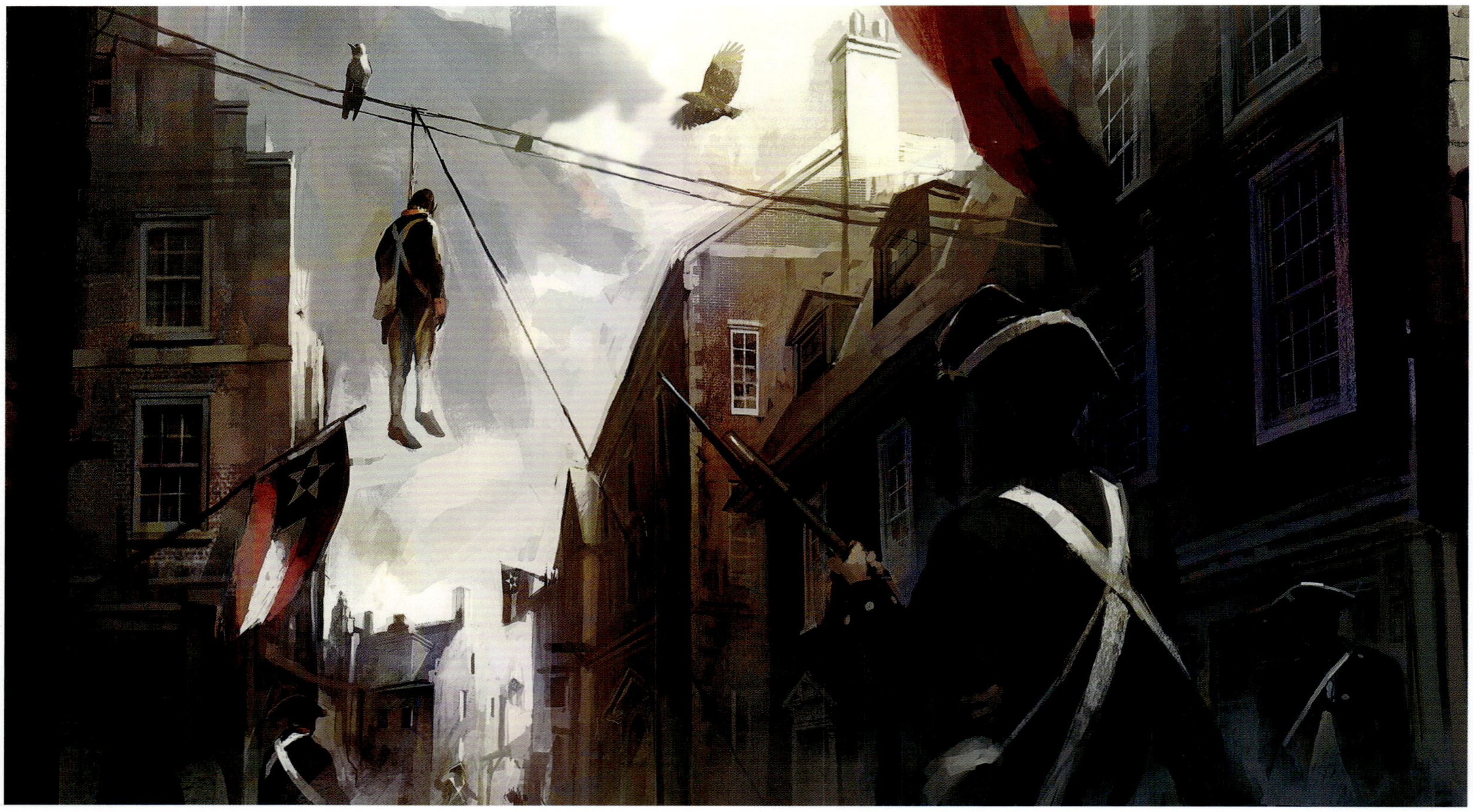

THE PATH OF TYRANNY

ABOVE: Artwork depicting the alternate history elements, including a flag with only one star (Guillaume Menuel).
OPPOSITE: Connor's new costume explored his connection to both the spiritual and the natural world (Guillaume Menuel).

Assassin's Creed III ultimately told a relatively compact and complete tale about Connor, his conflict with his own father, and the way the age-old Assassin and Templar war influenced the American Revolution. Thus, when it was time to explore additional downloadable content for the game, the developers at Ubisoft had the freedom to branch off in a surprising new direction.

Through the strange properties of one of the Apples of Eden, Connor is offered a glimpse of an alternate timeline in which the country's benevolent founding father, George Washington, was seduced by the power of the First Civilization artifact. Instead of leading the new country of America into democracy, Washington rises as a king, wielding his power to crush dissidents and rule with an iron fist. In this timeline, Ratonhnhaké:ton never adopts the name Connor and instead embraces his native background to tap into powerful animal spirits. Blinded by power, Washington builds his own massive pyramid in the heart of New York. Many of history's other familiar faces, like Benjamin Franklin, Samuel Adams, and Thomas Jefferson, are cast in new roles that match this history gone wrong.

The Tyranny of King Washington allowed Ubisoft's artists to let loose, traveling further into the realms of fantasy than any previous franchise entry had allowed. By stepping out of the established history, players gained superpowers that would feel out of place in the main game, and scenes included assassinations and other deaths that never actually happened. "It was very fun because of the freedom that we had in the DLC to take the world that we had established and create an alternate version," Raphaël says. "It's not only visual; it was in the new powers that the player could use with Connor. We were able to push the fantasy, because we were not in the spine of the franchise. So we could put an entirely different spin on the concepts that we created in the game."

Like any other installment, the art team had to do a lot of exploration to find the right tone to match the story. "We went in a very dark artistic direction in the beginning, but we found that it was too far," Raphaël admits. A subsequent pass added some of the glow and brightness from previous Assassin's Creed installments, seen in everything from the user interface to First Civilization lighting. "We were veering too far away from the franchise. So we brought in some contrasting light, the glowing light that is ever-present in the series." The *King Washington* DLC ended up feeling closely tied to the original game but with ephemeral and surreal undercurrents that matched well with the unusual story.

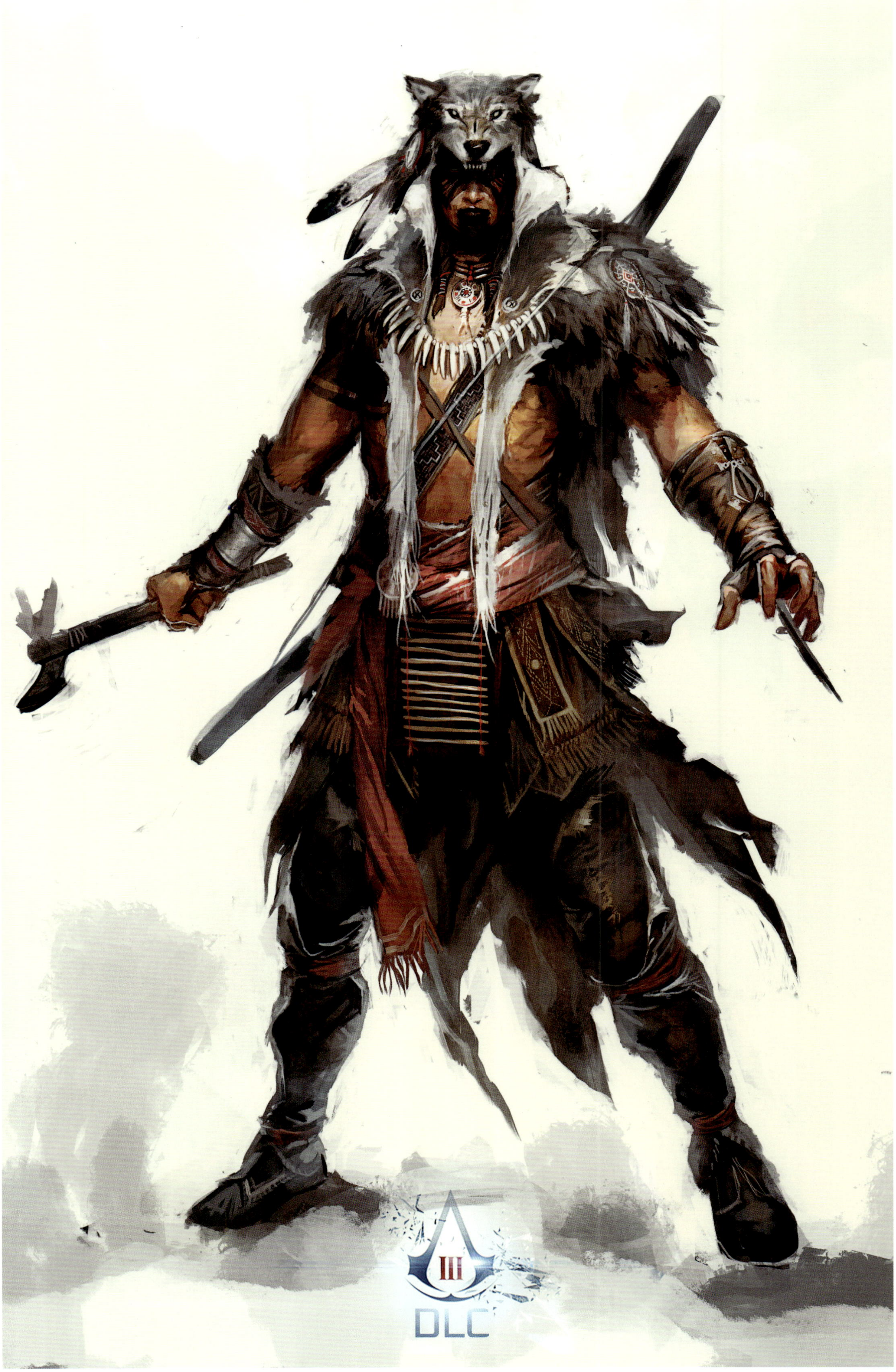
III
DLC

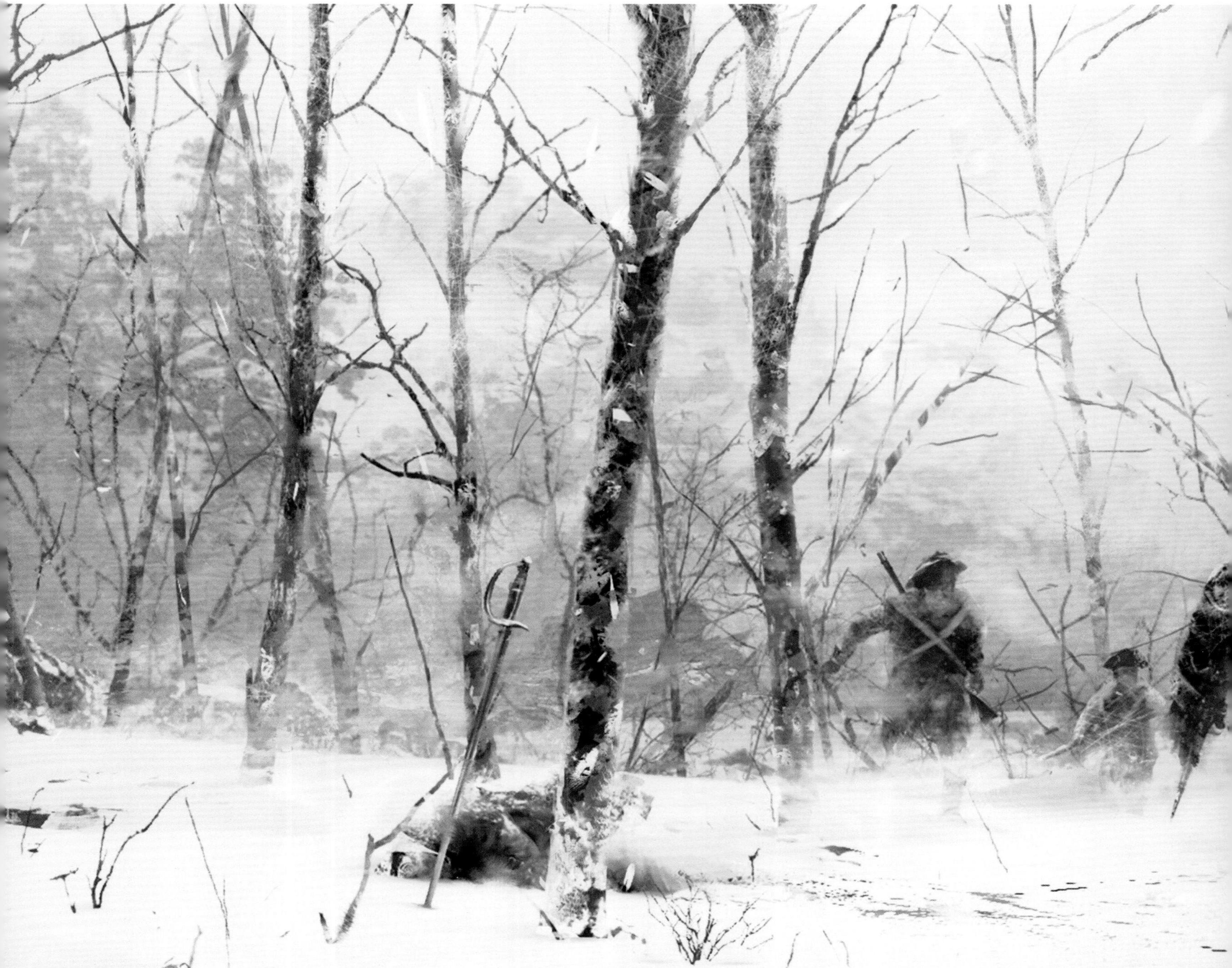

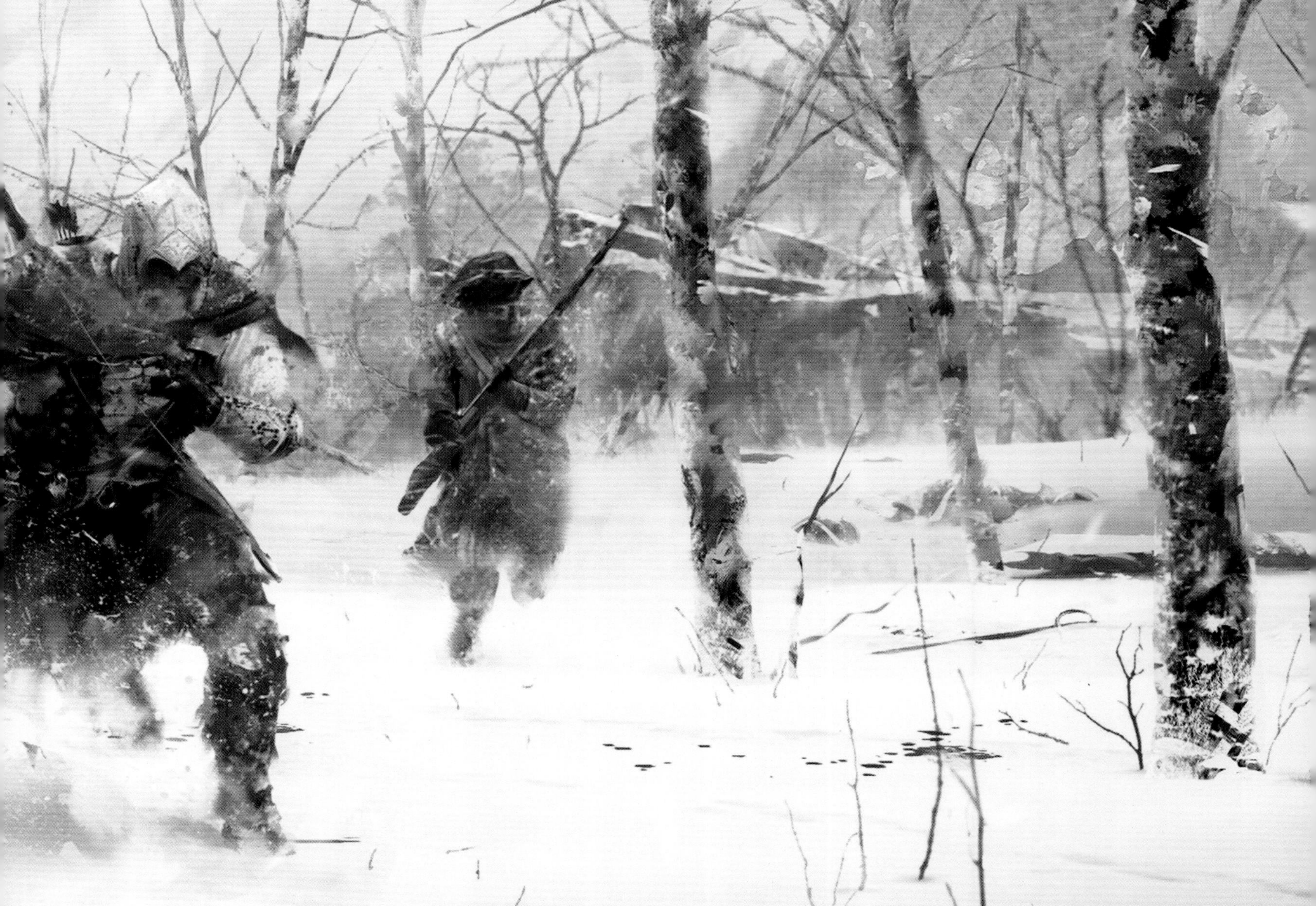

THESE PAGES: Award-winning artwork of Connor charging into battle through deep snow (William Wu).

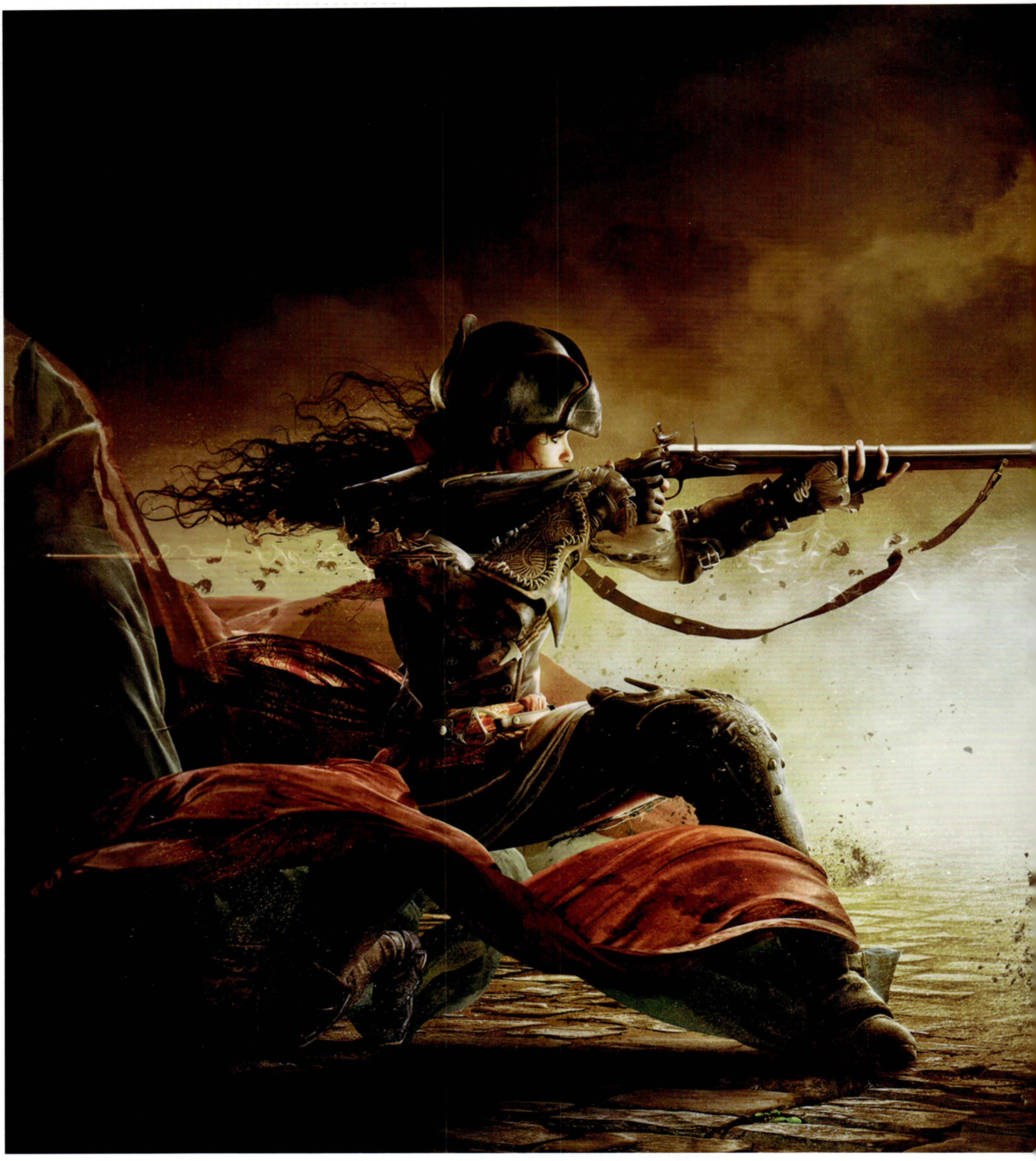

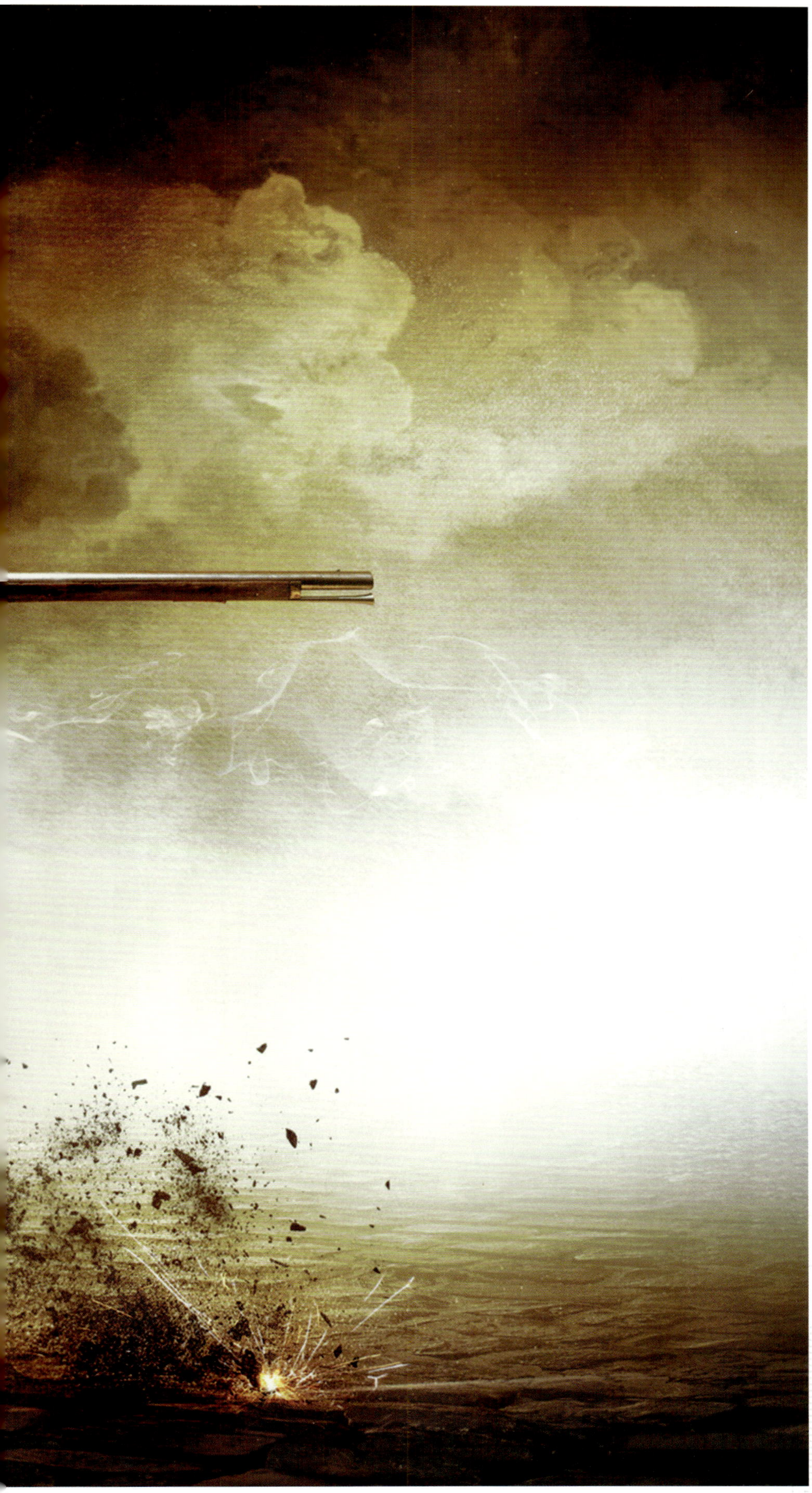

4 THE SEVEN YEARS' WAR

Part 1

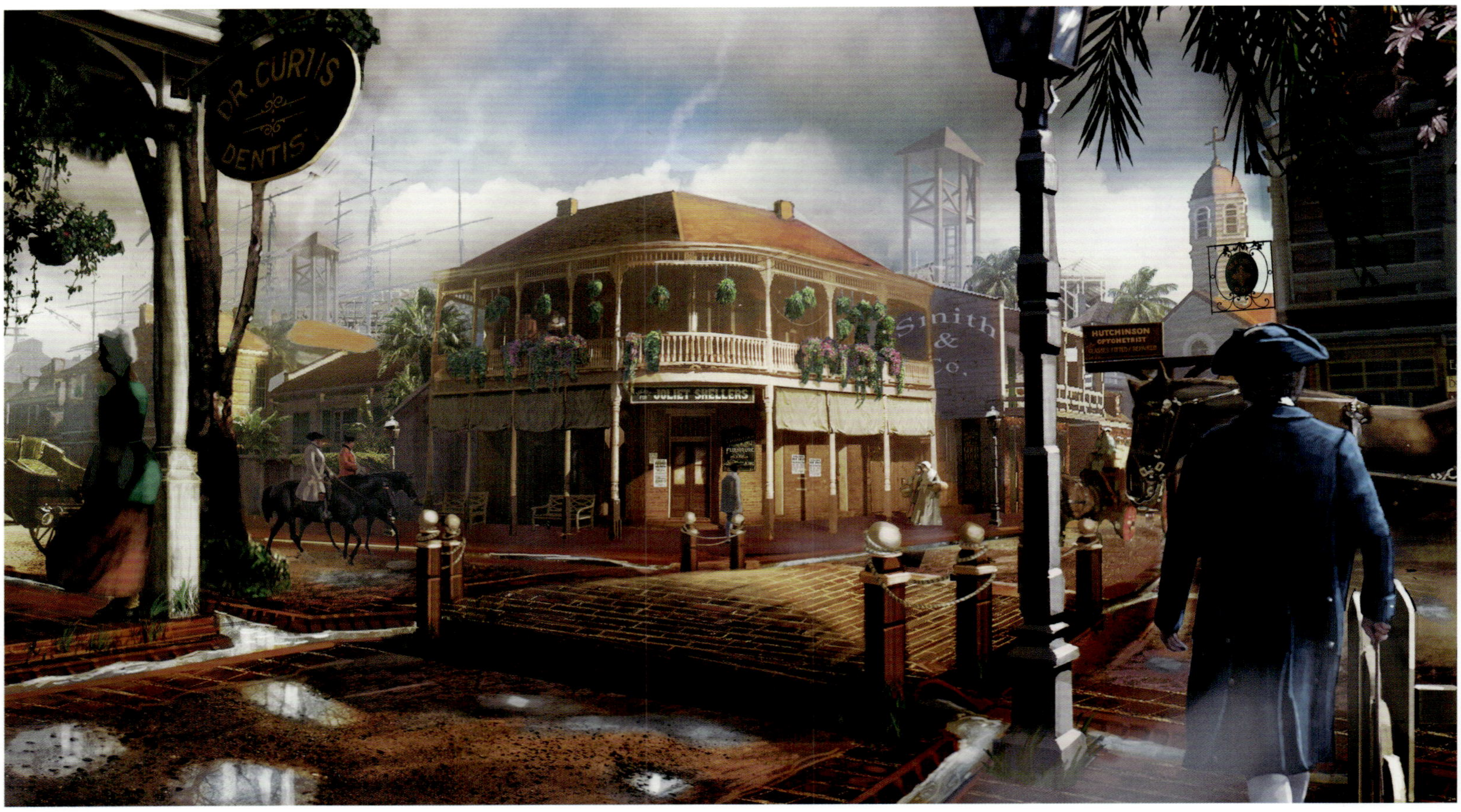

THE SOUTHERN CONNECTION

Originally released in 2012 as a portable game alongside *Assassin's Creed III* and re-released on consoles in 2014 to reflect an HD update, *Assassin's Creed: Liberation* charted a number of firsts. The lead studio was Ubisoft Sofia (Ubistoft studios are named after the cities where they are located), representing the first time that main development duties had passed from Montreal. It was also the first appearance of a female lead, and along with Connor's Native American heritage in *Assassin's Creed III*, *Liberation* served to further broaden the franchise's multicultural perspective. *Liberation* transported players to the southern shores of North America in the waning days of the Seven Years' War, also known as the French and Indian War. Originally a French colony, New Orleans had only been ceded to the Spanish Empire a few years before the game began. Aveline de Grandpré was a young woman at the time, a wealthy daughter of a French shipping magnate and his former African slave. By the time players meet her, Aveline had already trained as an Assassin and was using her newfound abilities to confront the greatest plague on liberty of the time: the evils of slavery. "We were trying to keep a consistency within the franchise, while also making something original," Raphaël says. "We wanted to introduce a new, fresh character to our assassins cast." Aveline's background as both a woman and a person of color were an important step for the franchise; the new character perspective invited creative opportunities for writers and artists alike. Aveline's story illustrated an eagerness to explore diverse protagonists and reflected a population of game players of similarly diverse experiences.

Liberation's gameplay and setting were a clear departure for the franchise but once again proved Assassin's Creed's ability to move into new arenas. On the artistic front, Aveline's adventures brought us the dangers of the Bayou, the charm of New Orleans, and a heroine who was always more than she appeared to be.

PREVIOUS PAGES: Aveline's design focused on her heroic and warrior-like qualities (Christopher Dormoy).
ABOVE: Concept of the wealthy area of downtown New Orleans (Eddie Bennun).
OPPOSITE: Aveline's costumes allowed her to blend in as both an Assassin and a noblewoman (Christopher Dormoy).

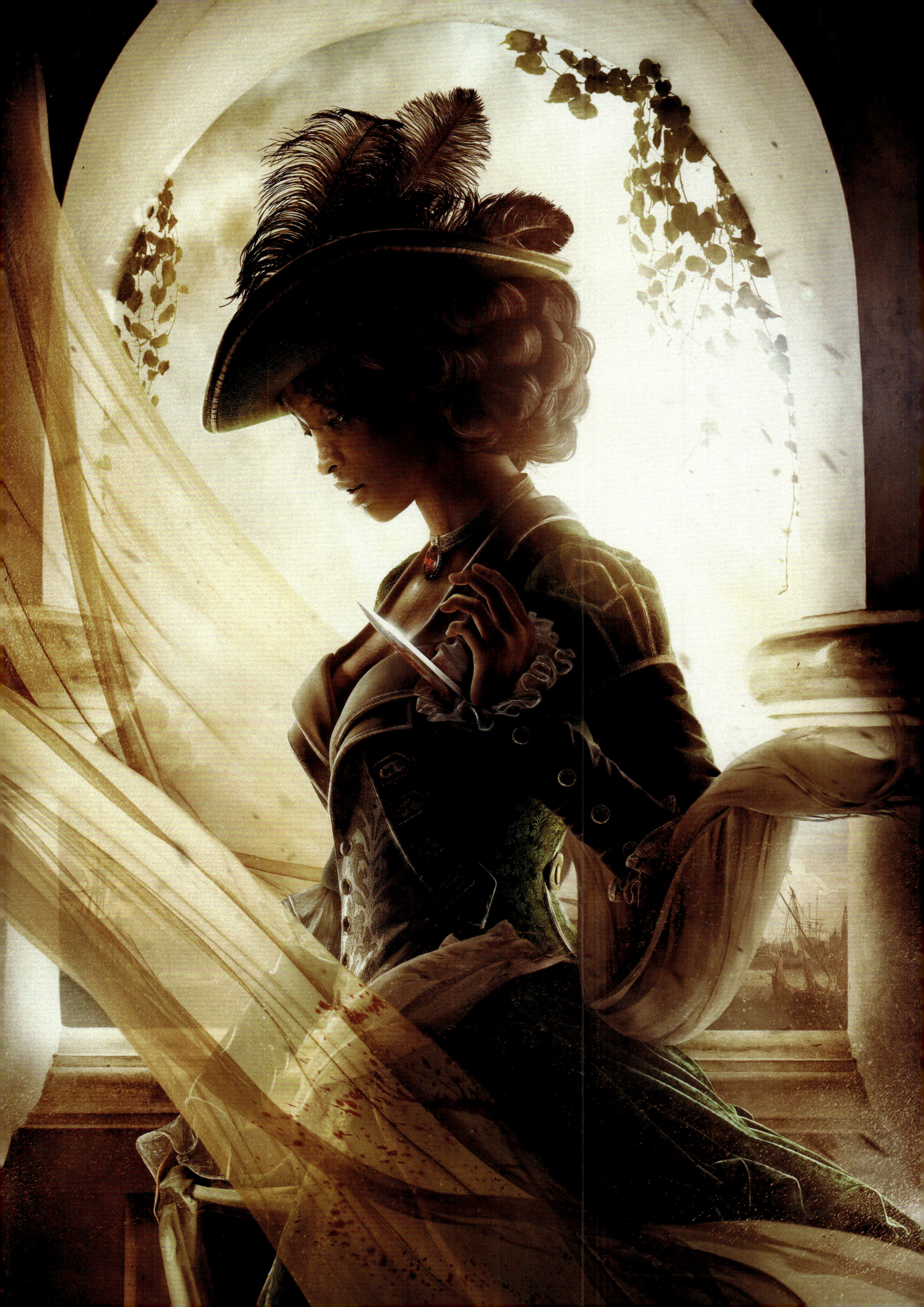

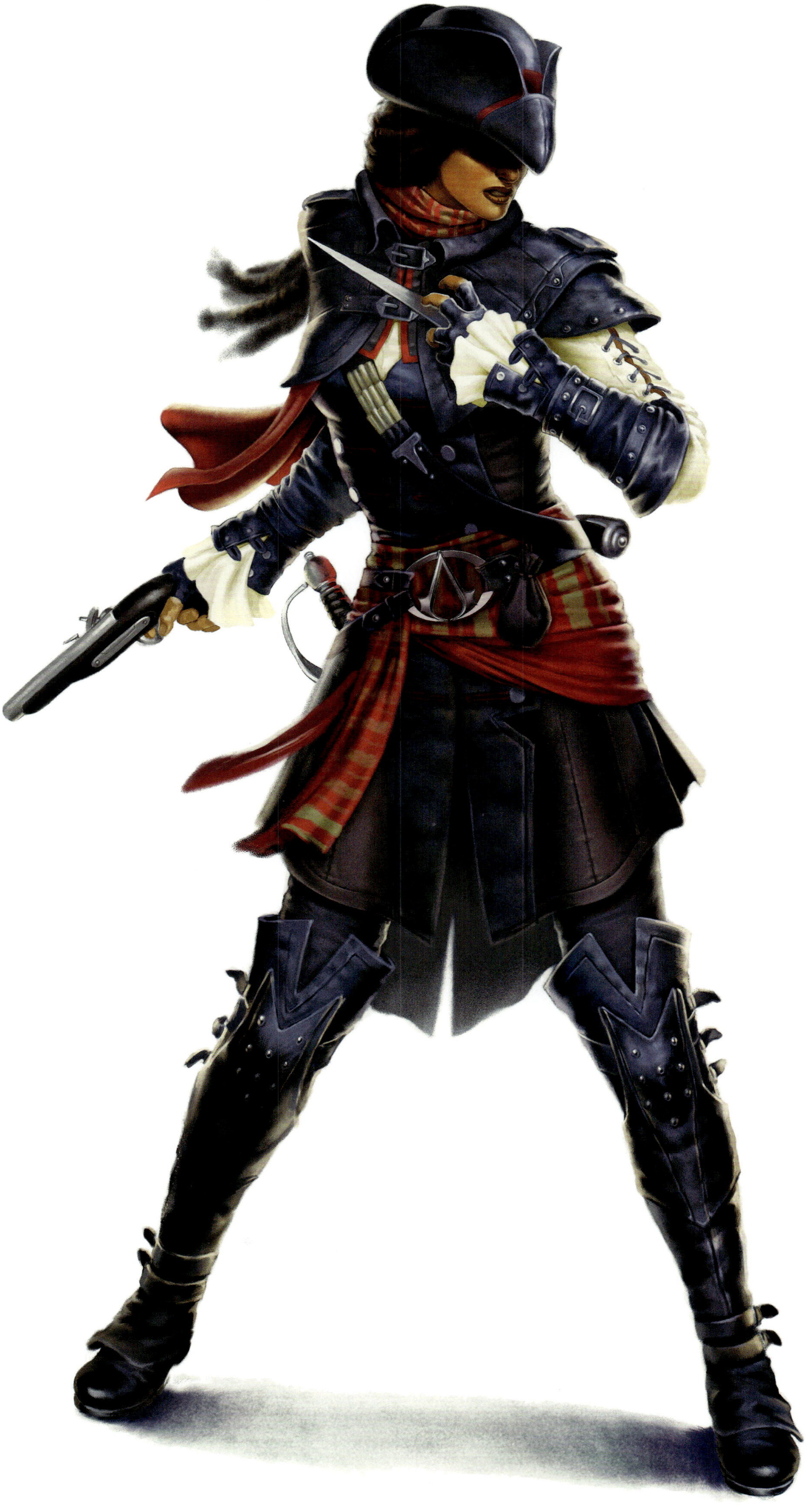

MULTIPLE PERSONALITIES

Aveline's mixed heritage established some clear conflicts from the very start. As a privileged lady of New Orleans, her fine dresses and cultured etiquette put her at home among the well-to-do. As a woman of color and the child of a slave, she was also keenly aware of the injustice that existed all around her, especially in regard to the ongoing ownership and trade of human beings prevalent in New Orleans during her time. Add in the integration of her training as an Assassin, and Aveline emerged as a perplexing individual. "Aveline's sensitive and contradictory personality made her a very complicated but amazing character to develop," says art director Eddie Bennun. "We faced the challenge of combining the typical-for-the-Assassins cold-bloodedness with virtues like compassion, self-sacrifice, and understanding."

Ubisoft artists and designers didn't shy away from Aveline's complexity but embraced it through a gameplay system that explored all her potential identities. "Our goals for Aveline were to have a typical deadly and agile Creed member, every bit an Assassin who was, at the same time, an emotional and graceful lady," says Eddie.

Rather than be a victim of her circumstances, Aveline capitalized on her background to succeed in her missions. Three distinct personas crystallized, each like a secret identity for a superhero, but no one of them a full representation of who she was. Artistically, these three identities manifested themselves through the outfits she wore, each granting her access to different places through which she'd need to pass. "We wanted each outfit to bring a very different gameplay experience based on action, stealth, and blending," Eddie says.

The well-dressed lady would be welcomed into society gatherings, but the limits of her elaborate dress would make roof-running and combat a near impossibility. The sophisticated lady of New Orleans persona was charming and free, refined and intelligent. The slave outfit, on the other hand, had Aveline adopting the very identity she fought so hard against, but it allowed her to mingle among others who had been enslaved and remain nearly invisible. Sequences in which Aveline adopted her slave garb depicted her as hardworking and understanding to a fault, but also hinted at ties to voodoo lore.

Finally, her Assassin outfit let her embrace her training. With her uniform on, she became a deadly killer, powerful and graceful as she moved silently from building to building or out along the dangerous paths of the bayou. The Assassin persona was also the one that needed to feel most connected to the wider identity of the franchise. Unlike that of most previous Assassins, Aveline's Assassin garb left off the hood, but her tricorn hat still alluded to the beak of a bird. Her color scheme was mostly new, but a red sash and touches of white recalled the Brotherhood's signature appearance. "The silhouette is very important," Raphaël says. "You have to take into account what the character communicates visually, so you have to play with the poses, the hood, and the profile. When you play the game, you don't see Aveline very often from the side, but you still have to consider what her silhouette represents." Aveline's three personas lent *Liberation* a different feel than any other game in the series. The sensation was almost one of playing three completely different protagonists that each emerged for their own impactful scenes.

OPPOSITE: Even without the iconic hood, Aveline is still recognizable as an Assassin through her hat's beak-like shape (Konstantin Kostadinov).

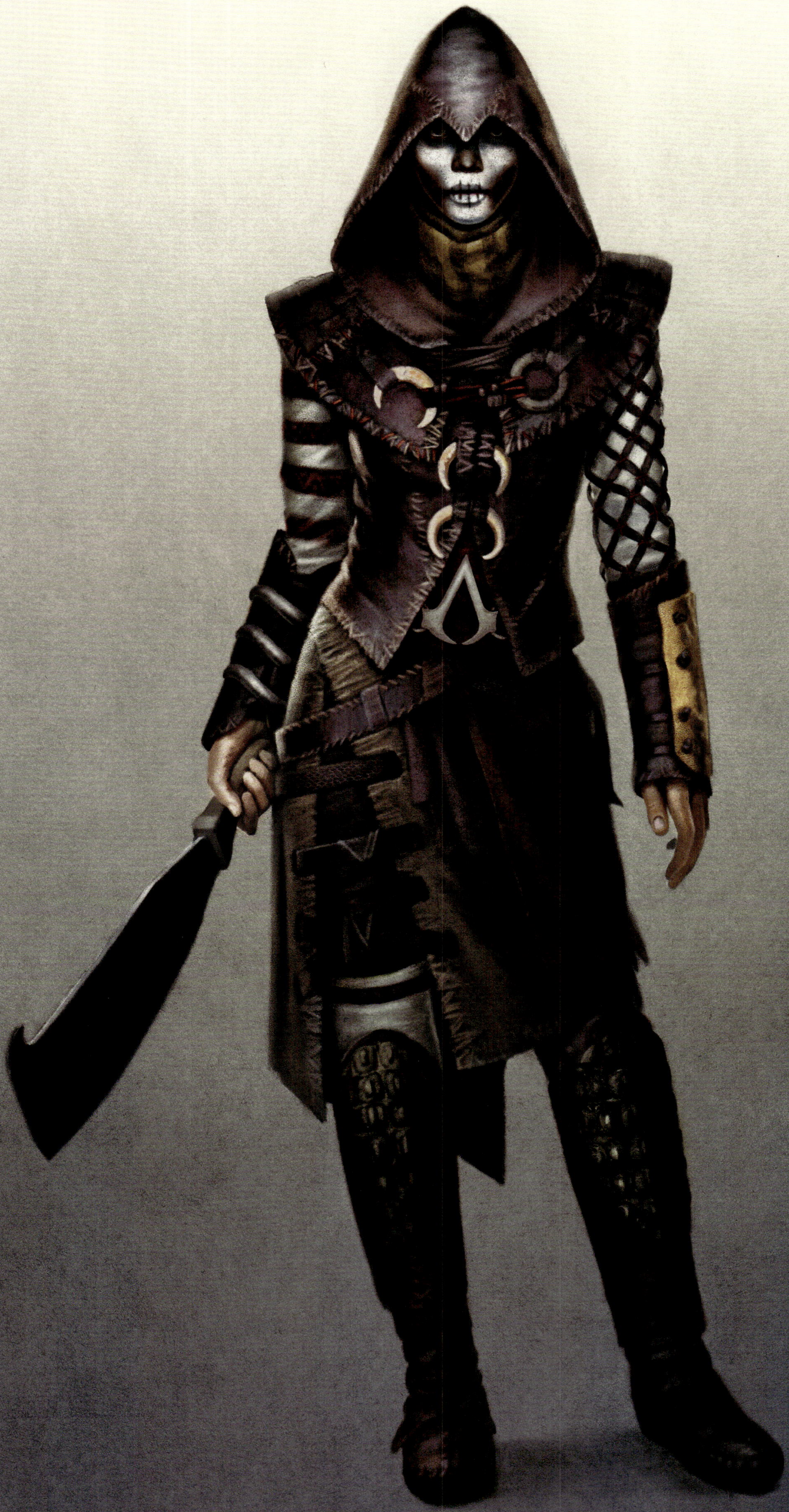

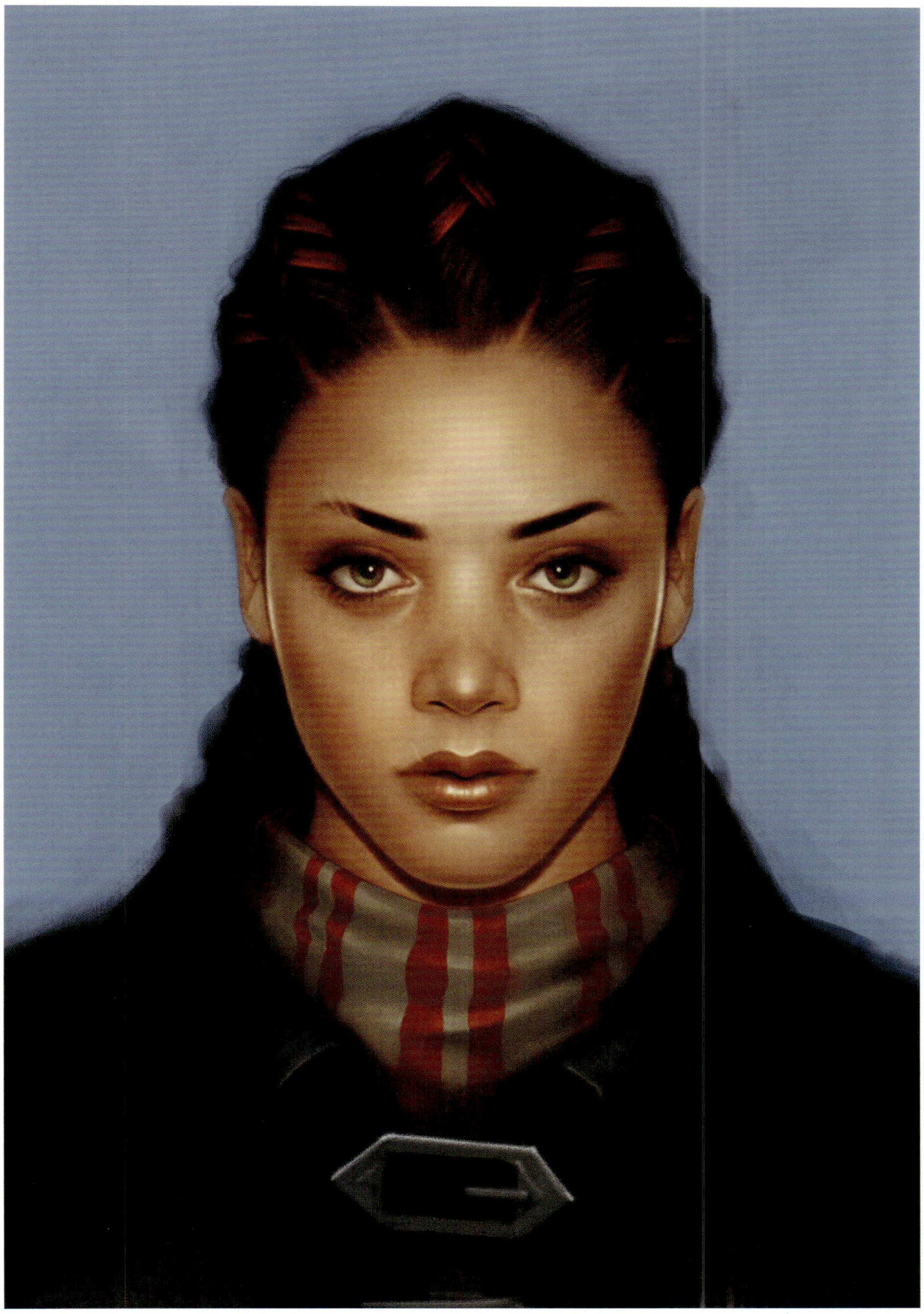

OPPOSITE: Concept of the Bayou Hunter outfit (Konstantin Kostadinov).
ABOVE: Portrait of Aveline (Borislav Mitkov).

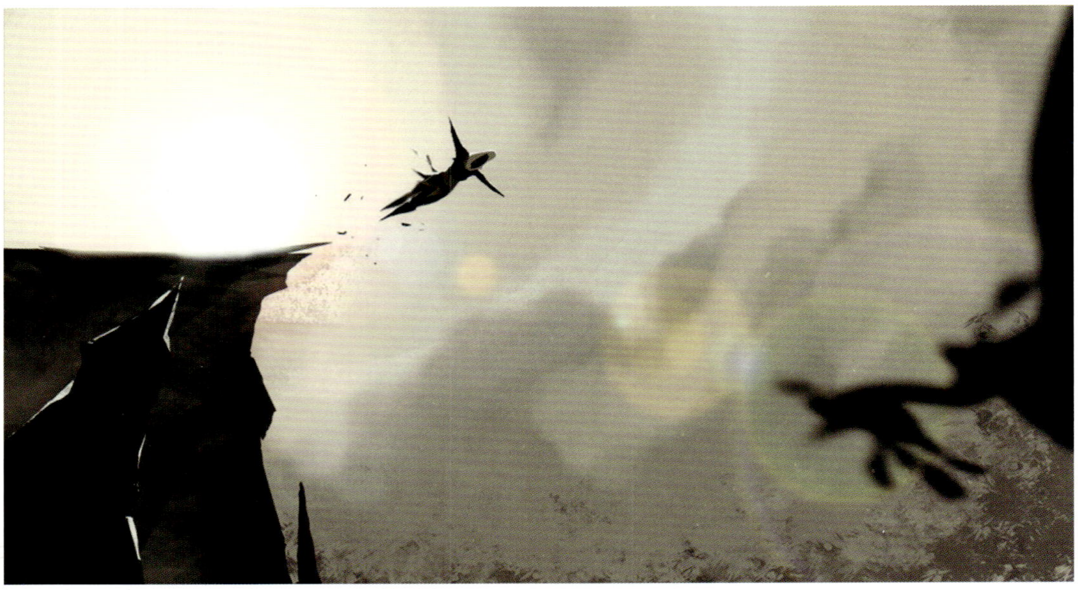

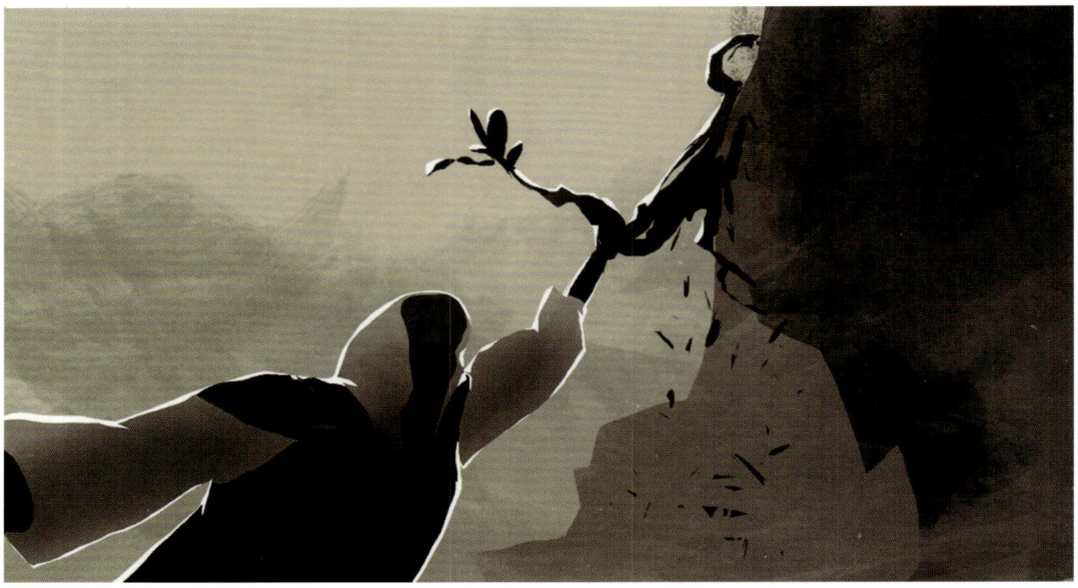

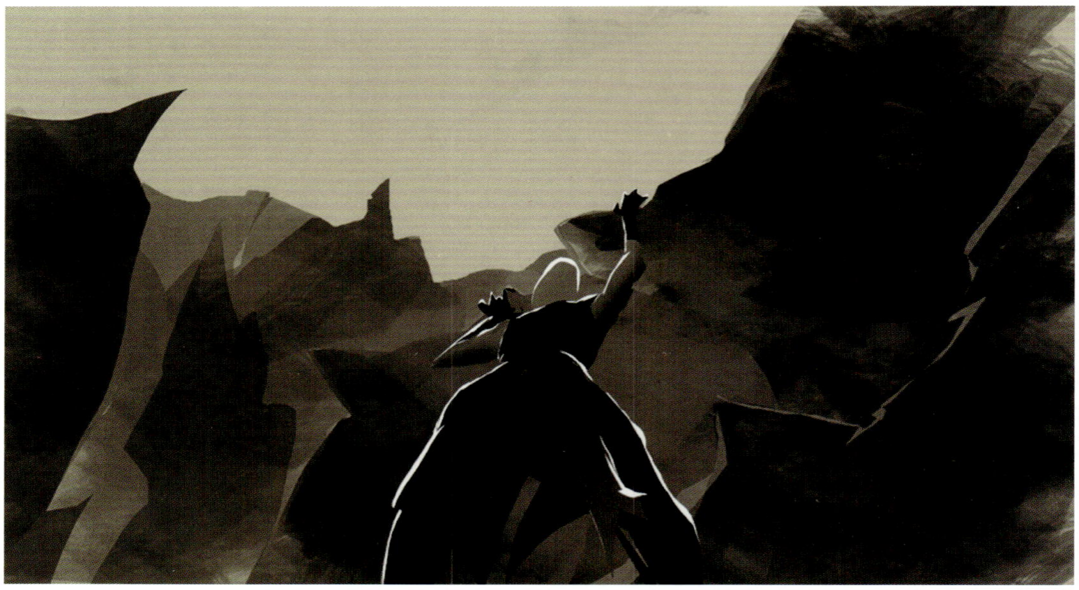

THESE PAGES: Newport storyboards (Ivan Koritarev).

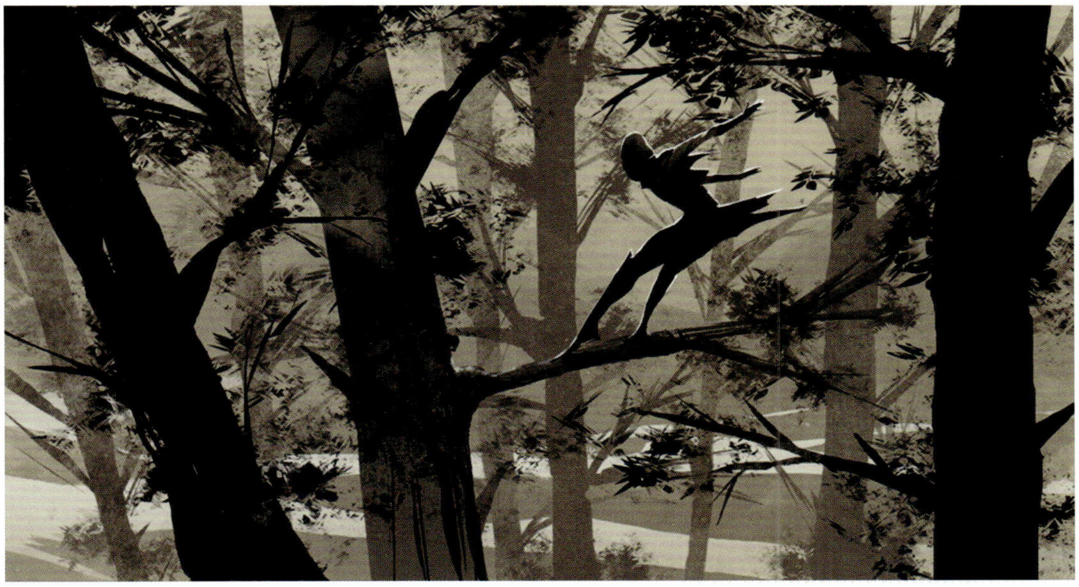

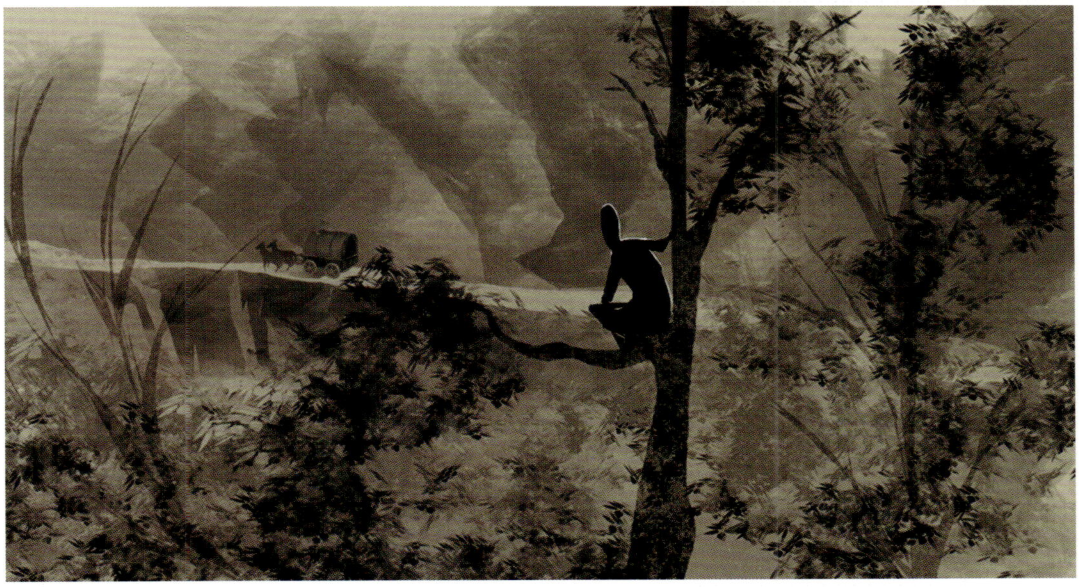

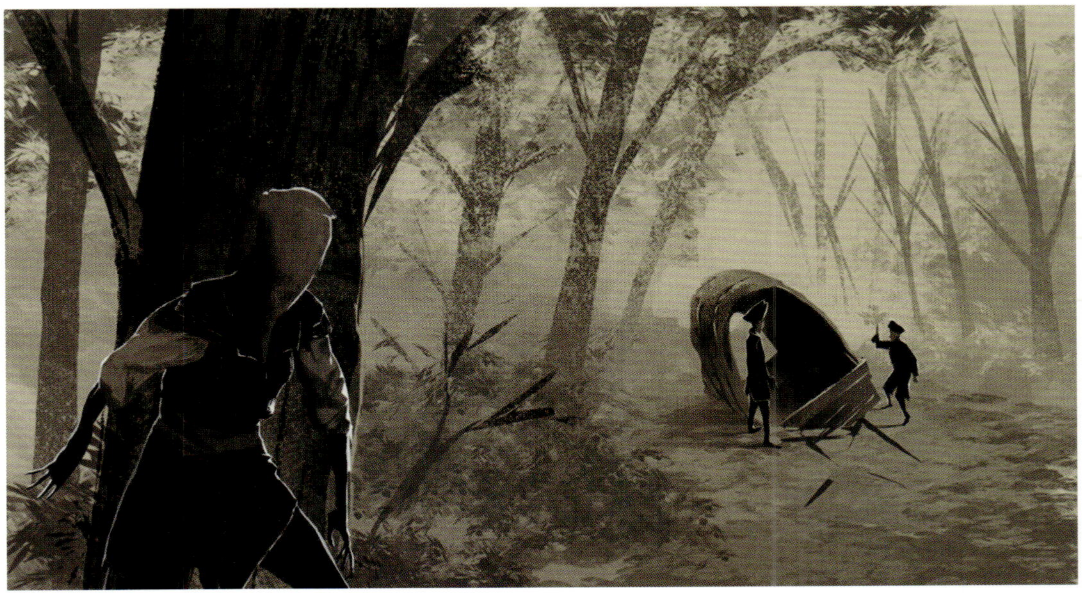

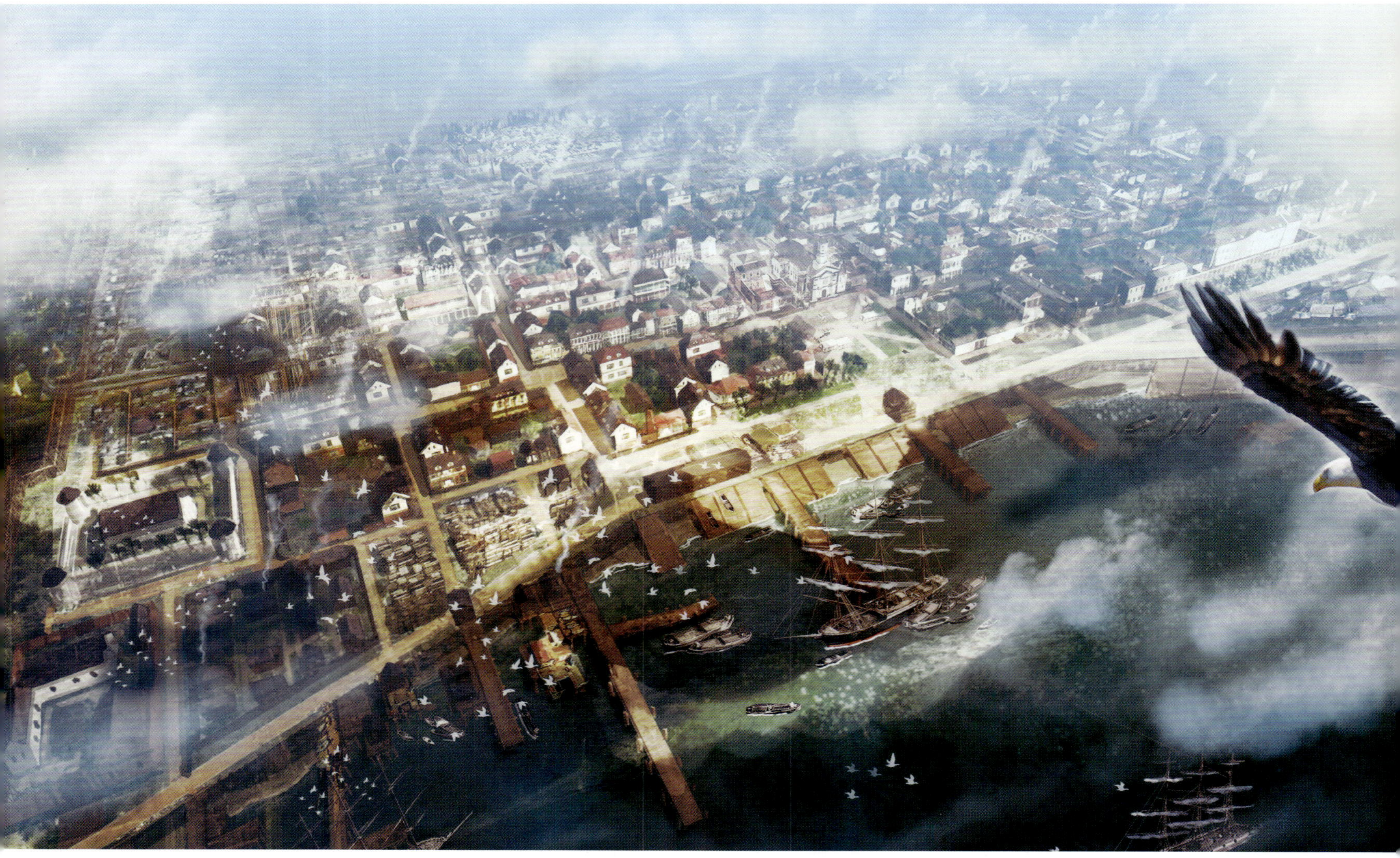

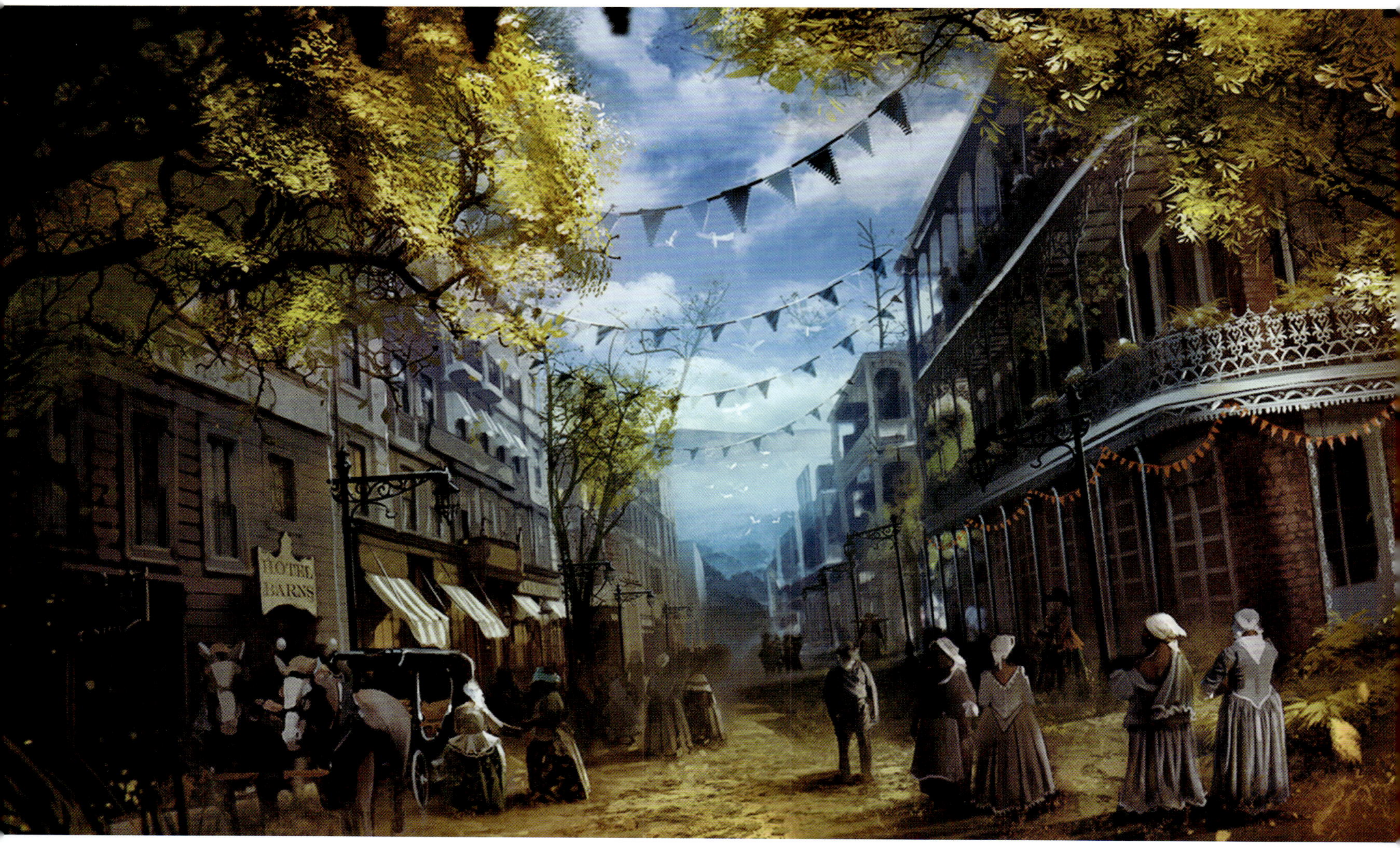
HOTEL
BARNS

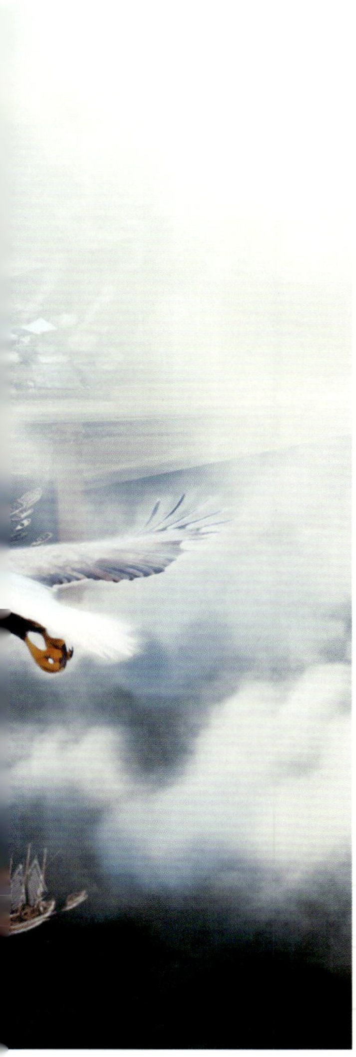

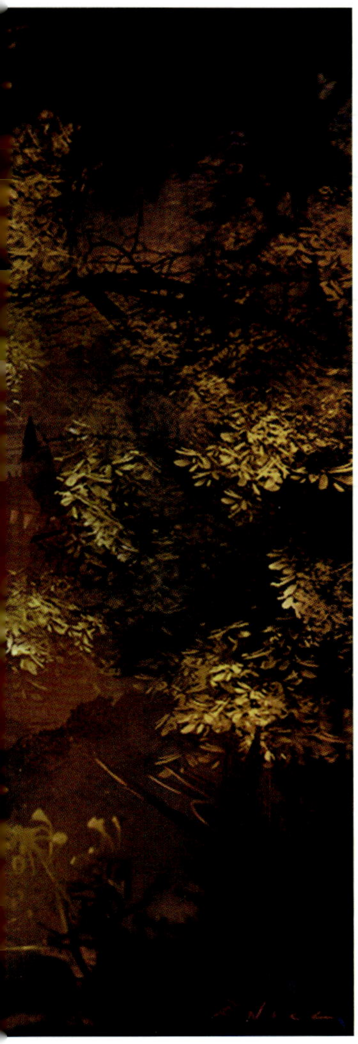

CITY BY THE SEA

New Orleans in the middle of the eighteenth century was a chaotic place defined not by individual cultures but instead by the strange ways those cultures had come together. Ubisoft developers embraced this diversity as they attempted to re-create the city.

The French citizenry were largely unaware that their city had traded hands in a treaty until their new Spanish leaders arrived to take charge. As the gateway between the Mississippi River and the Gulf of Mexico, New Orleans had also already emerged as a potent town for trade. Tragically, much of that trade was supported by slave labor. These conflicts and contrasts gave Ubisoft's artists plenty of room to create a memorable city. "New Orleans is a colorful, celebrating, and lively city, but also a city of contrasts, where freedom and slavery, Christianity and voodoo, luxury and poverty all coexist in one melting pot of different cultures," says Eddie.

For a starting place, Eddie and his team took a close look at New Orleans as it is today and then worked their way backward to craft a town that would eventually evolve into what they felt was an appropriate balance between historical accuracy and the right mood for the setting. "Modern New Orleans is distinguished by its unique architecture and style: open porches, steep rooftops, exotic plants and flowers," Eddie says. "Our goal was to represent the same, unique feeling back in the eighteenth century, showing the French and Creole influence and using the materials and construction styles typical for the time period." The resulting city, with its dirty streets and sometimes dilapidated buildings, felt authentic and lively, but the tension between liberation and imprisonment, rich and poor, was never hard to identify.

TOP LEFT: An eagle's-eye view of bright and colorful New Orleans (Eddie Bennun).
BOTTOM LEFT: A street scene with Colonial-style wooden buildings and a vibrant and lush color scheme (Nikolay Stoyanov).

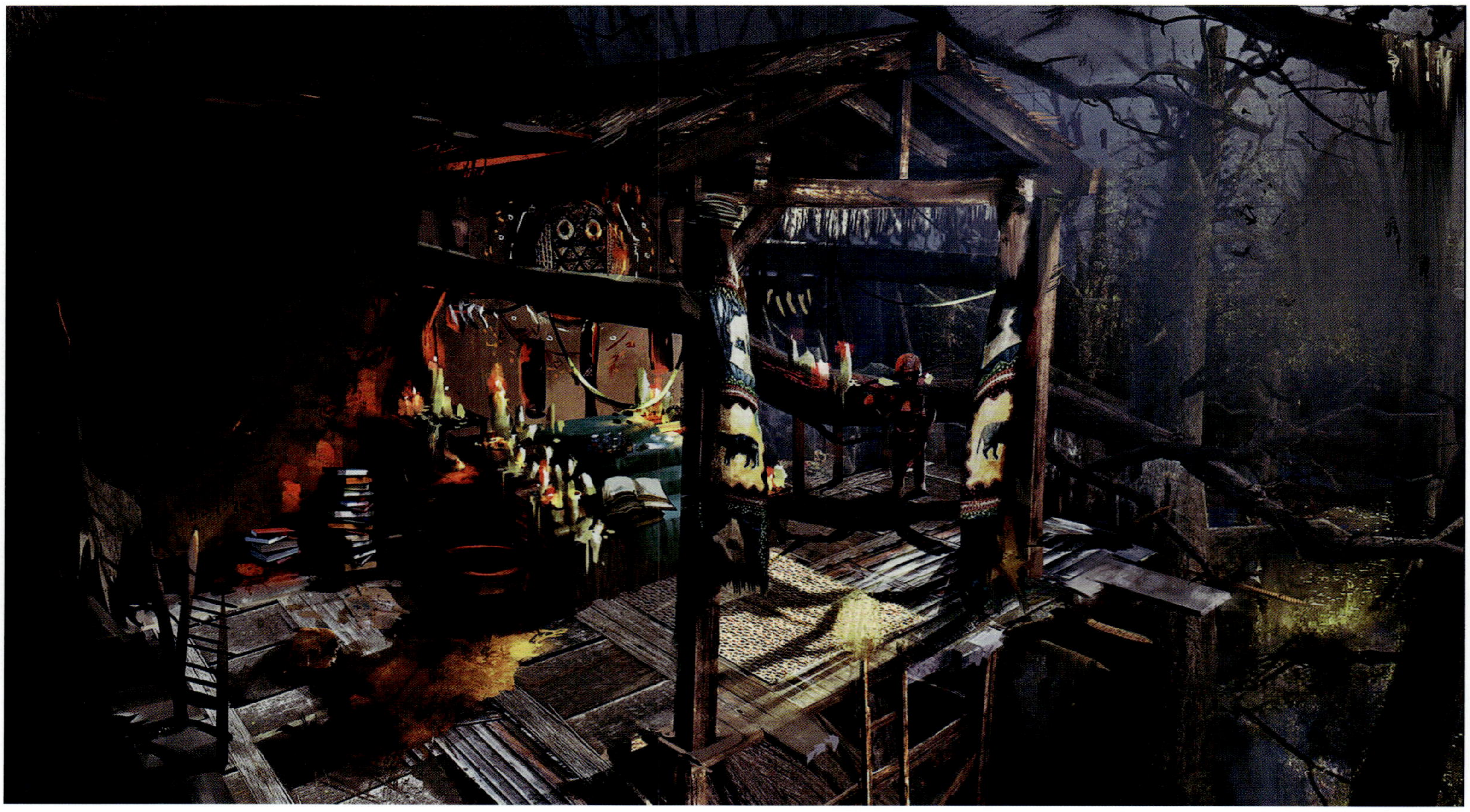

INTO THE BAYOU

Like its sister game *Assassin's Creed III*, *Liberation* ventured outside of the city to explore the wilderness. Whereas Connor wandered the pristine forests of the northeast, Aveline's travels took her into the marshes of the Louisiana bayou.

"The bayou is virgin territory—clean and unspoiled with serenity and mysticism wrapped together in one world and very much the contrast to New Orleans," says Eddie Bennun. The prevalence of open water throughout the swamps emphasized the importance of the new tree-running functionality, especially with the prevalence of alligators in the murky waters. Gray sky tones mixed with the bright and lively greens of trees and moss and provided an eerie and almost haunted quality to the locale. Aveline would use the creepiness to her advantage, terrifying soldiers with her blowpipe weapon, steadily convincing them that voodoo magic was at work.

While the bayou was open wilderness, Ubisoft's artists and designers managed to populate the large gameplay space with a number of distinct locales, including a small town filled with escaped slaves, an imposing fort, and a forgotten plantation overtaken by smugglers. However, the most mystical and intriguing spot was nestled deep within the marsh where Aveline's Mentor, Agaté, lived in an elaborate tree house that would become the site of a fateful confrontation between teacher and student.

TOP: Concept art of Agaté's hideout in the bayou (Nacho Yagüe).
OPPOSITE: The bayou's dark color palette and looming trees made for a dramatic and powerful experience (Nacho Yagüe).

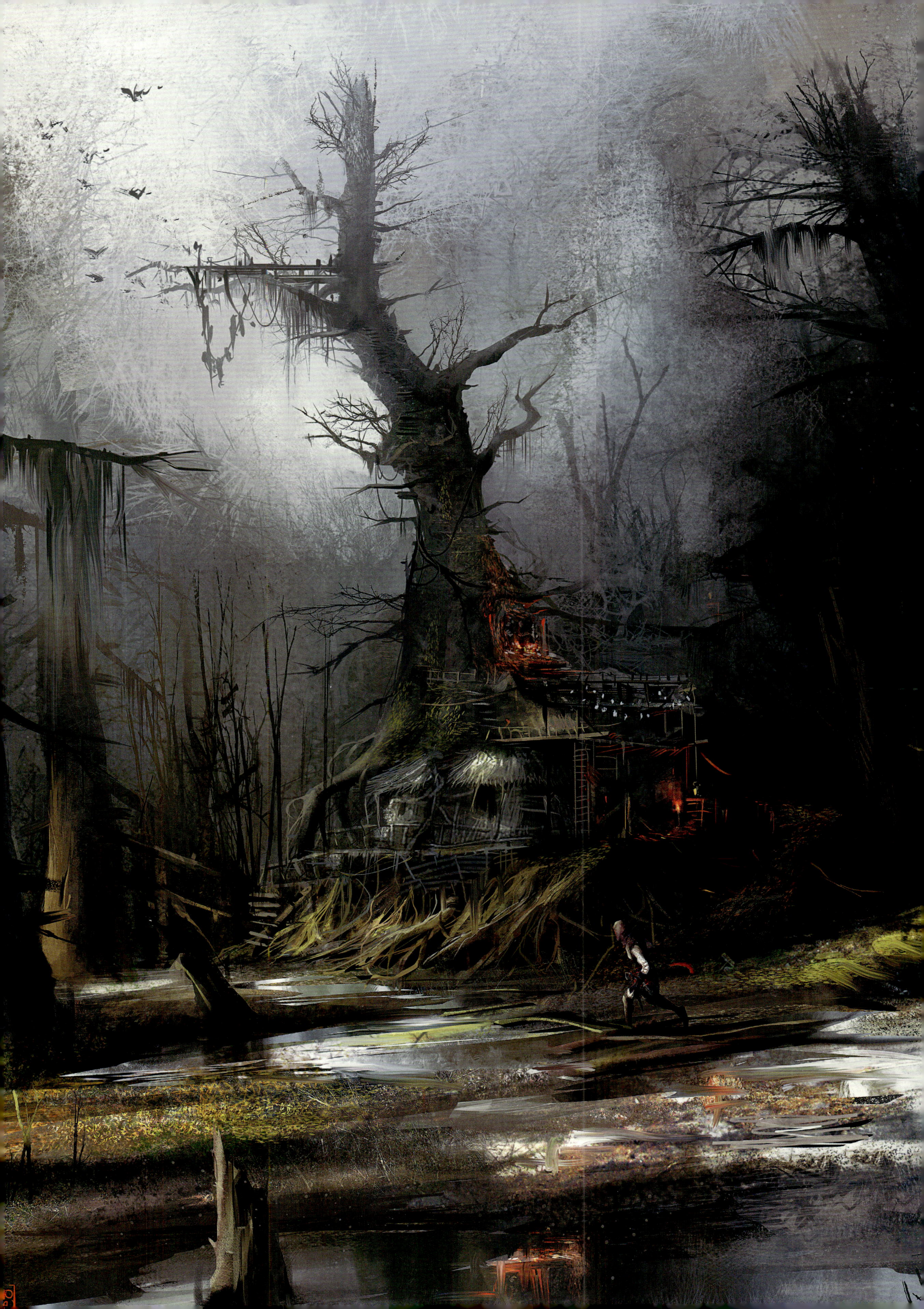

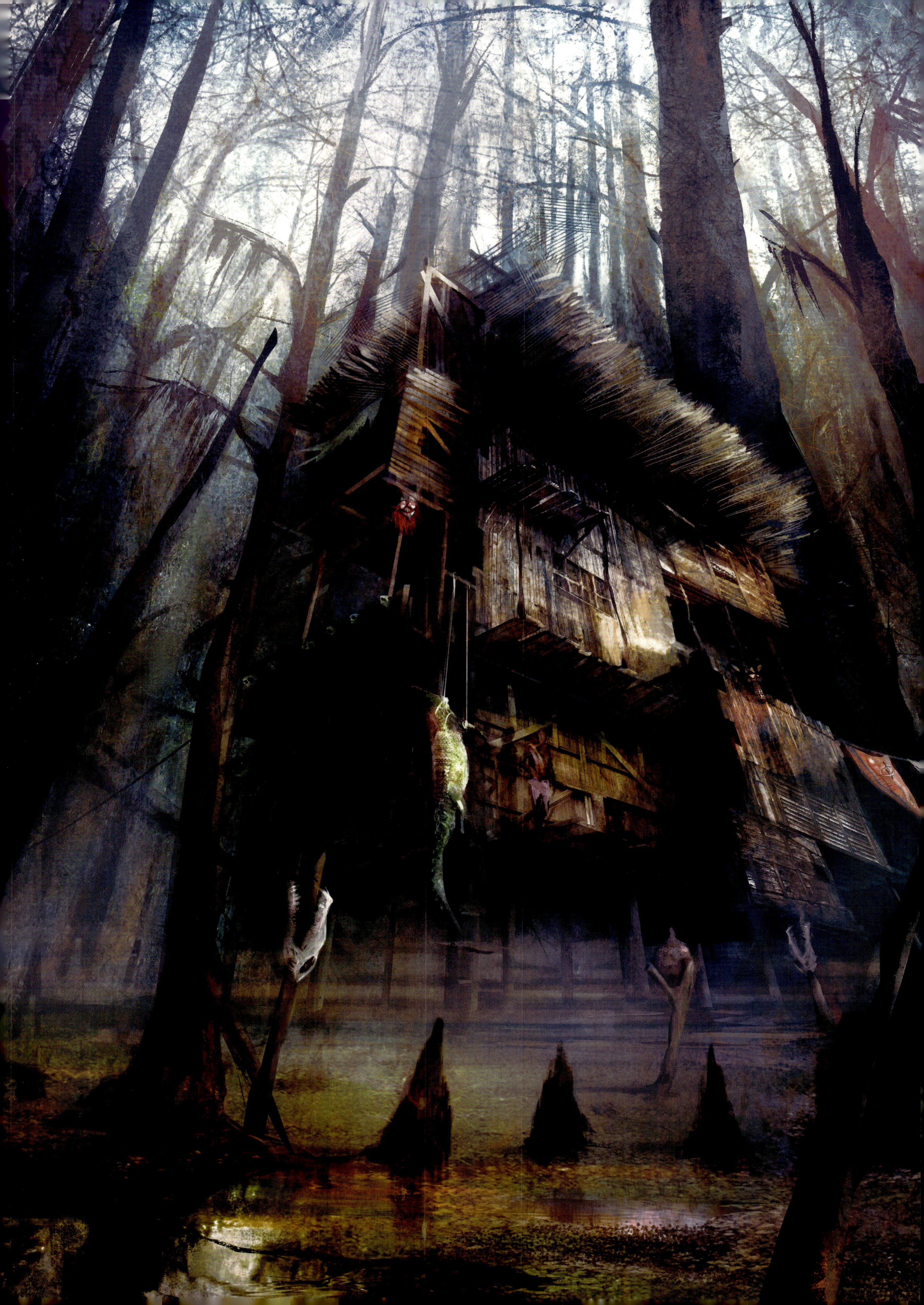

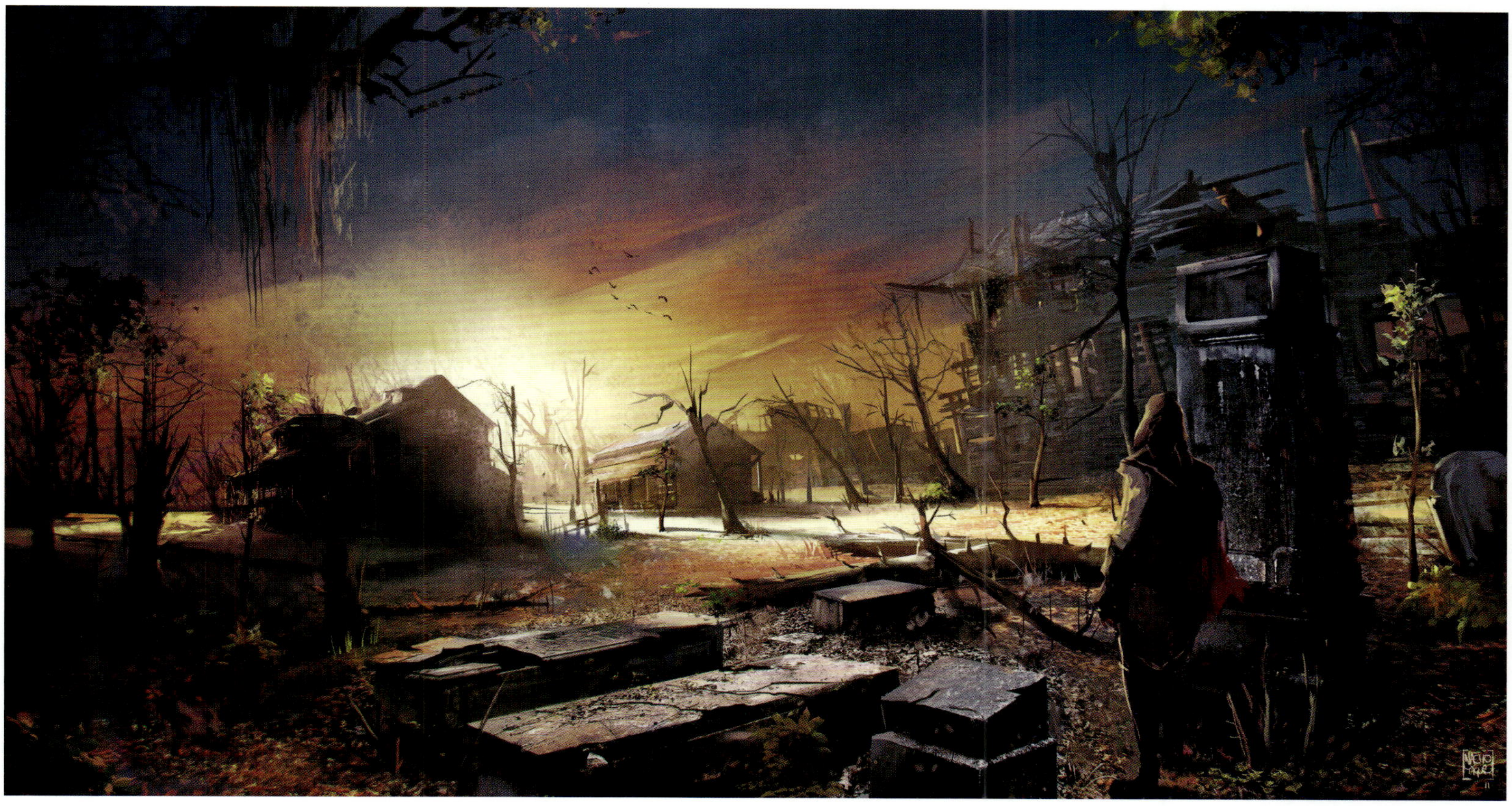

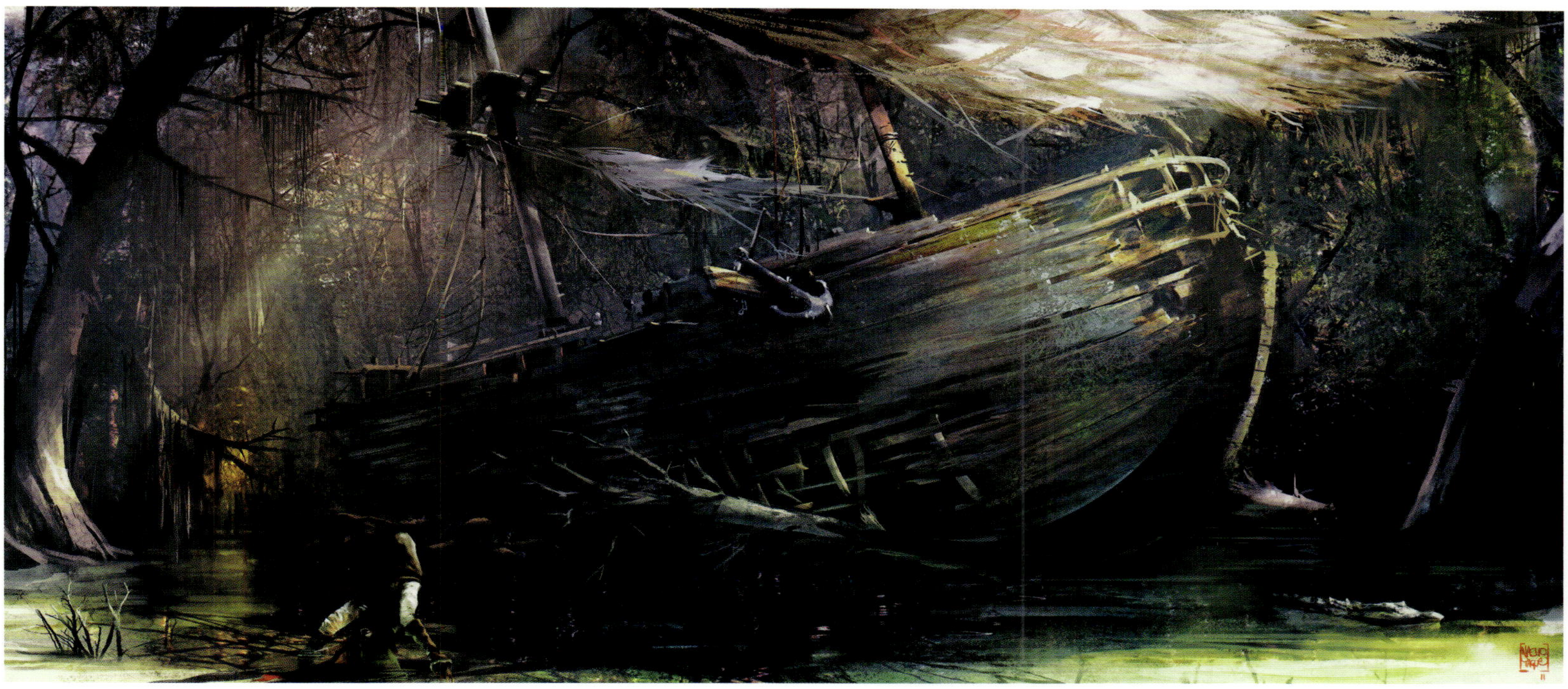

OPPOSITE: The upward angle of this composition makes Agaté's house a more imposing structure (Nacho Yagüe).
TOP: A graveyard in the swamp (Nacho Yagüe).
ABOVE: An abandoned ship in the bayou (Nacho Yagüe).
FOLLOWING PAGES: Early concept for Agaté's house (Nacho Yagüe).

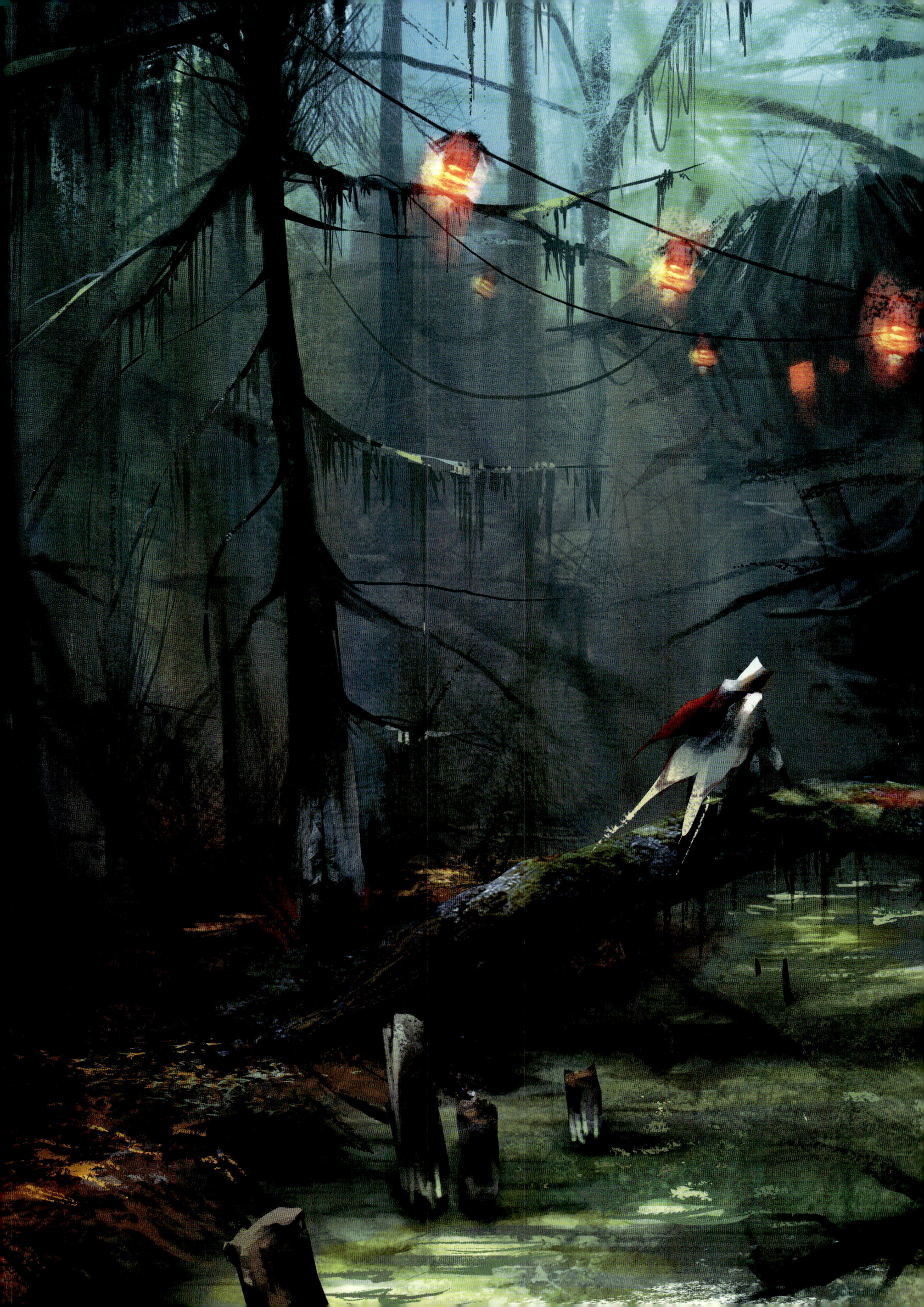

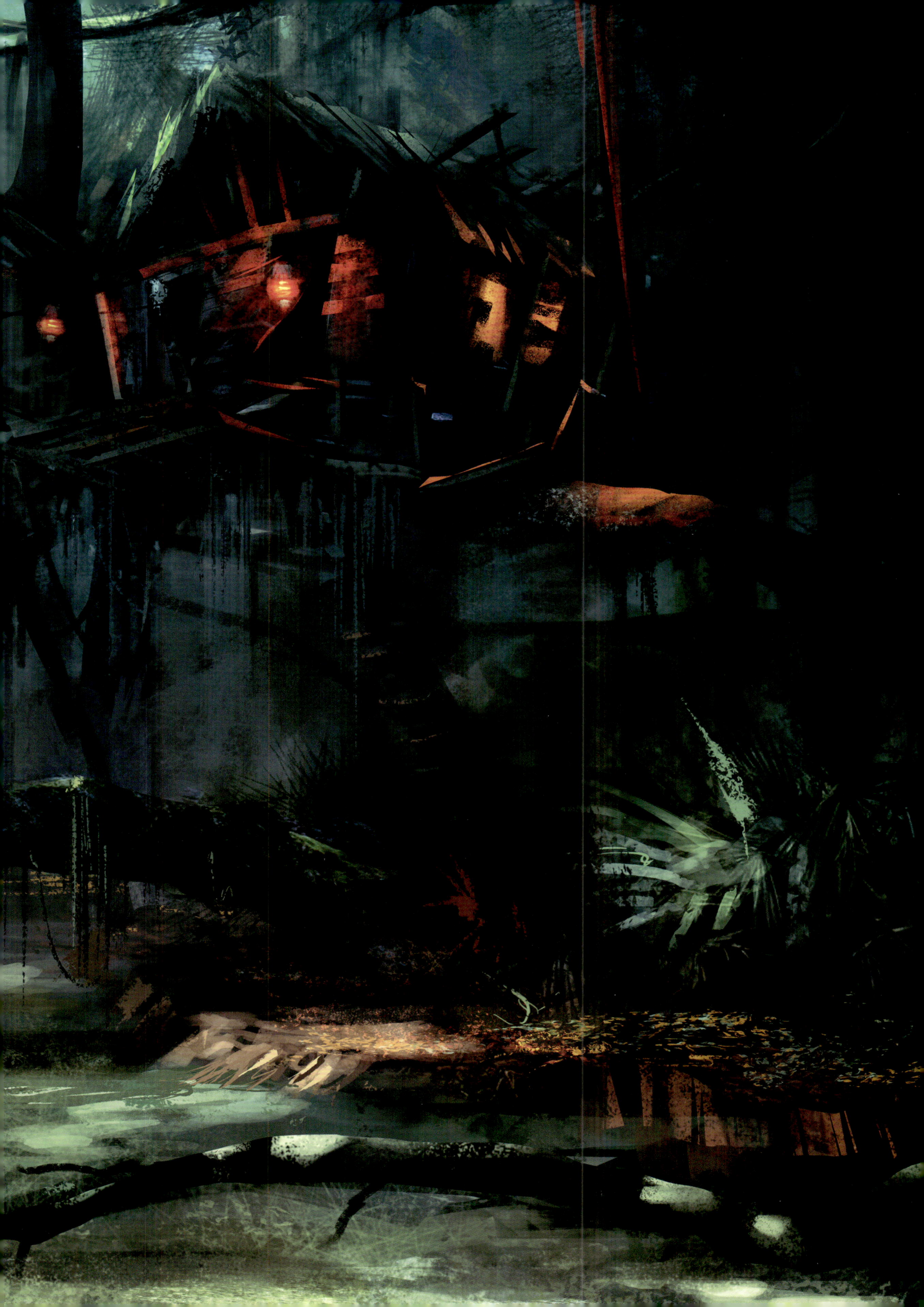

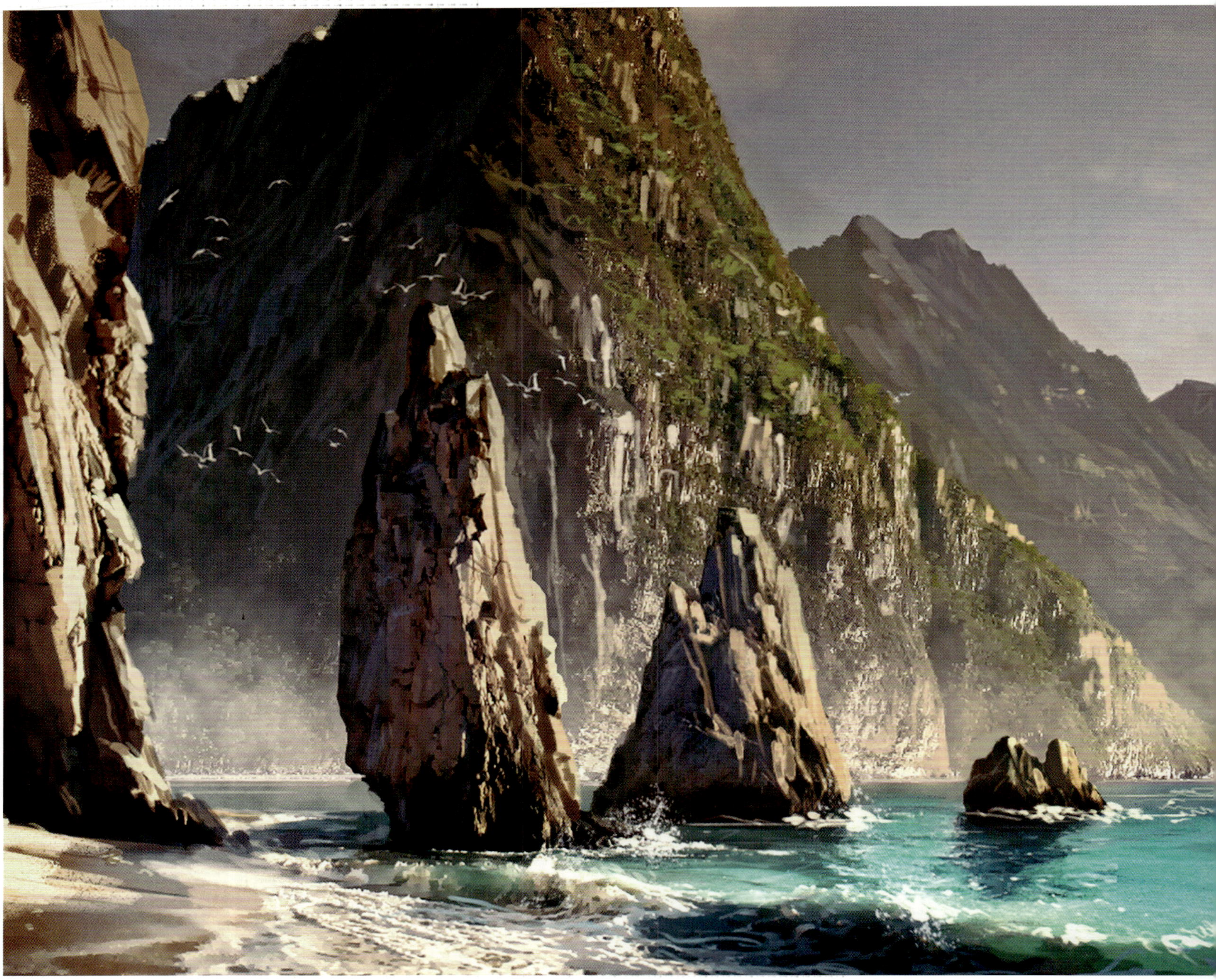

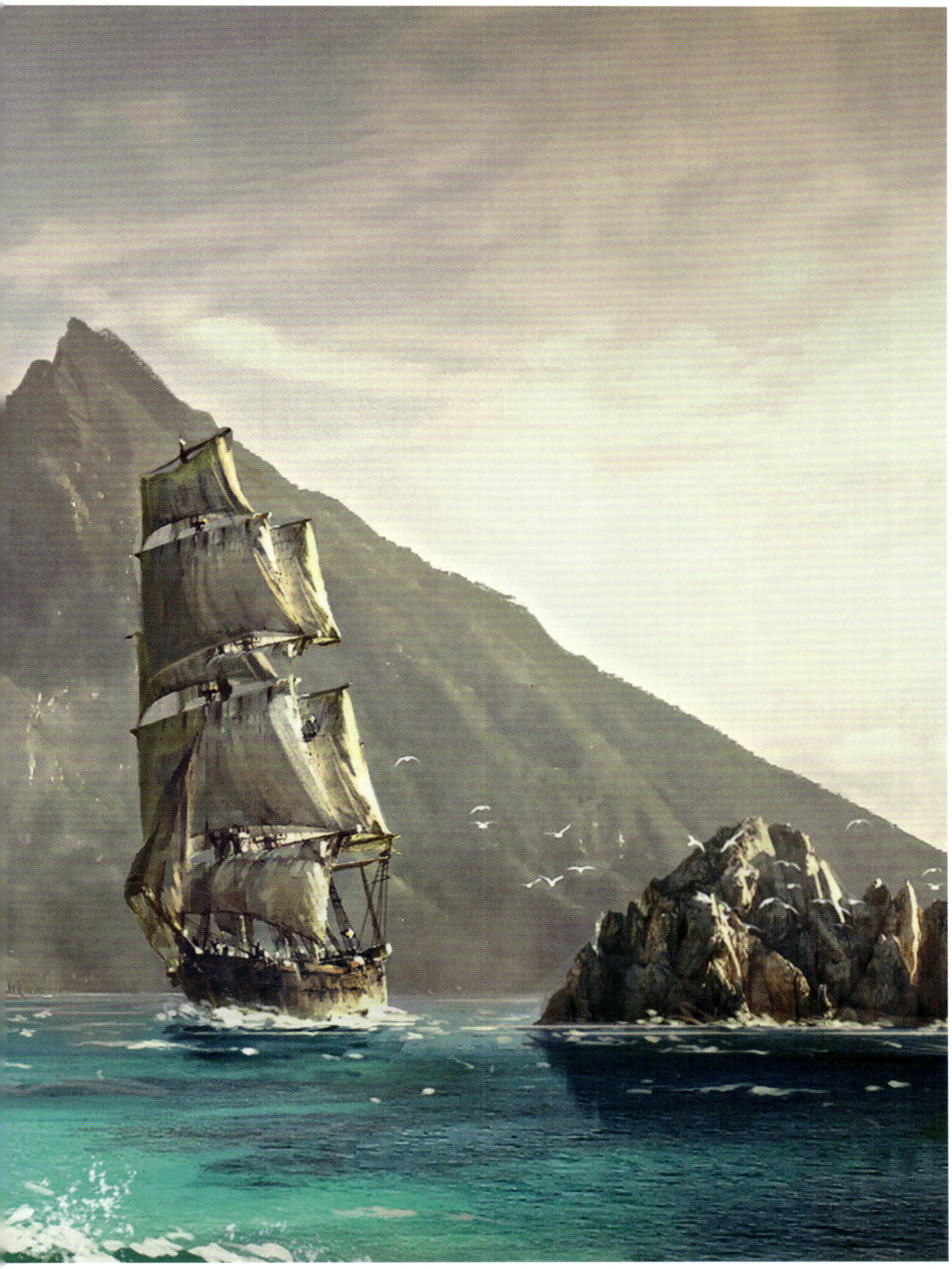

5 THE GOLDEN AGE OF PIRACY

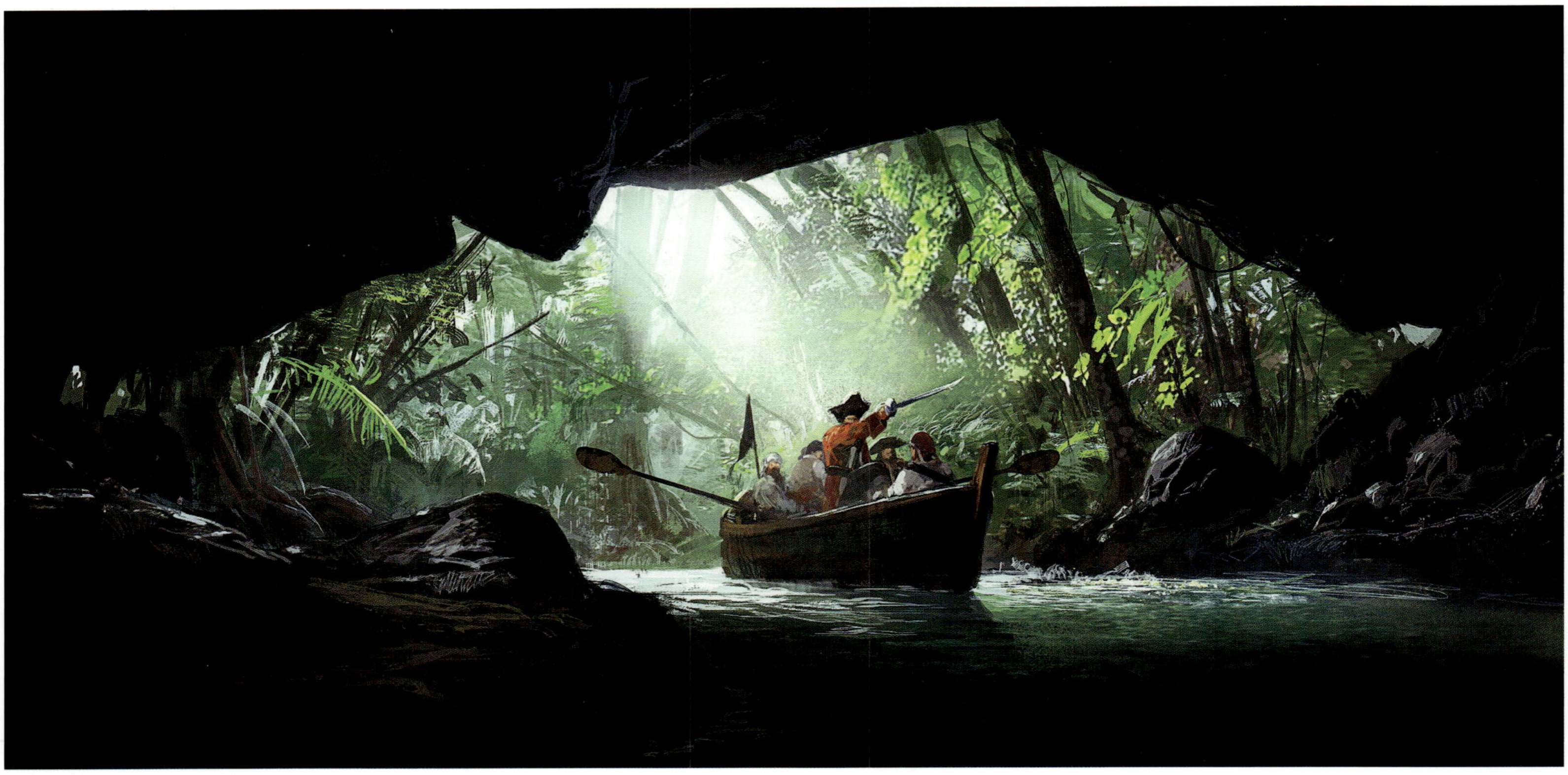

CHANGE OF SCENERY

Assassin's Creed III and *Liberation* had broken the rules. With their wilderness settings and new variations on gameplay, the franchise had wriggled free from the European urban setup that had dominated the early games and proven the concept and visual identity could go someplace entirely different.

Assassin's Creed IV: Black Flag was the next test of that flexibility. For the first time in a major console entry, the timeline jumped backwards in time from the late eighteenth-century American Revolution to explore the fabled pirates of the Caribbean who ruled the seas in the early 1700s. Small historical settlements like Havana and Kingston were to be the closest thing to cities. The new hero pushed against the boundaries of the word, spending much of the game denying the very Assassin's garb he had stolen. And the entire game would be built around the mechanics introduced as a side activity in the last game: sailing the high seas and engaging in naval conflicts.

The ambition behind such a vast open world was tremendous, and the scope of the concept art work required was equally overwhelming. The artists were up to the challenge. At this point in the franchise, the art team was producing enormous amounts of character and environment concepts and managed to keep pace with the demand. "*Black Flag* was the project for which I took on the role of creative director. I remember talking to executive producer Sebastien Puel about how incredible it was to feel the power of the collective team when all the different pieces of the development puzzle started to fall into place," Jean recalls. "We work with the best minds in the industry, and it's amazing when their forces are combined."

In choosing an artistic inspiration for *Black Flag*, there was no shortage of popularized visions of Caribbean pirates to choose from. However, much of the popular media is dominated by clichés or pure invention that has little to do with the historical tale of the short-lived pirate republic. Instead of embracing those fanciful stylizations, Ubisoft looked deeper into the historical record to craft a grittier vision for *Black Flag*'s setting and characters.

"As cool as the Disney treatment of piracy is, we aimed to be more mature, like an HBO version, to reveal the true harsh nature of piracy," Raphaël says. "For our inspirations, we read a lot of historical books and looked at artists such as illustrator and author Howard Pyle. His work is still very stylized, but it's closer to the historical reality of the time. No parrots, no hooks, but interesting, vibrant colors, fabrics, and fancy props that feel like trophies collected over the course of many adventures."

The art team's plentiful work helped inspire the rest of the development team. *Black Flag* released and became one of the most popular entries in the franchise, filled with awe-inspiring island vistas, hidden pirate coves, and a truly massive world to explore.

PREVIOUS PAGES: Exotic and mysterious islands ensure that the sea remains both beautiful and interactive (Raphaël Lacoste).
ABOVE: A captain leads his crew down a jungle river (Martin Deschambault).
OPPOSITE: Innovative, dynamic elements like animal life and waterfalls make the jungle a living, breathing environment (Martin Deschambault).

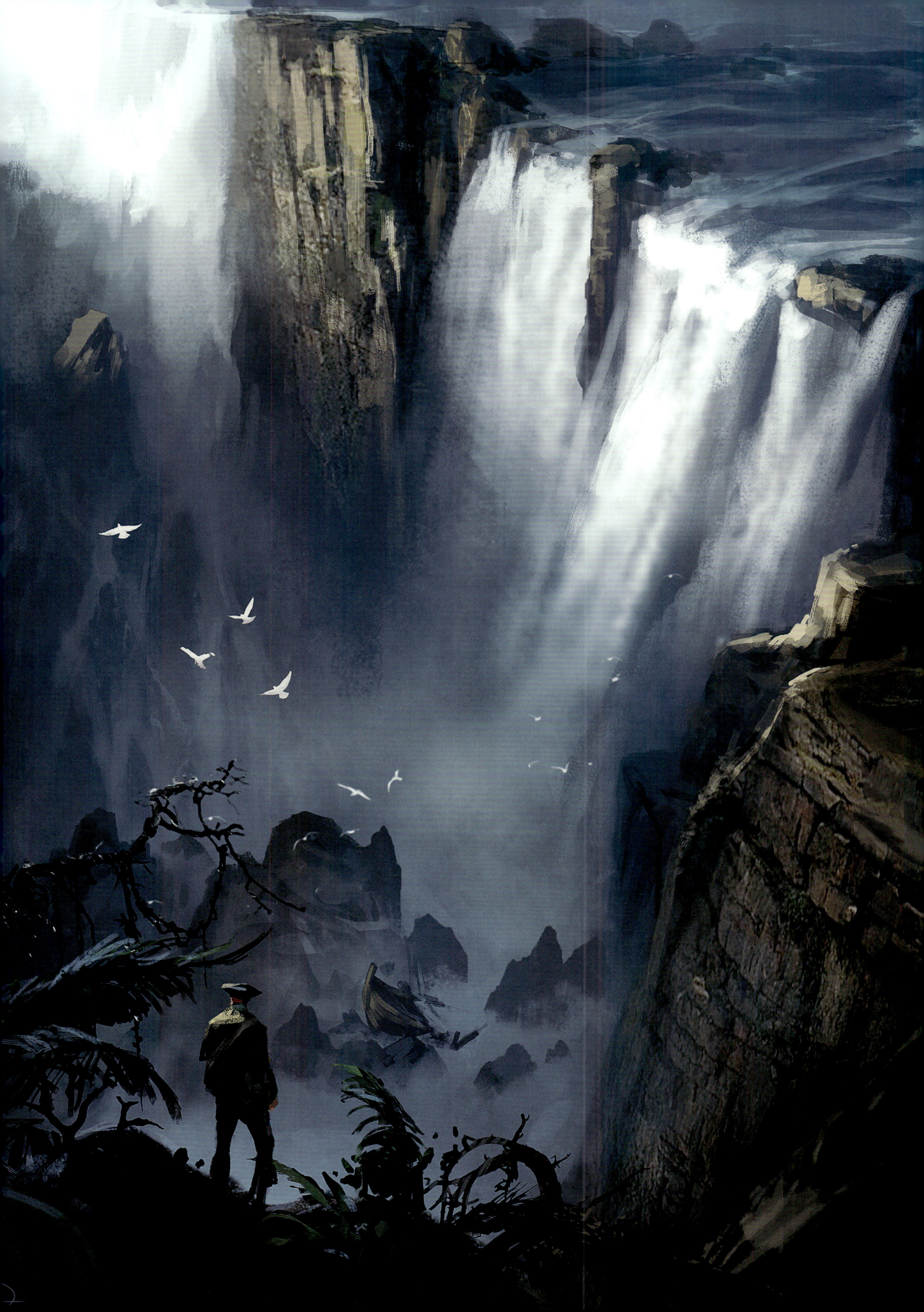

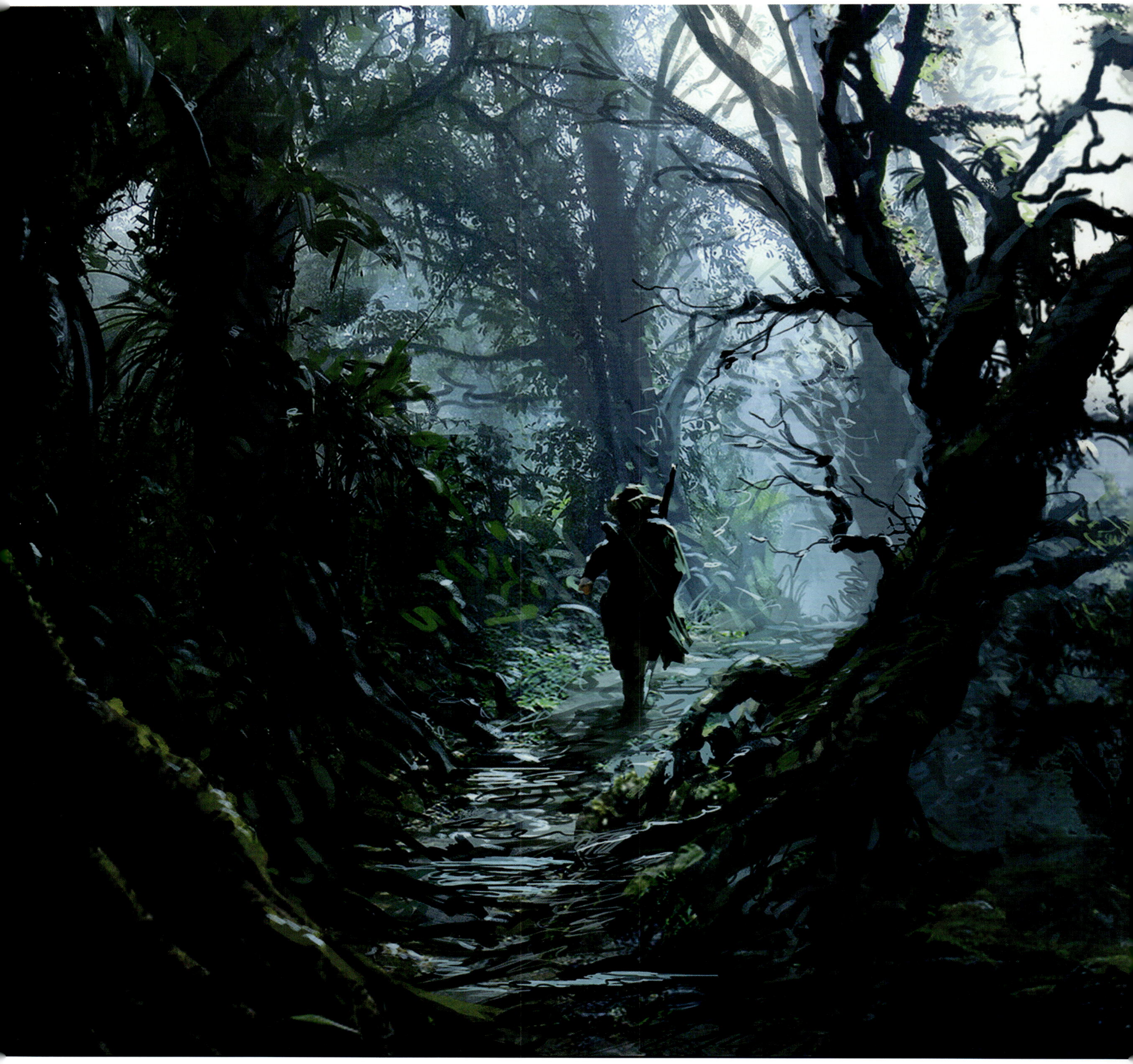

GUIDING VISION

Assassin's Creed has been lucky to harness the talents of several world-class artists to guide its artistic and creative direction. But as the franchise continued to gain steam and expand into new arenas, it became clear that a guiding artistic hand could help usher the franchise forward across a broad spectrum of different media. Raphaël Lacoste stepped up into the role of brand art director in 2011, as both *Assassin's Creed III* and *Black Flag* (upon which he served as art director) were in production. His eye for artistic presentation has helped to determine the visual style of the series ever since. "It's my goal to create the most credible and immersive environments, with diverse characters who are rich with life and experience," Raphaël says. "It is my hope for the art direction of Assassin's Creed to make people dream. I am not aiming to be too grounded, but to release the creative minds of the team and give them freedom to find different angles of interpretation and craft memorable moments."

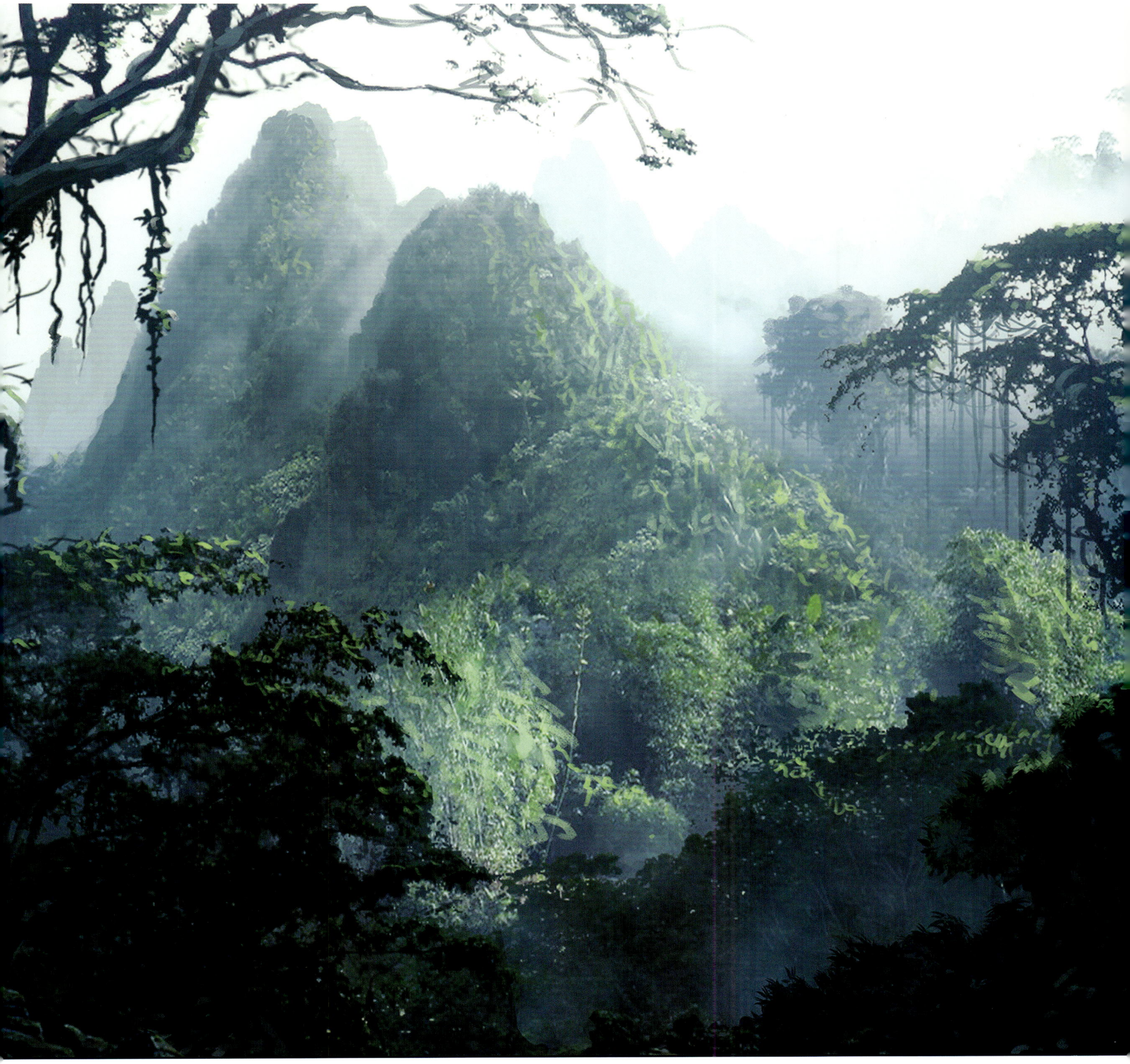

THESE PAGES: An artistic goal for *Black Flag* was to capture the feeling of exploration (Raphaël Lacoste).

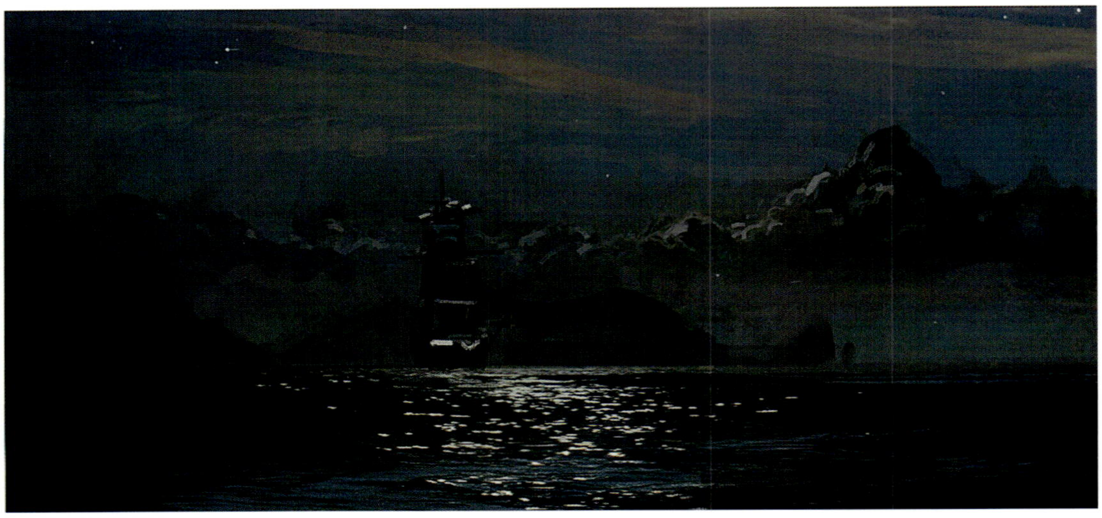
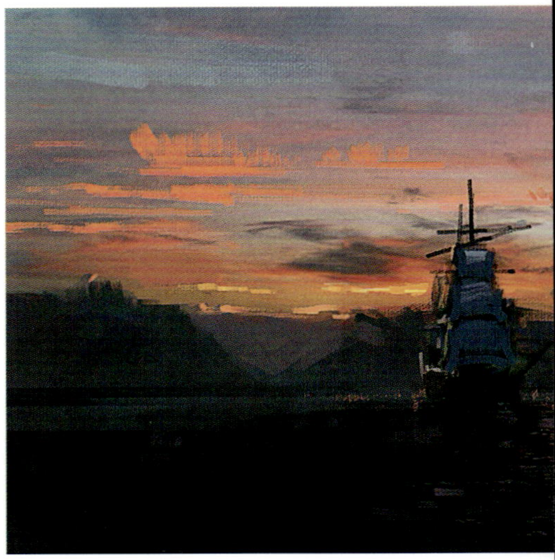
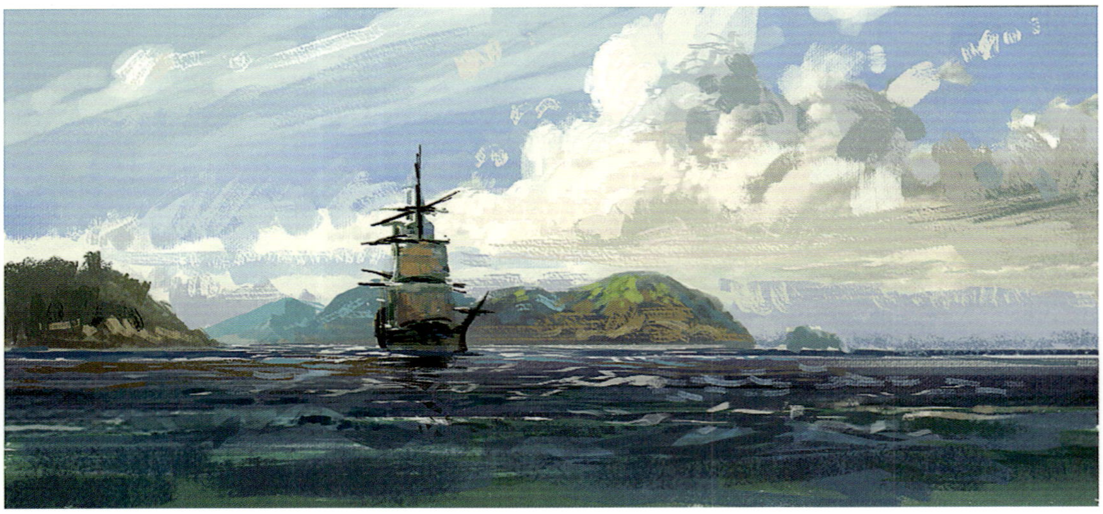
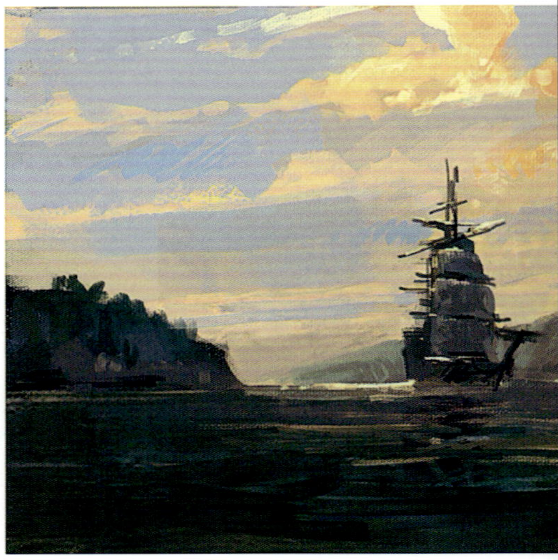
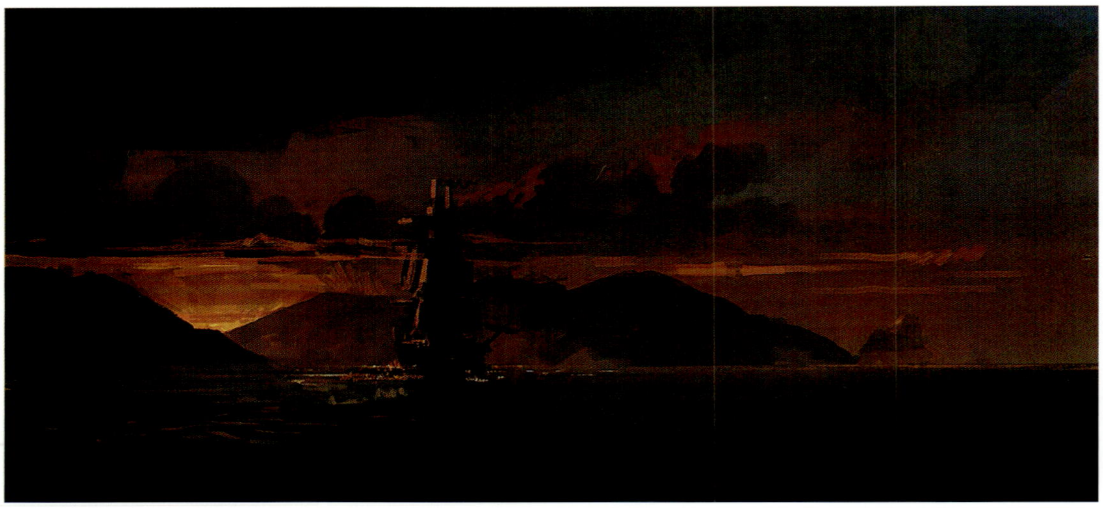
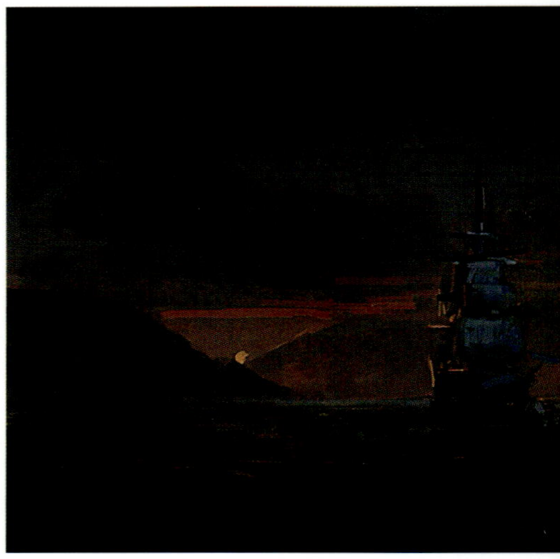

LIFE AT SEA

The anchor for both art direction and gameplay in *Black Flag* was the ship on the high seas. With freedom-loving pirates at the center of the experience, the contained naval conflicts of the previous game would not be enough. *Black Flag* needed a fully open world many times larger than anything that the series had tackled before, even if large stretches of that world were to be open ocean. The trick was to make sure it wouldn't be an empty, boring ocean. Ubisoft Singapore put a lot of work into making the ocean as realistic as possible, and and built upon the knowledge gained during the production of *Assassin's Creed III* to develop a groundbreaking ocean technology for the game.

With a dynamic ocean as a goal, the art team set to work. Open water couldn't be a static visual; any given moment needed to feel compelling and visually arresting. The water became a living, moving entity beneath the player. "What is really interesting about the tech of the ocean that was developed by Singapore is that the ocean is alive," Raphaël says. "It's not just a plane that fills

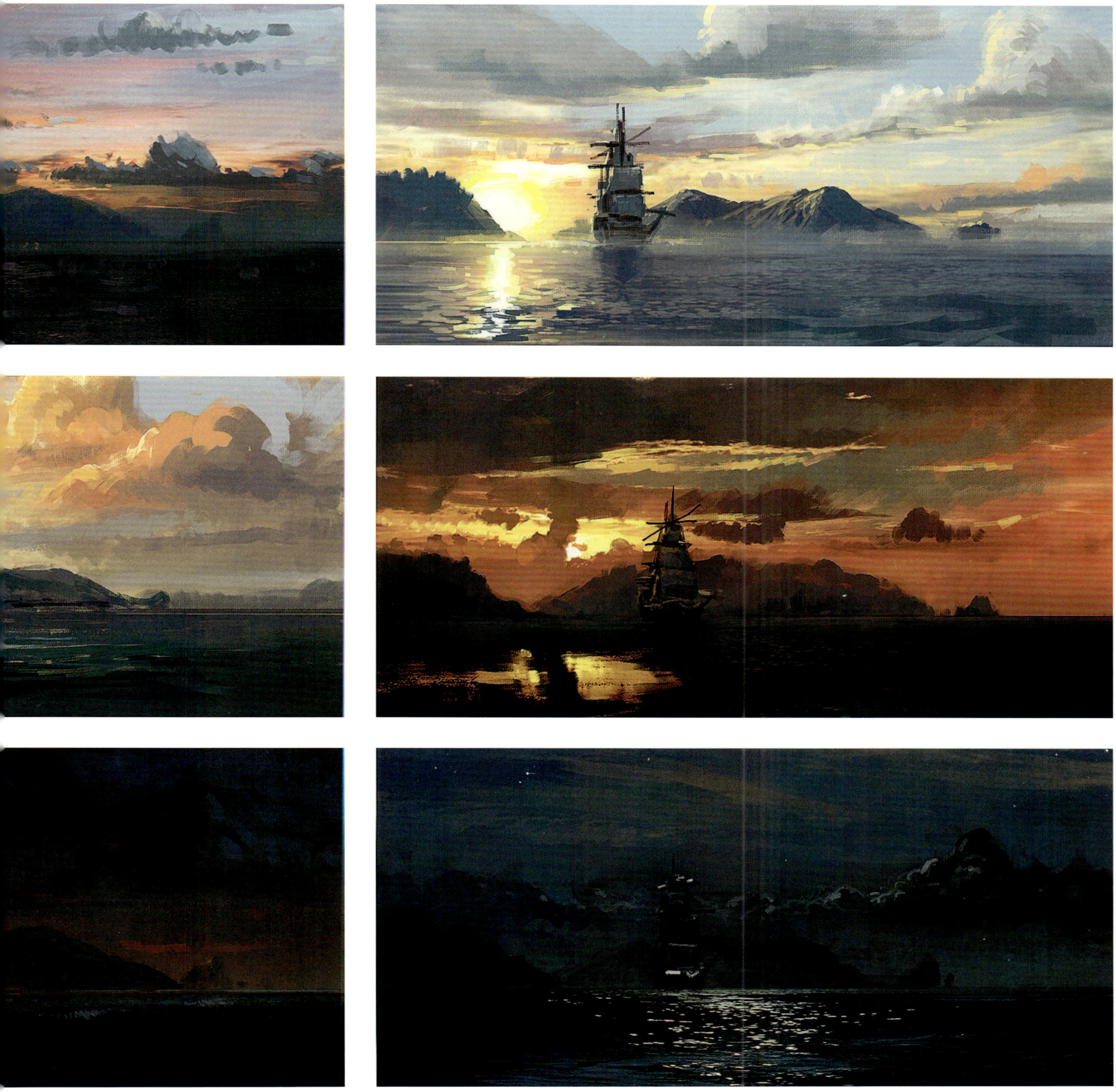

the space between the islands." Huge, rolling swells and tidal fluctuations rocked the player's ship from side to side. Devastating storms could arise at any time, ravaging ships caught in a passing rogue wave if the ship's captain didn't turn into the face of the rising swell.

The success of the ocean sequences wasn't just about beautiful water but also a gorgeous sky. "When you take to the seas, two thirds of the screen is the sky," Raphaël says. "We spent a long time designing key moments for the time of day. Every key moment was painted by an illustrator and was used as a reference for the lighters and the texture artists to make beautiful, epic skies during the game. Like the ocean, the sky was something that was living and breathing." Day would pass into night, offering spectacular views of the moon on the water, and nightfall could bring with it fog, leaving visibility limited and elevating the sense of mystery. Whether bright midday or the golden hours of dawn and sunset, the blue waters of the Caribbean provided an ever-shifting backdrop that could set virtually any mood.

THESE PAGES: Board of images setting visual targets for the sky and ocean at various times of day (Martin Deschambault).

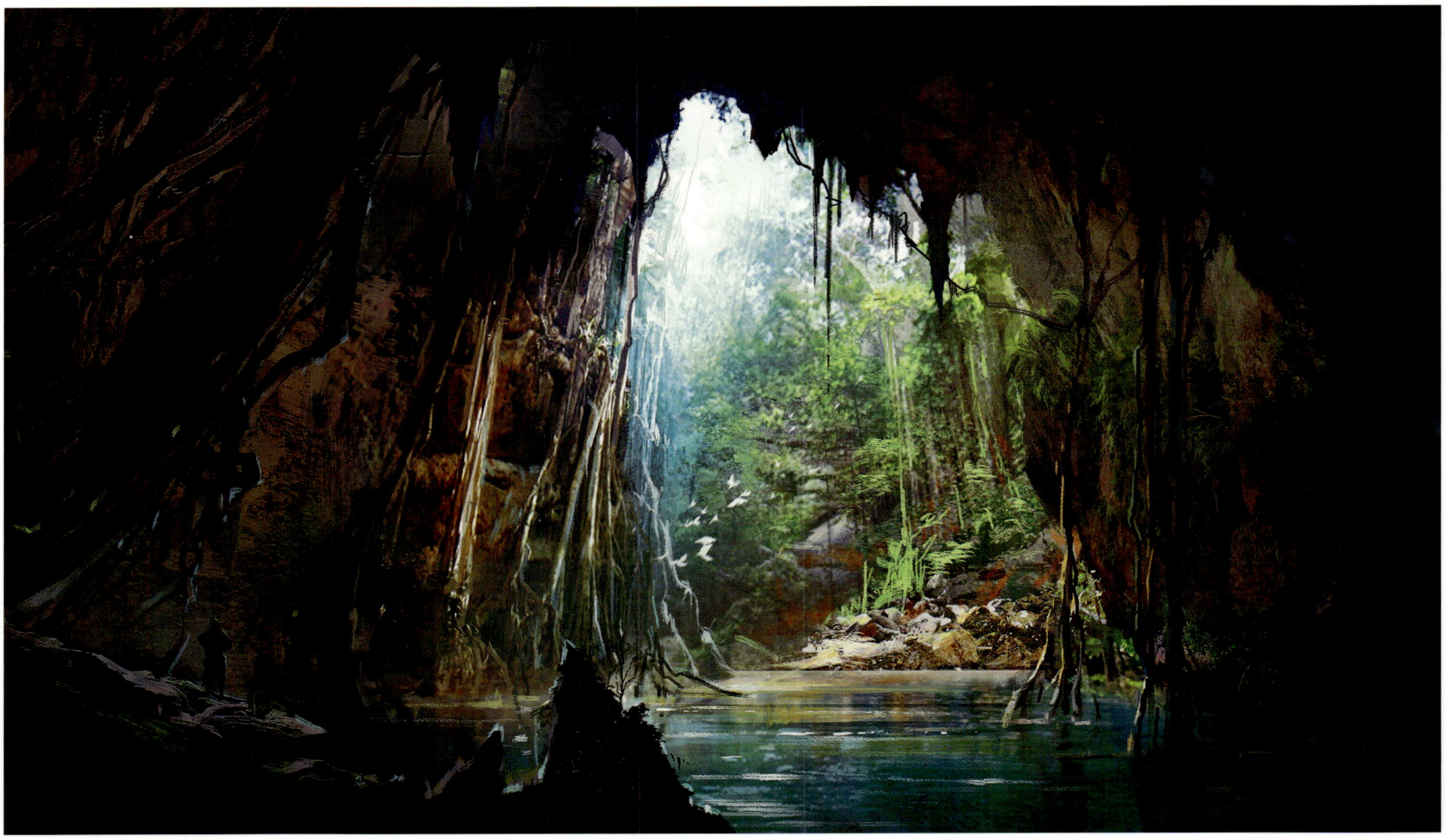

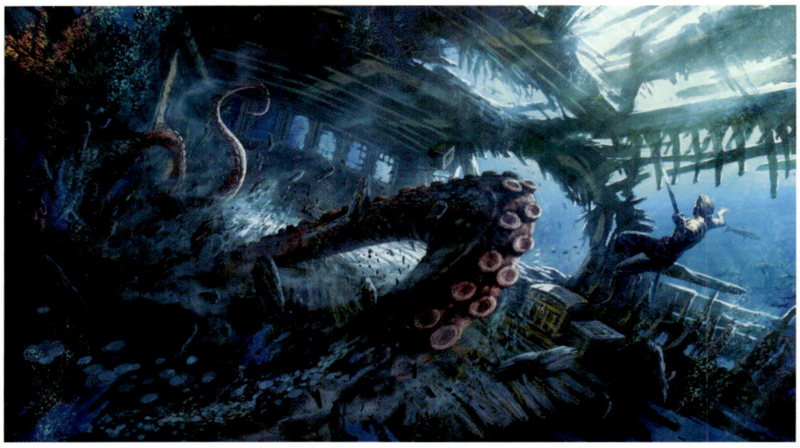

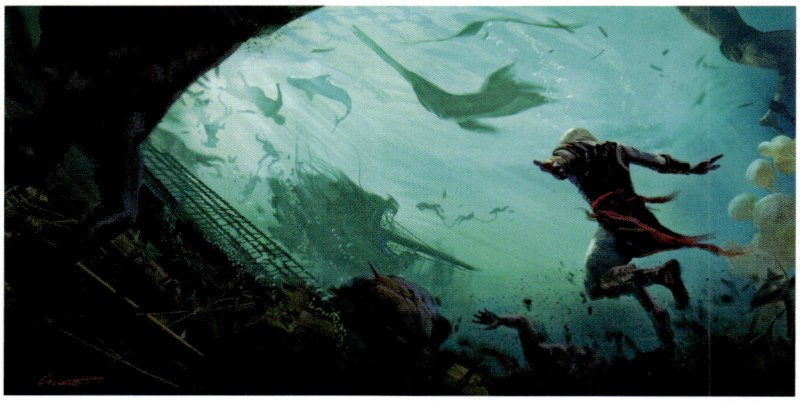

Like human crowds in cities and animals on the Frontier, the sea was filled with activity. Distant treasure ships crowded the horizon, tempting pirate captains with loot even when heavily armed escorts floated nearby. In brief, wondrous moments, whales would breach the water's surface, crashing back to the sea in a tremendous splash. Lost souls in makeshift rafts floated along the currents, hoping for someone to pass near enough to bring them aboard as new crewmembers. And always, the crew added the perfect soundtrack to the lapping waves, belting out bawdy shanties to pass the time. The sea was ripe with activity and adventure.

Some of the most bracing ocean exploits involved leaving the ship. Animal hunting took on a new scale with the opportunity to set out in a rowboat and try to bring down massive whales and sharks. Elsewhere, the masts of long-lost ships offered opportunities to lower the diving bell and search out wealth at the bottom of the sea floor.

By investing in the visual variety of sea creatures, ships, weather patterns, and even detailed underwater environments, the seas of *Black Flag* that could have felt barren instead seemed brimming with the potential for exploration and discovery.

THESE PAGES: Concept art depicting the immense and incredibly detailed underwater environment (Donglu Yu, Jing Cherng Wong, Hugo Puzzuoli).

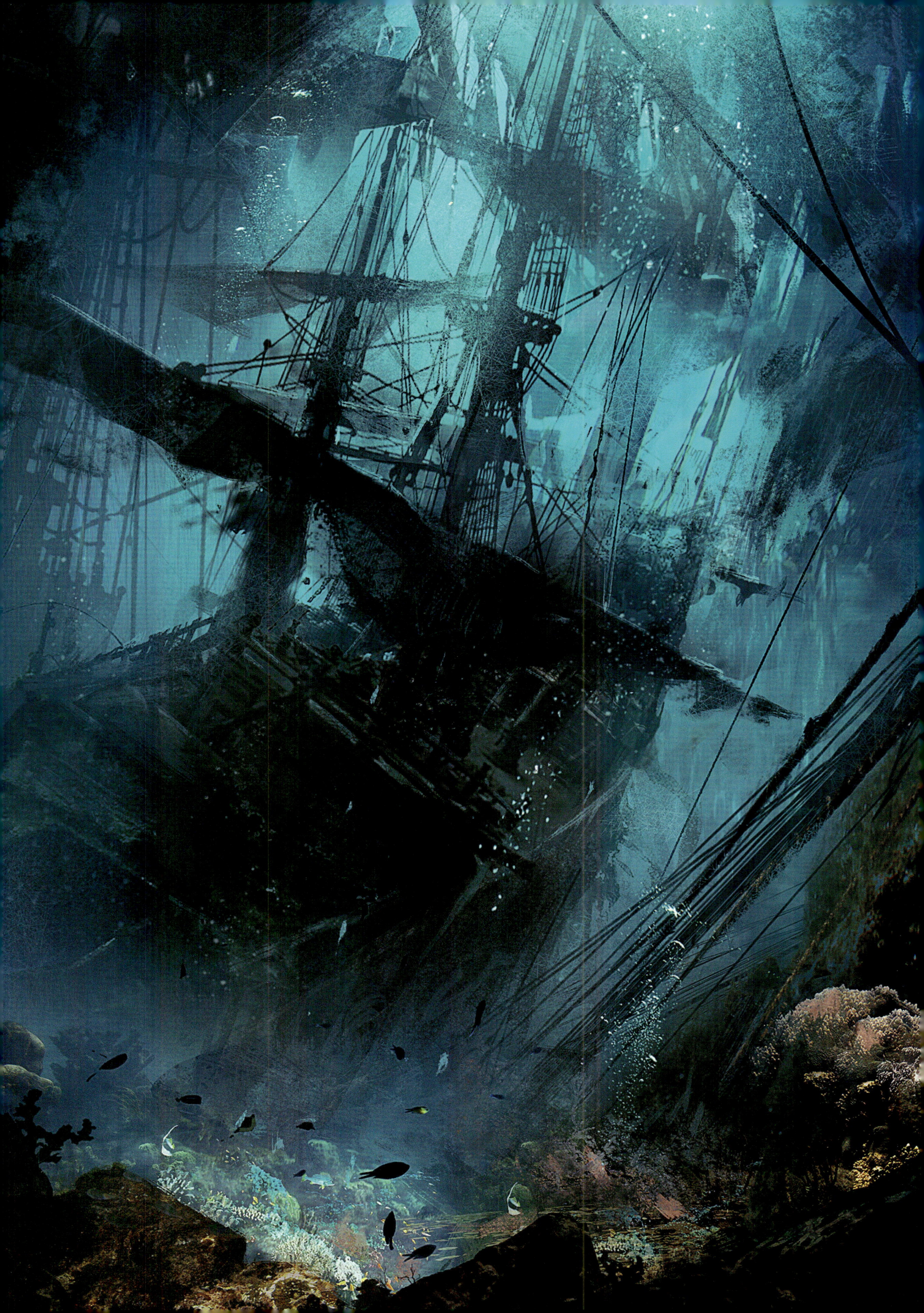

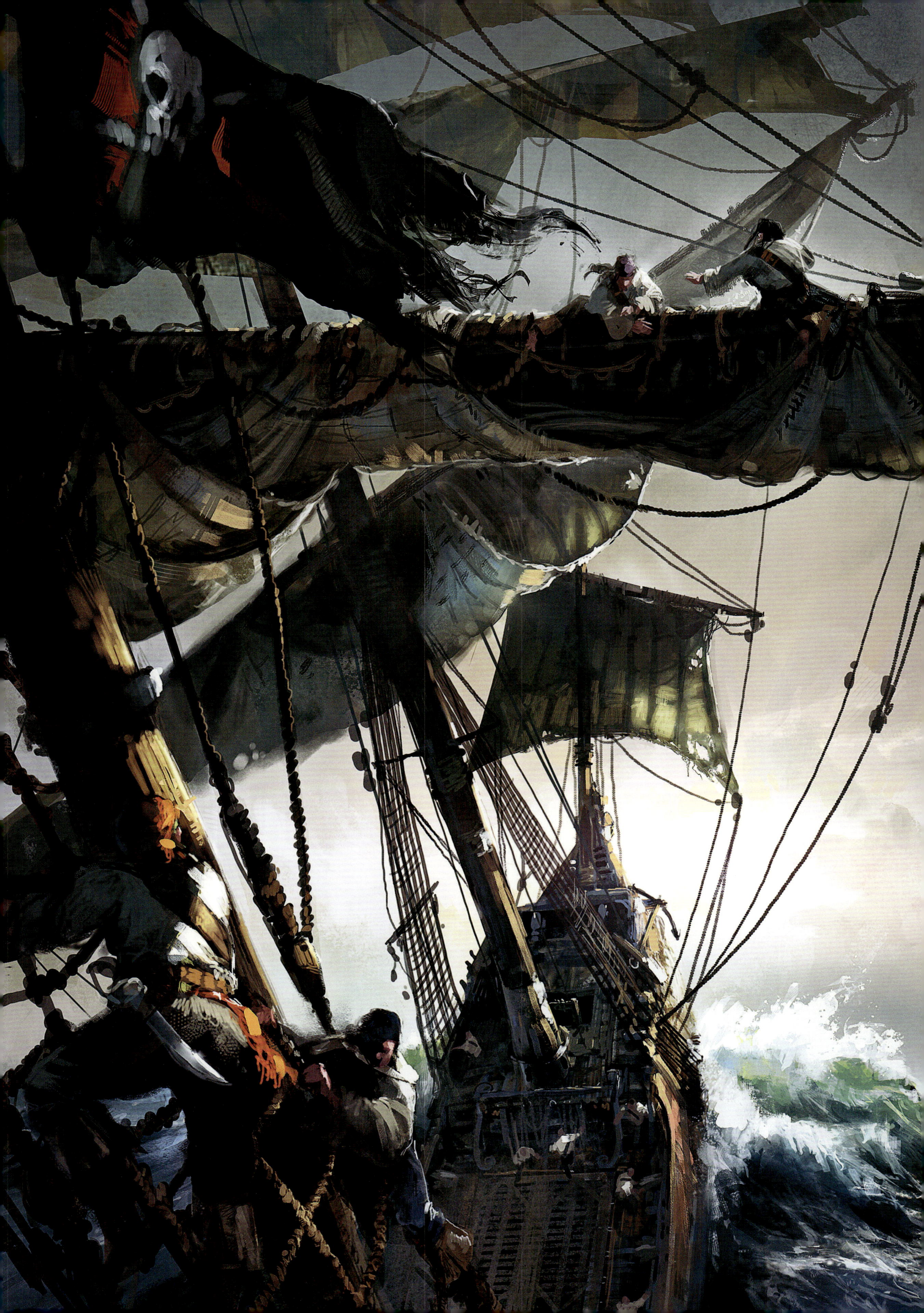

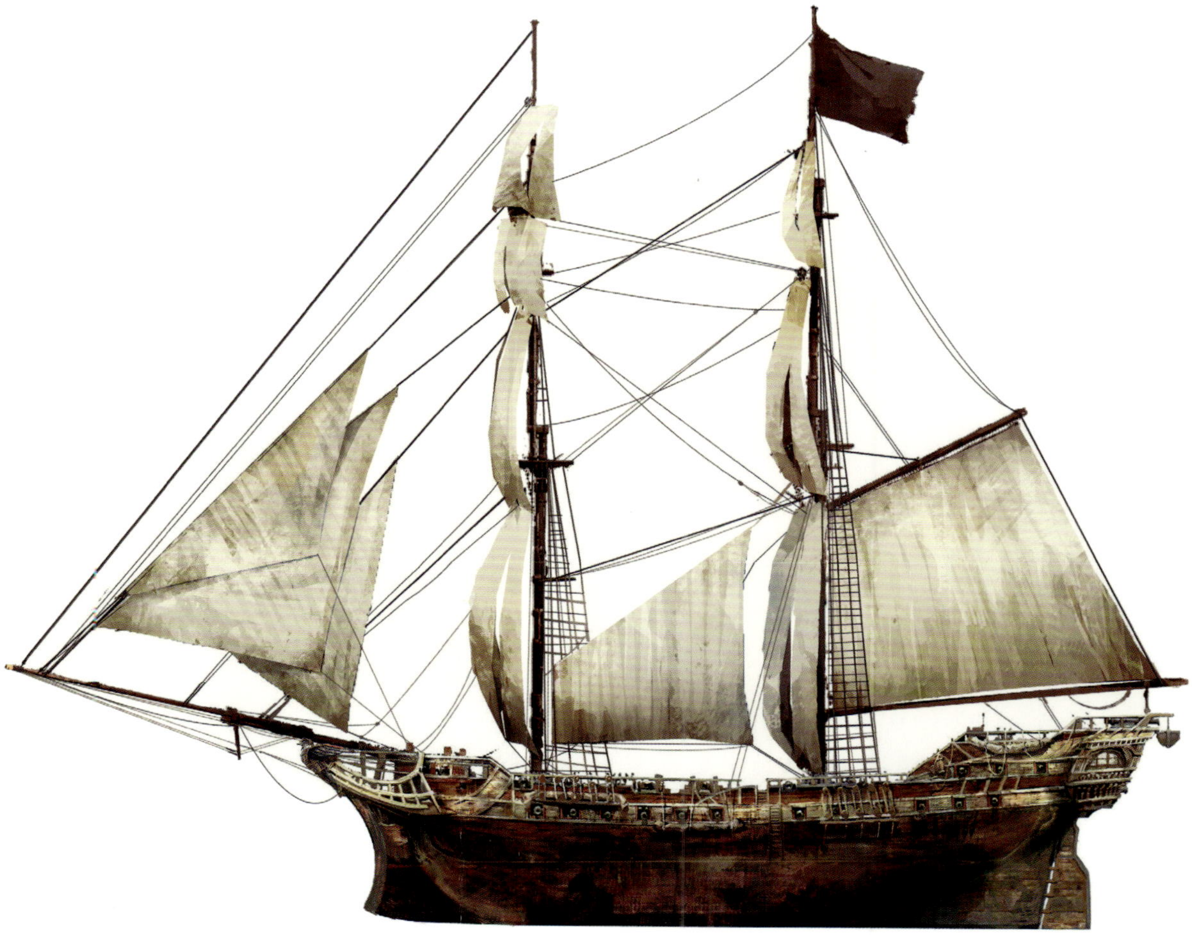

LAY ABOARD, LADS

The ships of *Black Flag* acted as extensions of their captains. Blackbeard's *Queen Anne's Revenge* was hulking and dark and somehow managed to look both filthy and magnificent. In contrast, Calico Jack's ship was brightly decorated and garish. Charles Vane's ship, the *Ranger*, is strange and macabre, decorated in whalebones. Every named ship in the game communicates its own character and adds to the narrative scope of encounters that might include it.

The same is true of protagonist Edward Kenway's the *Jackdaw*. As the ship players see the most, it needed to be a quintessential pirate vessel but also speak to the roguish qualities of its captain. The *Jackdaw* also had to feel distinct from what had been seen in the previous game with the *Aquila*. The team sought to build on the appearance of that signature ship from the previous game and created the *Jackdaw* as a realistic representation of a seagoing vessel during the early 1700s.

"Edward's ship, the *Jackdaw*, is an extension of himself," Raphaël says. "There's the folkloric symbolism of the bird, which is also the figurehead of the ship, but the design of the ship itself also reflects the Assassin. The ship is sleek. It's low and elegant. It moves like an Assassin in a crowd—agile, quick—and it can be very stealthy when needed." The *Jackdaw* as it appears in the final game succeeds through a basic design that feels simpler than some of the other ships depicted, but also because of its potential for modifications. As the game progresses, the *Jackdaw* advances as well, and each minor change to the wheel or addition of a ram or color change to the sails matches the core aesthetic.

No matter which ship showed up on screen, the pirate ships of *Black Flag* also worked because they became more than horizontal play spaces; the vertical potential of the ships was key. With cresting waves and dangerous seas, enemy ships could sometimes loom hundreds of feet over the player, crashing down into a battle from high above. As boarding ropes were flung away, the dramatic size differences between vessels became apparent, from small schooners to towering Man-of-Wars. Rather than having fights play out only on the decks, some ship takeovers demanded the ascension of high masts to take out carefully placed lookouts wielding dangerous rifles, echoing the cathedral climbs of earlier franchise entries. "Visually, I really pushed a lot to use the mast and the verticality," Raphaël says. "When two ships are locked together and boarding, it becomes a playable 3-D map in the middle of the ocean. You come to use the beams and the ropes, and it really becomes something that you have created on your own. Visually speaking, it was really important to maintain the fact that the ships are tall."

OPPOSITE: Artwork capturing the powerful experience of a ship plunging into the waves (Martin Deschambault).
ABOVE: The *Jackdaw* (Yong Jin Teo).

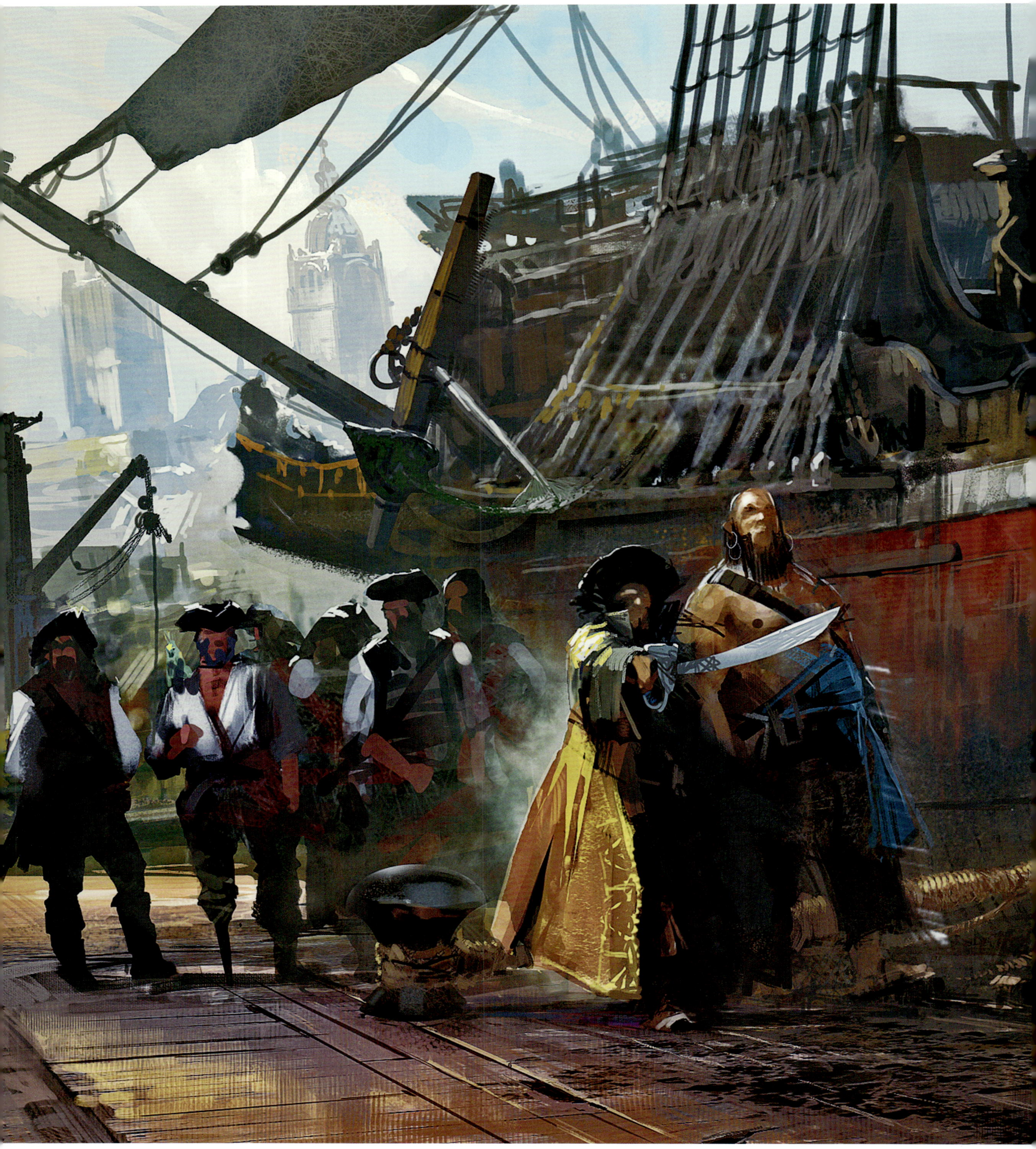

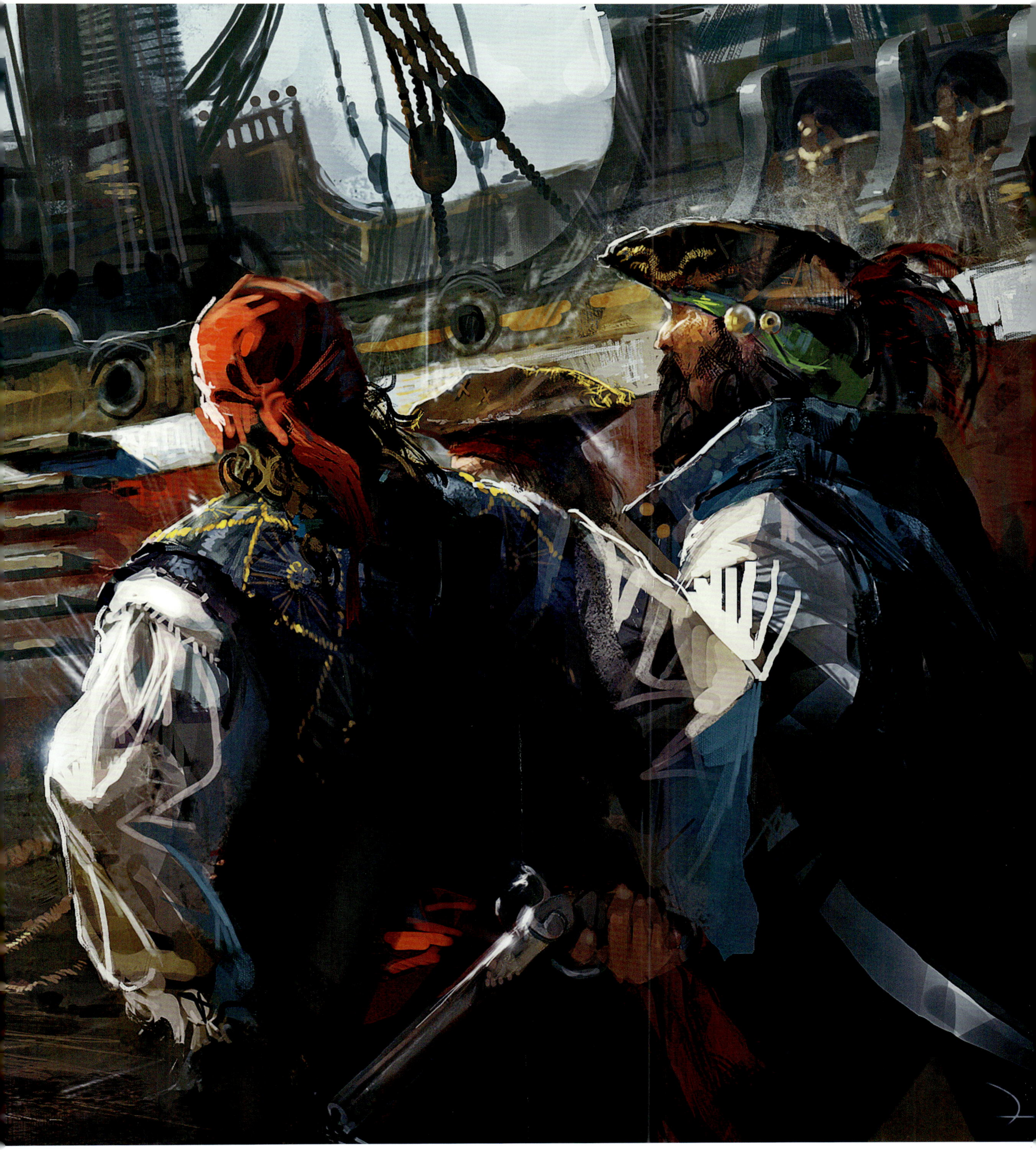

THESE PAGES: A standoff at the Havana dock (Martin Deschambault).

LAND, HO!

With dozens of islands, three small cities, and endless hidden coves, caves, and crannies, *Black Flag* had plenty of land to explore in between sea adventures. The many large and small landmasses needed to feel distinct from one another, while remaining true to the tropical tone of that part of the world.

The cities presented a particular challenge but also a great opportunity for creativity. Unlike cities such as Venice in the sixteenth century or New York in the late eighteenth, places like the settlement of Nassau had more limited historical data to inform their construction and tone.

Havana was the largest of the towns and the most cosmopolitan. "Havana is lush in its beauty as a Spanish Colonial setting," Raphaël describes. "The city's aesthetic, with many curves and round pillars and shapes in its architecture, is baroque in details and colors." Bright, vivid cloth draped the narrow streets of the Cuban capital, and the whole place felt alive and busy with trade. "For environment, the main goal at the beginning is to establish the mood and the composition of the environment," says Martin. "We try to focus on an interesting shape within the building or landmark to establish the main feeling of the game." The harbor was crowded and active, while farther inland, arches were draped in vibrant flower arrangements. Classic Spanish architecture offered an Old World feel, even as cutlass-wielding men of rough character made it clear that this was still a place on the fringes of lawful society. Some of the oldest parts of the city, like the beautiful Cathedral of Havana and the imposing fort, the Castillo de la Real Fuerza, were informed by the structures still standing today and offered a sense of authenticity to the city.

The British colony of Kingston, with its white-painted wood and pillars, would one day become the capital of Jamaica, but its earliest days were dominated by sugar plantations and the horror of slaves forced to work them. Beyond the city center, the sugar plantations and their workers offered a potent reminder of the worst crimes of the period, especially juxtaposed against the wealthy manor of Laurens Prins that sat near at hand. Across the bay, the fort at Port Royal provided the setting for one of *Black Flag*'s most powerful scenes. The military base was a prison and place of execution for pirates unfortunate enough to be caught.

The most ramshackle city to make an appearance was Nassau, the pirate haven and den of freedom (or criminality, depending on your perspective). "Nassau is in strong contrast with both Havana and Kingston," Raphaël says. "It is the pirate haven, a crooked patchwork of wooden constructions. It's dense, organic in every way, and you see that nature has not been completely mastered in this place in contrast to the well-manicured gardens of Havana. It's a gritty and tough place." The streets were dirty and seemed in places poorly organized. At the same time, the congenial people seemed pleased with their lot in life. Nassau offered the perfect backdrop for the pirate's home base—a place of freedom but perhaps without the planning necessary to be a lasting stronghold.

Beyond the three major towns, Ubisoft artists had enormous flexibility to craft interesting sites. The Mayan ruins provided a nod to the grand cultures that had populated these lands in earlier times. Small fishing villages dotted the coastline, and isolated islands might hide beautiful rock formations and waterfalls. Many of *Black Flag*'s most compelling locations captured the imagination not because they were great historical landmarks, but because they felt like secret hideaways yet to be trodden by human feet.

OPPOSITE: Concept of a street near the docks in Havana (Martin Deschambault).

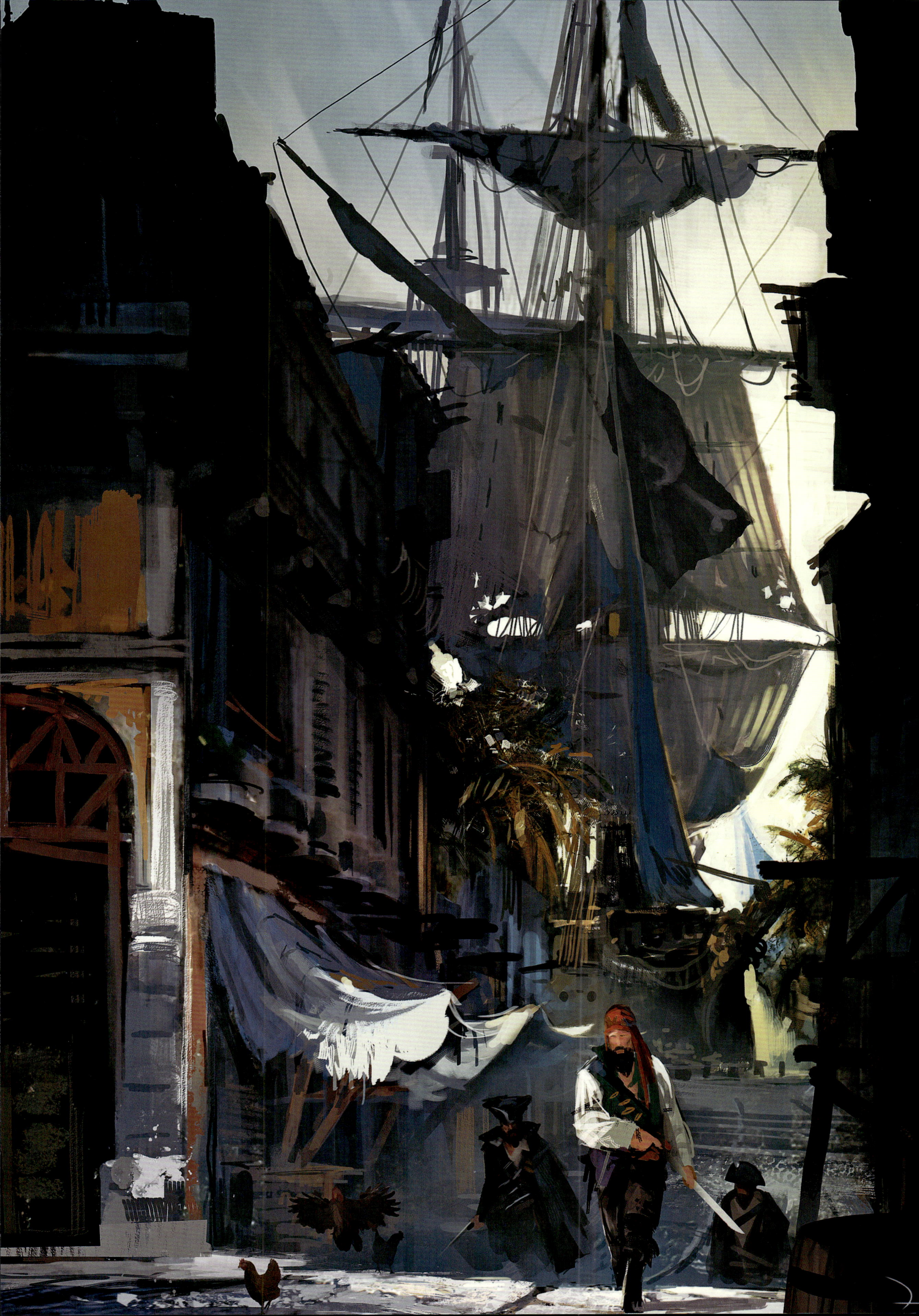

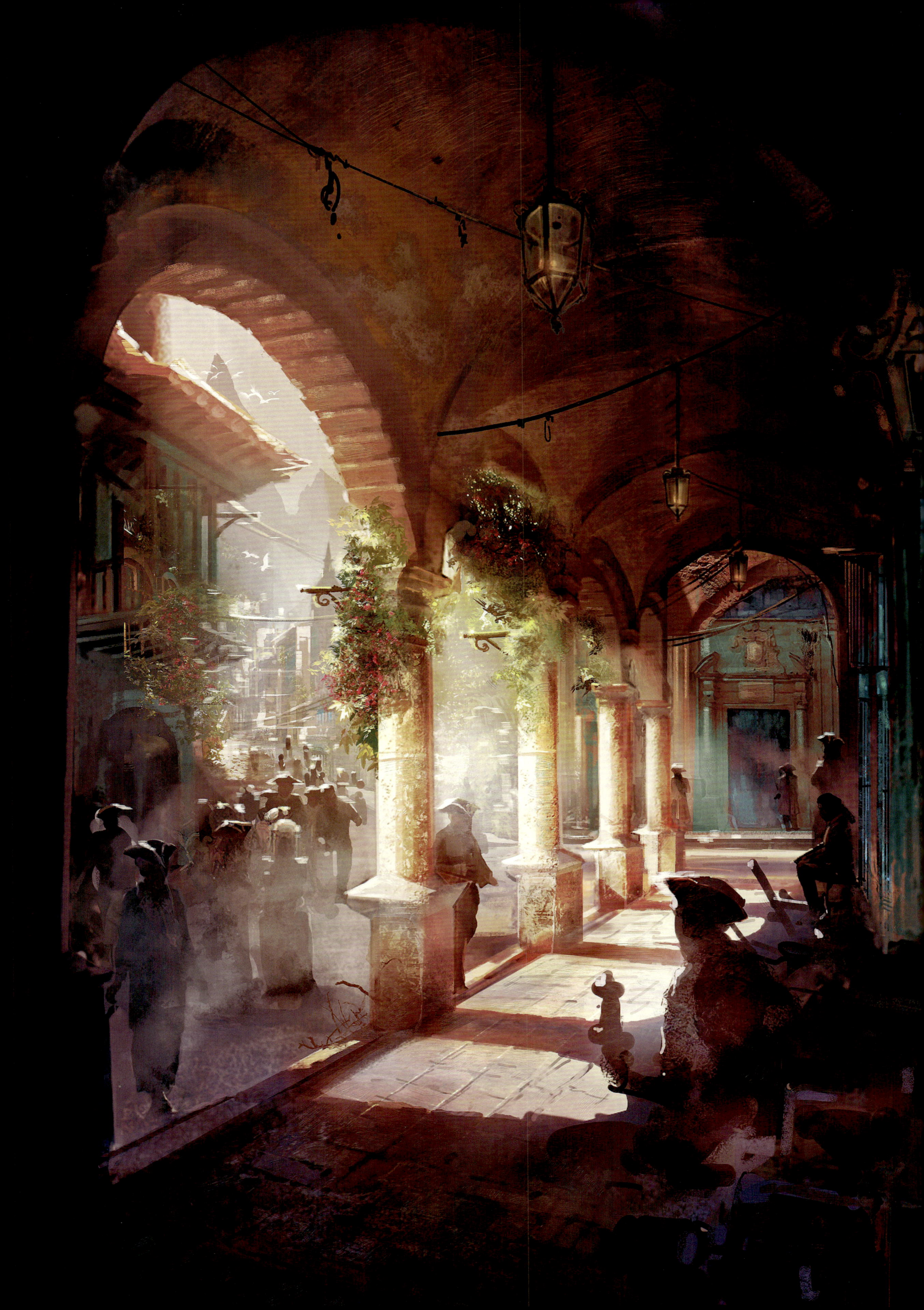

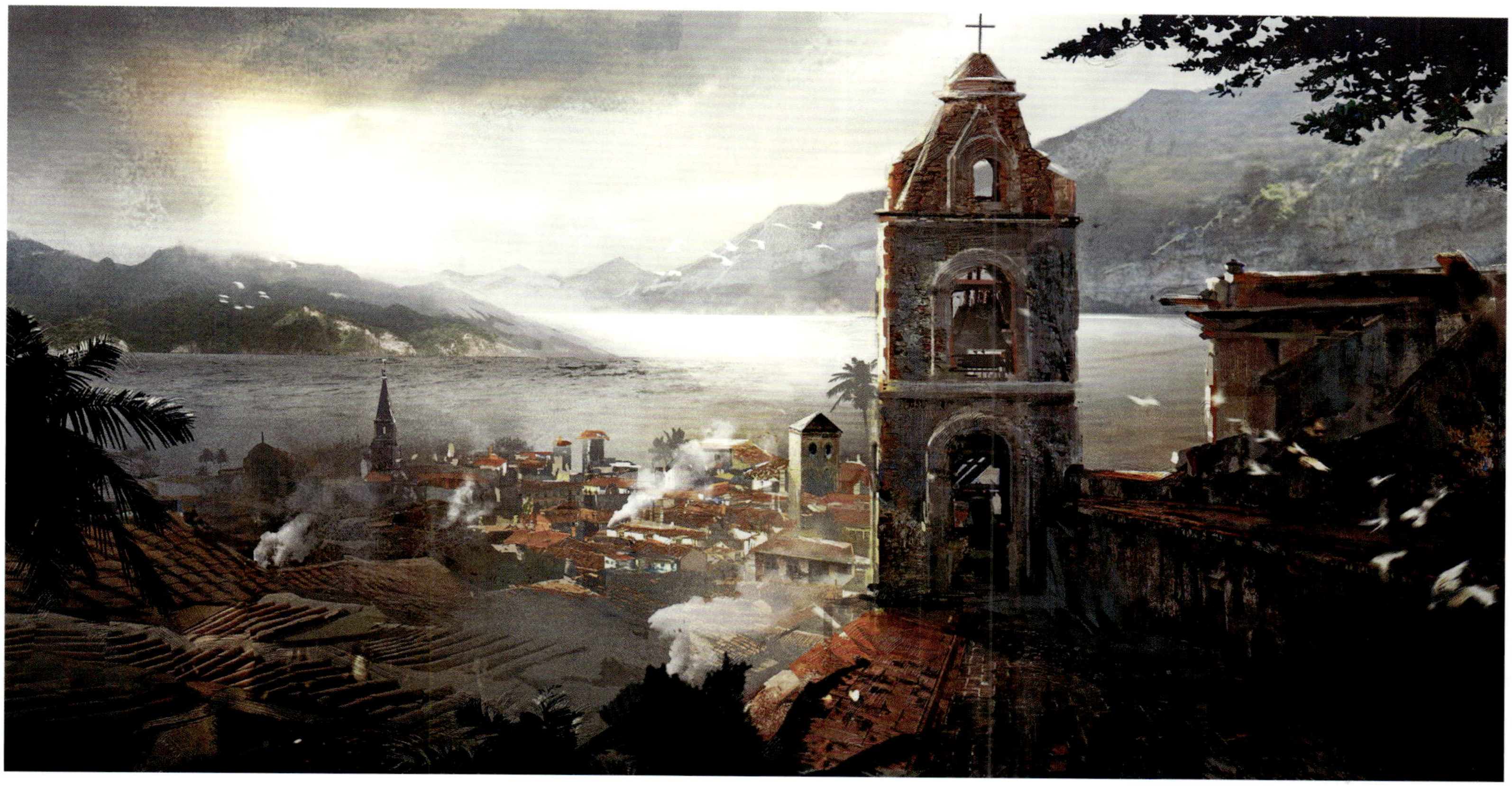

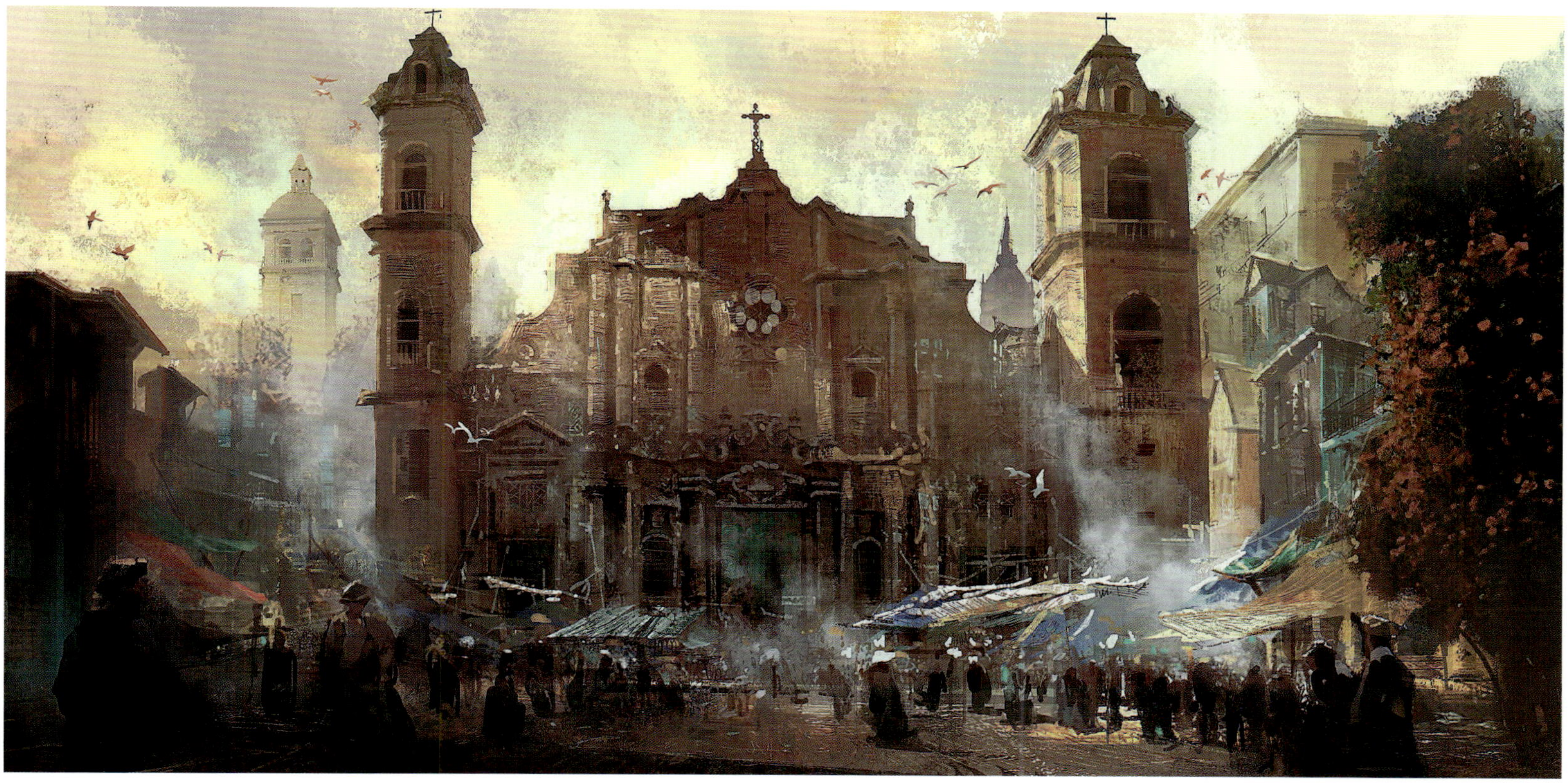

OPPOSITE: Lush and exotic, Havana featured bright lighting and a vibrant color palette (Donglu Yu).
THIS PAGE: Concepts of the Havana Cathedral (Donglu Yu).

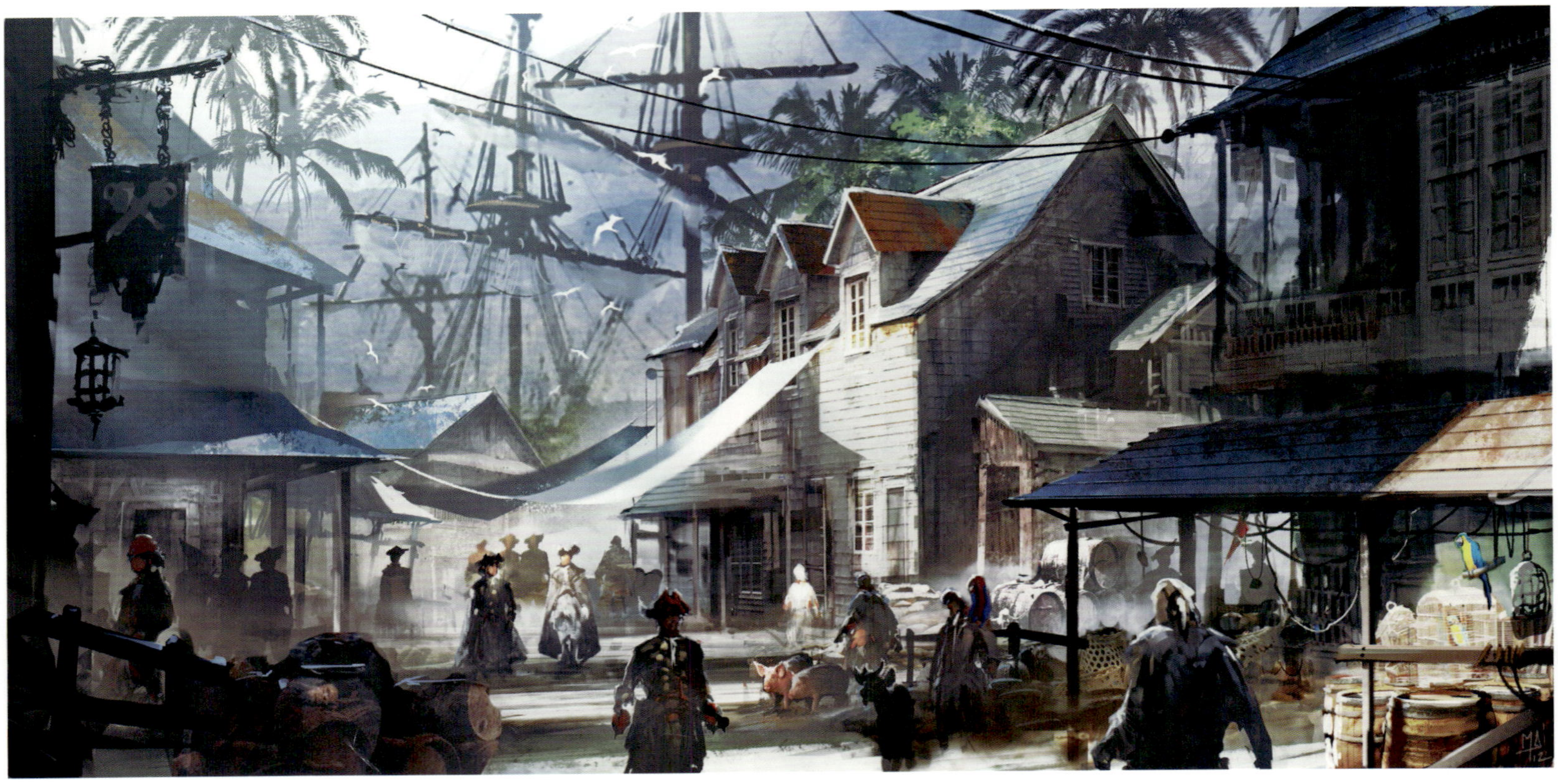

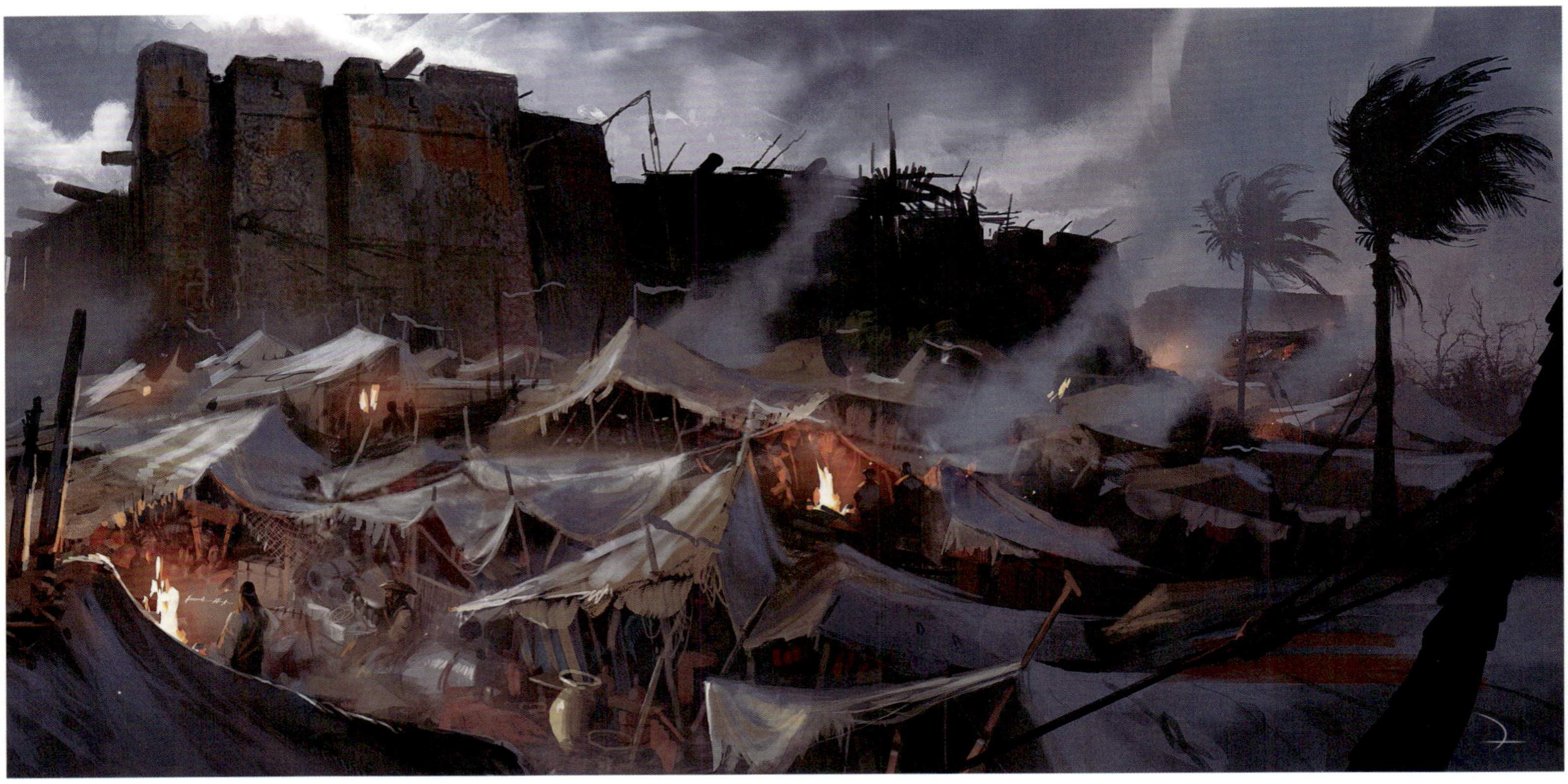

TOP: The street leading to the pier in Kingston (Maxime Desmettre).
ABOVE: A storm blows in over the fort at Nassau (Martin Deschambault).
OPPOSITE: Stairs alongside a Nassau market (Martin Deschambault).

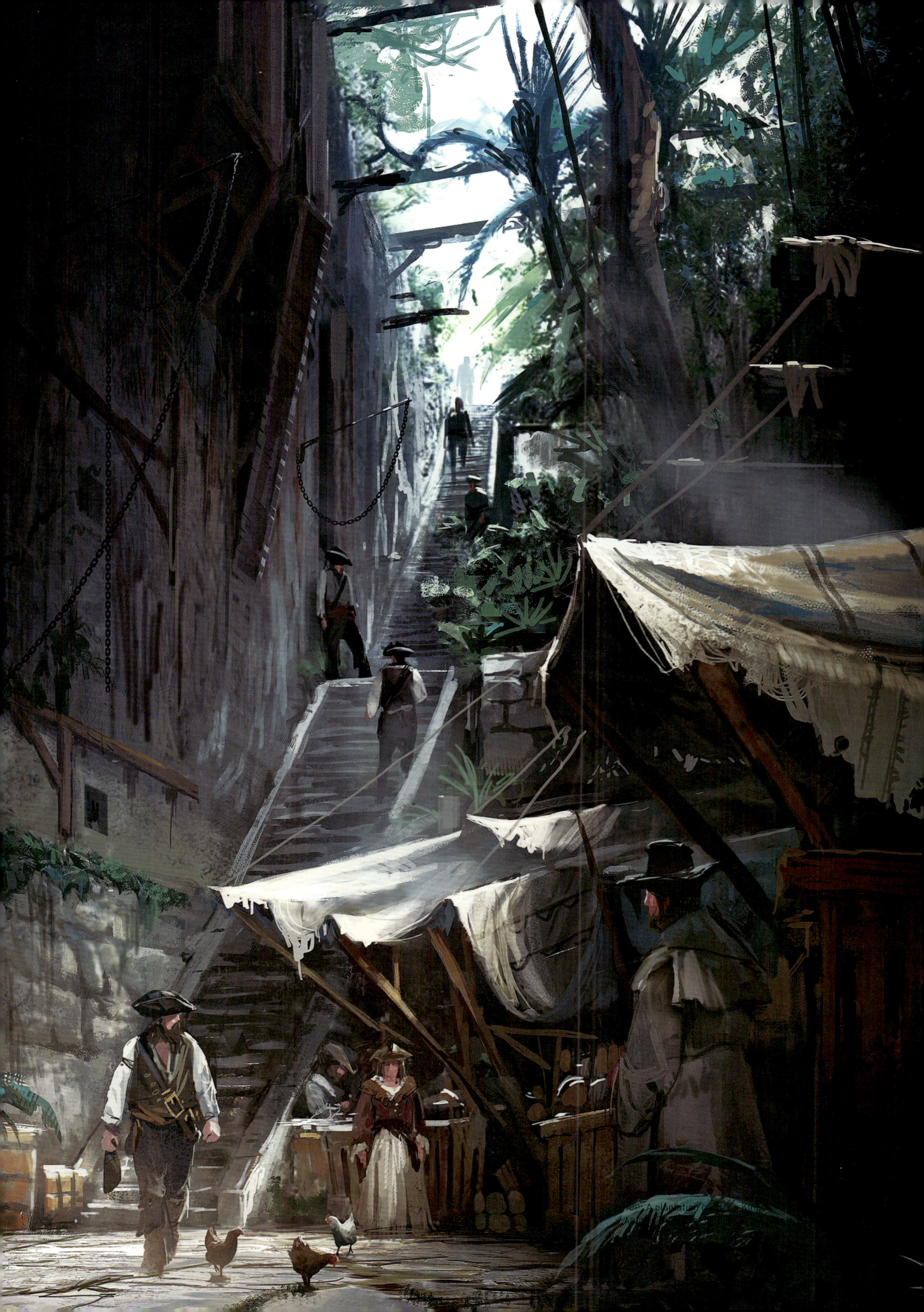

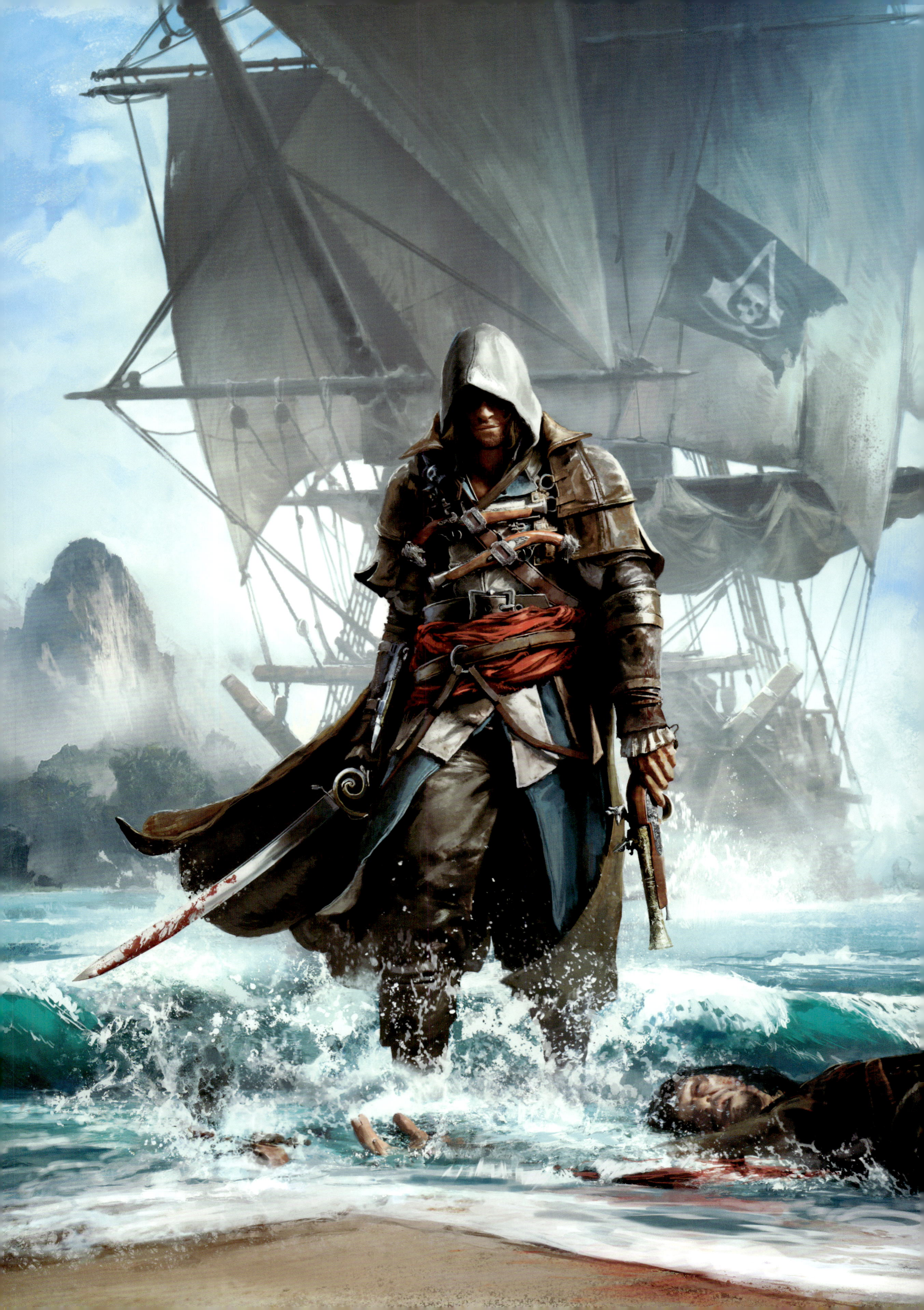

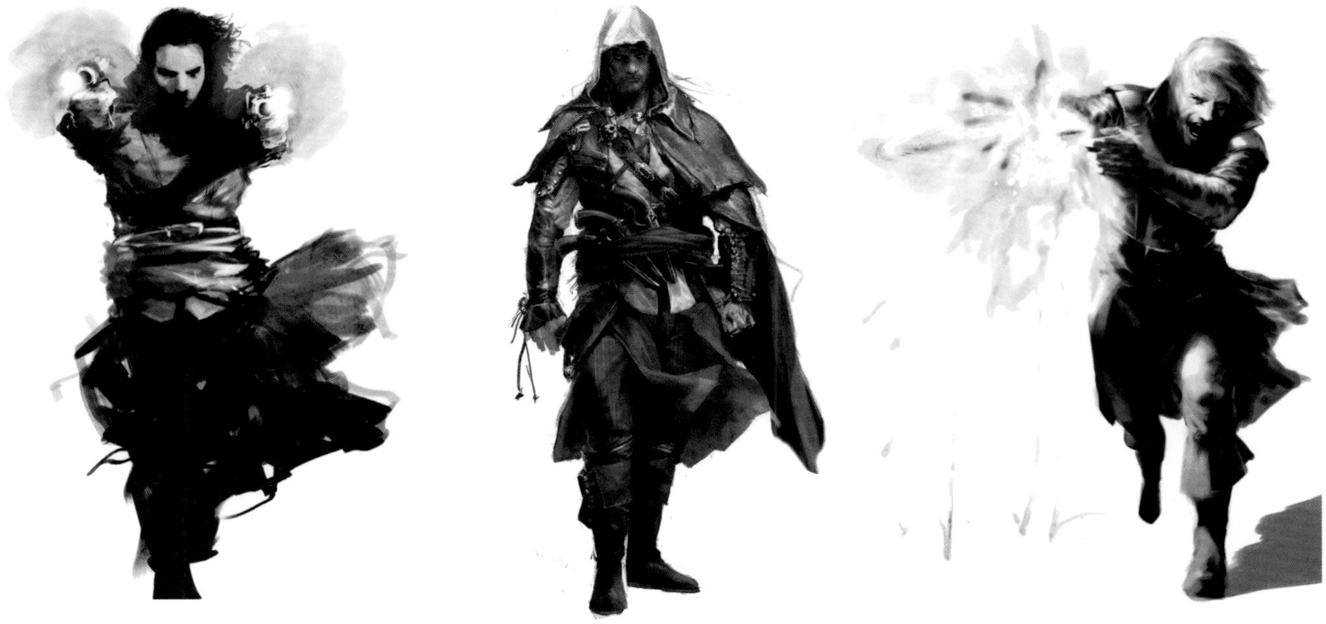

THE RELUCTANT ASSASSIN

Edward Kenway, the grandfather of Connor, may have eventually earned his place beside legendary assassins like Altaïr and Ezio, but he spent the majority of his adventure in *Black Flag* as a pretender to the Brotherhood. When Edward Kenway killed a shipwrecked Assassin, he had no idea that the man was already a traitor to the Brotherhood. The subsequent case of mistaken identity saw Edward looking out for himself and trying to find a pay day in the midst of a conflict that had far more world-shaking implications than he was willing to acknowledge. Only after years of loss and the sacrifice of his friends would Edward step up into his destiny, and in an odd twist, we only witnessed the beginnings of the good man he'd become as the story of *Black Flag* came to a close.

From an artistic presentation standpoint, Edward needed to stand between two very iconic and established visual archetypes. On one side, his stolen uniform needed to be unmistakable as part of the long lineage of the Assassin Order. On the other side, the mythology of the eighteenth-century pirate needed to come to the fore.

"Edward is selfish, reckless, and he takes what he wants," Raphaël suggests. "You see that in the design of his clothes. He doesn't wear the traditional Assassin's robe, which at times almost resembled a uniform, and his outfit is more like a patchwork of colors and trophies." The nature of his role as a pirate is also reflected in the design. "We were also dealing with some historical constraints: Pirates did not wear hoods; they made up their outfits by assembling different pieces collected here and there," explains Vincent. "In the end, it made sense: Contrary to all the previous main protagonists, Edward becomes an Assassin by accident, after stealing another Assassin's clothing." The long coat and hood reminded us of the Assassins we've met before, but perhaps his hood wasn't quite so pointed and eagle-like. The hidden blade peeked out beneath his sleeves, but the two pistols strapped to Edward's chest and the curved sabers in his hands reminded us of his unsavory tactics. He was unkempt and scattered, but hints of his eventual heroism shone through.

OPPOSITE: The lack of a beak on Edward's hood signifies his status as an unofficial Assassin (Martin Deschambault).
ABOVE: Various early research sketches of Edward (Vincent Gaigneux).

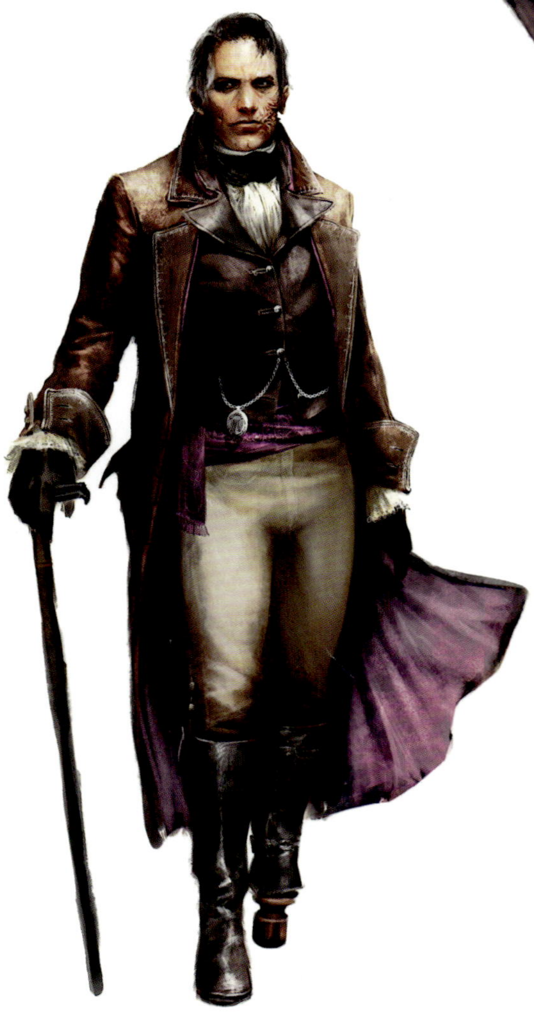

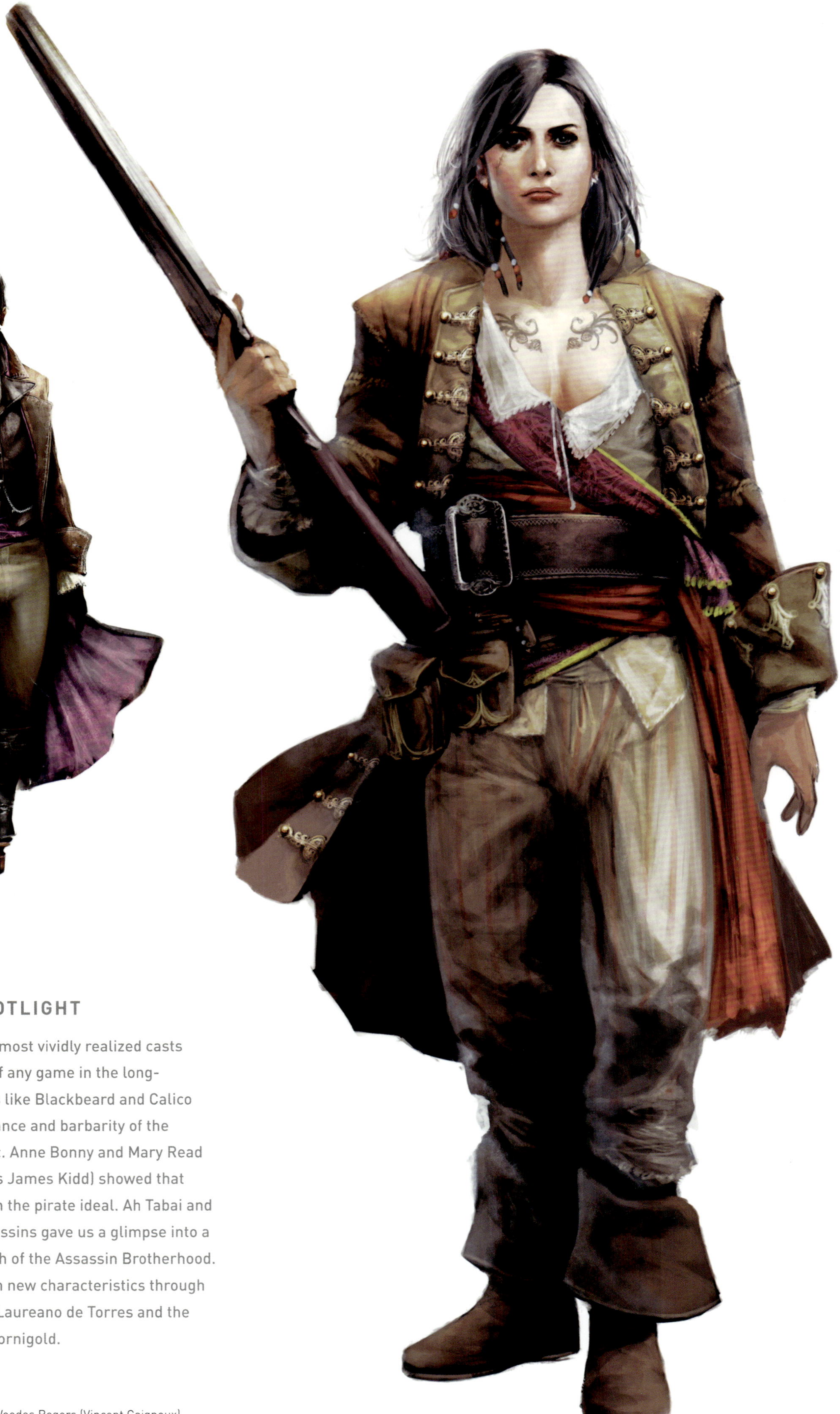

SHARING THE SPOTLIGHT

Black Flag had one of the most vividly realized casts of secondary characters of any game in the long-running franchise. Pirates like Blackbeard and Calico Jack showed off the brilliance and barbarity of the short-lived pirate republic. Anne Bonny and Mary Read (masquerading early on as James Kidd) showed that more than men believed in the pirate ideal. Ah Tabai and the rest of the Mayan assassins gave us a glimpse into a new, as yet unseen, branch of the Assassin Brotherhood. Even the Templars took on new characteristics through characters like Governor Laureano de Torres and the traitor pirate, Benjamin Hornigold.

ABOVE: Character art of the Templar Woodes Rogers (Vincent Gaigneux).
RIGHT: Early Mary Read concept (Vincent Gaigneux).
OPPOSITE: Iconic Blackbeard pose (Vincent Gaigneux).

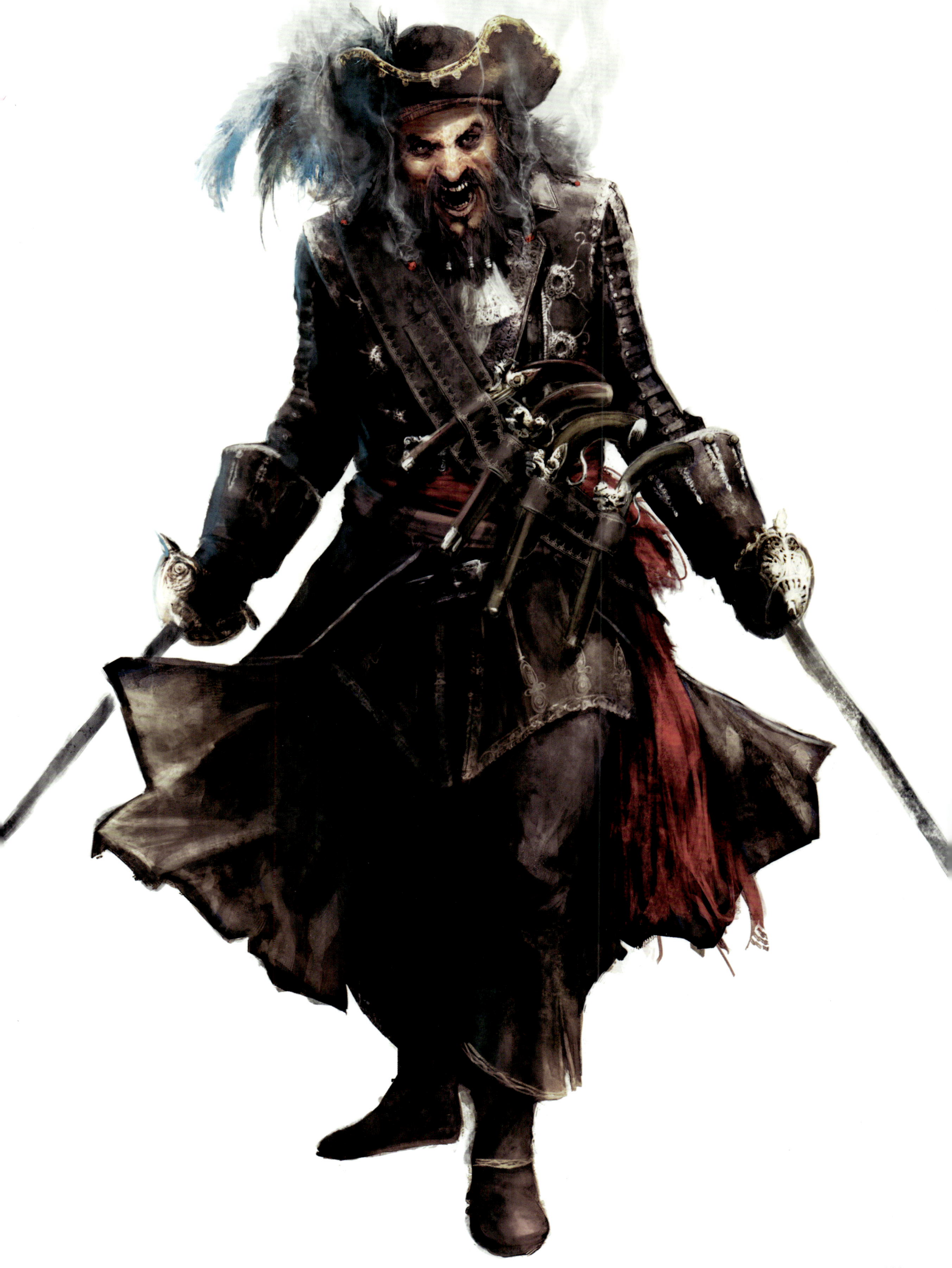

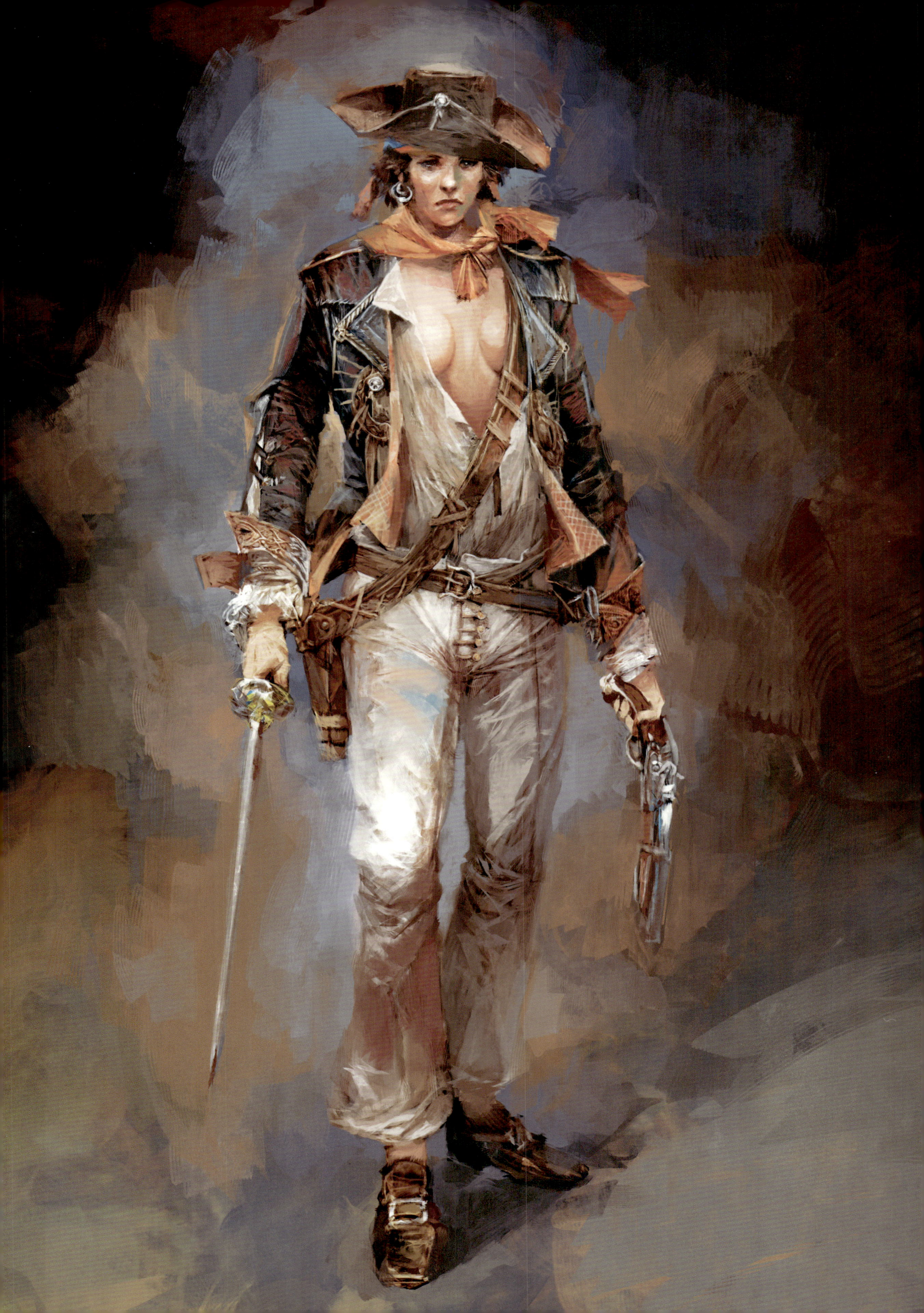

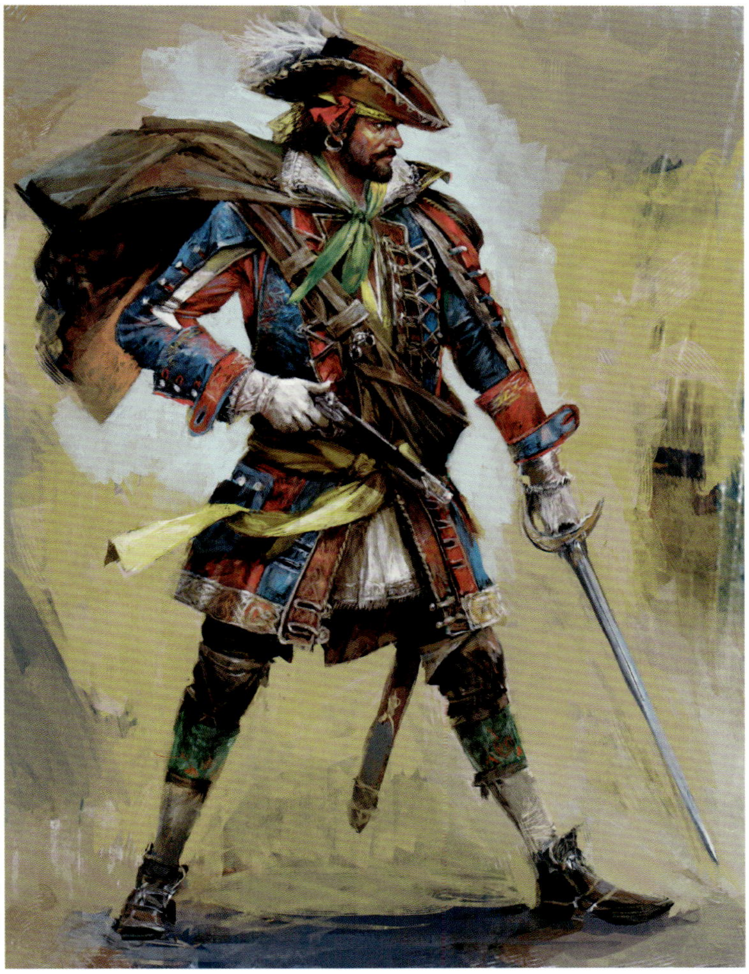

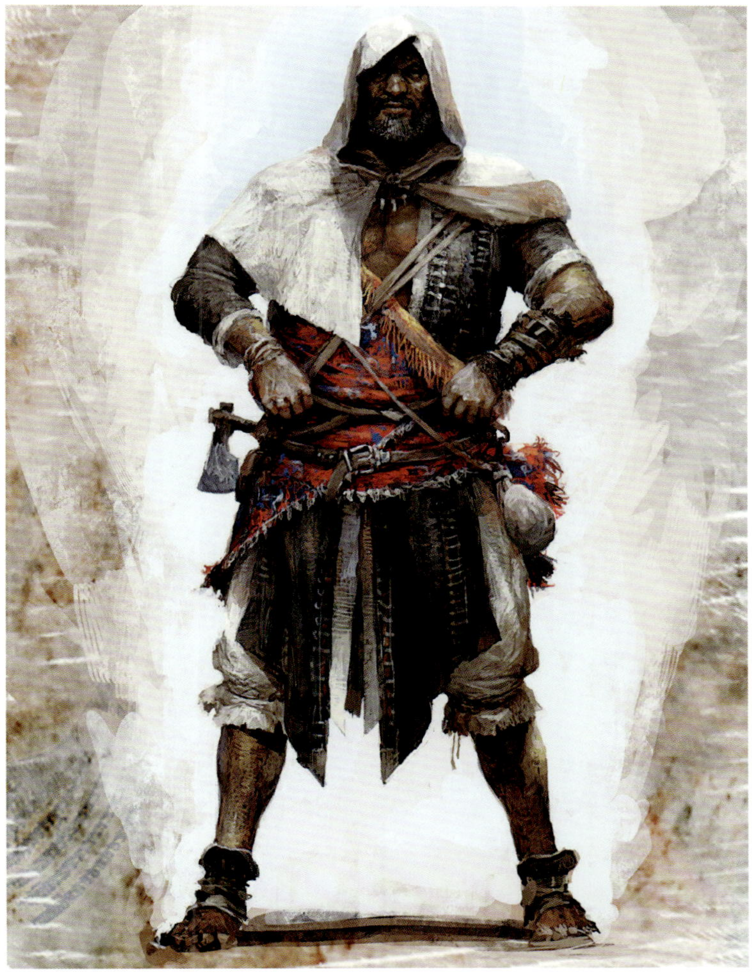

OPPOSITE: Early Anne Bonny concept (Patrick Lambert).
ABOVE LEFT: This design of Calico Jack features a variety of likely stolen fabrics that have been incorporated into his outfit (Patrick Lambert).
ABOVE RIGHT: Many pirate costumes featured Middle Eastern influences including silks, metal ornamentation, and other varieties of textures (Patrick Lambert).

THE PRICE OF LIBERTY

Throughout *Black Flag*'s lengthy campaign, one of the most riveting characters was the man who stood as quartermaster to Edward Kenway. Even playing second fiddle to Edward, it often seemed that Adéwalé's story had a life of its own. The Trinidadian pirate had risen up out of slavery, and even as Edward struggled to embrace the path of the Brotherhood, Adéwalé recognized the value of its tenets of freedom for all, and he departed to follow the Assassins.

Fifteen years of the in-game timeline passed after the close of *Black Flag* before the opening scenes of the game's downloadable expansion. The *Freedom Cry* DLC moved Adéwalé into the limelight as a main character. Fans had recognized the potential of the character and so did the artists at Ubisoft.

Says senior concept artist Vincent Gaigneux, "You can see in the art that he doesn't have the same weaknesses as the Assassins, so we could do some interesting things with the character. We had to have the character be more brutal, a lot of things that an Assassin couldn't be."

"When we saw the first concepts for Adéwalé as an Assassin, we were really excited," Raphaël recalls. "He was just the right guy—very charismatic and strong. The intention was to make a super powerful character whose motivation was all about revenge. You feel the presence and terrible consequences of slavery. Adéwalé is able to free a lot of people. He symbolizes their frustration, their anger, and their sadness." *Freedom Cry* found Adéwalé shipwrecked while on a mission for the Assassins near the Haitian town of Port au Prince. Forced to come face to face with the same ugly nature of slavery into which he'd been born, Adéwalé remained in the French colony for the following years and aided the Maroon rebellion that was striking back against the unjust slave masters.

Freedom Cry gave Ubisoft a chance to expand upon earlier discarded designs for Port au Prince that had fallen on the cutting-room floor for *Black Flag*'s main game. More importantly, the downloadable content pack gave Adéwalé a chance to prove his mettle in a starring role. The short but satisfying adventure felt rooted in the long-standing themes of the series; freedom and control could hardly find a more potent expression than in a close, hard look at slavery's horrible price.

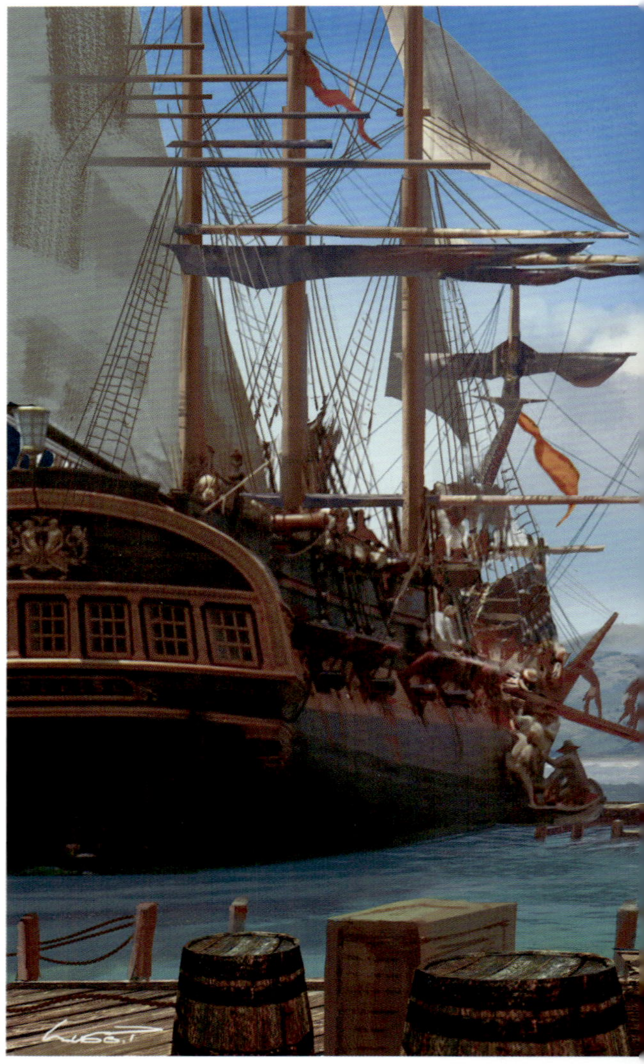

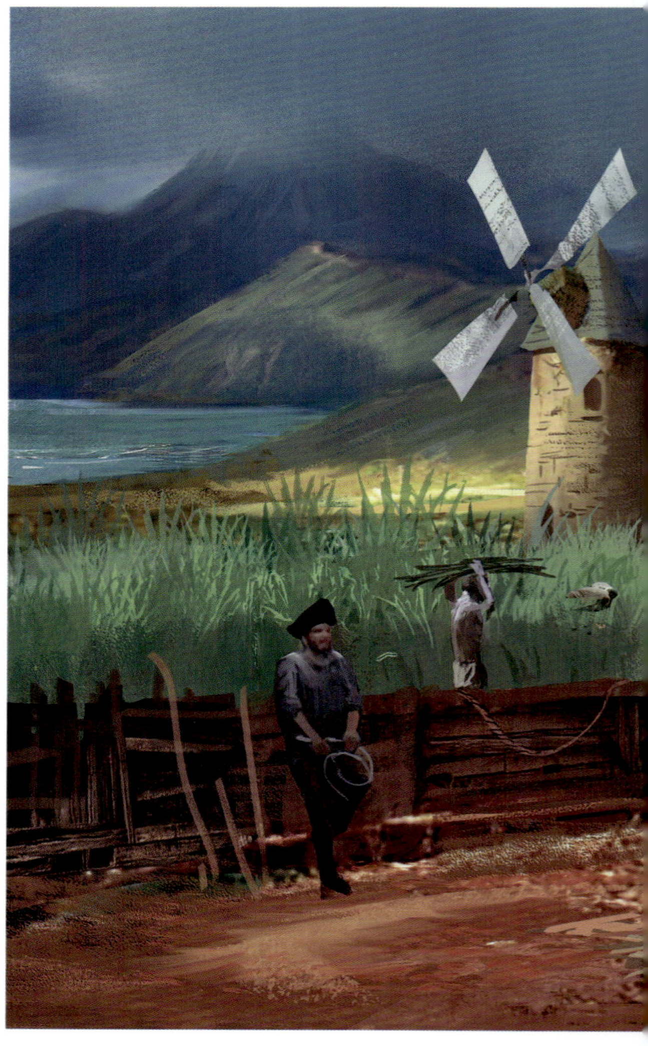

TOP RIGHT: Artwork contrasting the bright tones of the ocean and sky with the dark subject of a slave ship (Hugo Puzzuoli).
BOTTOM RIGHT: Plantation scene from *Freedom Cry* (Hugo Puzzuoli).

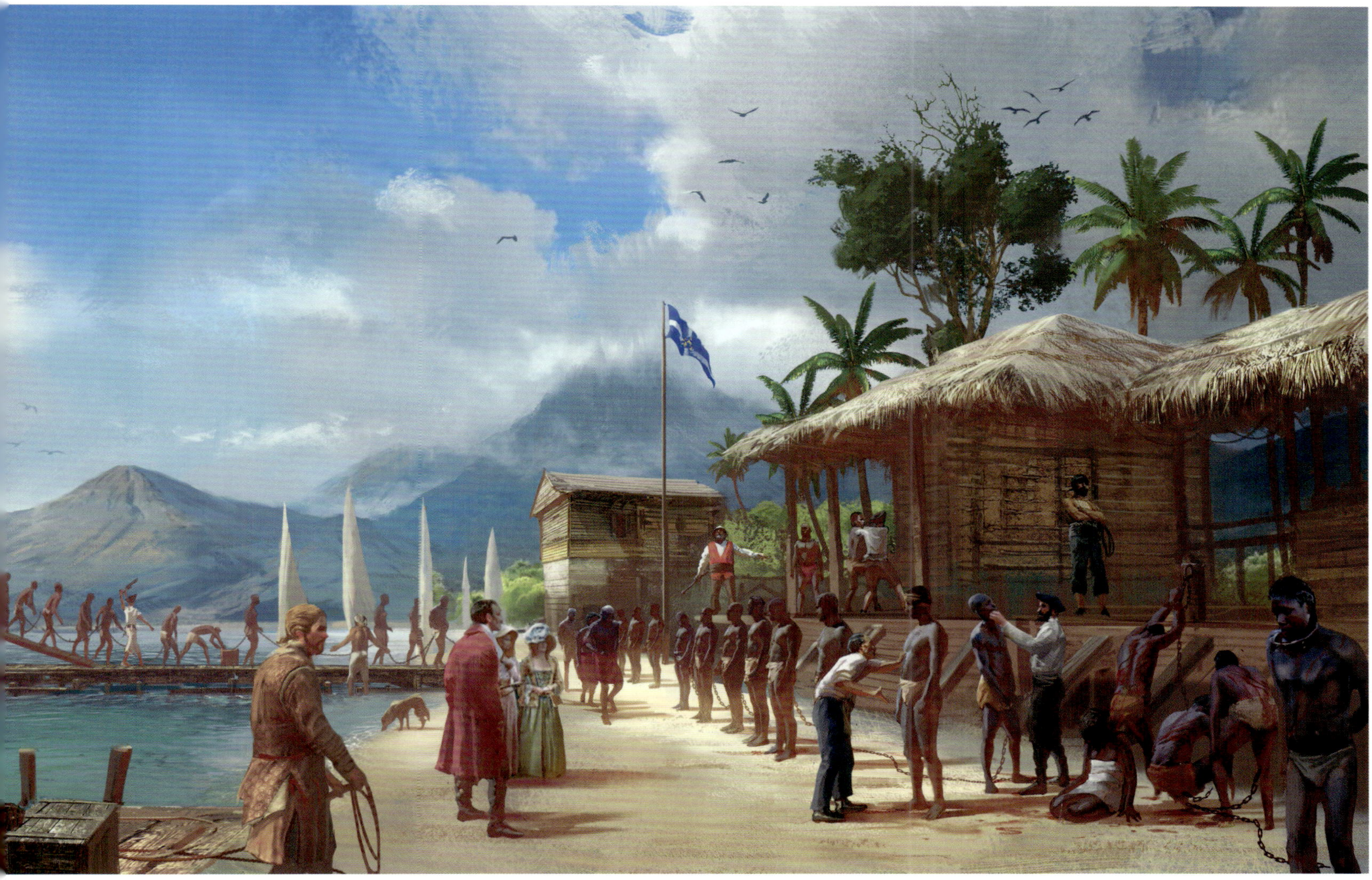

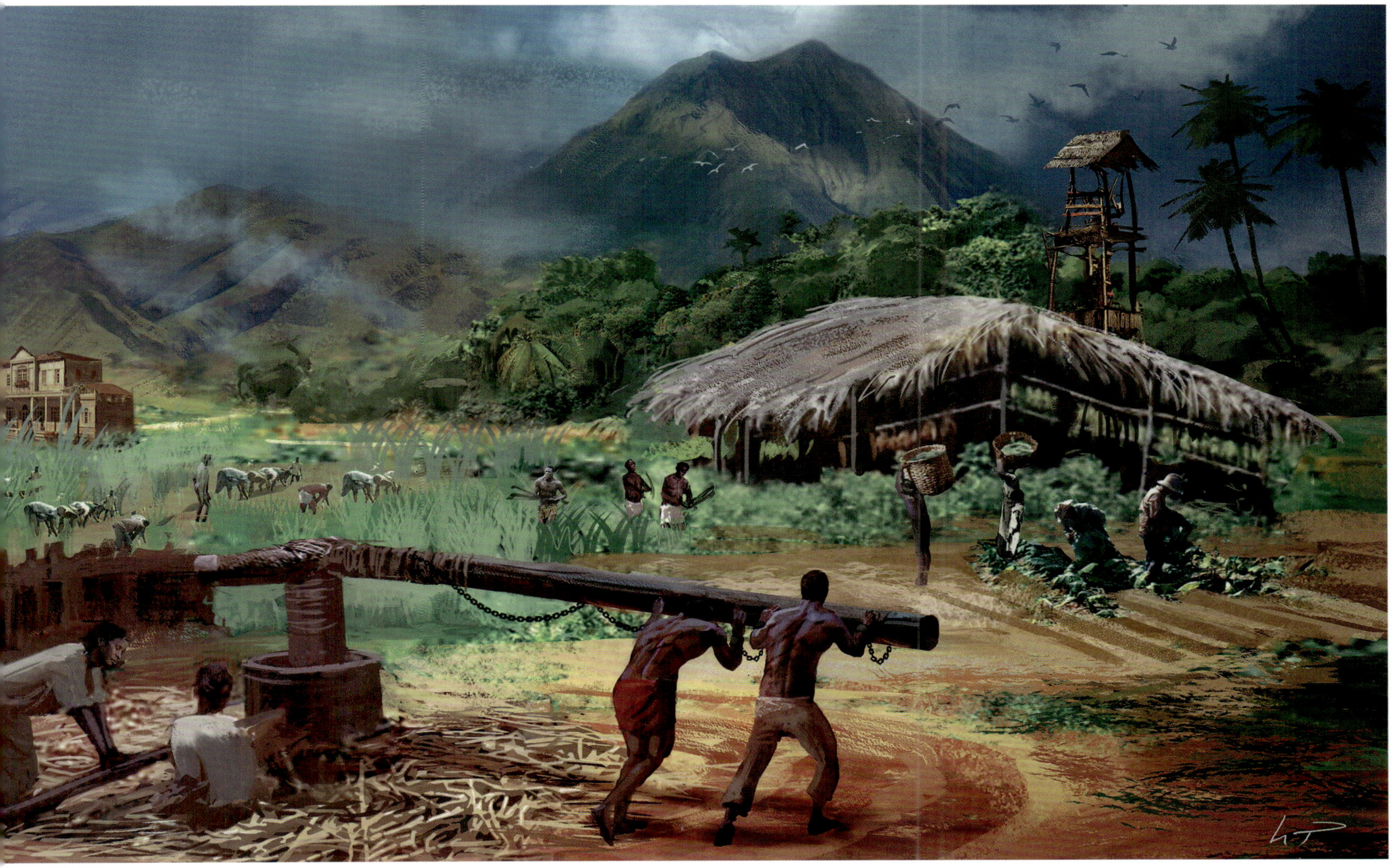

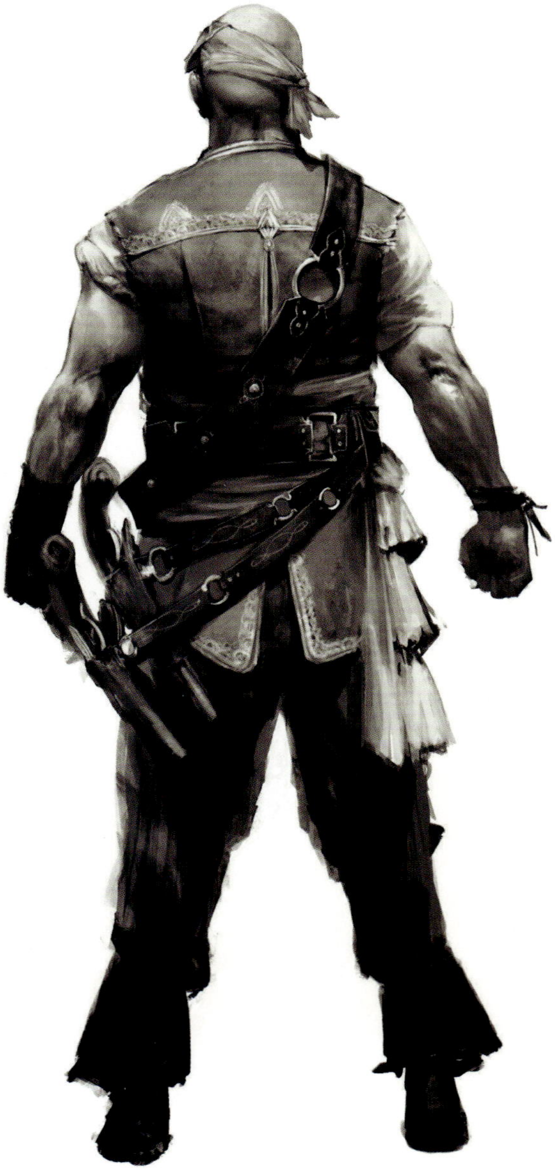

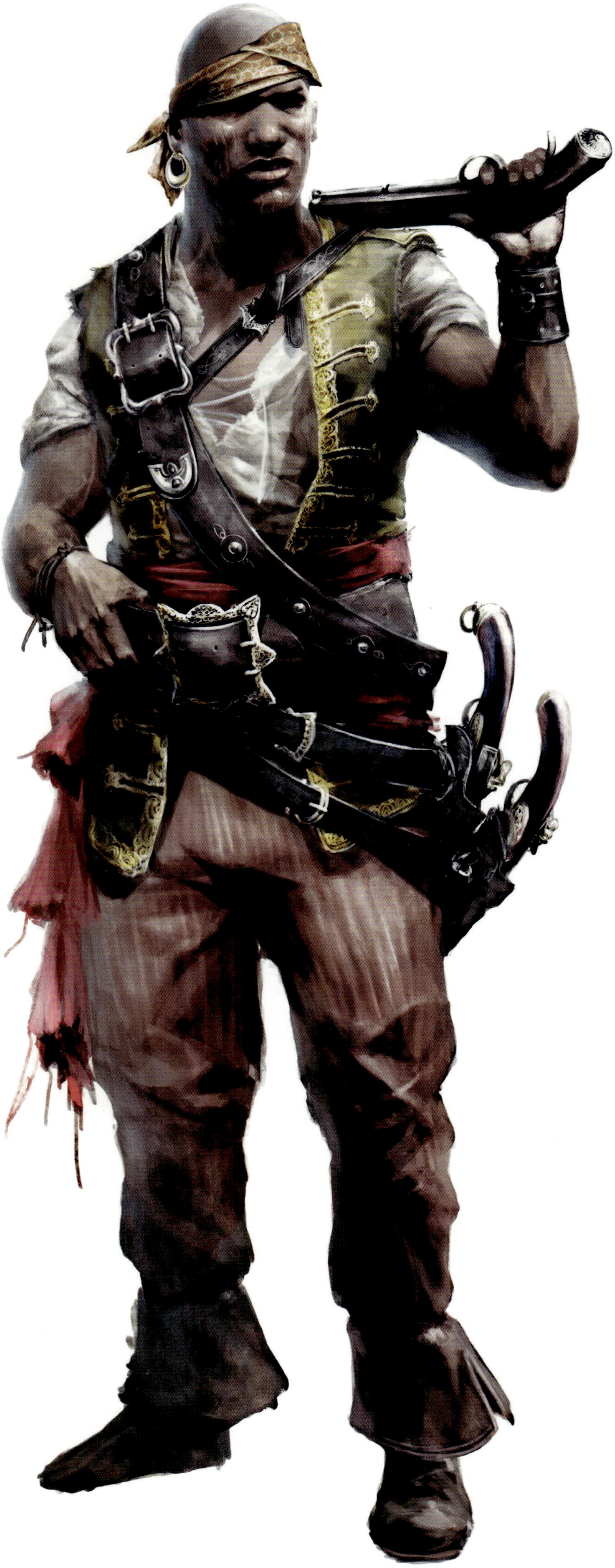

FROM SMALL BEGINNINGS

Adéwalé appeared in three distinct Assassin's Creed experiences, and in each we saw his steady advancement through the ranks of the Brotherhood. His earliest designs in *Black Flag* revealed a man of strength and quiet fortitude but without a guiding principle into which he could channel his energy. By *Freedom Cry*, players witnessed an Asssassin at the height of his power and conviction, willing to set aside his life abroad to help the strangers he met on the colony of Saint-Dominigue in Haiti. In his final appearance in *Assassin's Creed: Rogue*, Adéwalé is an older man who has fought for the Assassins for decades. He's saddened by the betrayal of one of the Brotherhood's own but remains unbowed even as that traitor ends his life.

ABOVE AND RIGHT: Adéwalé's pirate outfit (Vincent Gaigneux).
OPPOSITE TOP: Mayan temple concept (Hugo Puzzuoli).
OPPOSITE BOTTOM: Chilling scene of a sinking slave ship (Hugo Puzzuoli).

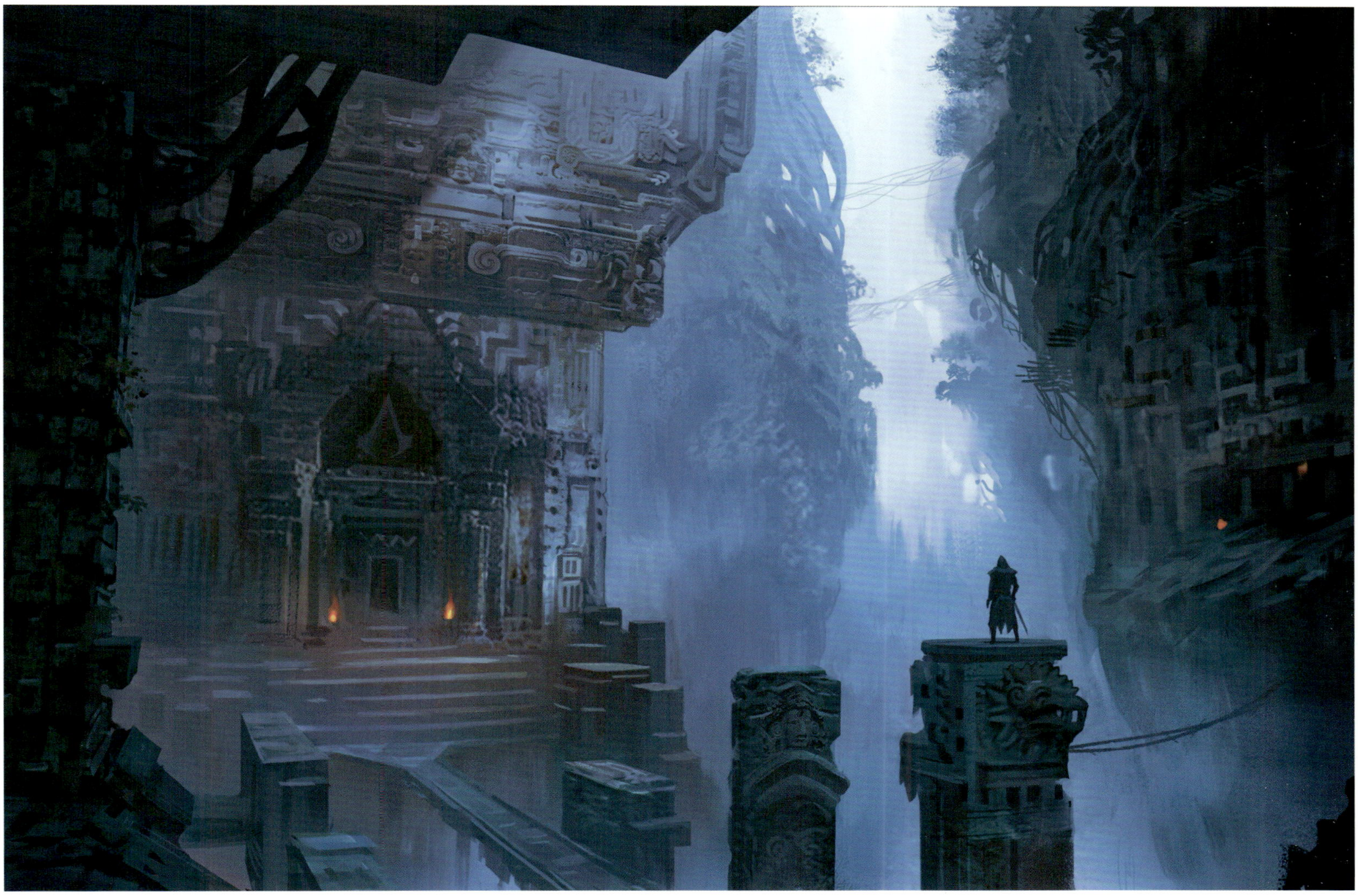

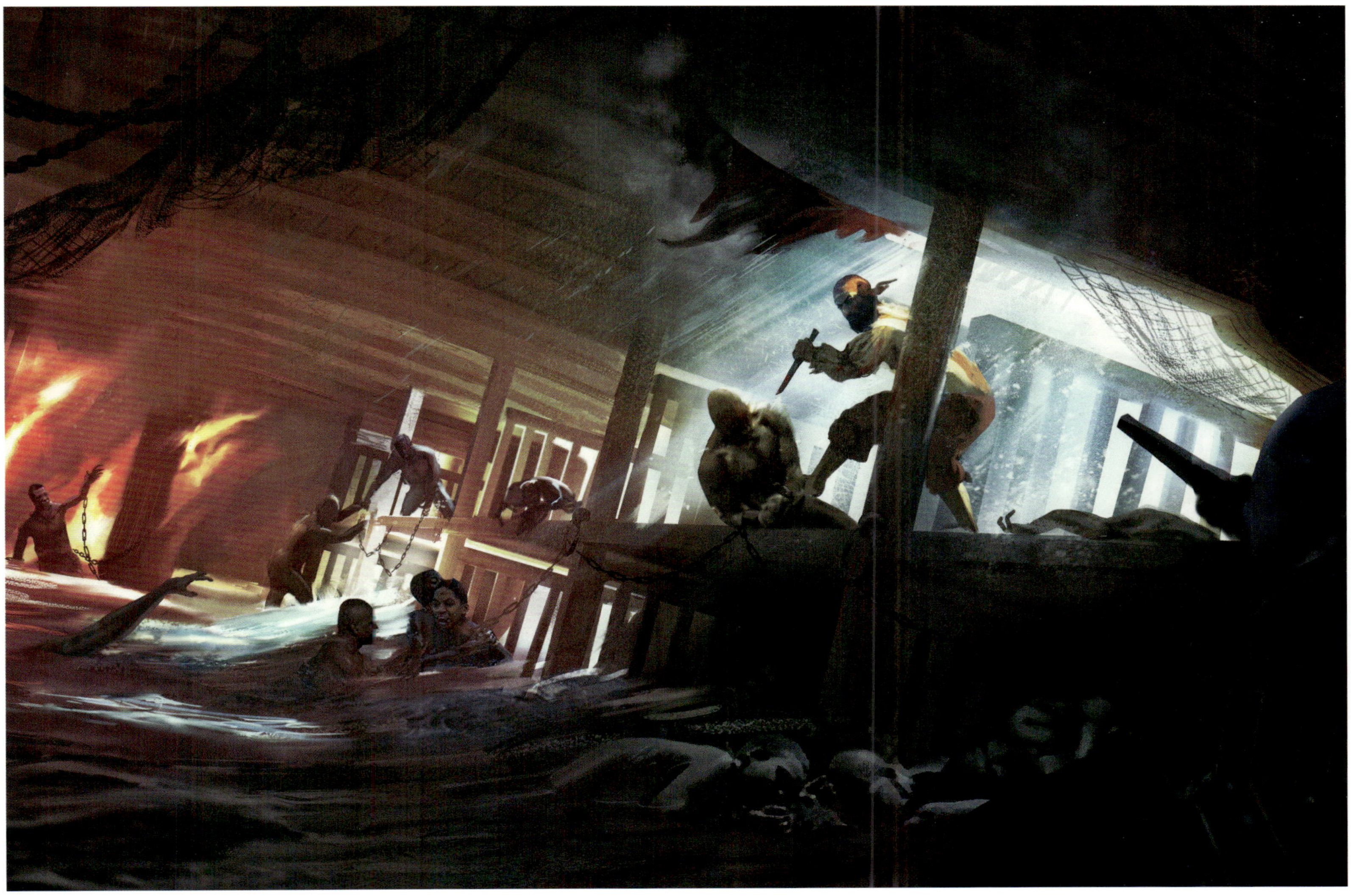

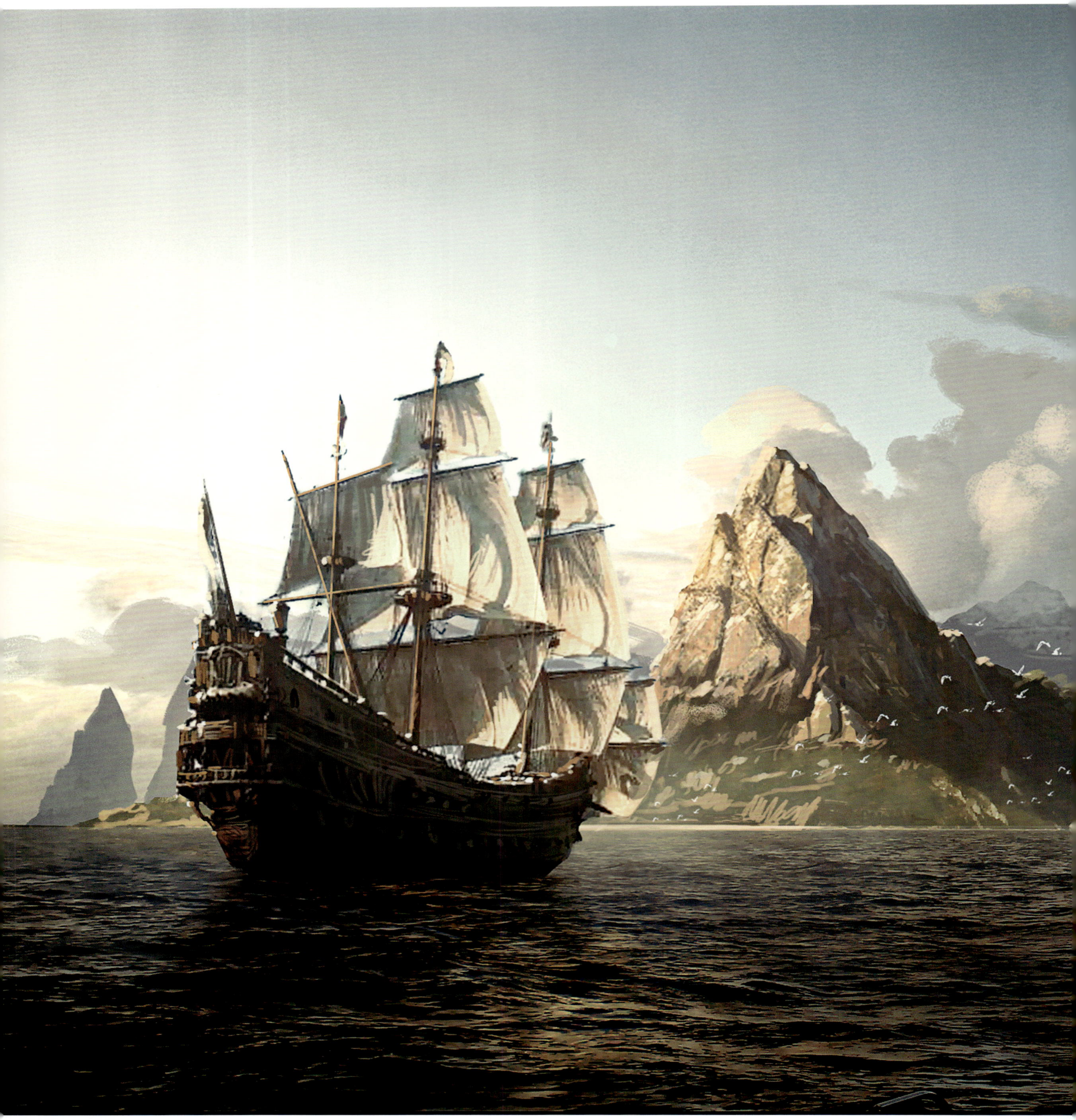

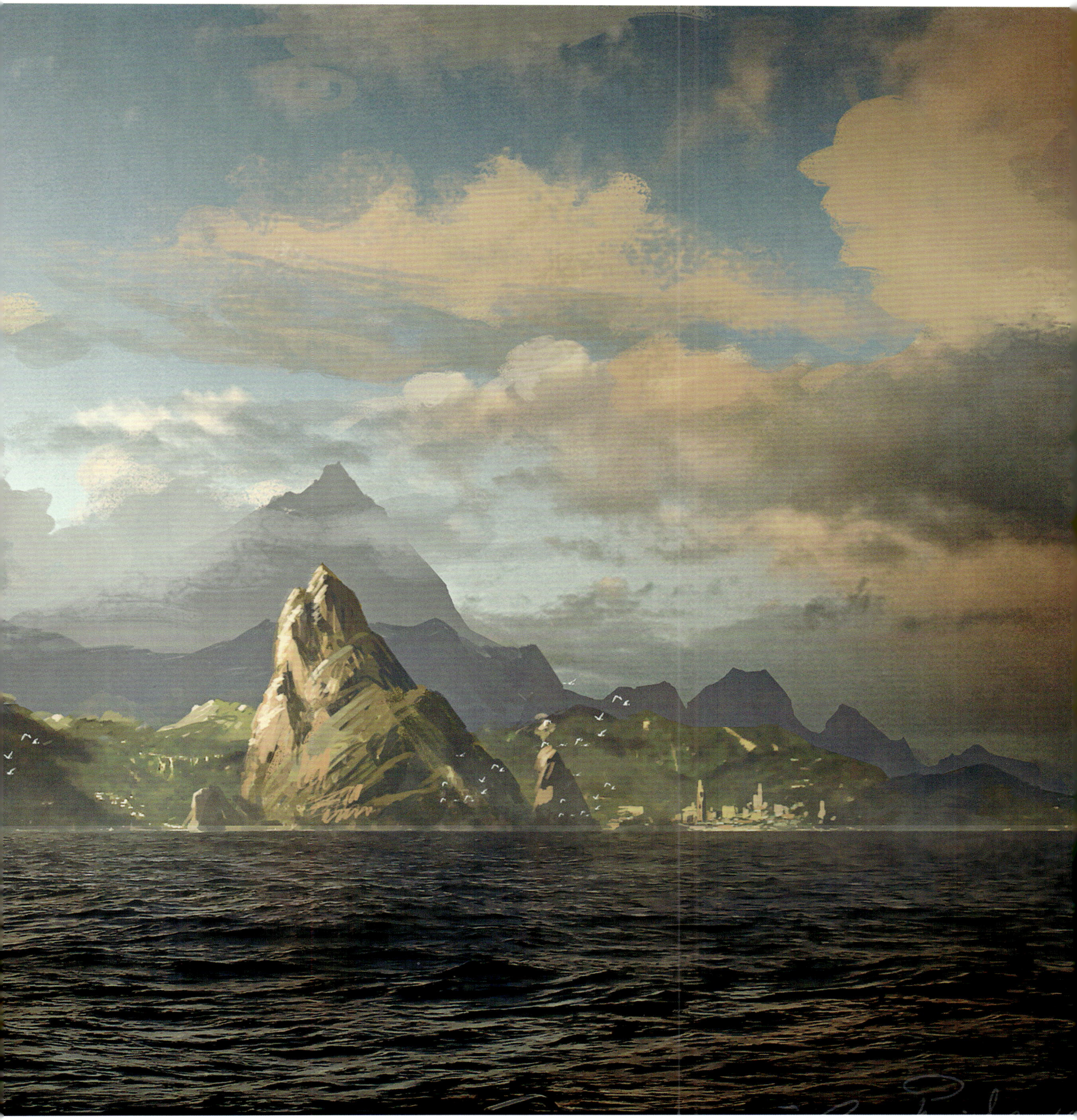

THESE PAGES: The vastness of the open sea contrasts with the dense jungles of the islands (Raphaël Lacoste).

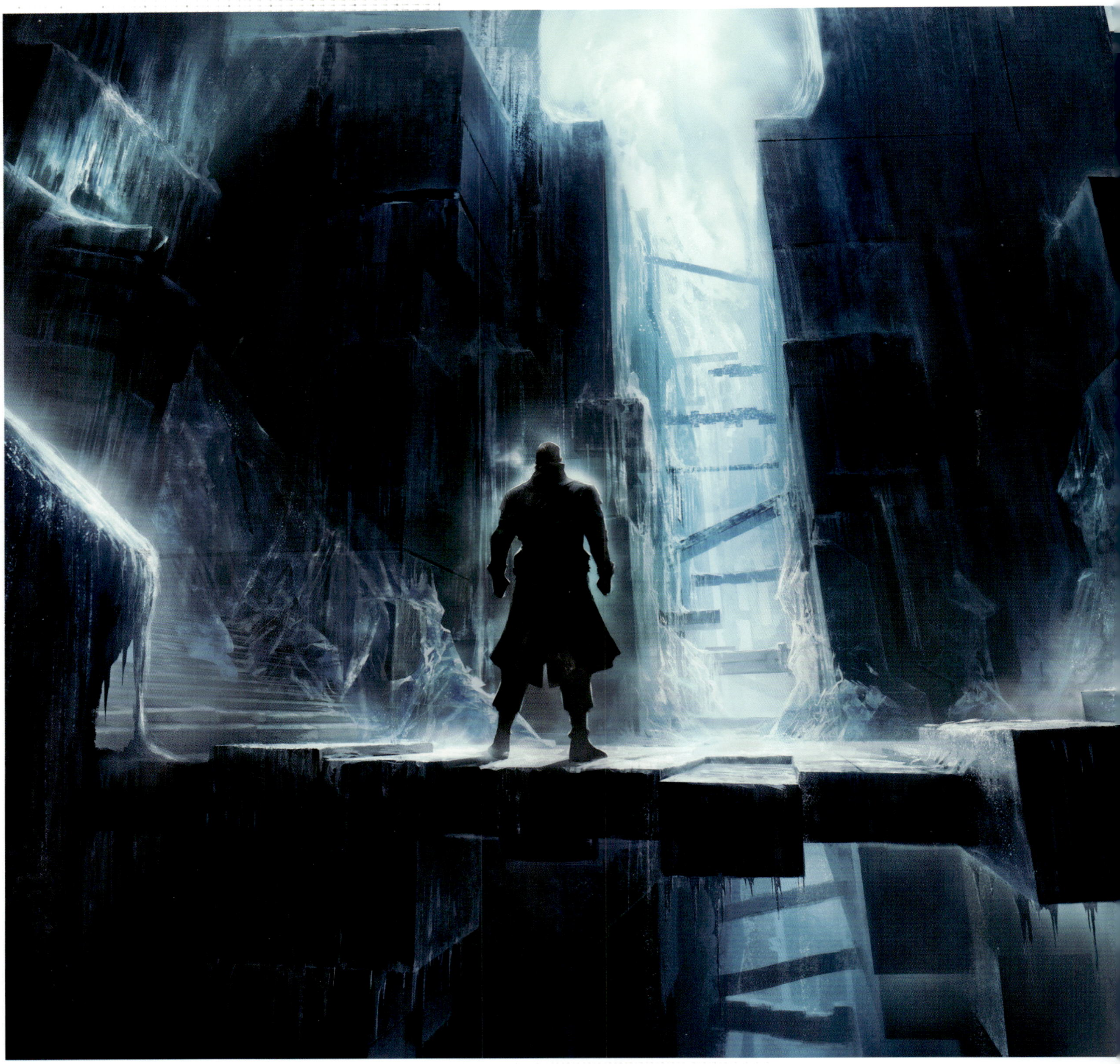

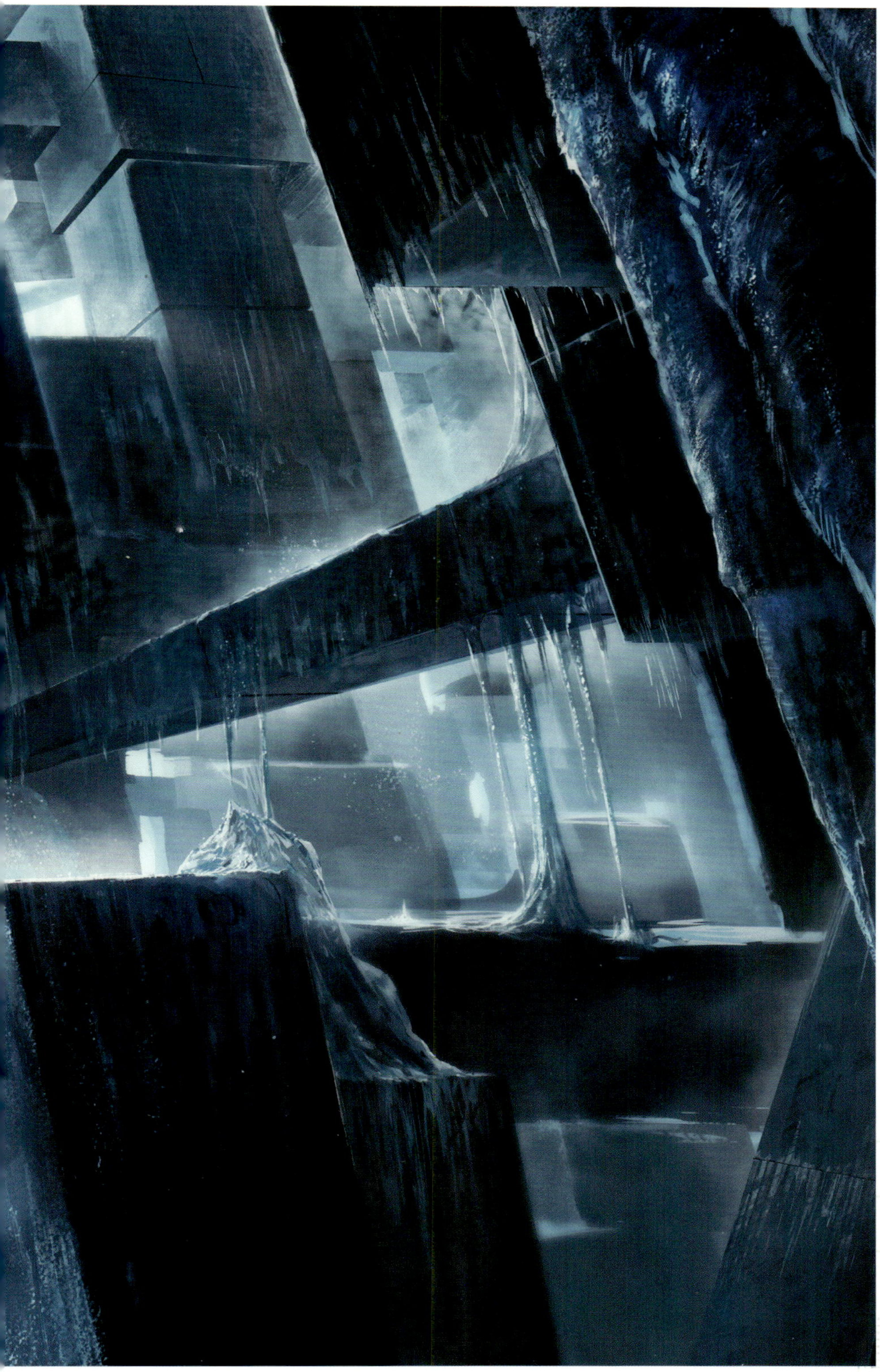

6 THE SEVEN YEARS' WAR

Part 2

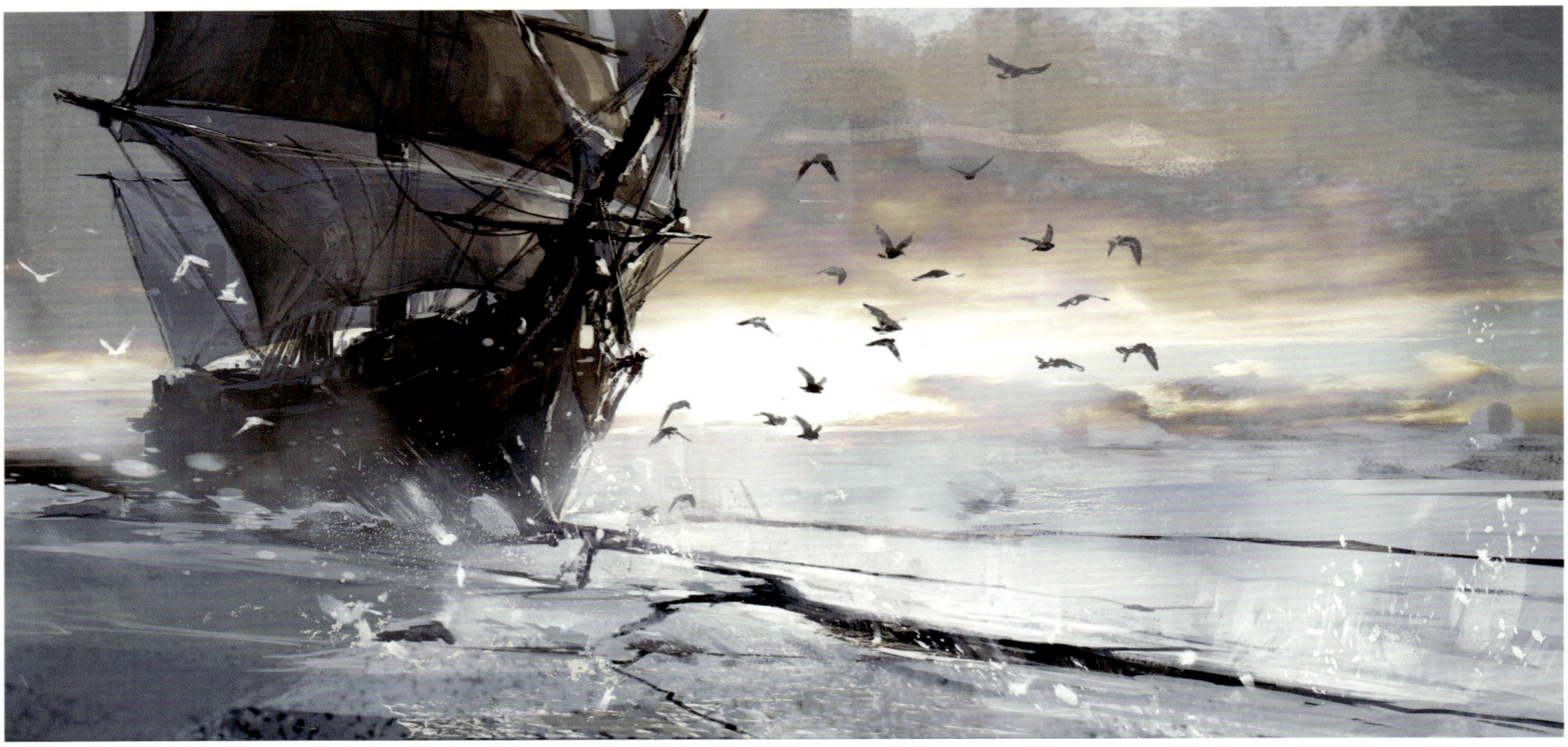

MISSING CHAPTER

Though *Assassin's Creed III* was released before *Black Flag*, the latter was set many years before the former. Both told relatively independent stories, yet when viewed together, the two left some questions unanswered. What had happened to the brave Adéwalé after his adventures in Haiti? And what sad series of events led to Connor's Mentor, Achilles, living alone in a mansion bereft of a Brotherhood to lead? The answers would come in a final act of the American saga called *Assassin's Creed: Rogue*.

Like *Liberation*, *Rogue* was set between the years of the other two console games based in the Americas, during the harrowing conflict called the Seven Years' War. Players followed the exploits of Shay Patrick Cormac, a young Irish immigrant from New York training as an Assassin beneath Achilles and the other members of the Colonial Brotherhood of Assassins. Shay's loyalty is tested and ultimately destroyed by the revelations that the Assassins may have been responsible for disturbing ancient artifacts that led to devastating civilian casualties. Exiled by his former allies, Shay finds himself drawn to the path of the Templars and sets out to hunt down the very Assassins he once called brothers.

Rogue has overtones of Greek tragedy as we watch our hero fall into the hands of the very organization the Assassins have opposed game after game. Shay undoubtedly heads to a dark place over the course of his adventure, but a subtler thread forces players to see the Templars as more than cliché villains and instead as nuanced characters with a clear purpose to their struggles.

Shifting allegiances and familial betrayals are fertile ground for artists, and the team at Ubisoft Sofia, under the art direction of Eddie Bennun, jumped at the opportunity to explore a character and story with such shadowy overtones.

PREVIOUS PAGES: A solitary image of Shay in a First Civilization temple (Ivan Koritarev).
ABOVE: Artwork showcasing the icebreaking ship feature (Kobe Sek).
OPPOSITE: Arctic concept (Guang Yu Tan).

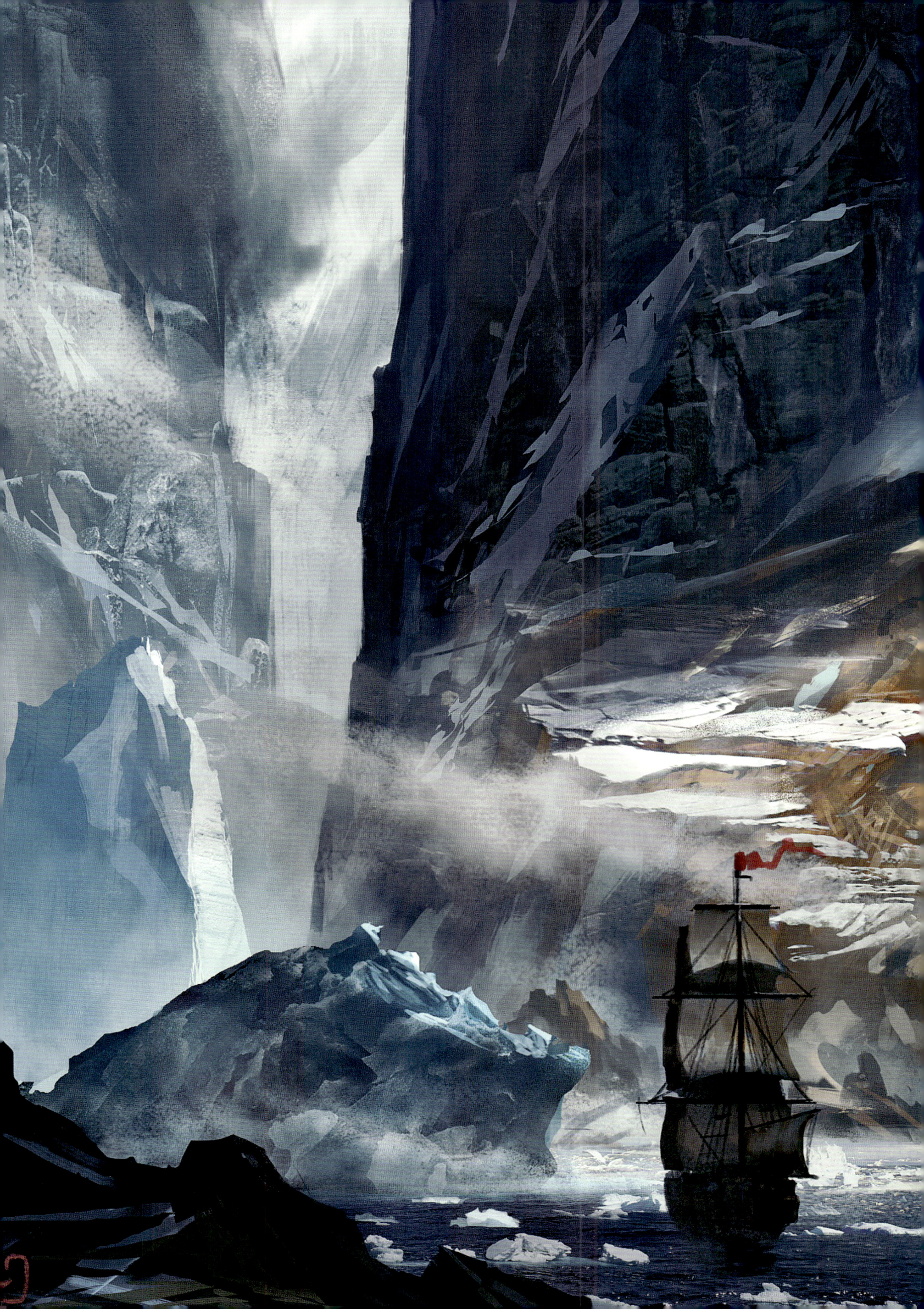

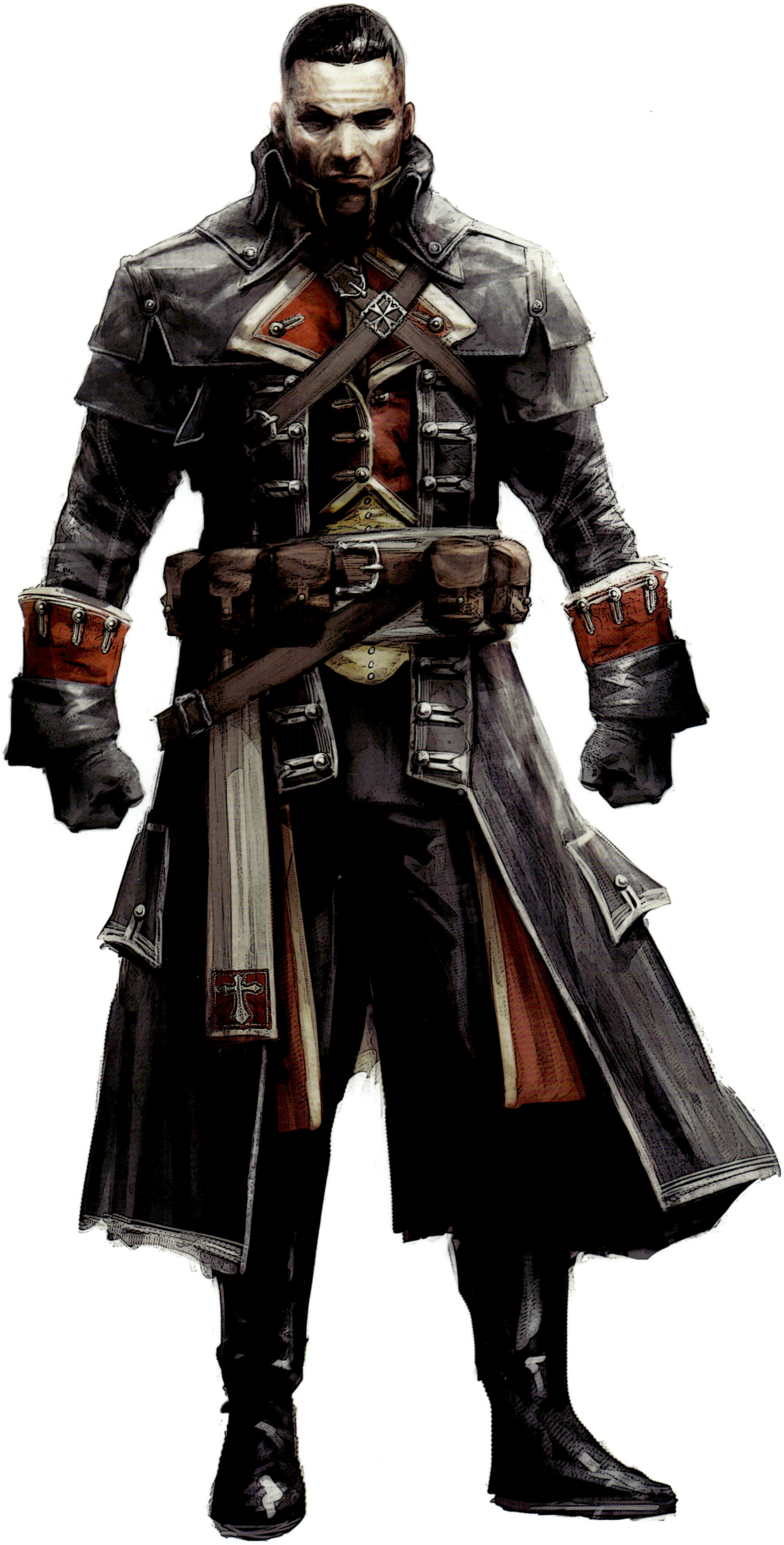

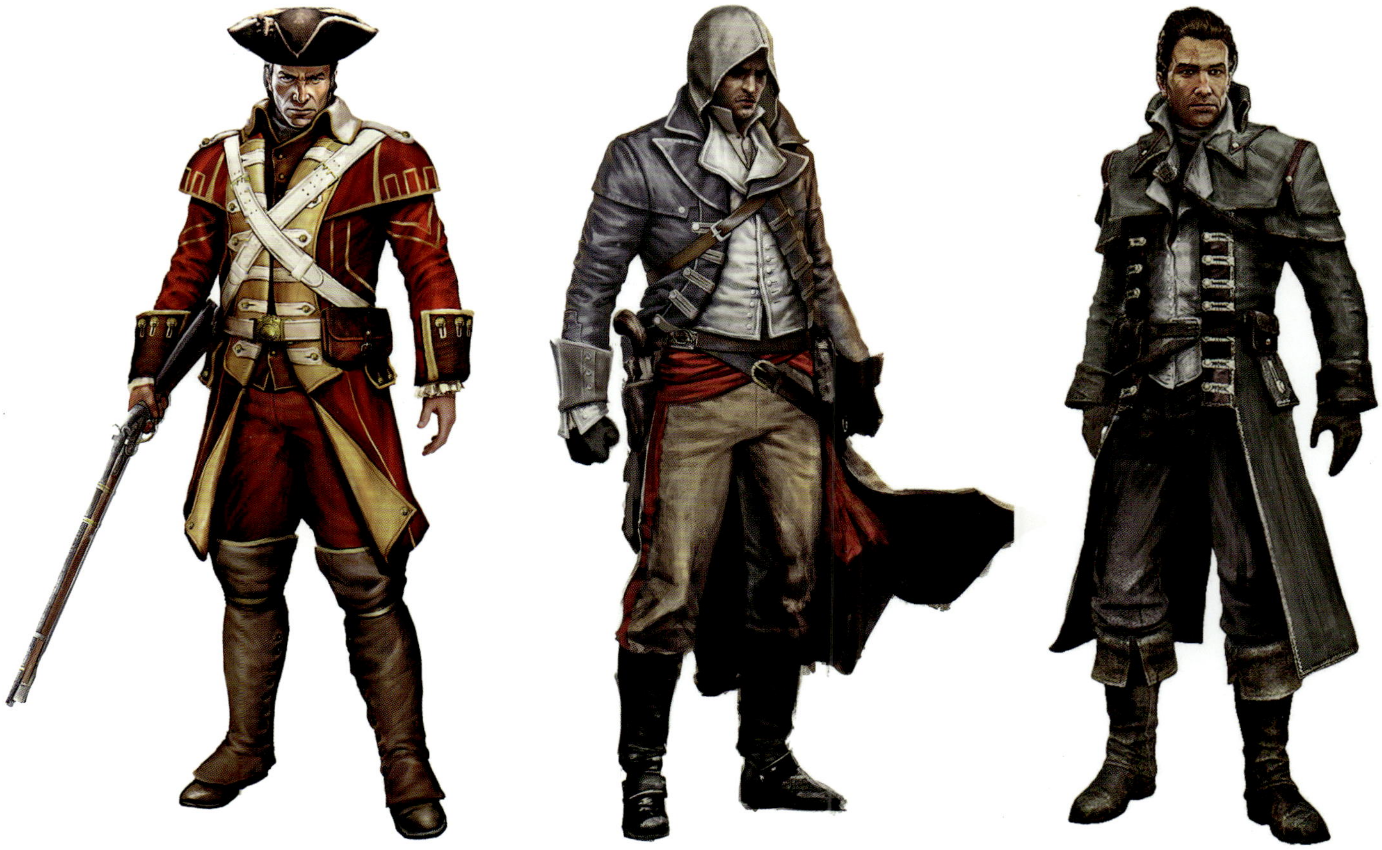

CHANGING SIDES

At the beginning of *Assassin's Creed: Rogue*, Shay Cormac was a member of the Brotherhood, but even the opening narration, peppered with nods to the Brotherhood's creed, made it clear that dark times lay ahead. The early hours go a long way toward establishing the friendships he had developed with his peers and teachers among the Assassins, making the tragedy of his betrayal more potent.

To reflect the shift, the team paid particular attention to narrative and dialogue-driven scenes, where Shay's changing personality could be communicated through voice, action, and appearance. "Shay's transition from an enthusiastic, loyal, almost naive young Assassin to a member of the Templar Order comes from his experiencing many inner conflicts, tough questions, and deadly situations," says Eddie. "In bringing this experience to *Rogue*, we used a cinematic approach in every scene, carefully matching Shay's emotions to the environment composition, weather, and light conditions."

Beyond cinematic sequences, the developers relied heavily on both character art and animation to communicate Shay's transition into a Templar. "One of the main goals for the art team was to show and support Shay's development visually, and we achieved this by using different outfits and animations as Shay's personality and allegiance changed," Eddie says.

In a medium as visual as video games, significant character evolution needed to be clearly expressed whenever the player saw Shay onscreen. "The main theme we had for that was chaos versus order," Raphaël explains. "Visually speaking, *Rogue* was reminiscent of *Assassin's Creed*, as there was a clear contrast between the very human, organic presentation of the Assassin and the linear, boxy shapes that defined the Templar. You can see that reflected in Shay. Visually, we reinforced the personality and development of his character in the story through the use of composition, colors, and lines. If you look at the character design evolution for Shay, it's very clear: darker colors and straight lines." By his final appearance in Paris, Shay bears little resemblance to the jocular man we saw in the opening scenes, and his recitation of lines from the Templar induction ceremony act as a fitting counterpoint to the game's opening lines drawn from the Assassin's creed. Whether players choose to see the Templars in *Assassin's Creed: Rogue* in their traditional role as villains or—for once—as heroes, there's no doubt that Shay's change of allegiance had led him to a dark and lonely place.

OPPOSITE: Shay's Templar outfit has a more structured, military look than his Assassin coat (Vincent Gaigneux).
ABOVE: Various Shay character art (Daniel Atanasov, Konstantin Kostadinov and Vincent Gaigneux, Konstantin Kostadinov).

THE MIDST OF DISASTER

Given Shay's close connection to his Assassin brothers, the story needed a dramatic event to trigger the sudden change of heart and his eventual fall into the arms of the Templars. History offered a calamity of fitting import to justify Shay's betrayal.

The 1755 Lisbon earthquake lined up perfectly with the desired time period of *Rogue*. The devastating natural disaster was one of the most deadly in recorded history, with tens of thousands believed to have died and nearly the entire city laid to waste. The event had political repercussions for the entire country of Portugal, curbing the Empire's efforts at colonization.

In the world of Assassin's Creed, the earthquake was triggered by Shay, who had been sent there at the behest of his Assassin Mentor to retrieve an artifact of the First Civilization. While the consequences were unintended, Shay would come to blame himself, Achilles, and the Assassins for their recklessness and turn from their path.

The Lisbon earthquake is one of the most astonishing moments in the history of the franchise. The horror of the city's fall is accentuated by the celebrations that precede it, as the earthquake occurred during the festival of All Saints' Day. "Lisbon is an Old World city with solid stone buildings, great landmarks, and mighty cathedrals—a perfect theater to experience the destructive power of nature and the Assassin Brotherhood's ambitions," Eddie says. An intense freerunning sequence sends Shay fleeing for safety through a city falling apart all around him. "To place the player in the very center of the disaster, we used shaking cameras, a panicked crowd, collapsing buildings, smoke, and fire," Eddie continues.

Shay's return to America shatters his connection to the Assassin Brotherhood and leads to his subsequent dismantling of the very organization he once served. The aftermath of Lisbon's disaster had a profound effect on the conflict between Assassins and Templars. As New York's chapter of Assassins is brought down by Shay, it paves the way for the rise of a Templar rite that would affect the American Revolution to come.

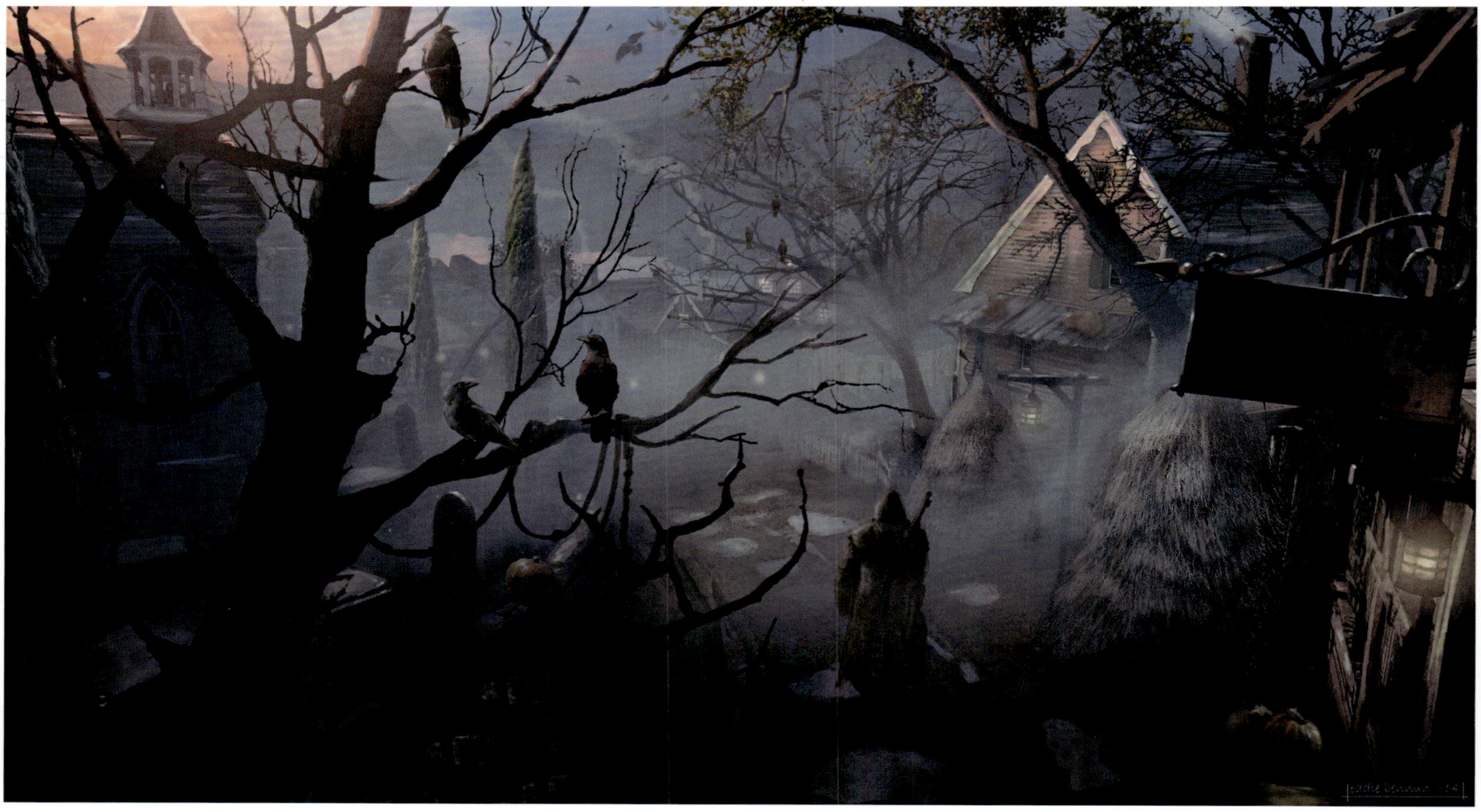

ABOVE: Artwork of Sleepy Hollow at sunrise (Eddie Bennun).
OPPOSITE: The collapse of Lisbon (Diana Kalugina).

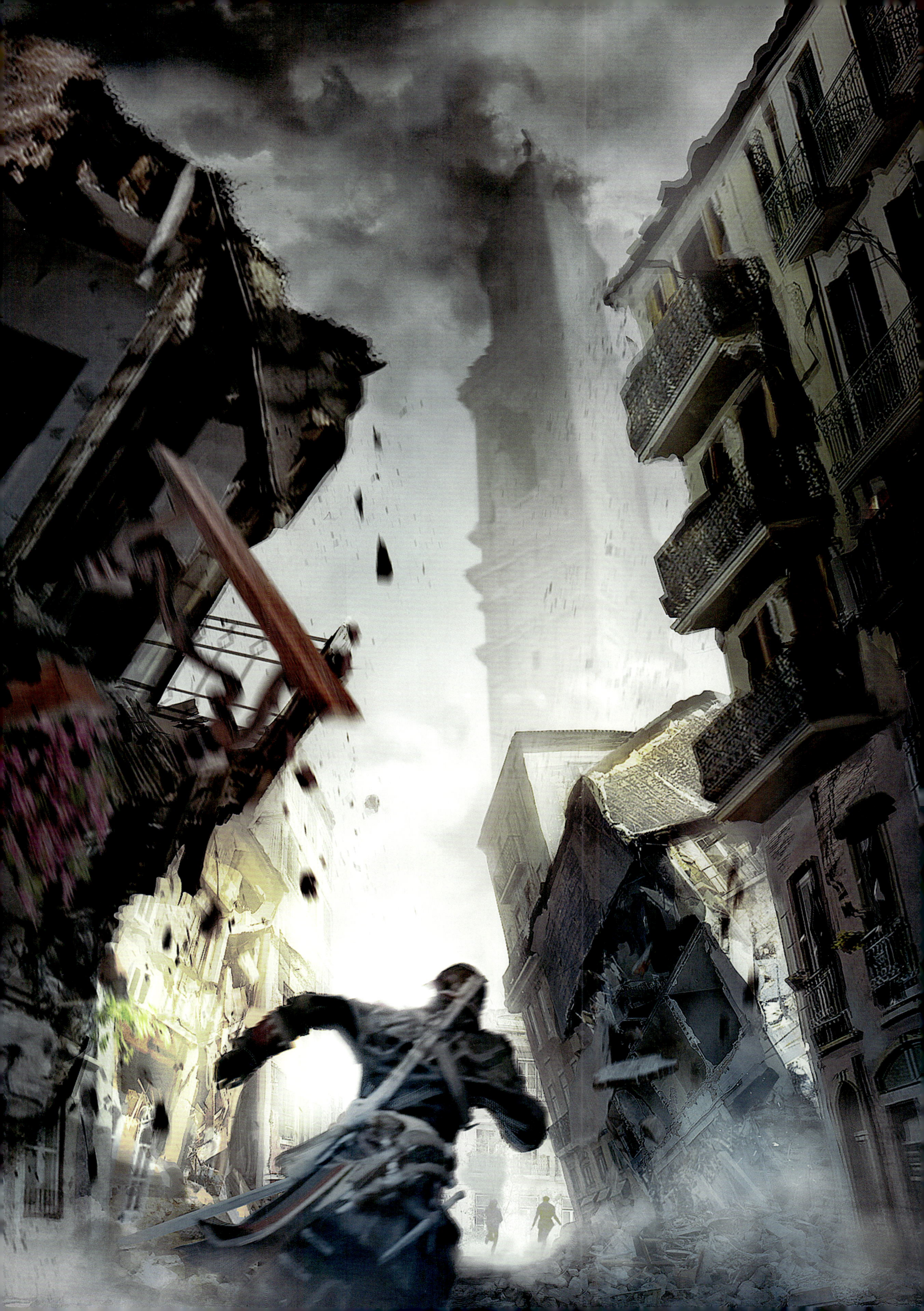

GOING NORTH

Rogue's story of betrayal and murder often left the player wondering if they were fighting for the right side. Shay's condemnation of the Assassins may or may not have been justified, but his cold and calculating assassination of former friends felt increasingly troubling as the game continued.

Few settings could have better reflected the antihero's emotional state than the seas of the North Atlantic, filled with craggy icebergs and harsh winds. The *Black Flag* team had embraced the lush vibrancy of the Caribbean islands, and the developers on *Rogue* created an open water setting at the other end of the artistic spectrum. Bright white snow and gray stone lined the shorelines, and the rare point of debarkation was usually to wander through the shattered and lonely hull of a long-forgotten ship.

Farther south, the pristine River Valley was a new experiment in Assassin's Creed environment design. The collection of interconnected rivers alluded to the Hudson River Valley but with only a tenuous connection to real geography. Tight waterways demanded careful ship navigation, but the numerous small ports and landing spots provided land exploration reminiscent of the Frontier forests of *Assassin's Creed III*. "We wanted to give the player an enhanced exploration experience in the American interior, so we populated the River Valley with settlements, forts, and native villages. Each of them was unique in theme and flavor, and many of them—such as Albany and Sleepy Hollow—still exist to this day," says Eddie. The art team looked to American pioneer experiences as inspiration to craft the valley and offer a semblance of green life and energy to contrast with the harsh nature of the North Atlantic sequences.

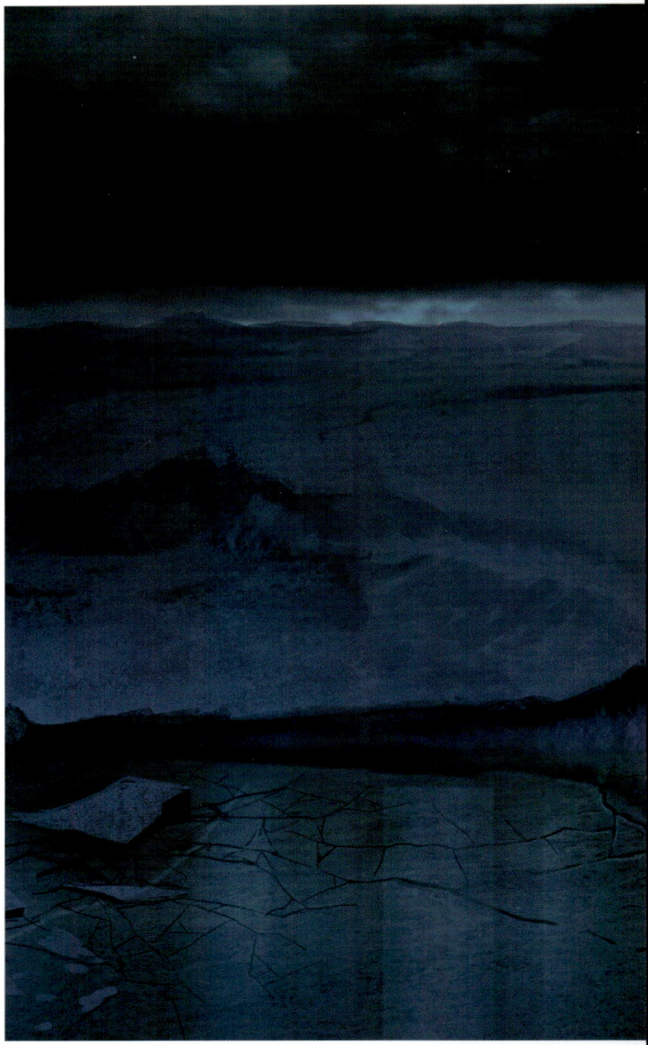

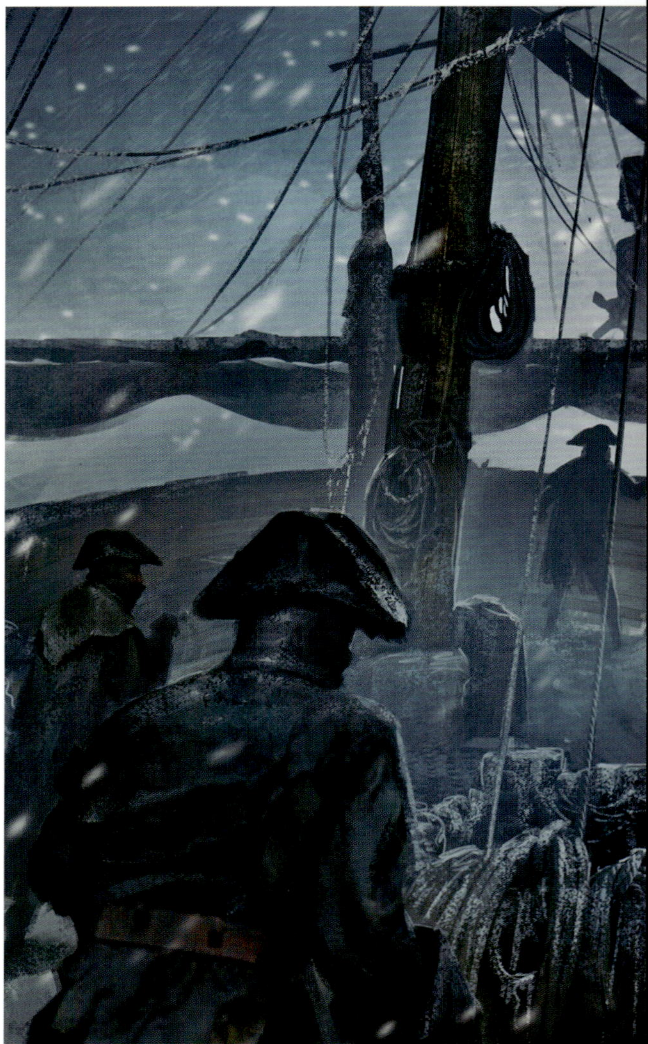

TOP RIGHT: Concept of a ship heading to the North Pole (Ivan Koritarev).
BOTTOM RIGHT: Artwork depicting the blinding snow and misty atmosphere of the Arctic (Ivan Koritarev).

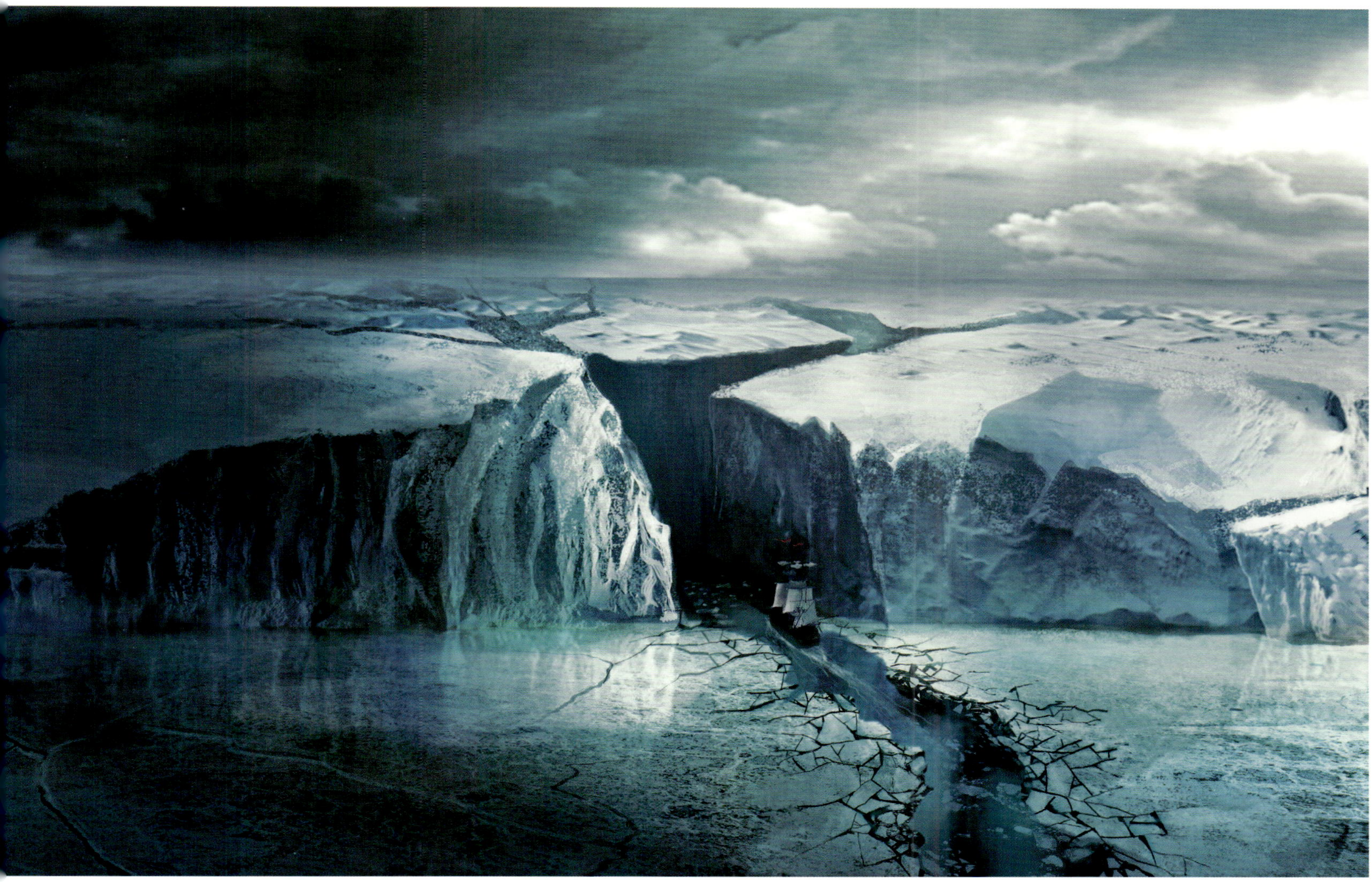

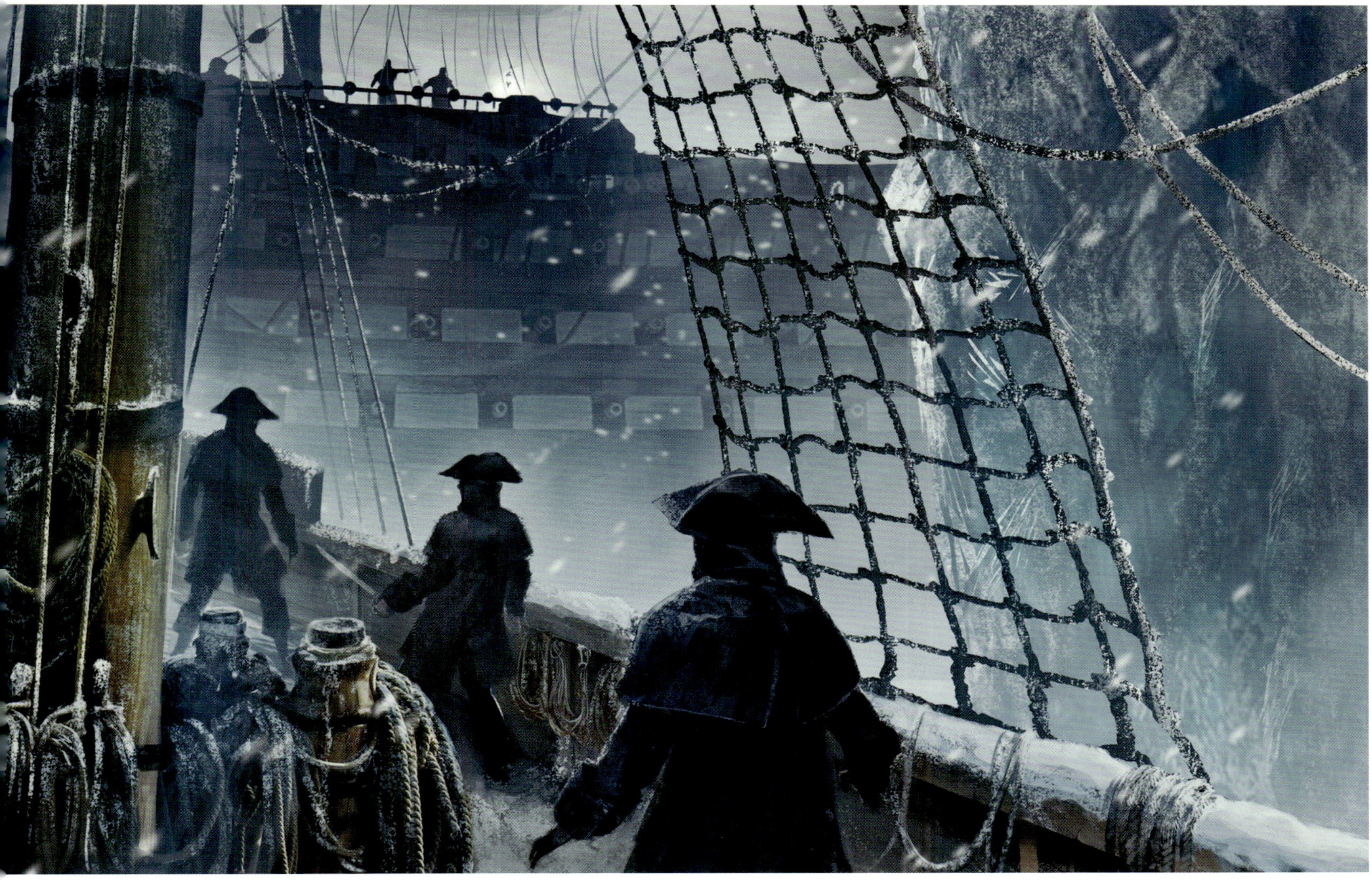

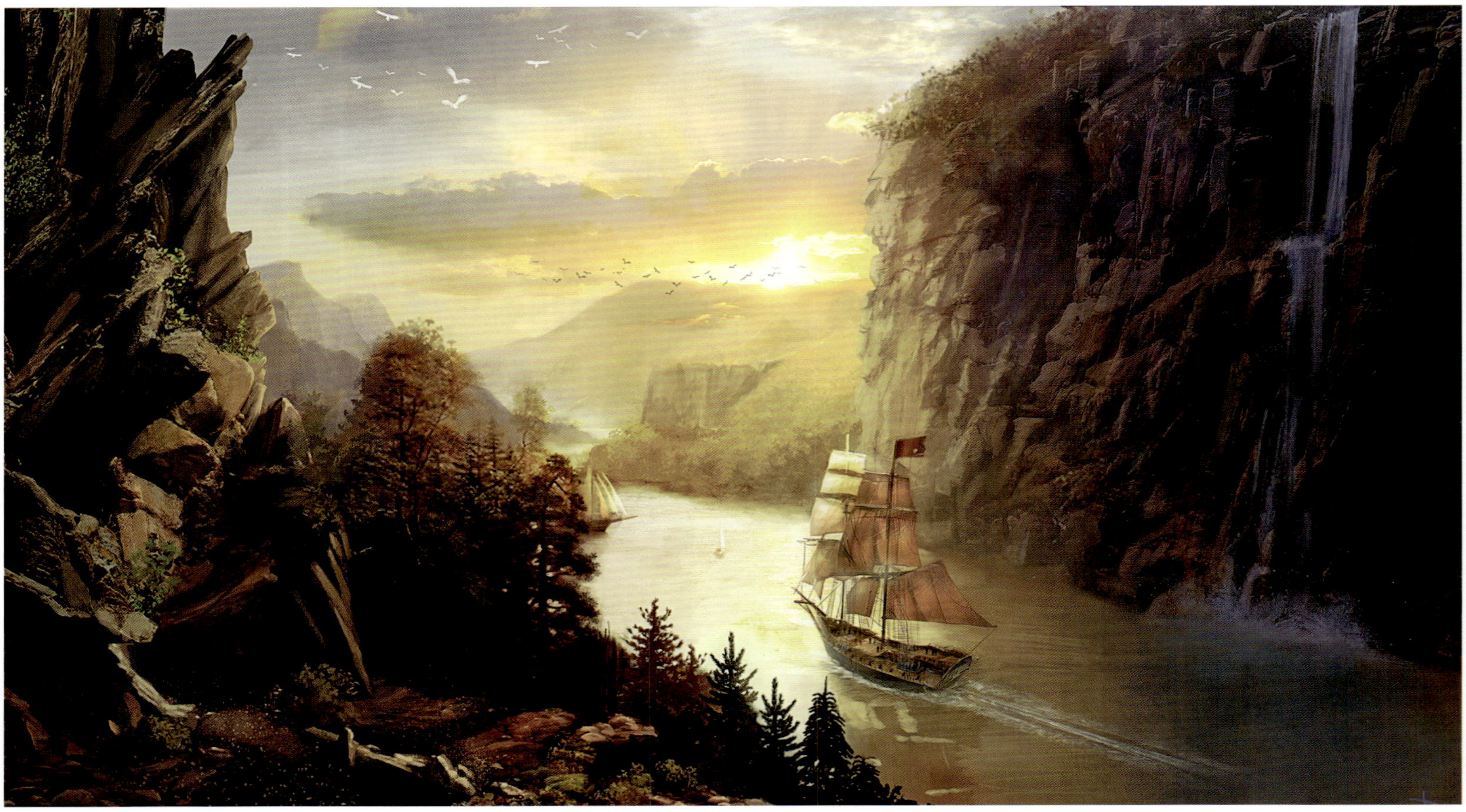

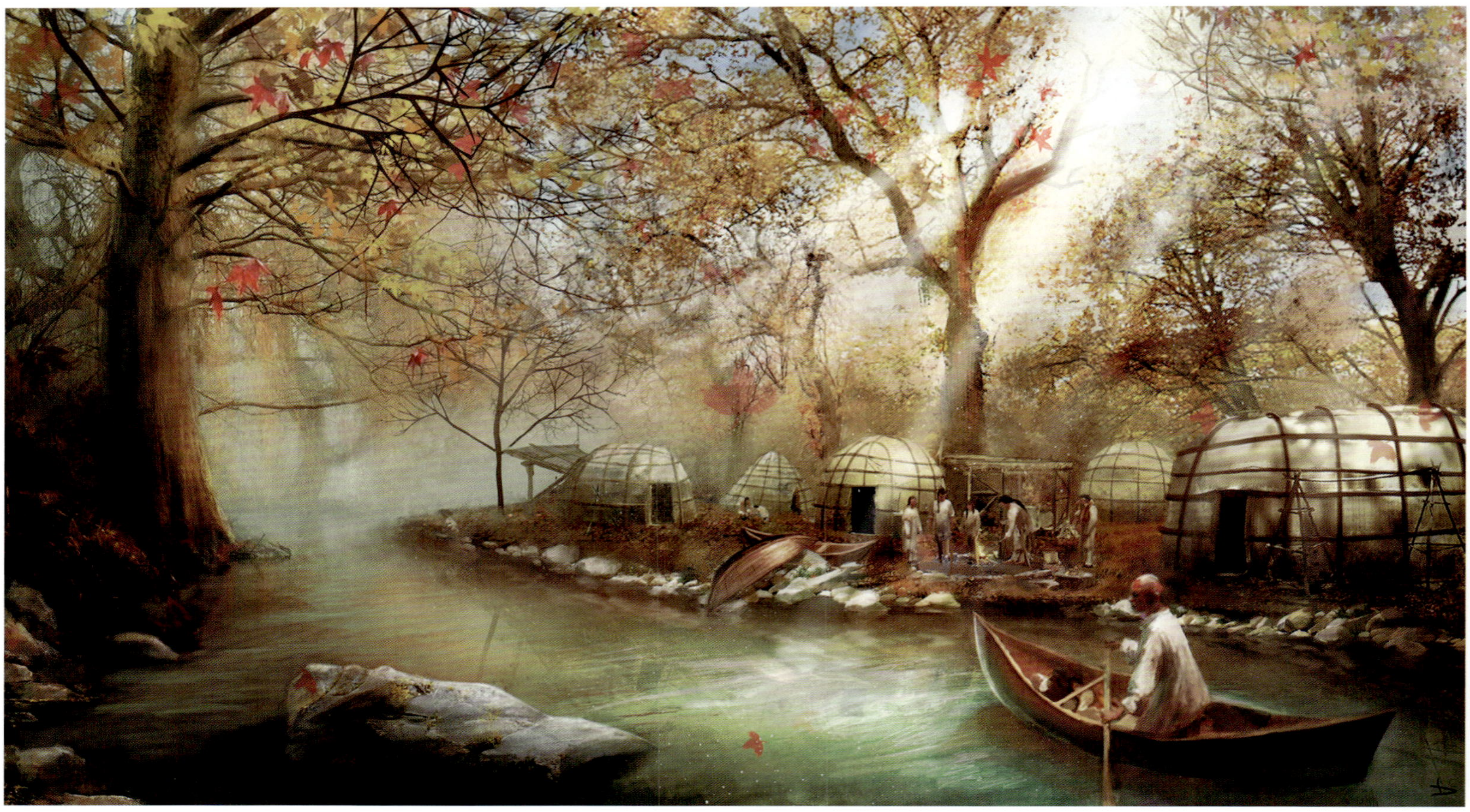

TOP: The foliage and sunny atmosphere of the River Valley contrast sharply with later Arctic scenes (Diana Kalugina).
BOTTOM: Artwork of a native village (Diana Kalugina).

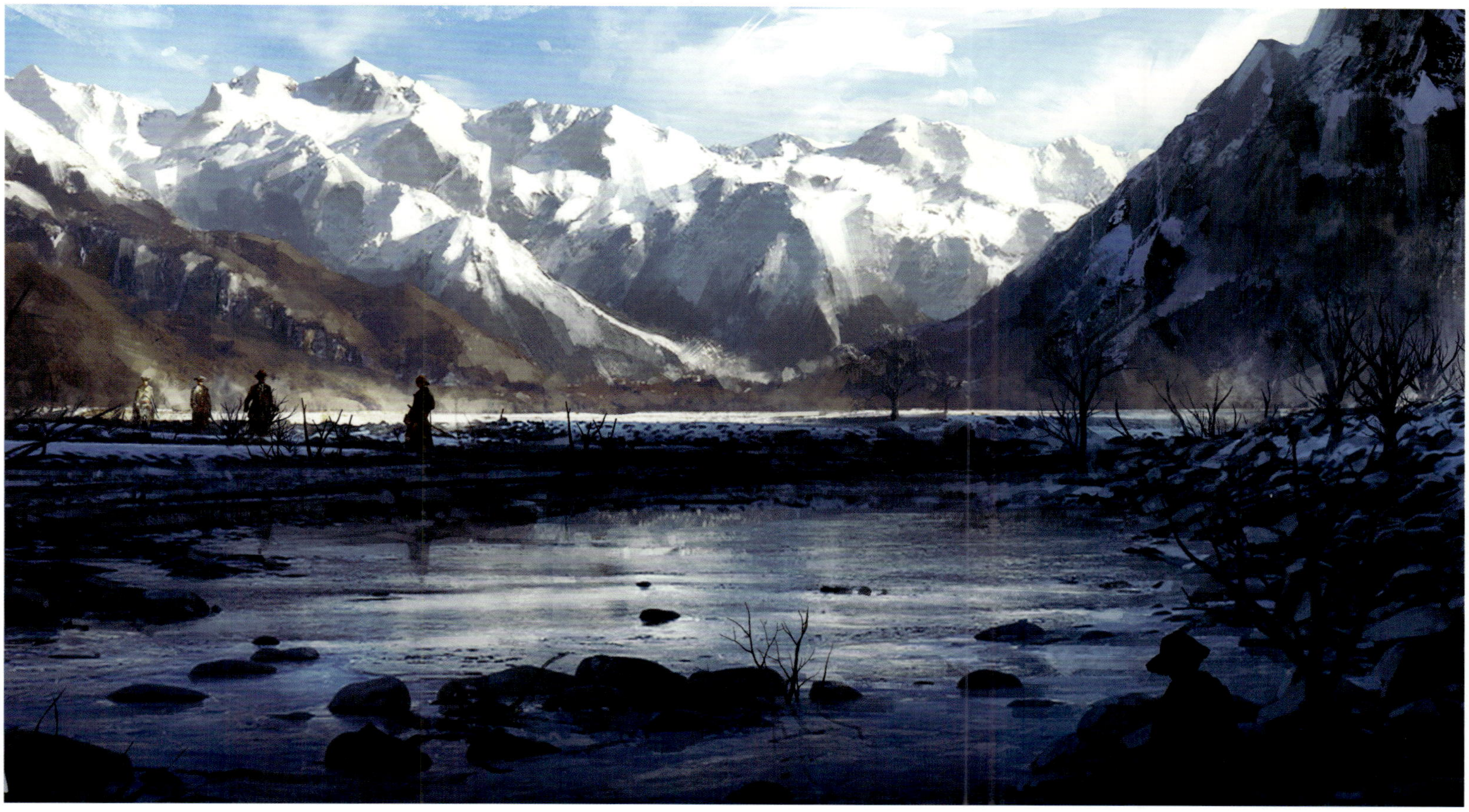

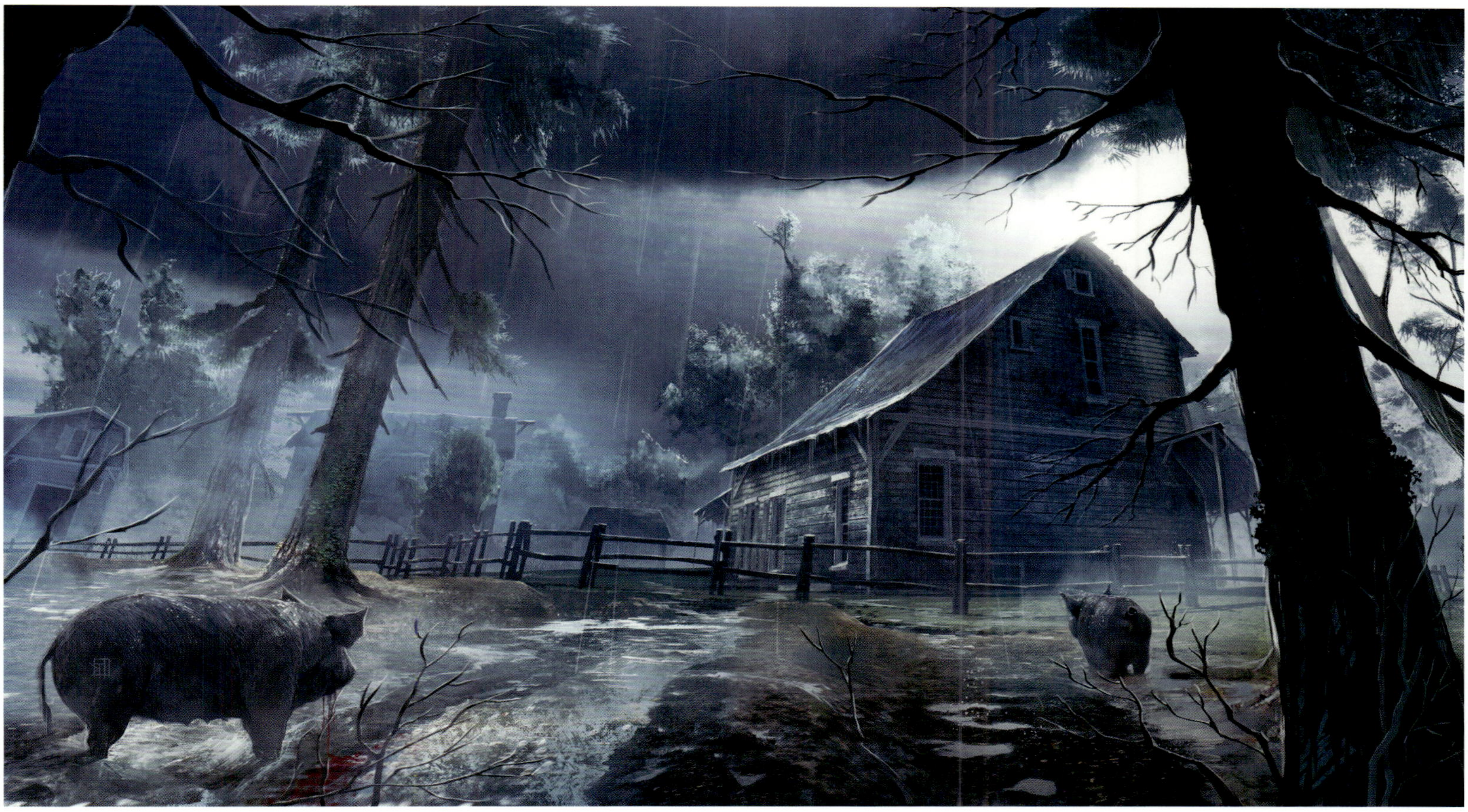

TOP: Concept of the floodplains (Max Qin).
BOTTOM: Stormy River Valley scene (Ivan Koritarev).

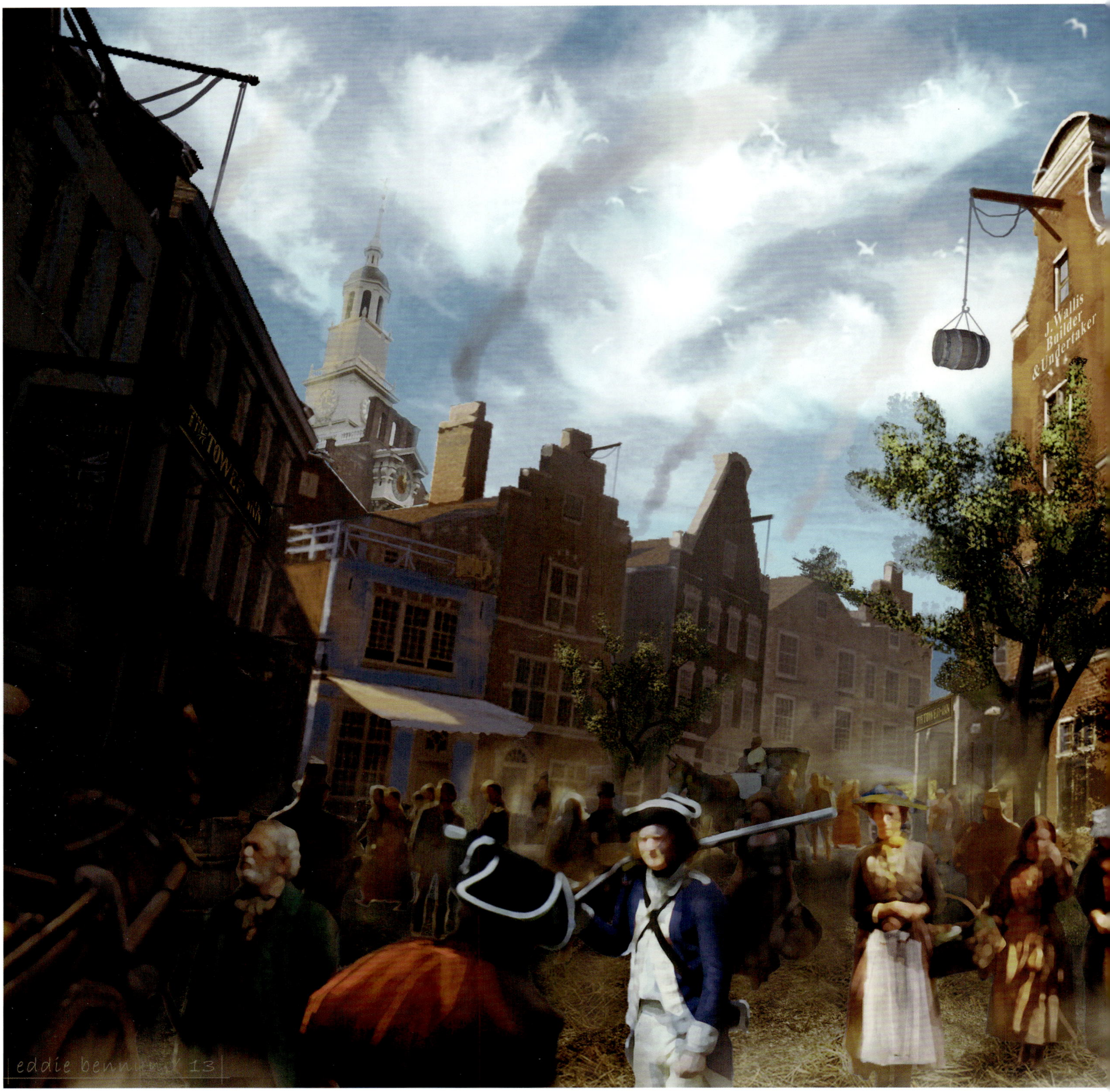

THESE PAGES: Artwork depicting a bustling New York street (Eddie Bennun).

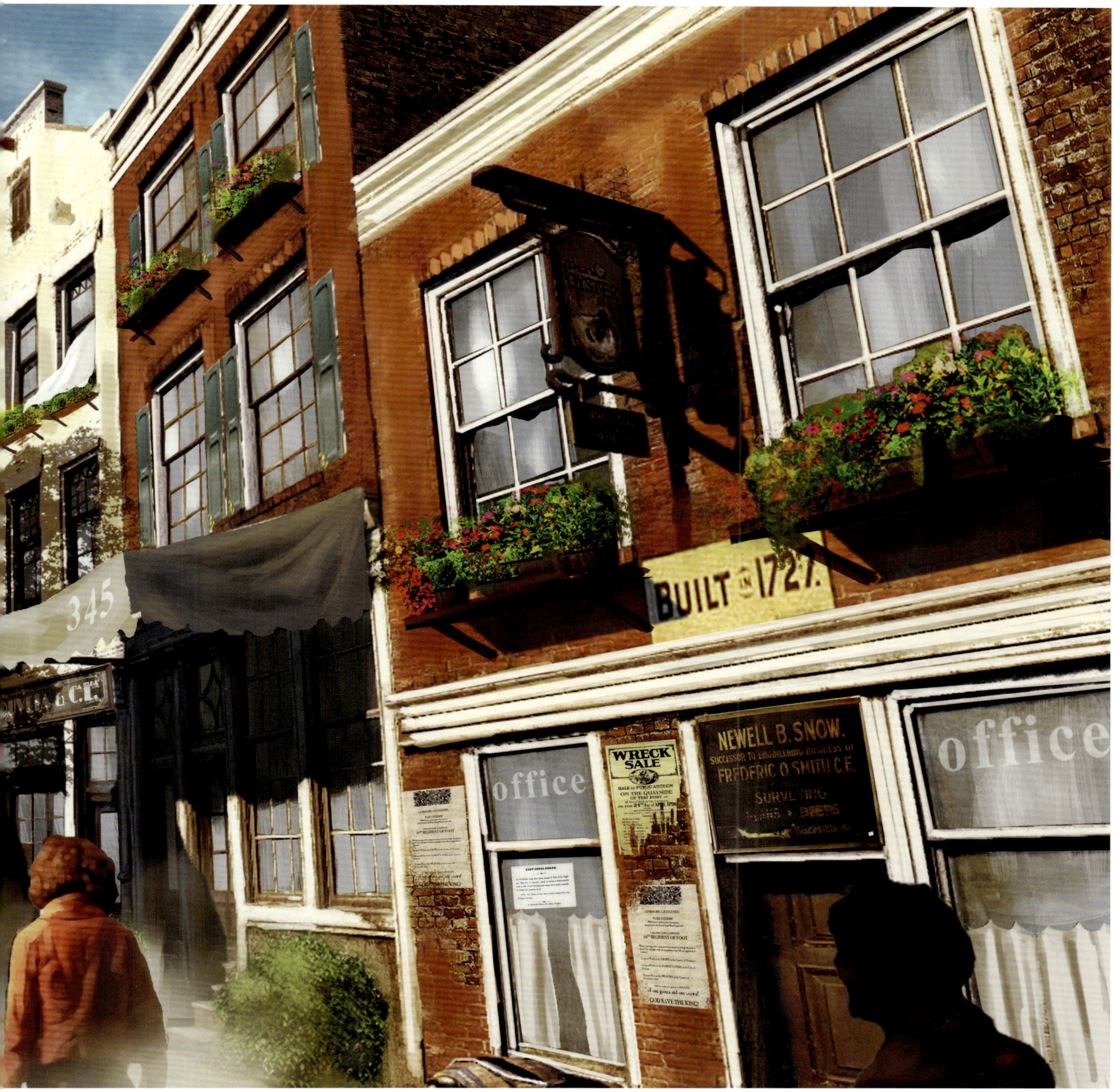

BACK TO MANHATTAN

Earlier in the series, *Assassin's Creed III* has already presented a portrait of New York as it appeared during the American Revolution, but *Rogue* offered the chance to visit several decades before. "The New York in *Rogue* is from an earlier period than that in *Assassin's Creed III*, and we wanted to express artistically the hopes and enthusiasm of the New World colony for a better life—a vivid, more colorful city that was growing in wealth," Eddie says.

In this still developing New York, the team also wanted to reflect the relative lawlessness of the period and populated the island city with dangerous gangs, all of whom were out to take Shay down. "We wanted to reflect the deadly New York gangs fighting for influence and territory," Eddie says. But in this history, those gangs had ties to the Assassins, leading to Shay often becoming the hunted party as he made his way through Manhattan's streets.

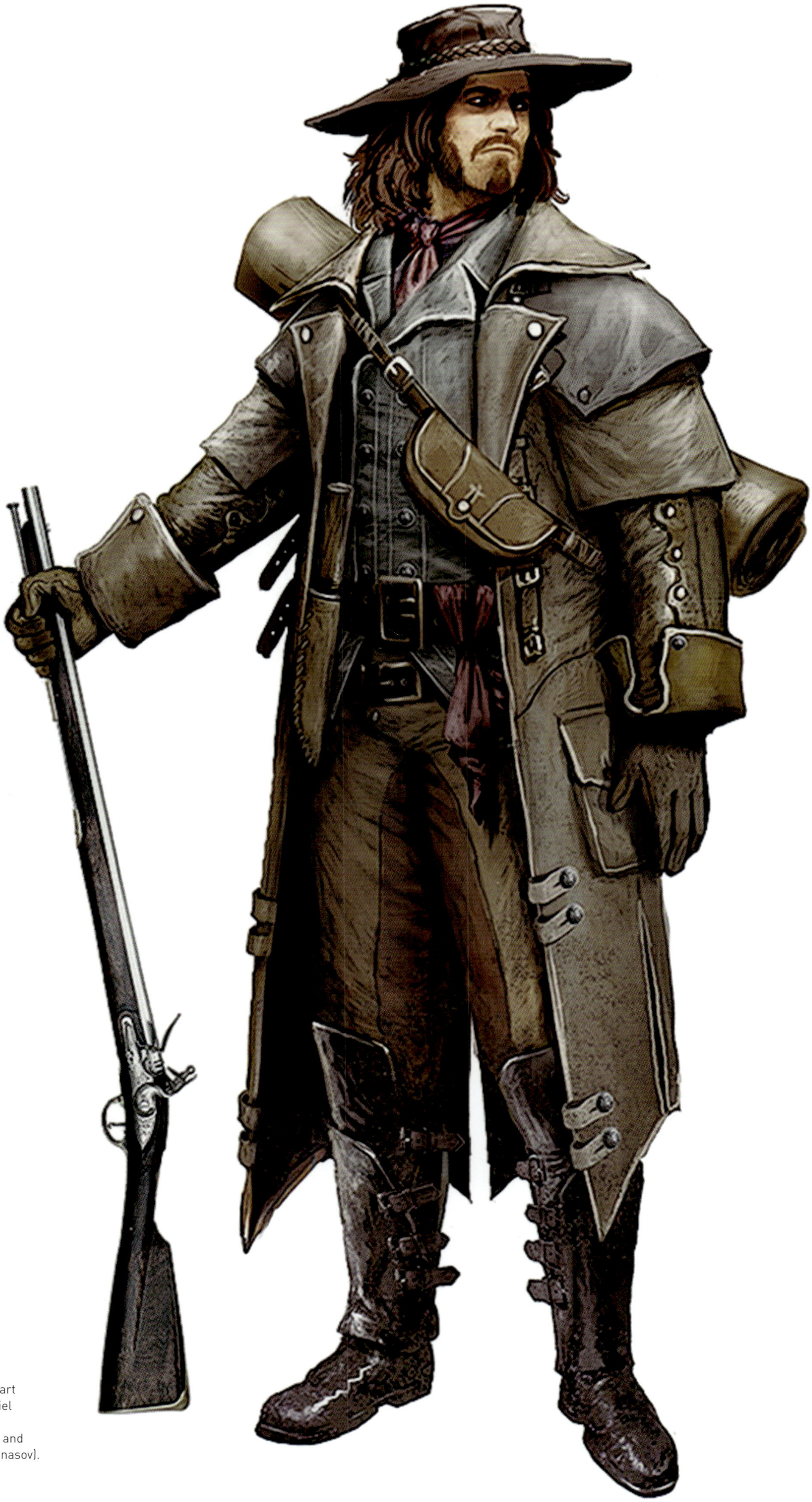

THESE PAGES: Character art of Christopher Gist (Daniel Atanasov), Jack Weeks (Konstantin Kostadinov), and Hope Jensen (Daniel Atanasov).

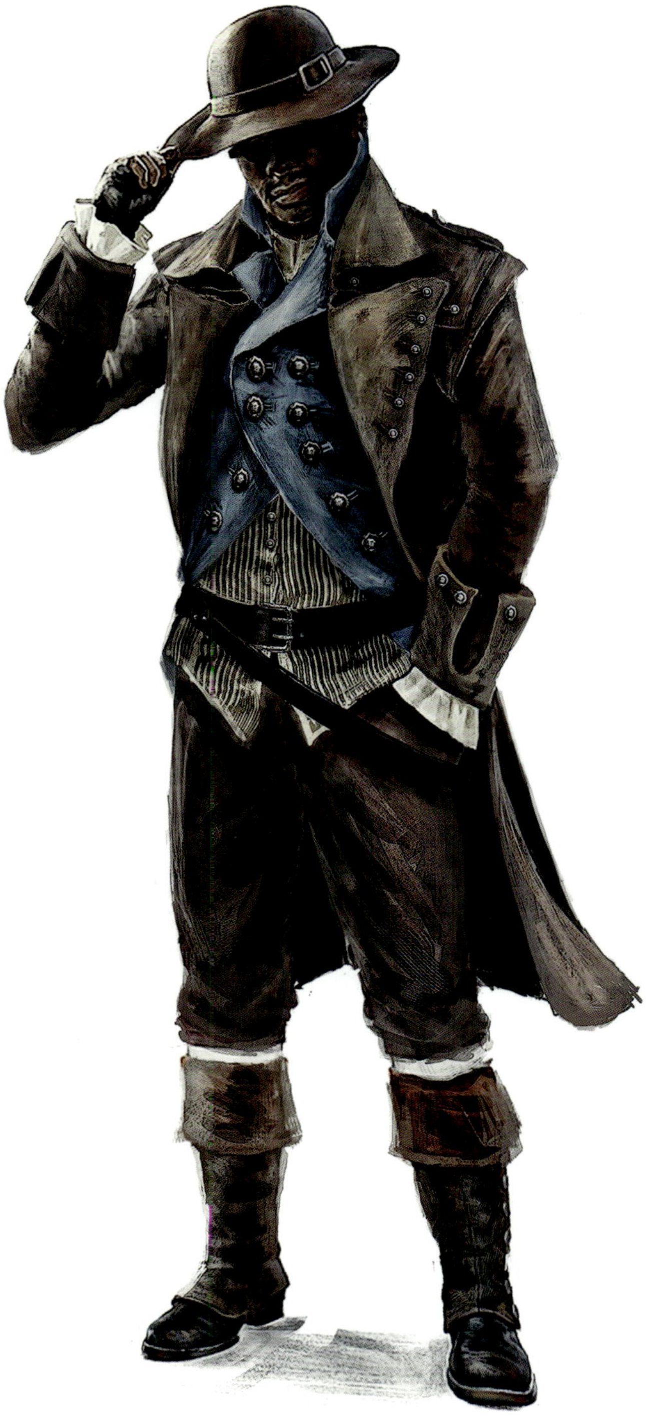

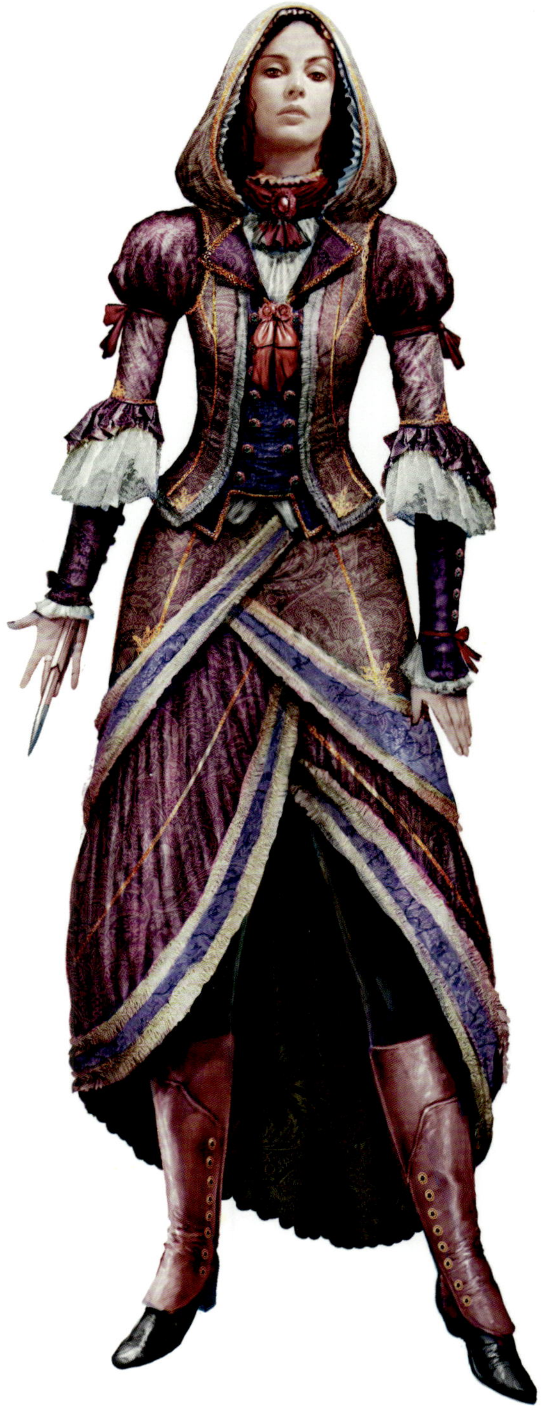

OPPOSITE SIDES OF THE WAR

More than many of the entries in the franchise, *Assassin's Creed: Rogue* presented a large cast of central characters that hailed from both sides of the Assassin and Templar conflict. The character art and conversations once again offered Ubisoft the chance to further refine the distinctions between the two competing groups.

On the Assassin side, characters like Liam O'Brien, Chevalier de la Vérendrye, and Achilles felt rooted in familiar Assassin iconography. A much older Adéwalé reinforced the men's resolve and commitment to the Brotherhood. Hope Jensen and Kesegowaase each moved further afield from the normal Assassin garb but maintained the obscuring hood in a nod to their commitment.

On the Templar front, varied individuals like Christopher Gist and Jack Weeks stretched the boundaries of a Templar's classic appearance, while William Johnson and Lawrence Washington felt more familiar in their immaculate suits. George Monro offered us the most sympathetic view of a Templar agent yet conceived. And, of course, the reappearance of Haytham Kenway provided a clear link to the events to come in the story of *Assassin's Creed III*.

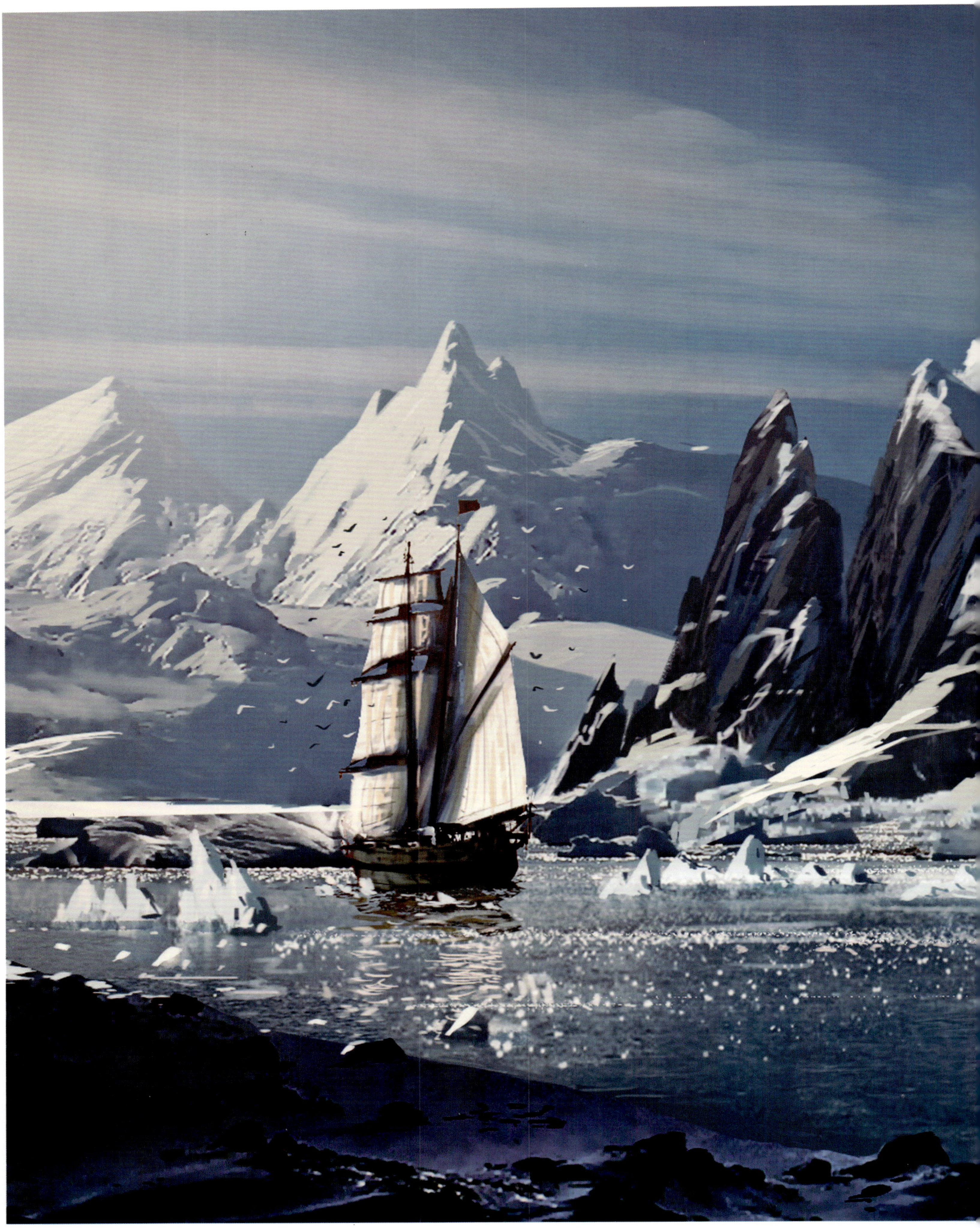

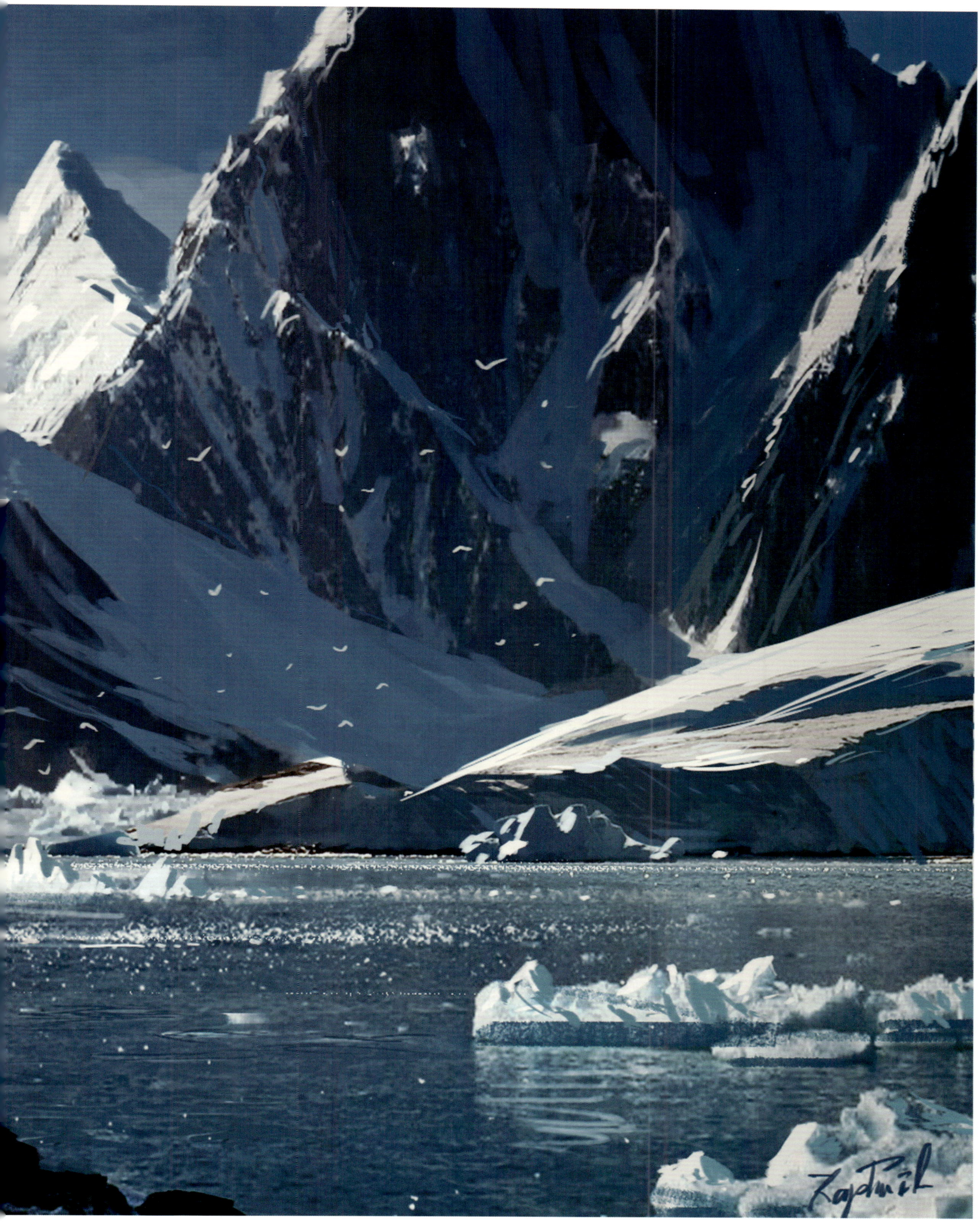

THESE PAGES: Although often a dark and bleak environment, the arctic offered stunning vistas of clear water and pure snow (Raphaël Lacoste).

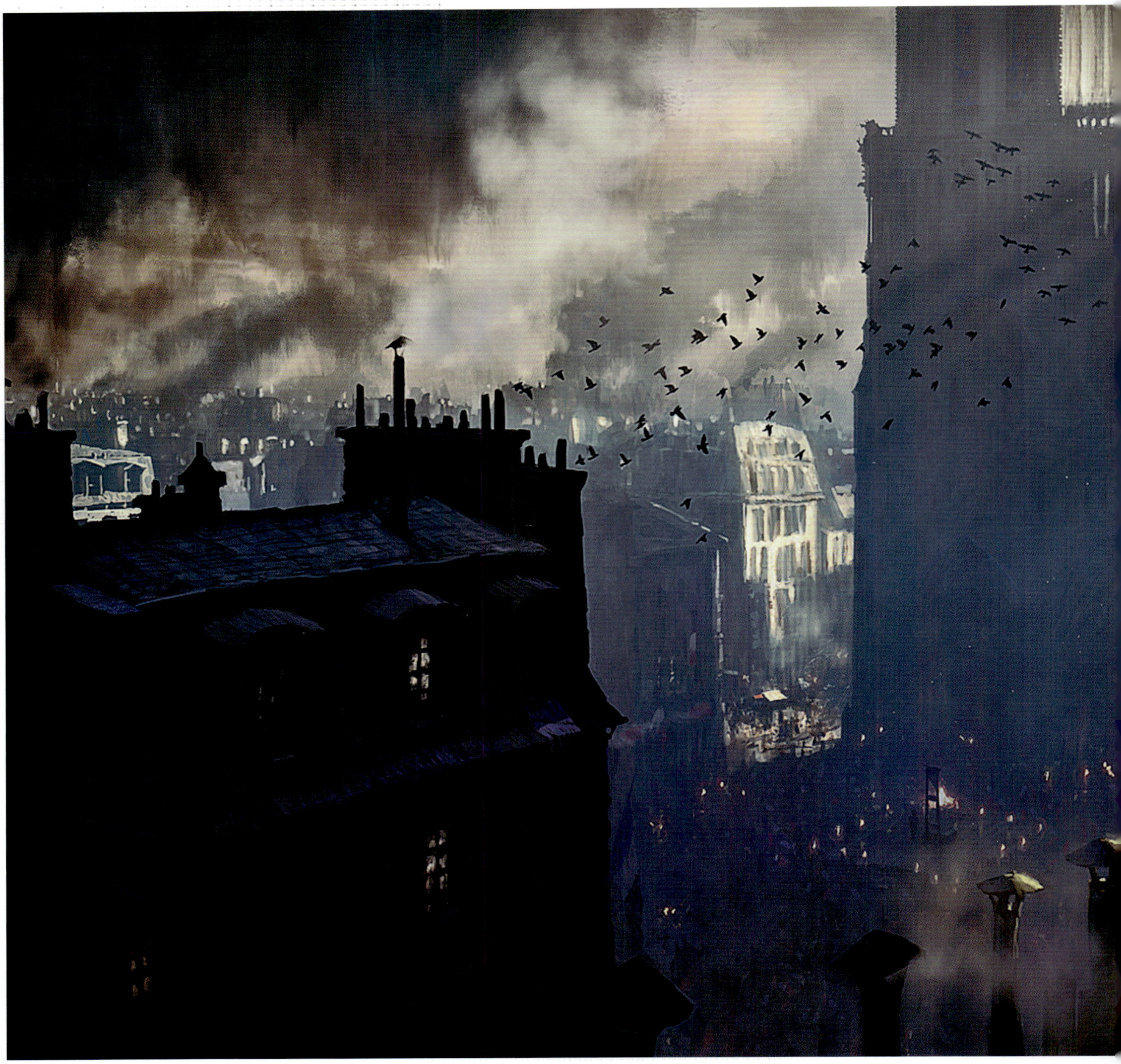

7 THE FRENCH REVOLUTION

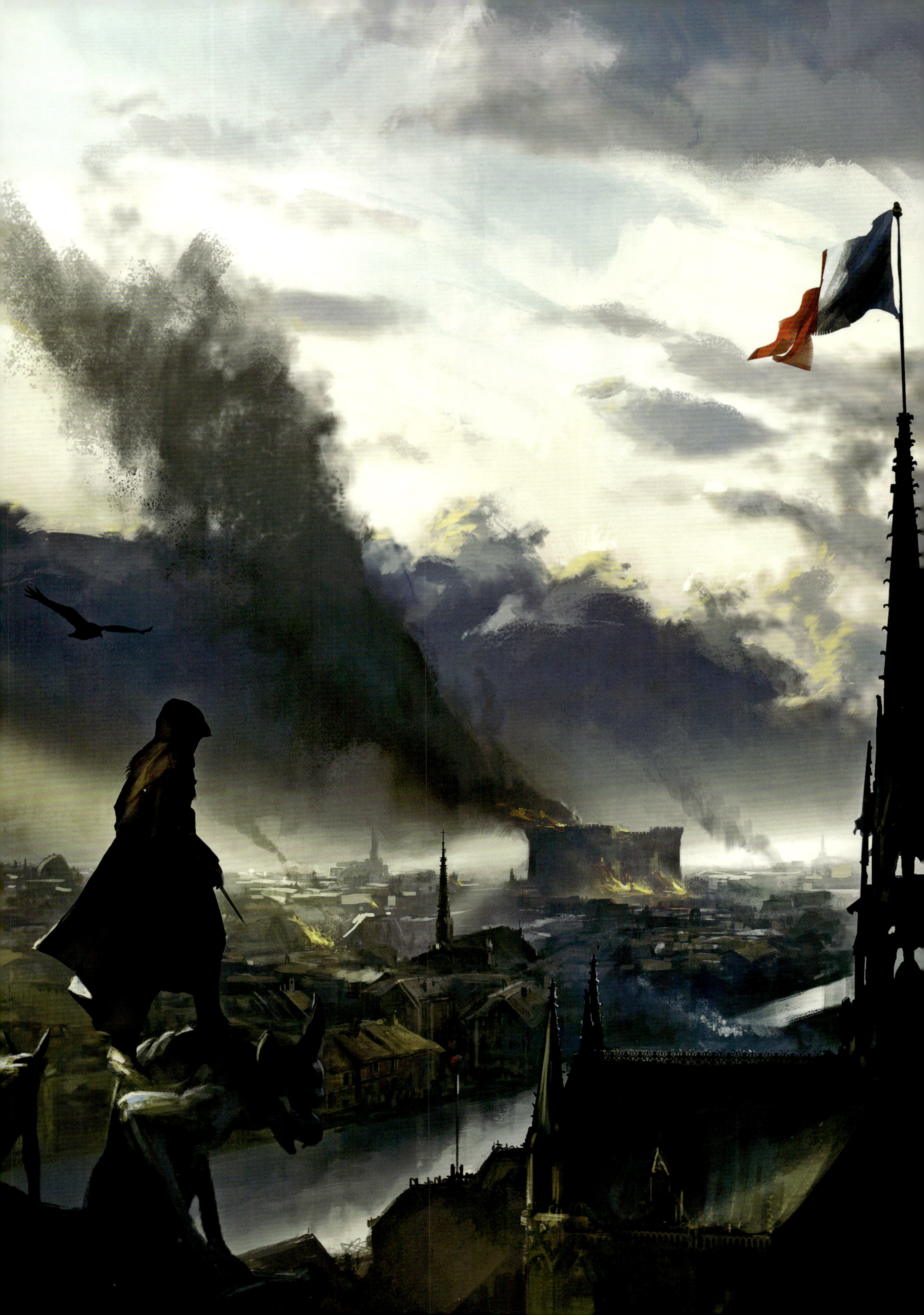

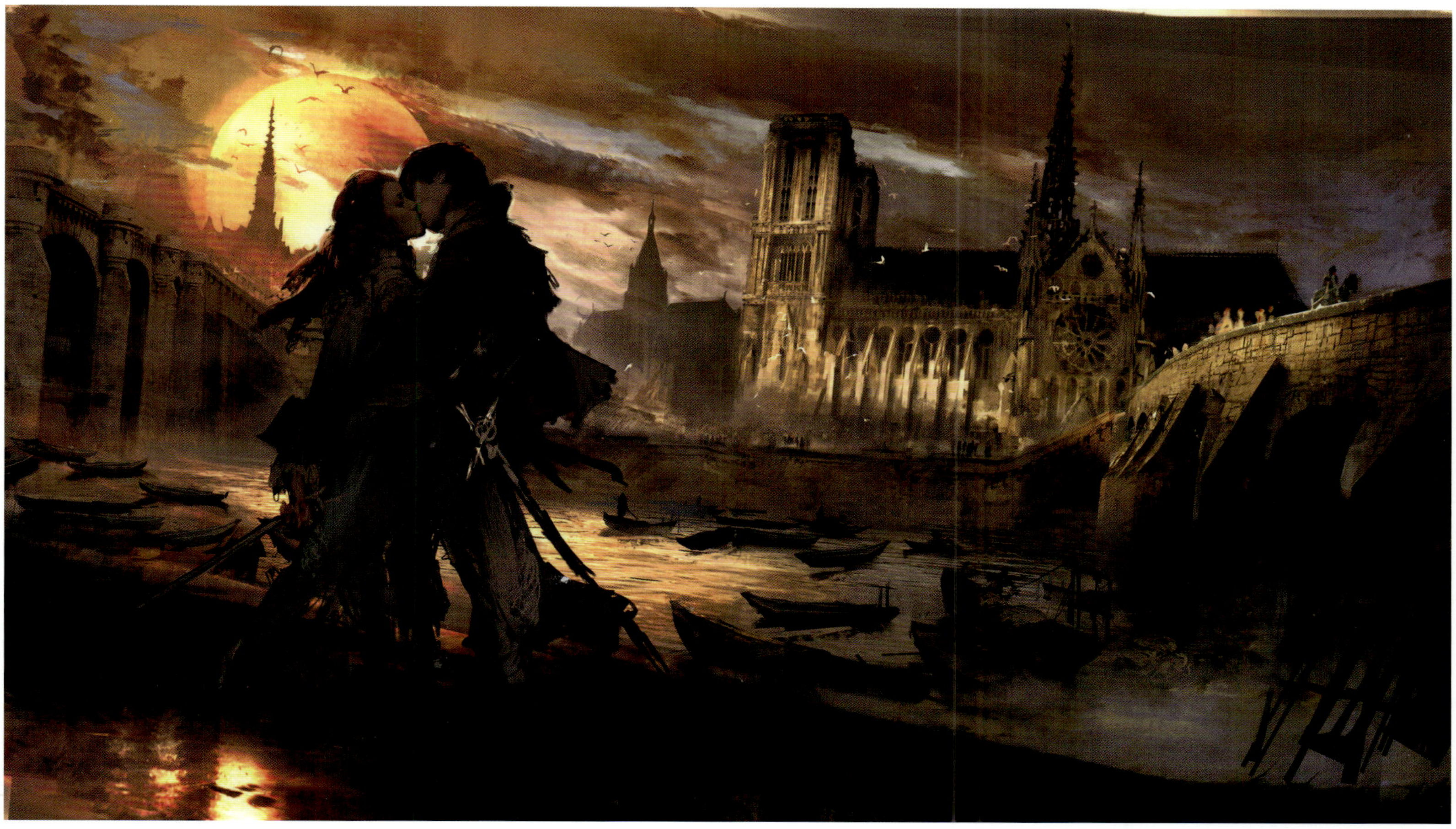

LOVE AND CHAOS

Assassin's Creed: Unity was set to be the first franchise entry built exclusively for a new generation of gaming platforms. With that new technical power came the responsibility for the art to keep pace. *Unity* needed to push the boundaries of what had come before and continue to expand the artistic potential of the series. Fortunately, the artists had a colorful palette with which to paint.

Knowing that *Assassin's Creed: Unity* would be a truly titanic artist c effort, the art team launched into concept work immeciately following the completion of *Assassin's Creed: Brotherhood*. Led by Mohamed Gambouz, the art team set to work shaping a vision for Paris in the midst of one of its most devastating moments of crisis.

The French Revolution could hardly be a more compelling and horrific tableau. By the time of open rebellion against the monarchy, Paris was one of the most beautiful cities in the world, filled with architectural wonder and a vibrant culture of music, food, and art. With the start of the revolution, the streets fell into anarchy, dominated by frenzied mobs and constantly shifting allegiances. The lines between rich and poor were laid bare, as nobles were dragged from their homes to the guillotine. Crime ran rampant, even as small sections of the city tried to ignore the chaos. In short, the artists couldn't have asked for more gripping imagery, but depicting the stark contrasts of violence and beauty would be a true challenge.

While the revolution played out over the course of the game, *Unity*'s other great artistic challenge was the depiction of a love story. The franchise had previously explored romantic entanglements for some of its protagonists, but no narrative thus far has been so fundamentally built on the relationship between two characters. Élise de la Serre and Arno Dorian met as children, and Arno's infatuation with Élise would ultimately drive his decisions, including his path into the Assassin Brotherhood. The star-crossed nature of their relationship drove *Unity*'s narrative, and the artistic links between the characters would go a long way toward making us root for them to make it against the odds.

PREVIOUS PAGES: Award-winning concept art contrasting the epic scale of the Notre Dame Cathedral with the guillotine below (Gilles Beloeil).
OPPOSITE: Smoke from the Bastille mixes with the heavy clouds in the sky, creating a dark, moody atmosphere (Martin Deschambault).
ABOVE: Artwork contrasting the devastation of the Revolution with the love between Arno and Élise (Maxime Desmettre).

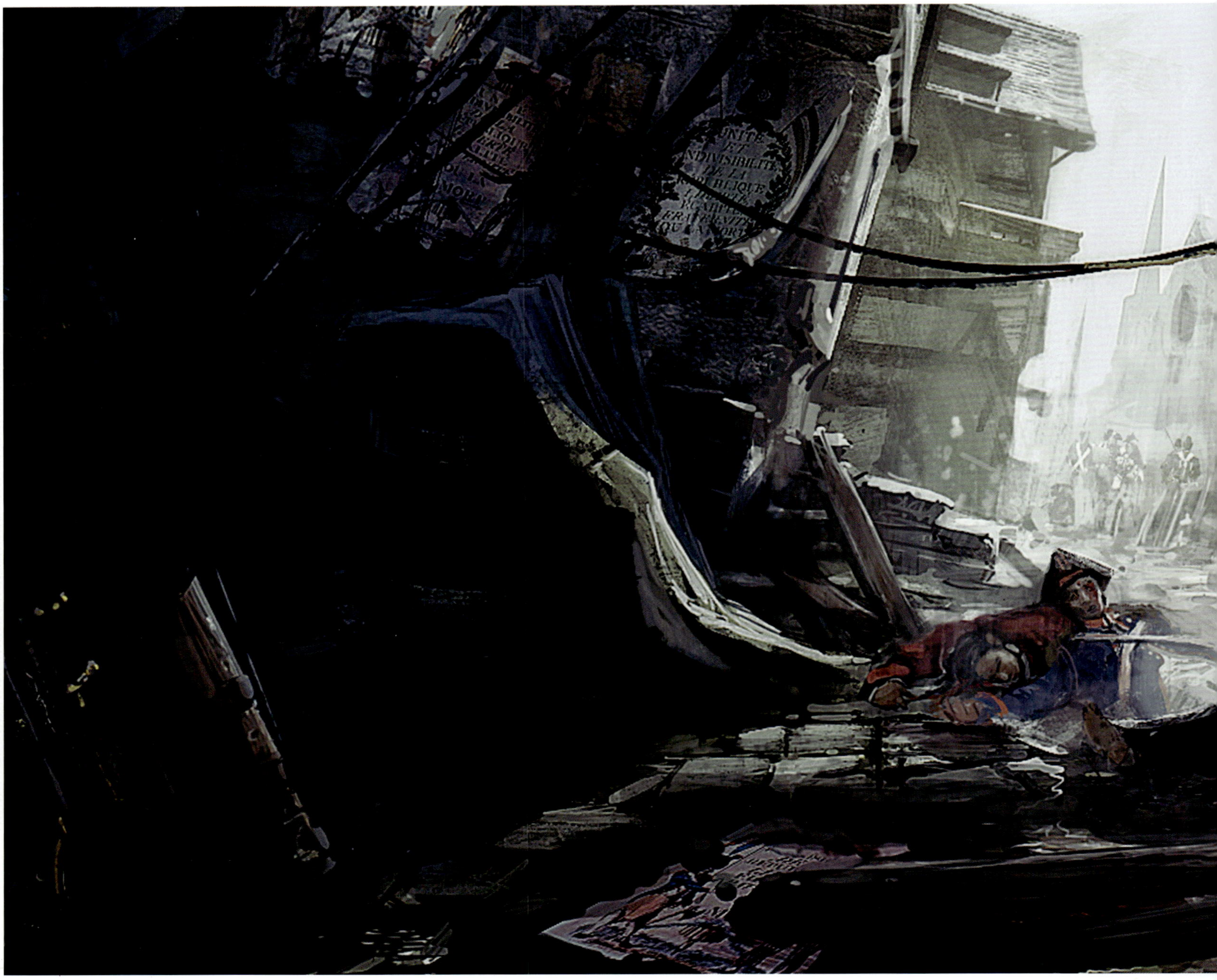

CAPITALIZING ON TECHNOLOGY

Assassin's Creed: Unity represented the franchise's first foray into an exclusively next-generation installment, and the art direction focused on taking full advantage of the new visual firepower. Mohamed charged the team to focus on three fundamental pillars that should be communicated in pieces created for *Unity*: light, smoke, and decay. "I pushed a mix of realism to increase believability, immersion, and stylization, as well as to give it some emotion and personality," Mohamed says. *Unity*'s artistic choices felt like a new step forward for the franchise, thanks to hardware that could more powerfully communicate the art team's vision. Paris had an edge of believability and immaculate detail. And the streets filled with crowded and lively revolutionaries were an artistic feat that couldn't have been accomplished on older hardware.

ABOVE: A nun prays over a martyr of the Revolution (Ludovic Ribardière).
OPPOSITE: Artwork depicting the violence of the mob (Ludovic Ribardière).

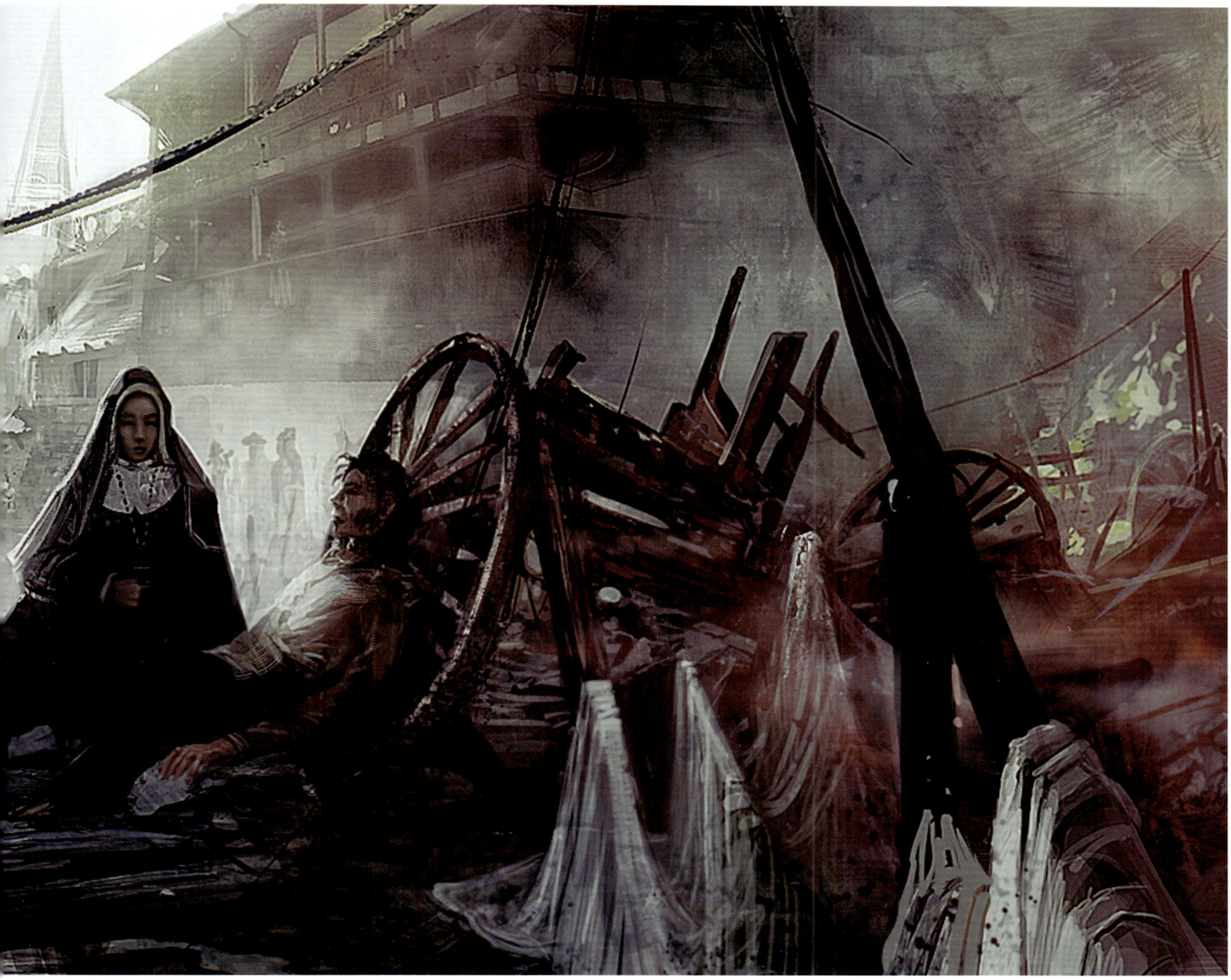

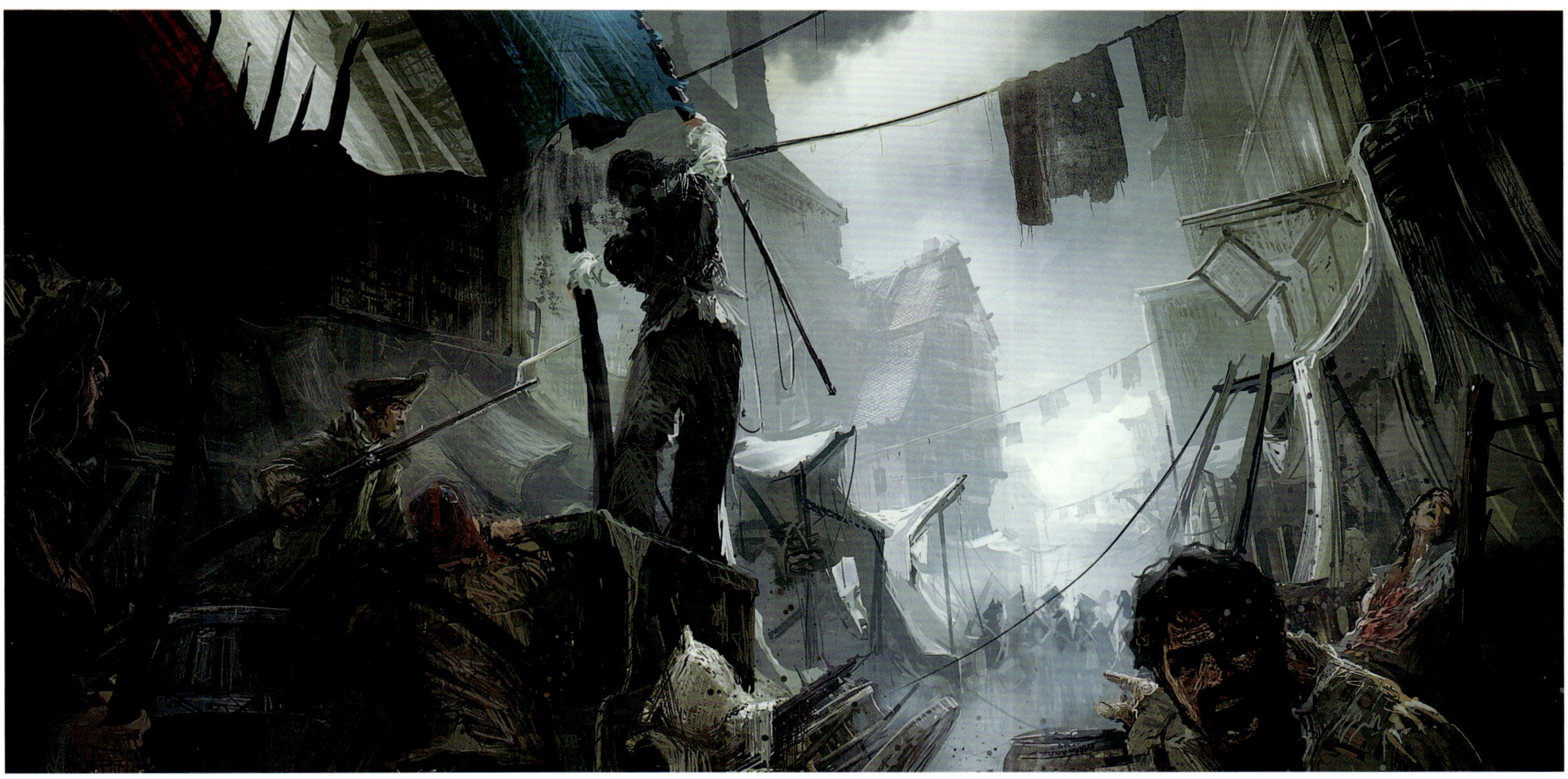

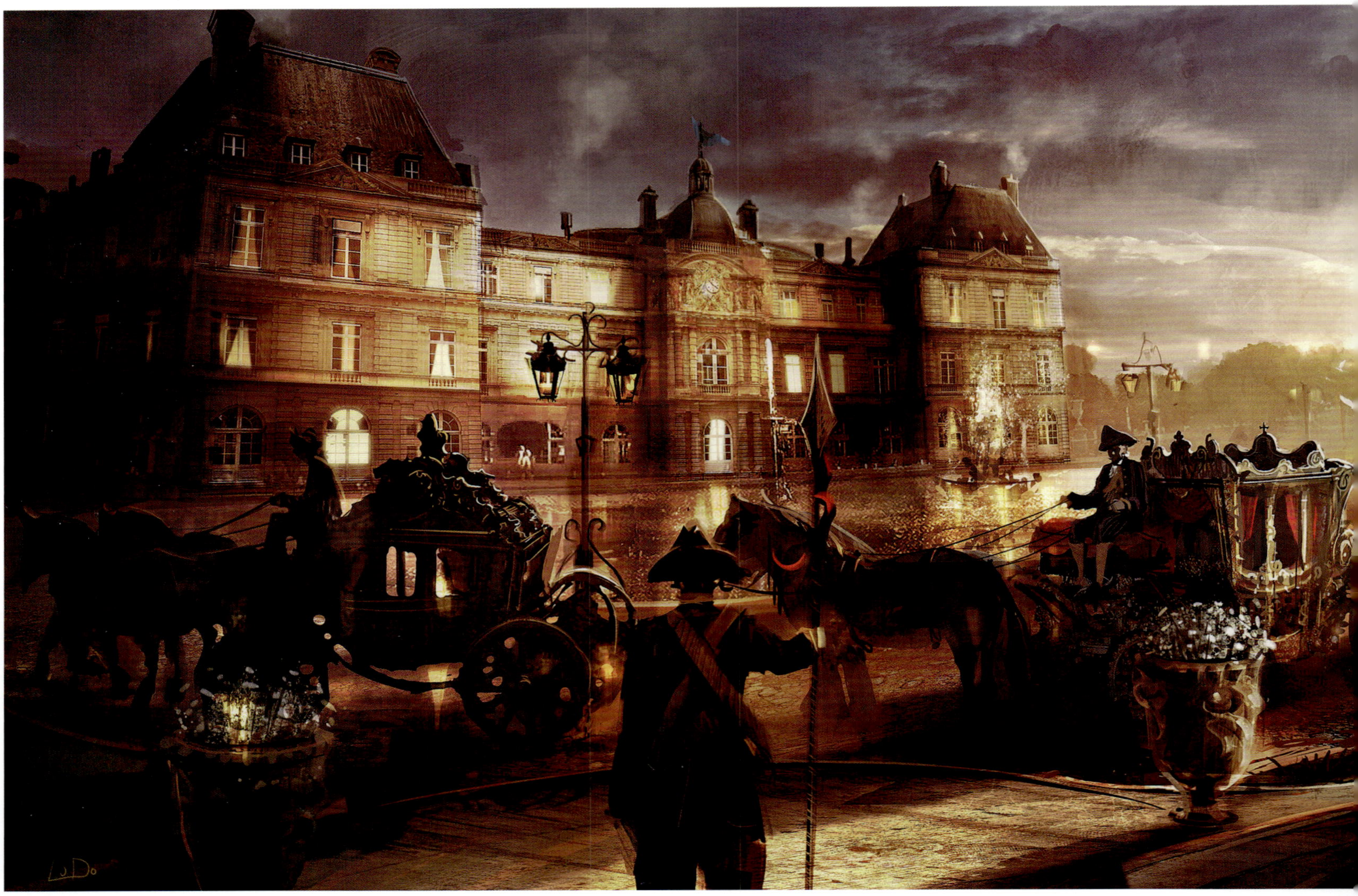

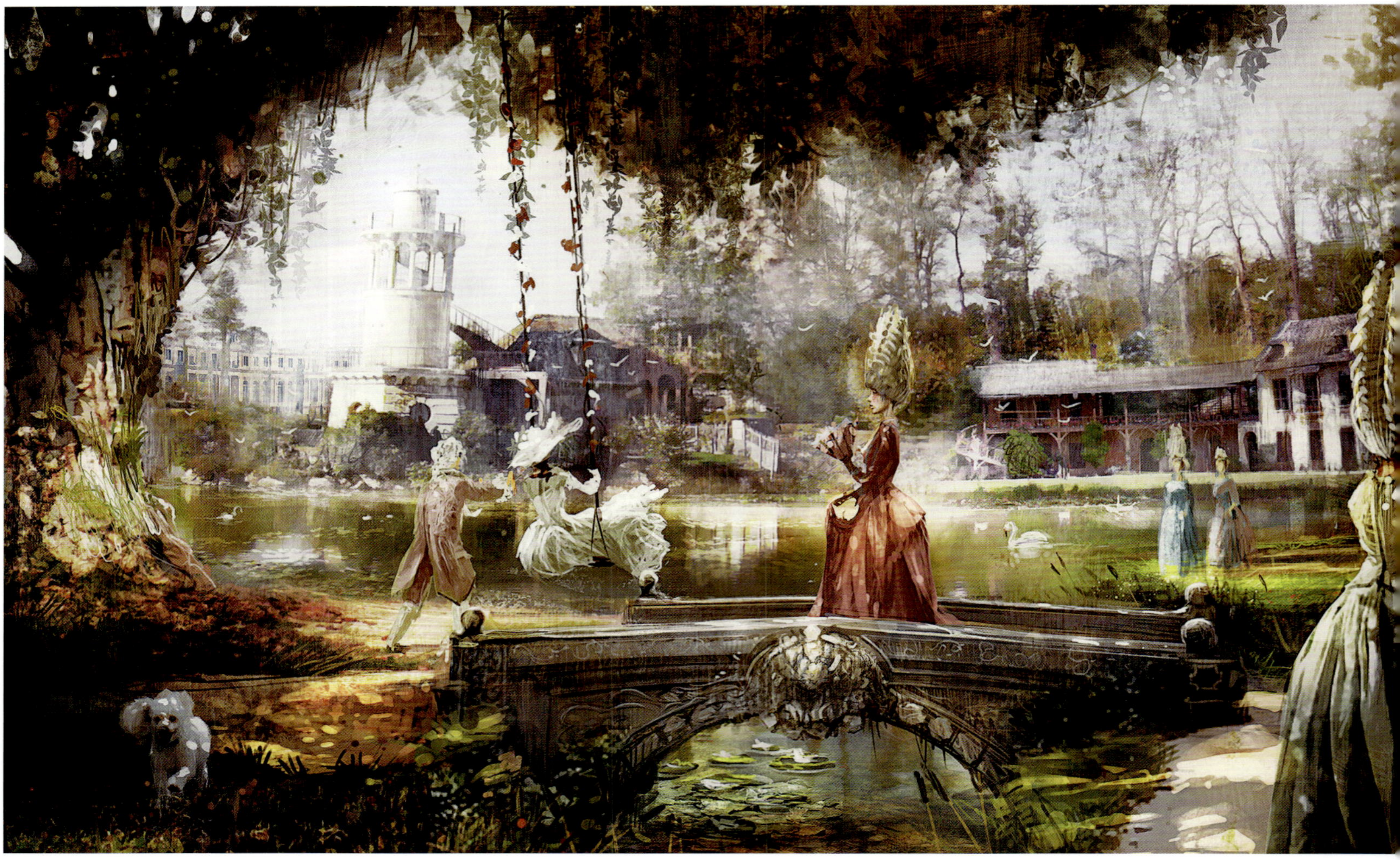

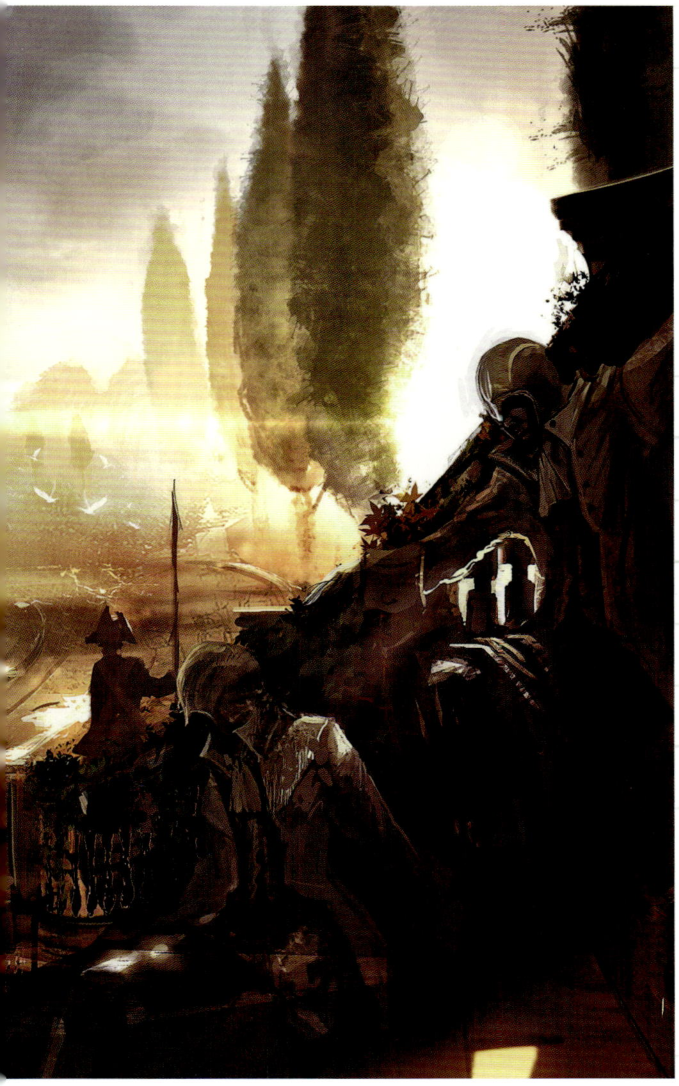

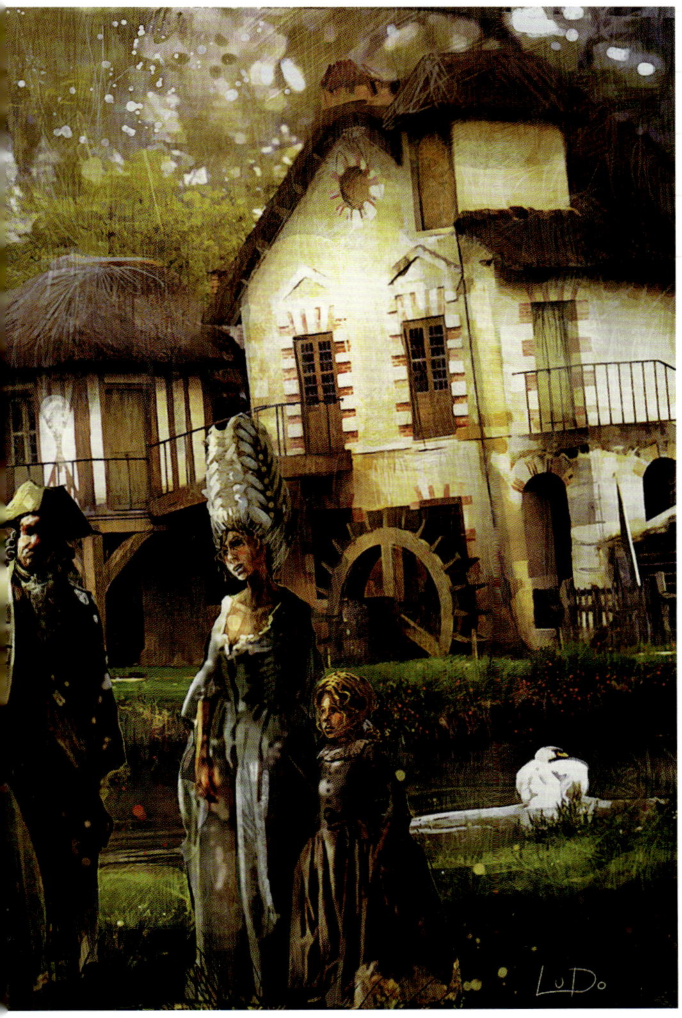

CITY OF LIGHT

Long before Paris became the first electrified city in the world, it gained its familiar appellation as the City of Light for its central role in the expansion of culture, art, and philosophy during the Enlightenment. By the time of the French Revolution, Paris was a hotbed of ideas and expression that shone out to the rest of the world.

In imagining this beautiful city on the brink of its greatest upheaval, Ubisoft's artists did what they always do: They looked to history for a starting point. More than any game in the franchise up to that point, *Unity* had the advantage of extensive historical data about the city, its inhabitants, and the descent into the Revolution that tore it apart. "The art team did a lot of work based on actual historical maps," Raphaël says. "They recreated an accurate layout of the city and its landmarks and continued to modify and adapt it to the needs of the game's level design." Beyond street layouts, the art of the period offered plentiful references to help inform the look of the city's many districts.

Early visualizations showed off picturesque avenues blanketed in vines and flowers, couples strolling along cobblestone streets, and inviting cafes and pubs. The lively elegance of the city needed to be apparent early on in order to accentuate the tragedy of what came next. More than any preceding game in the franchise, Paris had a cinematic feel. "It wasn't easy for the Unity art team to achieve the gritty, organic look of the city with the advanced features of the next-gen tech," Raphaël says. "Mohamed aimed for a visual direction that was very cinematic and was inspired by the movie *Perfume: The Story of a Murderer*." Beyond attractive street scenes, Paris was also home to architectural wonders. The problem arose that, more than any previous setting, eighteenth-century Paris had too many landmarks to comfortably represent within the game, due to the constraints of time and technology. "The biggest challenge was to make very hard choices in terms of what to prioritize when depicting Paris," Mohamed says. "We had to choose fifteen to twenty monuments and major city elements out of a hundred. So that was really tough—we wanted to have all of Paris and respect as much as we could the collective perception that people have of the city."

TOP LEFT: The golden light in this concept emphasizes the luxury and decadence of the Luxembourg Palace (Ludovic Ribardière).
BOTTOM LEFT: Marie Antoinette's idyllic village in Versailles (Ludovic Ribardière).

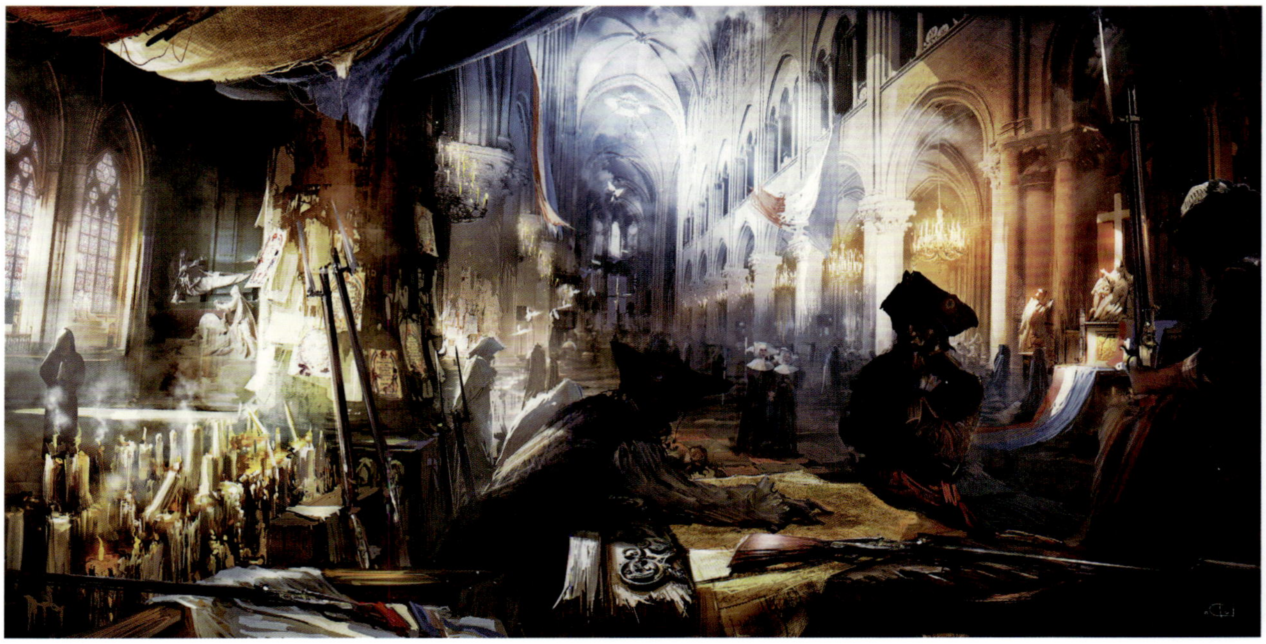

Along with the challenge of choosing the appropriate buildings to depict, the dilemma of building scale was a particular difficulty. Presenting every one of Paris' structures at a one-to-one scale would be impossible both from a technological and design perspective, so the art team spent countless hours investigating a middle ground that maintained an appropriate sense of majesty but without having the size of buildings override other development concerns. "We can't have everything within the scale of the city itself," Mohamed explains. "We'd have a location, and we'd put in 85 percent or 75 percent size of a building to keep the scale. It took a lot of work, a lot of trial and error. It was a compromise between our budget and the sense of scale that we wanted to present."

Like so many times before in the franchise, the tension between accurate re-creation and emotional grandeur was both a challenge and an opportunity to craft something truly remarkable. "Our descriptions are about maintaining the historical accuracy, while creating epic-ness and emotions—the artistic need to reinvent the reality," Jean says. "This is the balance we need to find, and that triggers more discussions." To help achieve balance, playing with contrasts is key. "There's an interplay of close and far, big and small, light and dark," explains Gilles. "These are the kinds of things I always try to do—put contrasts in my images like warm and cool, light and dark, far and close."

The Louvre would one day become a museum, but in those days it was a well-appointed palace. The Bastille presented an interesting challenge, as its prodigious walls were to be one of the early sacrifices to the Revolution. Ultimately, it was decided that the fortress offered too exciting a play space to tear it down completely. The similarly impressive Temple fortress provided the ideal place to serve as the Templar stronghold and infiltrating its interior one of Arno's most dangerous tasks.

Whether it was sprawling castles and palaces or small, second-story apartments, *Unity*'s biggest environmental triumph was the addition of interior spaces. Previous games had included select buildings that were open for exploration, but *Unity* took it to another level, with a full quarter of the game's structures available to enter. It was a titanic task that resulted in some of the most detailed and elaborate work yet completed for the franchise. Interior palace walls shone with splendor and were decorated in exquisite artwork. Shops were hung with individual tools of the trade. Quiet monasteries showed off utilitarian wooden rooms and simple artifacts of religious piety.

Some of the buildings were so detailed that it allowed designers to explore new gameplay dynamics. Murder mysteries demanded Arno carefully observe tiny details in houses, churches, and schools. Every visual clue had to be painstakingly created and placed. The success of these new mystery missions was dependent on both smart gameplay design but also clear visual communication.

Of all Paris's many gorgeous landmarks, both inside and out, no single location would take as much time and energy as the mighty Notre Dame Cathedral. Two of Ubisoft's developers spent a full two years together designing the church, which dominated the skyline from across the city. The huge exterior needed not only to impress with its size but also serve as an active and engaging play space—a freeclimber's paradise. Inside, shifting beams of colored light drifted down from high stained-glass windows, a testament to the cathedral's sacred purpose. However, the ground level told a different story. As the Revolution moved into full swing, the people of Paris occupied the nave, filling it with the detritus of the ongoing war. It was just one of dozens of ways players began to bear witness to a city falling into ruin.

TOP: Artwork depicting the occupation of the Notre Dame (Ludovic Ribardière).
OPPOSITE: Concept of the Rose Window (Ludovic Ribardière).

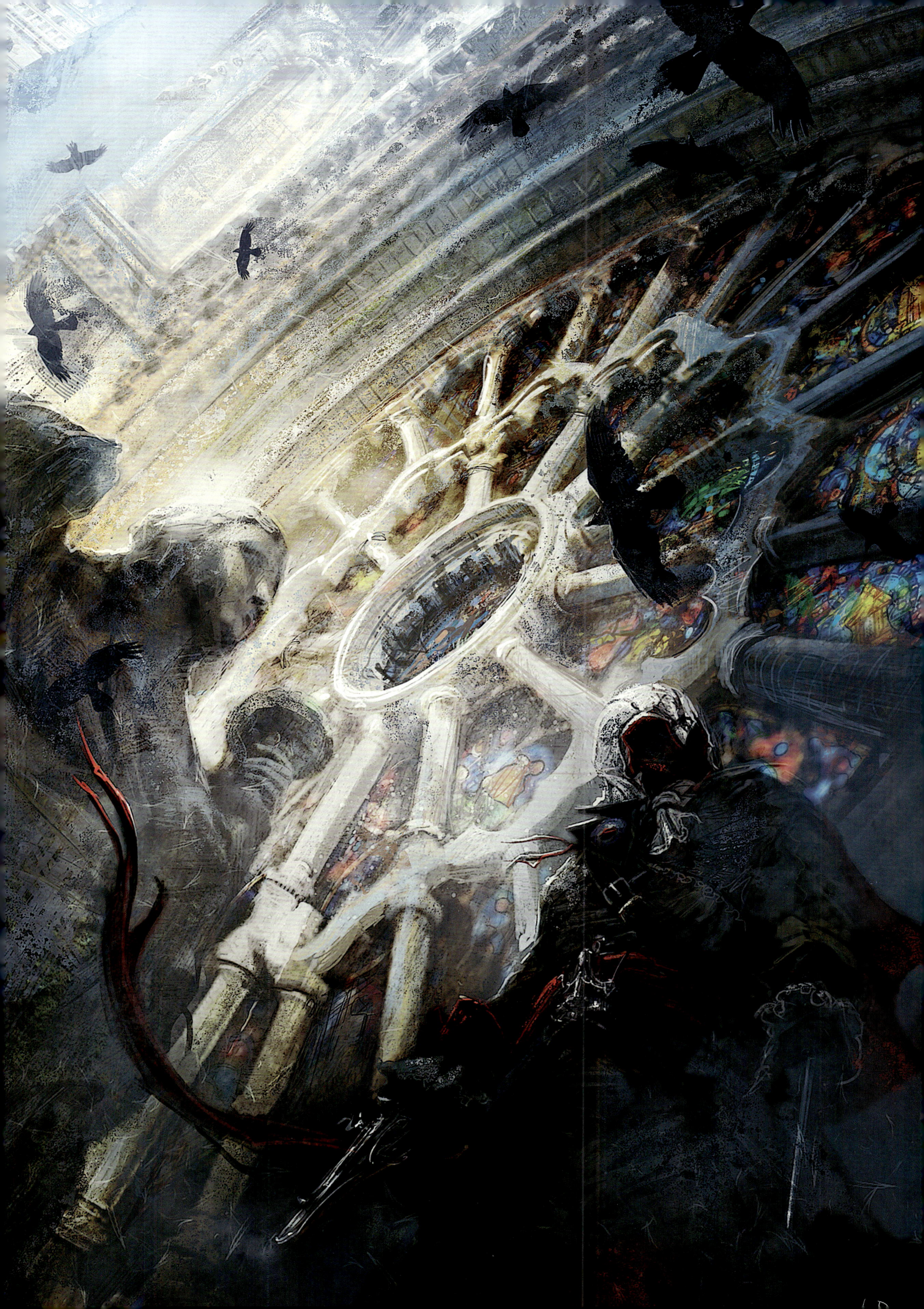

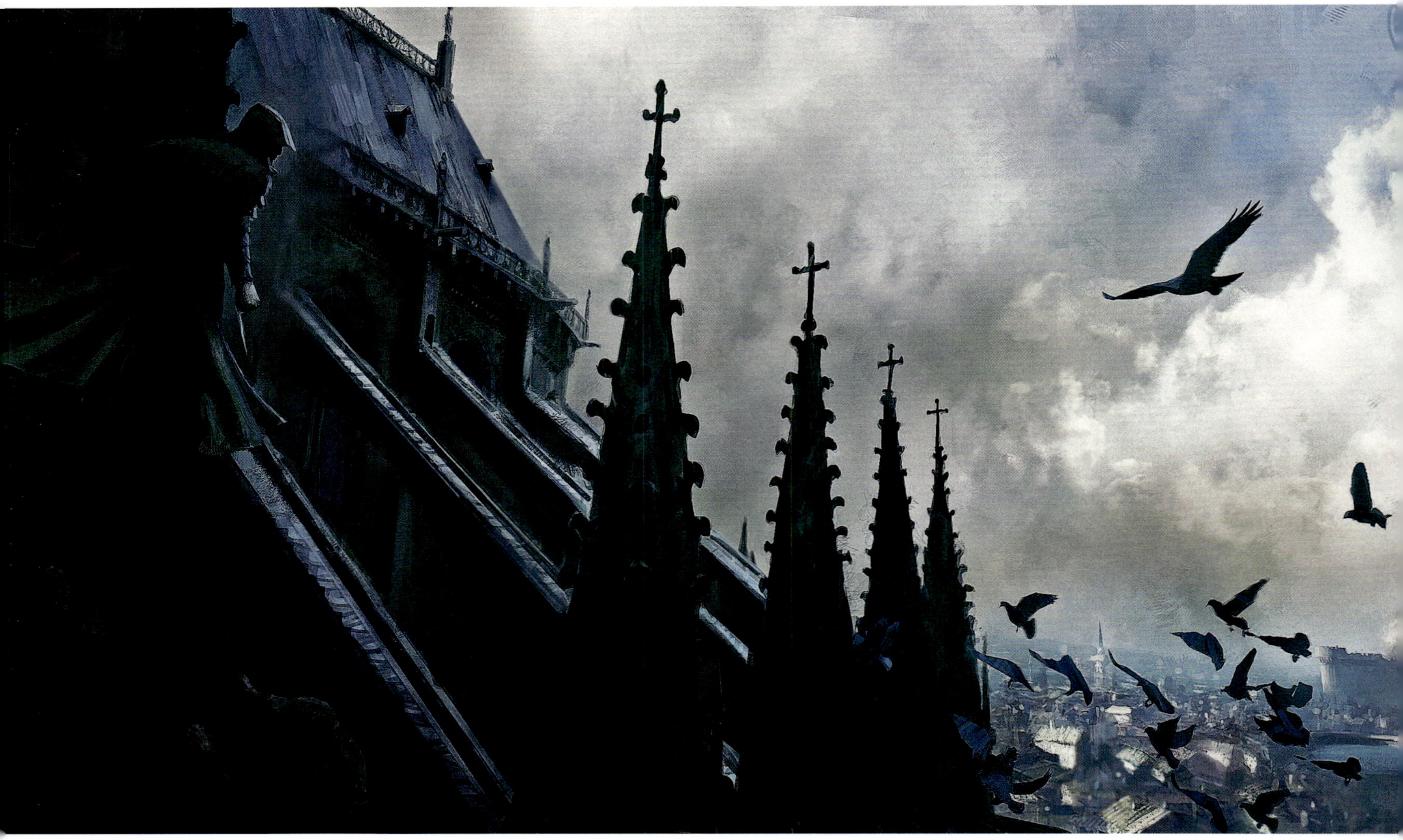

THE VALUE OF CONCEPT

Over the years since the inception of Assassin's Creed, hundreds of artists have produced thousands of individual concept art pieces for the team. But how does all that work specifically benefit the broader development goals? "The reason to do environment concept art is to show to the team the vision of the artistic direction," says environment artist Gilles Beloeil. "It's always easier to explain something visual with an image."

With concept art in hand, an art director can clearly communicate to the rest of the team an ideal form for the visual style of a given area or for the broader game. "The goal of the art is not always the same," Gilles continues. "Sometimes it helps to set the mood in a mission or to create a distinct feeling for a specific area. When we're in a big city such as Paris or Rome, for example, we have to feel the differences between the wealthy districts versus the poor areas."

In some instances, the team may be moving off course from a desired visual direction, and the art director might request a paintover in which an existing screenshot from the game-in-progress is provided to an artist and then painted over to illustrate a different mood, lighting, color palette, or style for the scene in question.

Whatever the reason for a given concept art piece's creation, the often hard-to-define look and feel of the final game owes a tremendous debt to the combined body of concept art produced for each installment.

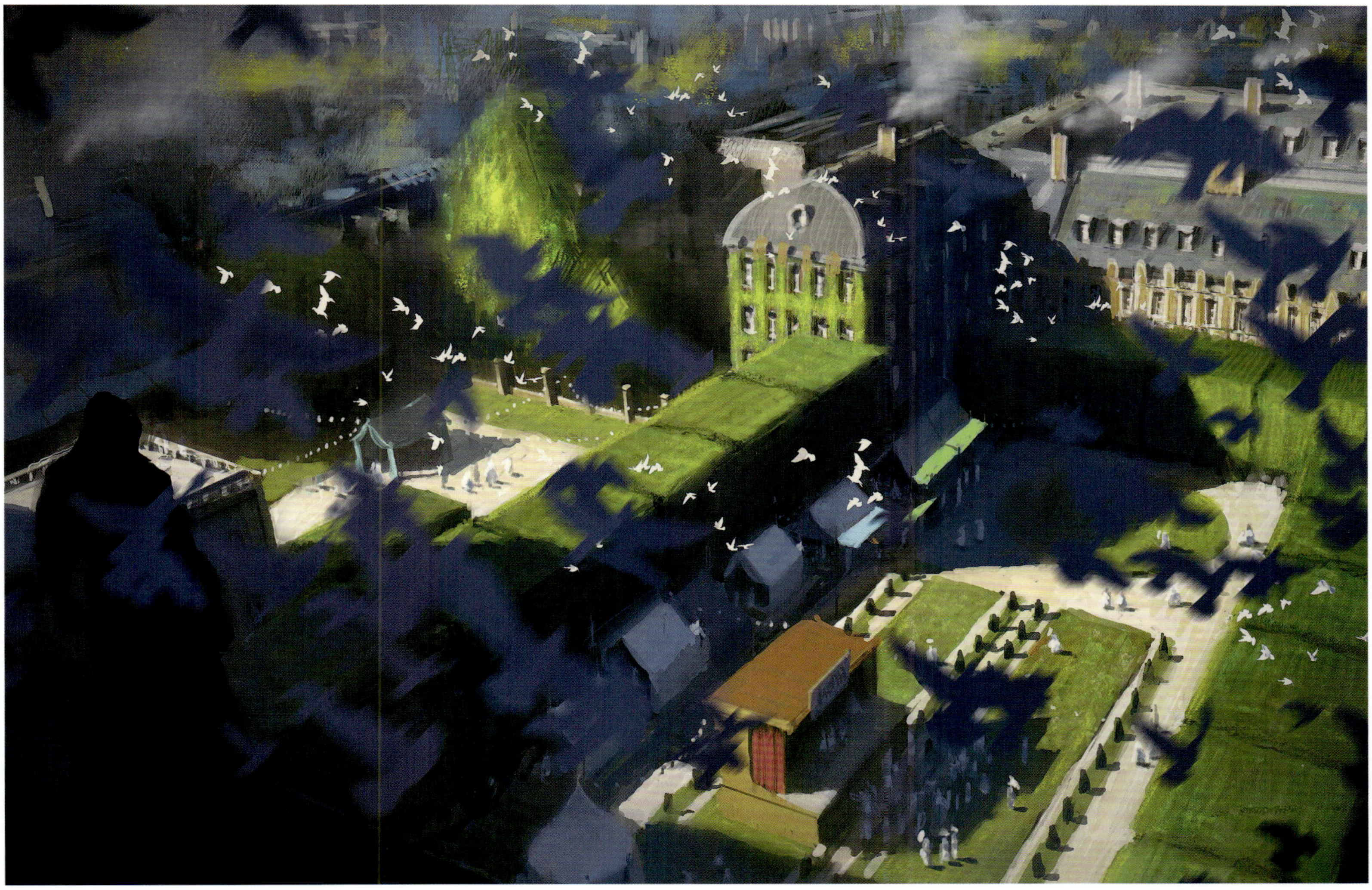

OPPOSITE: Arno atop the Notre Dame (Gilles Beloeil).
ABOVE: Impressionist-influenced illustration contrasting the dark movement of the doves with the sunlit calm of Le Marais below (Gilles Beloeil).

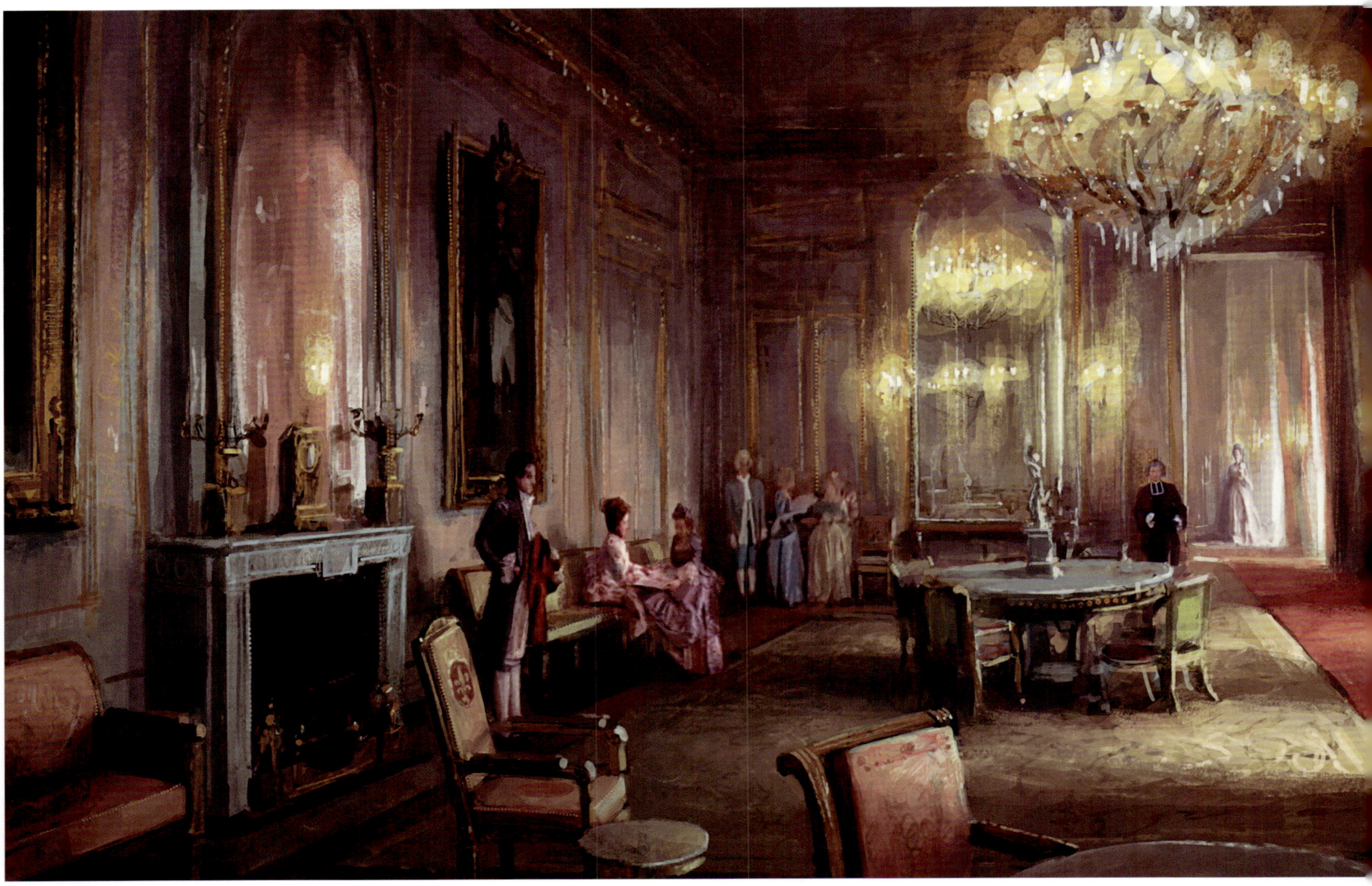

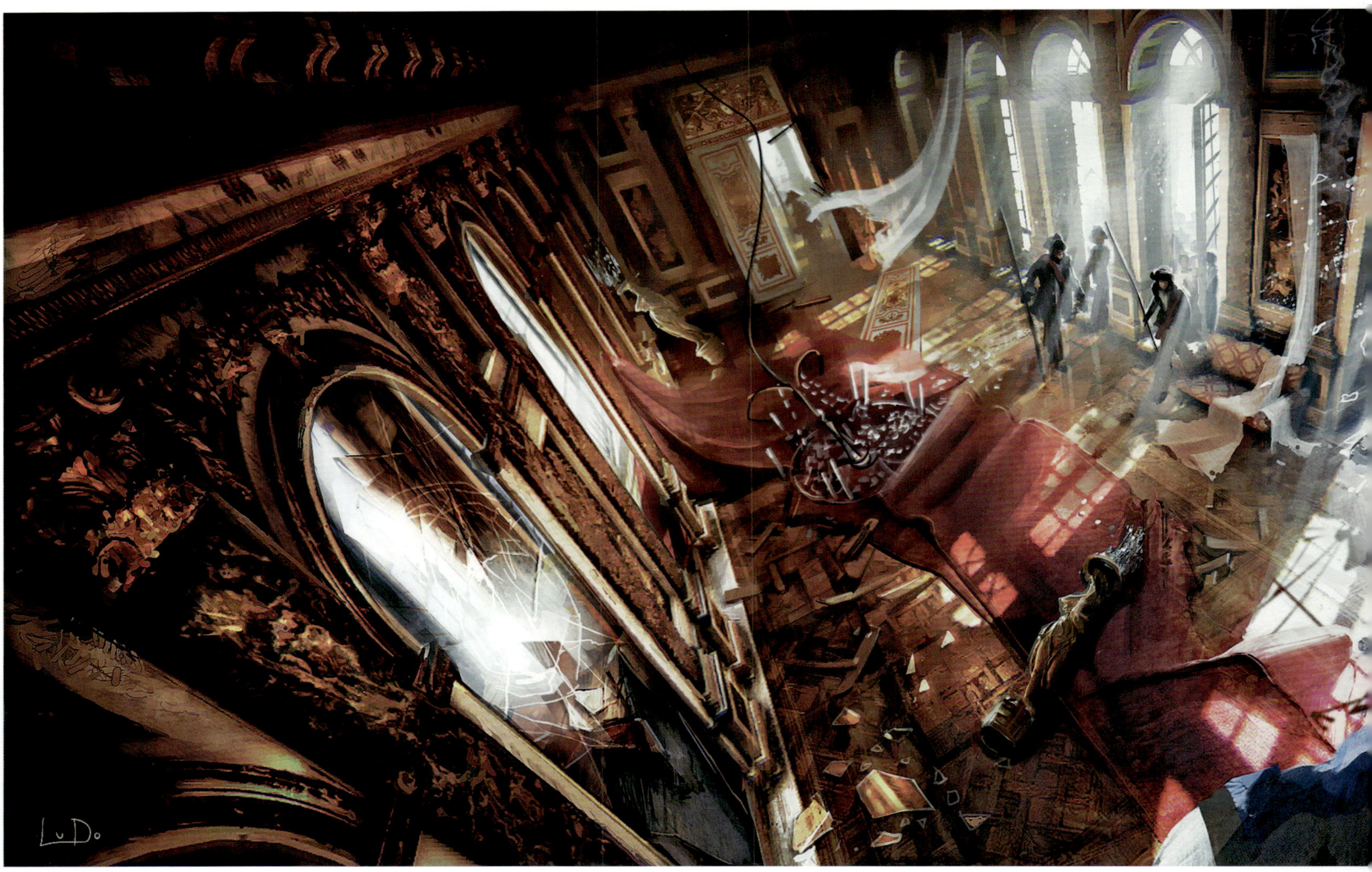
LuDo

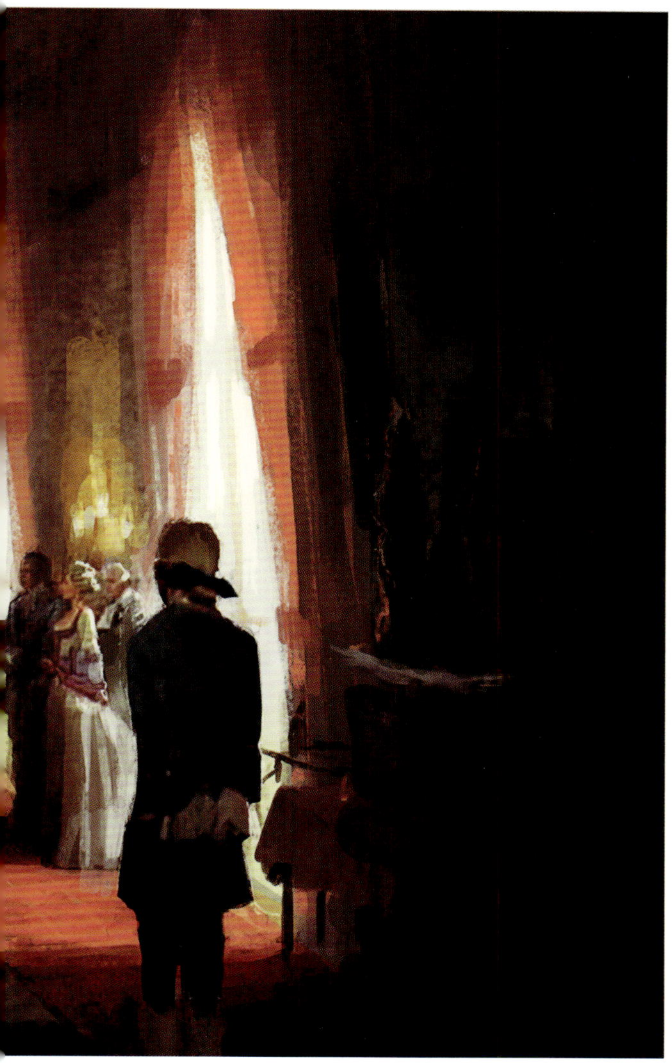

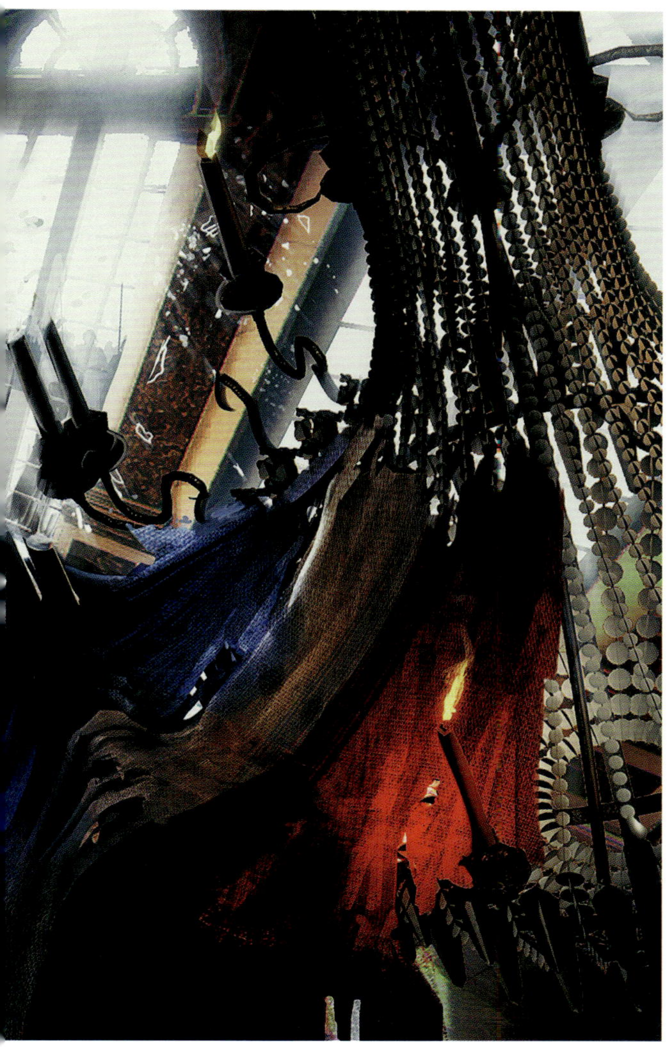

OPENING ACT

While most of *Unity*'s action takes place across the grand expanse of Paris, no story about the French Revolution would be complete without a glimpse at Versailles. The famously prosperous palace lived up to its reputation, both through its impressive façade and its sparkling interiors. The royal home and its environs would serve as a backdrop to Arno and Élise's first adventures and tragedies. Returning to Versailles later in the game, the change is shocking and disheartening, and the decay of the once opulent palace and its surrounding village echoes Arno's string of bad luck. It made for a stark and sudden change to an established location. For the most important location of Paris, a subtler transformation was in order.

TOP LEFT: A tranquil moment in a wealthy apartment before the storm of the Revolution (Félicien Nourry).
BOTTOM LEFT: The historical events that occurred in locations like Versailles would affect the tone and palette of the artwork (Ludovic Ribardière).

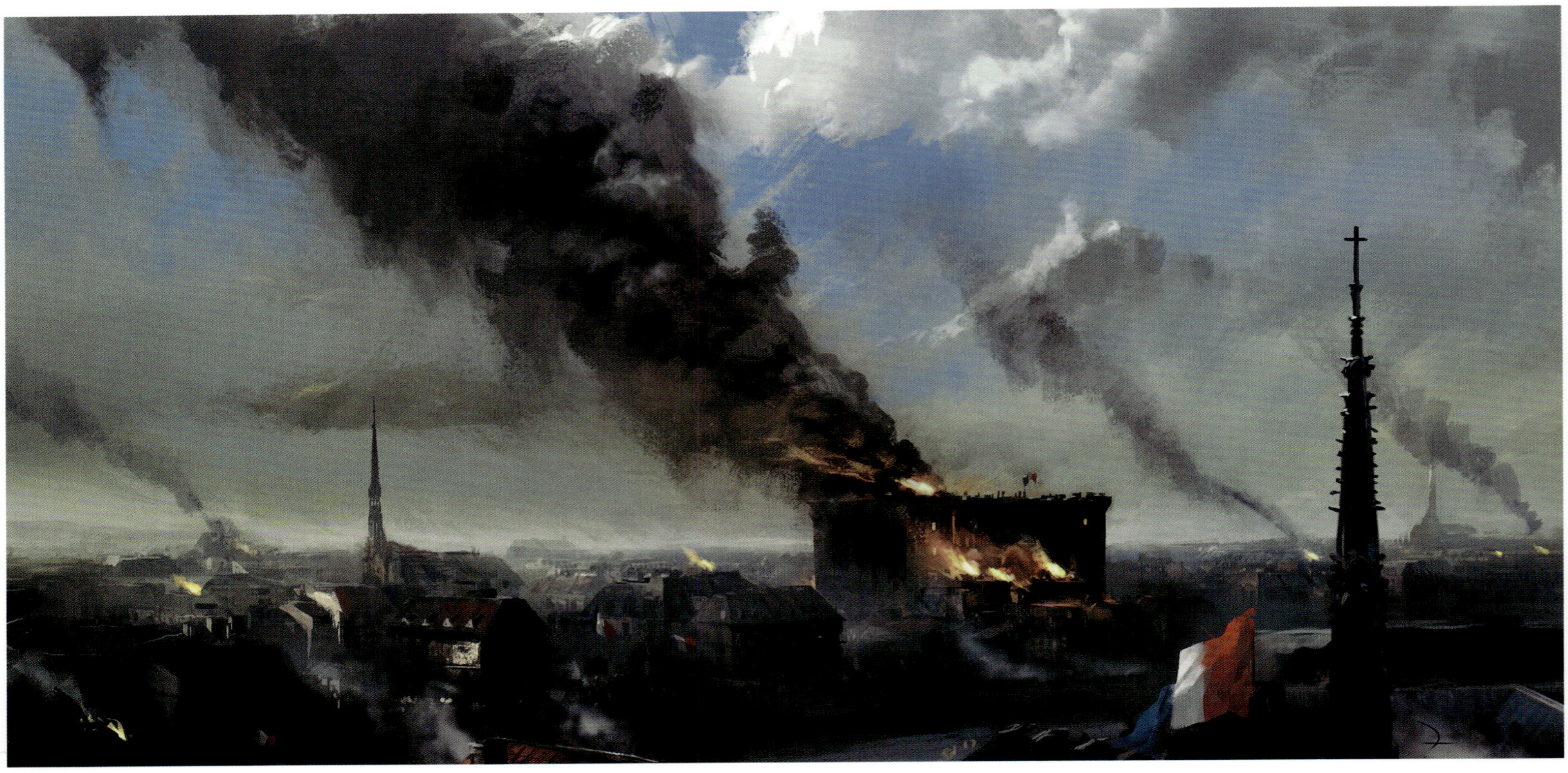

RUINED BEAUTY

The veneer of civility was ripped away by the tumult of the French Revolution, and the once pleasant streets of Paris transformed into battlefields. Previous installments had played with the idea of dynamic environments that changed over the course of the game, such as the revitalization of *Brotherhood*'s Rome. However, the scale of change depicted in Paris was to be of a different magnitude.

Some of the most striking art created for *Assassin's Creed: Unity* illustrated the clash between civilization and anarchy. A great cathedral rose in the distance, but nearby plumes of smoke told the story of brewing rebellion. A guillotine sits prepared to do violence in the center of a market square normally filled with life and activity. Paris became a sea of these contrasts, and the further into the game one explored, the more chaos began to overtake order.

As had so often been the case in previous installments, color could go a long way to depicting an appropriate mood. "Color is key when creating the feeling of transition into a more dramatic atmosphere," Mohamed says. "So we played with warm and cool colors." Early in the game many missions exhibited the rich colors of sunset, and as the city devolved into violence, the increasing presence of clouds and smoke helped to communicate the change. Beyond weather and lighting, the art team worked closely with level designers to ensure that each district helped convey the shift towards discord as the story played out. Arno's early missions were often confined to areas of relative peace and stability, but later missions took him into areas where unrest and turmoil were more apparent. "If you play the game as intended, if you follow the narrative, the order we chose for the locations flows from positive to negative," Mohamed says. "So you start in the richest and most colorful district and then after that, you end in a district that has a hazier atmosphere, especially at the end, which has a toxic mood to it."

However, the most potent tool for communicating the rising tide of anarchy was the crowd. The streets of Paris teemed with people, and their appearance spoke volumes. Early on, large crowds were simply an aspect of city life and encouraged players to move along the emptier rooftops when possible. At lavish parties, large gatherings of people wearing tailored suits and magnificent dresses were camouflaged to allow easy passage beyond watchful guards. As the Revolution progressed, angry mobs began to form, gathering around bonfires to watch effigies burn and leaders chant angry rhetoric. By the end, city dwellers were violent and overwhelming, pressing from all sides as they watched the formerly affluent and noble meet grisly ends. Afterwards, men and women would picket through the streets with the gruesome display of heads mounted on poles. As *Unity*'s story progressed and the months fell away, Paris felt less like a city and more like a war zone.

TOP: The storming of the Bastille would mark a dramatic shift in the tone of the game (Martin Deschambault).
OPPOSITE: Artwork depicting the Revolution's last riot. The golden light hints at the return of order and unity (Ludovic Ribardière).

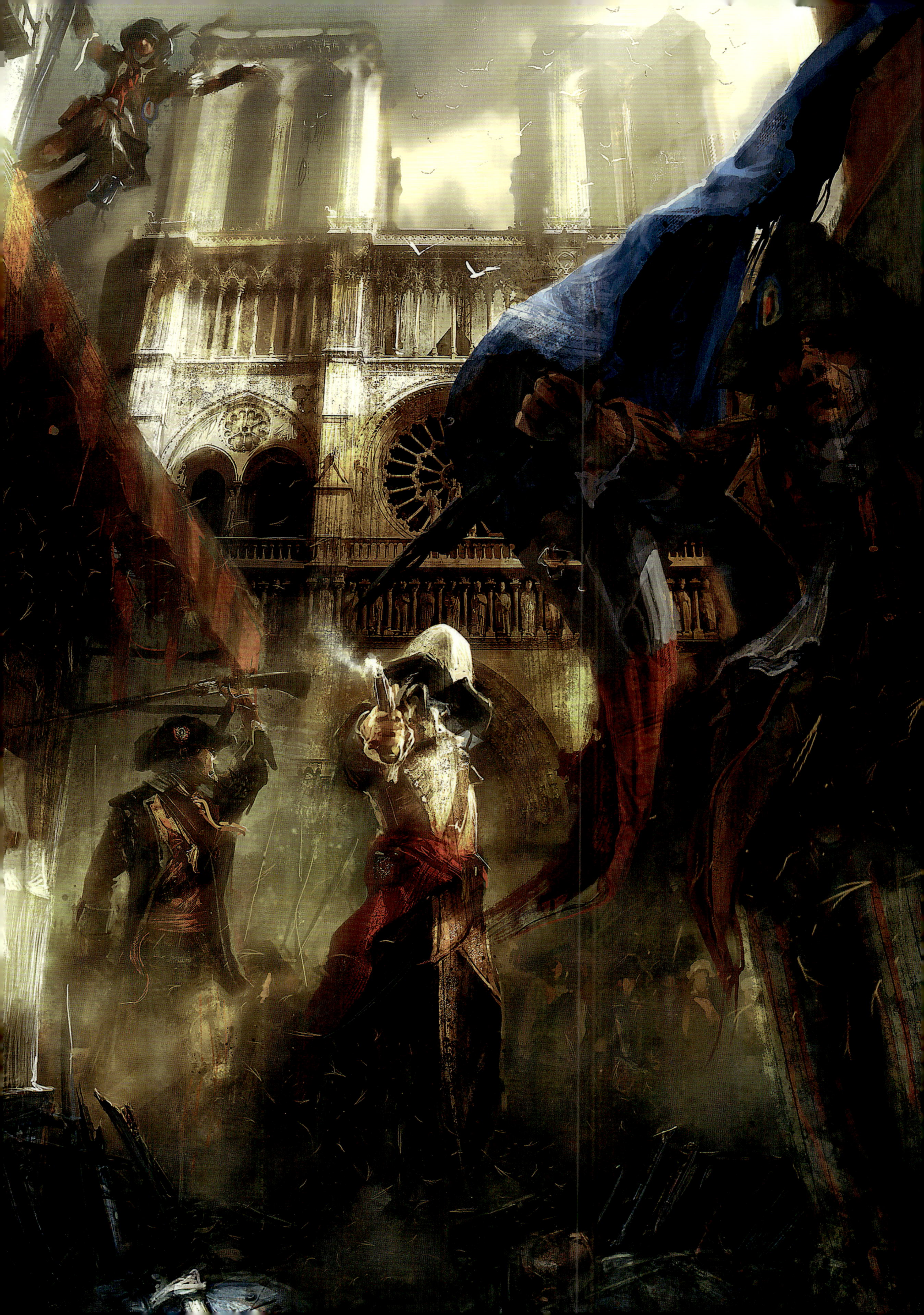

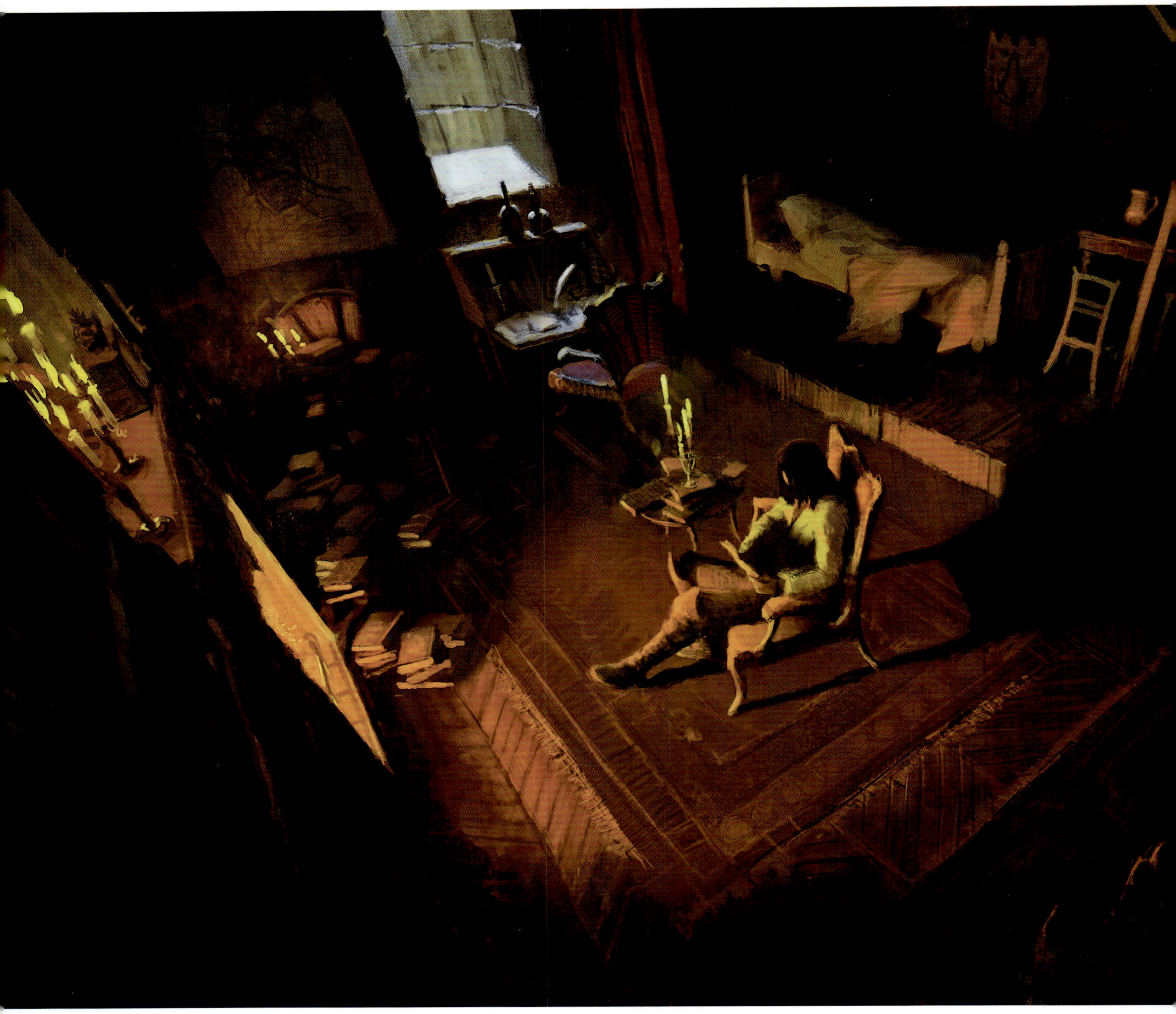

A SUITABLE FRONT

In what had by this point become a confident staple of the franchise, Arno needed a place to call home during his journeys about Paris. After the developers investigated the culture of the period, the plentiful cabarets and cafes led to a clear solution: Arno would revive and rehabilitate the Café Théâtre, which had fallen into ill repair.

With a consistent investment of livres, the Café Théâtre could transform from a derelict business into a thriving house of entertainment. However, the business was only a front to the rest of the lavish villa, which could become a house of luxury over the course of the game. Each rebuilt room offered new opportunities for exploration, including a number of secret rooms and passages. Arno's own upstairs apartments were particularly involved, as new mementos of his journeys would arrive to remind of missions undertaken over the course of the adventure. A few of *Unity*'s most poignant moments came as Arno paused from his trials to sit in his quarters and read the letters he'd received from his beloved Élise.

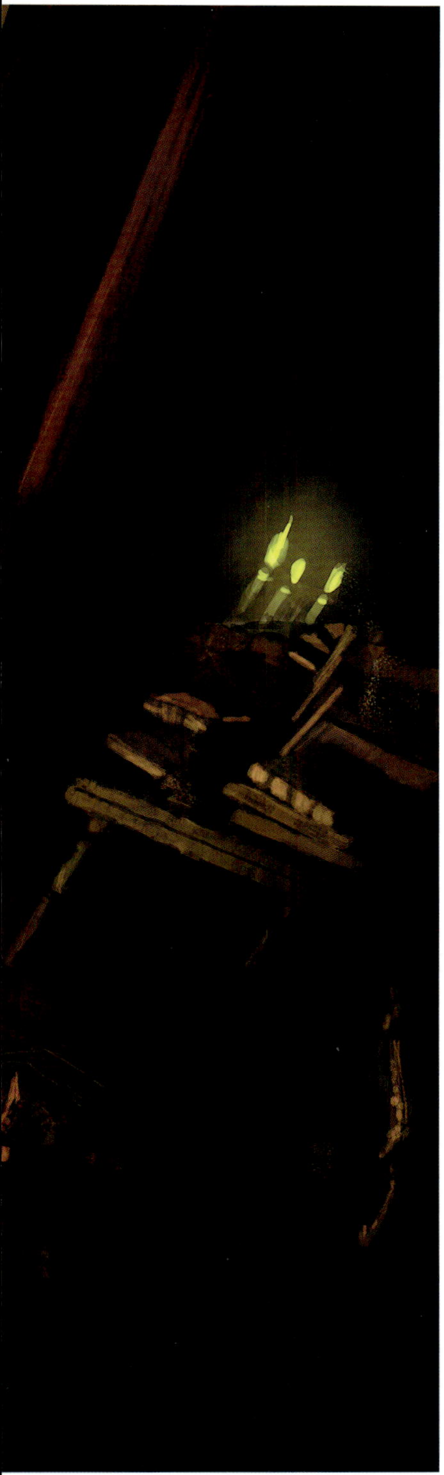

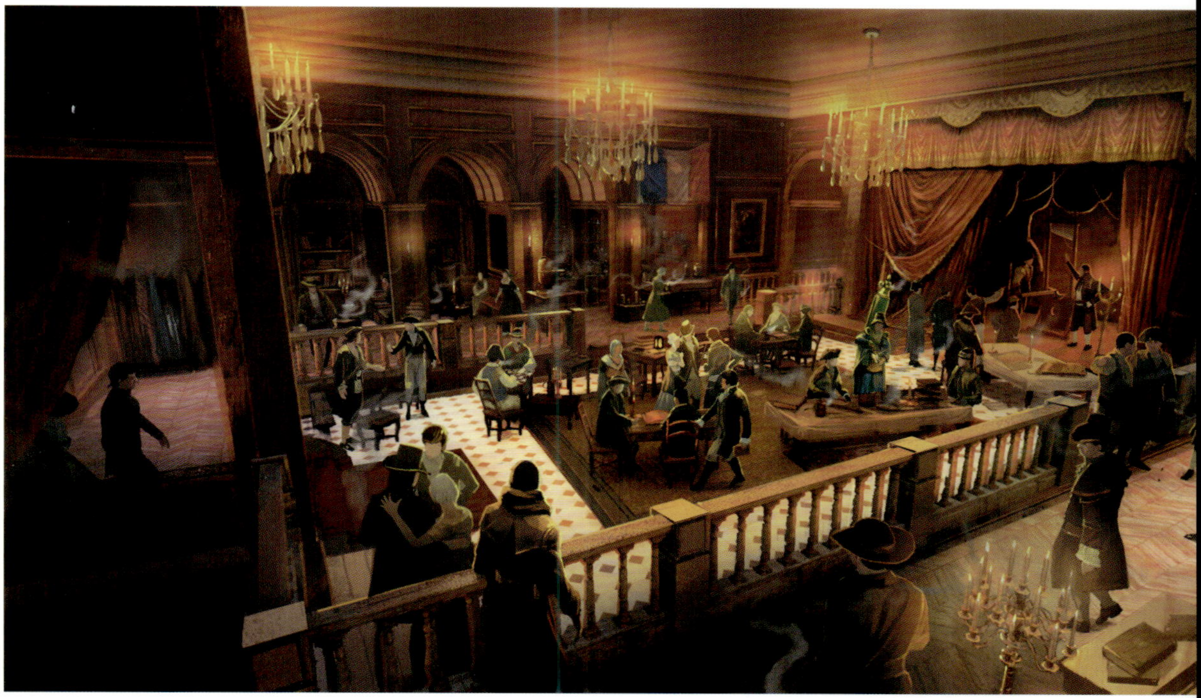

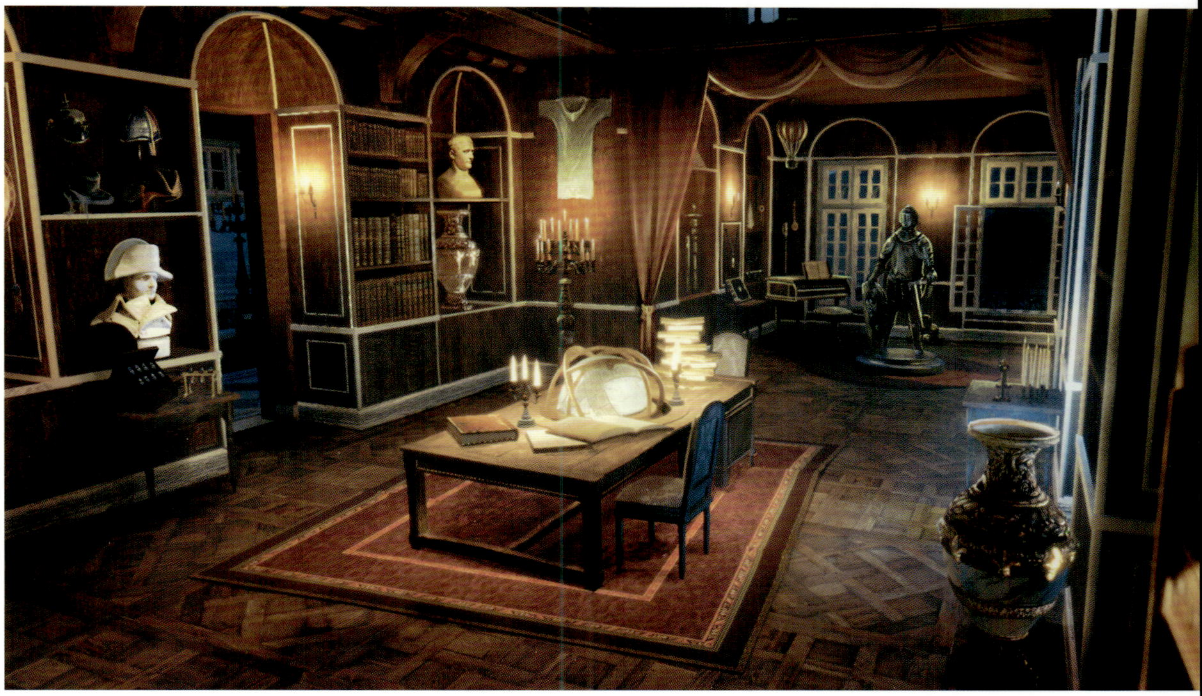

TOP LEFT: A wide shot of Arno's room, where the Assassin would retreat to read letters from Élise (Gilles Beloeil).
TOP: Artwork of the fully-repaired social club (David Alvarez).
ABOVE: The Villa's treasure room includes a globe, armor, and a bust of Napoleon (David Alvarez).

LOVE DURING WARTIME

In an interesting twist, the emotional core of *Unity*'s story did not lie in the tragedy of the Revolution but rather in the affections and tribulations of its two lead characters, Arno and Élise. The two met as children on the day Arno's father died and seemed forever linked from that point forward. Arno eventually found his way back to his father's path as a member of the Assassins, even as Élise was groomed all her life to take up the mantle of a Templar.

The earliest versions of Arno emphasized his position as a revolutionary, up to including the tricolor cockade on his uniform. This grim soldier of the Revolution gave way over time to a more noble countenance befitting his life prior to entering the Brotherhood. The dashing silhouette presented by his main outfit was slim and elegant, with more color than most of the central Assassin heroes that had come before. Even so, the classic hood and flashes of red kept the character tied to the long heritage. "When Ezio is in Constantinople, he has to blend in with the setting, so we designed the Ottoman fabrics of his clothes to harmonize with his surroundings," Raphaël remembers. "It's the same with Arno in Paris. Always keeping the spine of the brand through the hood, but the fabrics and design were created in accordance with paintings from the era and his social rank. We always try to make a clear connection between the setting and the character of the time period."

Unlike that gradual evolution of design that led to Arno's signature style, Élise came together with relative ease. Early designs came very close to what the team was looking for: a strong, rebellious young woman who would share the spotlight with Arno, even if the player never controlled her. "She's a very strong character," Mohamed says. "And she almost shares the main role with Arno, because for a lot of the game, there's this relationship in the duality between the two, and sometimes you practically feel that the story is told from her point of view."

Élise's link to the Templars demanded that the artists find a compelling uniform that matched the established aesthetic of the Assassins' enemies but that also felt heroic and original. Dark clothing tones stood in contrast with her fiery hair—as clear a signal as the artists had to communicate her tendency to stand apart from her fellows. Her willingness to shed gender norms in high boots and pants further established her defiant nature.

While players saw the world through Arno's eyes, it was the appeal and growing love between Élise and Arno that offered the story its potency. The cuteness of the two as children stealing apples, overdressed as nobleman and noblewoman, established their friendship. Stolen kisses as teenagers at a formal party told us instantly about the trajectory their relationship had taken since childhood. And a moonlit escape by hot air balloon offered the perfect mix of adventure and romance to make the player hope it might work out for the two lovers.

Even as the story established their chemistry, the way they appear throughout the game reinforces their connections as well as their differences. Arno is trim and buttoned-up, but graceful and likable in his demeanor and movements. Arno's silhouette features more diagonal lines and asymmetry in keeping with the established style of the Brotherhood. Élise is a barely contained firecracker, her red hair a not-so-subtle symbol of her own rebellious streak, but her style evokes the classic Templar look: "Although Élise has natural curves in her silhouette and flowing hair, the lines of her clothes are straight, horizontal and vertical, and convey that traditional military Templar vibe," explains senior concept artist Remko Troost. "There is no doubt she is different from Arno; she is a Templar." However, both share a tendency to wear blue as a central color—a simple reminder of their link to one another—and both exhibit small flashes of white and red, the familiar hues of the game franchise. Not coincidentally, red, white, and blue were also the hallmarks of the French tricolor cockade.

OPPOSITE: Environmental concept suggesting both the opposition and the unity between Arno and Élise. This image includes a placeholder crest for the game that would later be titled *Assassin's Creed: Unity* (Remko Troost).

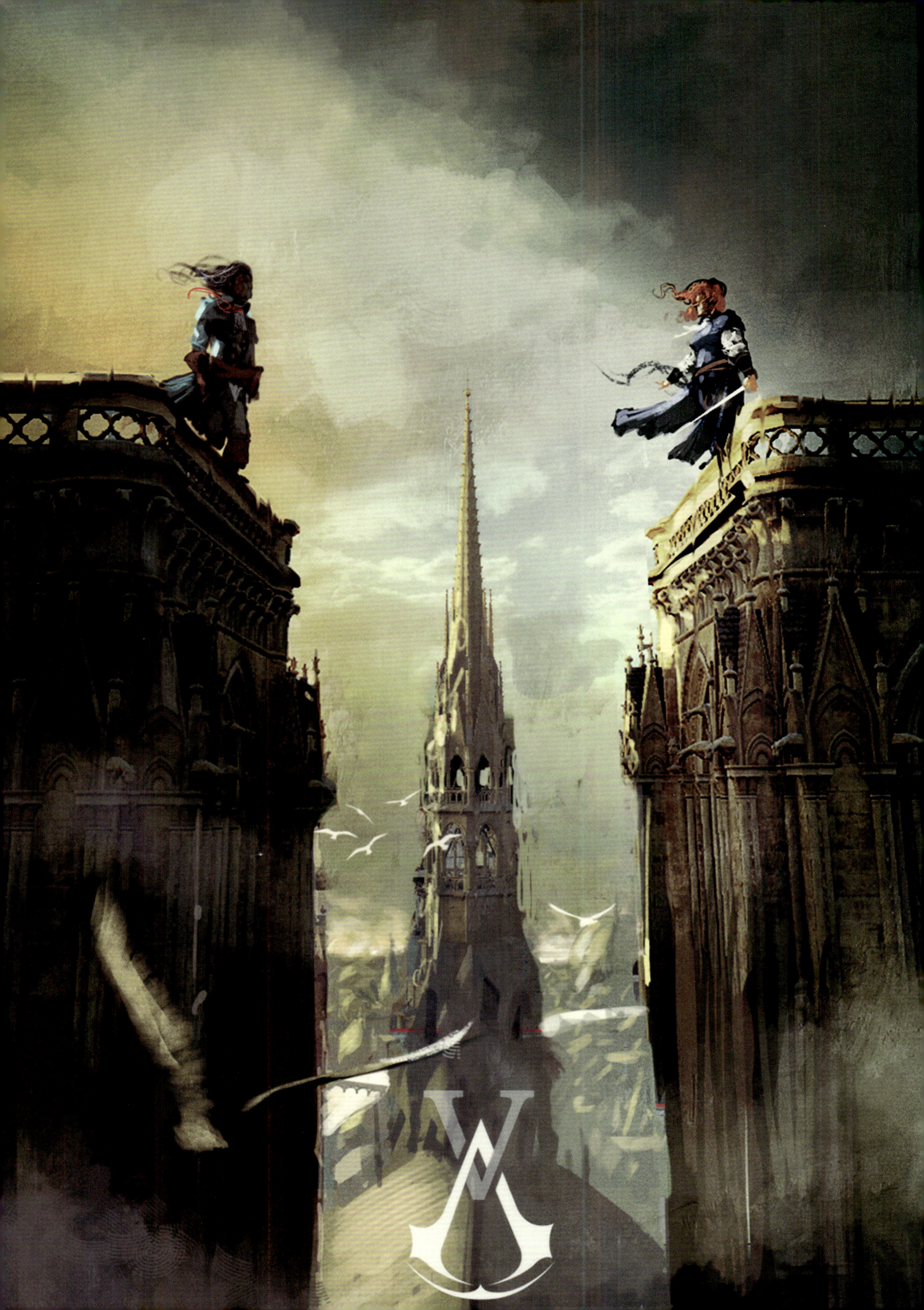

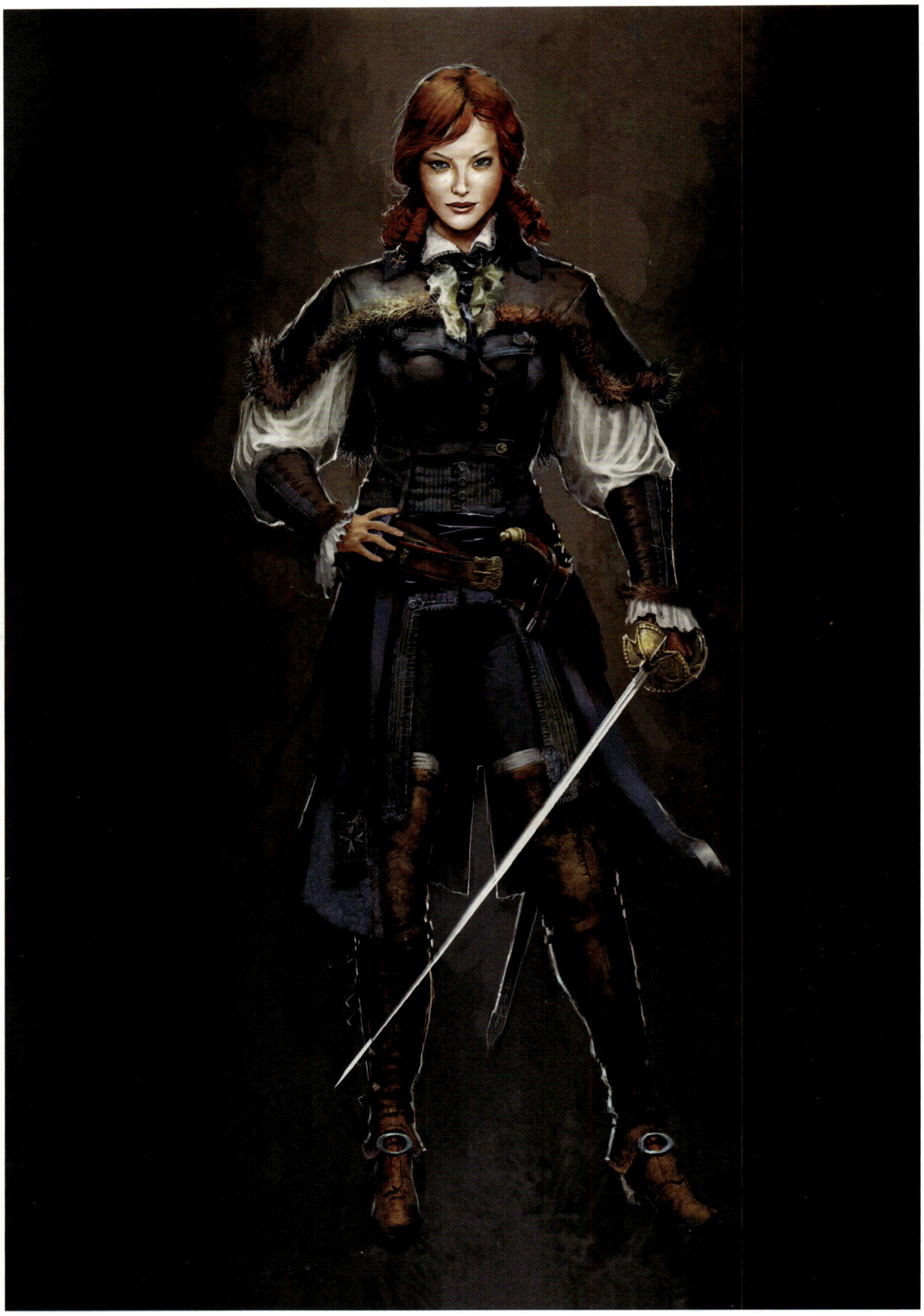

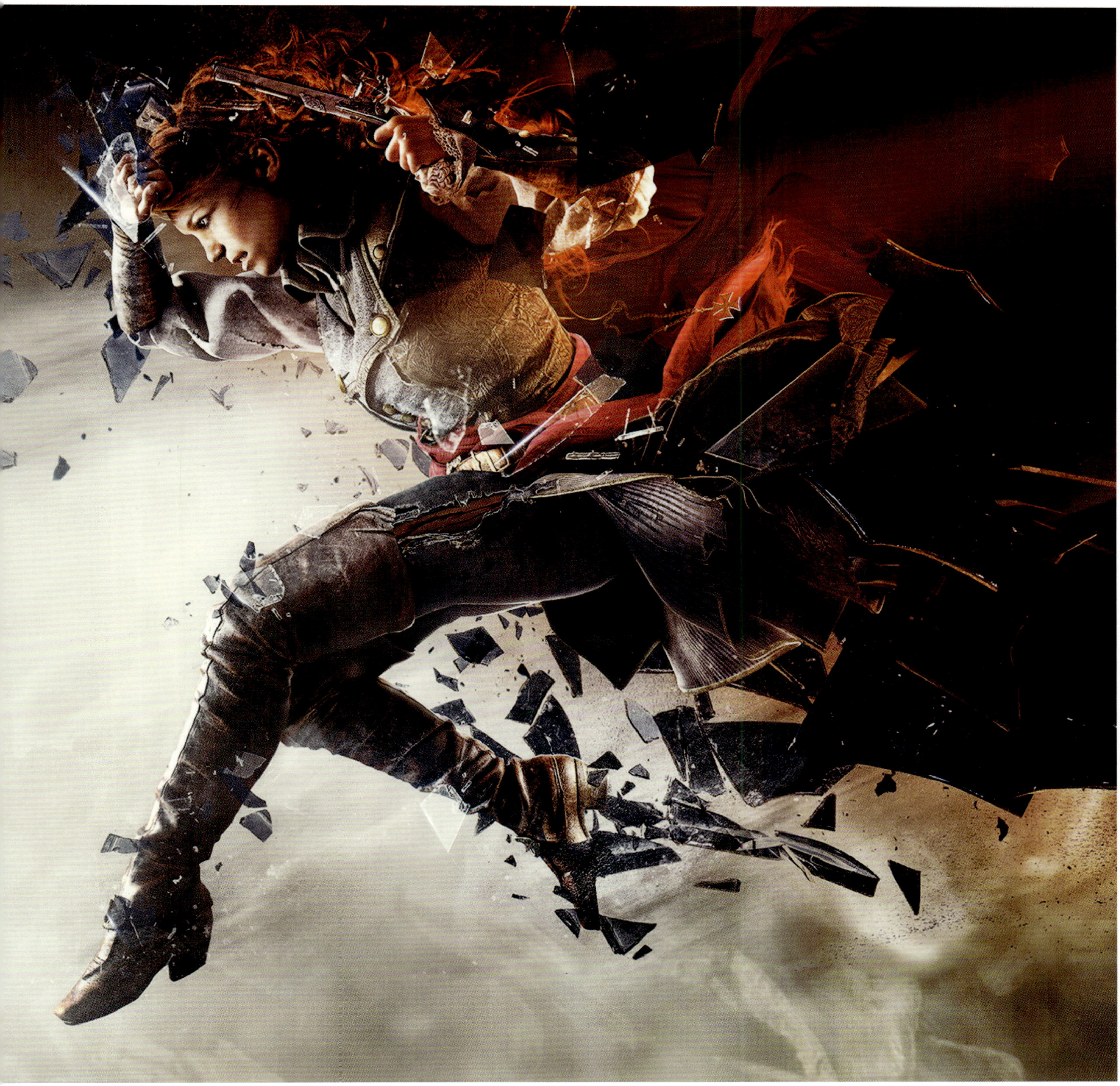

OPPOSITE: Élise character art (Remko Troost).
ABOVE: Élise's leading role in the game reinforced the Templars' strong visual style (Christopher Dormoy).

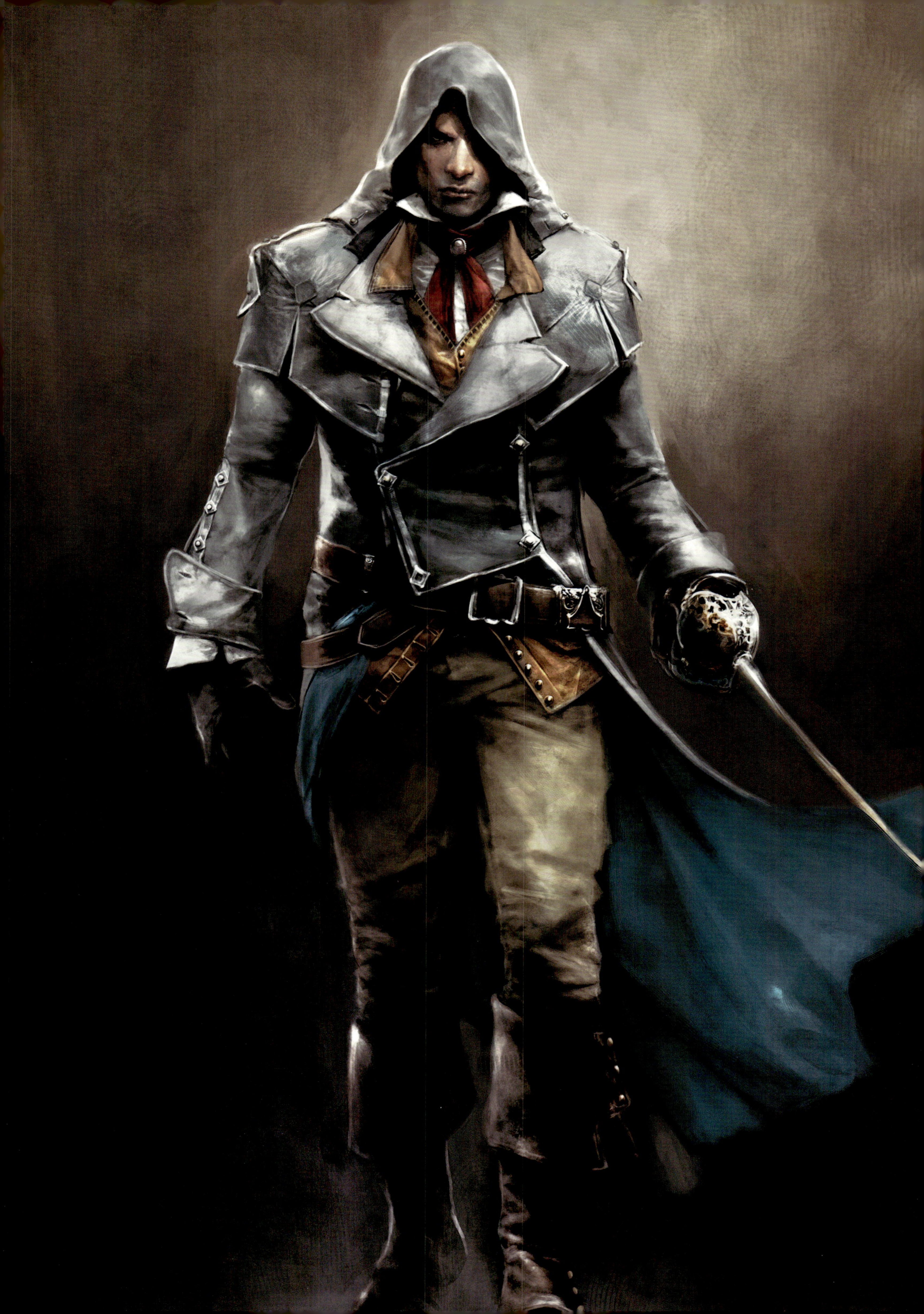

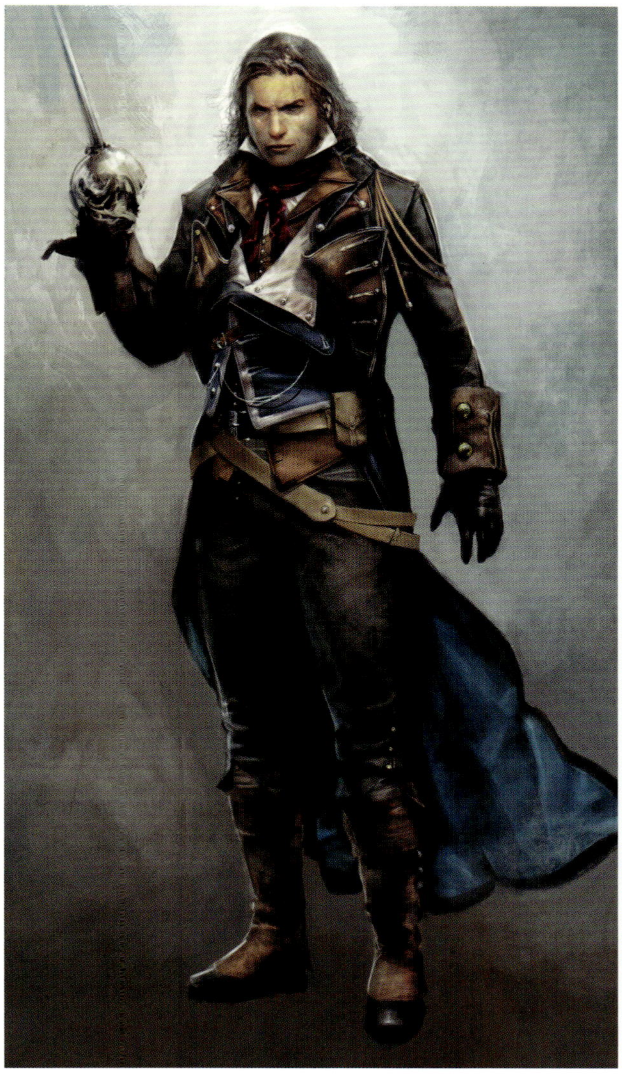

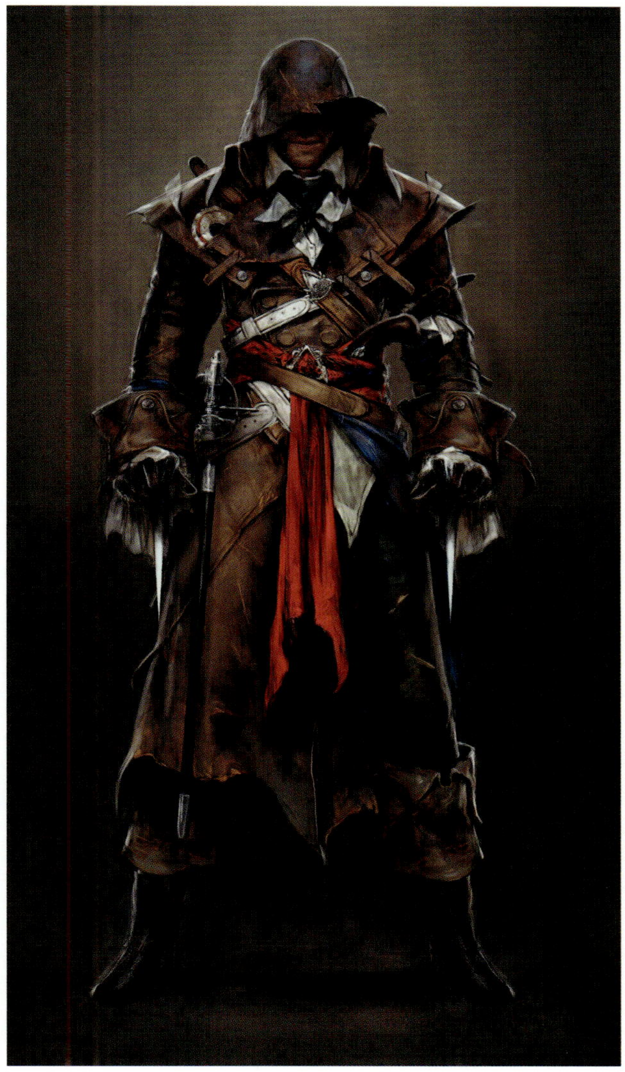

A PERSONALIZED HERO

Unity went further than any other game in the franchise toward putting control of the main character's appearance in the hands of the player. Arno could be equipped with everything from a slim rapier to a devastating polearm, and the choice of weapon not only changed the look of the character but the entire suite of animations that accompanied his actions.

Beyond armaments, the clothing on every body part could be altered among dozens of options. One variation made our hero feel like a military-minded soldier and another like a street criminal. Even the iconic Assassin hood had a large number of variations, letting Arno embrace the classic pointed tip or experiment with more modern variations on the theme. In addition to individual articles of clothing, the player could also swap entire color palettes that could be layered on top of whatever uniform had been chosen.

The new layers of customization served multiple roles. Over time Arno could adapt to appear as the perfect hero in the imagination of the player. Second, the costs associated with acquiring new weapons and armor pieces acted as an aspirational feature, a project to work toward the coolest-looking hero. Perhaps most importantly, the customization options helped each player stand apart when opting into *Unity*'s new cooperative game modes. Multiple variations on Arno Dorian might have been boring if they all adopted the same outfit, but a rainbow of colors and different apparel helped each player establish an identity in the online virtual space.

OPPOSITE: Character concepts for Arno emphasized his charm and swashbuckling attitude (Vincent Gaigneux).
ABOVE: Early Arno character art (Vincent Gaigneux, Jeff Simpson).

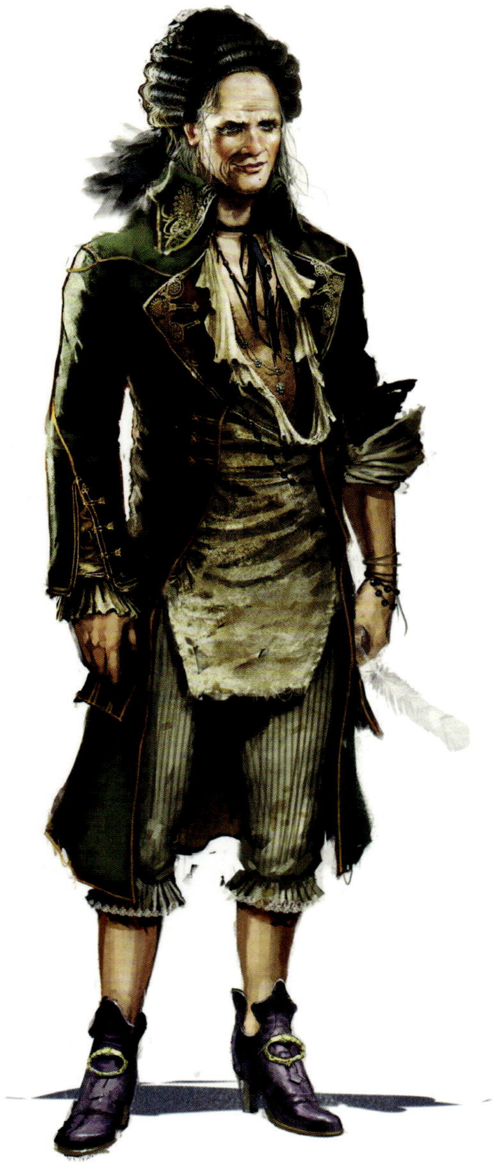

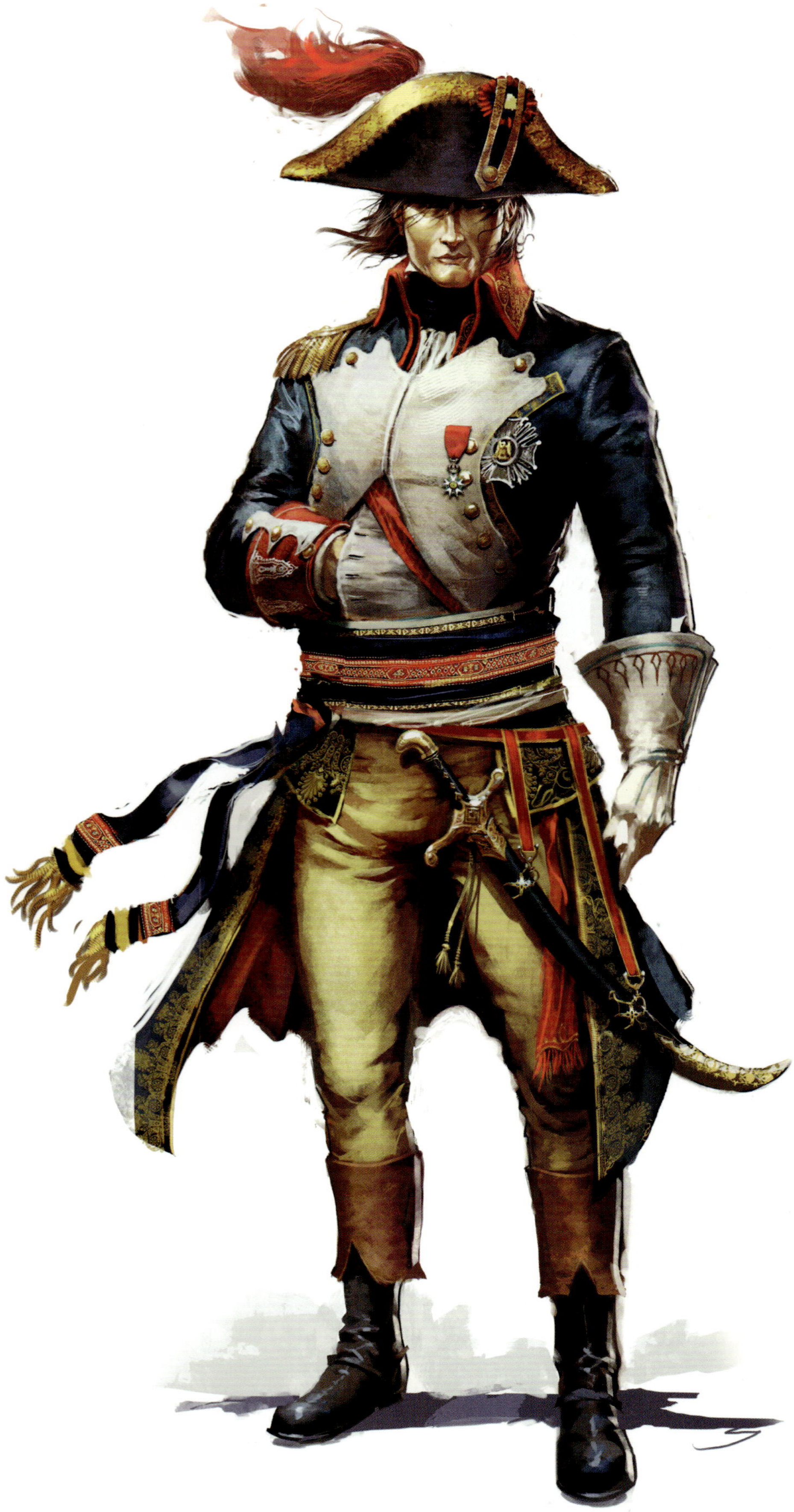

ARCHITECTS OF REVOLUTION

Like every Assassin's Creed installment, *Unity* provided the opportunity for new perspectives on familiar historical personages. The Marquis de Sade was an enigmatic portrait of a man torn between intelligence and hedonism. His presentation is seemingly slovenly and more than mildly perverse, and a glimmer of condescension and coldness rests behind his eyes. A young Napoléon Bonaparte has not yet risen to military superiority during the events of *Unity*, but his straight-backed discipline and fierce insight into people mark him as a future champion. We also meet the infamous Maximilien de Robespierre, whose fanatical devotion to the cause transformed him from erudite member of the bourgeoisie into a relentless and unmerciful dictator. Taken together, *Unity*'s secondary cast succeeds in the same way so many entries in the franchise have: by acknowledging the expectations players have been provided by history and then introducing a novel twist.

ABOVE LEFT: Marquis de Sade concept (Remko Troost).
ABOVE: Napoléon Bonaparte character art (Remko Troost).
OPPOSITE: Robespierre's highly structured outfit shows his rigid and uptight character (Remko Troost).

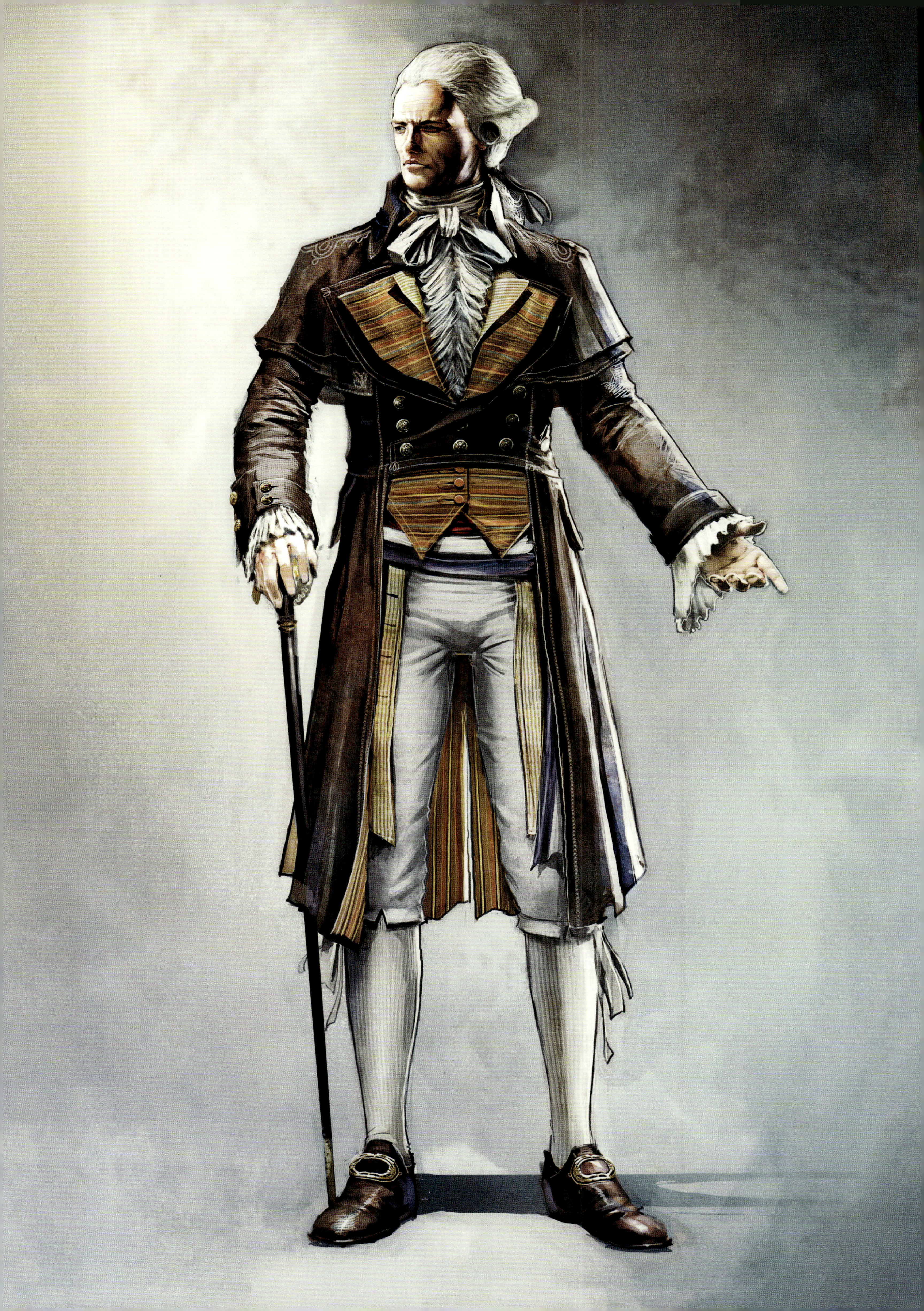

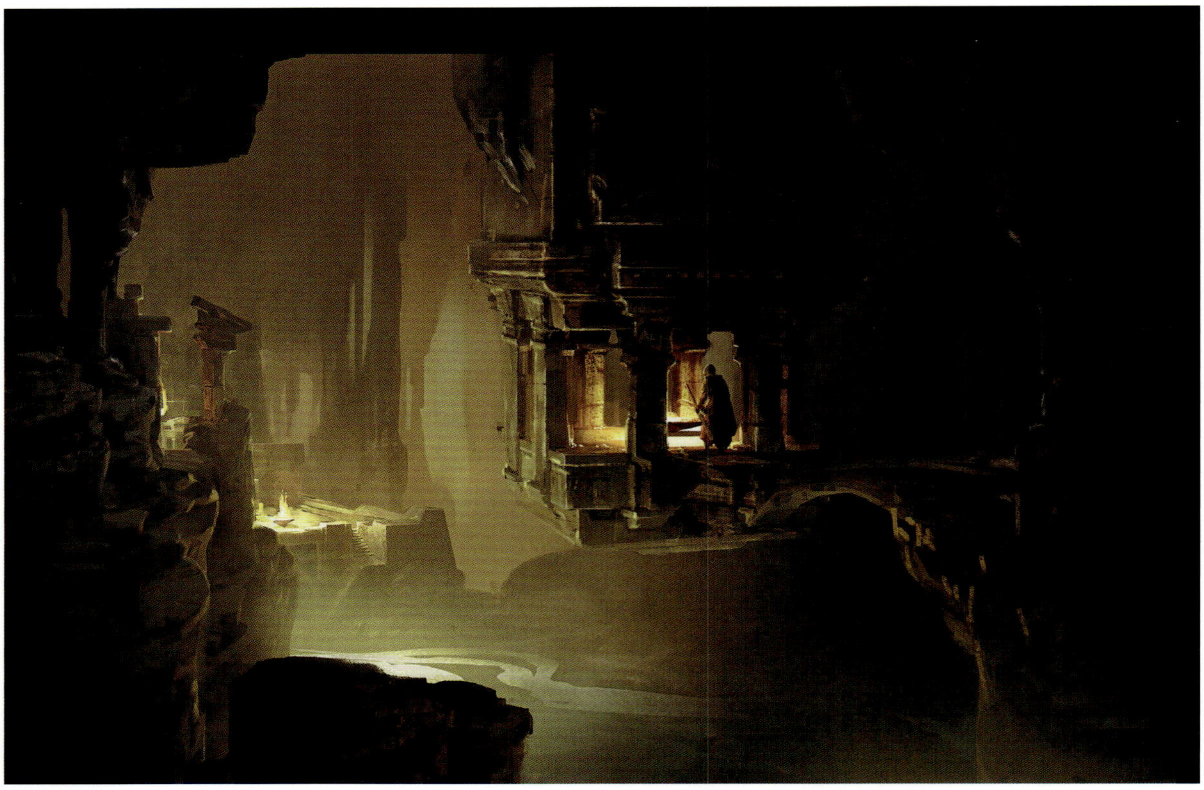

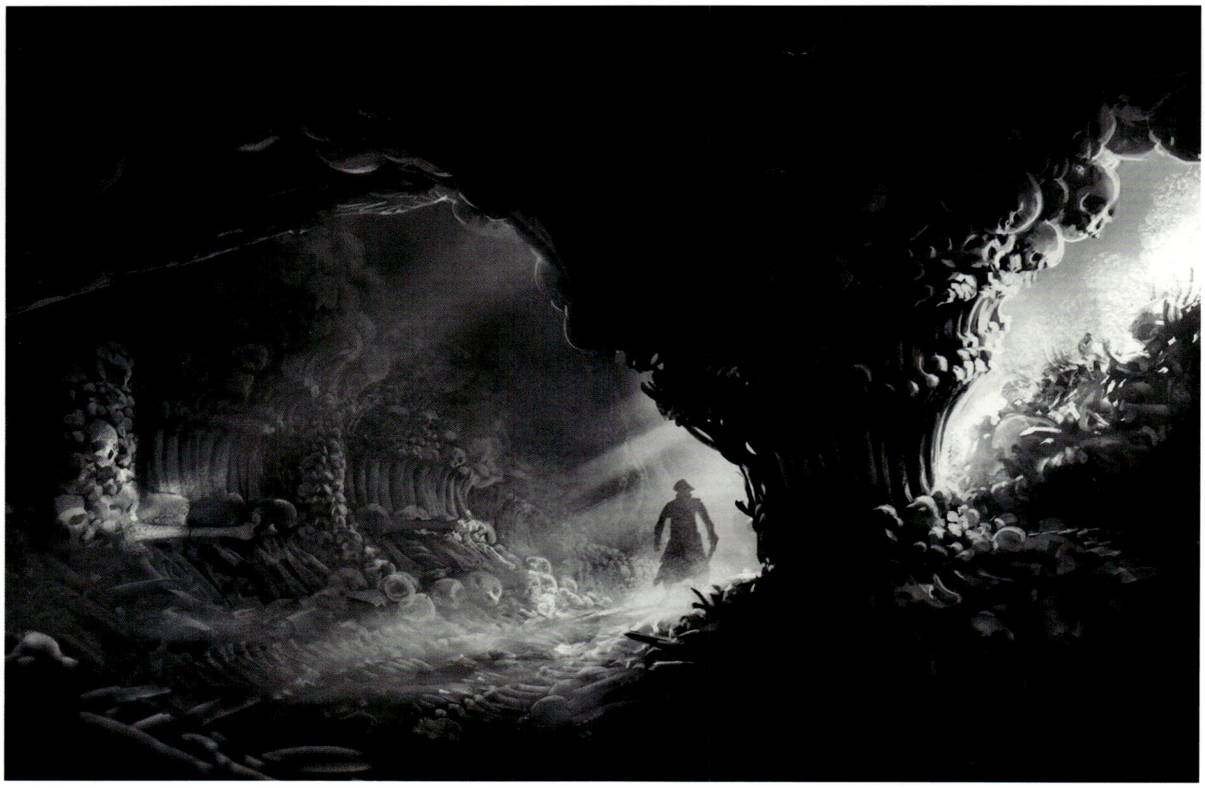

TOP: Concept art of an observatory chamber (Christophe Messier).
ABOVE: Tunnel made of bones in the catacombs (Christophe Messier).
OPPOSITE: Arno's *Dead Kings* costume changed his clean-cut, structured style to a more unkempt, rough appearance (Artist Unknown).

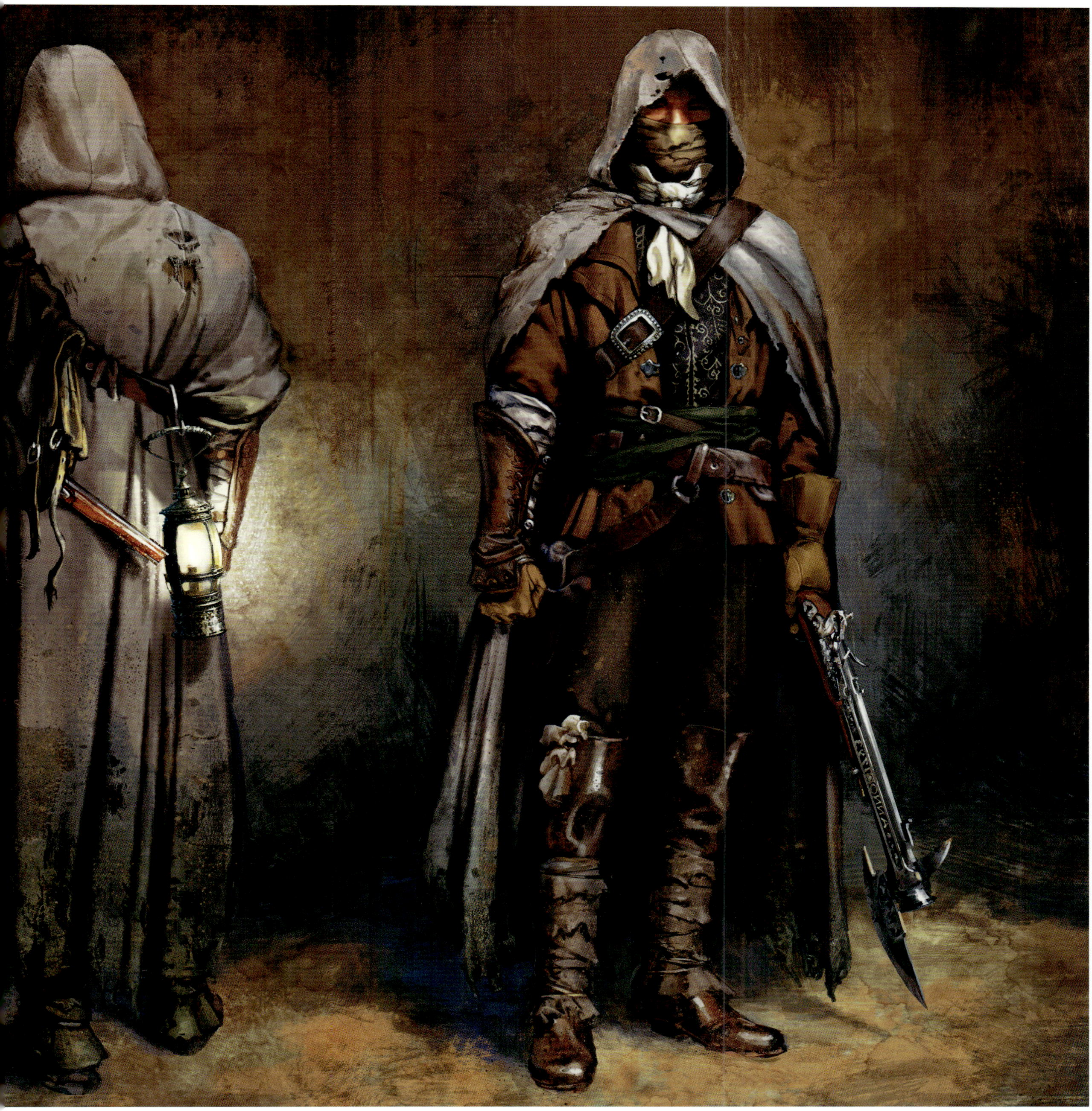

GOING UNDERGROUND

The catacombs beneath Paris were only explored through a few designated missions over the course of *Unity*'s storyline, but those moments revealed the vast underground network that stretched across the city.

The downloadable content pack called *Dead Kings* put the focus squarely on the exploration of catacombs, albeit outside of Paris proper in the run-down town of Saint-Denis. The story finds a disillusioned and bereft Arno ready to depart Paris for good after the tragedies he has faced during the Revolution. A mission from the Marquis de Sade sets Arno at odds against raiders aiming to sack the tombs of the French kings hidden beneath the city.

The dark storyline is echoed by an even darker environment. The catacombs have little of the resplendent lighting that defined Paris, and only a lantern's glare reveals the tumbled ruins and forgotten tunnels beneath the ground.

ANOMALOUS ACTIVITY

Through the power of the Animus and Helix technology, *Assassin's Creed: Unity* provided a look at Paris that extended far beyond the traumas of the French Revolution. "As we did the research, we found that Paris had so many historical layers that we thought that we could add other eras," Mohamed says. The history of Paris offered ample opportunities for discovery, even if other moments of time would be mere glimpses rather than full re-creations of the city.

In an opening scene prior to meeting Arno, the player witnesses an early pivotal moment in the conflict between Assassin and Templar. In 1307, Jacques de Molay is betrayed and burnt at the stake and becomes the last publicly known face of the Templar Order before the entire organization goes underground. Not only does the sequence provide the setup to Arno's quest later in the game, it also offers one of the only glimpses so far of the Assassin/Templar war in the years between Altaïr's adventures in the Third Crusade and Ezio's life during the Italian Renaissance.

Later in *Unity*, the mysterious Helix rifts offered players a chance to sidestep out of Arno's lifetime and briefly explore other moments in Parisian history, ostensibly on a quest to save Assassins who had become trapped within the simulation. The most magical and brilliant period depicted brought players to the bright and colorful days of the Belle Époque, a time of beauty and expansion in late nineteenth-century France depicted through flashing fireworks, colorful balloons in the sky, and the gleaming Eiffel Tower in the distance. The look for this golden age was in part inspired by the film *Moulin Rouge*, with its colorful theater style, flashy handbills and advertising posters, and celebratory decorations.

Another rift sent the player headlong into occupied Paris during World War II and offered the challenge of climbing the Eiffel Tower while under assault from German warplanes. The weight of oppression is accomplished with the nighttime setting accompanied by searing bright searchlights and flapping red flags. Mohamed cites Quentin Tarantino's *Inglourious Basterds* as a visual benchmark that he shared with the art team hoping to capture the same mood of crushing tyranny and evil. In one unused concept, we get to see more of Paris during World War II, as the glamour of a movie opening is contrasted with the threatening presence of the invading Nazis.

A third rift sequence hurled players back to a medieval siege of a Parisian fortress with catapult stones landing all around. "I told the team, in order to see Paris in the Middle Ages, they should see *The Messenger: The Story of Joan of Arc* by Luc Besson," Mohamed says. The looming fortress at the back of the scene instantly established the terror of an active siege, and the whole battlefield took on a frightening quality, thanks to the sight of spectral soldiers roaming the devastated plain.

Unbeknownst to most players, the team explored a fourth historical period. This last rift would have sent players headlong into the era of *The Three Musketeers*. Early seventeenth-century Paris would have undoubtedly provided a fun diversion and a clever counterpoint to the central tale depicting the Ancien Régime nobility at the height of its power in potent contrast to its ultimate fall during the events of the main game. However, as the constraints of production always force the development team to prioritize their wish list, this time period had to be cut, and the original scope of the other eras had to be narrowed down. "The time anomalies we wanted to include were radically different from each other. Each era was a lot of work because we had to rethink all the visual ingredients of the environments and make them feel unique," Mohamed admits. "It would have been impossible to do everything we wanted, because we couldn't just recycle assets. Every time period required distinct assets and a new approach."

Taken together, these explorations into other times provided visual variety and an exciting diversion from the ongoing story, and the team's artists embraced the opportunity to explore other moods and color schemes beyond their depiction of the French Revolution.

OPPOSITE TOP: Concept of a medieval Paris courtyard (Gilles Beloeil).
OPPOSITE BOTTOM: Digital painting depicting the Nazi occupation of Paris (Ludovic Ribardière).

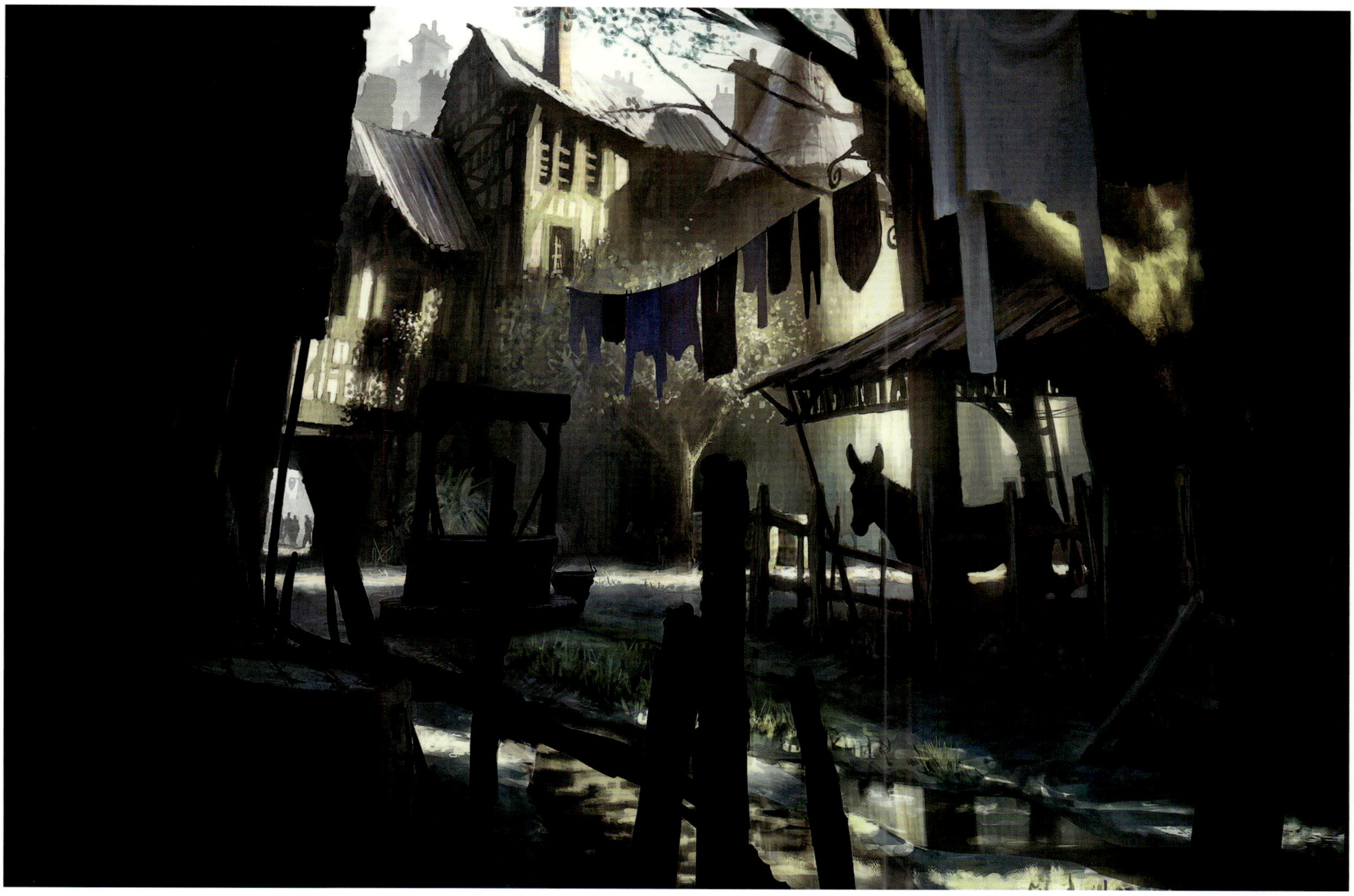

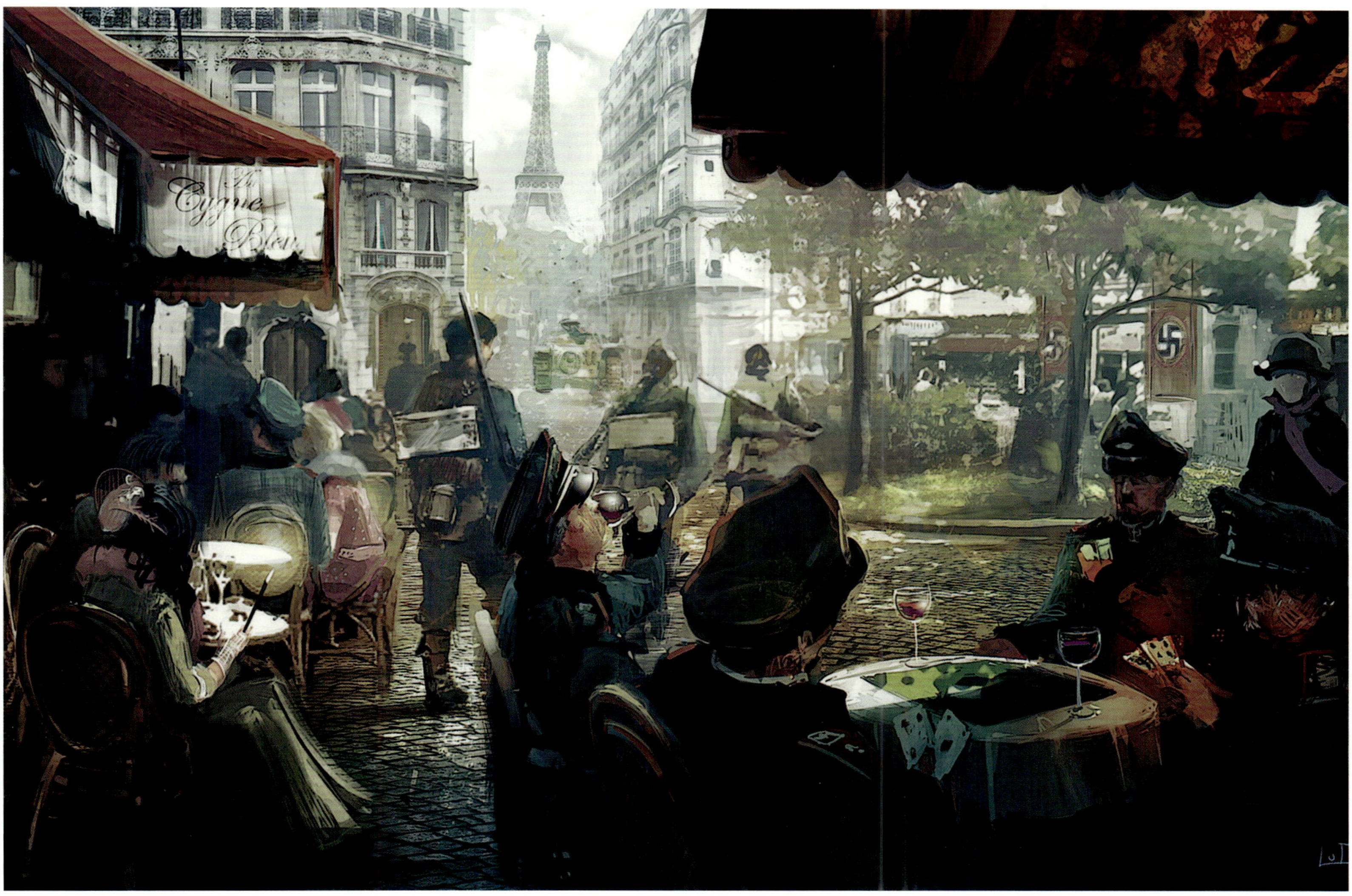
Cygne
Bleu

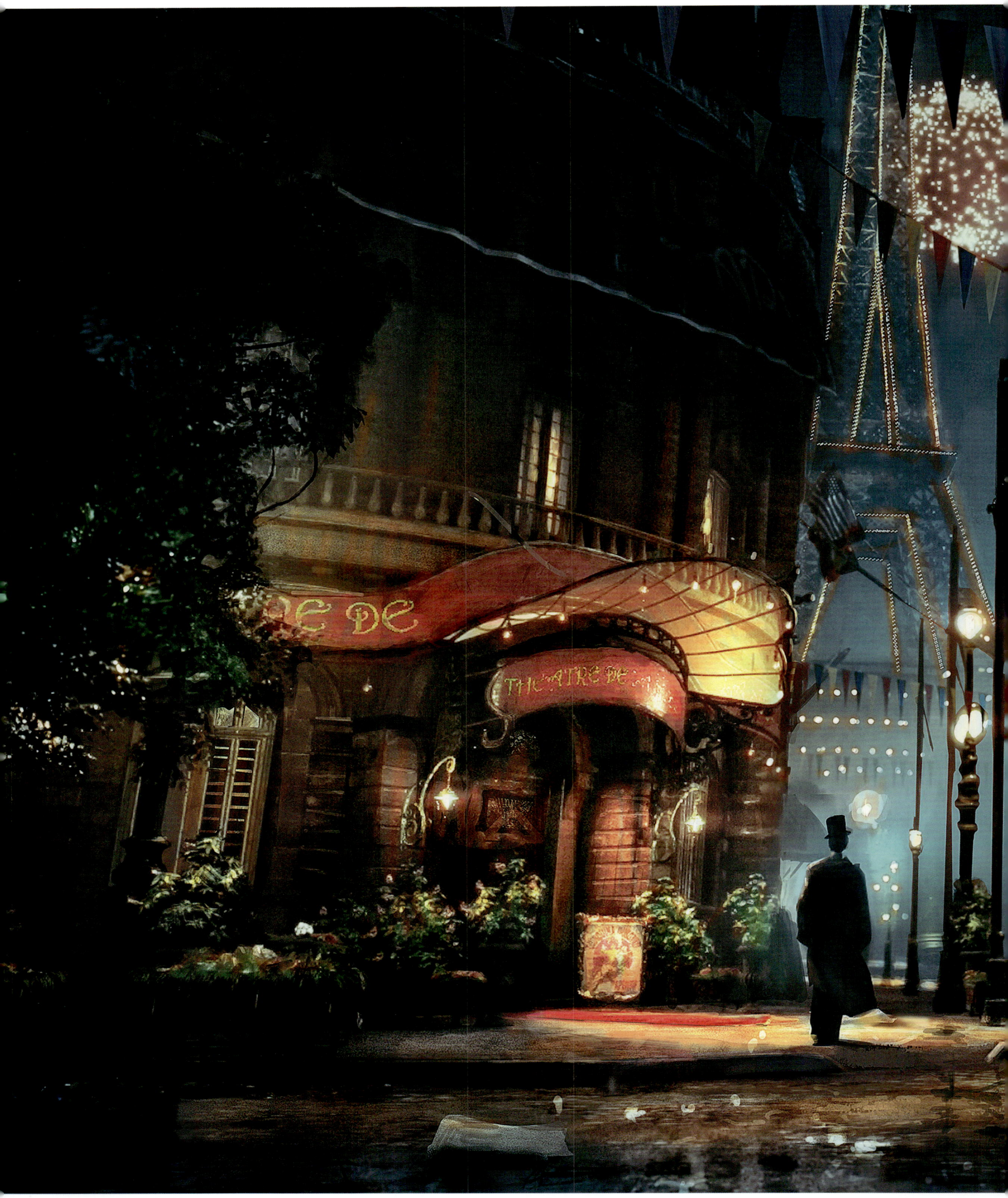
THEATRE DE

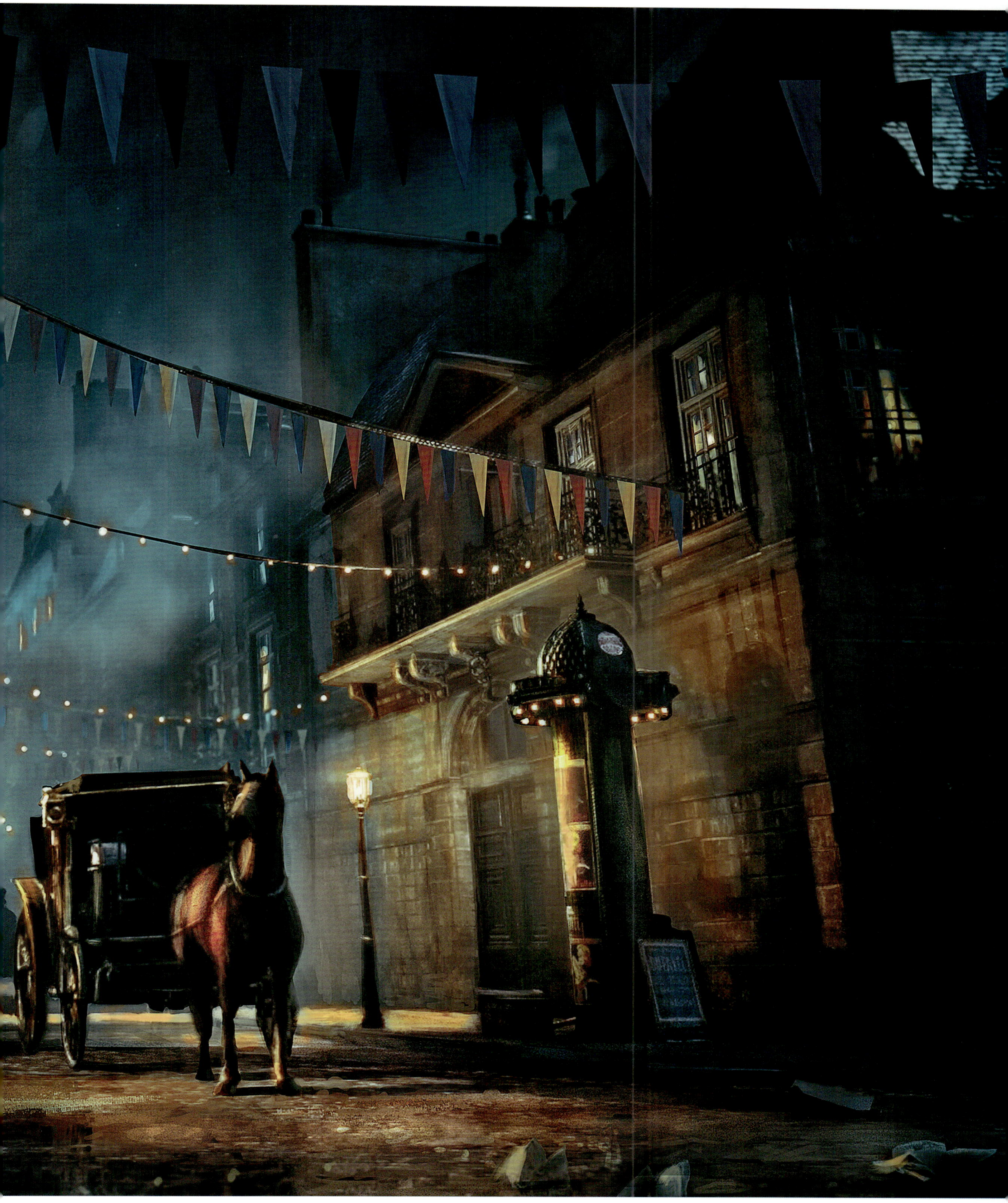

THESE PAGES: Concept highlighting the rich colors of the Belle Époque (Gilles Beloeil).

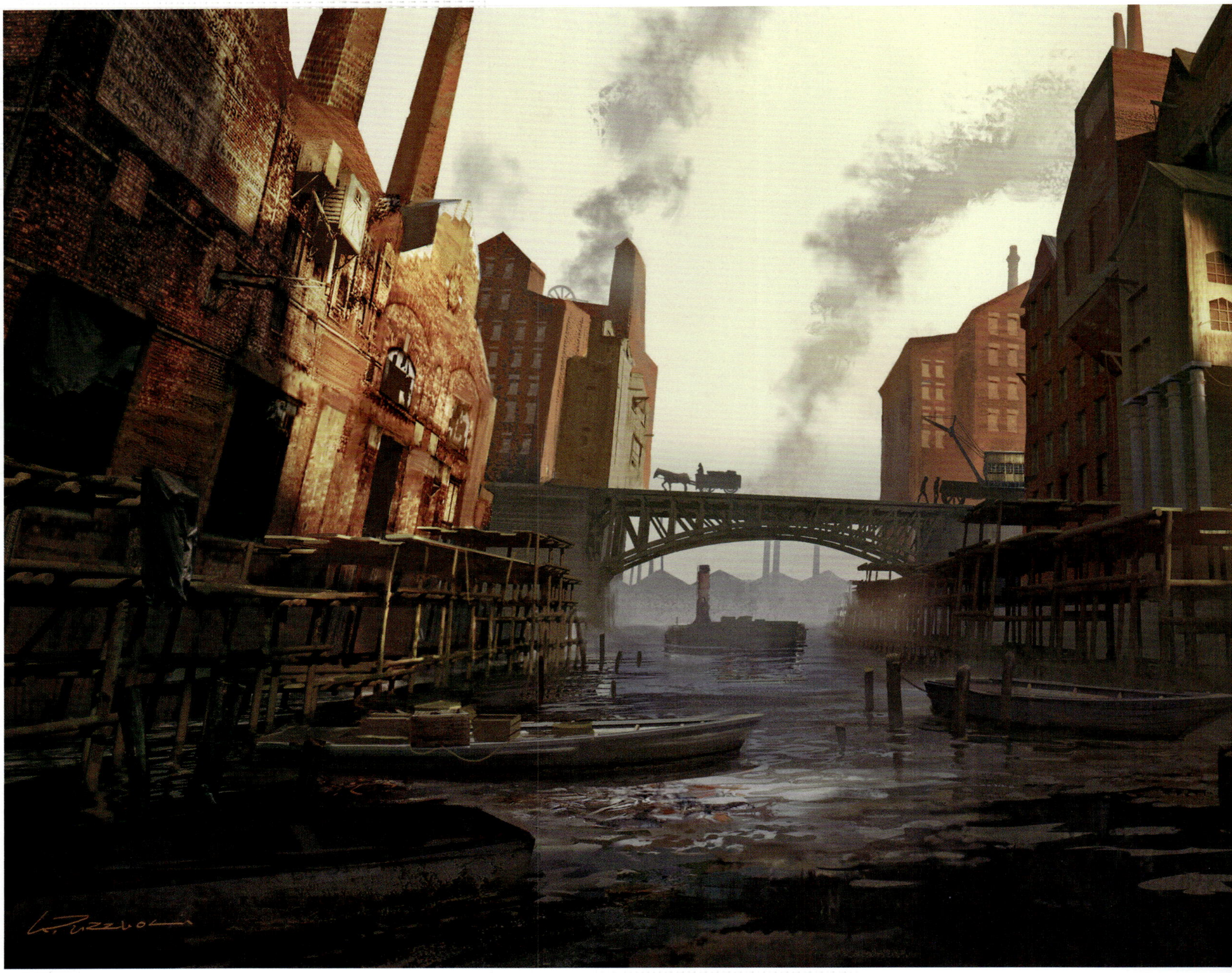

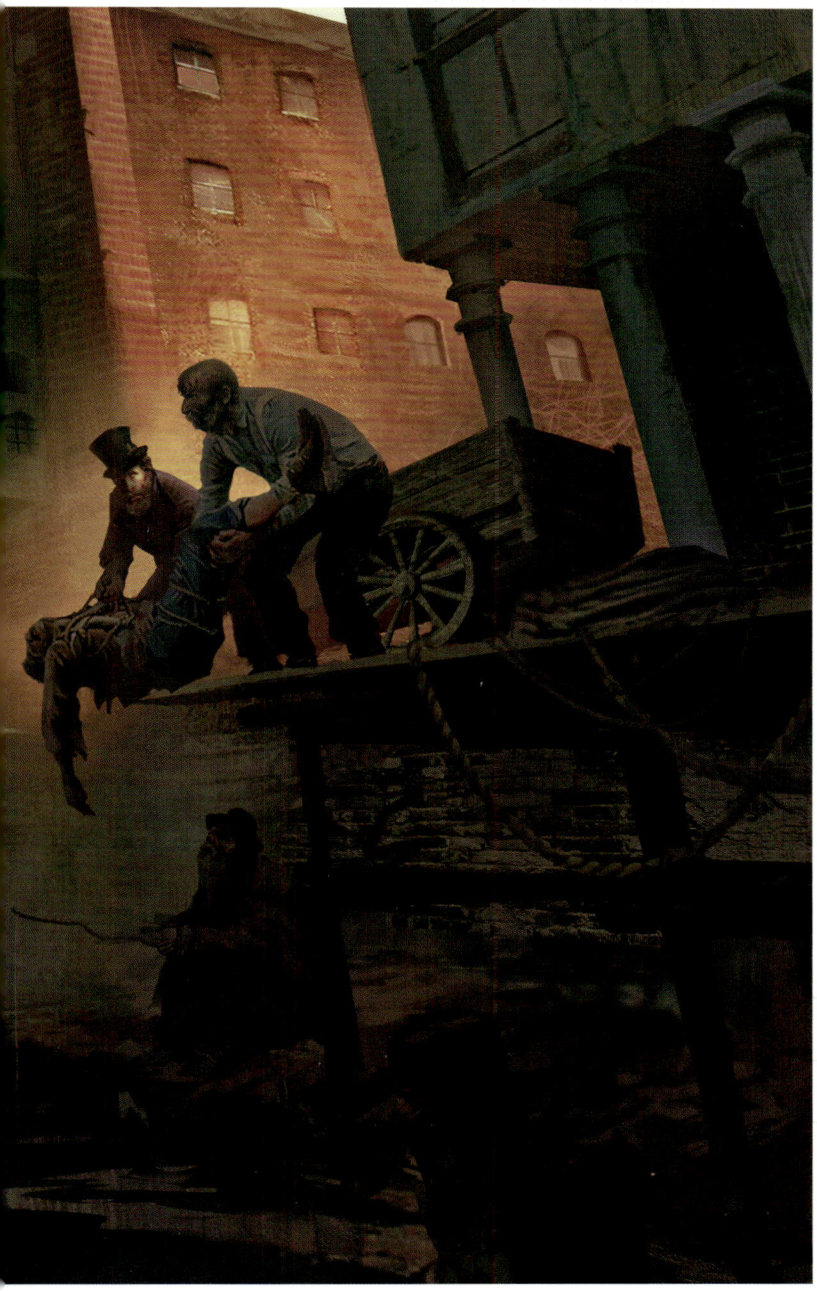

8 THE INDUSTRIAL REVOLUTION

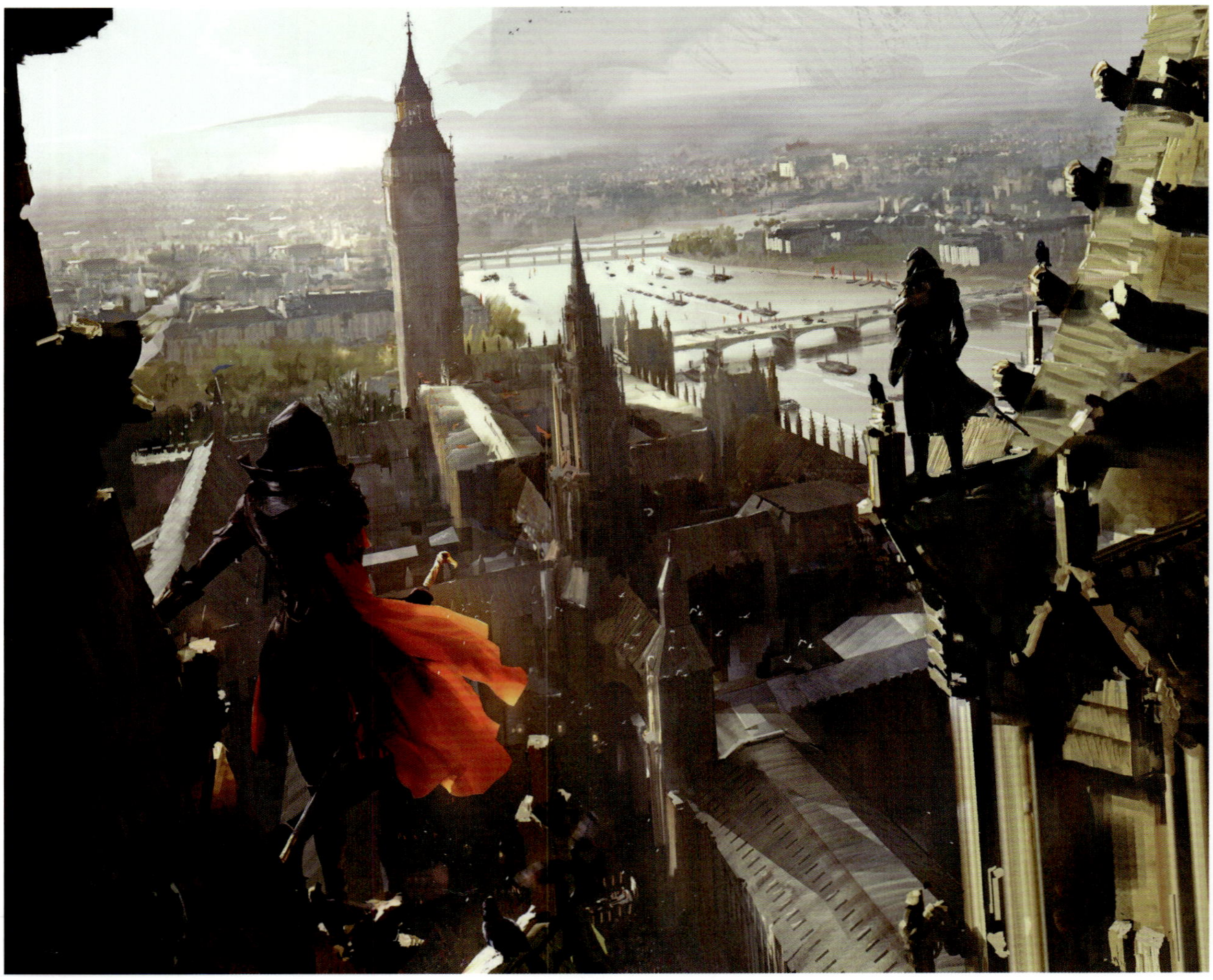

THE SEAT OF THE EMPIRE

The year is 1868, and London is the center of the world. Tumultuous times lay both ahead and behind for the sprawling British Empire, but in this moment, one nation at the edge of Europe is the head of a dominion whose body includes nearly a fifth of the world's population. "We have arrived at the gate of the modern age: the Industrial Revolution," says Thierry Dansereau, art director on *Assassin's Creed: Syndicate*. "So we see modern structures that are unlike anything we have seen before in the franchise." As *Syndicate* begins, the pivotal Industrial Revolution is in full swing, bearing with it the horrible burdens of poverty, pollution, and excess and the gifts of technology, transportation, and communication. After braving the high seas in the Caribbean, the frozen North Atlantic, and the birth pangs of democracy in America and France, Assassin's Creed takes us next to the center of the nineteenth-century world.

Like Ezio's adventures through the Italian Renaissance, no single conflict between nations or groups defines this moment in London's history. Instead, it's the broiling cauldron of profound cultural change that provides the backdrop. "The Industrial Revolution shaped the world as we know it today, like the creation of the middle class and capitalism," Thierry says. "Subjects like poverty, ecology, mass production, pollution, the banking system, and the way we live and consume products all arose during this era. Most of which we take for granted today was born in that period."

In this moment, the conflict between the Templars and Assassins remains as fierce as ever. The Templars see the chance to reach across the world and control it as never before, and the Assassins have never met a greater menace to society's freedom. The danger brings two heroes onto the stage of history to confront this rising threat presented by the Brotherhood's ancient foes.

PREVIOUS PAGES: Residents of the slums face the brutal gangs that control the area (Hugo Puzzuoli).
ABOVE: Artwork showcasing a vivid sunrise from atop Parliament (Tony Zhou Shuo).
OPPOSITE: Illustration contrasting the strong, faraway edifice of St. Paul's Cathedral with the smoggy atmosphere of the railways (Martin Deschambault).

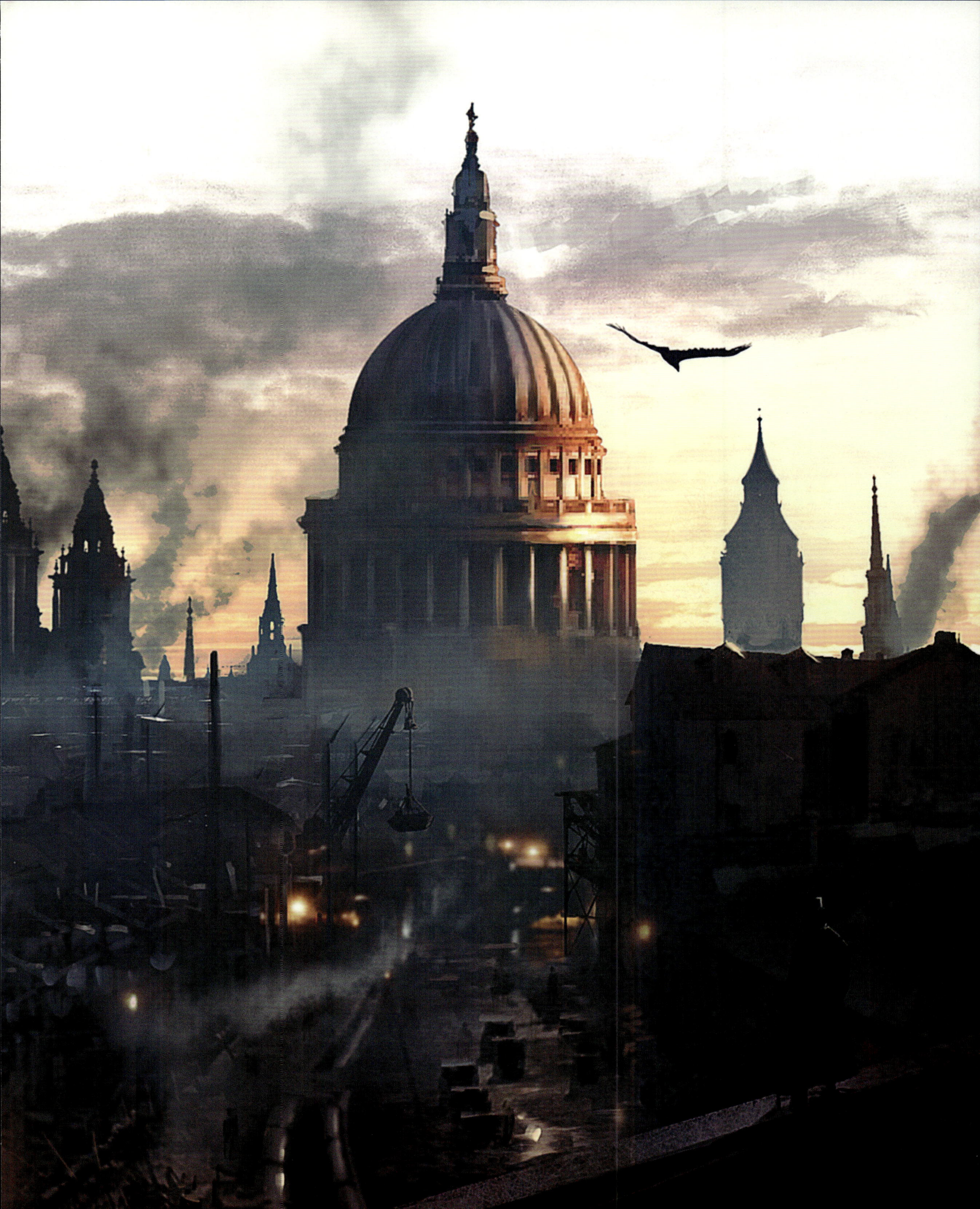

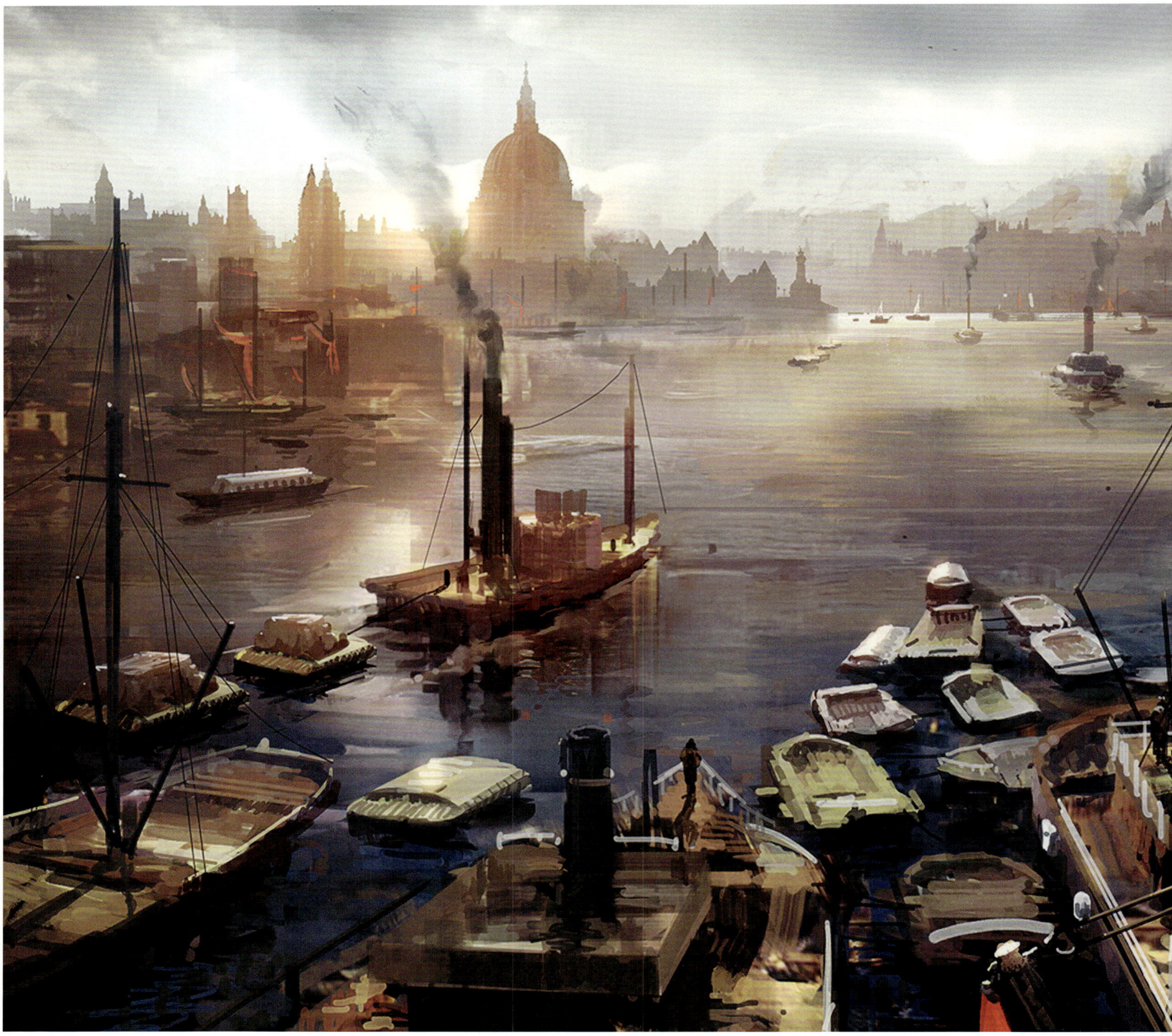

THESE PAGES: With its murky water and steam-powered boats, the Thames offers a varied and somewhat foreboding method of travel (Tony Zhou Shuo).

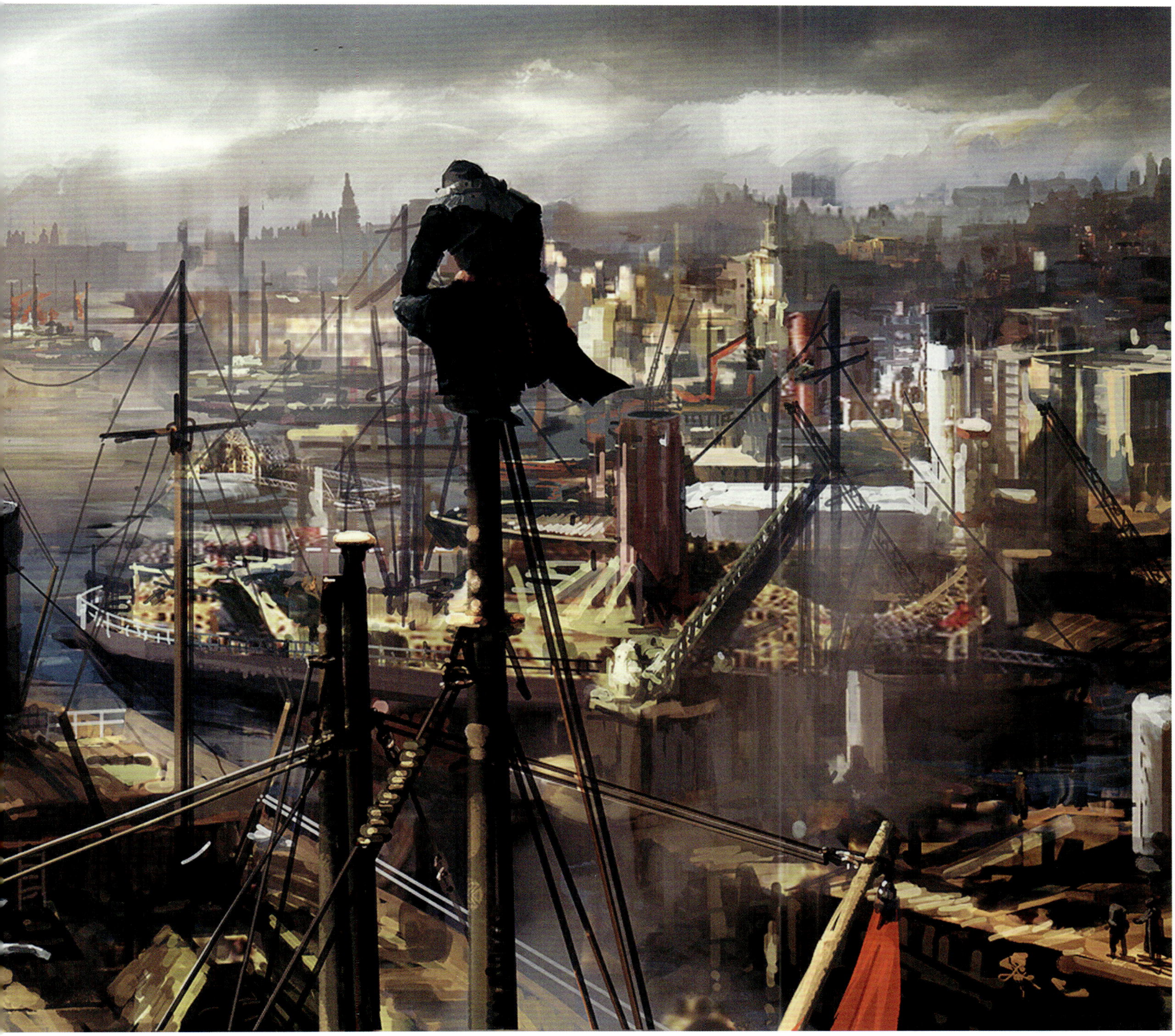

MATCHING ART TO HISTORY

Nineteenth-century London presents a dramatic and complex artistic backdrop defined by the contrasts between opulence and poverty. Industry is an ever-present aspect of daily life, and crime, disease, and pollution are rampant. In choosing an artistic direction for this new installment, Ubisoft's artists are embracing the dramatic shift in tone away from earlier games.

"Our main visual guideline is to create a colorful, saturated, and contrasted world," Thierry states. "Our London needs to also be dark and harsh in order to be coherent and accurate with the reality of the time period. We identified three pillars that will drive the artistic direction: contrast, evolution, and movement. Each pillar must be present in everything we produce."

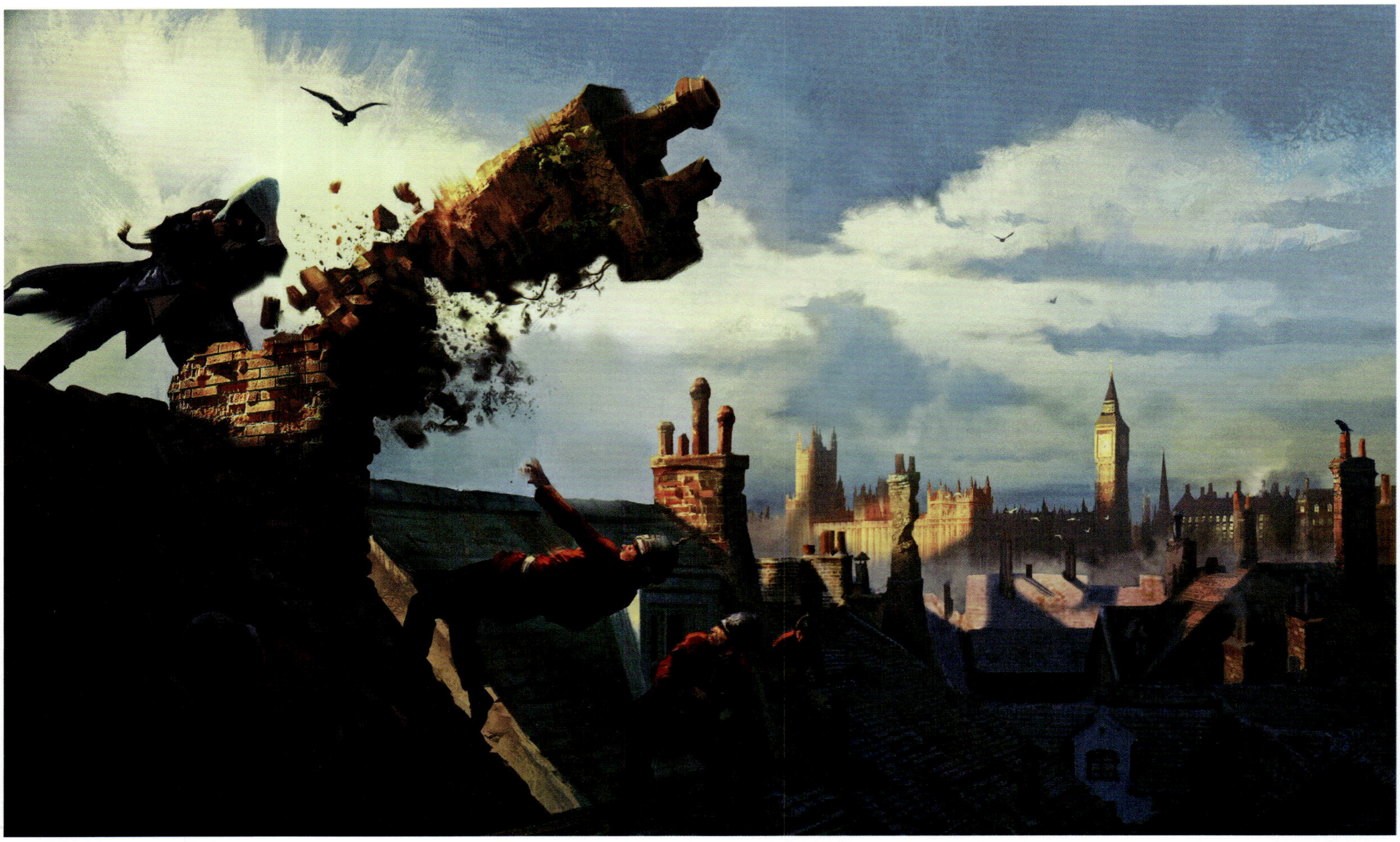

TWO SIDES OF A COIN

Twins Jacob and Evie Frye are no fledgling Assassins. As we meet our hero and heroine, the two have already stepped beyond the initiate's path and taken the Leap of Faith to become members of the Brotherhood once led by Altaïr Ibn-La'Ahad. *Syndicate* pulls back the curtain on this brother and sister ready to fight as soldiers in the age-old war between Assassins and Templars. The twins have proven themselves to the Brotherhood, but they now face the threat of a Templar intent on seizing control of the British Empire for himself and the overwhelming power of the Piece of Eden that might let him succeed. "When you control London, you control the Empire," Thierry says. The two siblings recognize the threat the Templars represent here at the center of the world's most powerful government and aim to stop them at any cost. "The Assassin's goal is to put an end to the control these people have over London and its people by any means necessary," Thierry says.

Artistically, Jacob and Evie allow for new opportunities in visual storytelling, as the game makers weave a story around two distinct personalities and styles. *Unity* gave us Arno and Élise as intertwined characters of central importance to the plot, but players only experienced Arno's life firsthand. The new protagonists of *Syndicate* are built with the opposite in mind. A single player will hop back and forth between Jacob and Evie, each with their own tasks and unfolding plots. "They will have their own missions, which means you can play both of them in free-roam in the world," Thierry says. Together the individual stories of brother and sister weave the framework of *Assassin's Creed: Syndicate*.

Jacob Frye is the rough-and-tumble sibling, a roguish and streetwise warrior striding through a world of gaslight and fog. In keeping with the times, his weapons are concealed. Blades and guns are unacceptable adornments for modern sensibilities, so they stay hidden behind layers of cloth. "Jacob is the brutal guy, the guy who takes all the risks and acts impulsively," Thierry says. "Jacob will break the bridge if he needs to but won't think about the consequence of his action." Visually, Jacob at first looks more like a street thug, and several distinct evolutions move him closer to the familiar garb of an Assassin, and richer materials communicate his growing influence across London. Regardless of his clothing, Jacob's look is meant to communicate his direct and often brazen approach to conflict; his missions might eschew classical Assassin orthodoxy, but they get the job done.

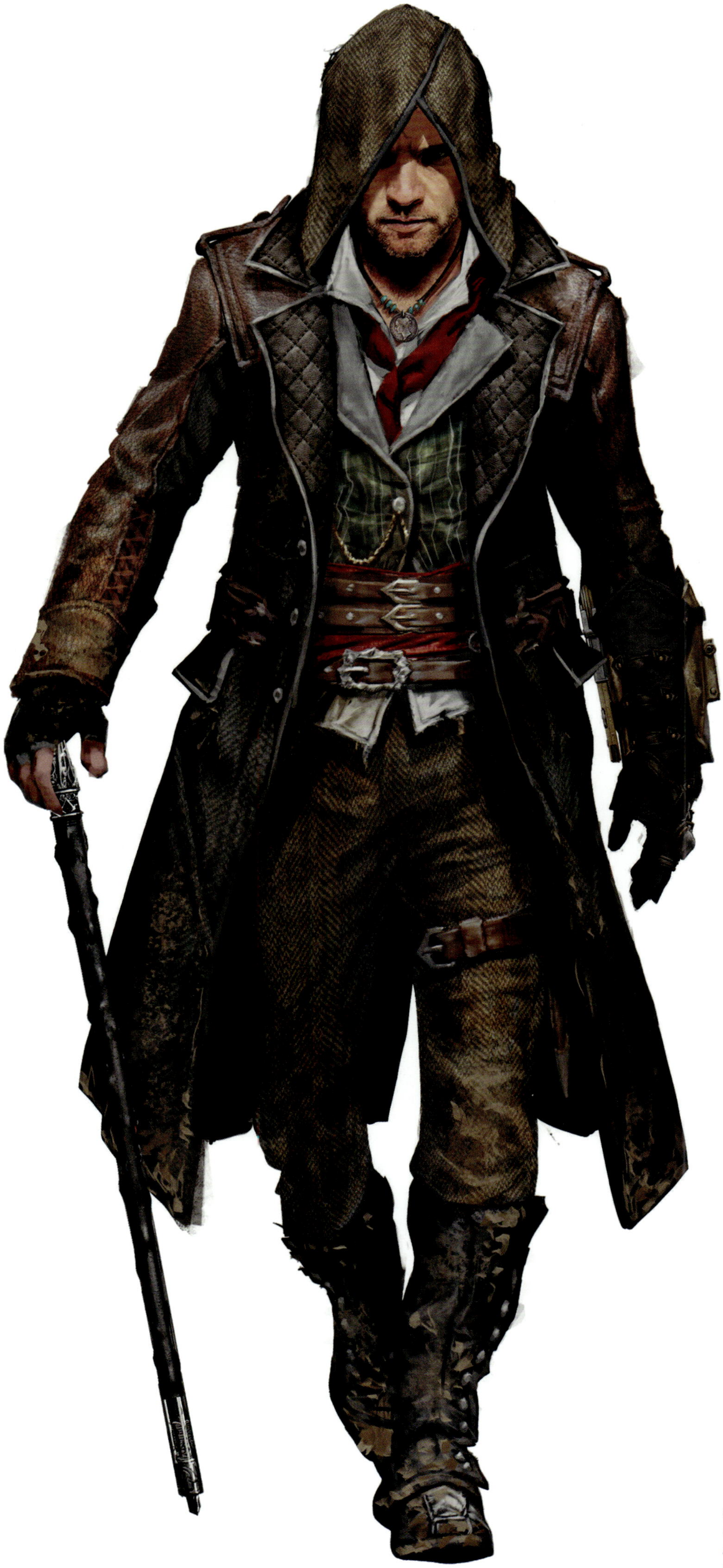

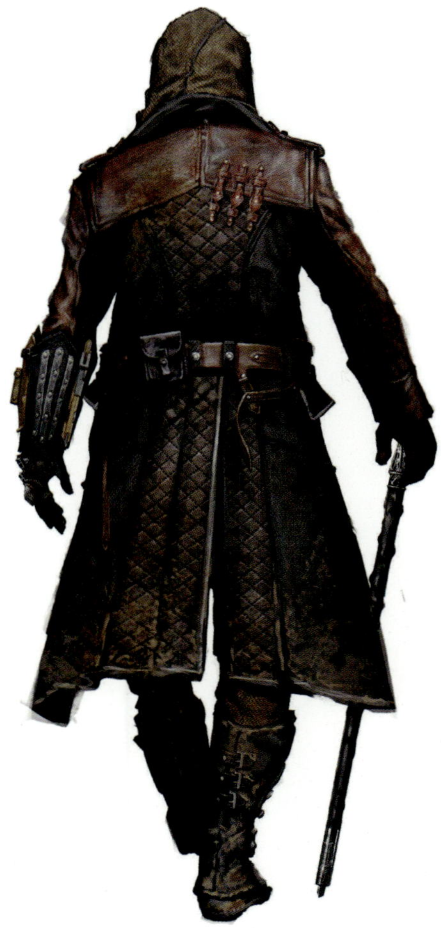

OPPOSITE: Concept art emphasizing Jacob's brash and unpredictable nature (Hugo Puzzuoli).
ABOVE: Inspired by a rock star motif, Jacob's outfits include sharp angles and layered textures (Grant Hillier).

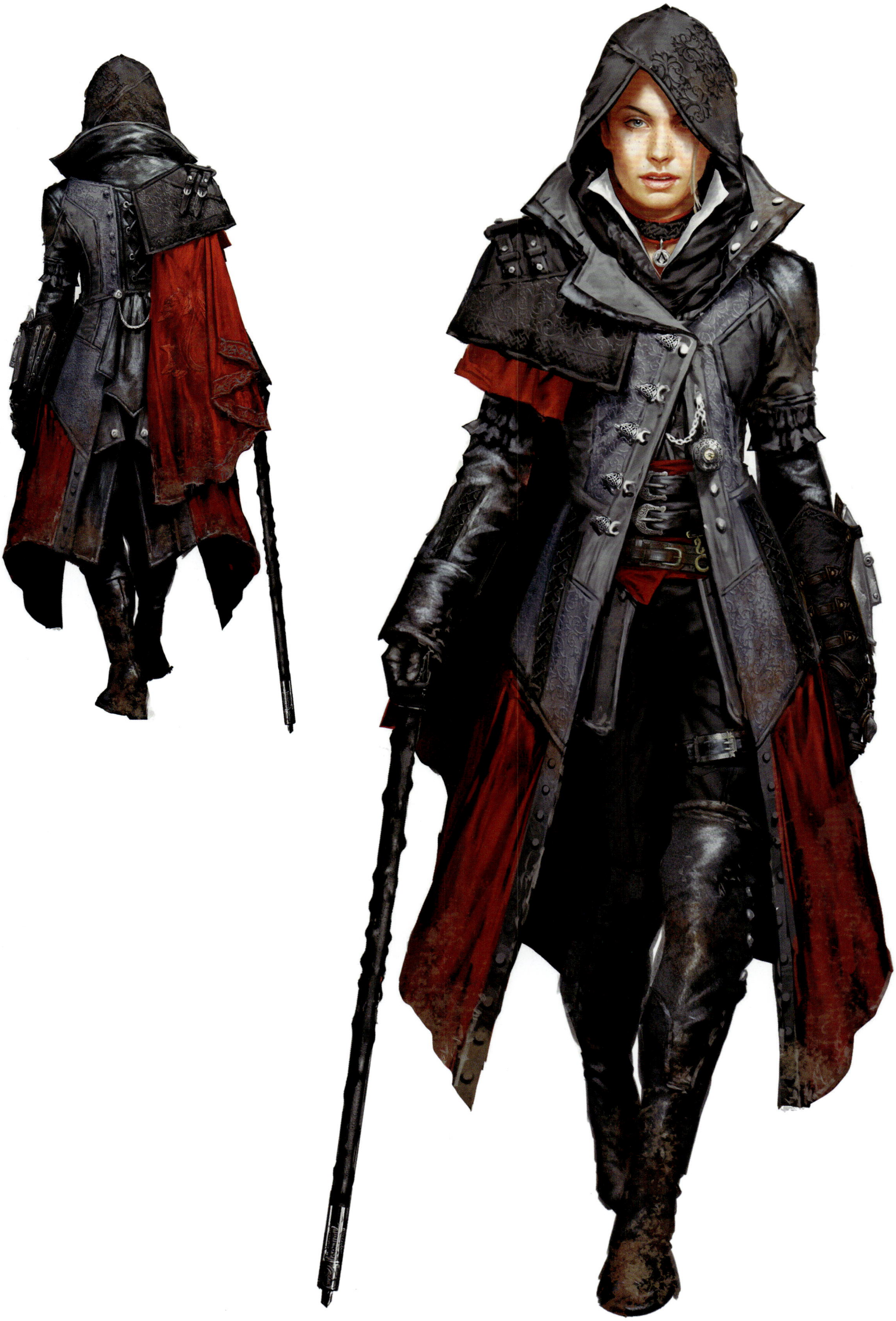

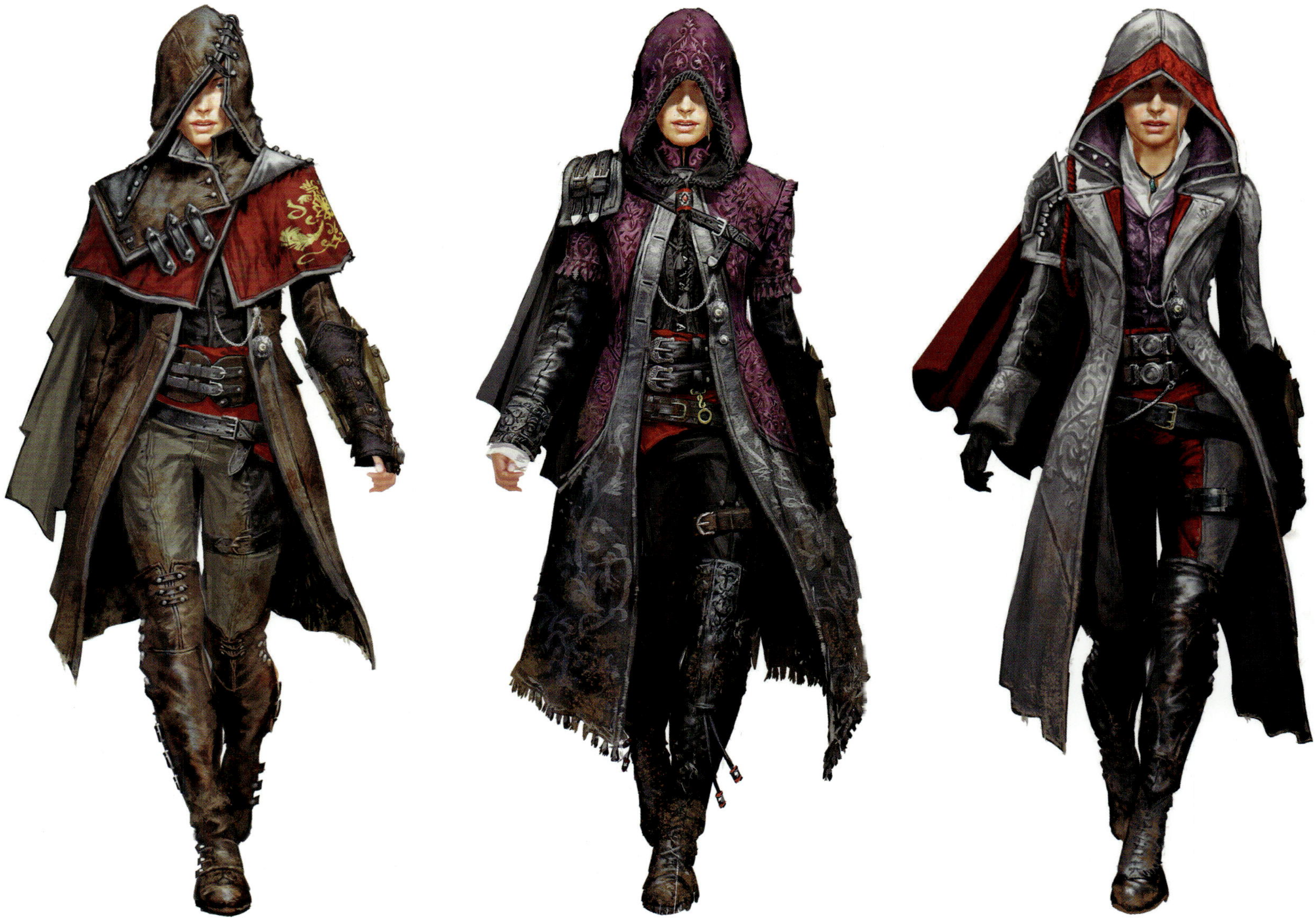

Jacob's sister, Evie, takes her cues from the greatest of the Assassins that came before. More subtle in her approach to danger, her missions are built around careful planning and surgical strikes. "Evie is more like the classic Assassin in our social setting," Thierry says. "She kills from the shadows, remaining unnoticed and invisible. Evie seeks a tactical approach while Jacob is more likely to pursue the high-impact solution." In keeping with that tradition, her visual presentation is more reminiscent of the classic Assassin outfits but with enough modern flair to feel dangerous and appealing to players and appropriately dark to keep her concealed on the soot-stained streets of the city.

Taken together, the two characters offer an opportunity for players to flip back and forth between two distinct fantasies and see the story play out from multiple perspectives. At the same time, the familial link between the Frye siblings ensures a unified story thread.

OPPOSITE: Evie's Master Assassin outfit (Grant Hillier).
ABOVE: Evie outfit variations with curved embroidery referencing the Assassin crest (Grant Hillier).

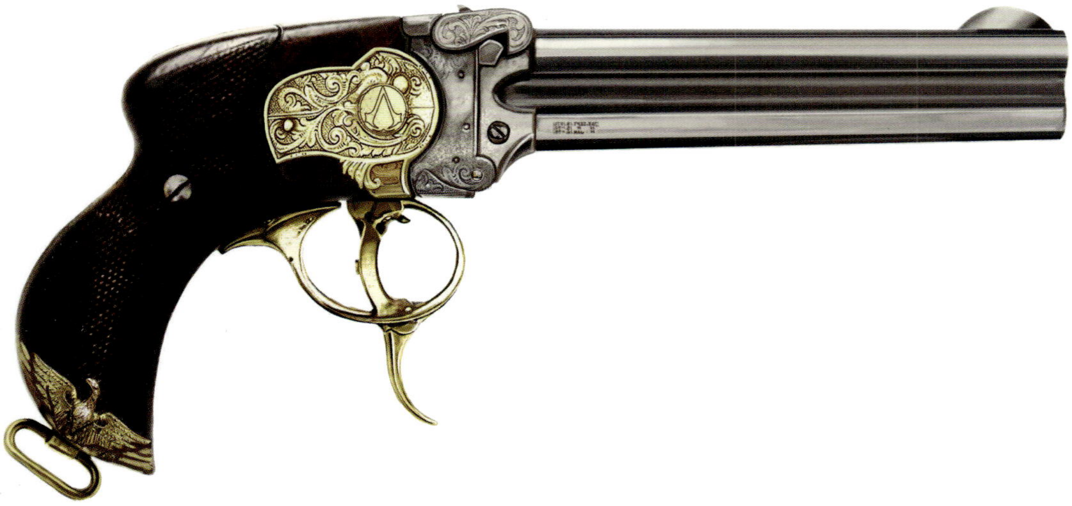
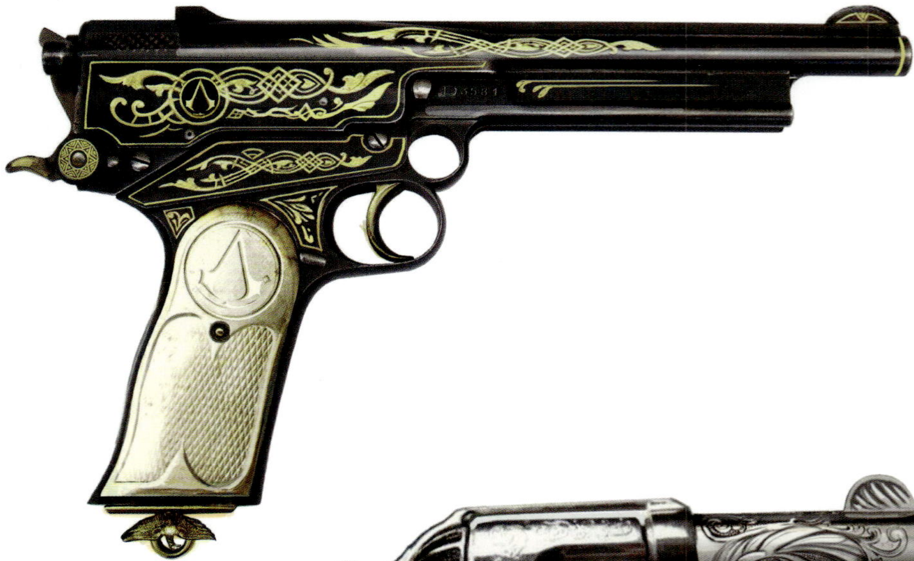
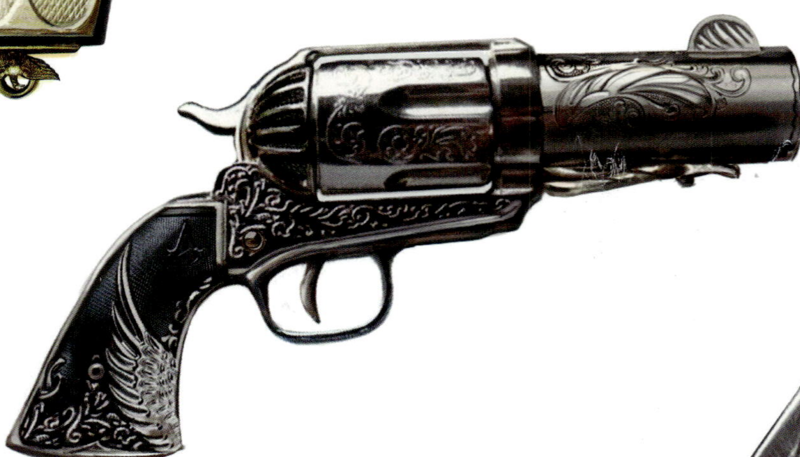
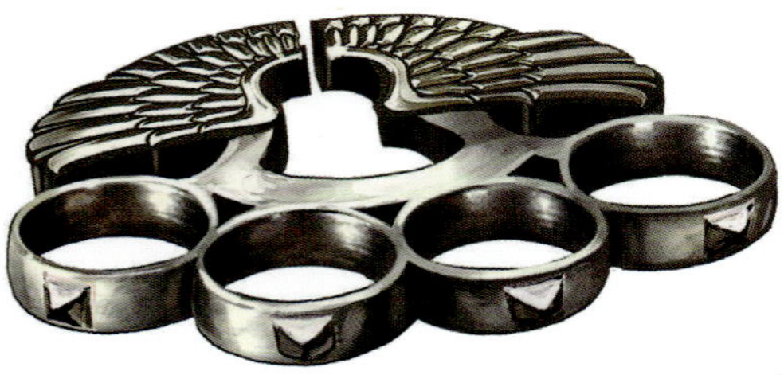
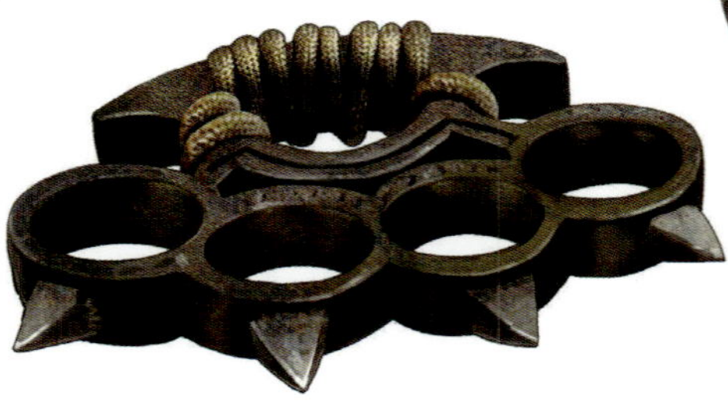
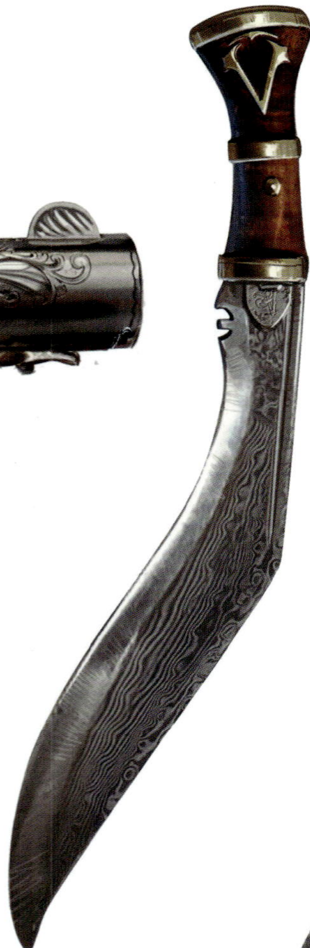
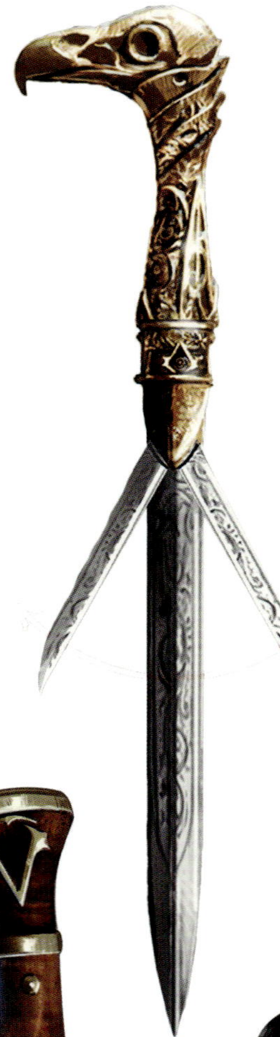
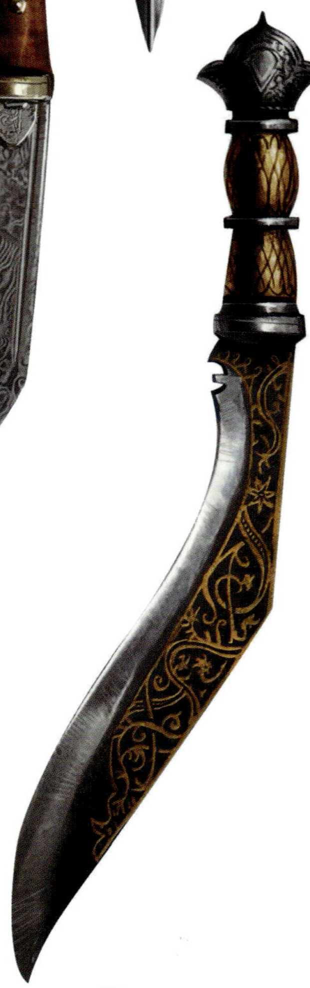
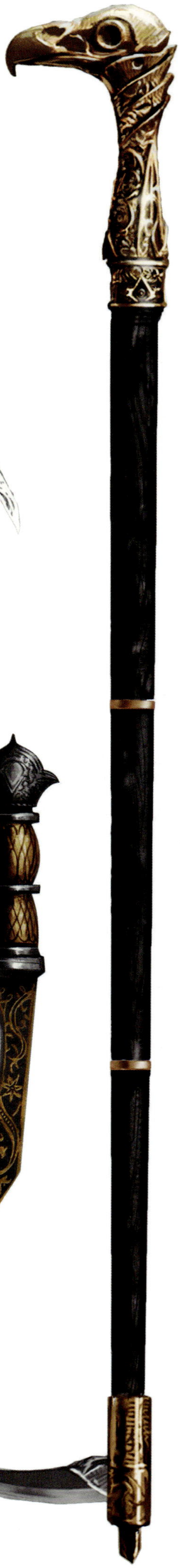

THIS PAGE: Weapon concepts for engraved pistols, knuckle dusters, the Indian kukri knife, and the cane sword (Caroline Soucy, Grant Hillier, Fernando Acosta).
OPPOSITE: Artwork for the Assassin Gauntlet with rope launcher (Grant Hillier).

A MODERN ARSENAL

Jacob and Evie have access to a variety of new armaments, and, because of the British Empire's long reach during the period, the weaponry comes from across the world. The cane-sword offers an understated way to transition from respectable London citizen to deadly Assassin. The kukri comes from distant Nepal via India and offers a brutal slashing tool for the most furious of melees. Brass knuckles present a potent edge in the fight club scenes that play out in the hidden backstreets of the city. And multiple swing-out cylinder and semi-automatic revolvers increase the range potential of our Assassins as never before.

However, as always, the new variation on the hidden blade is the real pièce de résistance of our Assassins' toolkits. While much of *Syndicate* avoids cliché nods to steampunk fiction, the Assassin Gauntlet flirts with that style, thanks to its multiple utilities and exaggerated design aesthetic. "The most steampunk-inspired element in the game is the Assassin Gauntlet," Thierry says. "It can do a lot of things: You can block with it; you can punch with it. It includes a throwing dart gun, the hidden blade, and a rope launcher. It will bring navigation in an Assassin's Creed game to a whole new level, because it changes the way you move through the buildings."

Grappling with the rope launcher is likely the biggest adjustment to gameplay, dramatically changing the options for traversal and free movement. High roof ledges are now easy to reach, allowing characters to slip between building levels in a moment. In addition, it solves the problem of the wide avenues that separate many of London's buildings; passing to the next block over is now a simple affair. "You are able to create zip lines to traverse large distances," Thierry says. "The London streets can be wide, and you are not always able to jump from roof to roof. The zip line solves that problem by allowing you to cross the street in no time. It's a great gameplay feature."

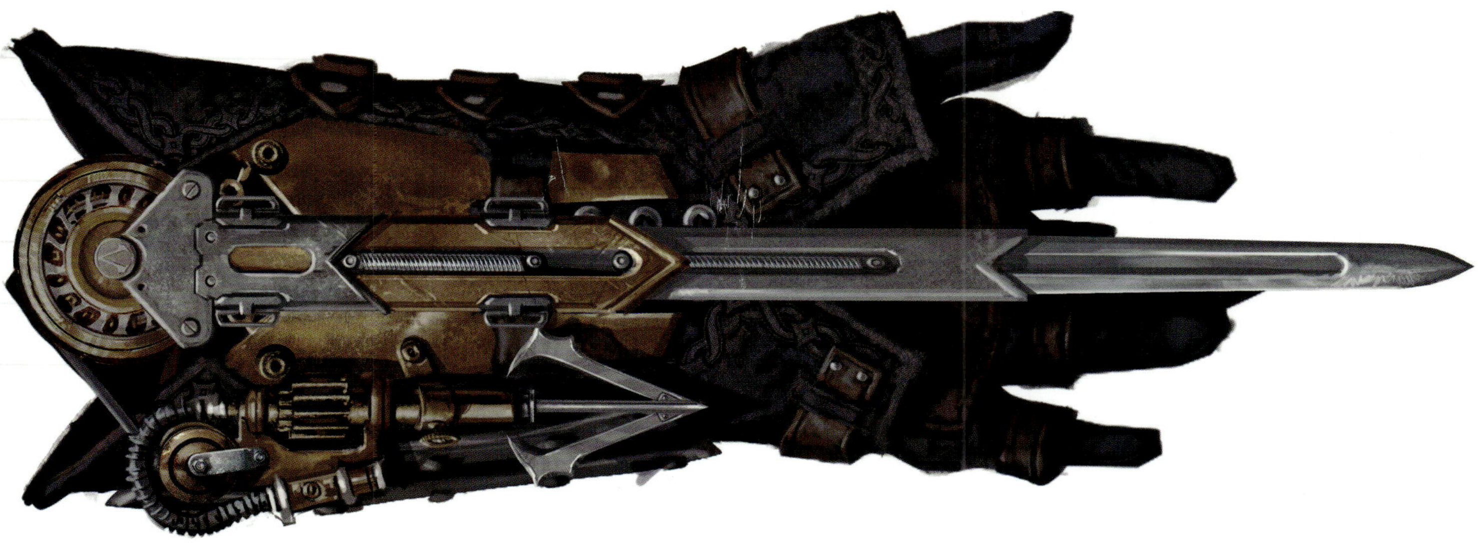

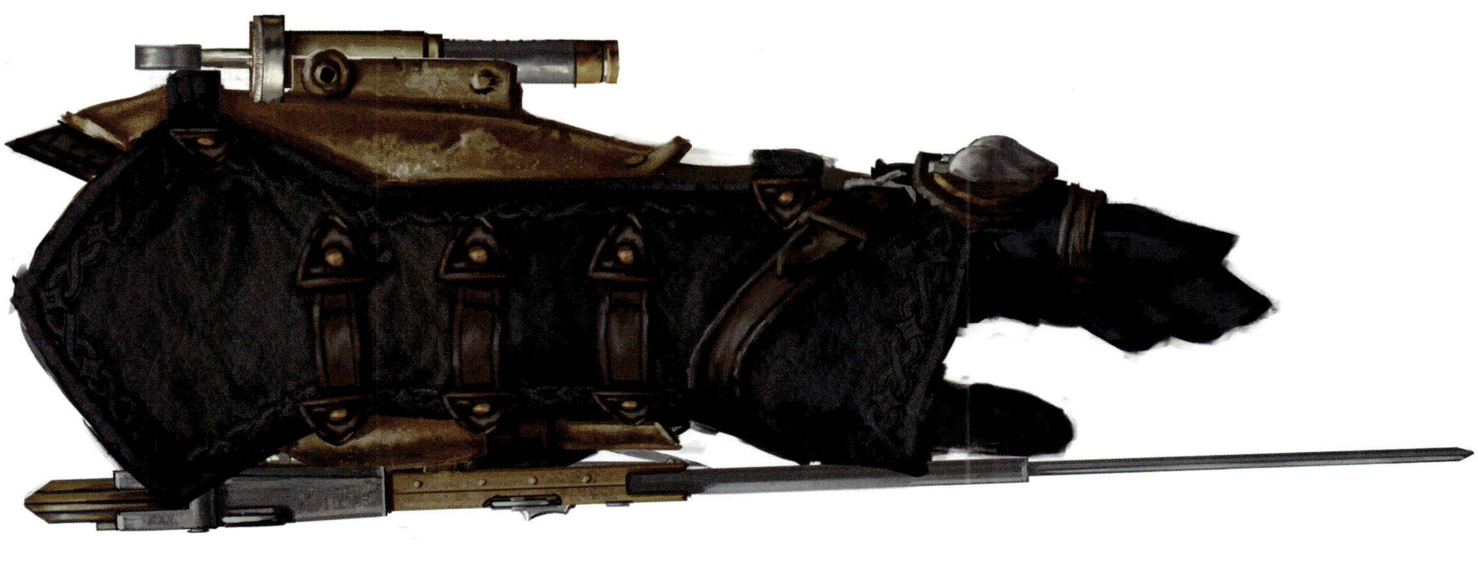

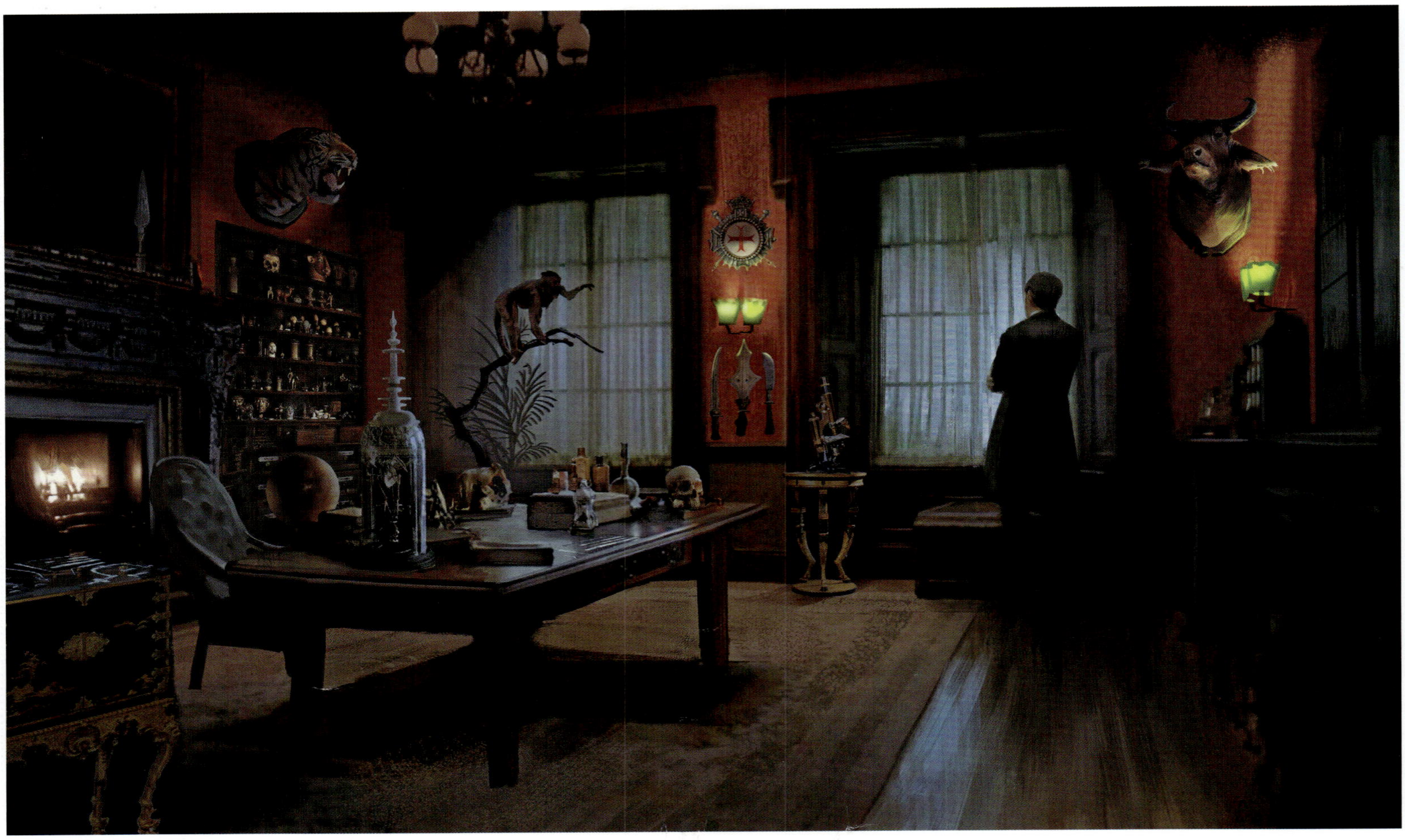

A WORTHY TARGET

ABOVE: Starrick's world is one of economical power and manipulation of both the natural world and humankind (Hugo Puzzuoli).
OPPOSITE: Crawford Starrick's slicked hair and dark clothing were designed to give him a severe, menacing look (Grant Hillier).

Some entries in the Assassin's Creed saga have played with indistinct and shadowy opponents or abandoned the concept of a central antagonist entirely. That's not the case with *Assassin's Creed: Syndicate*. Crawford Starrick is a clear antagonist to the Frye siblings but one with a complex agenda of his own. The ambitious rail baron is a well-known public figure in London, but his real duties are the ones he performs as the Grand Master of the British Rite of the Templar Order. His autocratic leanings establish him as a clear target, but his deep commitment to the Templar cause and their view of humanity's needs make him believable and relatable.

Starrick's severe look underscores his no-nonsense personality. Slicked back hair gives him a controlled style and imposing aristocratic overtones. His piercing eyes establish his potent charisma and dangerous political potential. "Exaggerating certain aspects of his personality helps," says concept artist Grant Hillier. "The mustache, for example, or the hairstyle, which is slicked back and shaved on the sides to give him a severe look. The dark, round eyes, the penetrating stare—these features give him added menace. He's very intelligent, but he's using it for sinister purposes."

It's Starrick's canny political instincts that make him untouchable and dangerous to the Assassin siblings—the man is a master of manipulation with unrivaled ambitions. "We wanted to give our main antagonist a lot of personality and charisma. A good villain has to be as strong as your main hero," Thierry says.

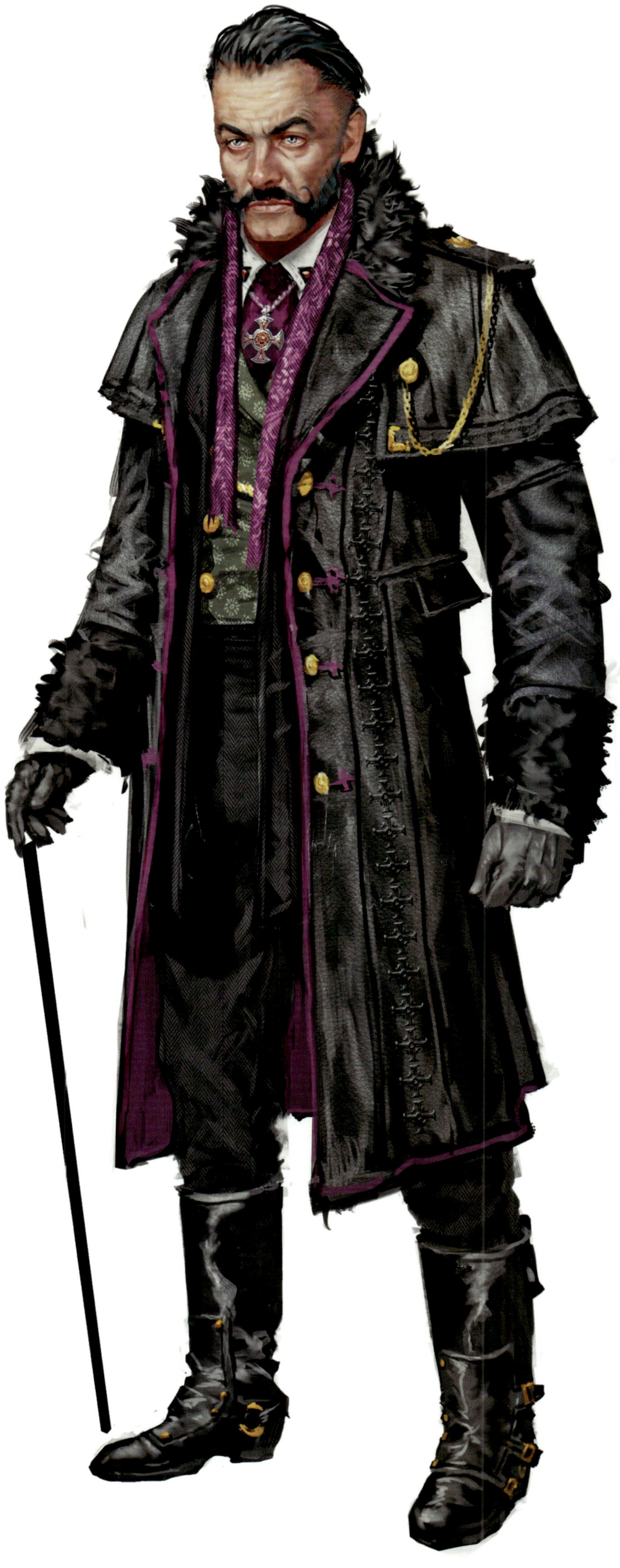

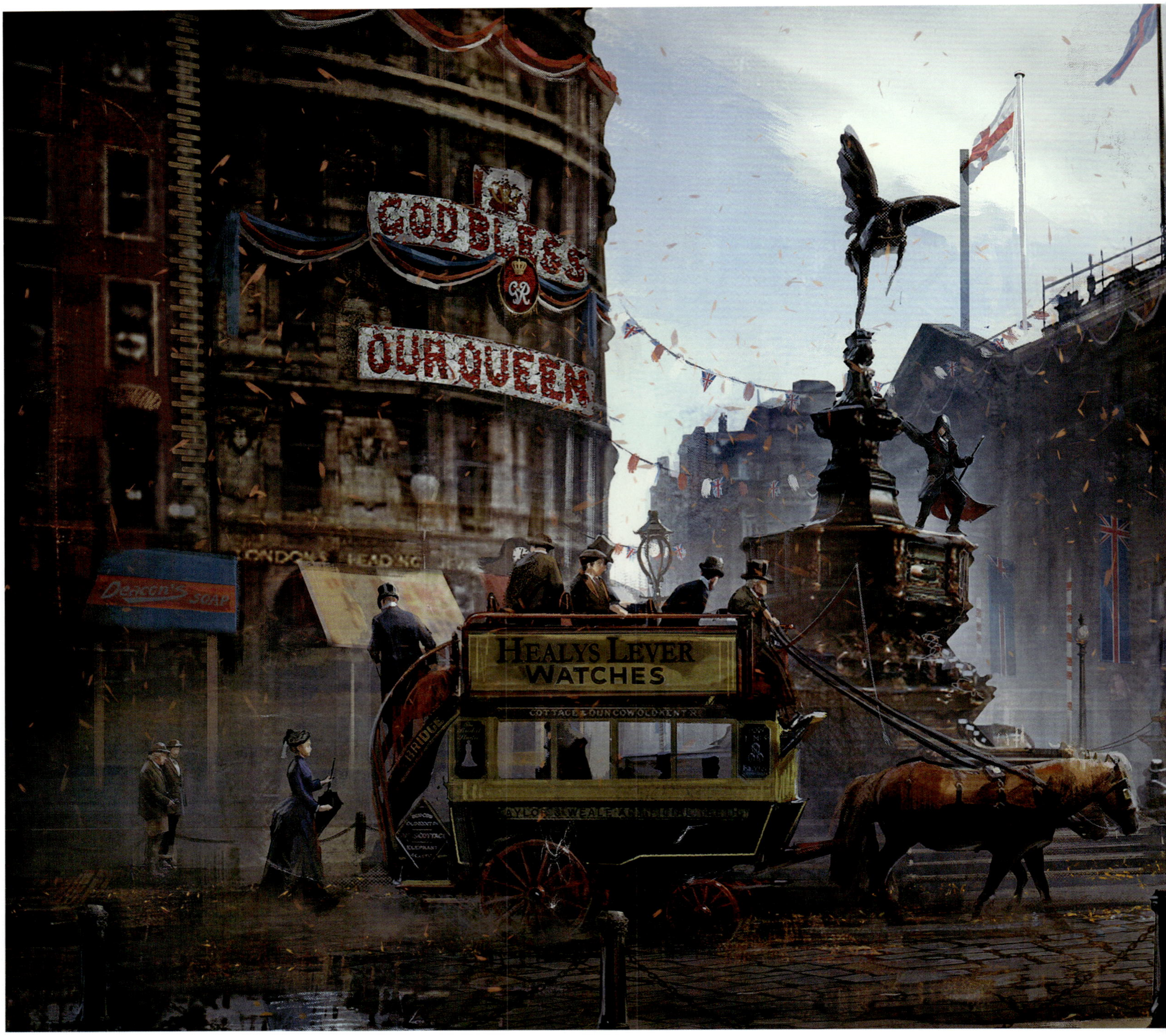
GOD BLESS
OUR QUEEN
Deacon's SOAP
HEALYS LEVER WATCHES

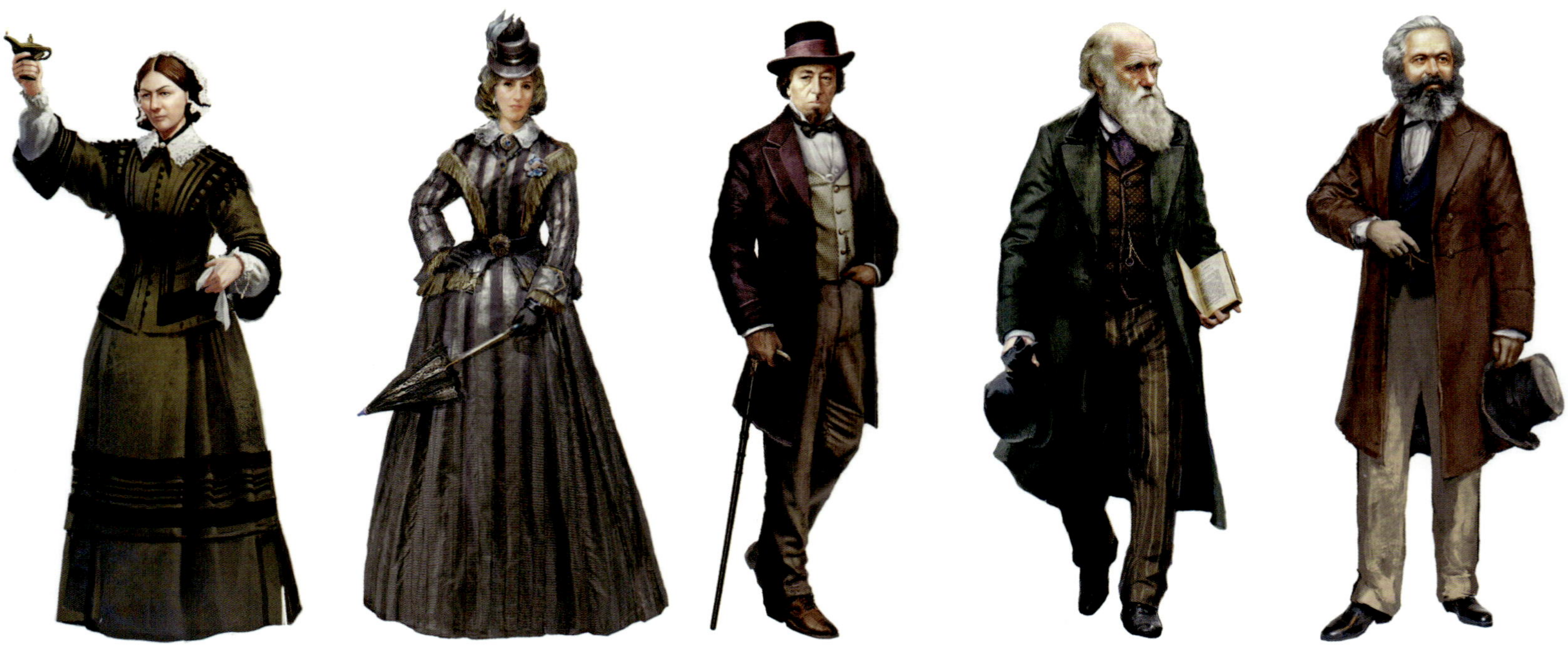

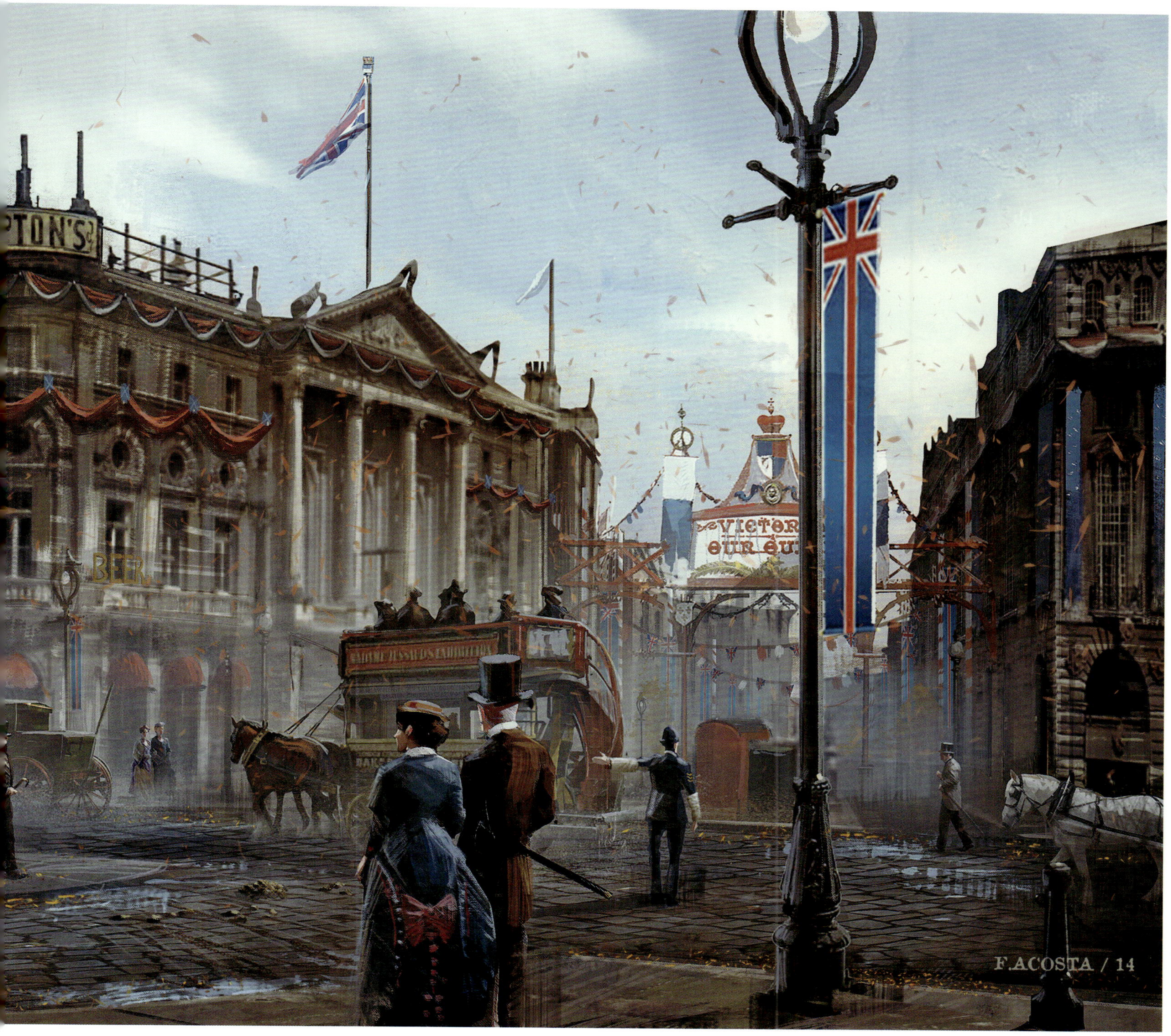

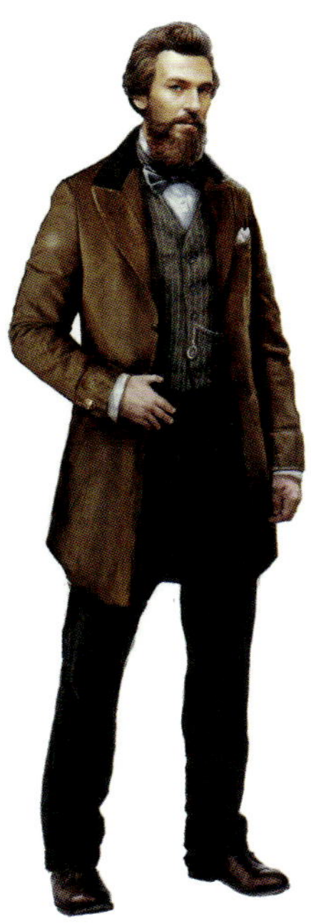

HISTORY'S FINEST

Evie, Jacob, and Starrick are fictional constructs, but like all the Assassin's Creed games that came before, *Syndicate* is filled with familiar faces from the pages of history. Alexander Graham Bell is still a young man in 1868, not yet settled in North America and already busy with the sound experiments that will birth the telephone. Charles Dickens still has stories and novels to write about the highs and lows of London life. And Charles Darwin has already published many of the controversial books that will so profoundly affect the interpretation of science and religion in the coming decades. Victorian-era London is awash in fascinating people to meet, get to know, and influence; Evie and Jacob's adventures bring all these and more into the limelight.

ABOVE: Highly recognizable locations, such as Piccadilly Circus, were recreated using photographs from the Victorian era and modified to fit the Assassin's Creed aesthetic (Fernando Acosta).
BOTTOM LEFT: Character art of Florence Nightingale, Marie Anne Disraeli, Benjamin Disraeli, Charles Darwin, Karl Marx, and Alexander Graham Bell (Fernando Acosta, Yu Li Qing).

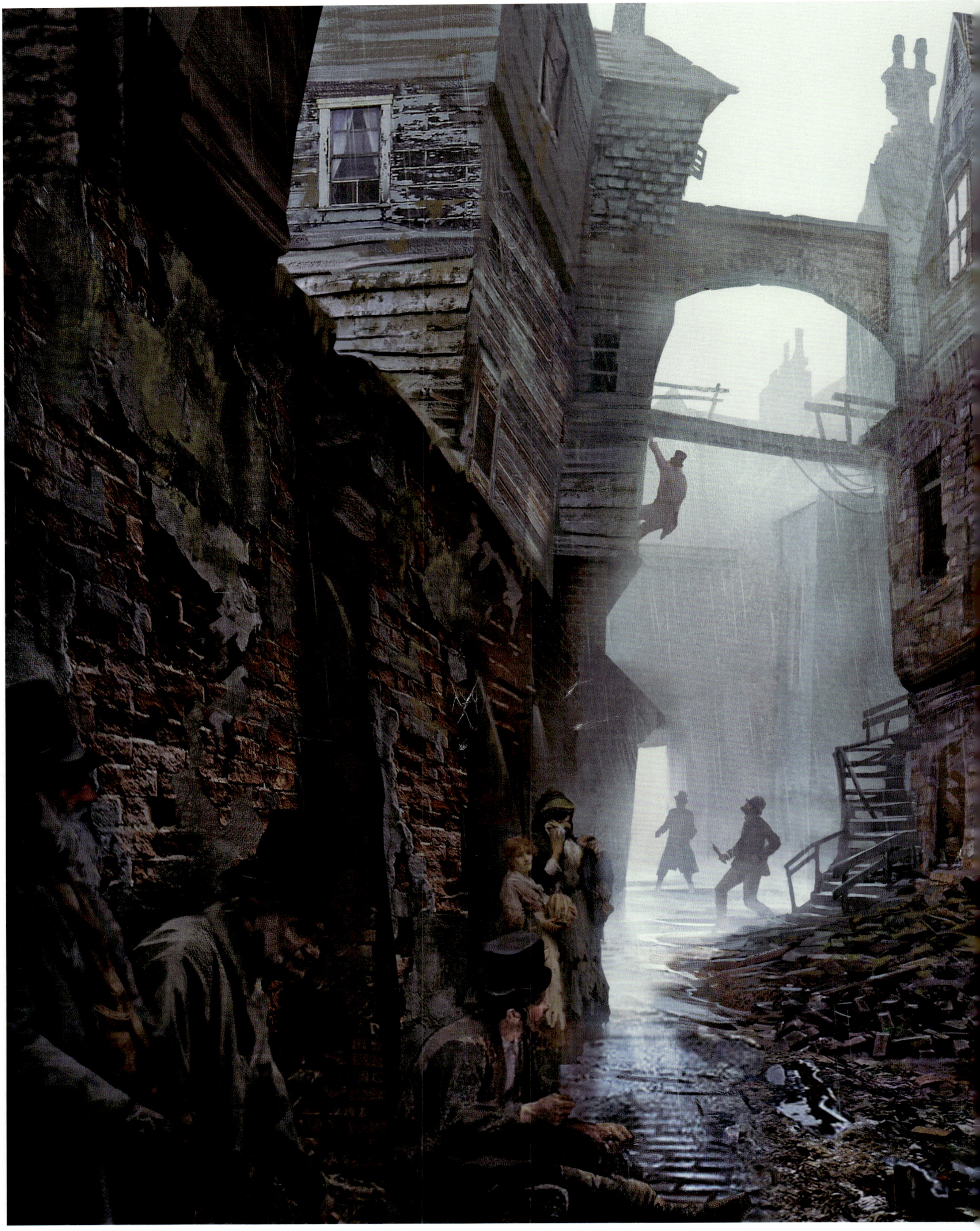

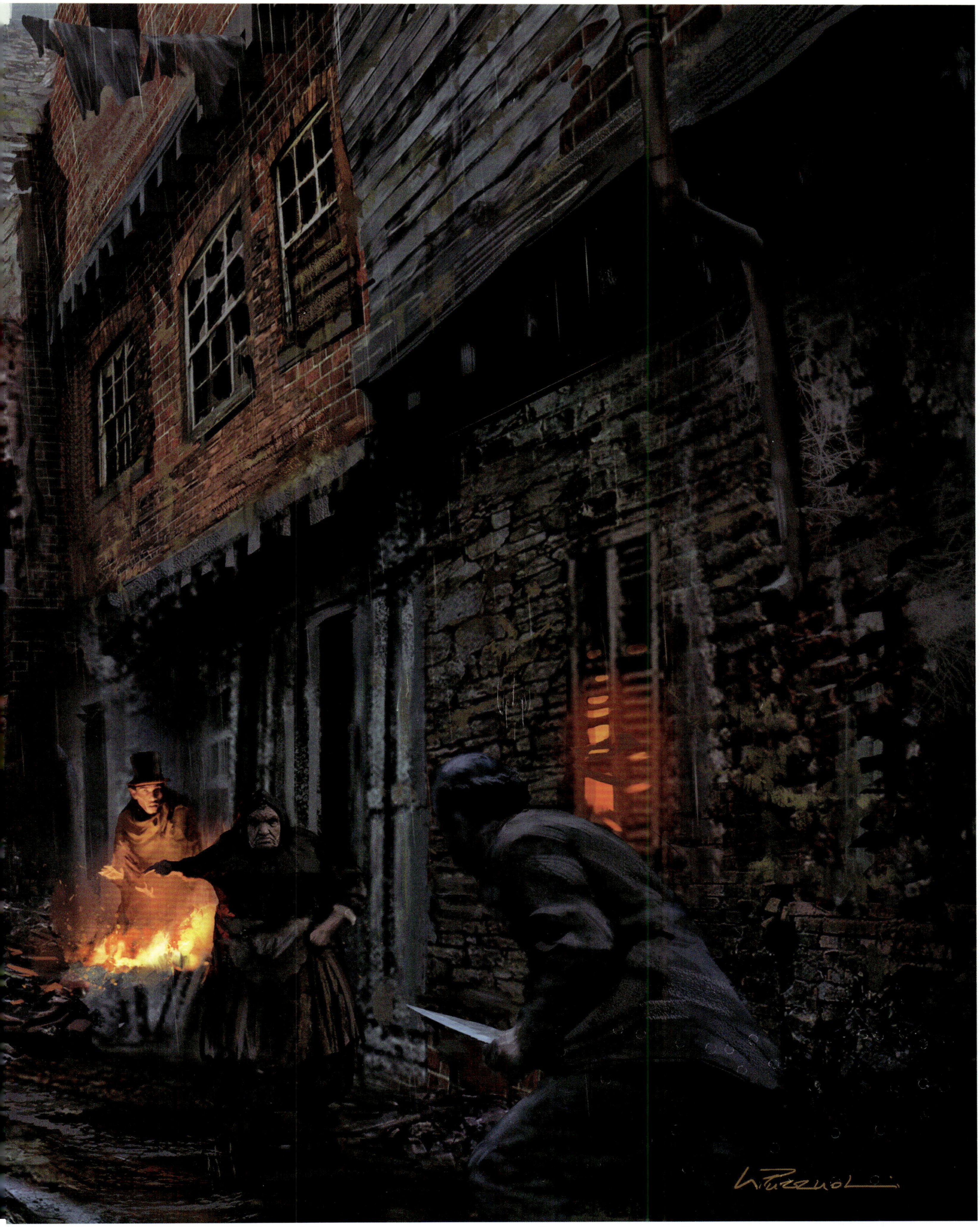

THESE PAGES Award-winning artwork showing the soggy, narrow streets of the slums (Hugo Puzzuoli).

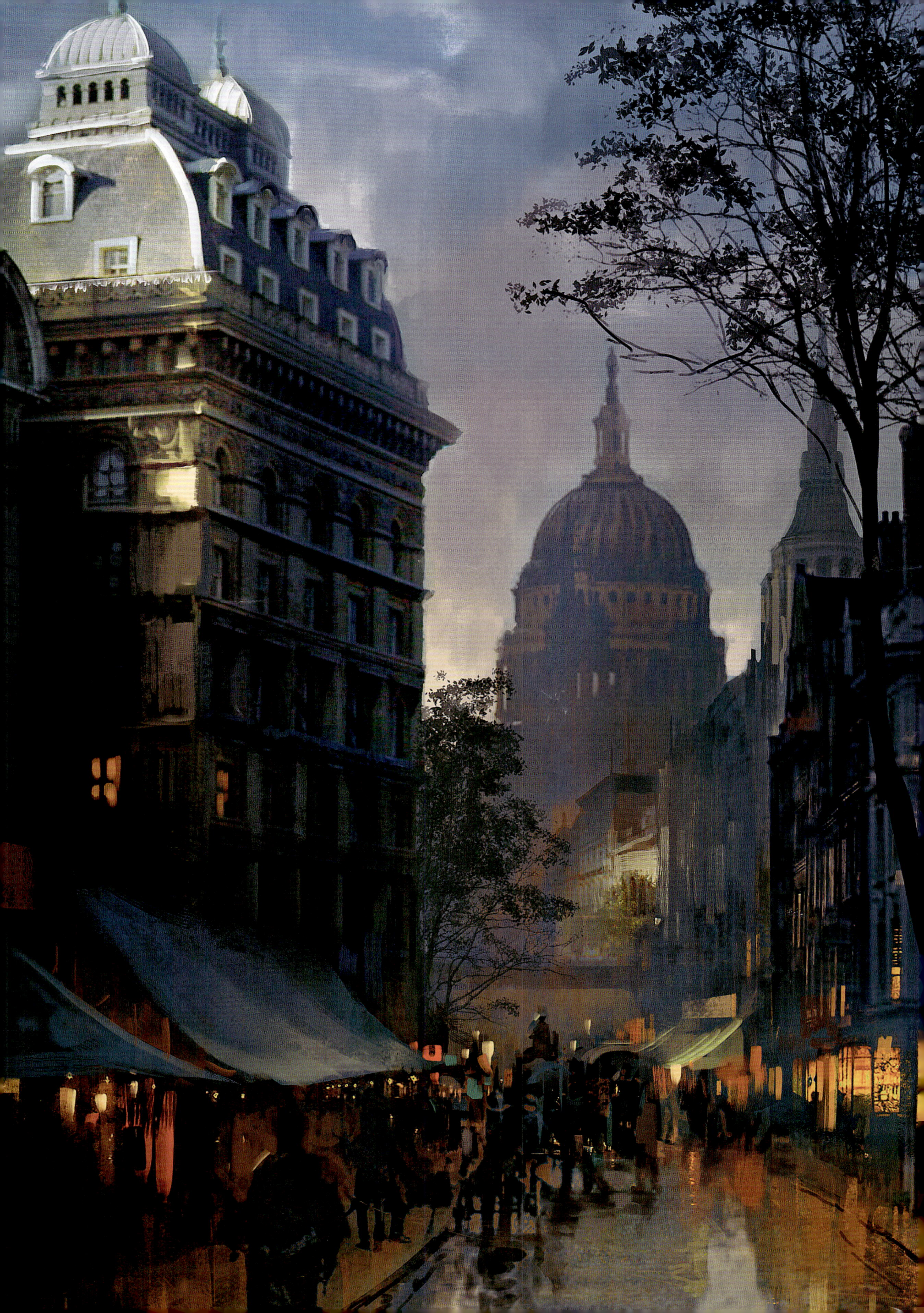

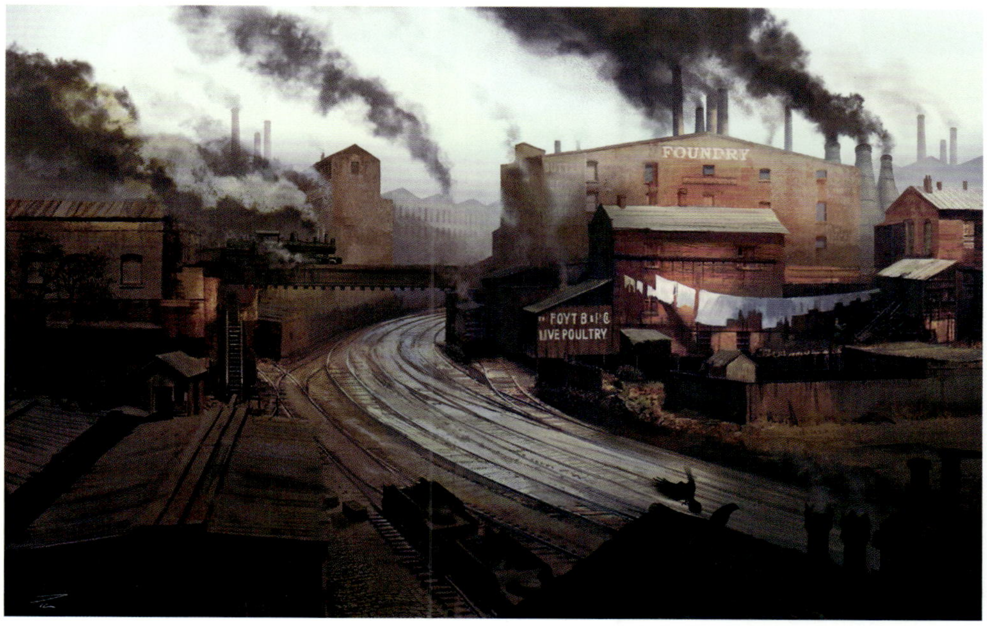

A CITY OF INDUSTRY

Nineteenth-century London is a city of contradictions. The splendor and color of Buckingham's gardens and the majesty of architecture like that of the Bank of England reveal opulence and pomp, even as workhouses and smoke-spewing factories reveal degradation and poverty. Of course, the incongruity makes for an ideal game setting, filled with opportunities for artistic contrast.

No laws of the period governed the expansion of industry, so grit and smoke fill the streets and choke out the sky, leaving many neighborhoods a swirling mass of fog and soot. The dark eddies of vapor make London's streets darker and gloomier than in the Assassin's Creed games that have come before, but the new atmospheric quality would lose its novelty if it was everywhere. Instead, pollution is integrated into *Syndicate*'s weather system, coming and going to help communicate shifting time and to accentuate moments of storytelling when desired.

Even where smoke doesn't darken the streets, rain often keeps the streets reflective and shiny, especially with the flickering gaslights that dot the streets at regular intervals. Gaslights make nighttime a more viable play space and encourage players to notice the dynamic adjustments as day fades to night and back again. "Gas changed the way the night was perceived by civilians, because the darkness was less fearsome," Thierry says. "The night became an occasion for entertainment, and people could get out on the streets and go shopping and see shows. This is something new that we wanted to play with in terms of light and entertainment venues." The passage of time is a major component of the visual presentation, and players witness the shifting eddies of sunlight and artificial light, pollution and natural weather, and the changes in street life as the hours pass. The physically based lighting system presents an incredibly realistic rendering of objects and the way light plays across them, and that light shifts as the time of day changes. So, when Big Ben reads 2:00 A.M., the darkness outside reflects it.

Along the street, a more reactive and attentive crowd pays attention to danger and steers clear, especially since in this age, active vehicles surge along thoroughfares, affecting the flow of pedestrians. "We have improved the artificial intelligence of the crowds, so you will notice their behavior seems more natural and purposeful," Thierry says. "Since we now have vehicles, people are not walking in the middle of the street. They are walking on sidewalks, and they will look before crossing the street—right and left—to avoid being hit by a carriage. That gives the sensation that the crowd is more alive and active."

An interconnected set of rails carries steam-driven trains across the city, and the constant sound of their passage is a regular accompaniment to life. These trains are more than eye candy. The train system offers new options for quick traversal through London, and players can move on and off of their moving platforms and cars with ease. "We have a total of seven train stations, which are massive," says Thierry. "And there is a large network of railways in *Syndicate*. The idea was to make it work systemically within the city, so there is always an opportunity to jump onto a moving train at one point and get off at another." That new flexibility for interacting with moving platforms extends to the famous River Thames, where the crowded waterway is always in motion with passing boats. Instead of looking for the nearest bridge, Jacob or Evie can leap from one moving ship to the next.

OPPOSITE: Environment art of entertainment venues in evening lighting (Martin Deschambault). ABOVE: With their bleak smokestacks and stained bricks, factories add a harsh element to the tone of nineteenth-century London (Hugo Puzzuoli).

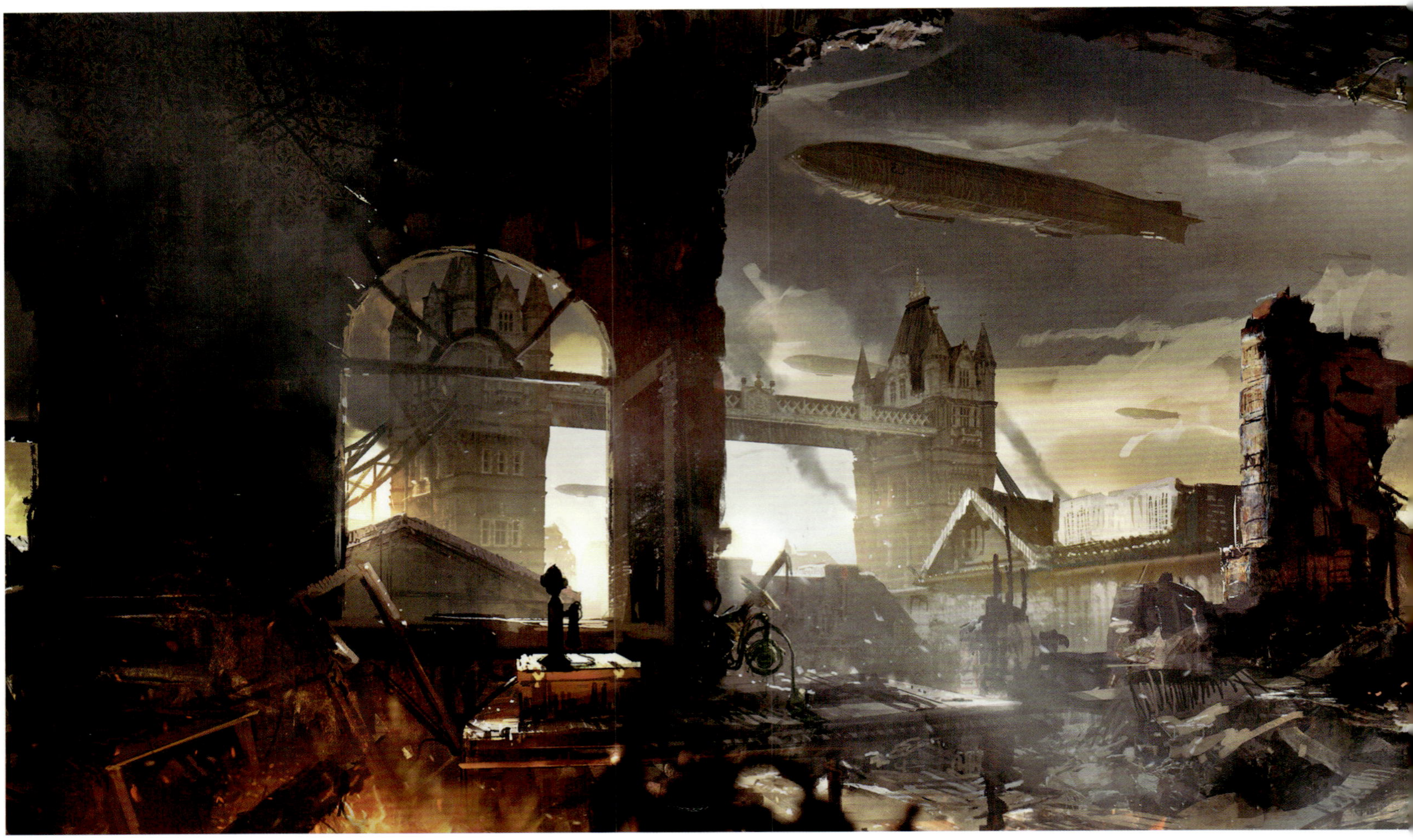

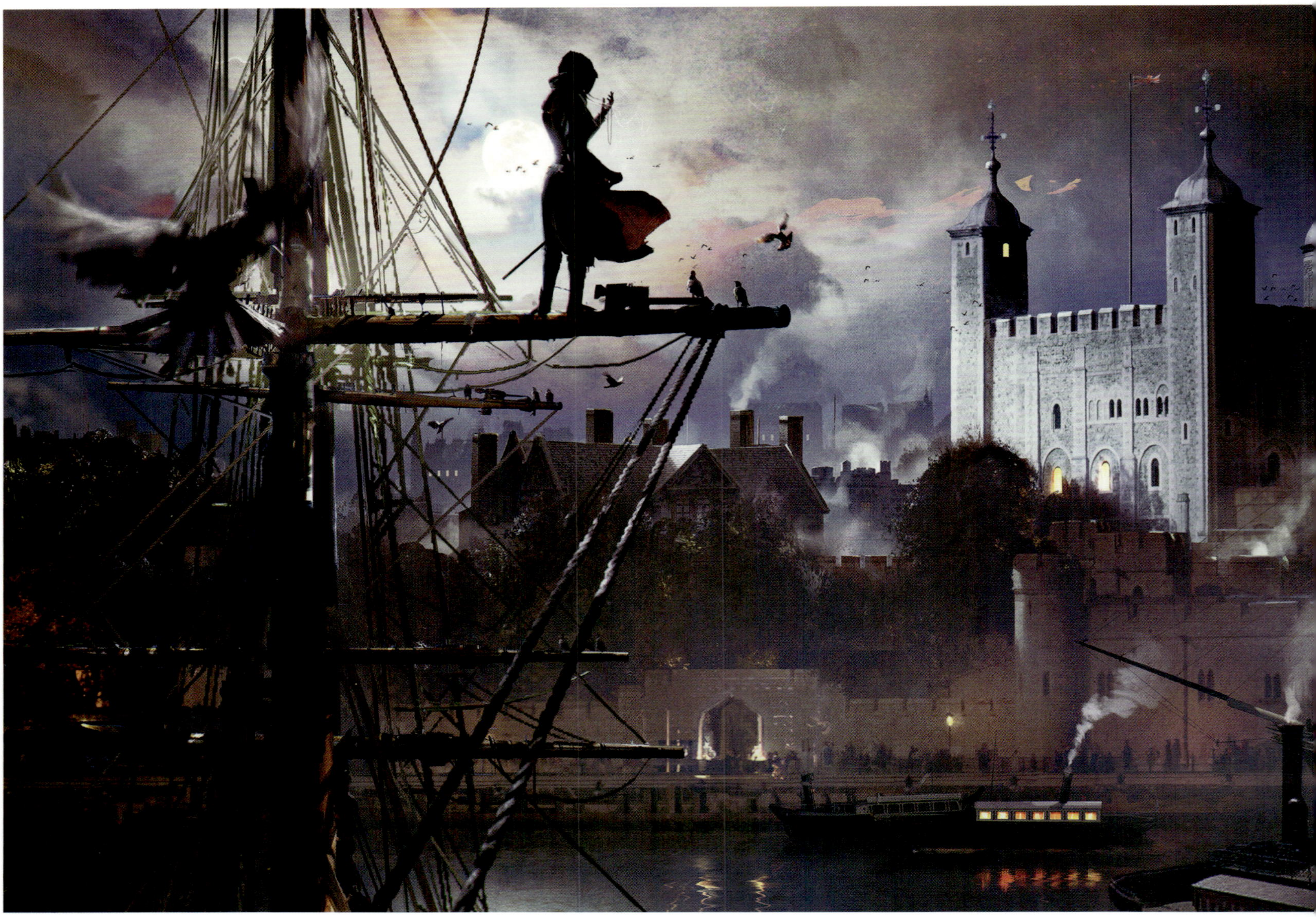

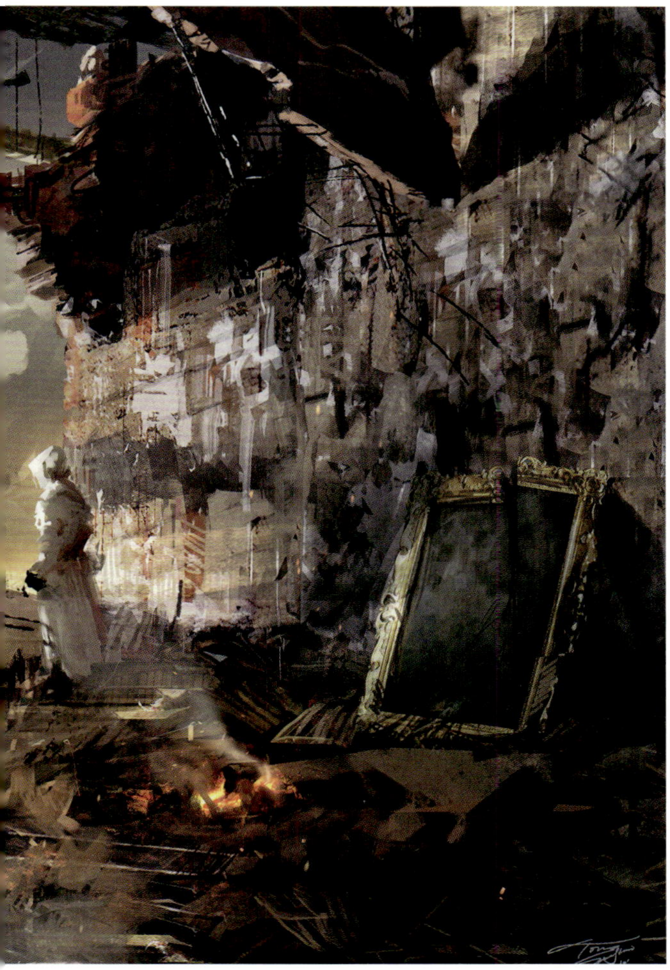

STEPPING THROUGH TIME

Following up on the success of the feature in *Assassin's Creed: Unity*, *Syndicate* once again allows players to explore an entirely different epoch through the integration of a time anomaly. The sequence takes us several decades beyond the Industrial Revolution and into the dark days of the Great War. "We go into the World War I setting, and the player meets Winston Churchill and assassinates German spies," Thierry says. While modeled on the rifts we've seen before, this new breach through time offers a more open gameplay experience. "The time anomaly is more of a sandbox approach. So you aren't running through a defined parkour; it's going to be a mostly a freeroaming experience," Thierry explains.

In addition, there's a deeper interaction between encountering the anomaly and then returning to the main timeline during the Victorian era. During the World War I encounter, players visit the Tower of London before it's been opened to them in the main game, lending an air of freshness and excitement to the mission.

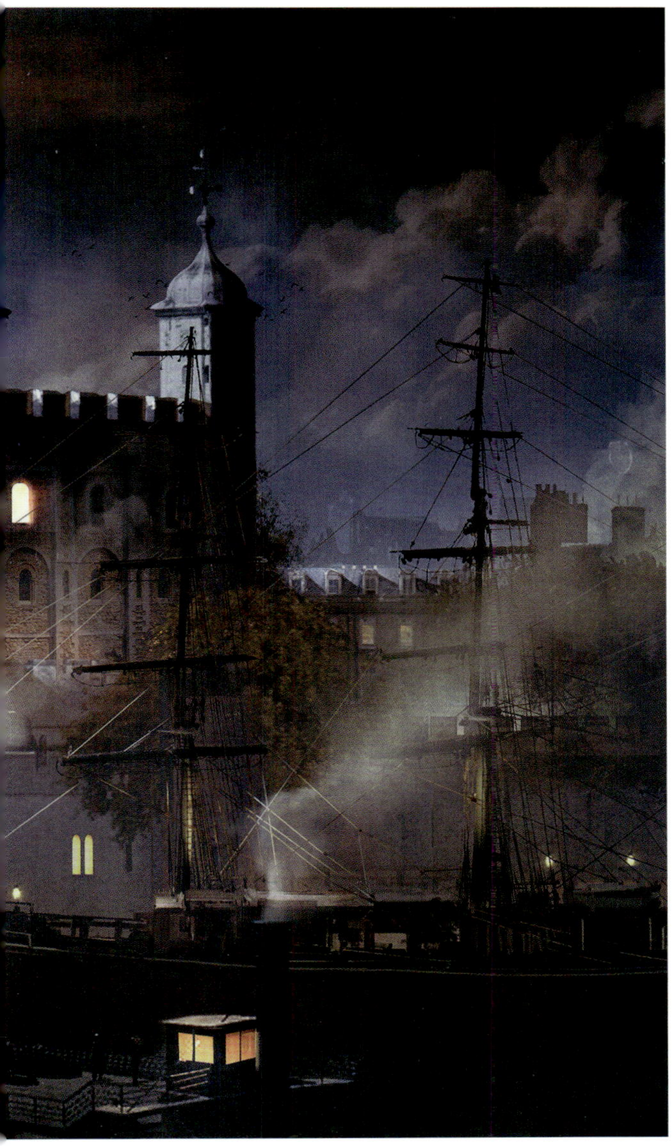

TOP LEFT: An Assassin looks to the Tower Bridge from the ruins of a wealthy home (Tony Zhou Shuo). BOTTOM LEFT: A scouting mission at the Tower of London (Tony Zhou Shuo).

LIKE BEING THERE

In its march through history, Assassin's Creed has hit another turning point. In the investigation of nineteenth-century London, photographic evidence is available as reference. Where previous games relied primarily on paintings, sketches, and written descriptions, *Syndicate* can instead refer to photographic material that details London as it was during this moment in time.

"We are fortunate enough to have tons of photographs taken directly from the time period," Thierry says. "And I mean tons. We have literally thousands of pictures." The broad availability of photographs from the period is both an opportunity and a challenge to the team. Knowing exactly the way a place looked isn't hard, but choosing how much latitude to take from the historical record feels like a larger decision than before.

In addition, the available photos have another limitation; they're all in black and white. "It is more of a challenge than using a beautiful painting with full colors, because while using the reference, the challenge of the photo is to use it as a style," says concept artist Hugo Puzzuoli.

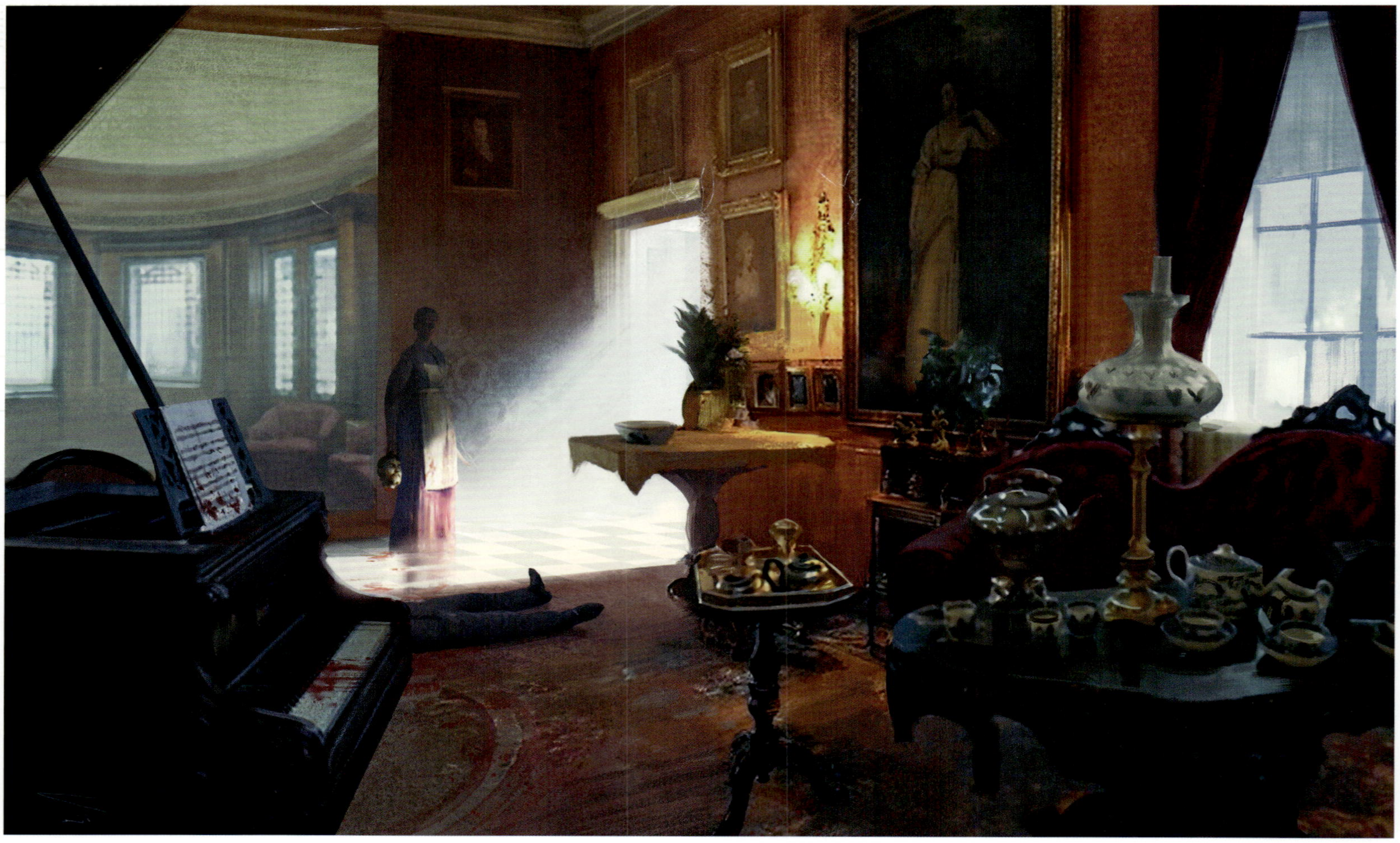

ABOVE: A disturbing scene lurks beneath the luxurious façade of this wealthy home (Hugo Puzzuoli).
OPPOSITE: Jacob creeps through the Bank of England's library (Fernando Acosta).

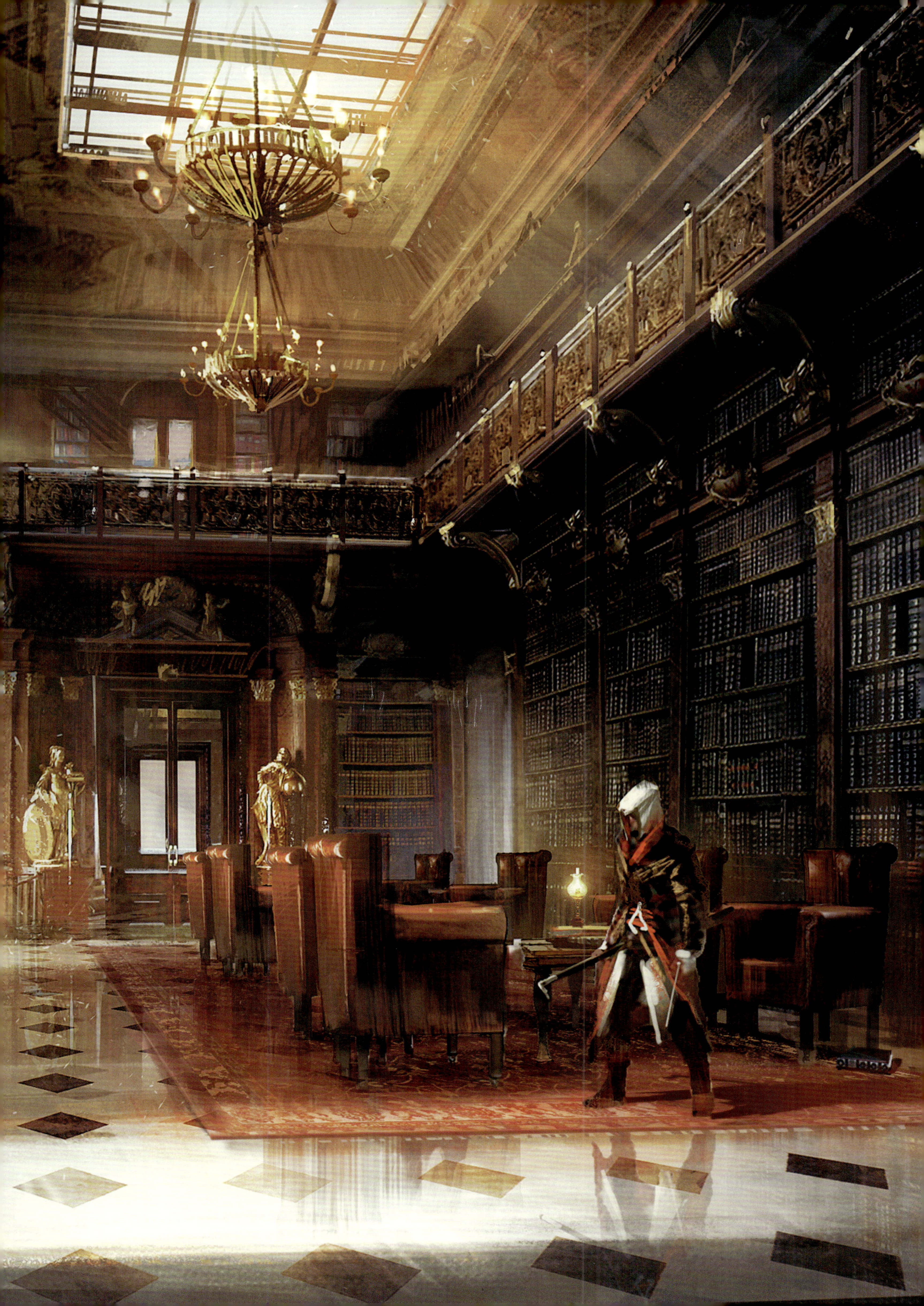

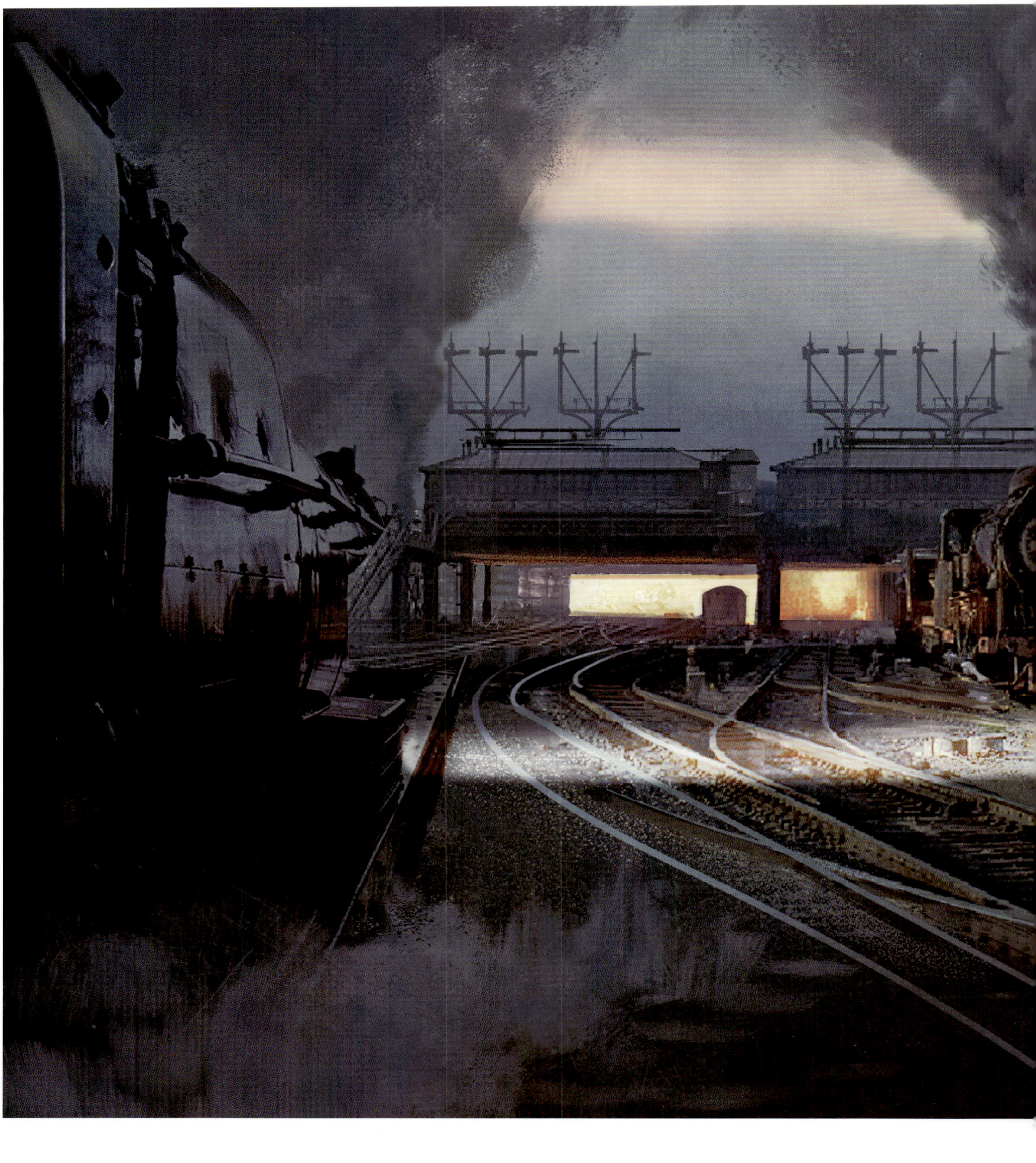

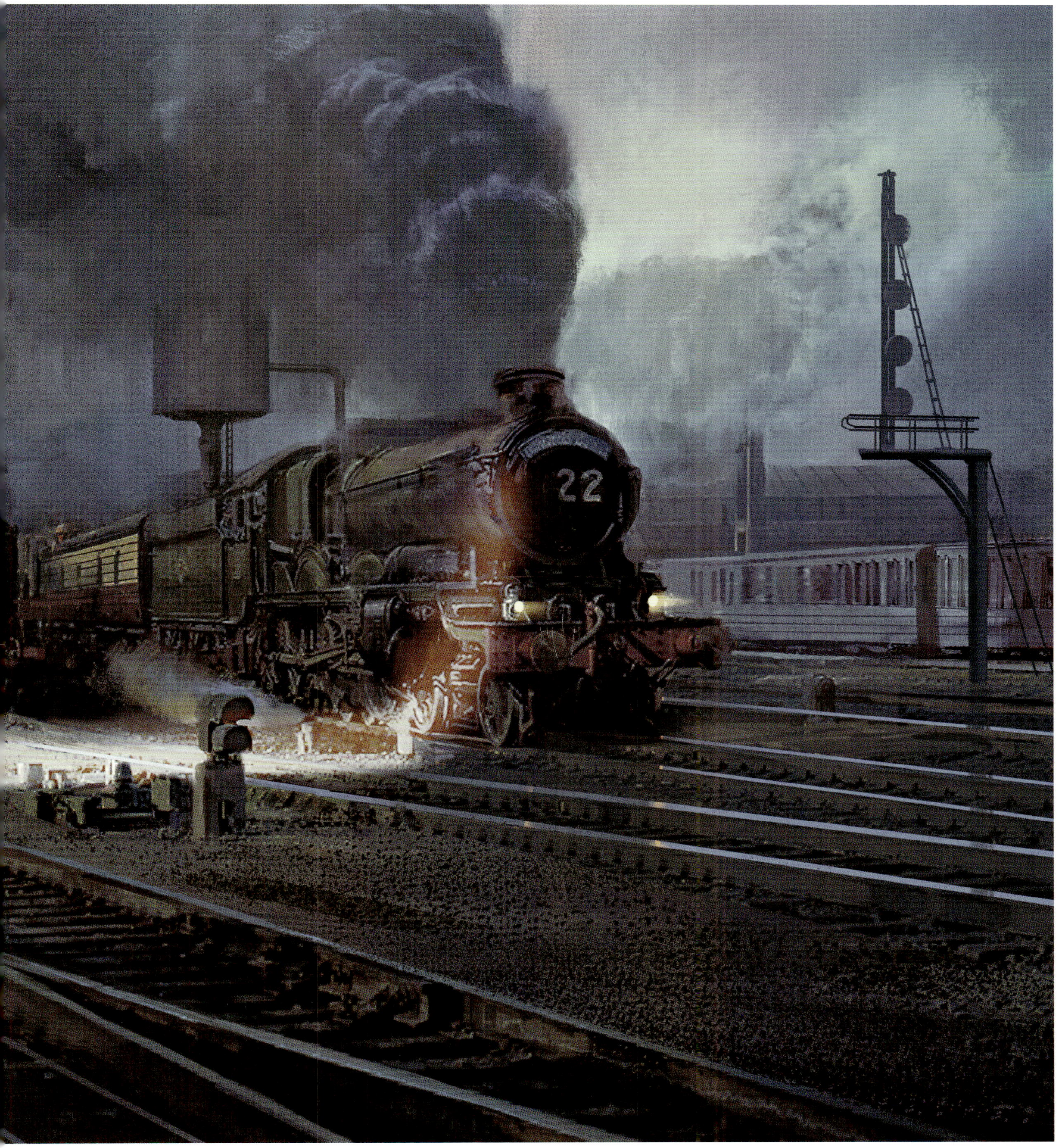

THESE PAGES: The art direction highlighted steam trains as an iconic part of the Industrial Revolution (Hugo Puzzuoli).

THE RISE OF MODERNITY

After so many entries spread across so many places and times, *Assassin's Creed: Syndicate* steers into uncharted visual territory. The art style established years ago with the first game still informs many things about the direction of this latest project, but sometimes it's in specific rejections of style elements that *Syndicate* finds its own voice.

The stark white colors and brighter tones of previous games have been overridden by the fires of commerce and production, and both the streets and the characters that inhabit them are darker than ever before. Some of the churches and cathedrals that dominated previous eras remain, but now many of the biggest buildings to explore are huge factories. These ironworks, gasworks, and breweries offer potent traversal and platforming challenges in highly secular spaces instead of religious ones. "We chose to make our factories like our cathedrals," Thierry says. "*Assassin's Creed: Unity* had some amazing interiors, which really stood out as an artistic feature that matched the setting. For *Syndicate*, it's the factories that define the mood of London during the Industrial Revolution. I was inspired by something I read about the nature of factories. They are like monsters, and if you could analyze their personalities, they would all be classified as psychopaths. They don't care for the environment or their people; they are all about production at all costs."

Syndicate also uses its visual palette to study the deep class struggles at play during this pivotal moment in society's expansion. Dickensian environments and situations abound as Jacob and Evie travel to overrun poorhouses or take on missions to save children from labor and slavery. We see the profound differences between rich and poor by moving through the city's many districts. Neighborhoods like Westminster and Buckingham are resplendent with palaces and gardens, metropolitan areas like Lambeth and the Strand showcase city life, and Whitechapel reveals the depths of poverty inflicted on the city's most afflicted citizens. Whitechapel workers of the period had a life expectancy of twenty years, compared to some seventy years for a resident of the Westminster district. Players will see that discrepancy in the crowds, with a higher percentage of older people in rich districts and greater numbers of younger crowds in poorer neighborhoods. Artists depicting the city's distinct boroughs have the latitude to express the crushing poverty sitting side by side with the world's richest women and men.

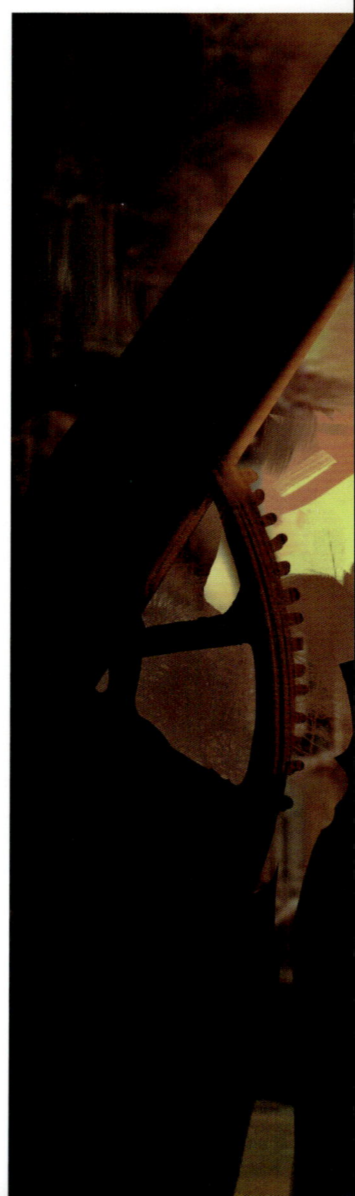

TOP RIGHT: London includes three types of factories: ironworks, gasworks, and breweries (Hugo Puzzuoli).
BOTTOM RIGHT: This concept shows the factory as a consuming and unfeeling entity (Hugo Puzzuoli).

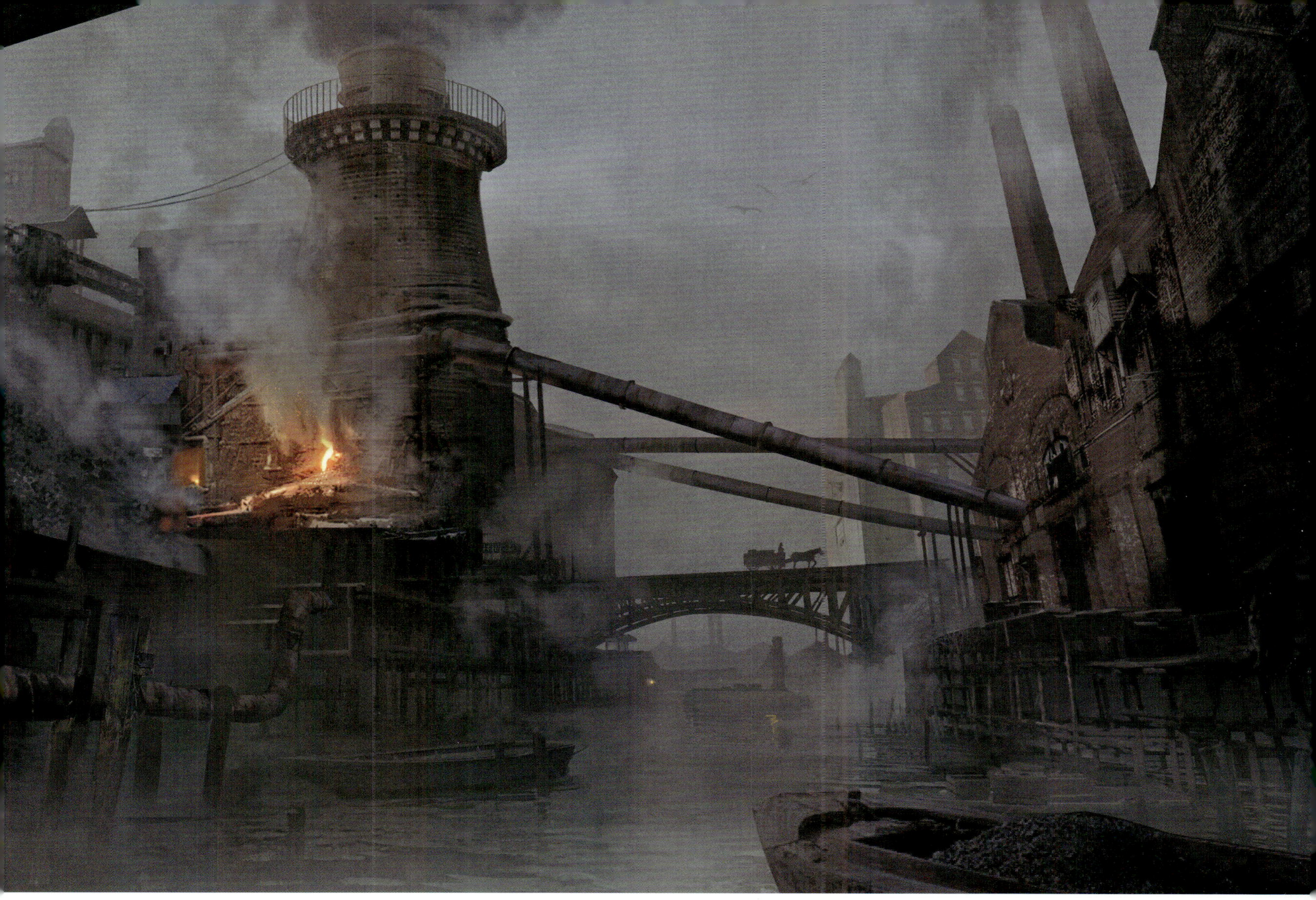

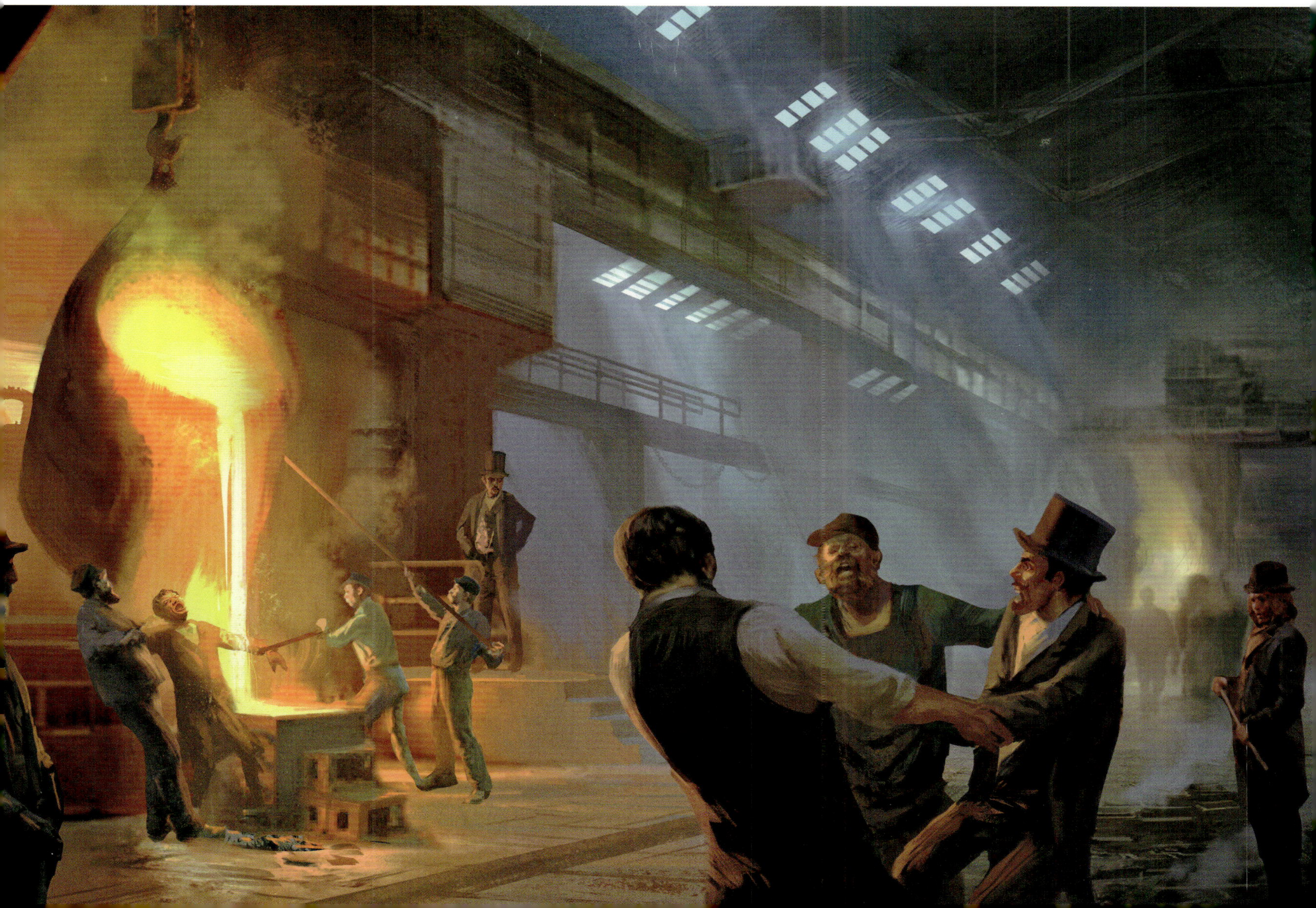

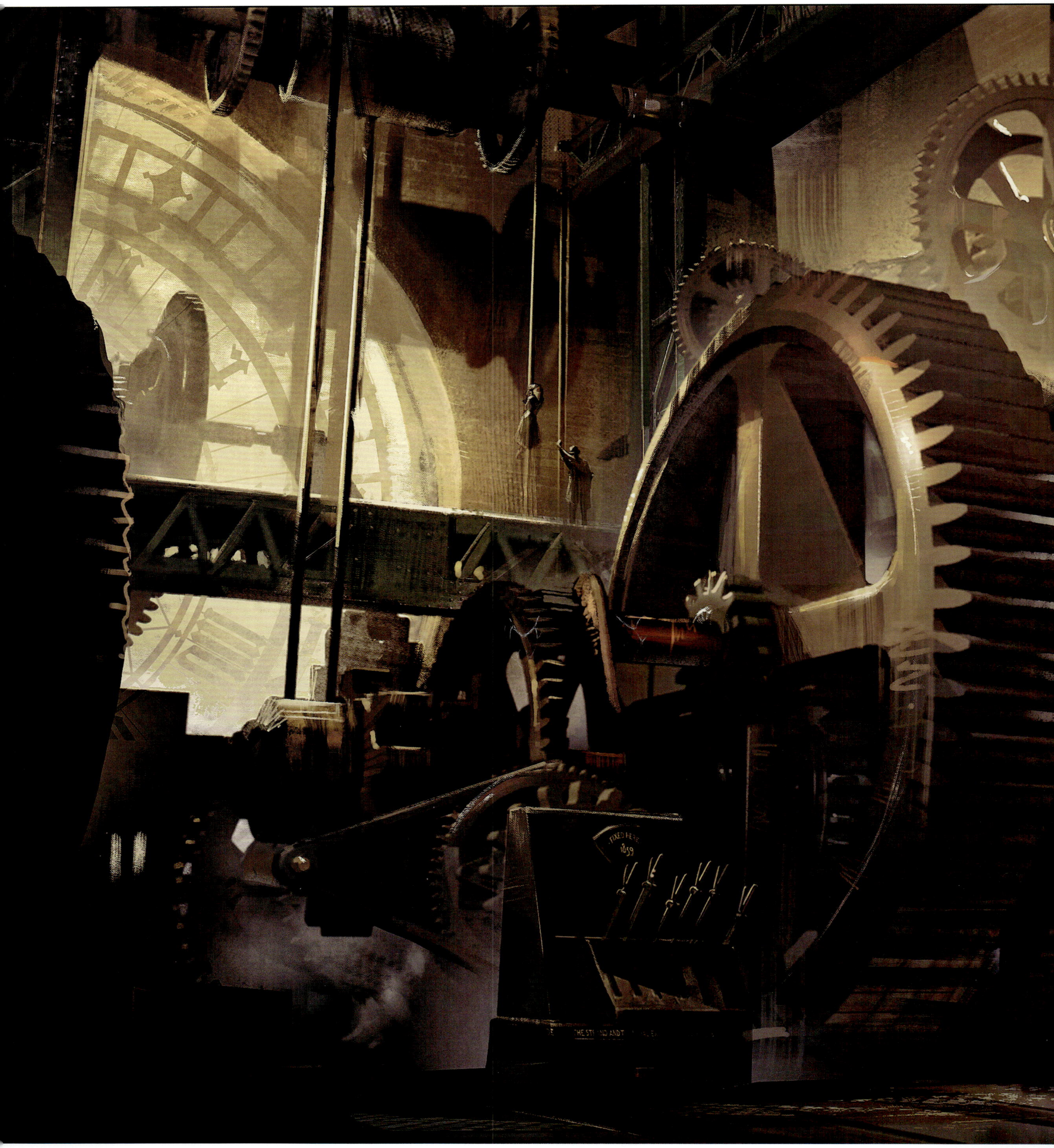

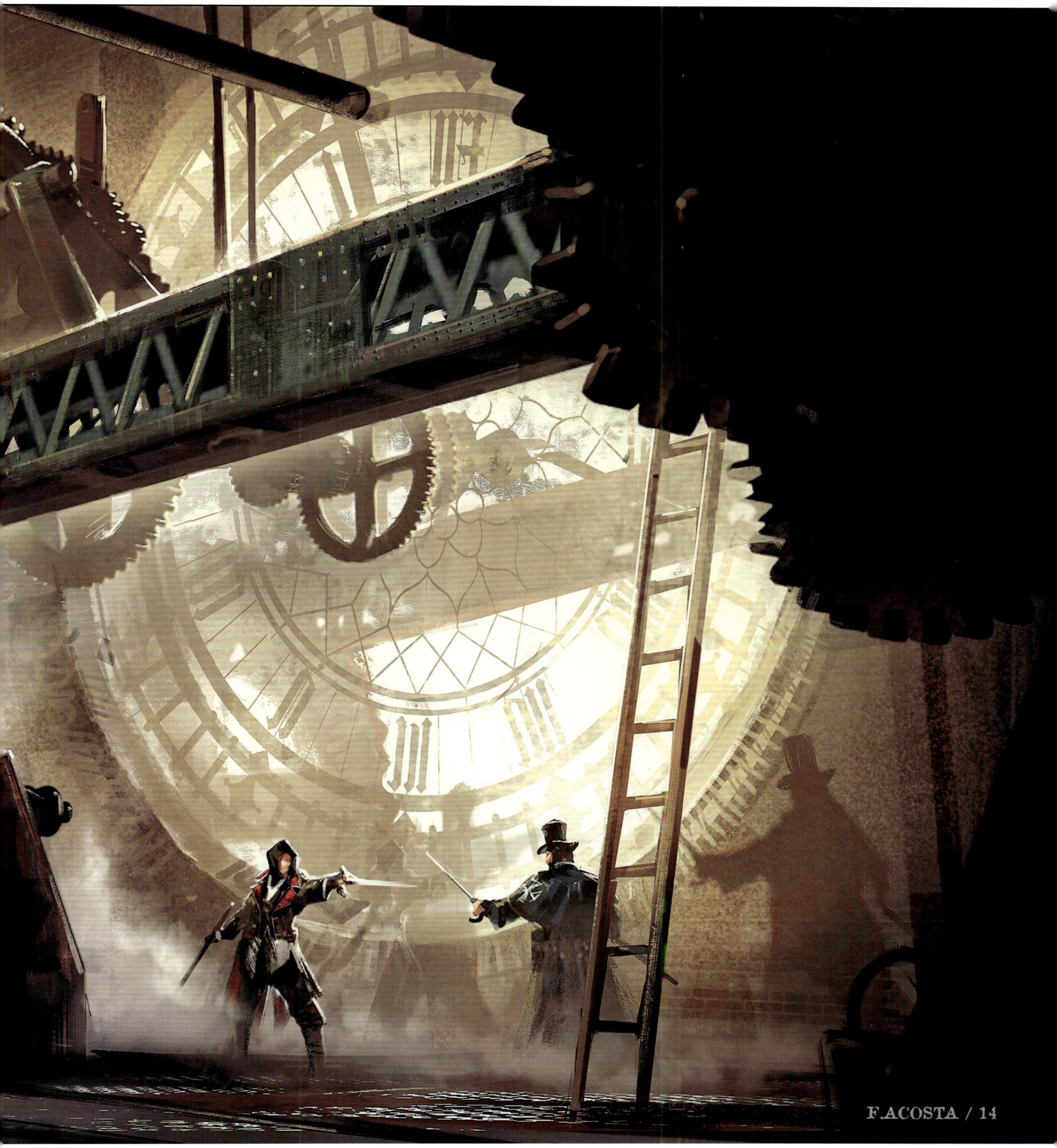

THESE PAGES: Artwork of a duel inside the face of Big Ben (Fernando Acosta).

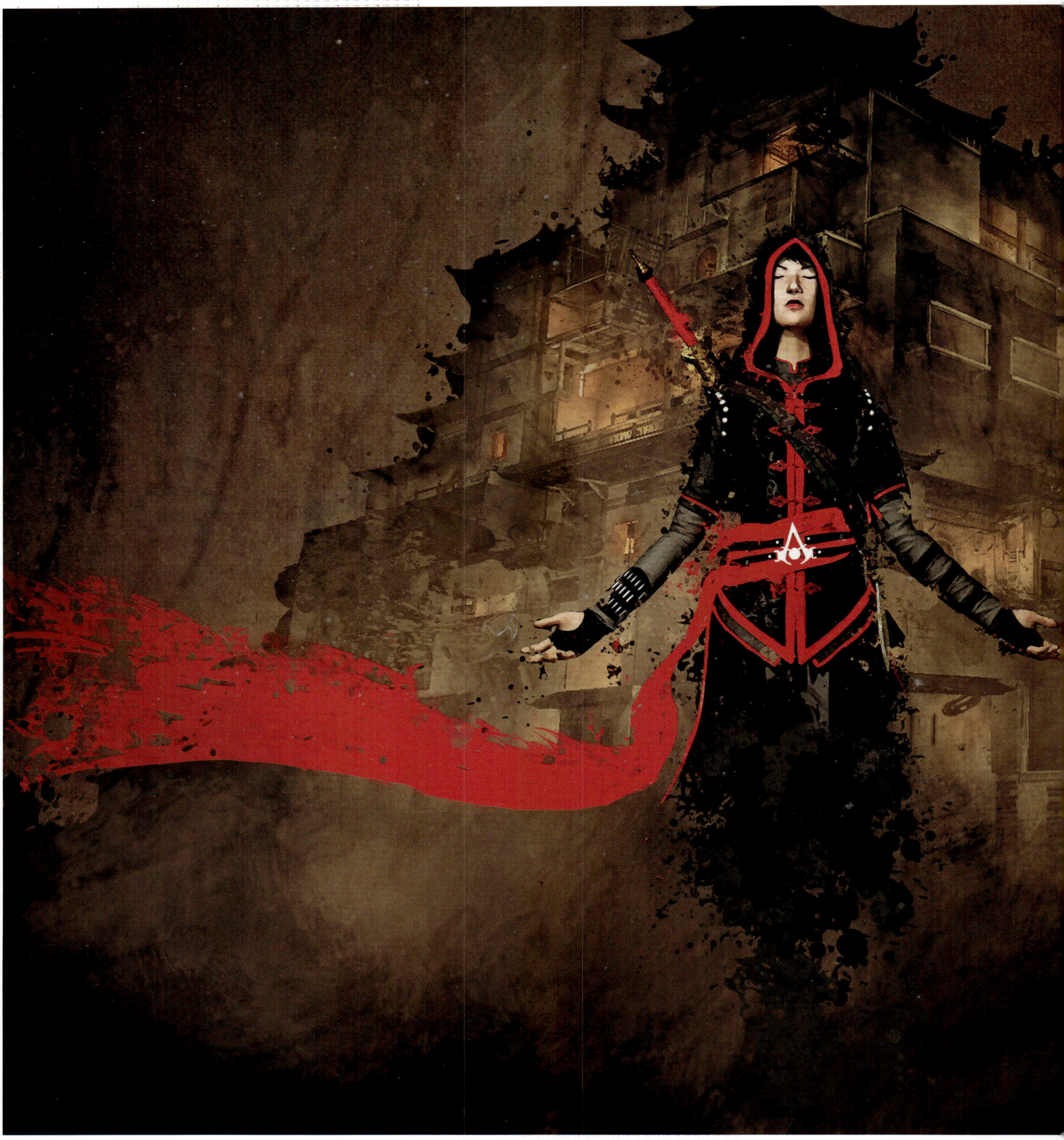

9 CHRONICLES

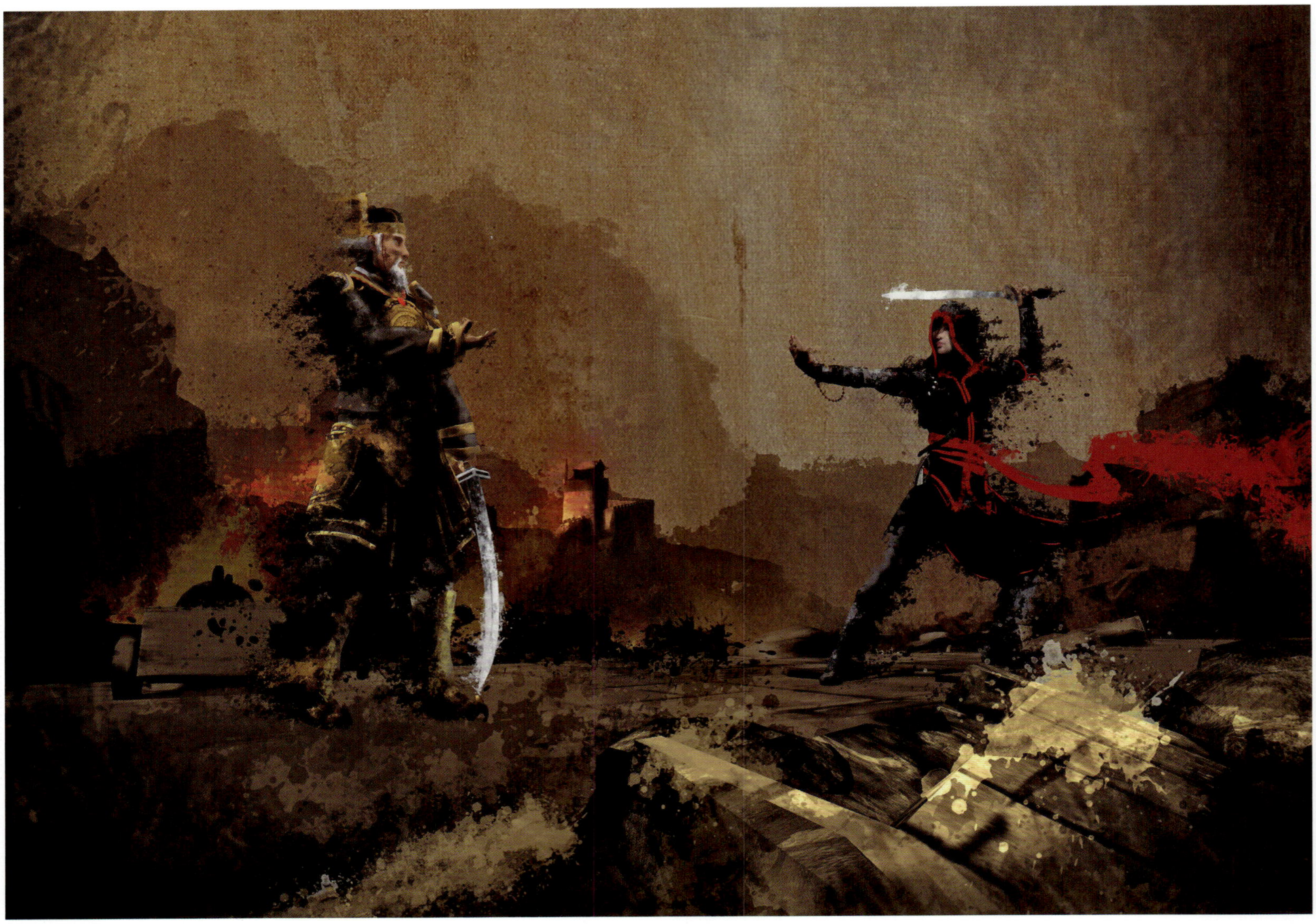

A NEW PERSPECTIVE

As Assassin's Creed has grown, opportunities continue to arise for new angles on the story. The latest venture has been the *Chronicles* games, which takes characters initially introduced in other media and pulls them into the game space.

Dispelling the assumption that every Assassin's Creed game needs to maintain the same large-scope treatment as *Black Flag* or *Syndicate*, the *Chronicles* games are smaller scale. In the past, linear level progressions have had more in common with classic action/platforming games than open-world 3-D adventures. "The idea for *Chronicles* came to life over a dinner I had with Julien Cuny, who was the brand content director at the time," explains Aymar Azaizia, who now holds that position. "We were talking about our shared love of platformer games and how cool it would be to have a 2.5-D platformer game for Assassin's Creed in a radically different art style. It was easy to imagine how a game—or even multiple games like this—could bring a new spin to the brand, something independent and fresh. We looked at each other and said, 'Why not?'"

Even while venturing into new gameplay styles, the *Chronicles* games maintain the DNA of the brand. While it may be a two-dimensional playspace, freerunning, stealth, and assassination remain core to the gameplay. Lead characters might offer a new cultural twist, but familiar visual cues like the hood and hidden blade remain intact.

PREVIOUS PAGES: *Assassin's Creed Chronicles* provided an opportunity for a variety of new artistic formats (Ben Blethyn).
ABOVE: Shao Jun faces off against Zhang Yong (Ben Blethyn).
OPPOSITE: Shao Jun's sash adds a fantastical element to the watercolor artwork (Ben Blethyn).

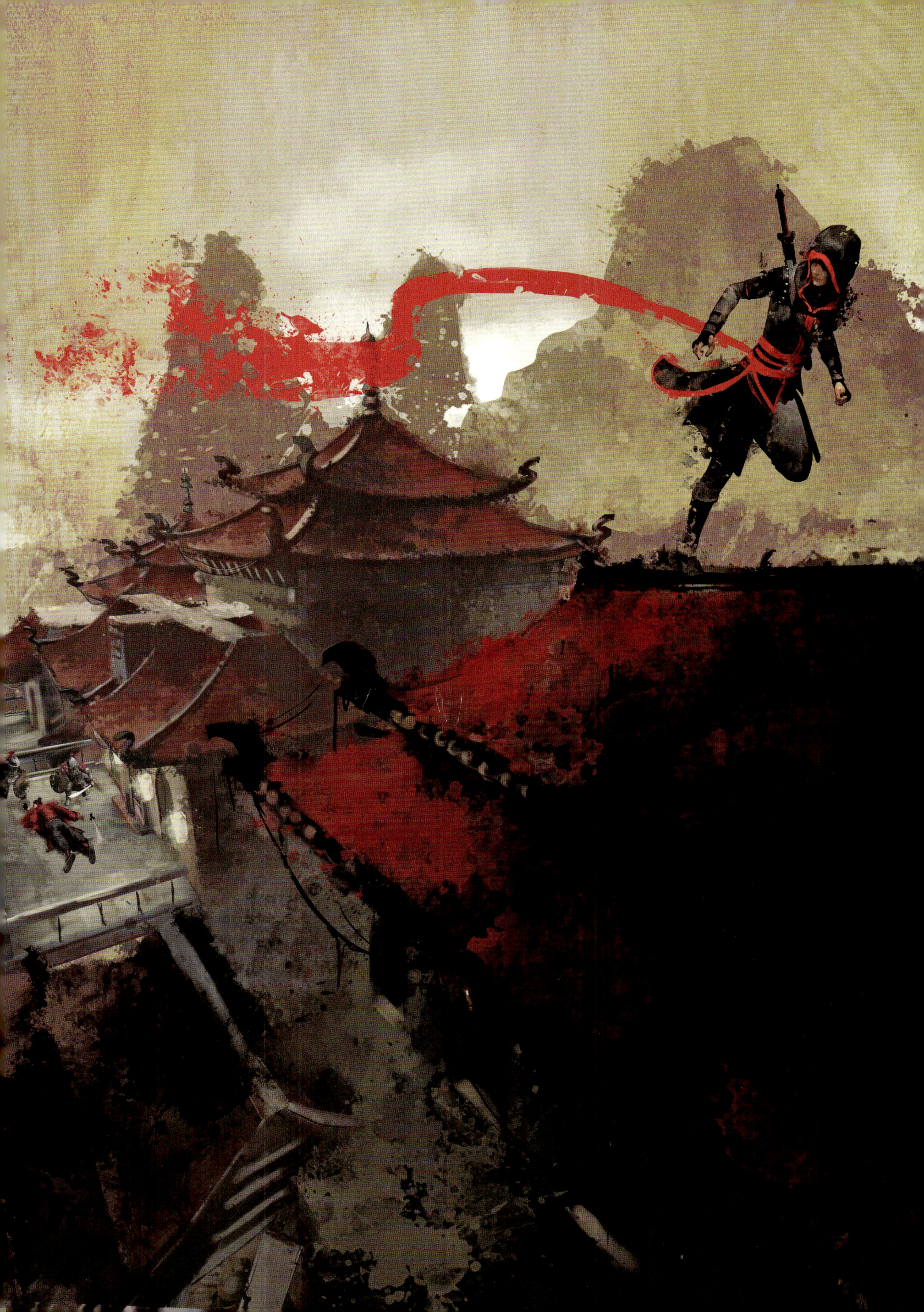

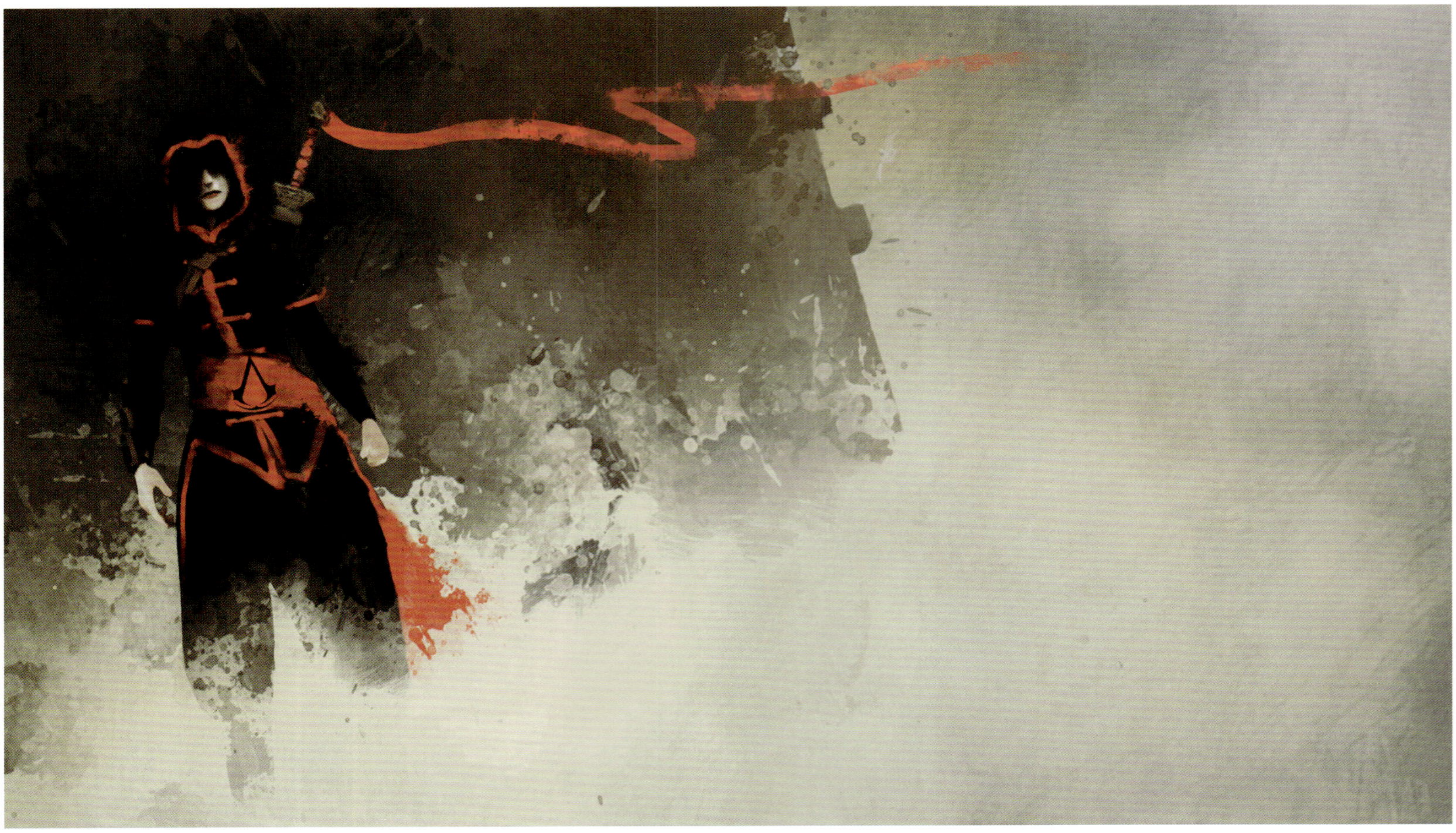

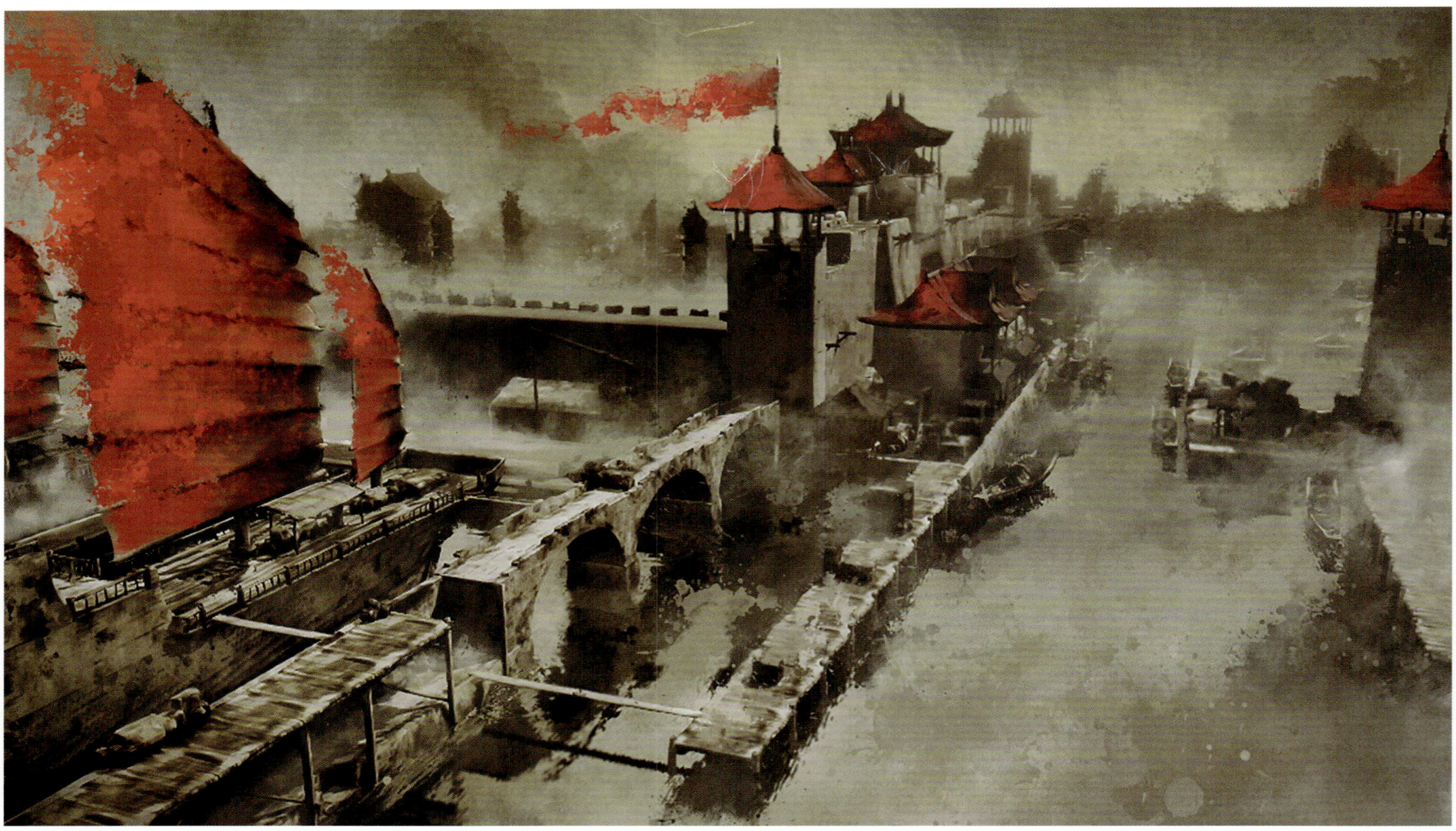

THESE PAGES: Concepts for this game fuse the traditional Chinese inks with more contemporary, loose styles (Ben Blethyn).

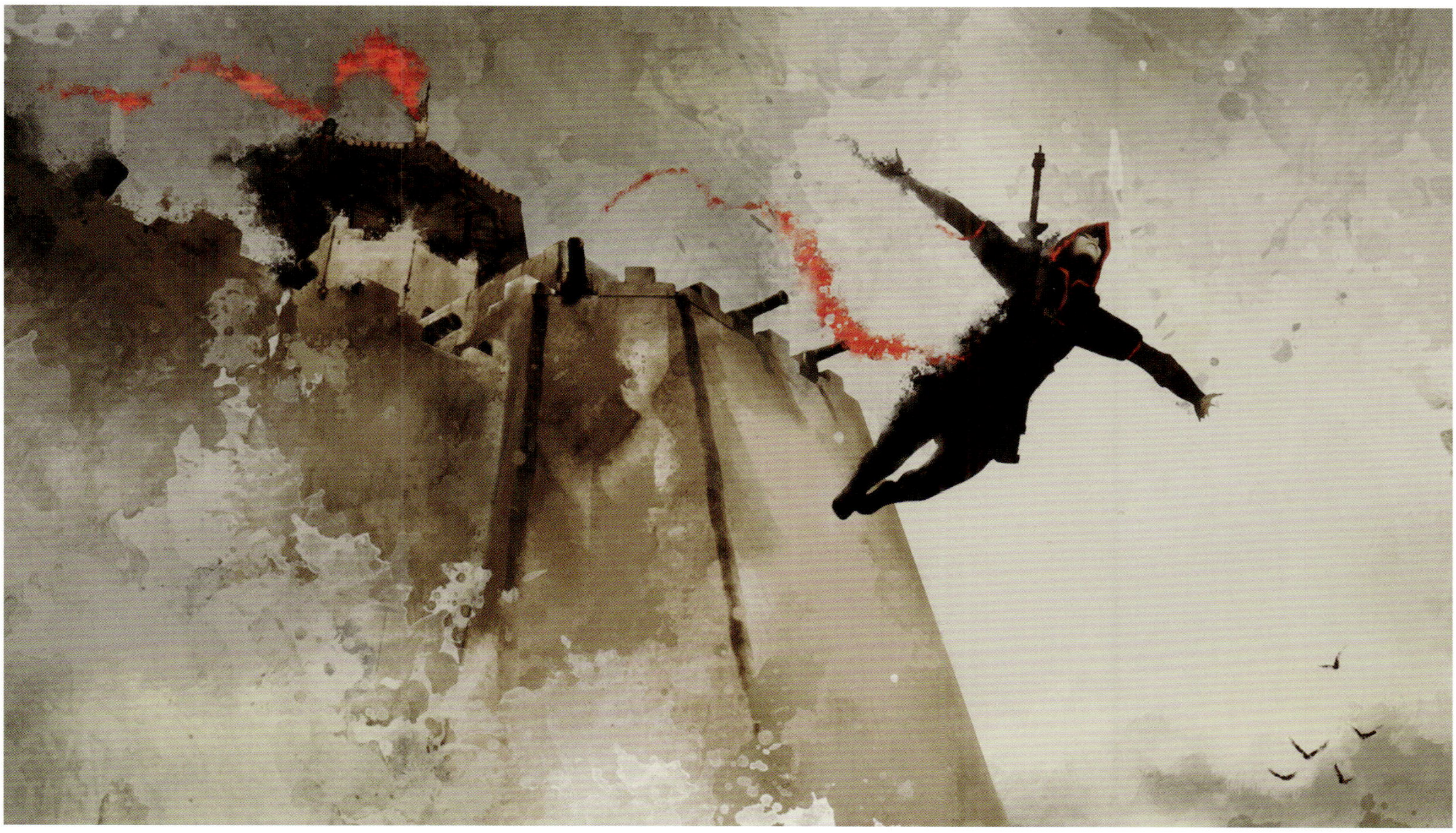

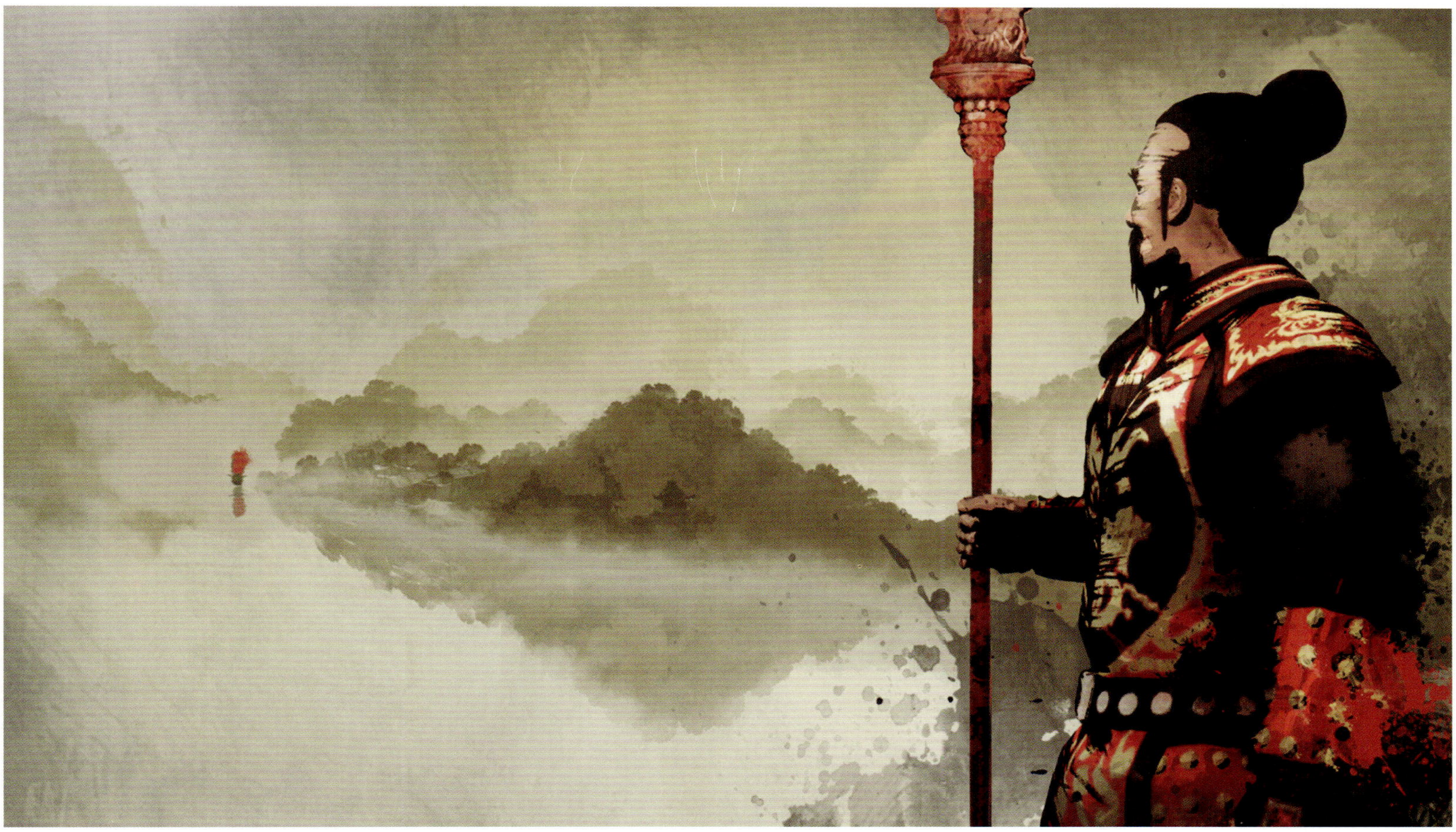

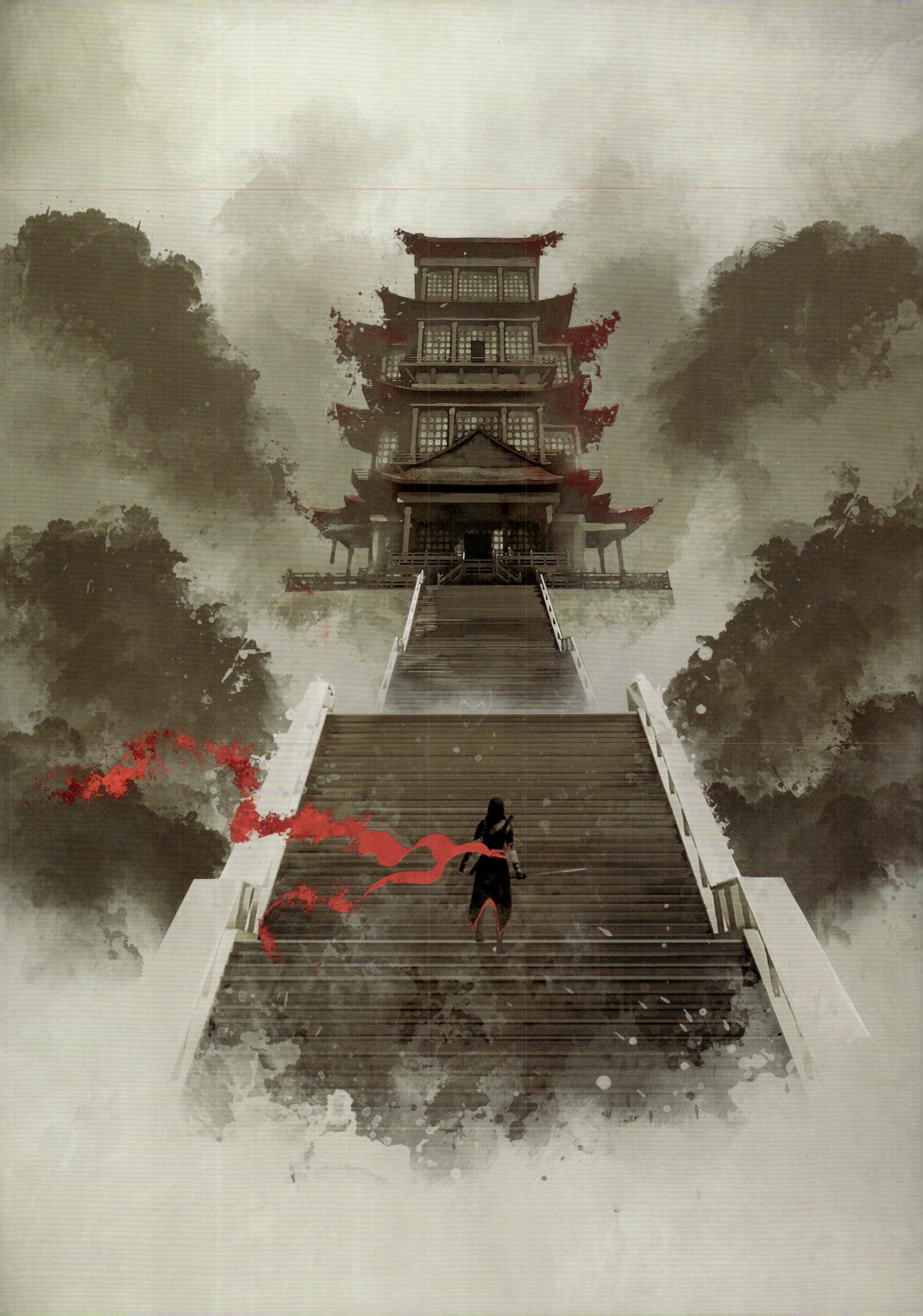

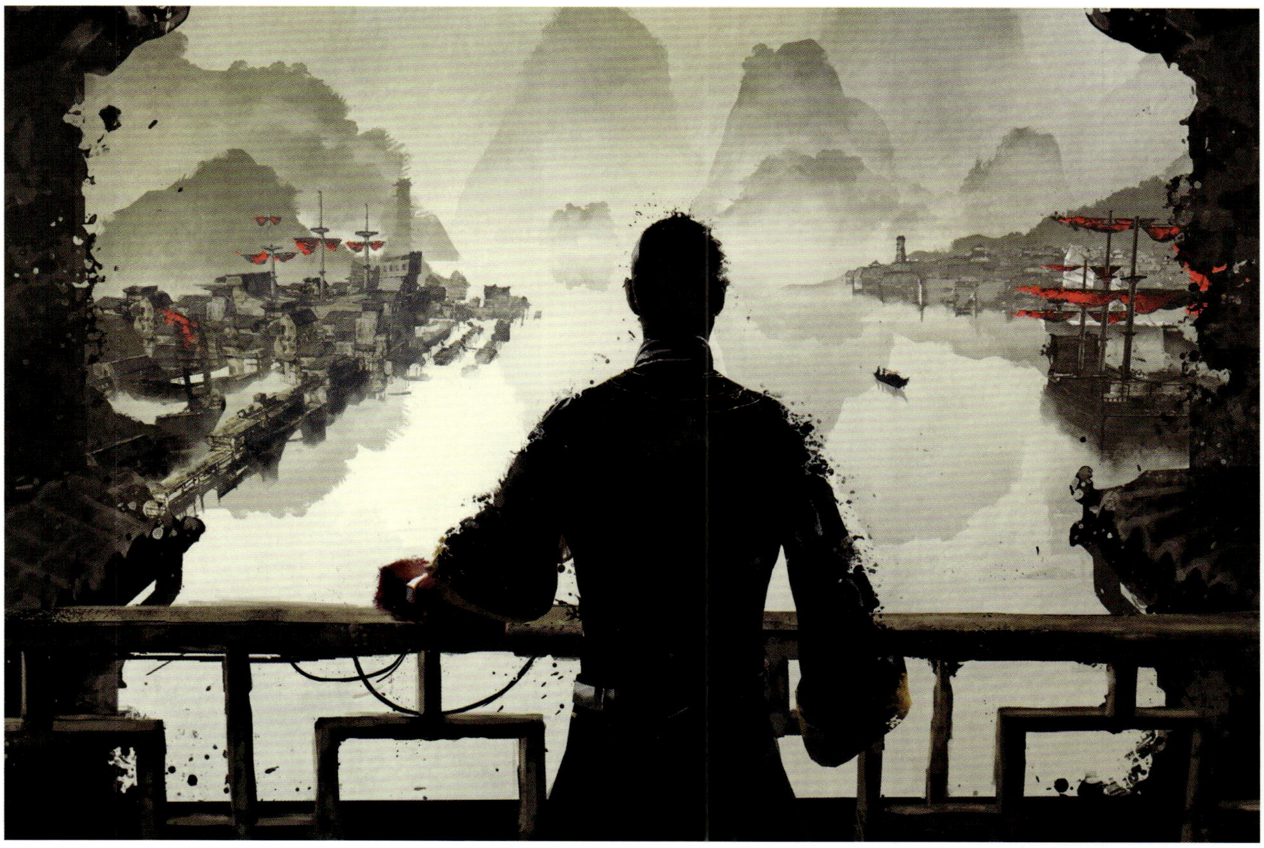

TO EACH THEIR OWN

The idea for a new branch in the Assassin's Creed game chronology was exciting, but the prospect of starting from nothing was daunting. "One of the most crucial steps when creating a new Assassin's Creed medium is to define who your Assassin is," Aymar says. "Creating a new Assassin from scratch can be a very lengthy, difficult process, and we knew we had Assassins that were already known and popular with very little to no screen time." By tapping into existing fiction to provide leads for the *Chronicles* games, Ubisoft was able to focus on fully realizing each setting and gameplay while adding new layers of depth to the lore. The team set out with a plan to more deeply explore a character fans had been eager to learn more about for years: the Chinese Assassin and Ezio's one-time protégé, Shao Jun.

Shao Jun is a character we briefly meet in the animation short, *Embers* (see Chapter 2). "She is a young Chinese Assassin that traveled from the far east of China to Italy to meet this legendary Mentor, the retired Ezio, and ask him to help her in her cause," Jean says. "Through some discussions, I think Ezio tries to make her realize what being an Assassin is really about and to not be confused about the real objectives of the Brotherhood. But then we don't know that much about her. All we know is that she goes back to China and tries to revive the Brotherhood there." The *Chronicles* game picks up from there, detailing Shao Jun's adventures in her homeland and her confrontation with the corrupt Chinese emperor.

As the idea for *Chronicles* grew, Ubisoft looked to its internal UbiArt Framework team to move forward, but their expertise with 2-D production was already devoted to existing projects like *Valiant Hearts* and *Rayman Origins*. Instead, Ubisoft quietly sent out the call for third-party developers and found an ideal partner. "The pitch Climax Studios sent us was really impressive, as they nailed down exactly what we were hoping to see for *Chronicles: China*," Aymar says. "What they presented to us was a multilayered level design with a unique art style inspired by the art of the Ming Dynasty that was still distinctly Assassin's Creed, so we were very excited to move forward with them."

Chronicles: China is deeply inspired by classic Asian watercolor art and colors, in particular the Chinese inks of the Ming Dynasty that were part of Climax's initial pitch. The art style melds that historical artistic inspiration with an impressionistic quality and layers in parallaxed vistas for a smooth and arresting presentation. "Another one of our references and inspirations was the introductory cinematic of *Street Fighter IV*, as we were so impressed by how they chose to reintroduce this franchise in a unique way that was still loyal to the characters and style of the *Street Fighter* franchise," Aymar says.

THESE PAGES: Fluid and evocative, these artworks feature beautifully minimalistic vistas (Ben Blethyn).

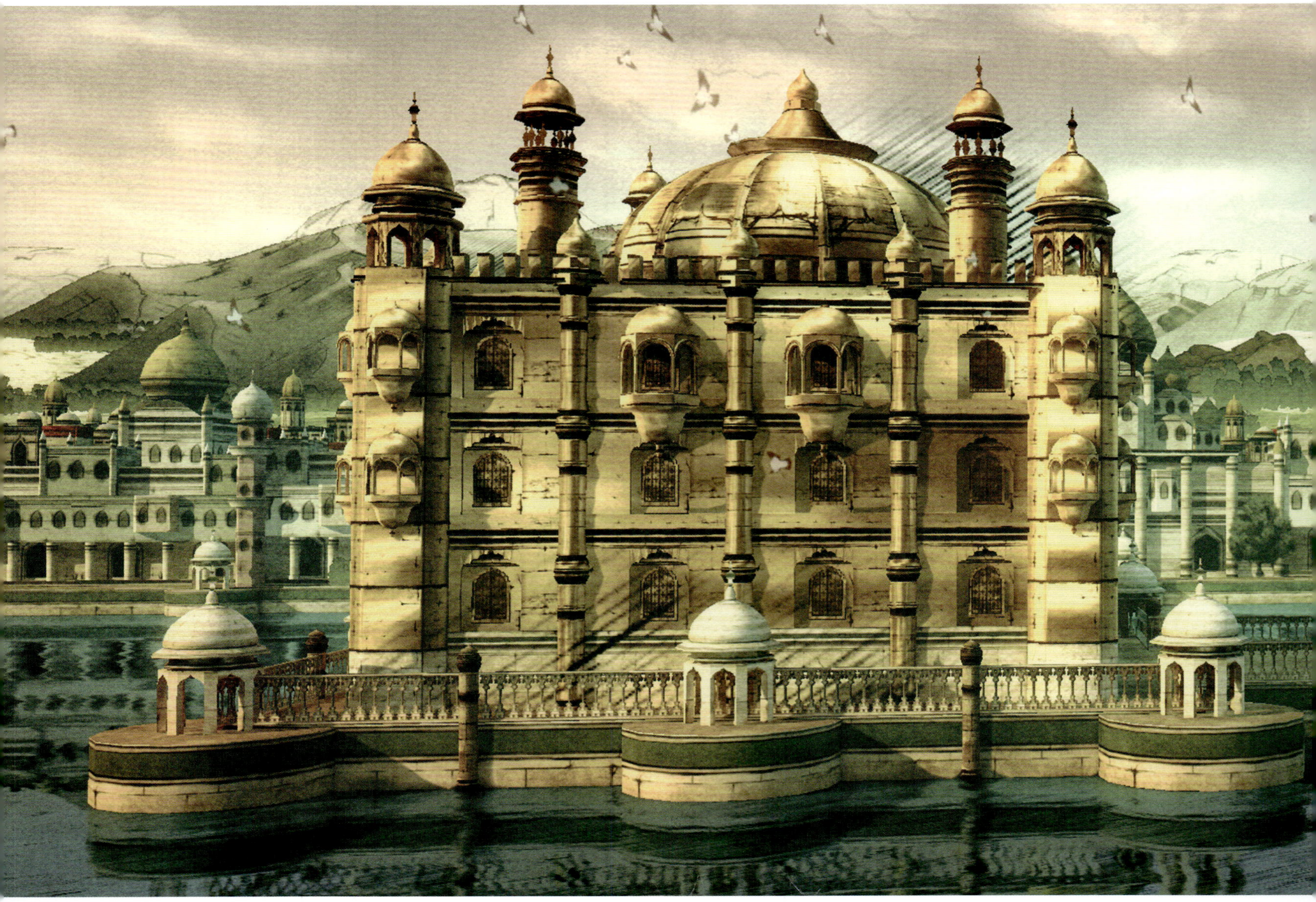

THESE PAGES: During development, the art style is continually being refined. This world panorama was used to balance the visuals between levels and establish the flow of the game (Saul Marchese).

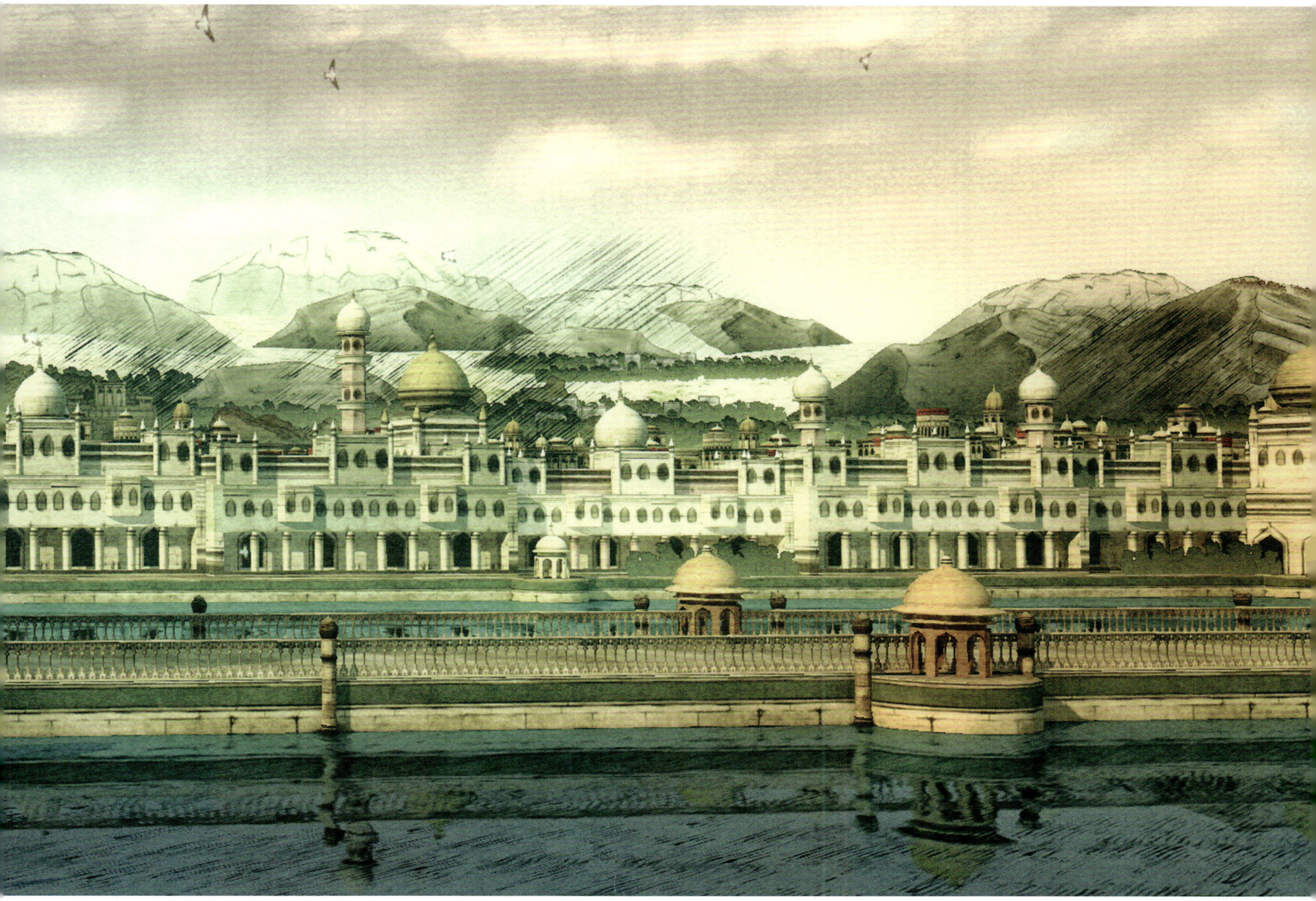

BECOMING A TRILOGY

As Shao Jun's game began to coalesce, it was clear that the *Chronicles* concept had the potential to become something more. "We knew we could push to make a series of games like this, each with its own distinctive art style, tone, and lore," Aymar says. Climax Studios came back with a pitch for an Indian-themed story, which lined up perfectly with plans for the graphic novel, *Assassin's Creed: Brahman*, which at that point had yet to release.

"The setting would offer a perfect contrast to the China episode of *Chronicles*, with dense, saturated colors, and the protagonist of *Brahman*, Arbaaz Mir," Aymar says. "Although *Brahman* and *Chronicles: India* share commonalities when it comes to style, they also had a lot of differences as we adapted to the medium we were working with." Arbaaz Mir is an intriguing lead. The Indian Assassin gets caught up in the search for a diamond that happens to be a powerful Piece of Eden and eventually becomes embroiled in a romance with the Indian princess Pyara Kaur.

For artistic inspiration, the team at Climax combined two distinct styles to find a colorful artistic vision that still feels grounded and accessible. The colors and culture of the Sikh Empire deliver a curved, shiny aesthetic. These influences meld with a Western journalistic perspective alluding to the British rule of the period and the many British lithographs and illustrations of India that emerged during the period. The resulting art direction is a profound shift from *Chronicles: China* but still draws on an illustrative quality to maintain consistency.

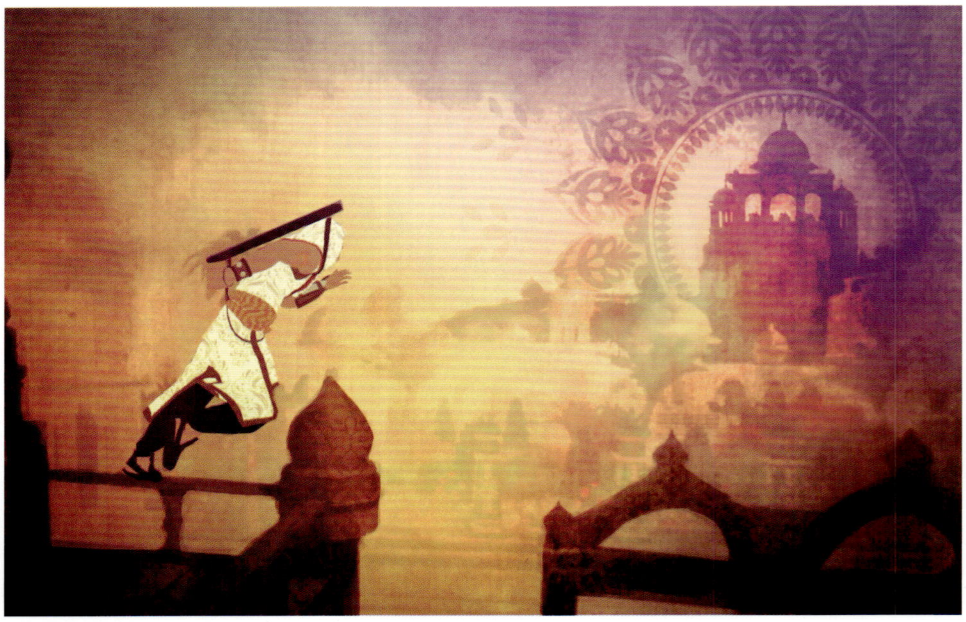

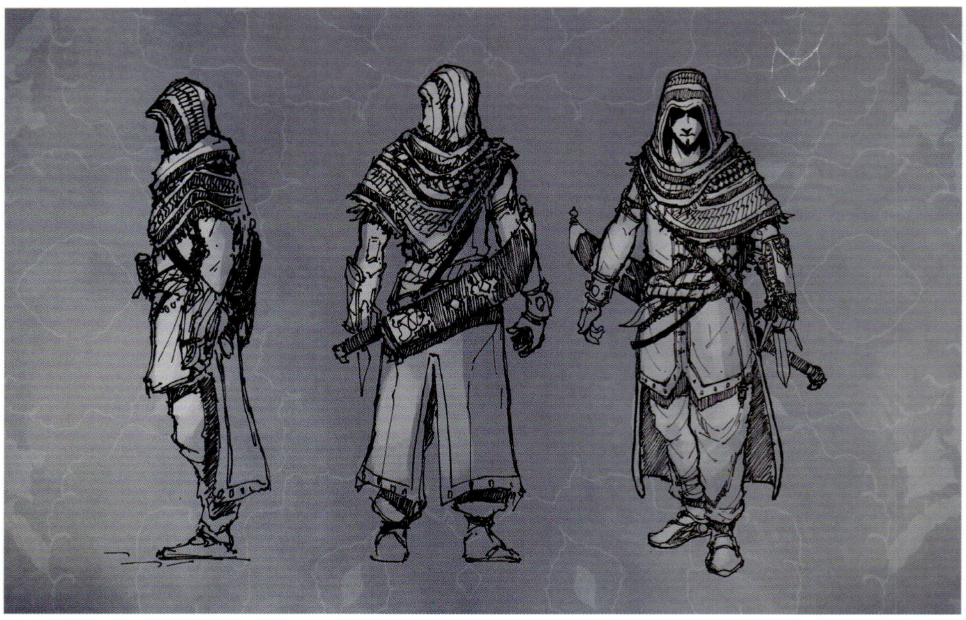

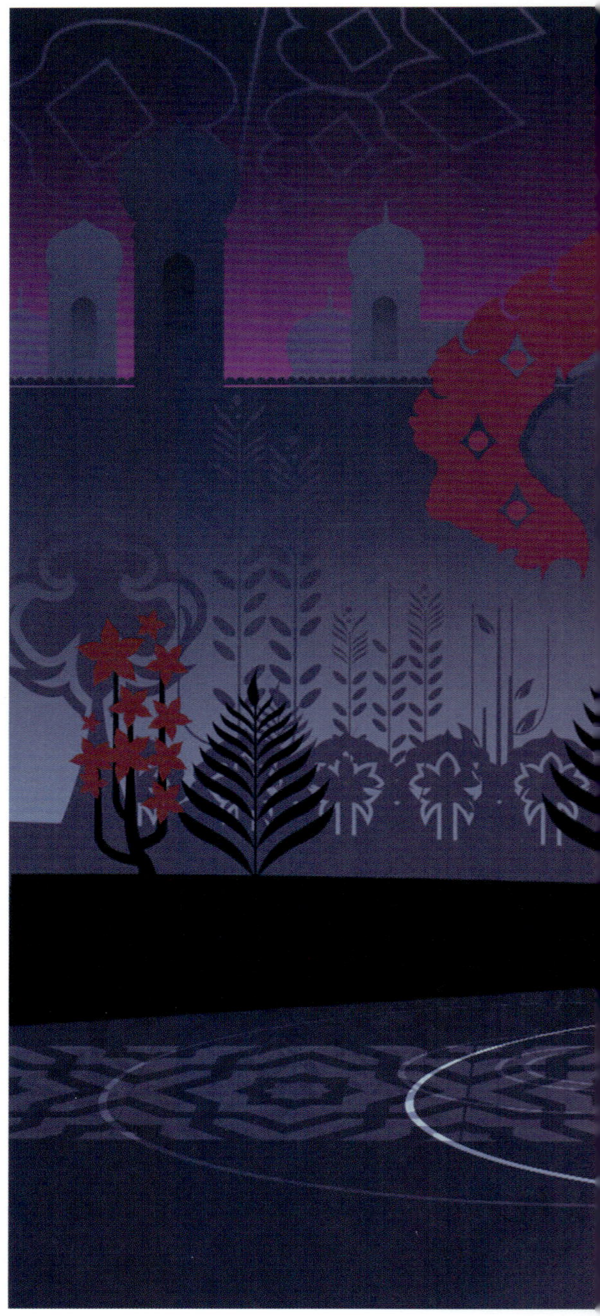

TOP: An early narrative concept demonstrating how the use of silhouette, pattern, and color can create a rich, atmospheric scene (Glenn Brace).
ABOVE: Final sketches for Arbaaz Mir (Ben Blethyn).
OPPOSITE: Exploration of the use of depth and the parallax backdrop (Saul Marchese).

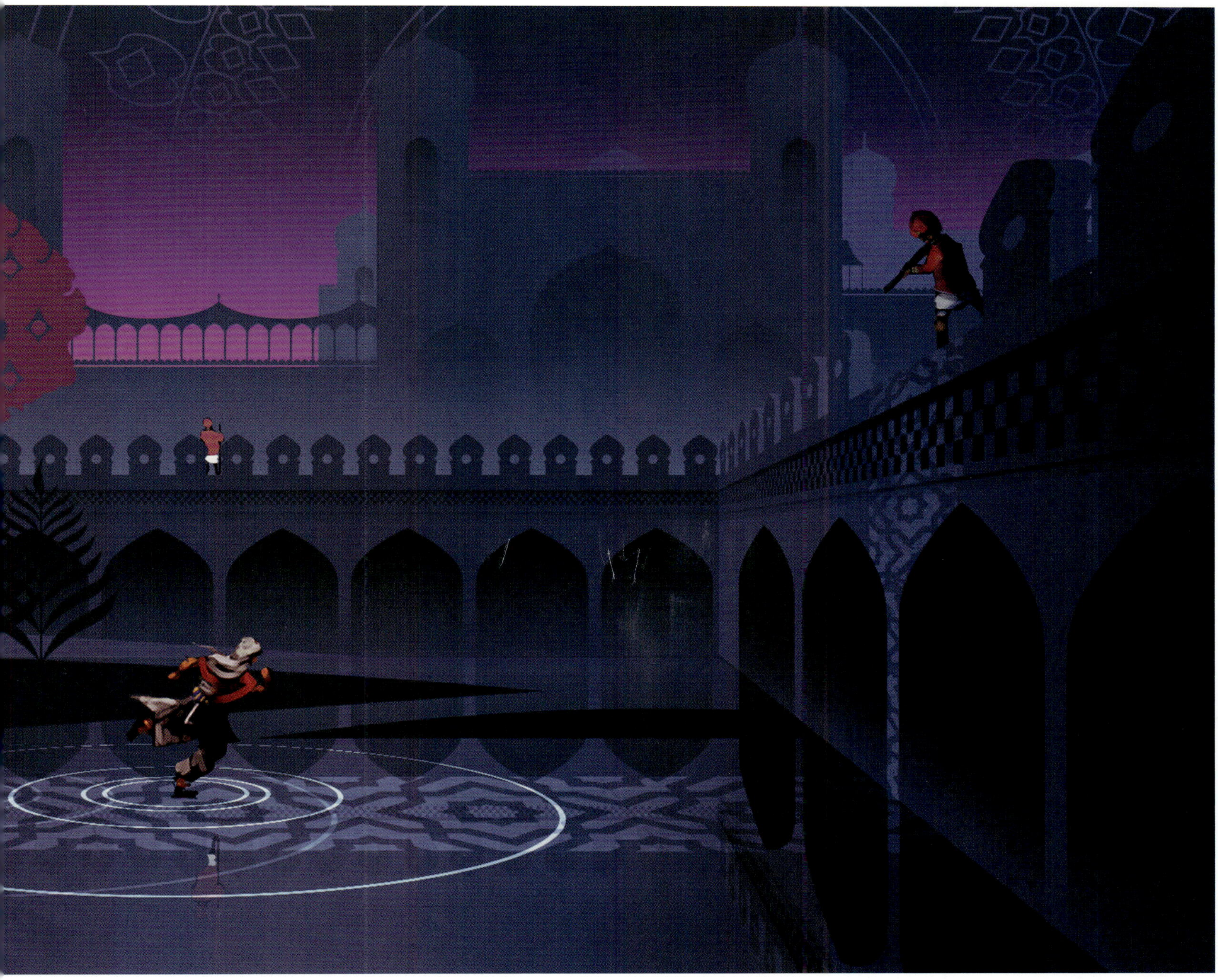

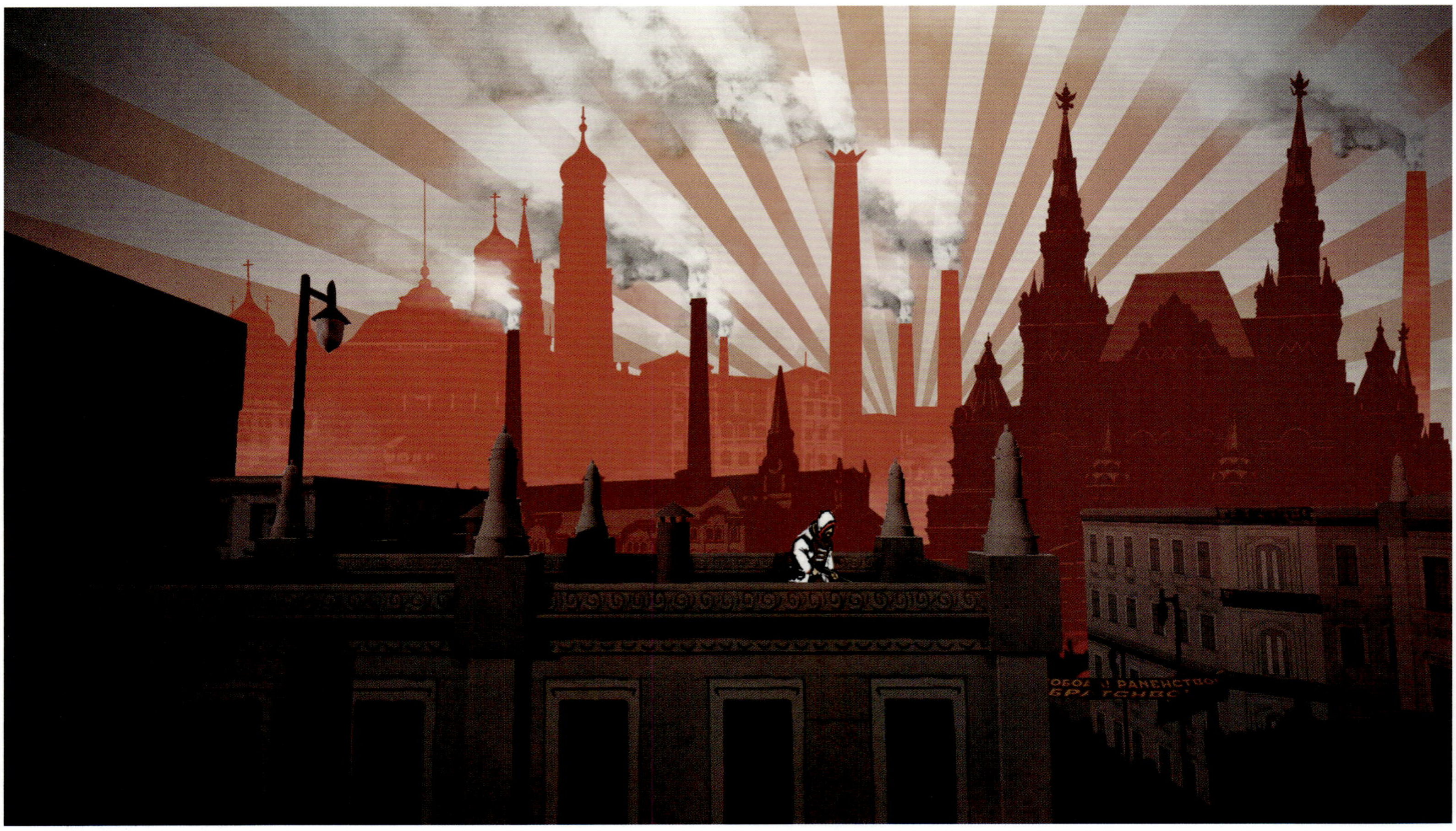

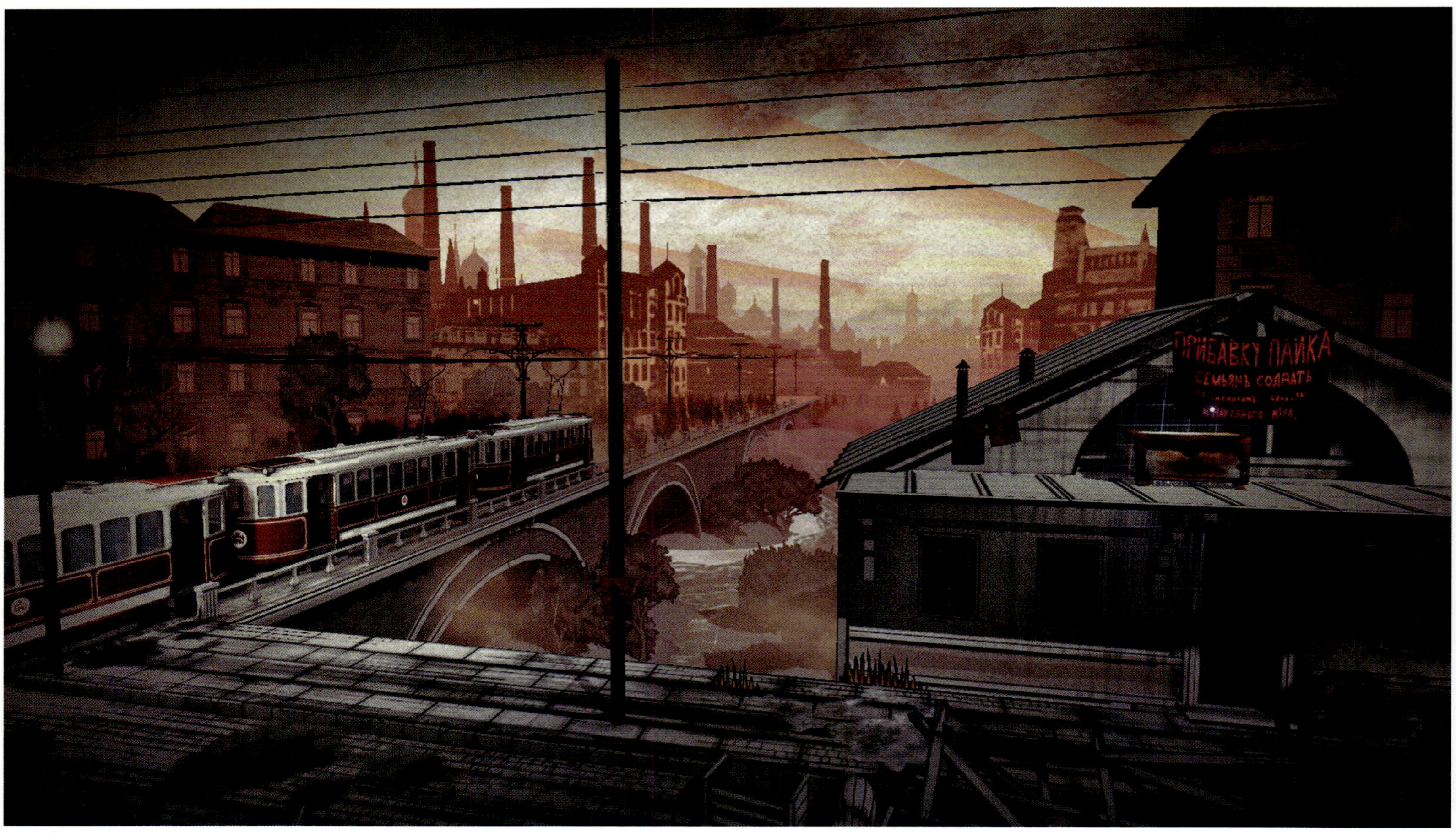

THESE PAGES: The art for *Chronicles: Russia* was guided by the concepts of civil war, the death of an empire, and the rise of its people (Saul Marchese).

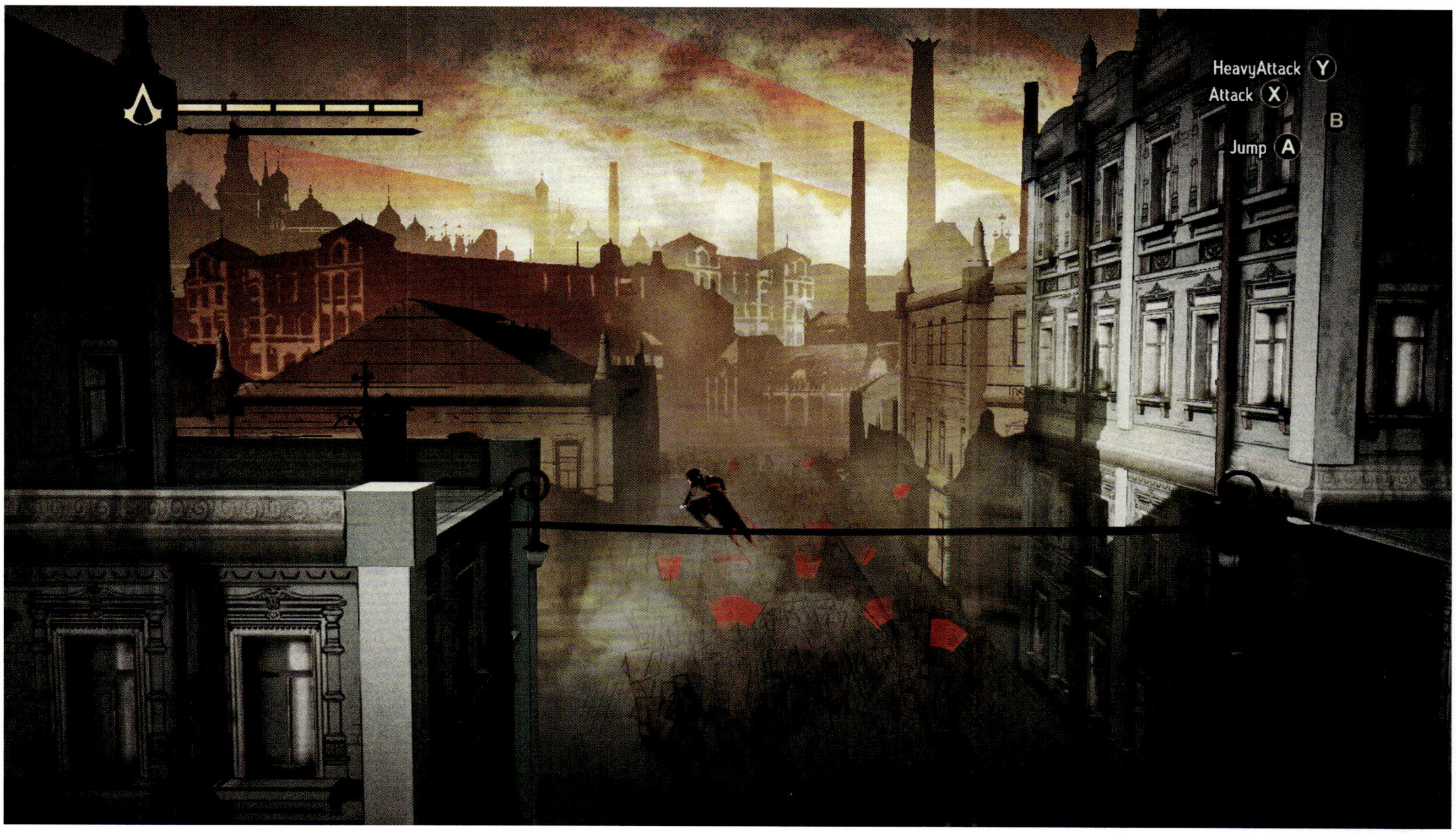
HeavyAttack Y
Attack X
B
Jump A

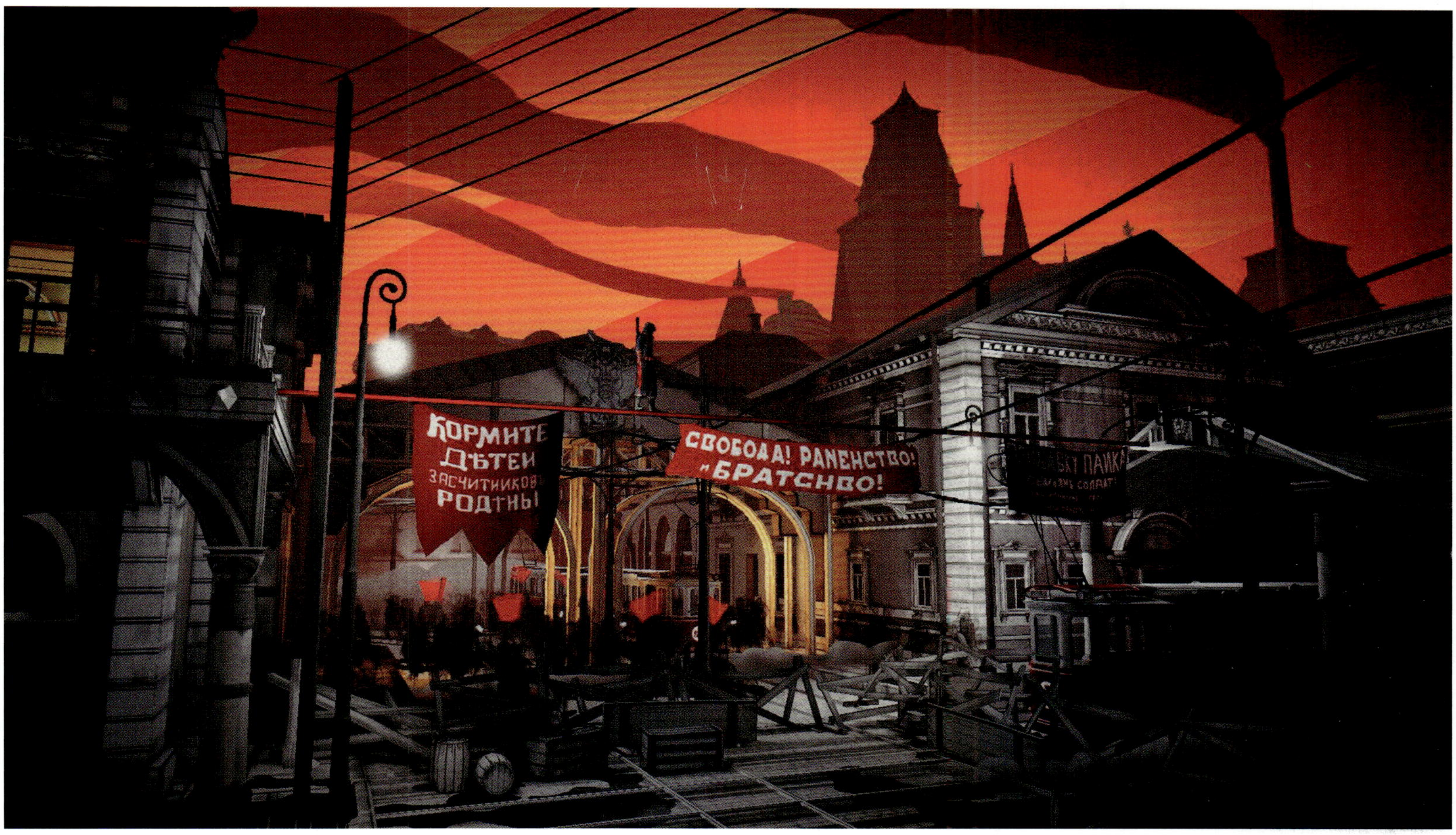
КОРМИТЕ ДѢТЕИ ЗАСЧИТИКОВ РОДТНЫ
СВОБОДА! РАNЕНСТВО! И БРАТСНВО!

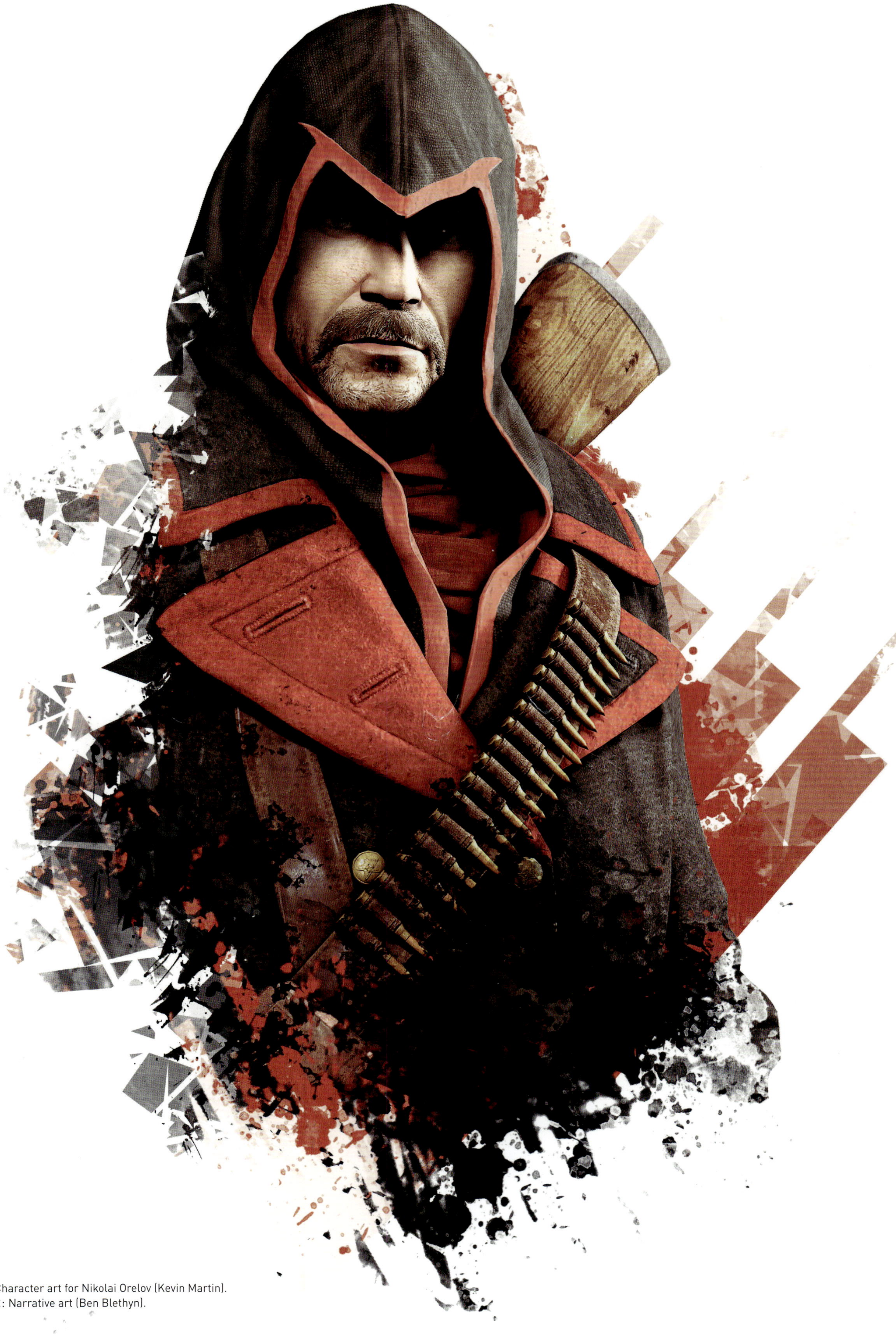

ABOVE: Character art for Nikolai Orelov (Kevin Martin).
OPPOSITE: Narrative art (Ben Blethyn).

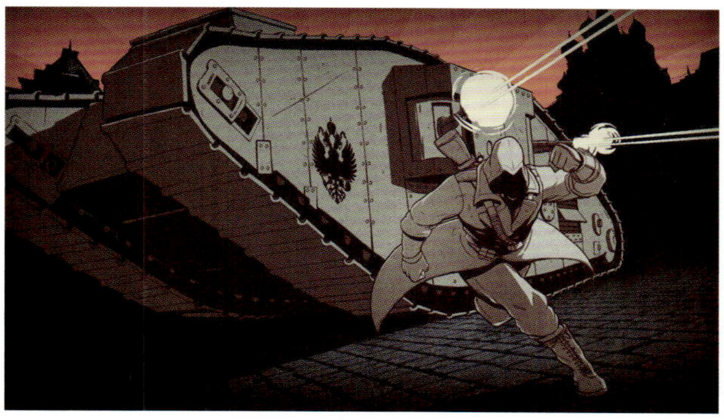

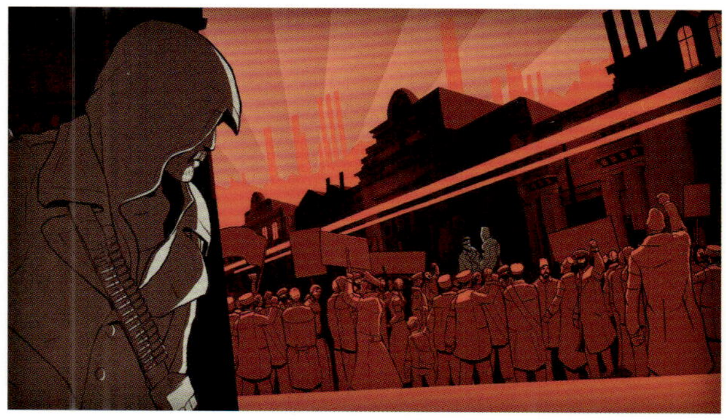

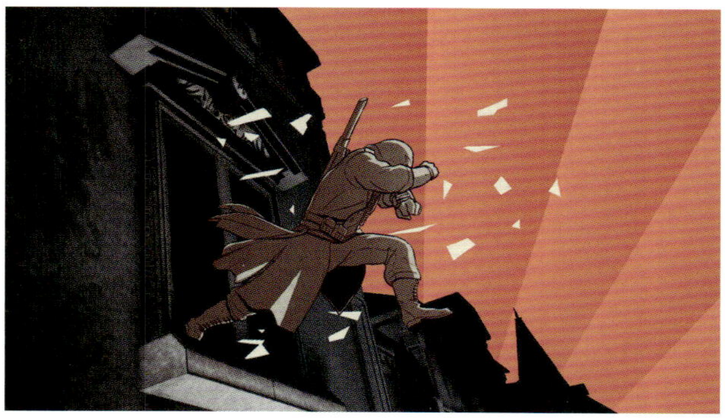

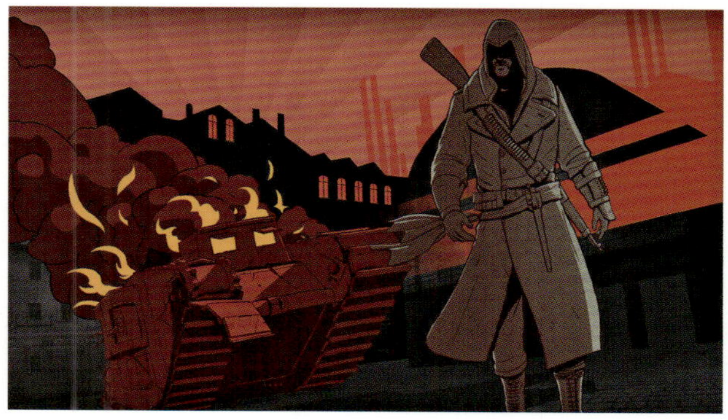

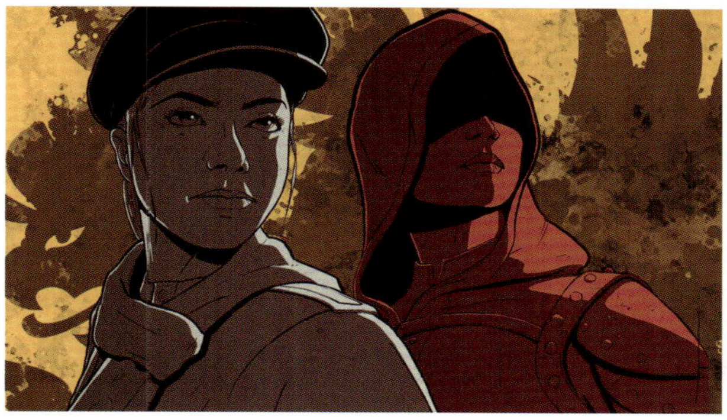

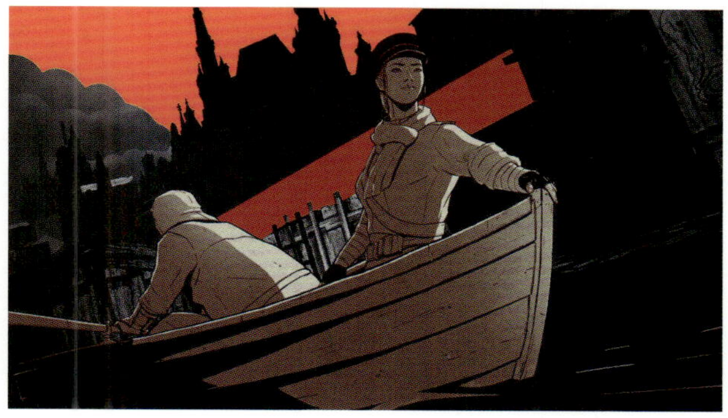

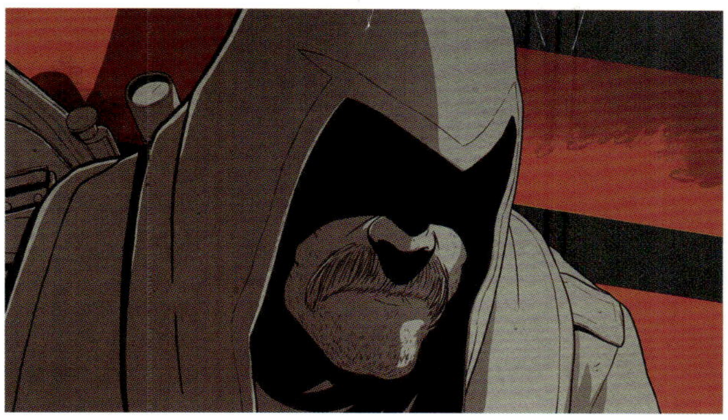

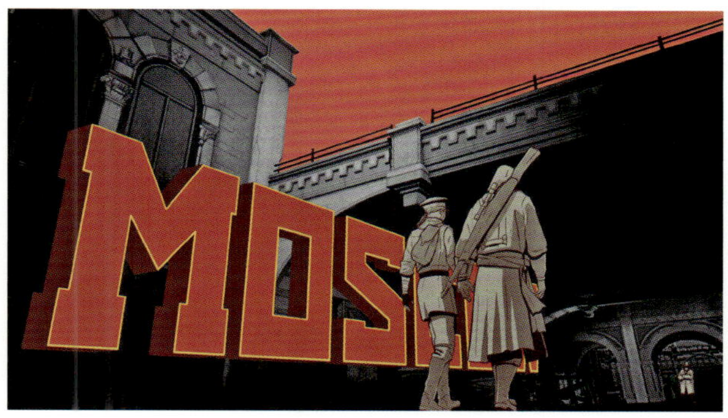

With two strongly imagined projects underway, it was natural to extend the *Chronicles* banner to become a trilogy. The successful integration of a graphic novel character from *Brahman* led Ubisoft and Climax to select Nikolai Orelov, star of the earlier comic series *The Fall* and *The Chain*, to be the hero of *Chronicles: Russia*. Taking cues from the first two entries, chief art inspirations came from the culture in question. "The art team was inspired by Russian Constructivism and propaganda posters, while still maintaining a fun, clear game and level design," Aymar says. The late nineteenth and early twentieth centuries allowed the team to explore how industrialization and technology brought optimism to the Russian cultural identity. *Chronicles: Russia* borrows liberally from photo montage, propaganda art, and technical line drawing to expand upon Orelov's story.

No matter the setting, the focus for *Chronicles* is on maintaining a consistency in the Assassin's Creed world and finding new perspective on the history-spanning conflicts and conspiracies. "That's the richness of the franchise: to have so many variations without losing its soul or spirit," says Jean. "It's also about consistency. It makes sense; it's linked. Especially when you talk about human history, everything has to make sense. That's something that we try not to forget."

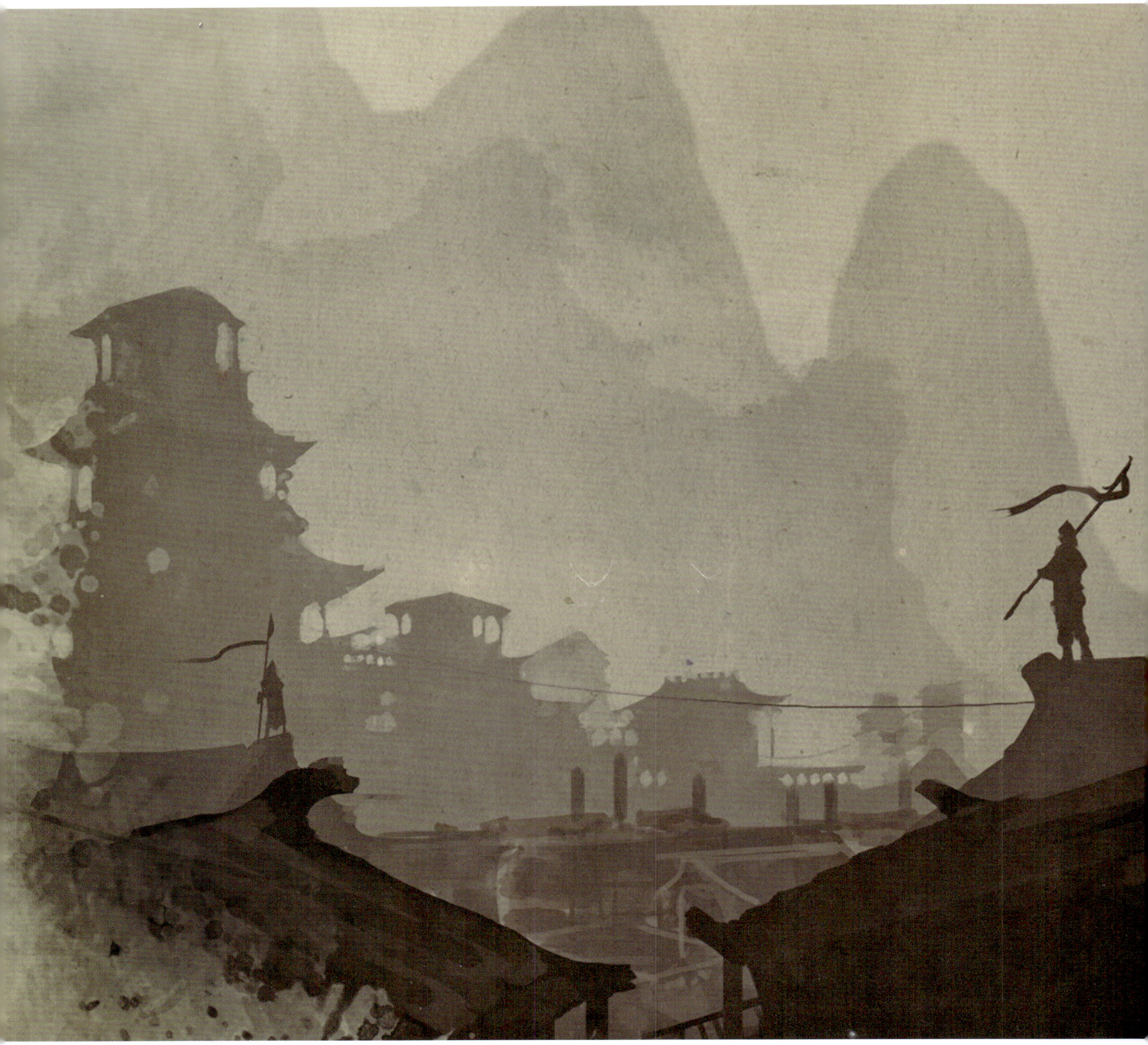

THESE PAGES: Shao Jun's movements and poses were inspired by Chinese kung fu masters (Ben Blethyn).

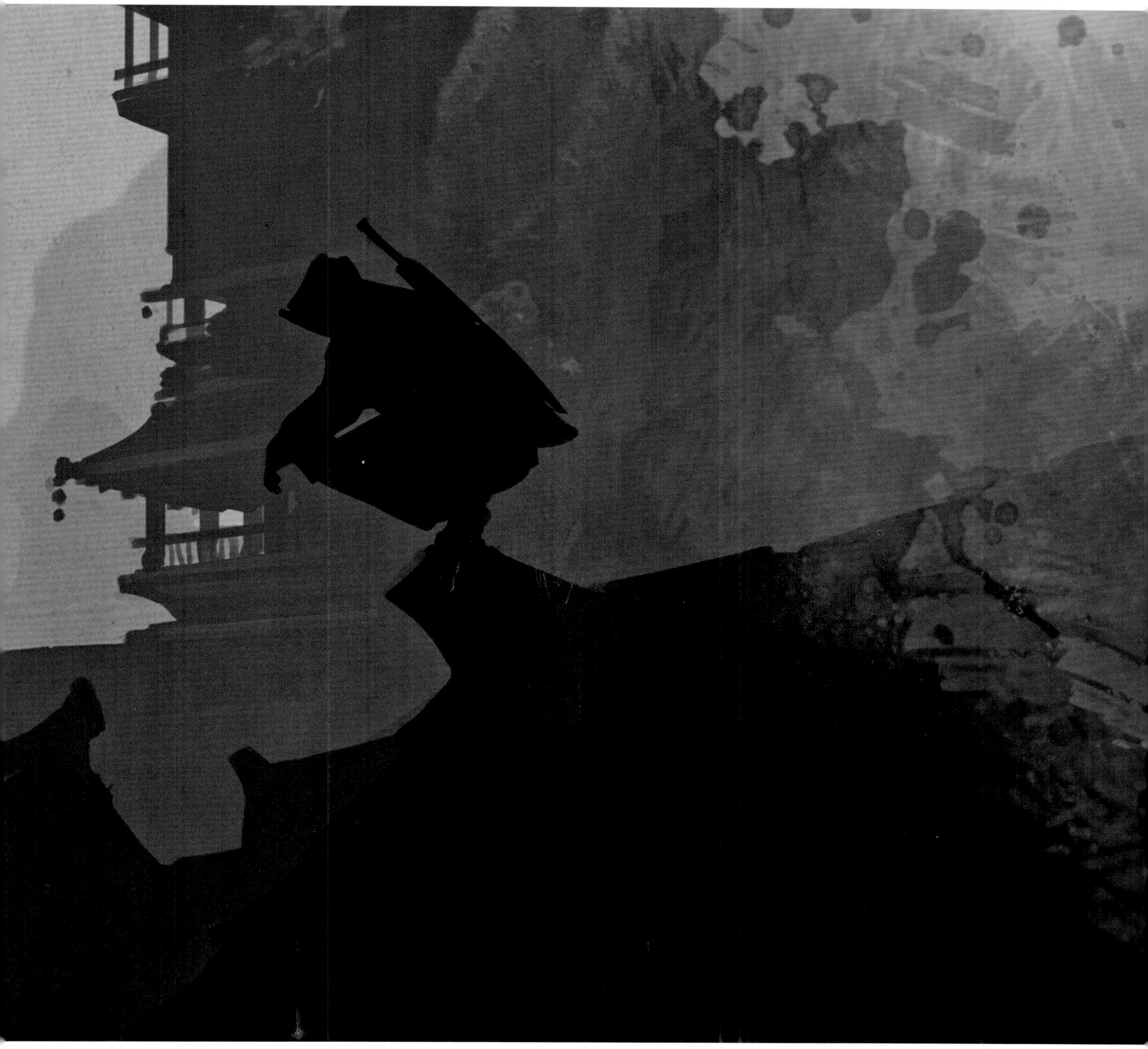

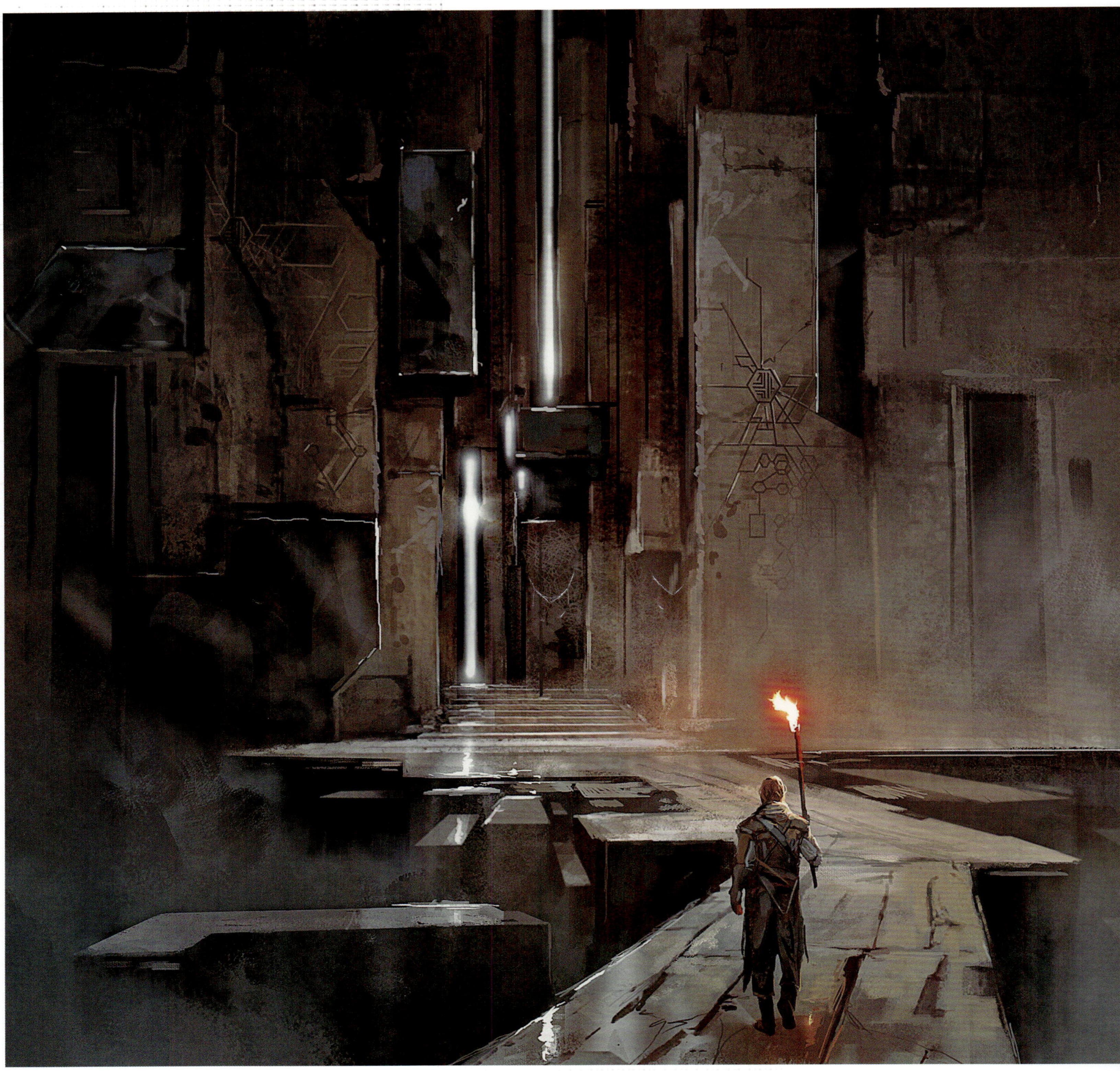

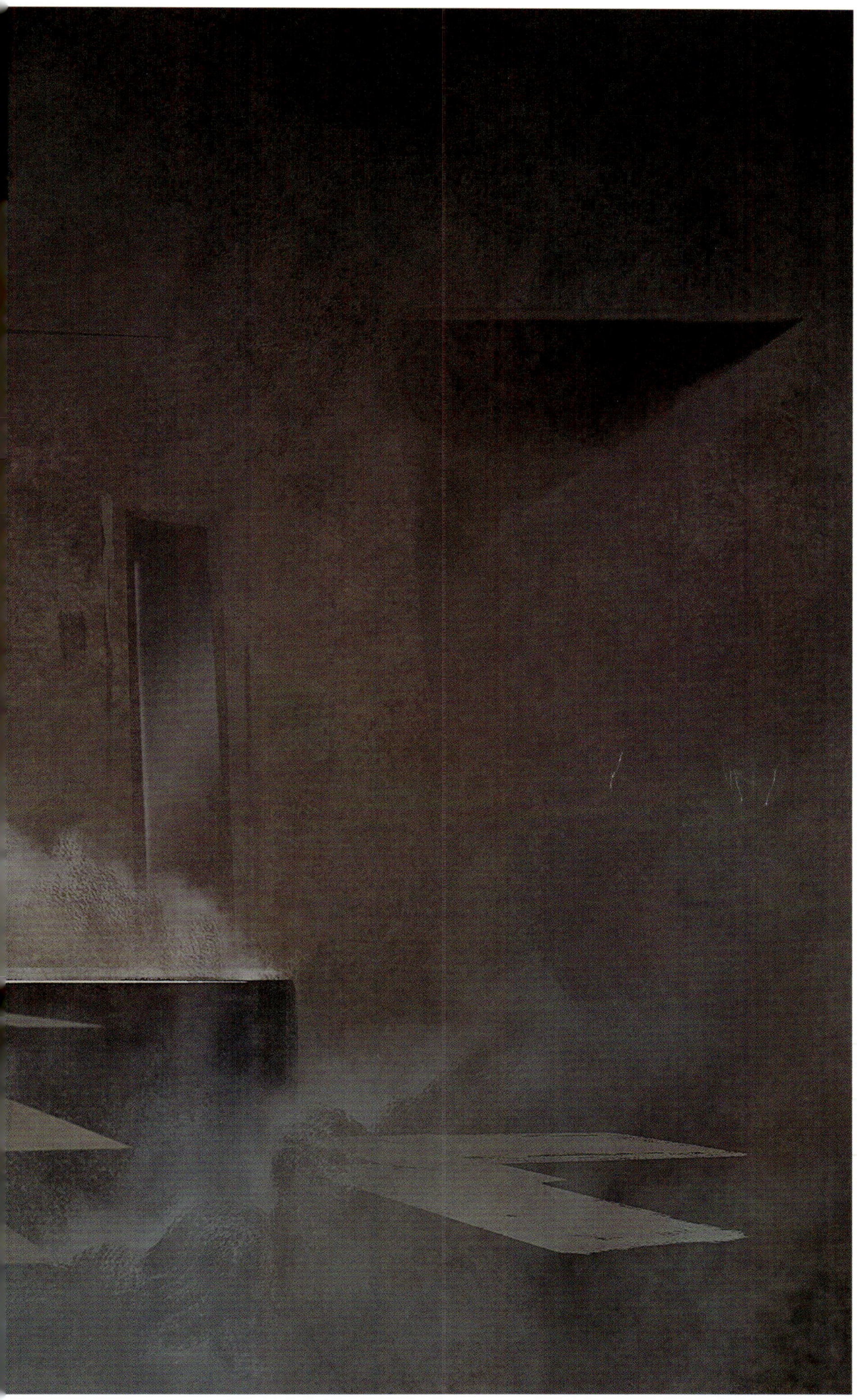

10 THE WORLD BEFORE

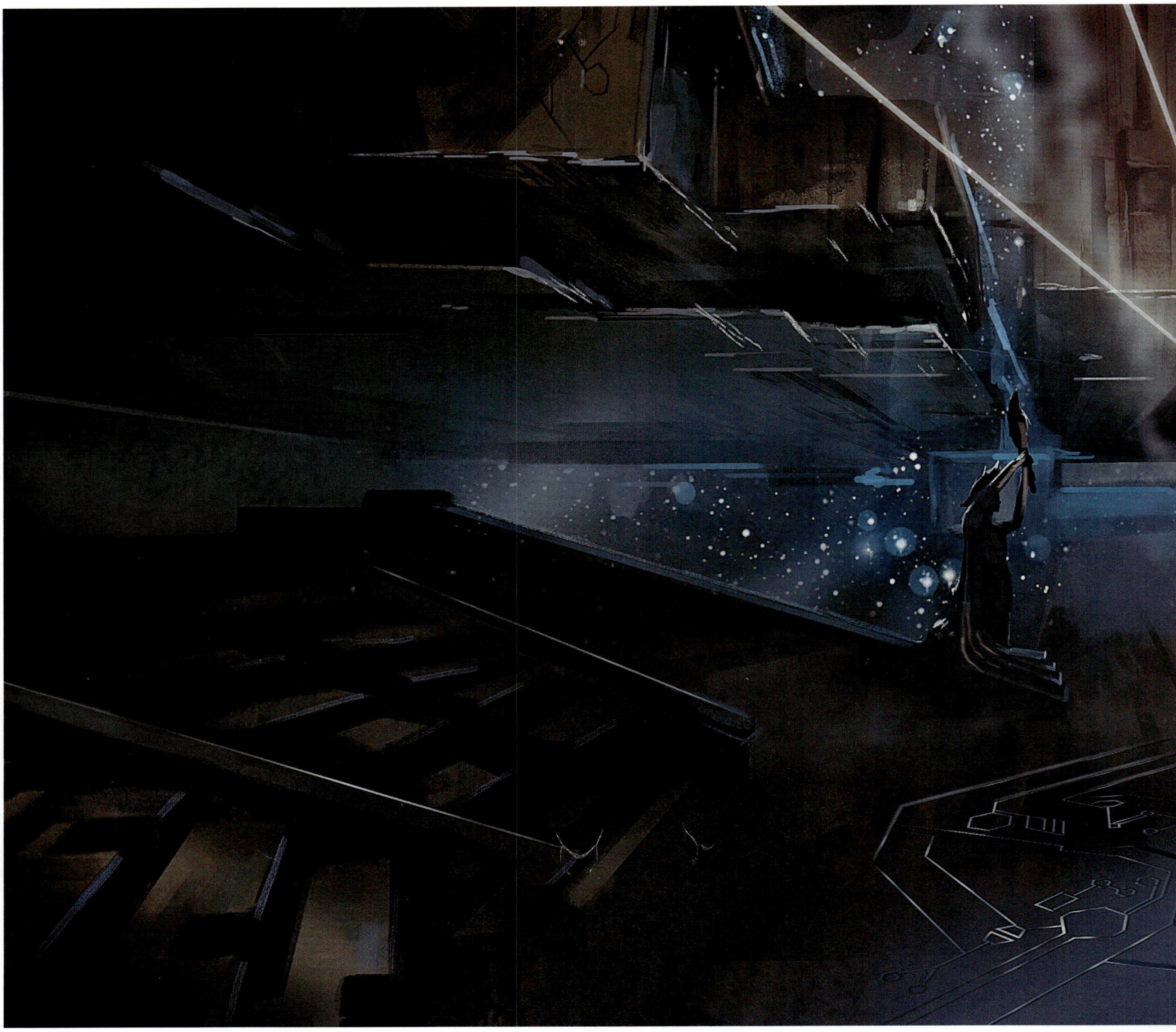

THOSE THAT CAME BEFORE

Introduced in the first game and threading its way through the entire Assassin's Creed mythology, the First Civilization is central to the allure and mystery of the entire franchise. With each installment, fans learn more about the strange, god-like beings who once ruled the planet, along with their immensely powerful technology, which outstrips even the ingenuity of modern humanity. However, in the earliest days of the franchise, the First Civilization was a big idea with only a loose conception of what it might mean to the franchise. "We didn't have a very clear vision in the first *Assassin's Creed* game of what this First Civilization would look like," Raphaël says. "With each game, we developed the concept of the First Civilization further. We researched and imagined various representations and progressively narrowed down the look of these beings and their world."

For fans, few aspects of the series garner so much debate as the First Civilization. Just a glimpse of its architecture or objects is enough to set off discussions and speculation. Ubisoft has unwrapped the riddle of the First Civilization with agonizing slowness over the years, but after nearly a decade of reveals, a picture of this powerful precursor civilization is coming into focus.

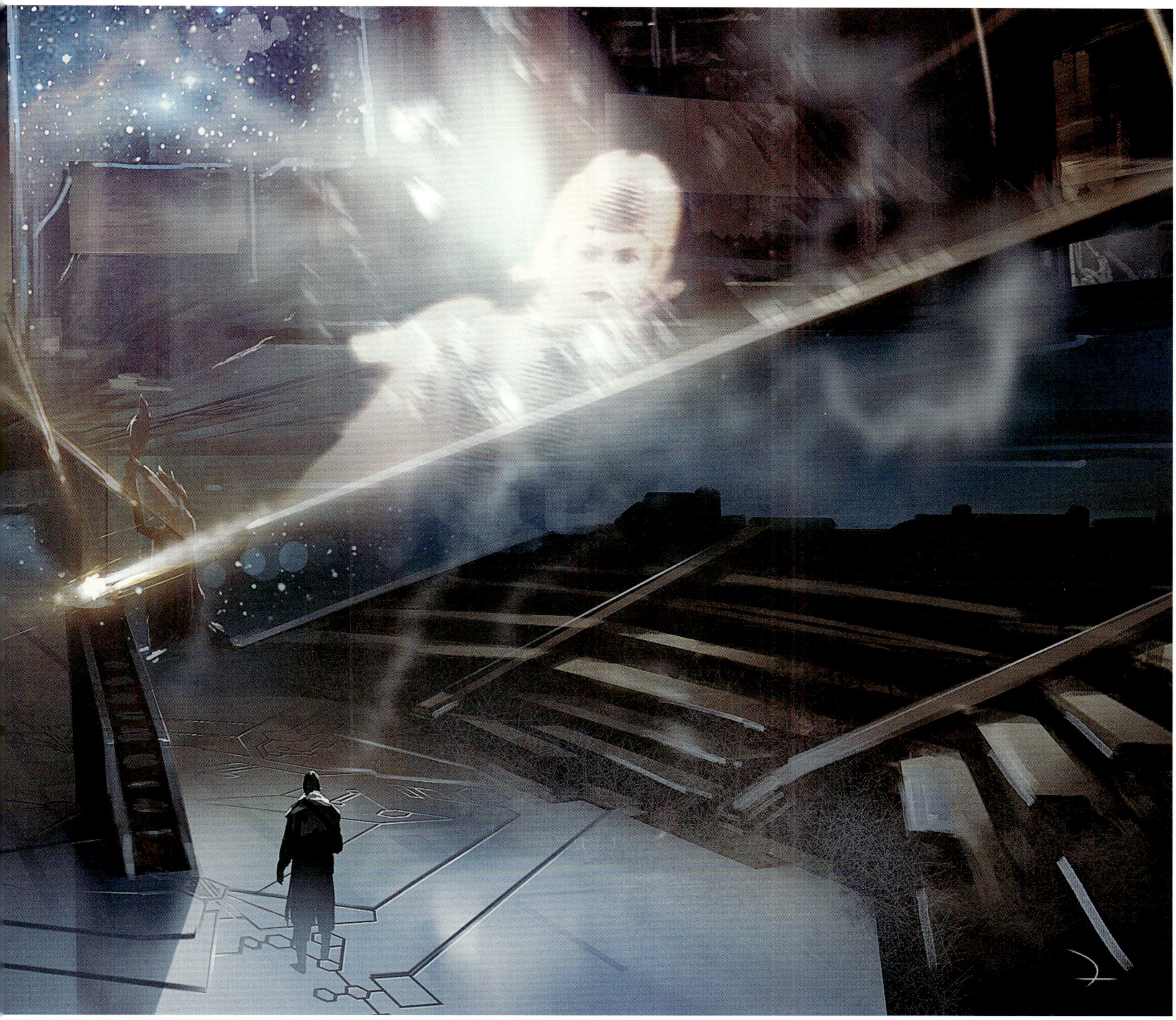

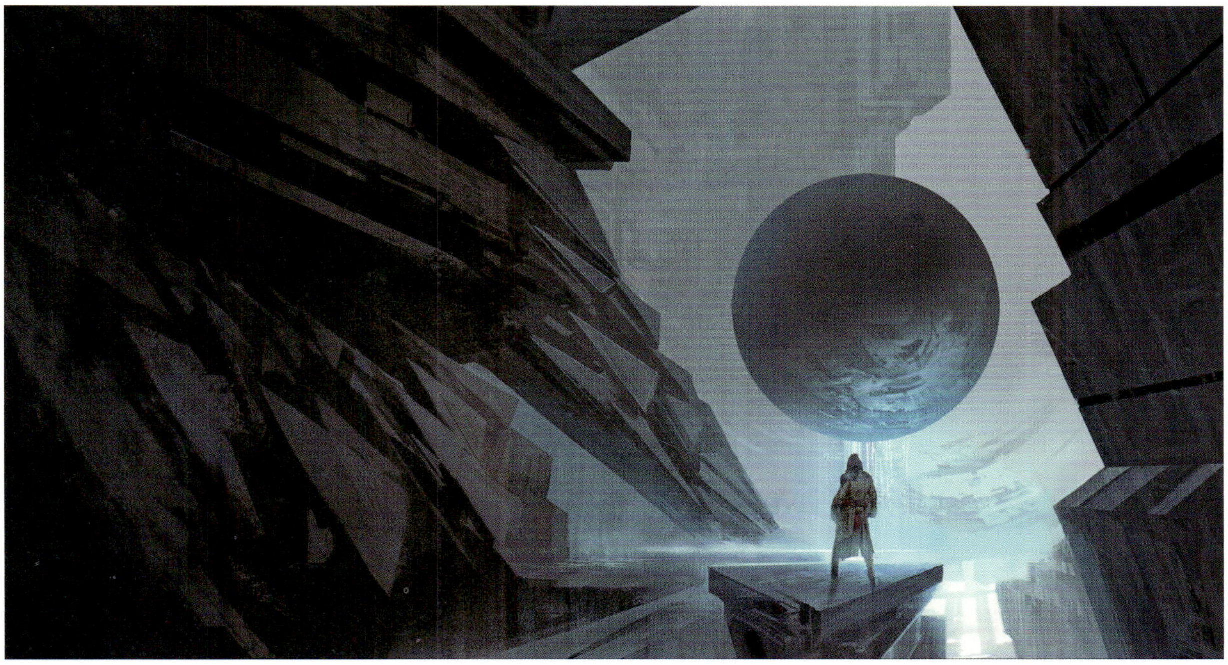

PREVIOUS PAGES: The Observatory from *Black Flag* (Martin Deschambault).
ABOVE: Main chamber of the Observatory (Martin Deschambault).
LEFT: Initial research for a First Civilization artifact that didn't make it into *Syndicate* (Hugo Puzzuoli).

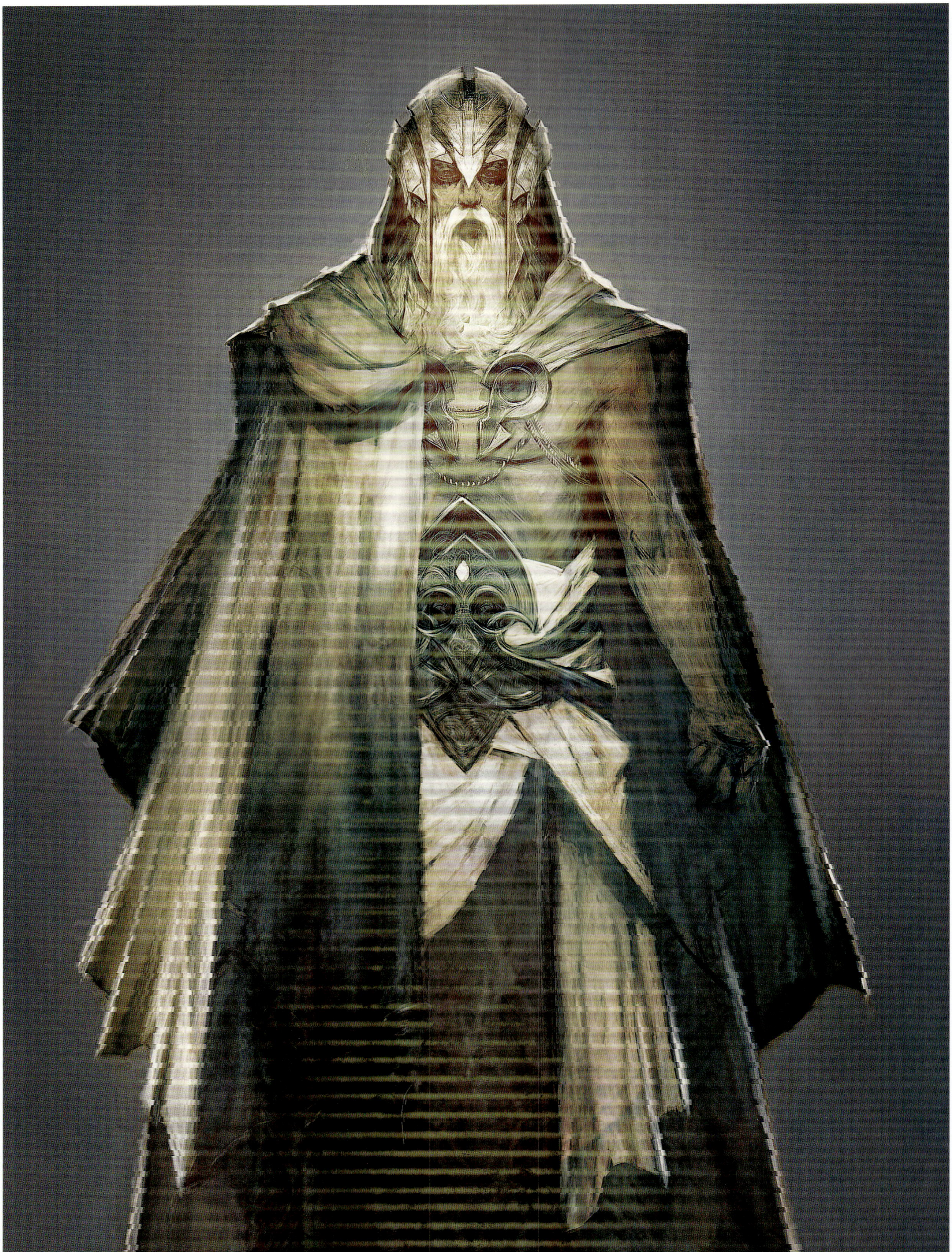

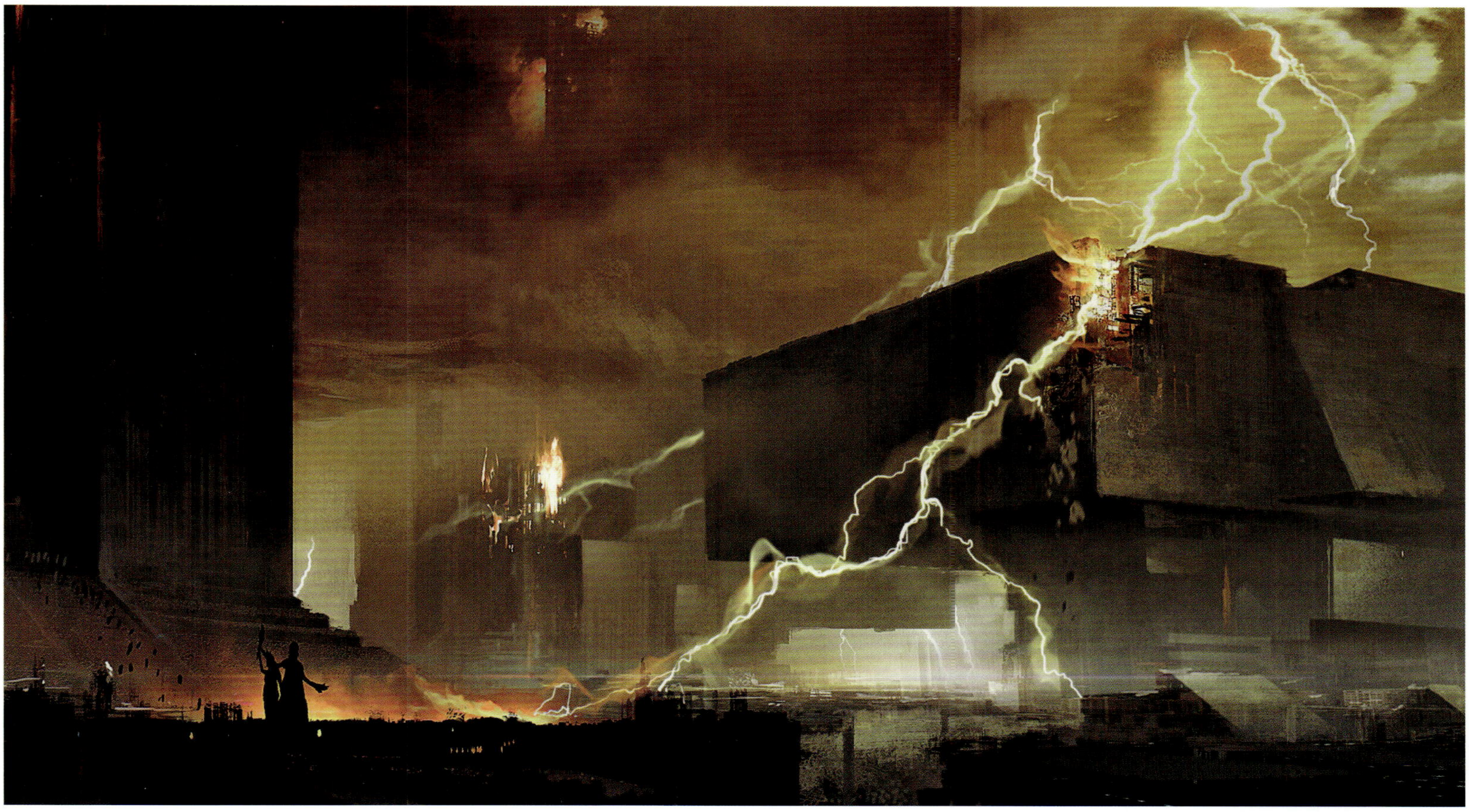

HUMANITY'S ORIGIN

While much of Assassin's Creed embraces the true events of history and seeks to play within that framework, the First Civilization was an exception. By suggesting that a powerful race of beings predated humans, Assassin's Creed gained an exciting twist of science fiction to go with its historical conspiracies. "The First Civilization artifacts can easily be interpreted as magic, but it's really very advanced technology impossible to be fully understood by normal human beings," Mohamed says.

Over the course of the games, we learn that our incredible predecessors looked like us for a reason: The scientists of their society created humanity as a lesser servant race. Led by a charismatic leader named Eve, the humans broke free of enslavement during a devastating war. Soon after, a massive solar flare struck our planet and brought a conclusive end to the First Civilization, paving the way for humanity to inherit the earth.

Even so, the scattered First Civilization relics have guided some of the greatest people and events in human history. These Pieces of Eden helped build empires, shatter armies, and herald scientific enlightenment. Perhaps more importantly for purposes of the games, the lost fragments of power provided a perfect set of MacGuffins, clever plot devices to fuel the never-ending conflict between Assassins and Templars.

OPPOSITE: Concept for Tinia, also known as Jupiter (Jeff Simpson).
ABOVE: Illustration of the destruction of the First Civilization (Martin Deschambault).

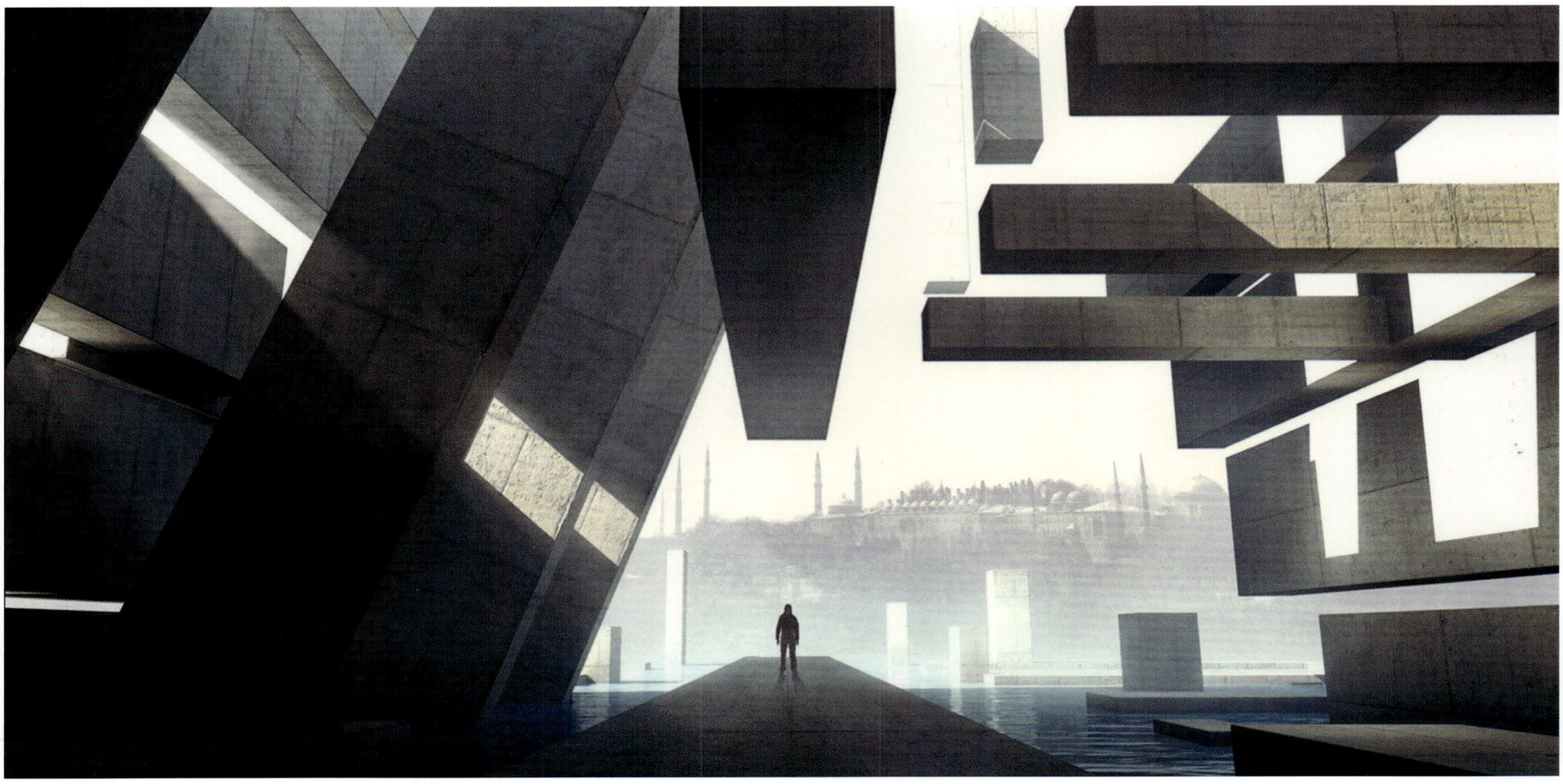

A STYLE ALL THEIR OWN

ABOVE: First Civilization architecture is characterized by overhanging, blocky structures and self-illuminating ambience (Raphaël Lacoste).
OPPOSITE: Artwork of Animus Island (Gilles Beloeil).

The first *Assassin's Creed* revealed little in the way of visualizations for the precursors. Each passing installment helped fill in the gaps, and visits to extant First Civilization ruins gave shape to these people who had previously only existed in the imagination of fans. "This is where we are able to add some sci-fi elements," Raphaël says. "We keep the present-day and historical parts very grounded, but we have more freedom when it comes to the First Civilization. I really hope one day we can have a big part of the game set in their era."

First Civilization architecture is defined by a sense of immensity and overwhelming scale. Huge rectangular blocks meet each other at sometimes surprising angles, and the mathematics of how everything fits together don't seem to add up. Environmental artist Gilles Beloeil explains, "When I worked on *Revelations*, the intention was for the Animus Island, the mysterious 'safe mode' of the Animus, to resemble First Civilization architecture. Even though the Animus Island was part of Abstergo technology, it's clear that it was subject to the influence of First Civilization intelligence. The creative director wanted me to look at an Escher painting. He wanted something a bit disorienting. So the scale is really crazy and things are floating upside down." Often, overhanging blocks reach out farther than they should, and hard right angles dominate the view. "I like the poetry of this kind of presentation," Raphaël says. "It's very simple. There is a playing around with atmosphere—a mysterious, huge shape seemingly floating in the air." Diffuse light seems to float down without a clear point of origin, and floating sigils of light indicate long-lost technology as it comes alive.

"The style was strongly inspired by French landscape artists who created beautiful paintings using the most interesting aspects of the elements of nature," Raphaël says. "They played with proportions and atmosphere to create very interesting compositions."

Another primary source of ideas was modern Japanese architecture. "The focus on poetic simplicity and empty space is keenly felt in the temples and hideaways of First Civilization technology. The minimalist, monolithic architectural qualities were a big inspiration for us," Mohamed says.

The Assassin's Creed art teams would also look to an odd amalgamation of primitive civilization architecture as seen in Egyptian and Mayan monoliths and pyramids, and the glowing bright lights of science fiction movies like *Tron*. By combining all these disparate inspirations, the First Civilization began to establish its own identity.

While their architecture might have seemed alien, the actual people of the First Civilization seemed more inspired by classical mythology. Draped in togas and robes, standing tall and statuesque, characters like Juno, Minerva, and Jupiter were clear analogues to ancient gods, implying that whole religions had sprung up around the last surviving members of this lost culture.

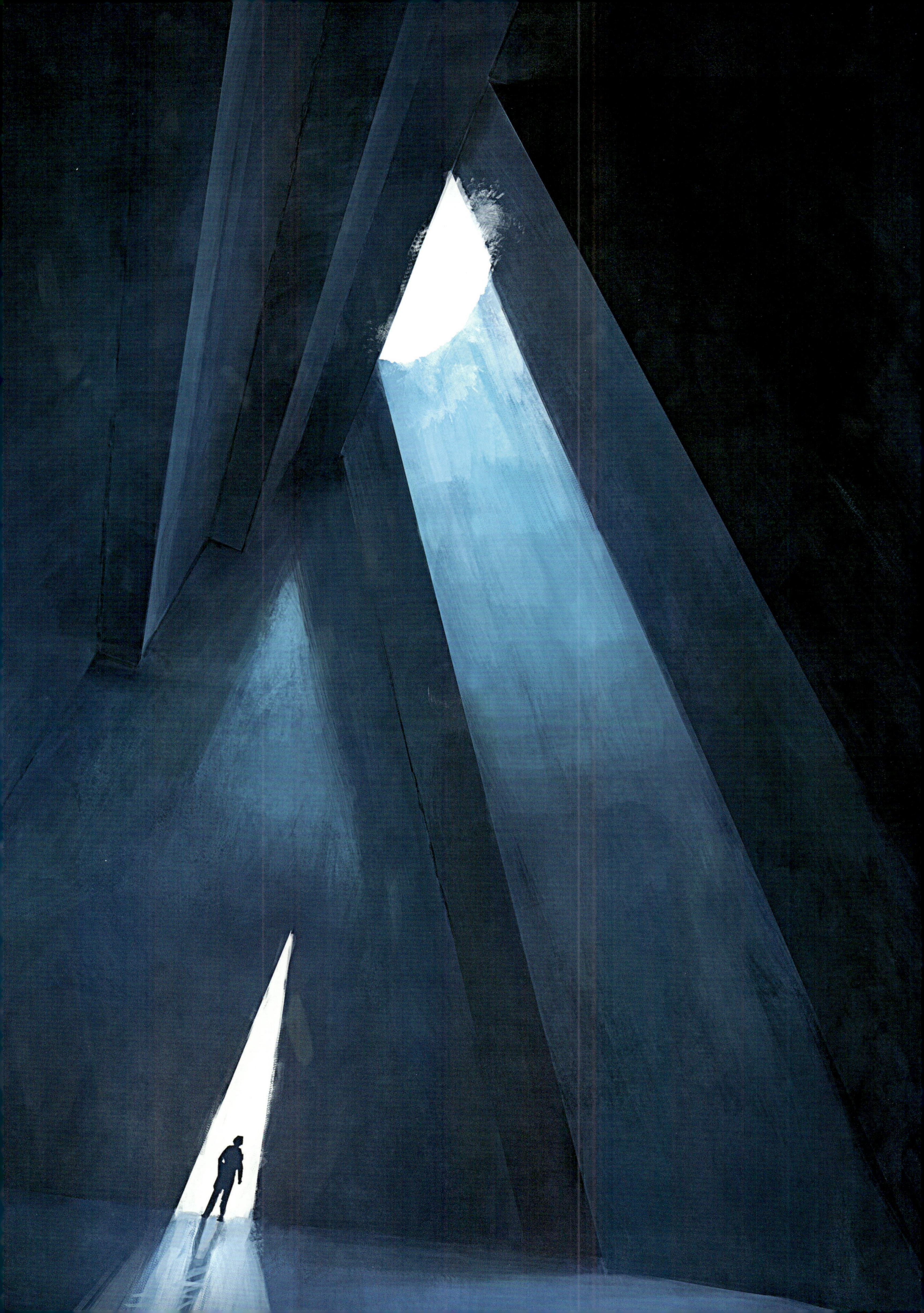

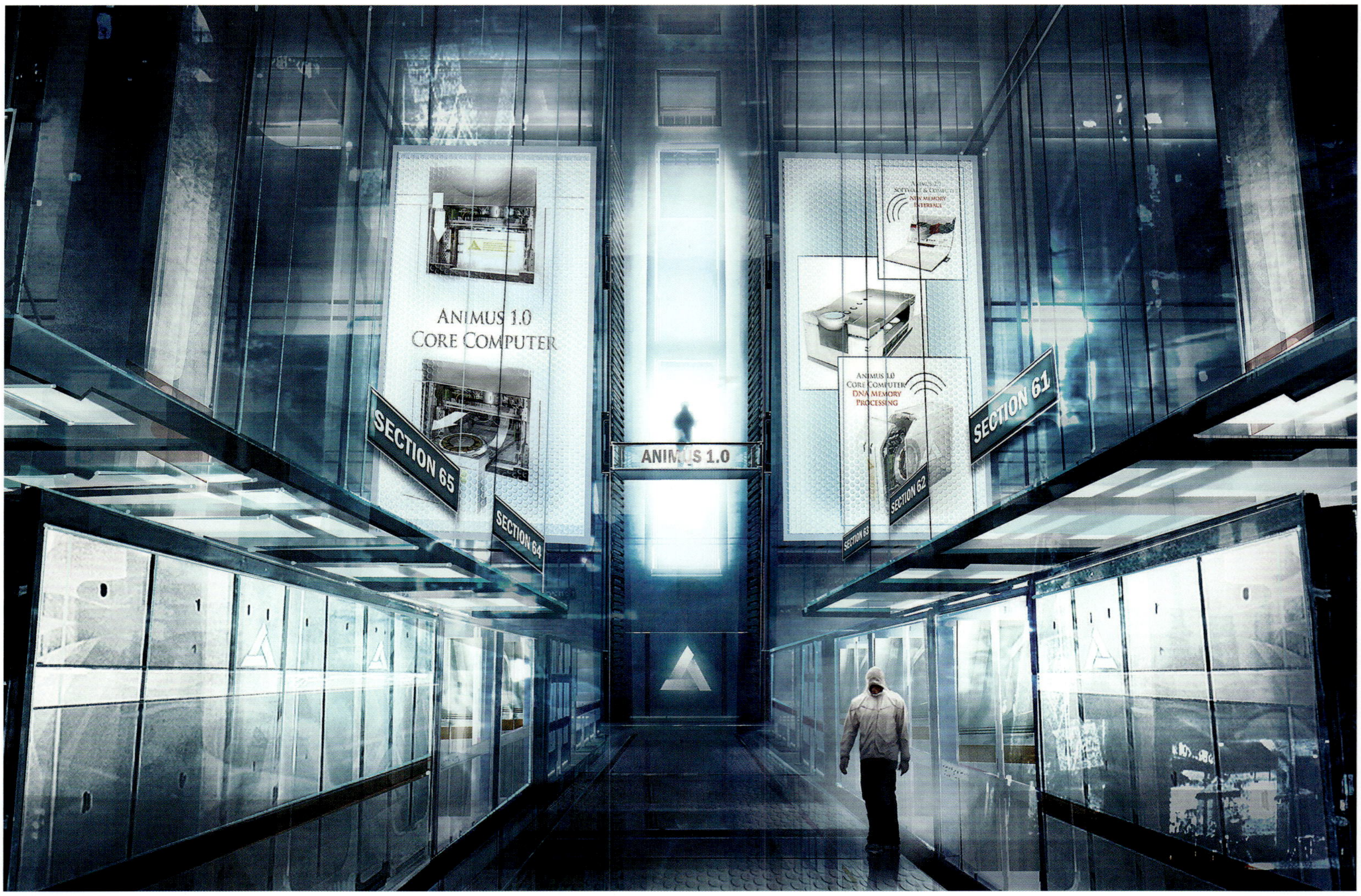
ANIMUS 1.0
CORE COMPUTER
SECTION 65
SECTION 64
ANIMUS 1.0
NEW MEMORY
INTERFACE
ANIMUS 1.0
CORE COMPUTER
DNA MEMORY
PROCESSING
SECTION 61
SECTION 62
SECTION 63

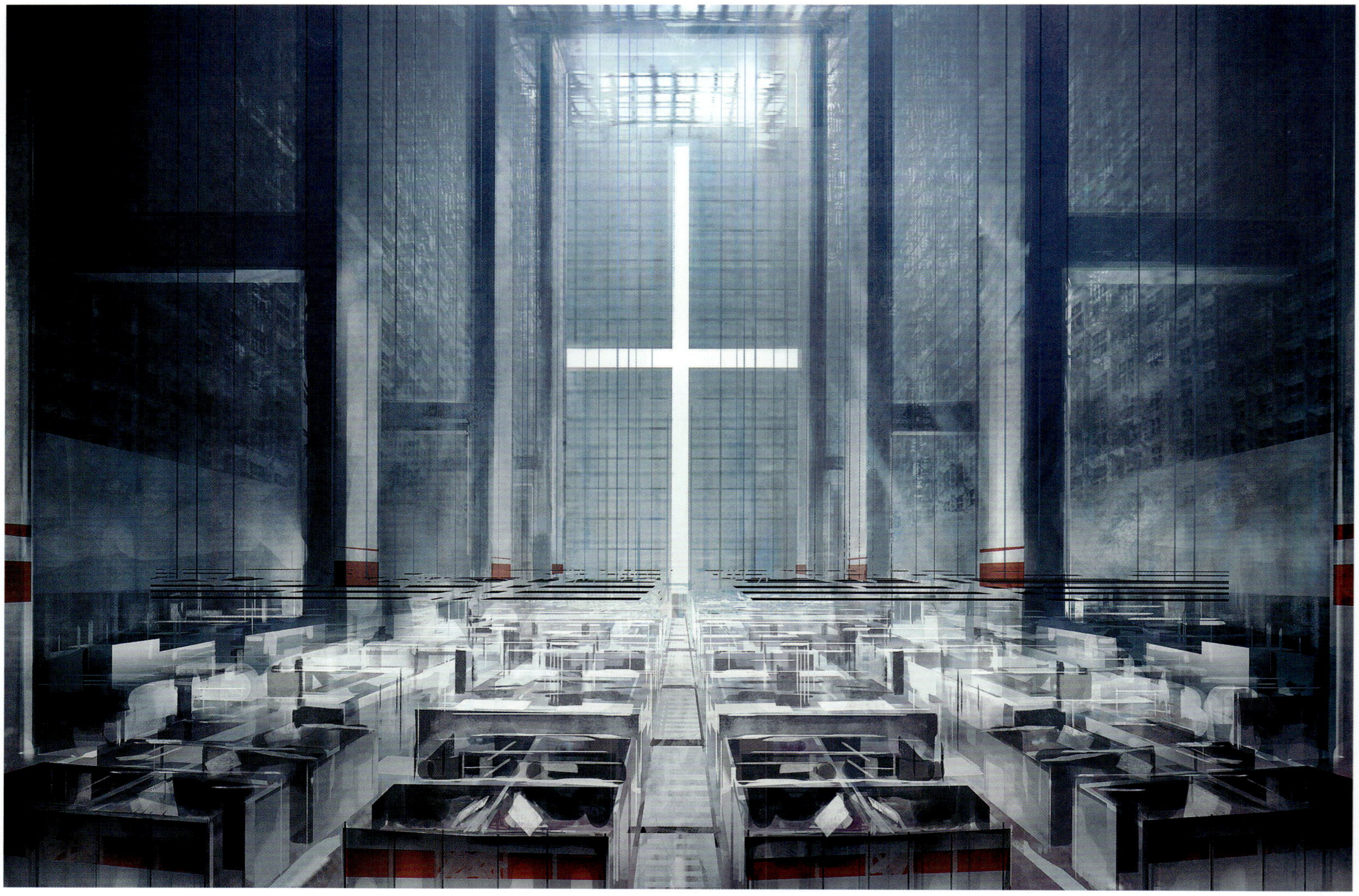

HIDING IN PLAIN SIGHT

While the First Civilization provided a science fiction layer to the Assassin's Creed universe, the existence of Abstergo Industries helped ground the series in the present day. As the modern-day commercial front for the Templar Order, Abstergo persists through each of the games as an ultra-powerful international company with ventures in everything from computers and aerospace tech to entertainment and medical research.

From the first glimpse of a locked white experiment room in the first game, Abstergo feels sterile and monolithic. "The Abstergo Industries buildings are almost like religious sites but very cold," Raphaël says. "The presence of a vast power is palpable: the power of the Templars. This is enhanced by visual details like the huge scale of the pillars, which are out of proportion, cold, and unwelcoming." The company is a modern-day bogeyman: an analogue for all the giant corporations that seem to govern the processes of our lives and guide us down a path of profit and success that ultimately only serves a select few at some unfathomable top of the pyramid.

Abstergo visuals are rooted in the Templar Order from which the company emerged. Bright white walls and hard, straight lines still govern the style, while the occasional cross imagery offers reminders of the original uniform. "Everything is connected to the Templars visually: the straight lines, the square shapes, even the cross," Raphaël says. "This is what we use a lot in the design of the characters, but also in the design of the environments that are connected to the Templars."

Mohamed recalls a clear connection being drawn between the First Civilization and Abstergo. Both seem daunting and dangerous, overwhelming and hard to understand. "I always thought that it would be cool to have some similarities between them in terms of architectural style," Mohamed details. "That is why, for both, I usually refer to modern Japanese architectural style for the primary inspiration. For anything related to accessories, design, objects, I usually use Apple, how they are purified, simplified, and minimalistic in design."

In more recent games, we see a softer and yet more subversive side to Abstergo through the introduction of Abstergo Entertainment. The threatening nature of the company isn't so heavy-handed here, with visual displays that are more friendly and public-facing. "In *Black Flag*, we entered Abstergo Entertainment, the division of Abstergo Industries that was also responsible for the development of *Liberation*. We used ourselves, Ubisoft, and companies like Google as sources of inspiration," Raphaël explains. "We introduced brighter, more saturated colors and warmer materials like wood instead of cold concrete everywhere." However, the overpowering nature of the company is still apparent through its expensive skyscraper headquarters and the towering server farm at the company's heart.

This growing entertainment division introduced a meta-quality to the franchise narrative, supplanting Ubisoft with Abstergo Entertainment as the supposed publisher of the games about historical figures like Aveline and Shay Cormac. Abstergo Entertainment plays into the ongoing conspiracy theory themes at the root of the Assassin's Creed story, even as brief scenes set within the company serve to remind players that a First Civilization intelligence continues to haunt Abstergo's network, a looming threat for a future game.

OPPOSITE TOP: Abstergo Industries' blue lighting and harsh angles create a cold, impersonal atmosphere (Donglu Yu).
OPPOSITE BOTTOM: An office room from *Assassin's Creed II* shows hints of Templar iconography (Martin Deschambault).

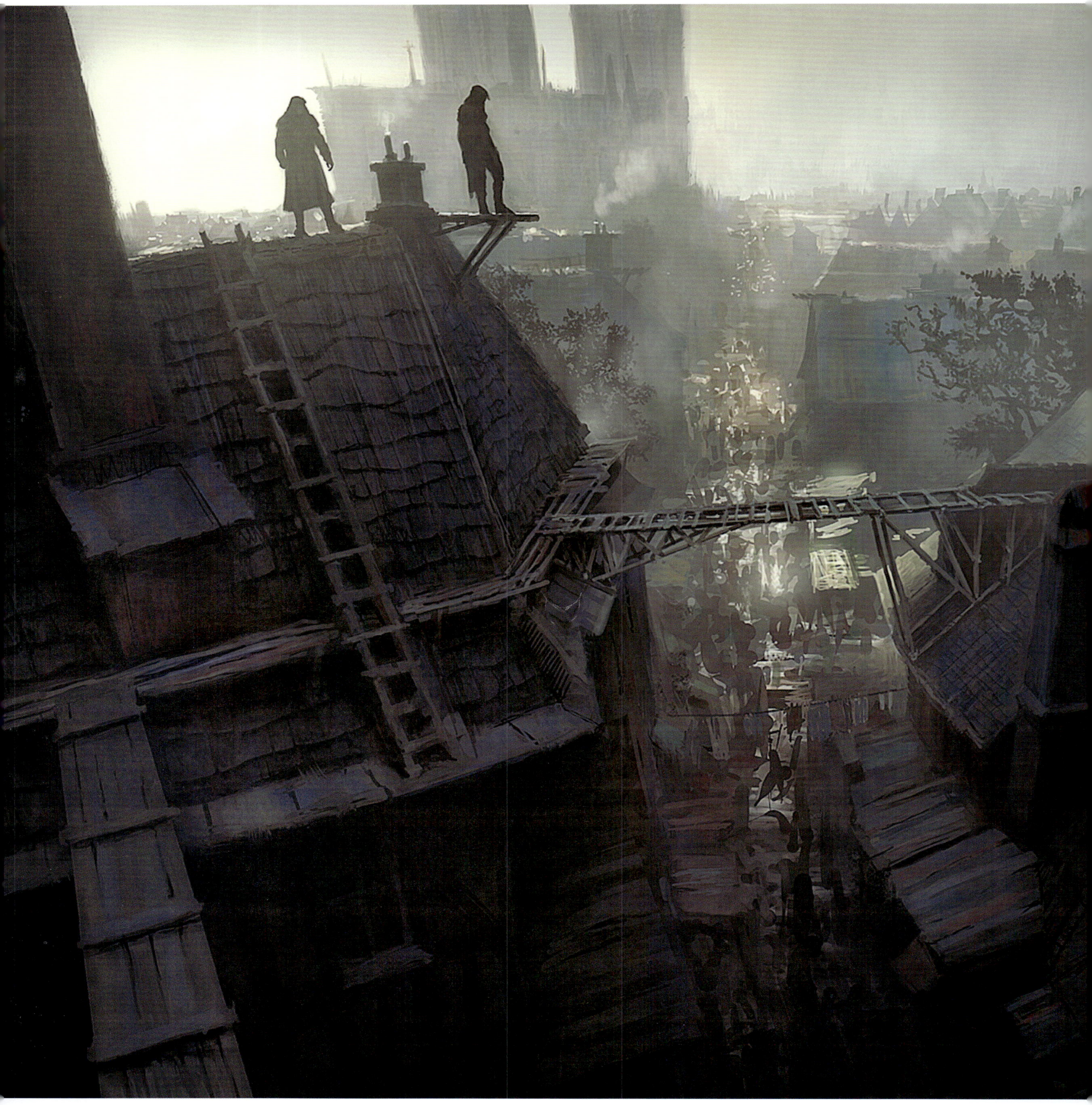

THESE PAGES: Artwork of a cooperative multiplayer vista from *Assassin's Creed: Unity* (Gilles Beloeil).

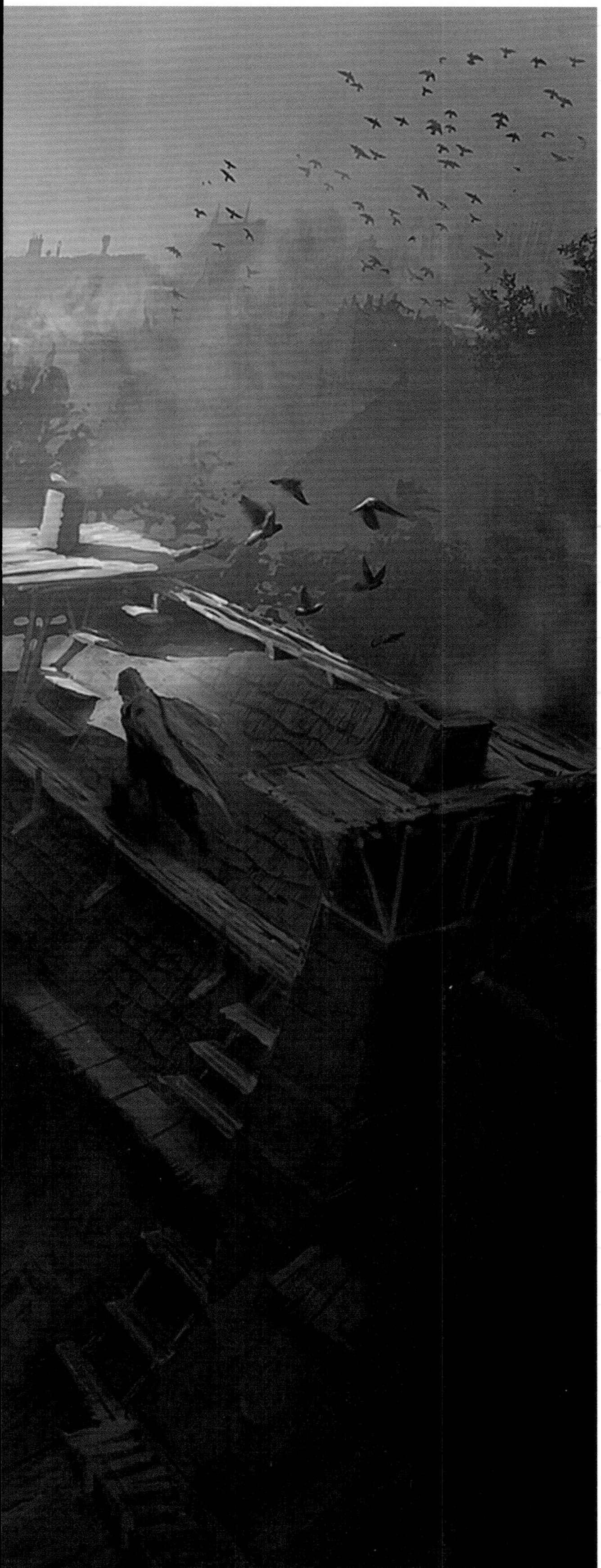

IN TRAINING

Beginning with *Assassin's Creed: Brotherhood* and continuing on through *Black Flag*, Ubisoft introduced a new branch of storytelling in which Templar recruits were placed into the Animus and, through the Bleeding Effect caused by experiencing ancestral memories, trained to confront modern-day Assassins. The story setup allowed for a new competitive multiplayer game mode and freed the multiplayer development teams to craft an array of new characters, locations, and scenarios to populate the world.

In *Brotherhood*'s and *Revelations*' multiplayer storylines, players were treated to new Renaissance locales, like the posh Castel Gandolfo and the rocky island of Mont Saint-Michel in Normandy, France. Creative characters like the beautiful but deadly Courtesan, the distracting Harlequin, the hunchbacked Nobleman, and the hooded and macabre Executioner each offered their own twist on familiar Templar and Assassin visual styles.

With *Assassin's Creed III*, the multiplayer levels stayed in time with the campaign storytelling by heading to North America and suggesting that the multiplayer experience was now a branch of Abstergo Entertainment's public game platform. The Colonies offered new cat-and-mouse arenas at Boston Harbor and along the icy coastlines of the Northwest Passage, among others. Native American warriors like the Coyote Man and Silent Shadow were pitted against the Colonial Preacher and Hessian soldier.

By the time *Black Flag* rolled around, the structure of new characters and locations could dive into the Caribbean tropics and revel in some truly colorful characters and locales. The Dandy and Duelist hunted the Mercenary and Navigator through the pastel streets of Martinique and the old stone city of Saba Island.

Subsequent installments moved away from the competitive multiplayer conceit, but the years of its inclusion provided some of the series' most unusual and creative character concepts and landscapes.

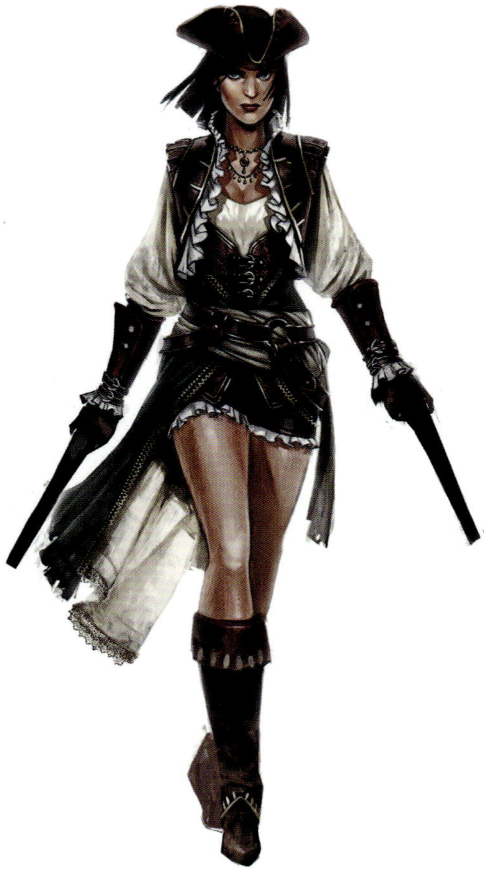

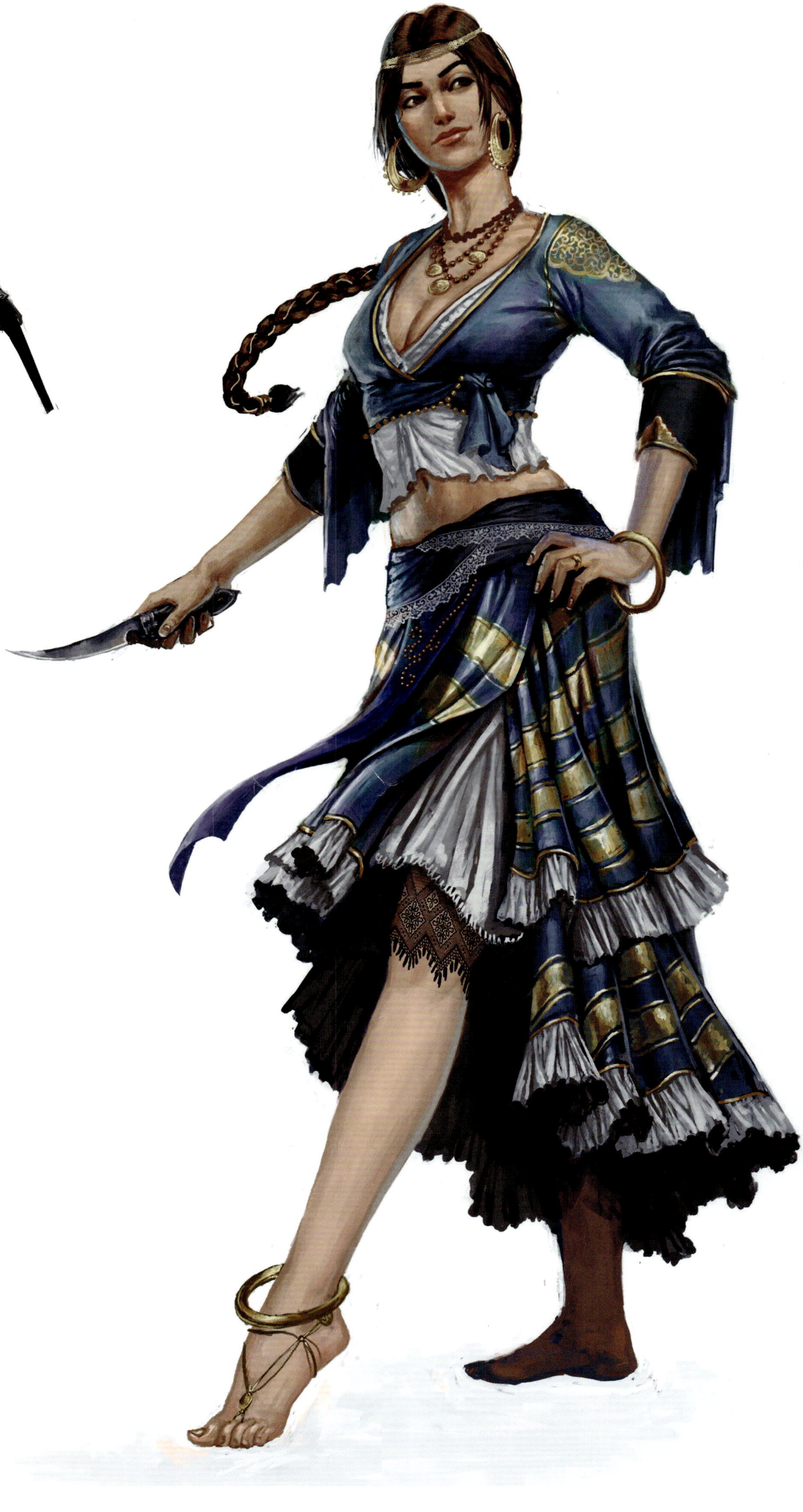

TOP LEFT: Art of the Captain's daughter from *Assassin's Creed IV: Black Flag* (Rémi Farjaud).
RIGHT: Character art of the Trickster from *Assassin's Creed: Revelations* (Johan Grenier).

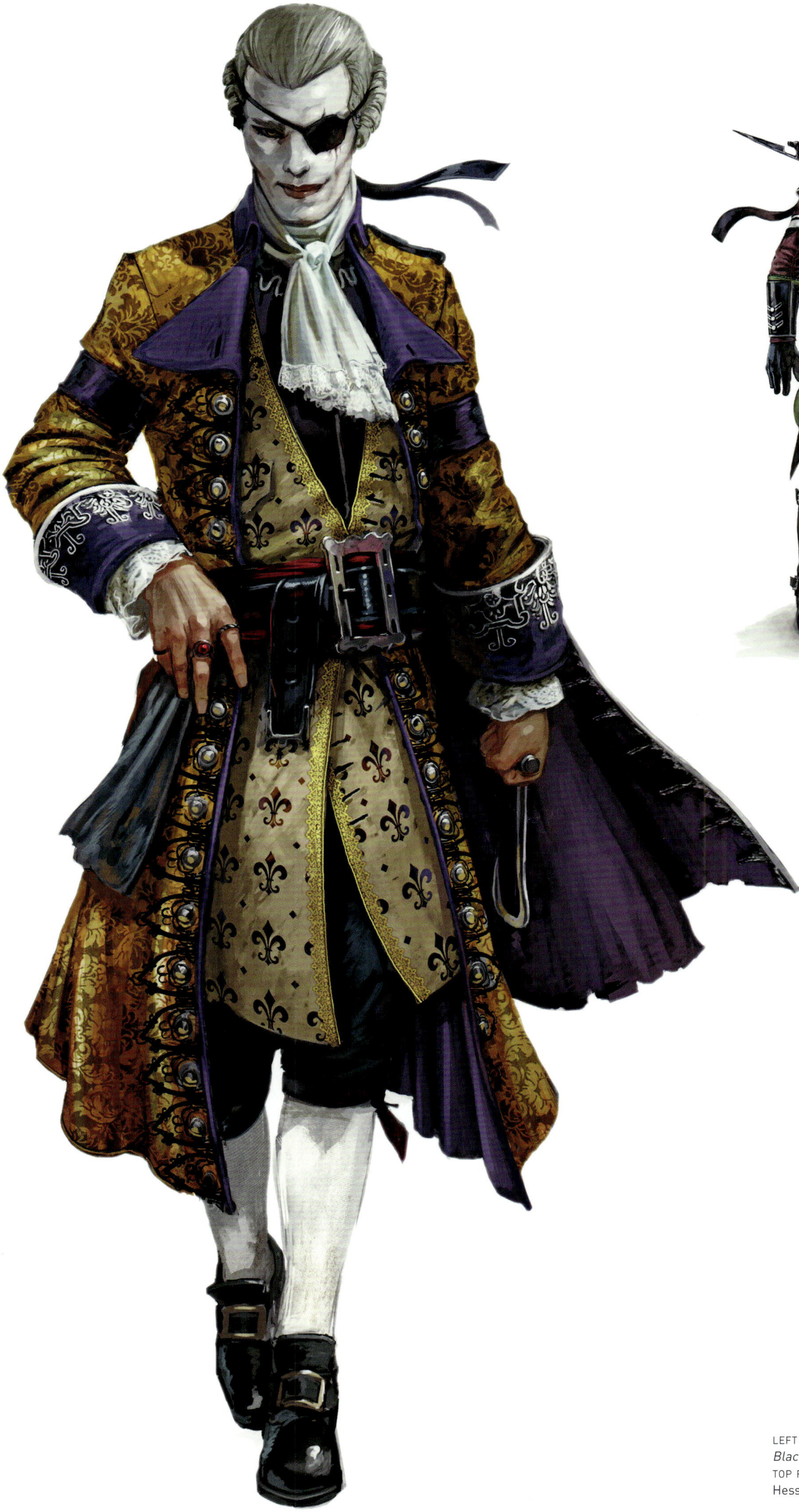

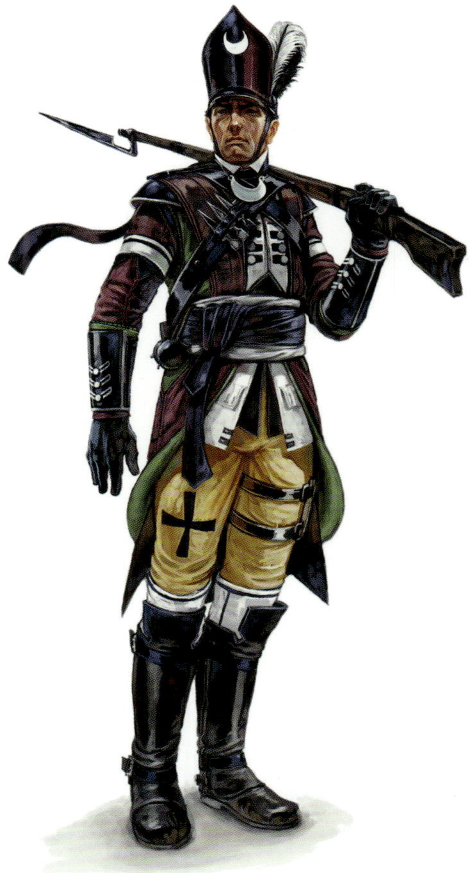

LEFT: Artwork of the Noble from *Assassin's Creed IV: Black Flag* (Antoine Rol).
TOP RIGHT: Character art of Gerhard von Stantten, a Hessian solder from *Assassin's Creed III* (Antoine Rol).

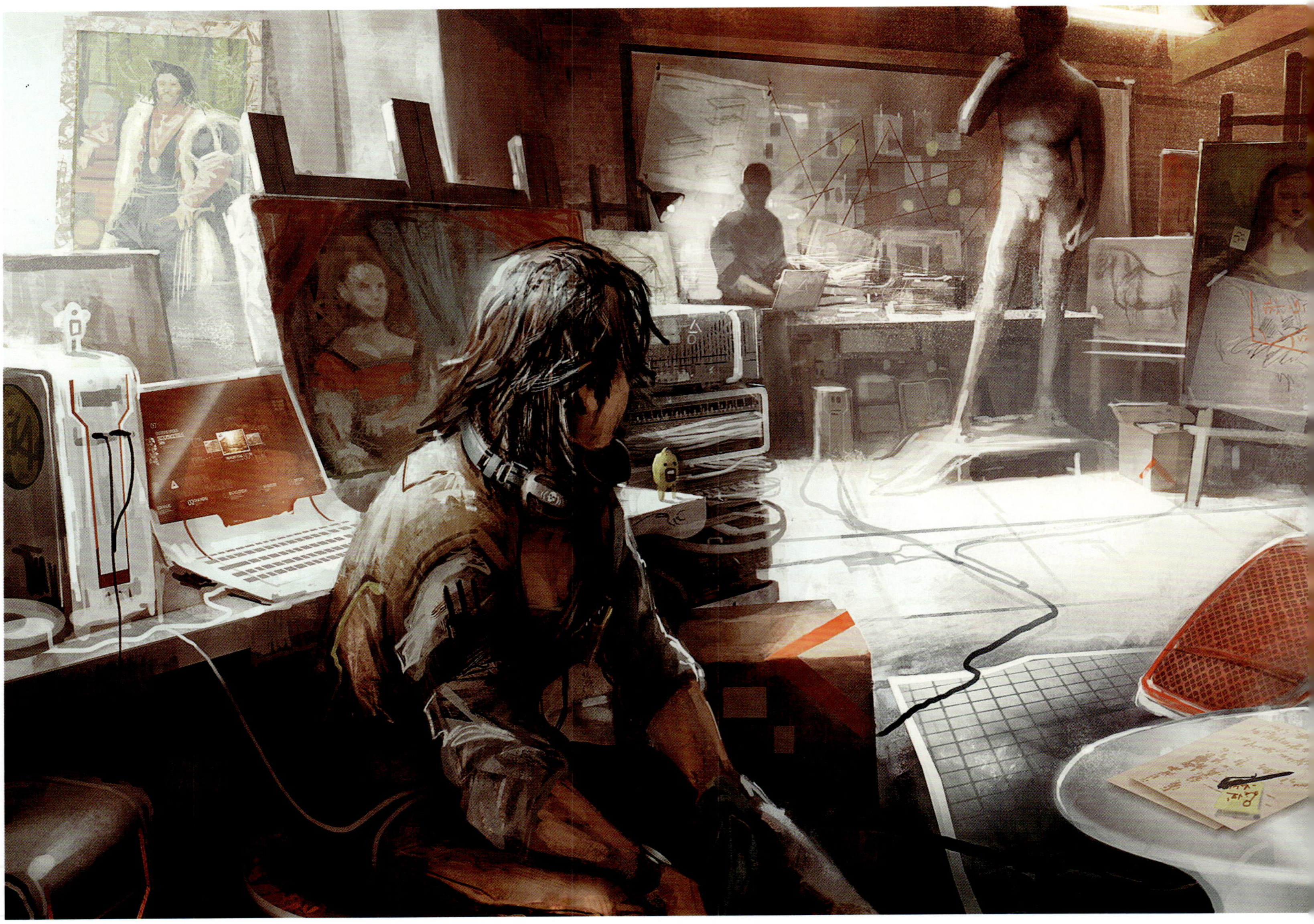

THE UNDERDOGS

The various epochs of human history on display throughout the Assassin's Creed storyline have shown that one side of the war or the other often gains an upper hand. Ezio's defeat of the Italian Templars drove them away to Constantinople. *Unity*'s Paris found the Assassins and Templars in a sort of cold war treaty status. In the modern day, there's little doubt who is winning. Under the guise of Abstergo Industries, the Templars have infiltrated every part of daily life around the world. Meanwhile, the Assassins are an endangered species, scattered to the winds after the murder of their most recent Mentor and struggling to survive in the shadows.

Like any underdog, the Assassins are easy to cheer for. Hidden bunkers and clandestine communication networks make them feel smart and dangerous. The few modern Assassins that we meet suggest that members of the Brotherhood are now counterculture revolutionaries, the people who aren't willing to accept the status quo. In other words, the Assassins of the modern-day world come across as unbearably cool.

The modern-day Assassins needed to feel distinct from their Abstergo enemies, so the environments in which players interact with them feel organic and less organized, especially as the laboratory setting of the first game moved into the apartment hideout of the second. Where Abstergo feels impenetrable and hierarchal, the Assassins exude youth and creativity. "Between the present day of *AC1* and *AC2*, we went from blue and cold to much warmer," Mohamed says. "So I stuck to the same structure for *Assassin's Creed II*, focusing on a warmer and intimate feel, because you move to a modern-day Assassins setting and an Assassin's Animus. The apartment with the red bricks, for example, is a total departure from that cold and clinical look that you have in *Assassin's Creed*."

As the carryover modern hero between the first five games, Desmond Miles is an everyman pulled from obscurity and given purpose through his interaction with the Assassin Brotherhood. His simple, casual style was

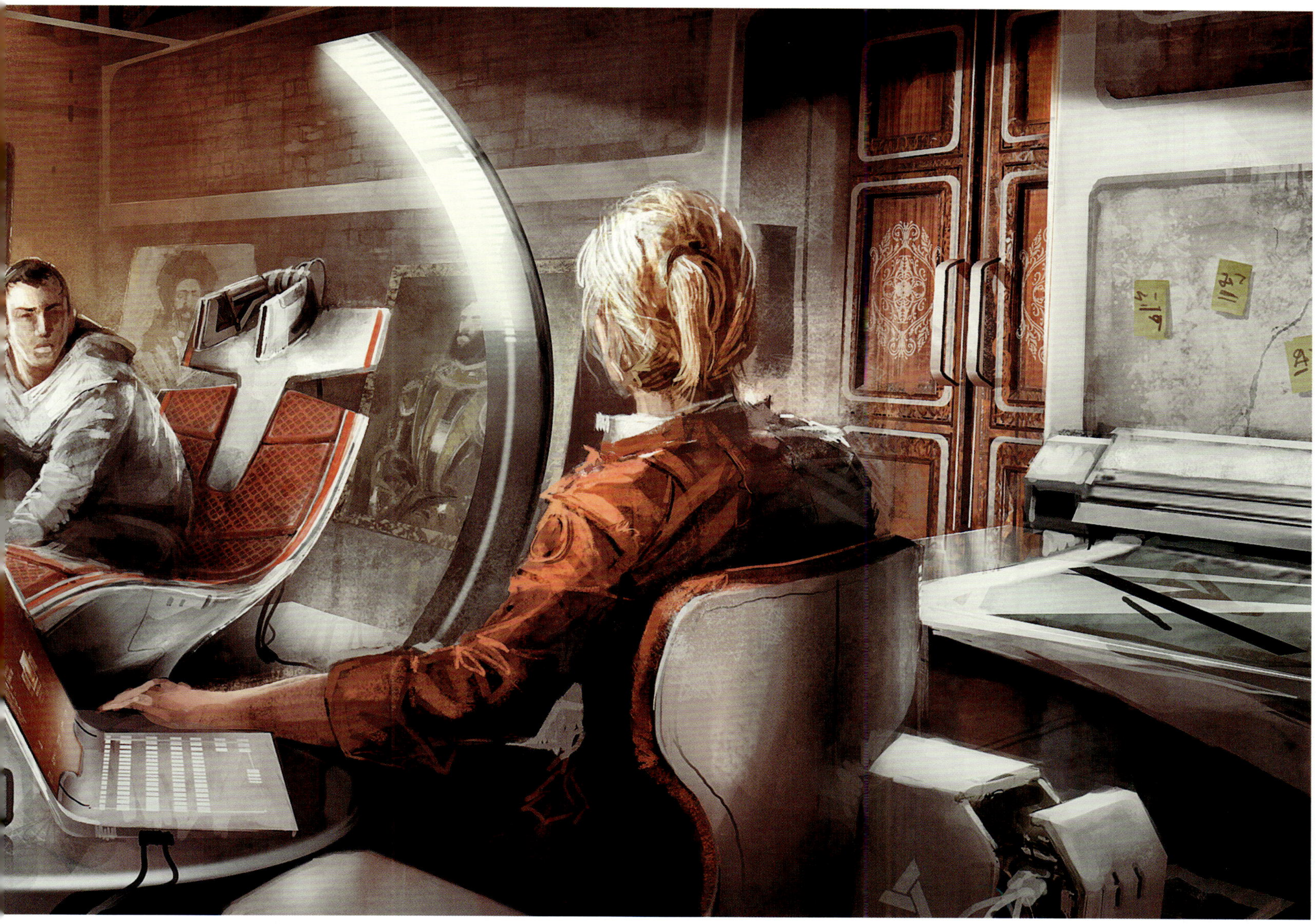

meant to feel like an extension of the potential game player. "We wanted to create a character that you can make a connection with," Raphaël says. "Desmond is not a superhero or villain who looks like a caricature. He is a regular guy you would see on the street. I think it's better for player immersion to stay grounded with these real, identifiable, modern-day characters."

And so, when Desmond began to acquire the skills of an Assassin and continue on to save the world, he acted as an extension of the player's engagement in the story. Over time and the course of multiple games, Desmond's style morphs. Even as he moves from lab experiment to deadly hero in his own right, the character's visuals echo the shift. By the time he's heading out on missions to confront Abstergo, his raised hood and hidden blade make him the equal of his ancestors.

While Desmond acts as a stand-in for the player, his fellow Assassins help to further consolidate our understanding of the Assassins place in modern-day culture. Rebecca Crane is a technical genius, single-handedly co-opting Abstergo's technology and improving on it. Her casual style and cool demeanor are a contrast to the character of her verbal sparring partner, Shaun Hastings. The buttoned-up British analyst and historian provides a dose of sarcasm to keep the mood light, and his wit carries over into database entries that might otherwise seem dry and academic. In later games, Desmond's father, William, adds an element of family drama and also a glimpse into the Assassins' leadership in the wake of the Mentor's death. While we only meet a few present-day Assassins, their personalities are enough to establish the Brotherhood as a group of brilliant, flawed, and compelling characters.

In the most recent games, the clandestine work of the modern-day Assassins has been harder to detect, especially as we learn more about the machinations of Abstergo and its entertainment branch. But even from the shadows, it's clear that the Assassins continue to get the upper hand when it really counts over their more overtly powerful enemies.

THESE PAGES: The modern-day Assassins' version of the Animus has a warmer and less sterile appearance (Martin Deschambault).

LIVING HISTORY

"The way we treat the past in terms of artistic direction can be different from one game to another, and that is really interesting because it allows us to explore and to evolve," Raphaël says. "This is what I like about the franchise. We have different locations and historical periods, but we are also free to bring variety to our artistic directions. At the core of the franchise, what connects all the games together is the Animus and the contrast between the present day and the past."

Whether in the hands of the Templars or the Assassins, the Animus technology (and later the Helix entertainment platform) has been the glue that ties together past and present and establishes a plausibility to the time-spanning fiction that would otherwise be absent. In its earliest incarnation, the Animus felt like a prototype computer program. Computer code faded to a bright white field, and then architecture began to populate into view. By the second installment, the Assassins had stolen the tech for themselves, and more organic touches began to creep into the Animus art style.

Some of the most arresting visuals to arise out of the Animus technology came from *Assassin's Creed: Revelations*, in which Desmond Miles wandered a strange island within the Animus framework as his real-life body tried to recover from a coma. The Animus island itself was filled with high stone arches and ruined structures that recalled First Civilization architecture. Further exploration of the island brought Desmond (and the player) into absurd, Escher-esque labyrinths of memory and physics gone awry.

As the Animus technology moved from experimental prototype to public-facing Abstergo consumer product, the visualization continued to transform. Now the artists had an excuse to make menus and UI interactions that felt more gamelike, since the fiction implicitly suggested that the player was encountering a piece of software built by Abstergo Entertainment. Even so, we still are treated to the glitches of Helix anomalies and other breaches in the code, not to mention the ever-present reminder that a First Civilization intelligence is hiding somewhere within the tech, a ghost in the machine.

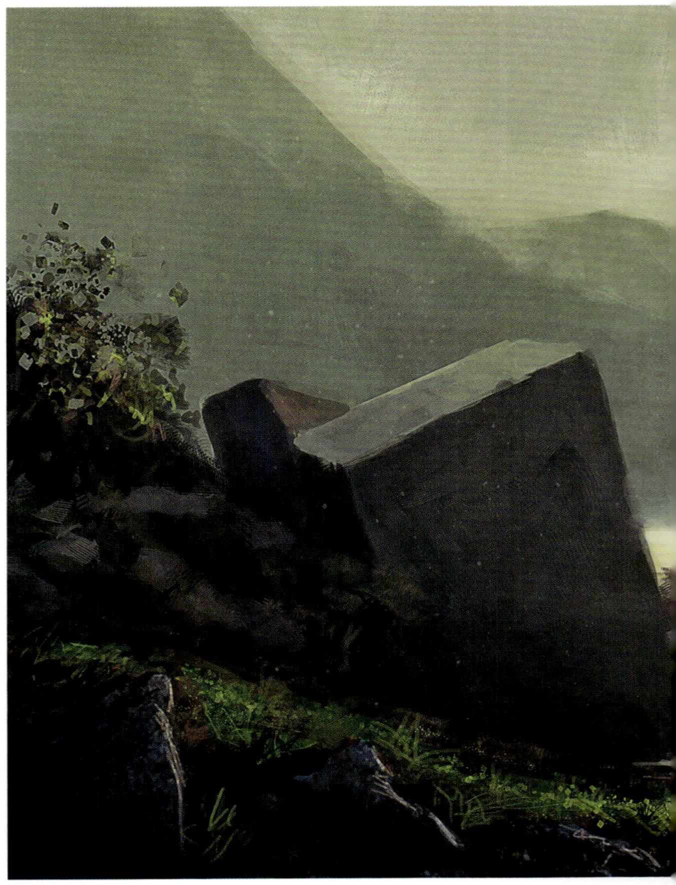

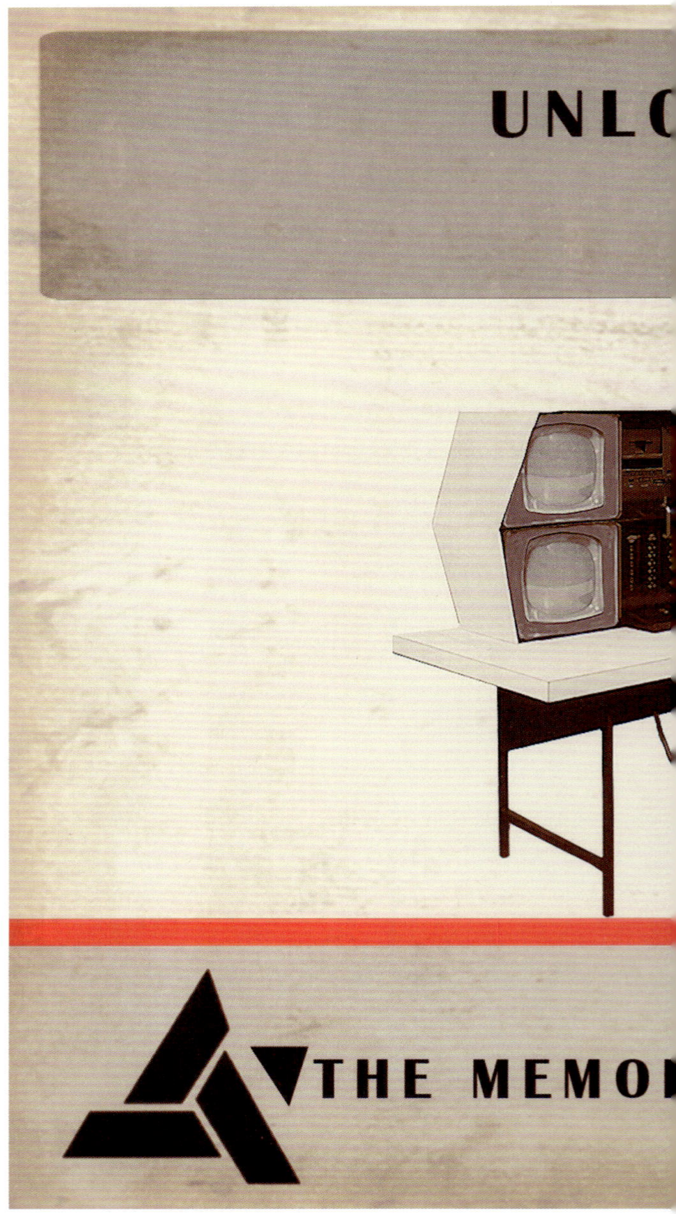

TOP RIGHT: Early concepts of the Nexus Portal from *Assassin's Creed: Revelations* (Gilles Beloeil).
BOTTOM RIGHT: Animus prototype advertisement from 1960.

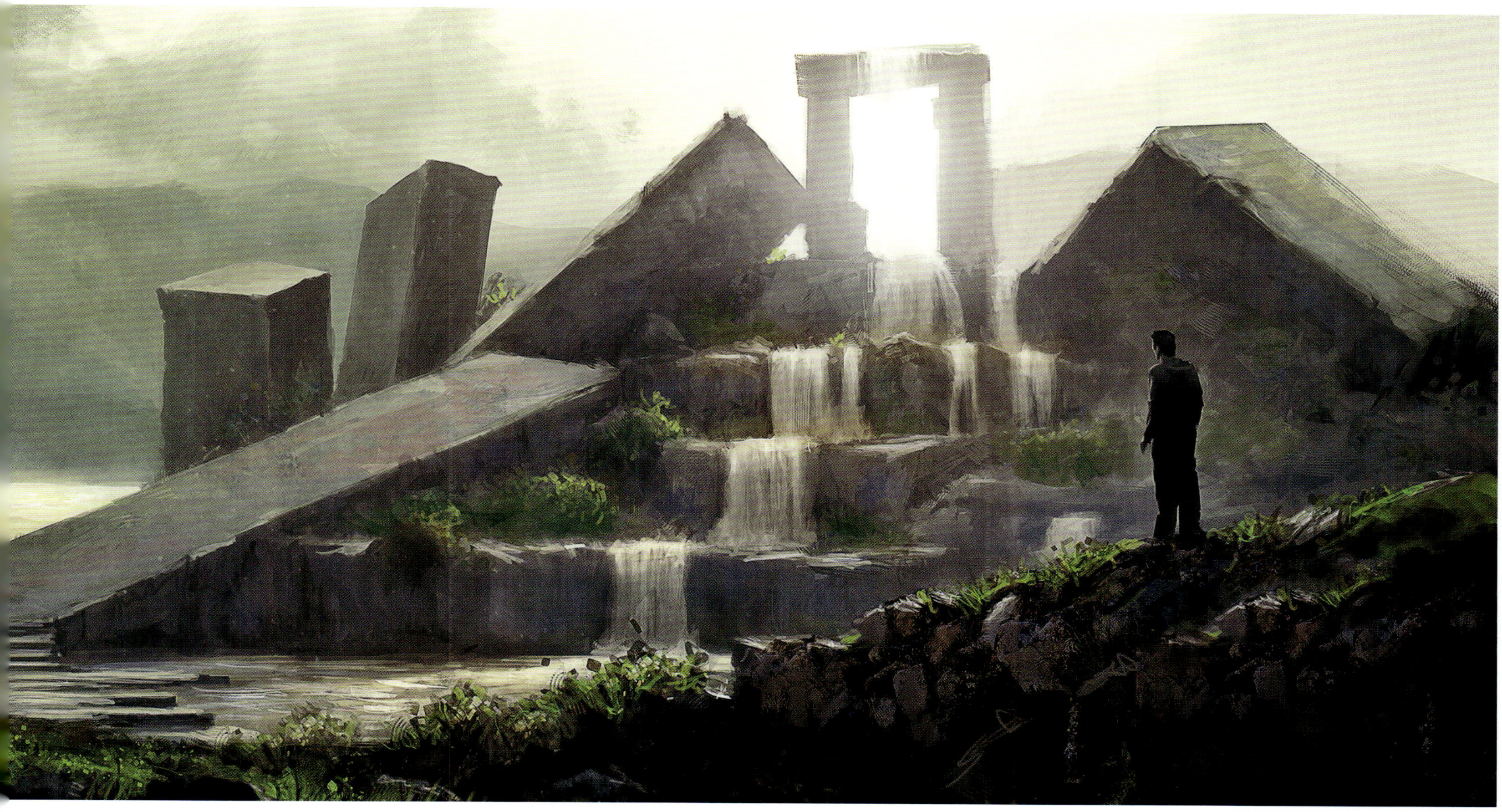

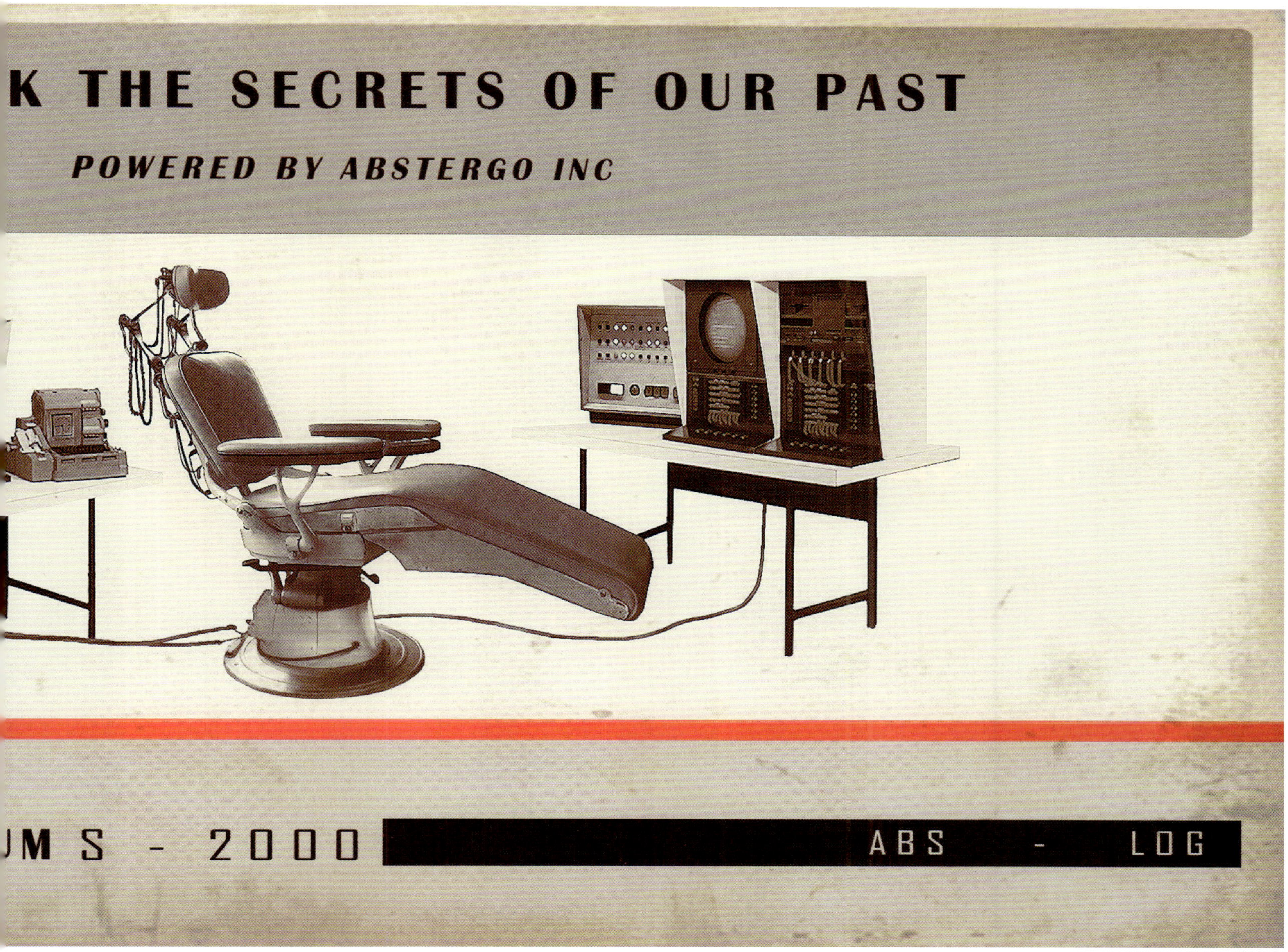
K THE SECRETS OF OUR PAST
POWERED BY ABSTERGO INC
JMS - 2000
ABS - LOG

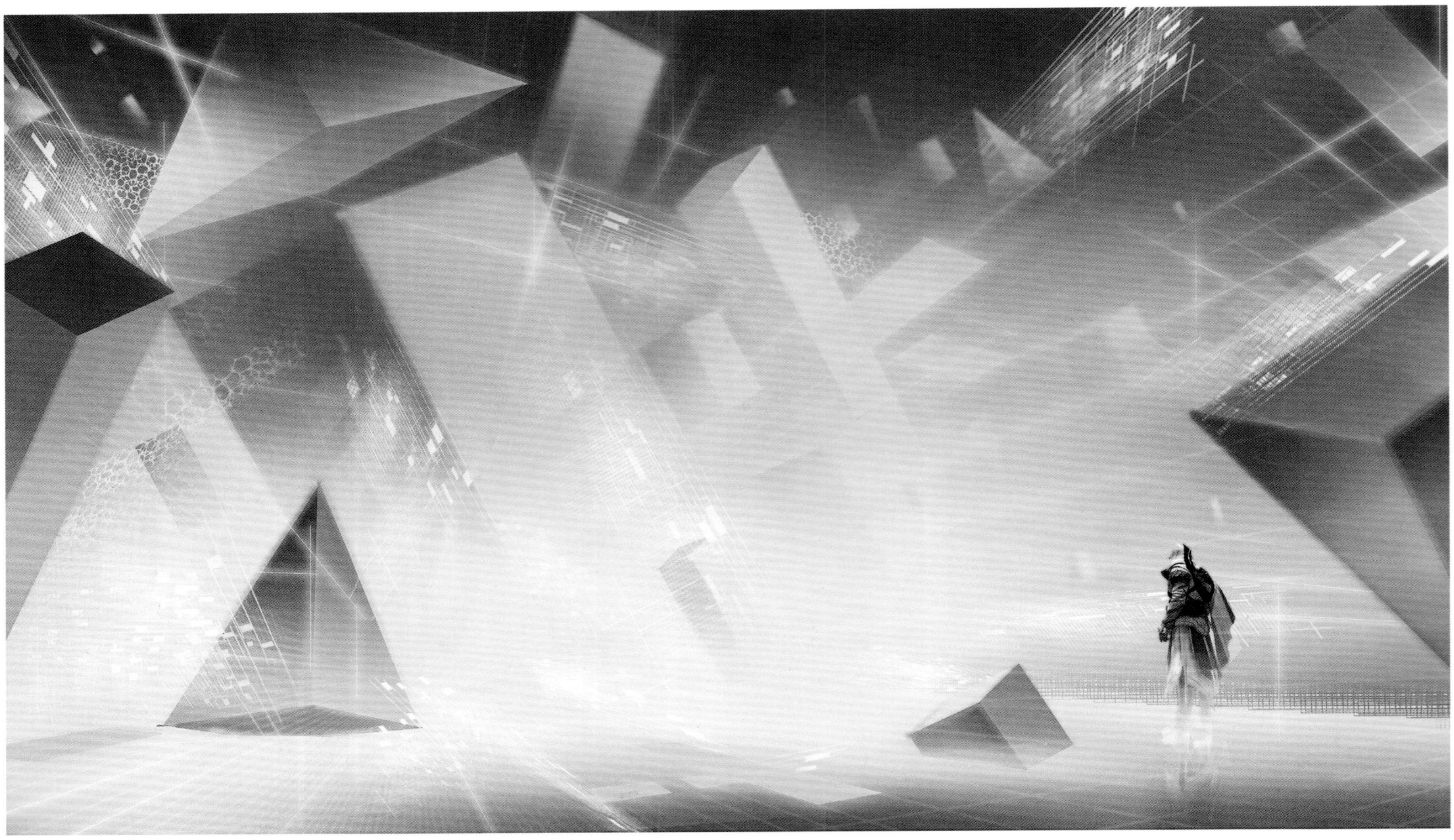

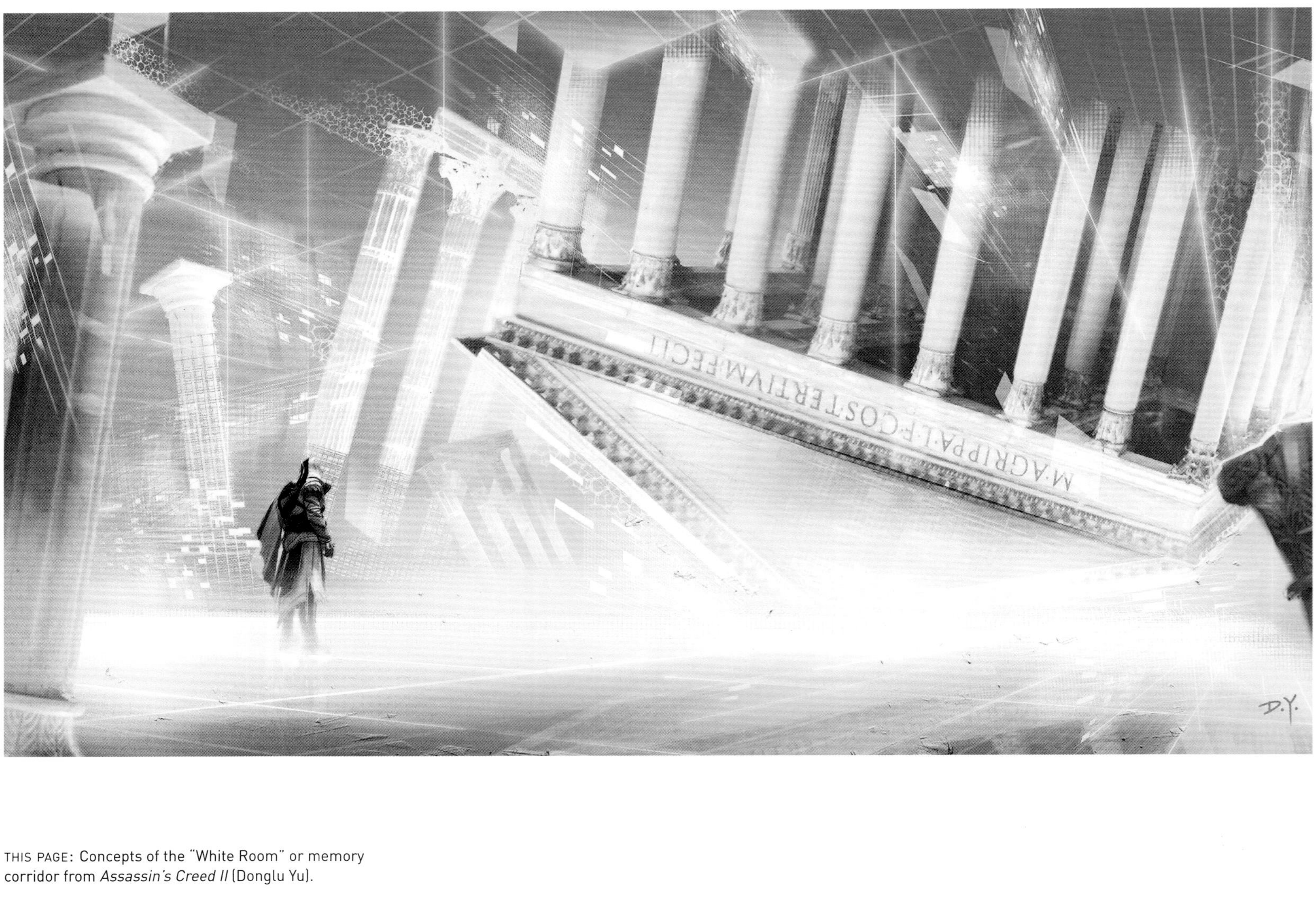

THIS PAGE: Concepts of the "White Room" or memory corridor from *Assassin's Creed II* (Donglu Yu).

PRESENTATION IS EVERYTHING

While fans may be able to rattle off the towering historical landmarks of each Assassin's Creed entry or the backstory of their favorite hero, they're less likely to recall the specifics of the user interface and presentation design that framed each narrative. However, the UI's subconscious effect on player experience can profoundly influence the emotions evoked in any given game. Moreover, clearly designed menus, maps, and databases are the difference between frustration and enthusiasm for any game as complicated as Assassin's Creed entries tend to be.

With each installment, the team at Ubisoft has evolved the front-end and menu experience to match events of the narrative. "Each Assassin's Creed game has its own signature style when it comes to presentation direction," says Brent Ashe, presentation director on *Brotherhood*, *Revelations*, *Assassin's Creed III*, and *Liberation*. "The menus, UI, and the HUD are always an abstract distillation of the themes of the game."

The first *Assassin's Creed* game originated the clean and bright aesthetic that would dominate later iterations and was rooted in the idea of the Animus as an experimental platform or operating system. By the second game, Abstergo's technology had been acquired by the Assassins, and the user interface reflected the change. "It had to be radically different from the presentation style of *Assassin's Creed I*, because in the narrative we switched from menus that were generated by an Abstergo-built Animus to menus generated by an Animus that was based on stolen tech and upgraded by the Assassins," explains Brent.

By the time of *Brotherhood*'s release, a new challenge arose. The single-player campaign played out using the Assassin's version of the Animus, while the new multiplayer modes were meant to be Abstergo training experiences; the user interfaces needed to be distinct. To reflect the shift, the multiplayer menus harkened back to the first game in the series. "When you start the menu in *Assassin's Creed: Brotherhood*, you experience some menu glitches," Brent says. "This is the menu screen switching back and forth between the Assassins' Animus and the Abstergo Animus. Most players probably never even noticed it, but we did this to emphasize this narrative consistency. There's a narrative reason for everything we do, even when it comes to menus and user interface."

For *Revelations*, Desmond had fallen into a coma, and once again the trappings around the game maintained the threads of the story. The normal "white room" aesthetic flipped to a darker, glitchier inverse of the familiar style. *Assassin's Creed III* represented Rebecca's upgrade to the Animus technology, as well as sharp new angles and shards—a subtle homage to the natural Frontier environments and rugged lead character of Connor, trapped between warring cultures.

Meanwhile, *Assassin's Creed III*'s multiplayer and *Liberation* showcased the first appearance of an Abstergo Entertainment product. The public-facing arm of Abstergo had to be more colorful and appealing than Abstergo's internal products, with a goal of subverting public opinion against the Assassins and secretly taking their very genetic identity. "It made sense to adapt the presentation style to be less clinical and more appealing to players in order to reach as many consumers as possible and obtain their genetic information," Brent describes. The new presentation style evolved with *Black Flag*, maintaining the colorful and cinematic presentation style but adding underwater overtones to match the pirate milieu. Those same water tones carried over into *Rogue* but with a more sinister and dark vibe, reflecting Shay Cormac's troubling turn away from the Brotherhood.

Unity offered a new challenge with the fictional introduction of the Helix platform and allowed for a new UI concept to show up in the early minutes of the game: a queue of entertainment products that offered Abstergo's skewed twist on previous adventures. "Abstergo Entertainment's Helix was definitely inspired by the popularity of Netflix," says presentation director Shaci Mallak. "Helix was Abstergo Entertainment's way of moving from a gaming audience to going mainstream. We wanted the player to get that initial feeling of seeing a variety of entertainment programs but with an Abstergo twist." After completing the Jacque de Molay opening sequence, the Assassins hack in and reveal Abstergo's true intentions to the player. Consequently, much of the remaining portions of *Unity* feel like a high-tech evolution of the Animus from *Assassin's Creed* and the subsequent multiplayer training programs.

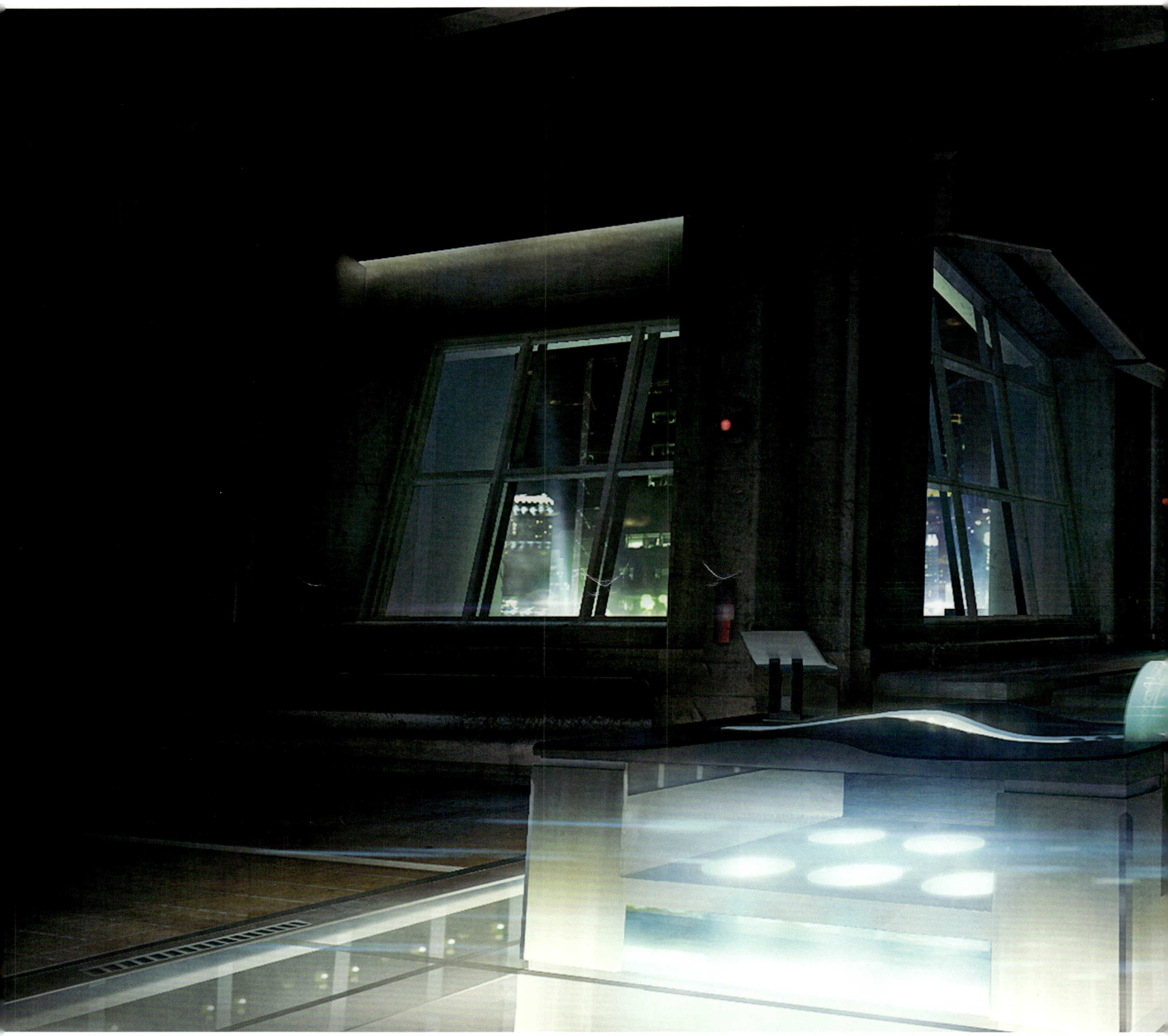

THESE PAGES: Artwork of Warren Vidic's office (William Wu).

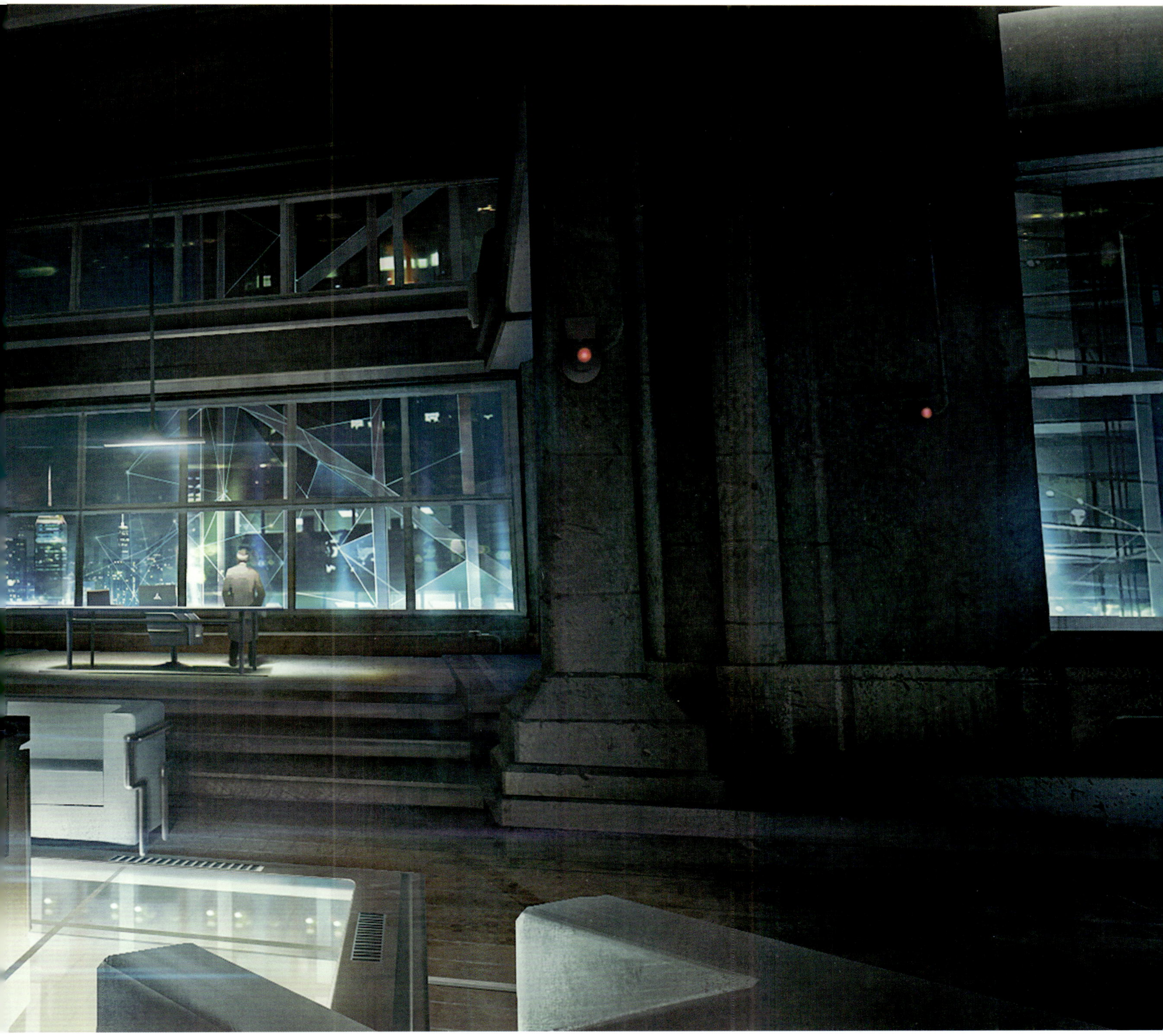

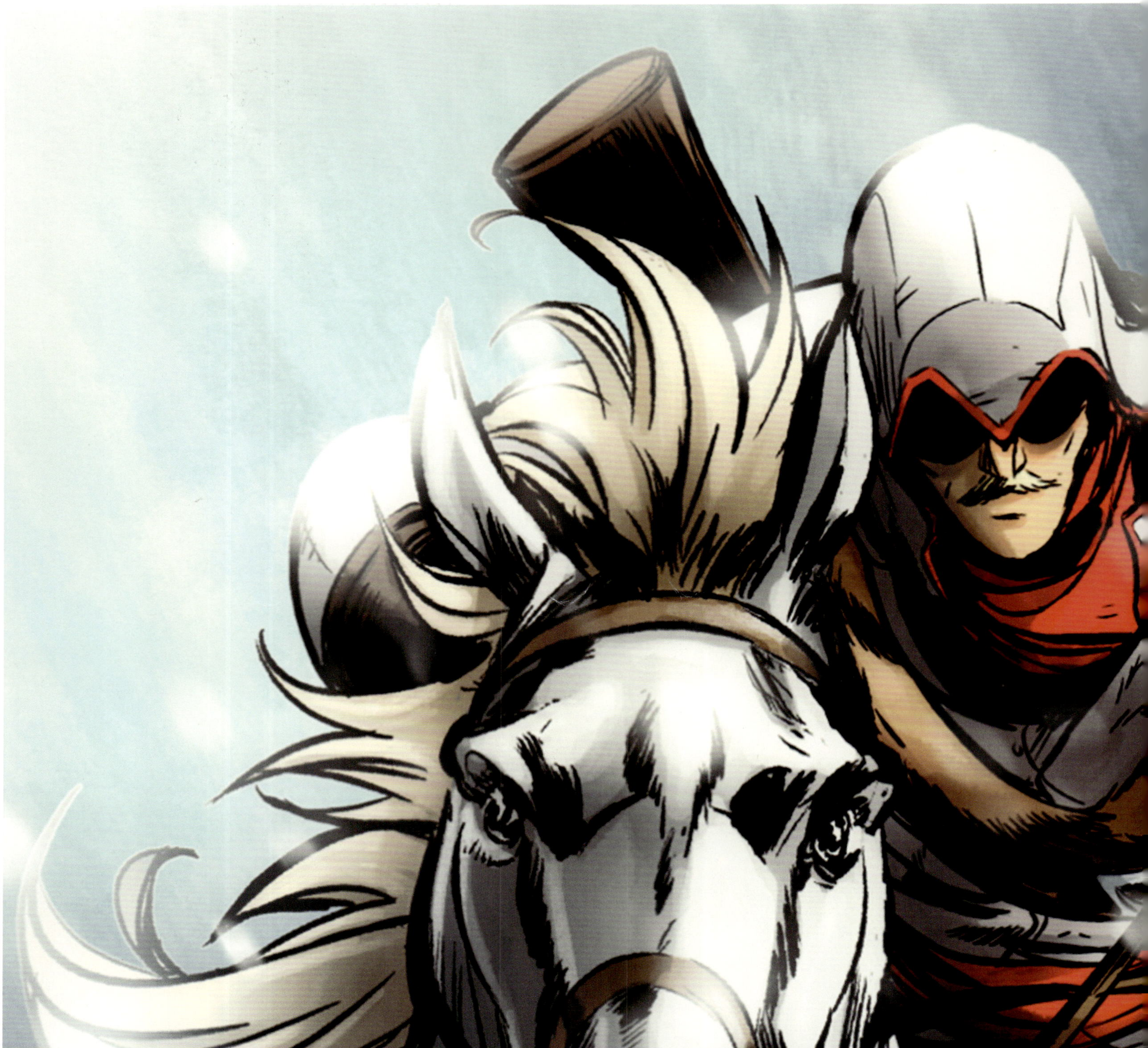

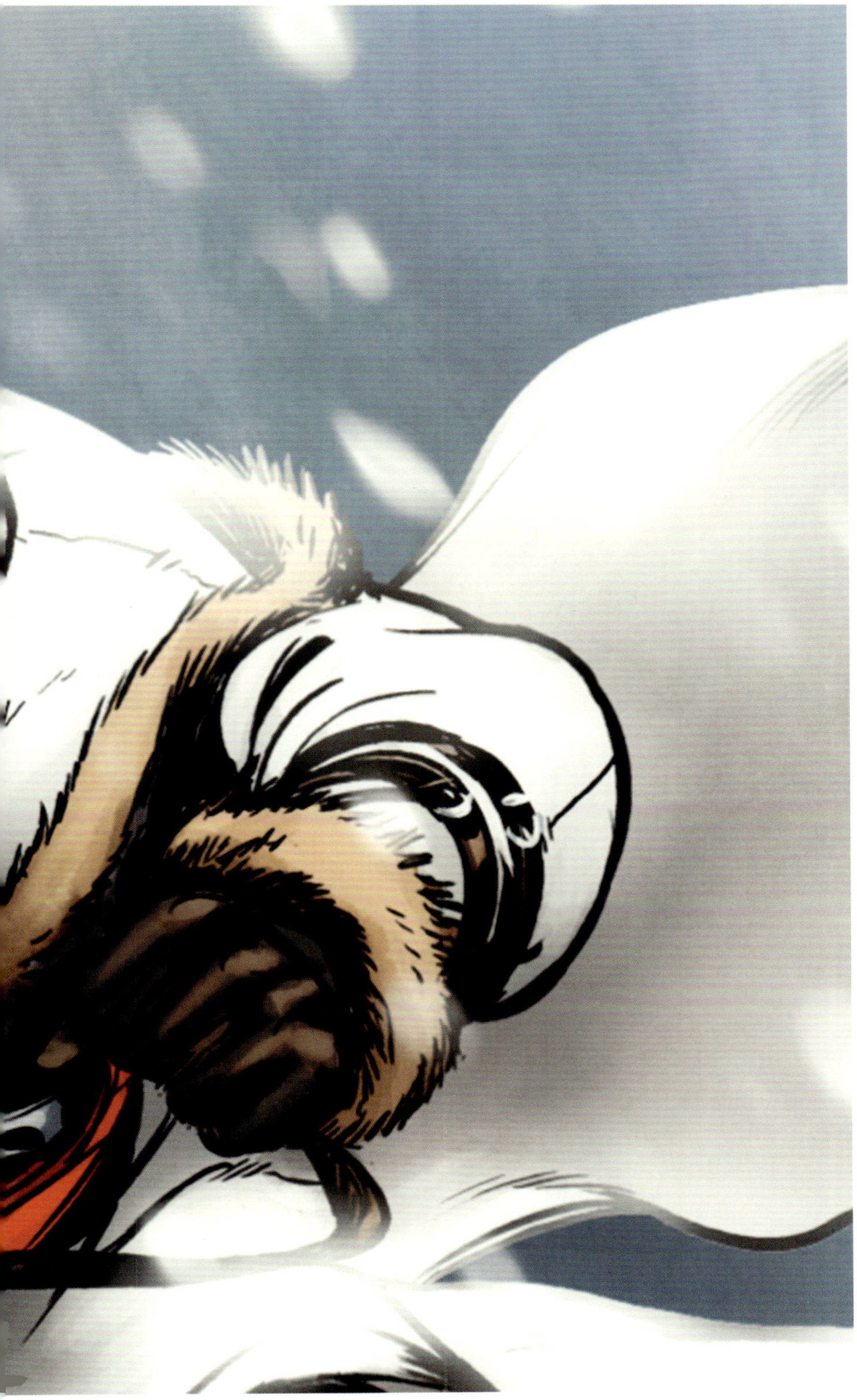

11 BEYOND GAMES

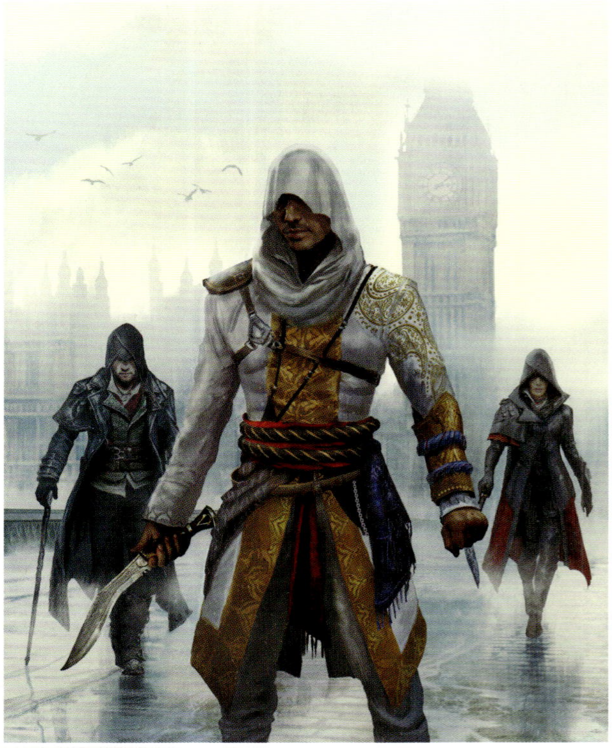

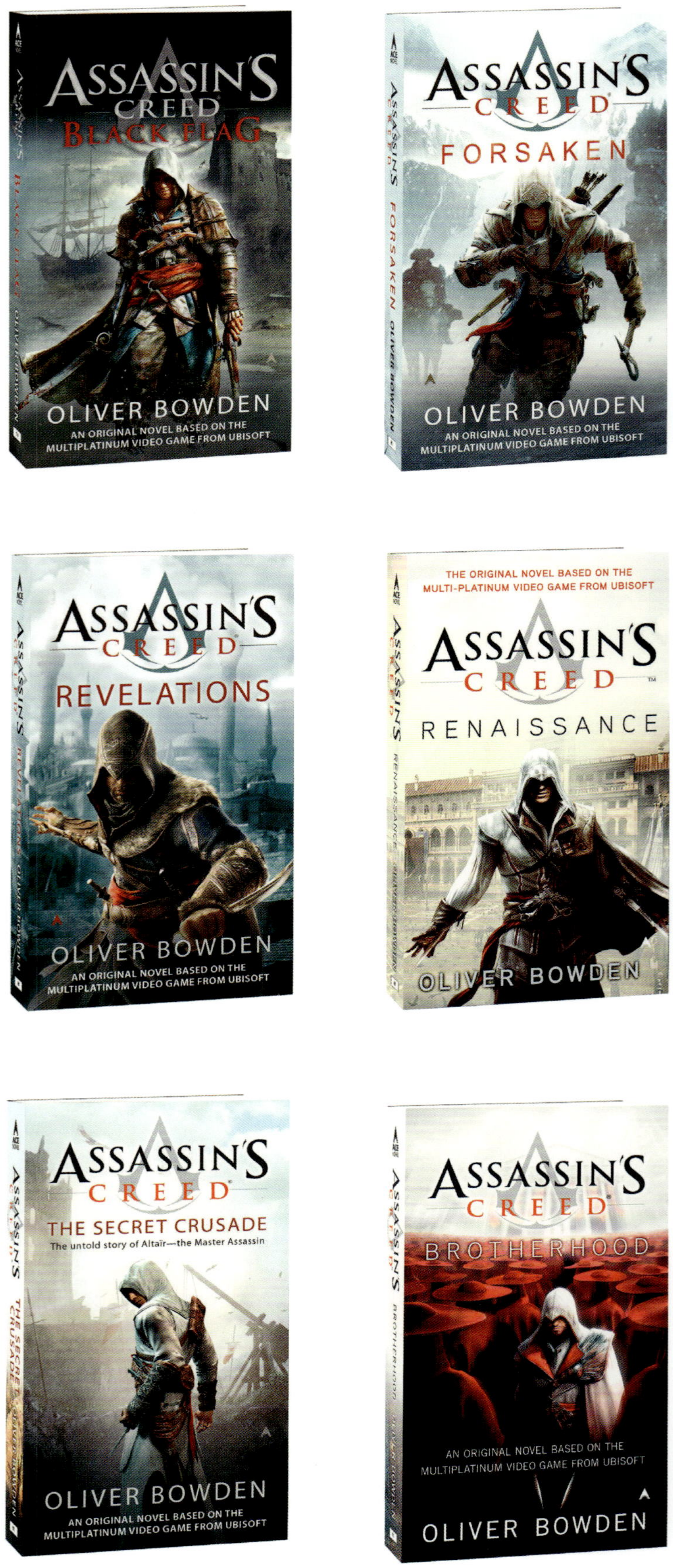

CROSSING MEDIA

Assassin's Creed has always been first and foremost a game franchise, but its storytelling and artistic potential makes for an easy transition into other media. Outside of games, new creative voices have added their own characters and storylines into the mix or new perspectives on established settings and heroes.

Over time, Assassin's Creed has broadened its reach into numerous media beyond games, with an eye toward engaging with franchise fans in whatever format excites them. "We try to aim to develop projects and products that both enrich the lore and also invite newcomers to step into our universe and explore," Aymar says. "The presence of Assassin's Creed in a variety of different media and products makes the brand stronger, as long as we safeguard the lore's consistency and respect its rules. Some fans prefer to dive into the novels; others like to collect all the statues or dress themselves in Assassin's Creed gear. The point is not for everyone to have everything Assassin's Creed, but that there's a part of Assassin's Creed for everyone."

Over half a dozen novels by Oliver Bowden have accompanied the release of major Assassin's Creed games over the years. Some of the books, like *Renaissance* and *Black Flag*, directly retell events depicted in the main games. Others reach further afield; *Forsaken* tells the story of Haytham Kenway's childhood, while *Unity* retells the game's story from Élise's perspective. While the nature of the medium has produced only a small number of accompanying art pieces, the few visuals that were created illustrate the imaginative scope of these tales.

PREVIOUS PAGES: Comic art of Nikolai Orelov from *Assasssin's Creed: The Fall* (Karl Kerschl and Cameron Stewart).
ABOVE LEFT: Original concept for the cover of the latest Assassin's Creed novel: *Underworld*. *Underworld* tells the story of Henry Green, an important character in the game *Assassin's Creed: Syndicate*, before he meets Jacob and Evie Frye. Henry, born Jayadeep Mir, is the son of Pyara Kaur and Arbaaz Mir, the protagonist of the graphic novel *Brahman and Chronicles: India*. The design of his costume strongly reflects his background, and stands out in the environments of London during the Industrial Revolution (Hugo Puzzuoli and Grant Hillier).
ABOVE: Covers of the Assassin's Creed novel series.
OPPOSITE: The iconic poses of Edward Kenway, Connor Kenway, Altaïr Ibn-La'Ahad, and Élise de la Serre come to life in statue form.

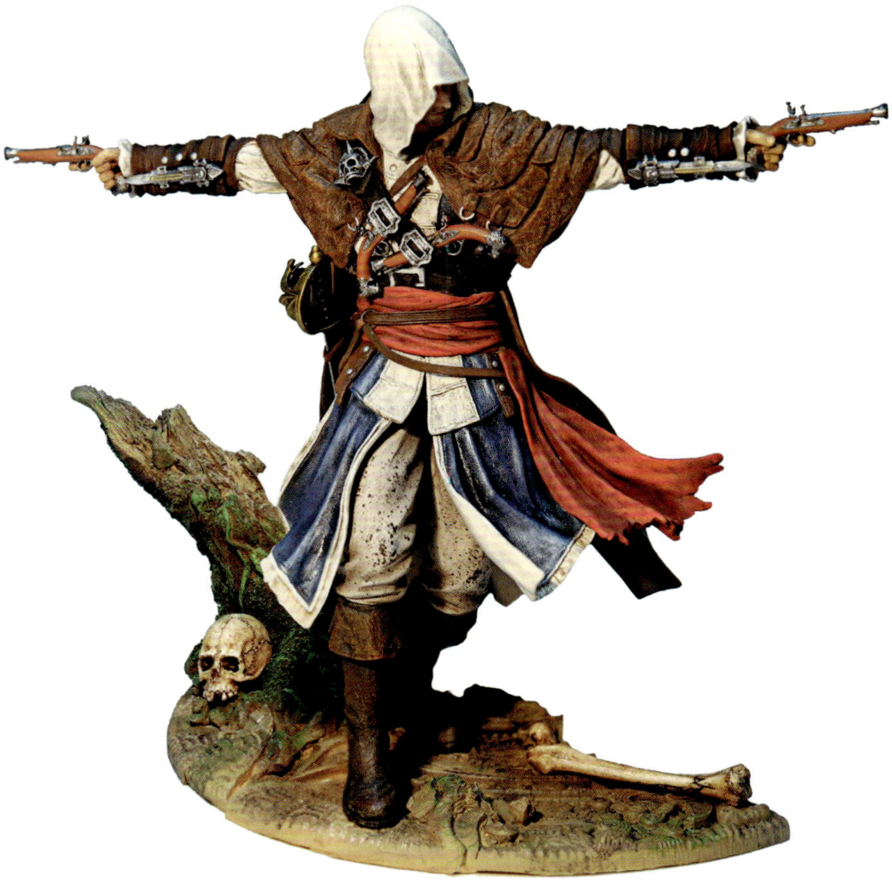

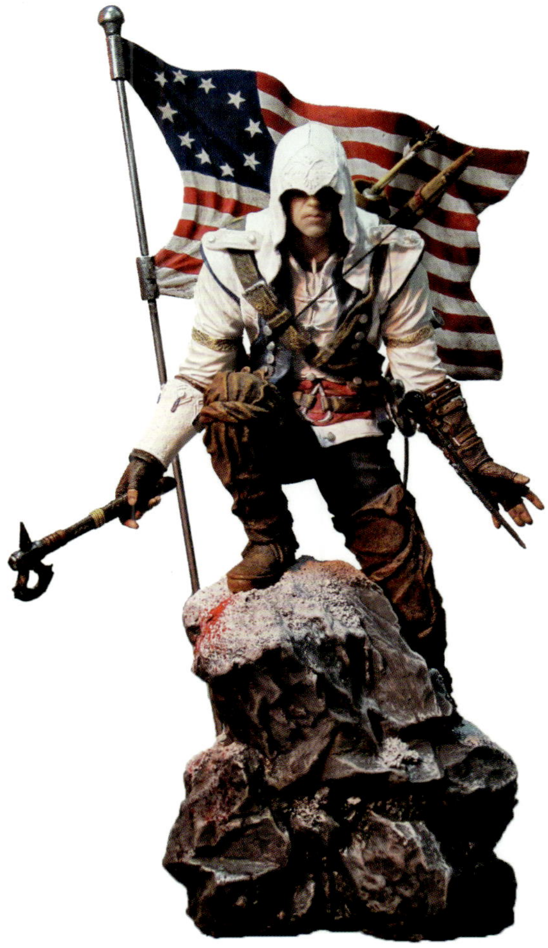

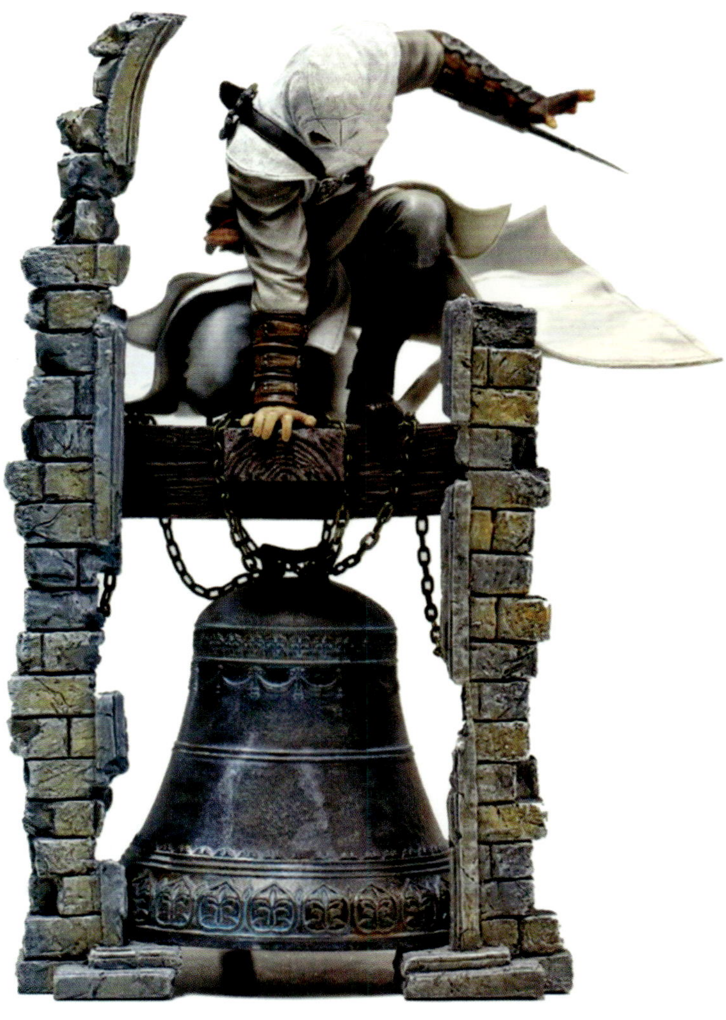

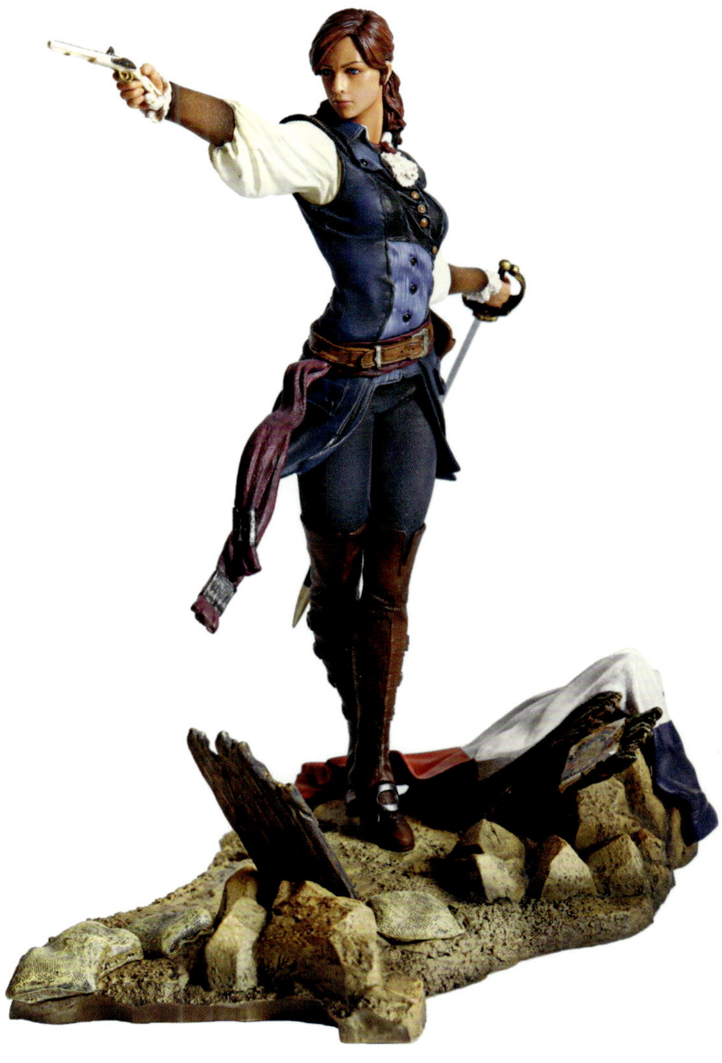

EZIO'S PREFACE

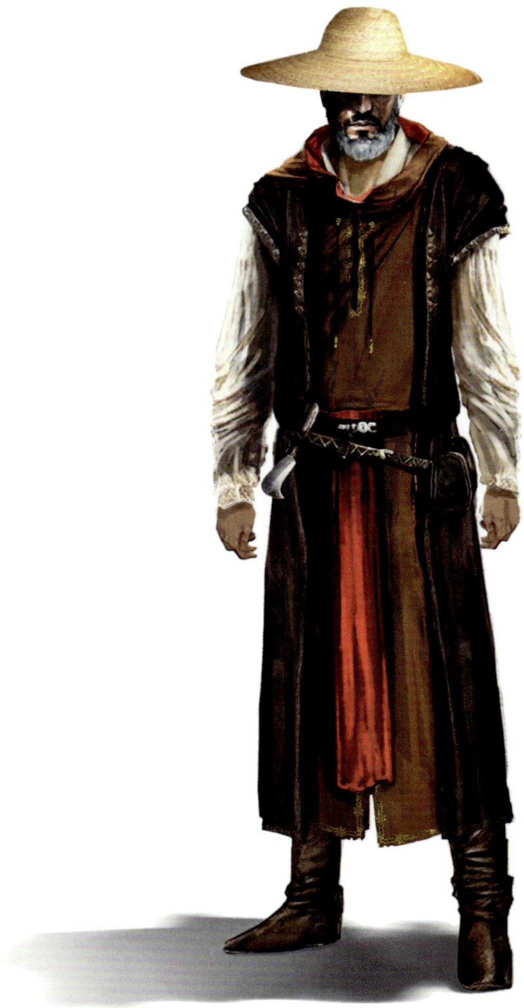

One of the earliest ventures outside of games came through the short film *Assassin's Creed: Lineage*. The three-part story acts as a preface to *Assassin's Creed II*, following Ezio's father, Giovanni, as he travels across Italy tracking the beginnings of the conspiracy that will reveal itself in the console game.

The film was important on a number of levels, most significantly for presenting live actors in the roles of characters that would later appear in animated form in *Assassin's Creed II*. The elaborate costuming and choreographed fight scenes evoked the feel of the games, and freerunning sequences and tailing missions were a clear homage to those interactive activities.

While the investment in live action was considerable, re-creating Renaissance Florence, Rome, and Venice was impossible. As a result, some of the photo-realistic backgrounds of *Lineage* were actually matte paintings crafted by some of the same concept artists building out the world of the games.

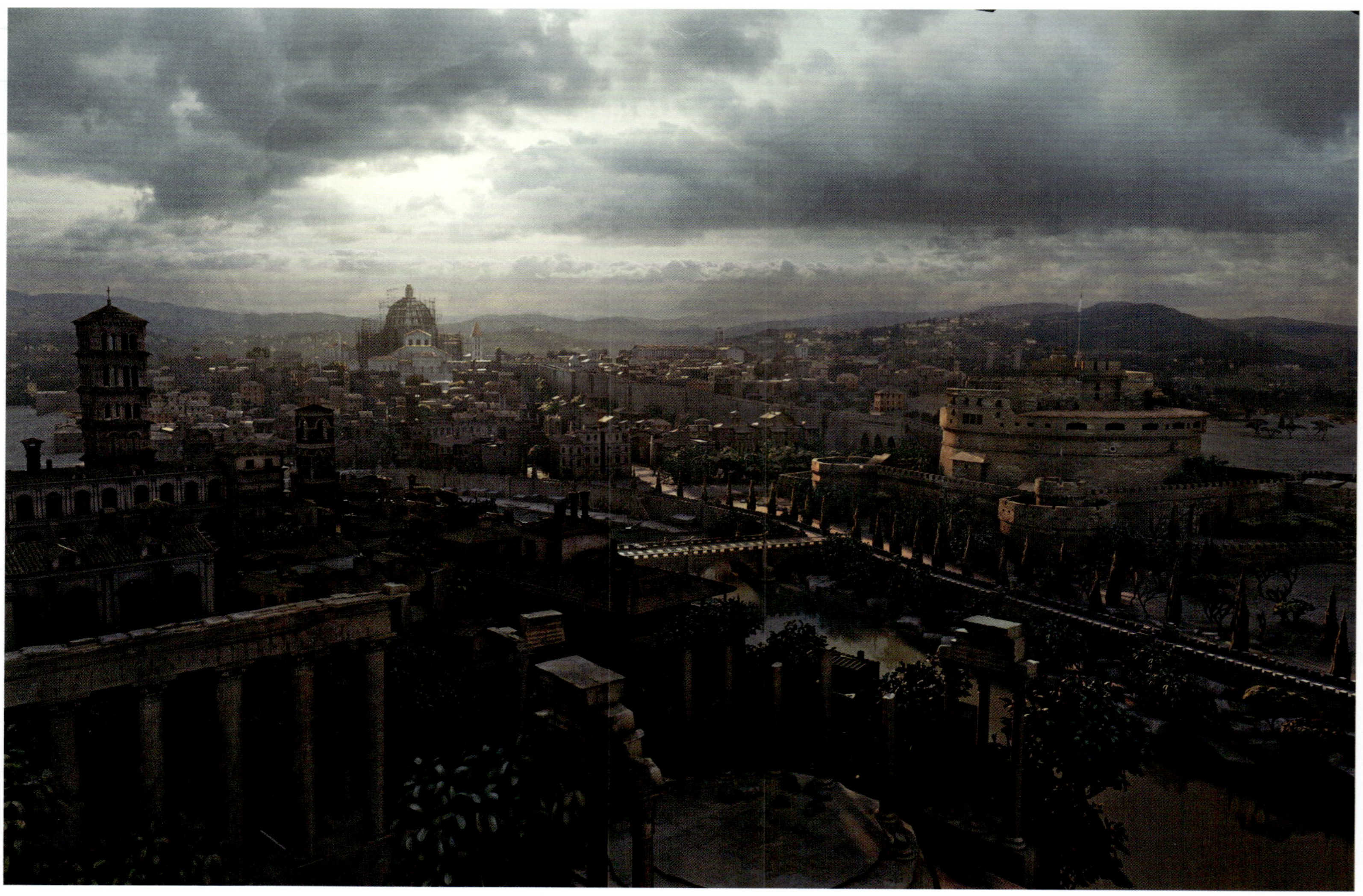

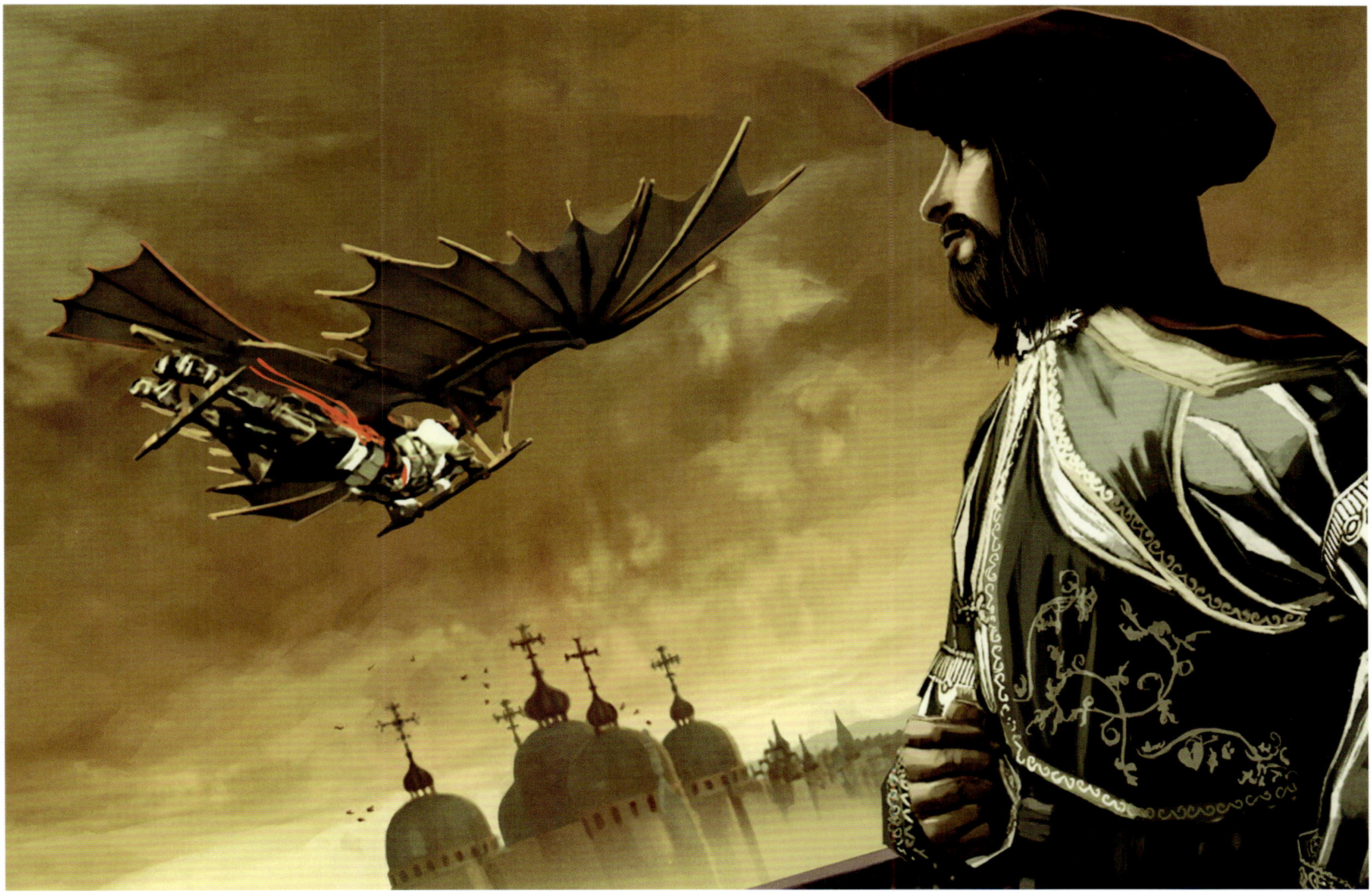

THE RISE OF CESARE BORGIA

Set directly prior to the events of *Brotherhood*, *Assassin's Creed: Ascendance* was an experimental animated short with a surprising and distinct visual style. The film follows Ezio as he investigates the rising threat of Cesare Borgia, illegitimate son to Rodrigo and the central antagonist of *Brotherhood*. Through short narrative vignettes, Cesare's villainous and conniving nature is revealed, from his ruthless conquering of much of Italy to his brutal treatment of the very allies who helped him rise to power.

The short film strove in every way to feel like a part of the universe of the broader game series. Sound effects, music, and even voice actors were drawn from the game, lending authenticity. The animated backgrounds were drawn directly from 3-D locations within the world of *Brotherhood* and then subsequently painted over to match the film's animation presentation.

While *Ascendance* felt like a natural extension of the game universe, its painterly art style was unique. "The general direction was to create a look and feel that reminds us very much of the paintings of the era," explains *Ascendance* art director Nicolas Drolet in a "Making Of" documentary about the short. *Assassin's Creed: Ascendance* was meant to evoke the sensation of staring at a Renaissance painting from Botticelli or da Vinci but one that moved freely in 3-D.

The success of the animated venture undertaken with *Ascendance* helped to fuel enthusiasm for *Embers*, the pivotal final chapter in Ezio's story (see Chapter 2).

OPPOSITE TOP: Character art of an older Ezio from *Embers* (Nicolas Drolet).
OPPOSITE BOTTOM: Matte painting of Rome from *Lineage* (Gilles Beloeil).
ABOVE: Concept art of Leonardo da Vinci and the flying machine from *Assassin's Creed: Ascendance* (Artist Unknown).

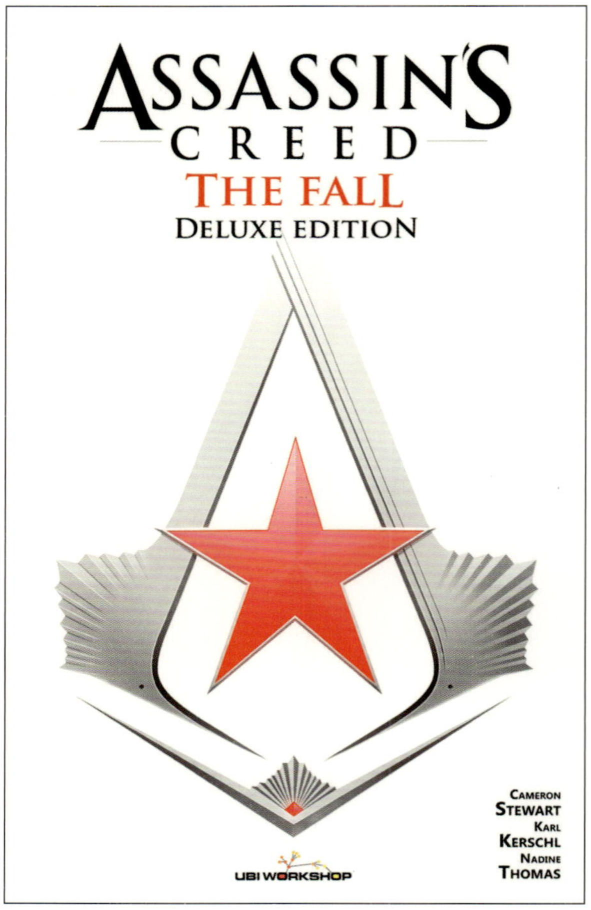

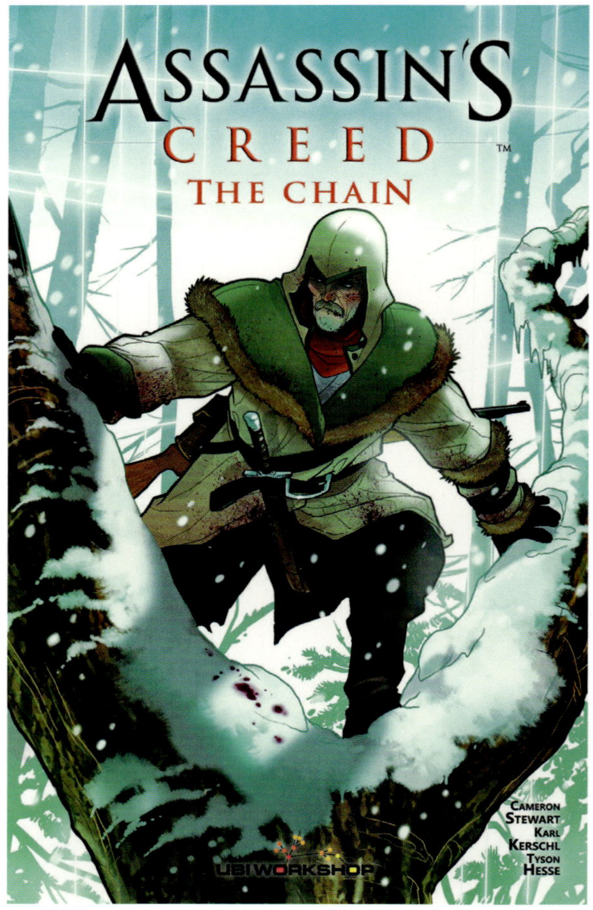

NEW MEDIUM, NEW HEROES

With its stylish costumes and nearly superheroic characters, it was no surprise that Assassin's Creed quickly made the transition over to the world of graphic novel storytelling.

An entire line of French comics have uncertain ties to the canonical story of the franchise. Nonetheless, the series contributed some memorable imagery of both the modern day Assassins and delved into time periods the games have never touched. The early volumes explored the tale of an Assassin named Aquilus and his adventures in ancient Rome, taking readers as far back as any character so far established in the fiction. A second set of volumes was similarly off the beaten path, primarily delving into an Egyptian Assassin in the fourteenth century.

Later English-language comics became much more integrated into the growing storyline, beginning with *The Chain* and *The Fall*. "We were trying different things, and it made sense to do a graphic novel that would really tie into the brand's lore," Aymar recalls. "It was incredibly important to us to find the right partners to do this, because we knew how delicate the integrity of the brand's lore could be. We already noted the work of comic artists and writers Cameron Stewart and Karl Kerschl, but when we found out their studio was located one block away from the Montreal production studio, we knew it could be a great collaboration."

The two multivolume graphic novels wove an intricate plot with a profound impact on the modern-day status of the Assassins. In the past, we learned the story of the Russian Assassin Nikolai Orelov and his encounters with the Templars of Siberia in the waning days of the nineteenth century. Orelov's story is framed by the modern-day story of a troubled young man named Daniel Cross. The eventual reveal that Cross is a double agent for the Templar Order leads to the death of the Assassins' Mentor, which in turn establishes the dire straits of the modern-day Assassins seen in the games. A second volume offered a touching story about Orelov and his son years after his initial conflicts in Russia, while in the future, we learned more about Daniel Cross' struggles against the Animus Bleeding Effect and his continuing betrayal of his former Brotherhood. Cross was so central to the events of the modern-day story that his fate was ultimately resolved within the games in the final scenes of *Assassin's Creed III*.

Assassin's Creed: Brahman introduced yet another thread into the weave, launching readers back to India in the 1830s. The story followed the Kashmiri Assassin

TOP LEFT: The deluxe edition of *Assassin's Creed: The Fall* included ten extra pages for the sequel (Cameron Stewart, Karl Kerschl, Nadine Thomas).
TOP RIGHT: Cover art for the first volume of *Assassin's Creed: The Chain* (Cameron Stewart, Karl Kerschl, Tyson Hesse).
OPPOSITE: Assassin Arbaaz Mir takes out an enemy in *Assassin's Creed: Brahman* (Cameron Stewart and Karl Kerschl).

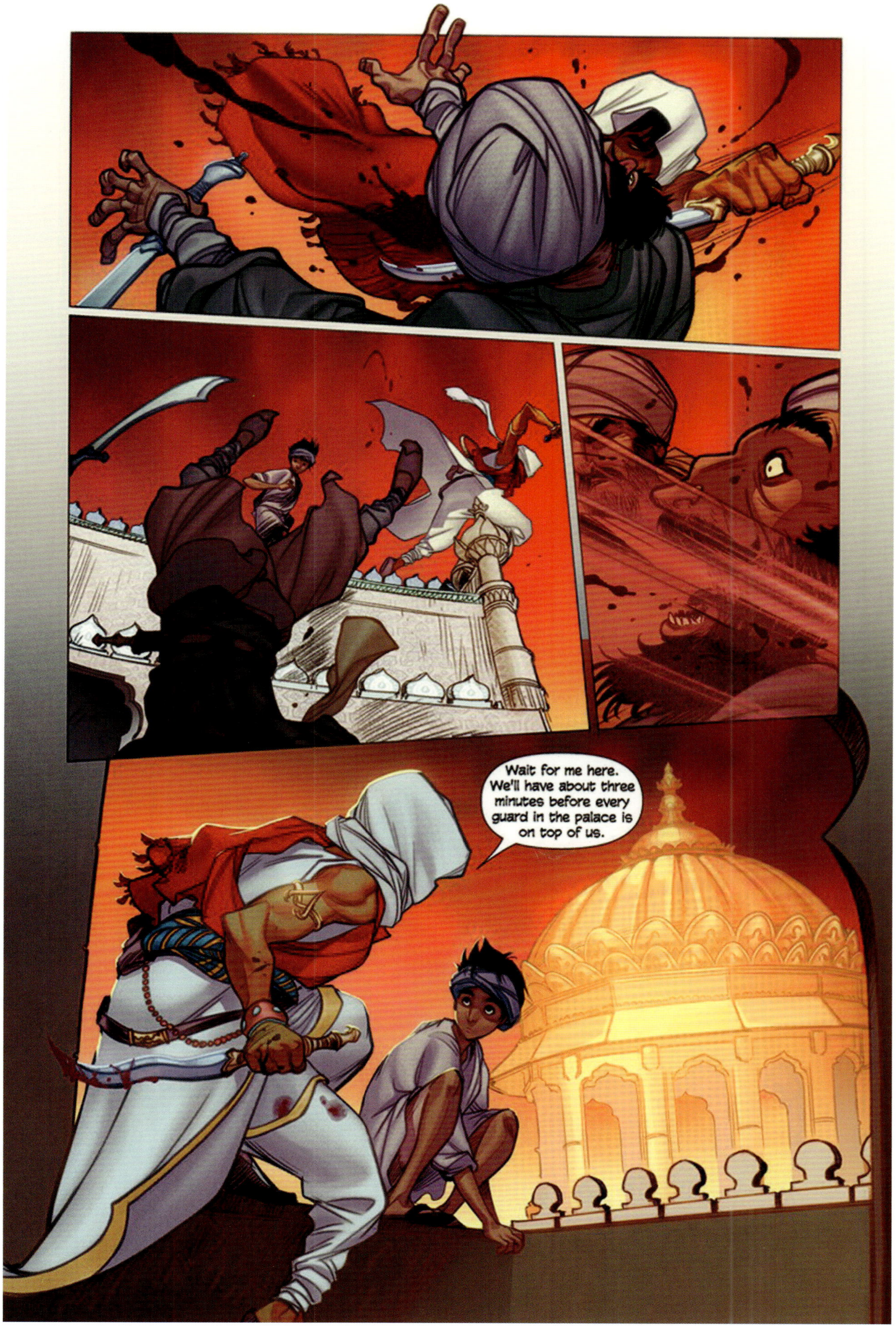

of the time, Arbaaz Mir, as he seeks out a powerful First Civilization artifact, only to have it revealed that the artifact carries a warning for Mir's descendant, the Indian movie star Monima Das, about the terrible danger presented by the resurgent artificial intelligence of Juno. "We felt this story was again a tale that might not have worked in one of our main games but fit perfectly in a graphic novel," Aymar says. "Arbaaz Mir's look was rich and colorful, like his personality. He is probably the closest to a Han Solo character of all our Assassins, meaning he is not the typical honorable warrior, but more of a rogue with a big mouth."

Both Orelov's and Mir's adventures created such a distinct visual flavor that both have been tapped as installments of the new *Chronicles* games (see Chapter 9).

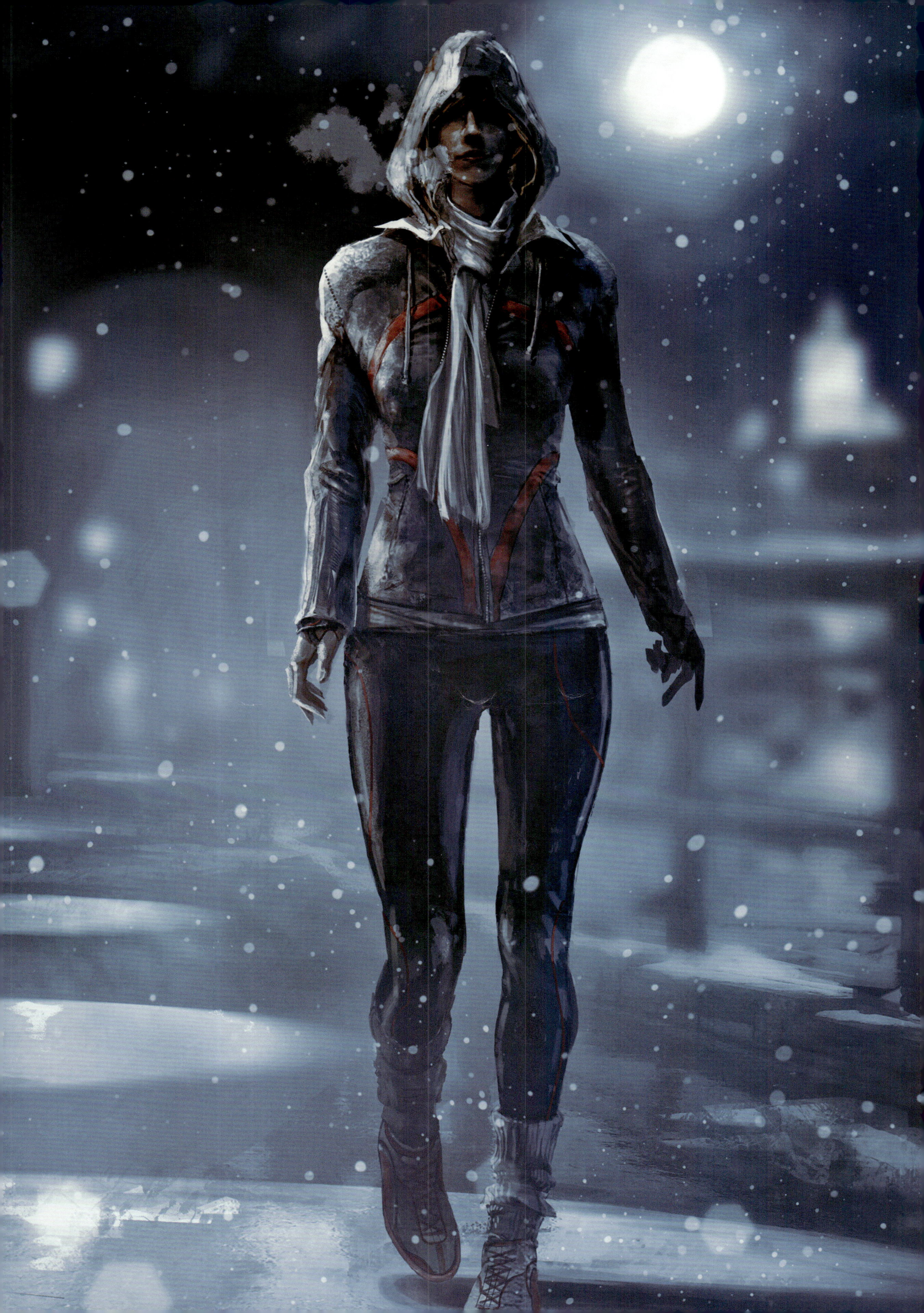

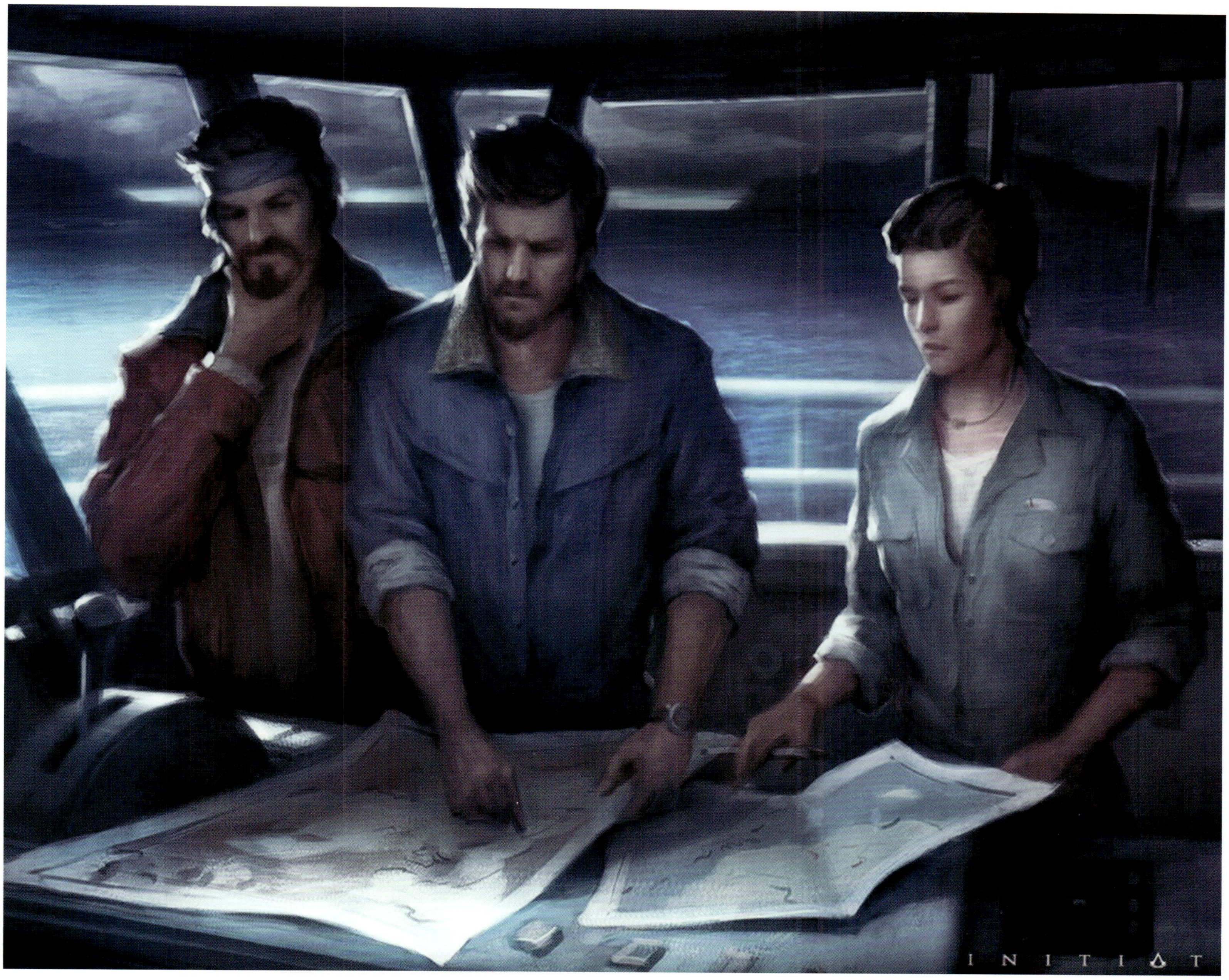

BLURRED LINES

Ubisoft has always flirted with the space between reality and fiction, and few branches of the mythology explore the gray space like *Assassin's Creed: Initiates*. The real-world website offered a place for fans to dig in and embrace the fantasy beyond the games. While the form and visuals of the *Initiates* website shifted over the years, the project grew to allow a linked experience between games. Hidden files offered new insights into Desmond's adventures. New branches of fictional history were uncovered, such as the life of Adéwalé's grandson Eseosa as an Assassin during the Haitian Revolution. And a shared profile allowed the most enthusiastic fans to earn bonus content in the games and broaden their knowledge of what happens between major game entries.

"With *Initiates*, our goal was to create a community portal for dedicated Assassin's Creed fans," Aymar says. "We merged a lot of different concepts, and we aimed to target players' progression, unlockables, profiles, unique game content, and new storylines, all at the same time. It was clear we tried to do too many things at once, which made the accessibility of *Initiates* suffer. Nevertheless, some amazing art, stories, ideas, and people came from this initiative, which will have a huge positive impact on our brand."

OPPOSITE: Concept of Galina Voronina, a modern-day Assassin from Russia (Oliver Donato).
ABOVE: Artwork of Eric Cooper, Gavin Banks, and Susan Drayton aboard the *Altaïr II* (Namwoo Noh).

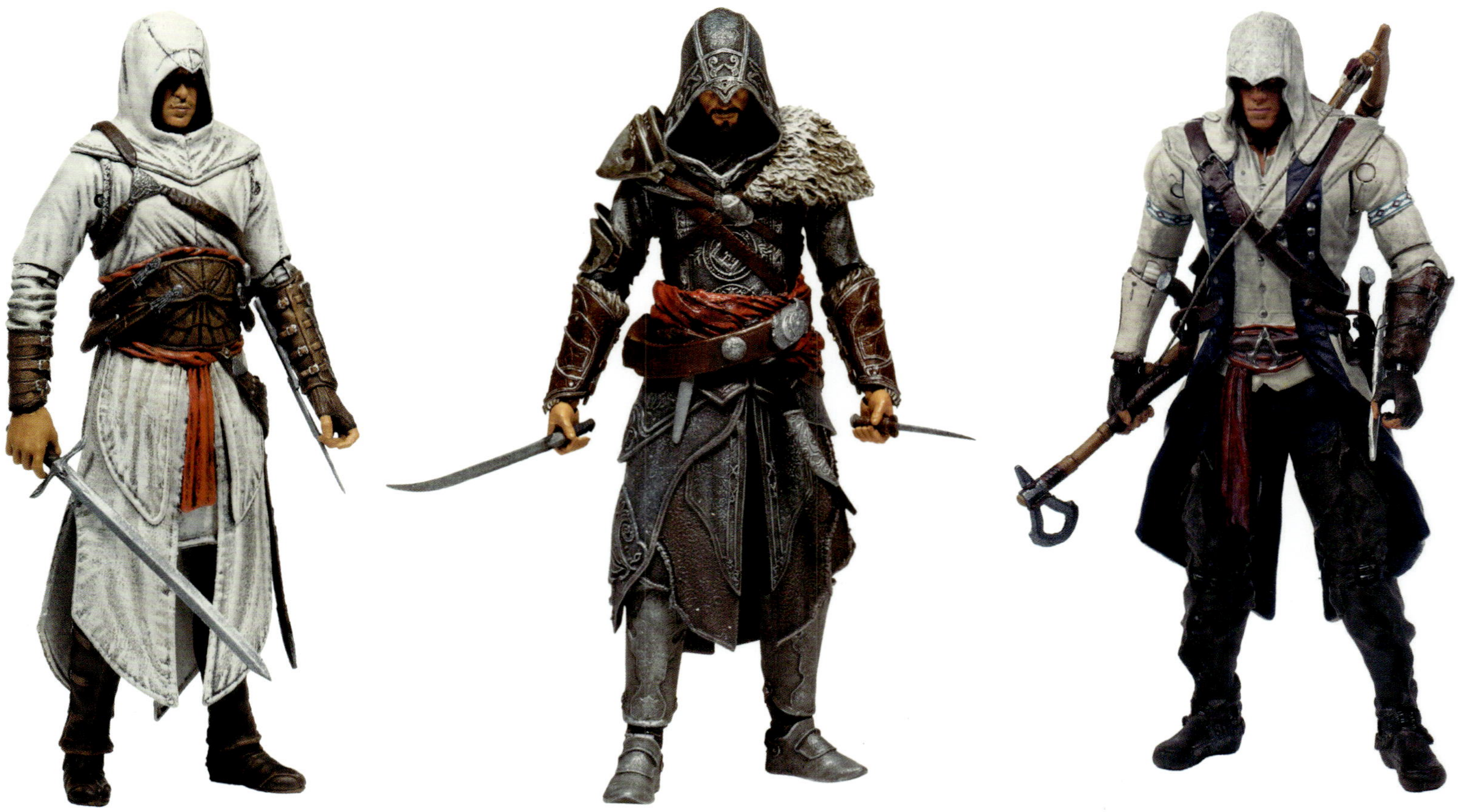

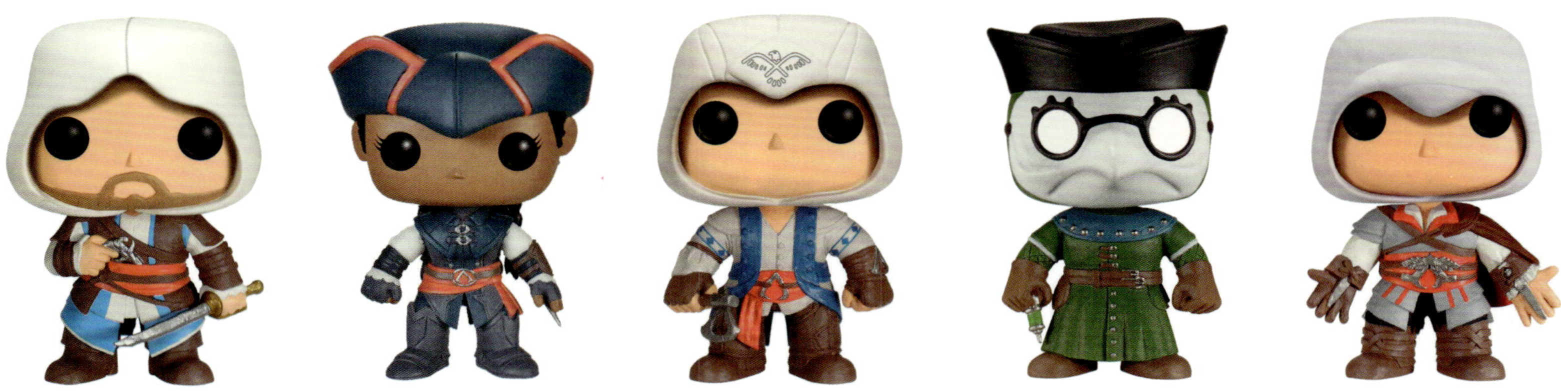

GIVEN FORM

A natural impulse for fans is to seek some tangible object for their enthusiasm. So it comes as no surprise that Assassin's Creed has spawned a broad array of collectible toys, figures, and statues crafted by some of the most talented toy makers in the world. Ubisoft's own UbiCollectibles, McFarlane Toys, Play Arts Kai, and MEGA have each created expressive molds that manage to capture the essence of the many heroes and heroines that the Assassin's Creed franchise has crafted.

"When it comes to Assassin's Creed licensing and merchandise, we try to find partners who are already aligned with us in terms of their way of working," says Aymar. "We love it when a company can bring their own creative vision to the table while still respecting the brand."

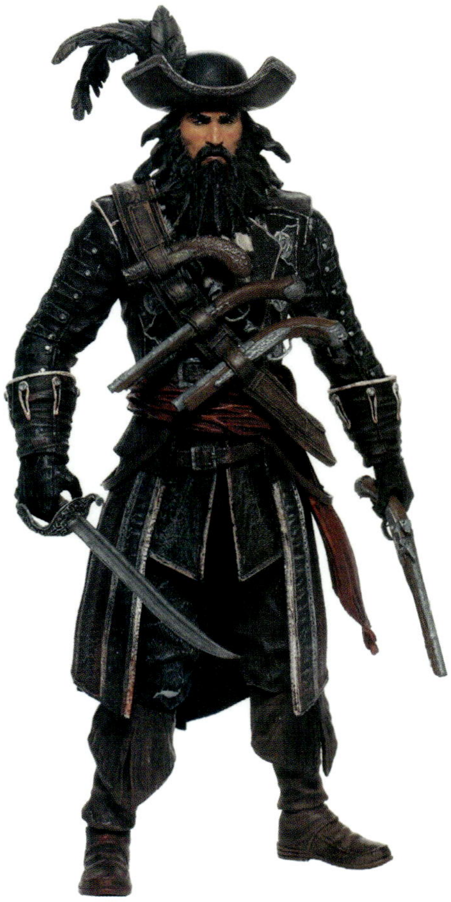
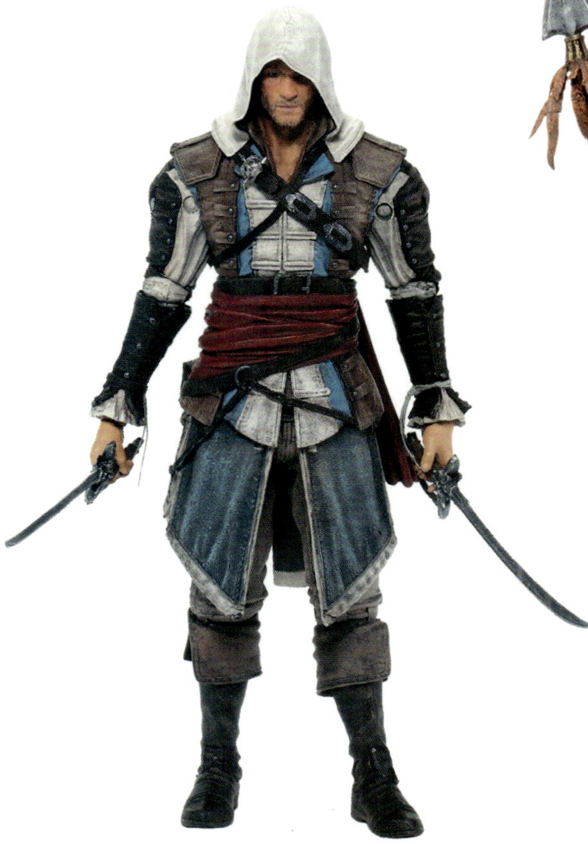
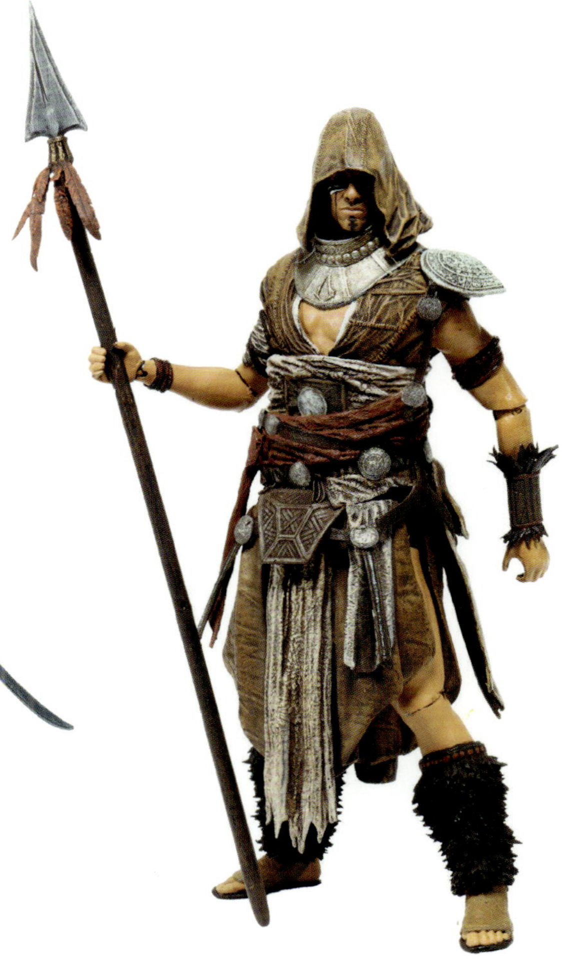
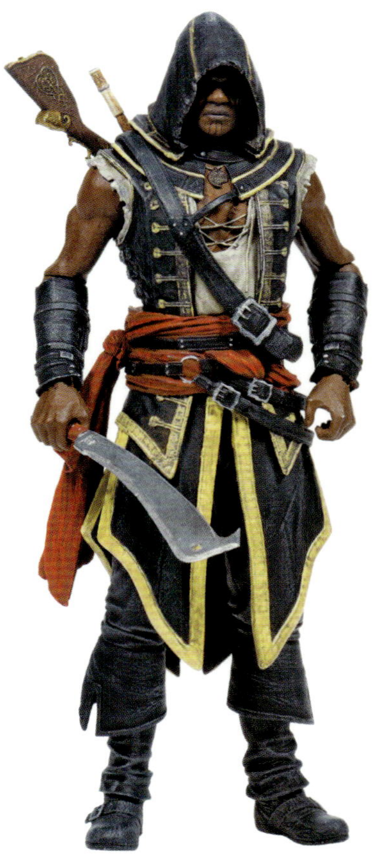
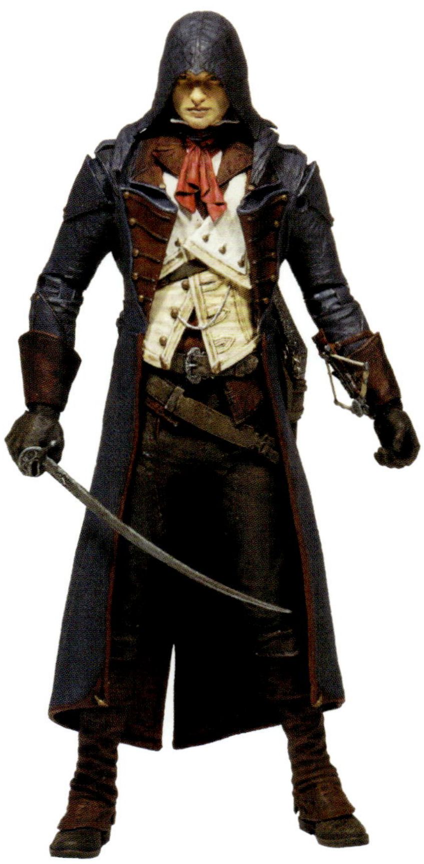
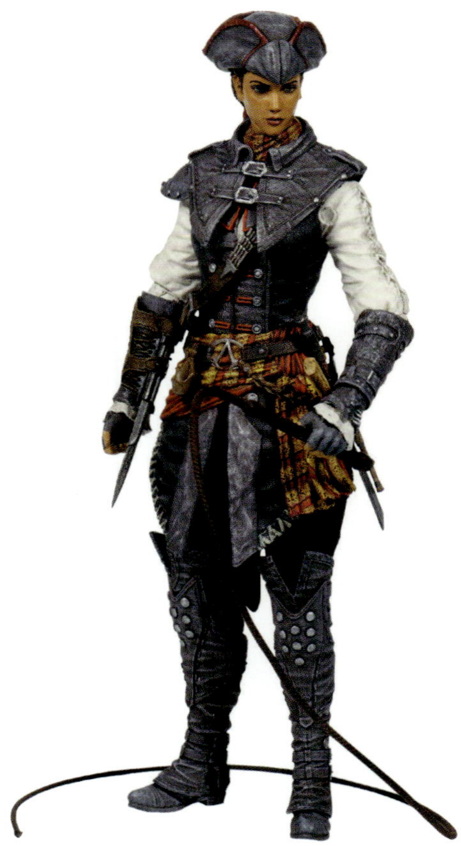

OPPOSITE TOP AND ABOVE: Collection of McFarlane figures.
OPPOSITE BOTTOM: Funko Pop! figures of Edward, Aveline, Connor, the Plague Doctor from the *Assassin's Creed: Brotherhood* multiplayer mode, and Ezio.

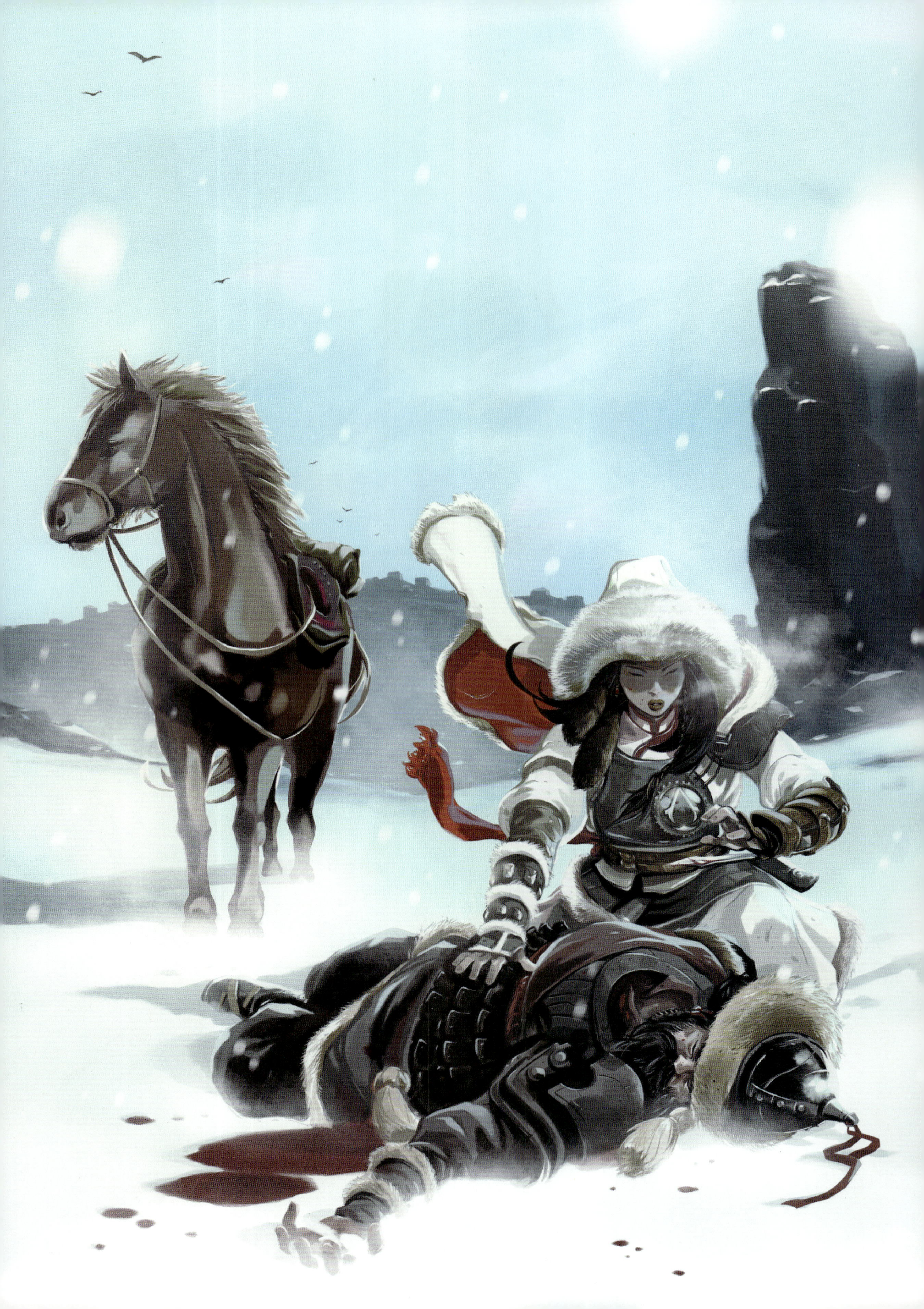

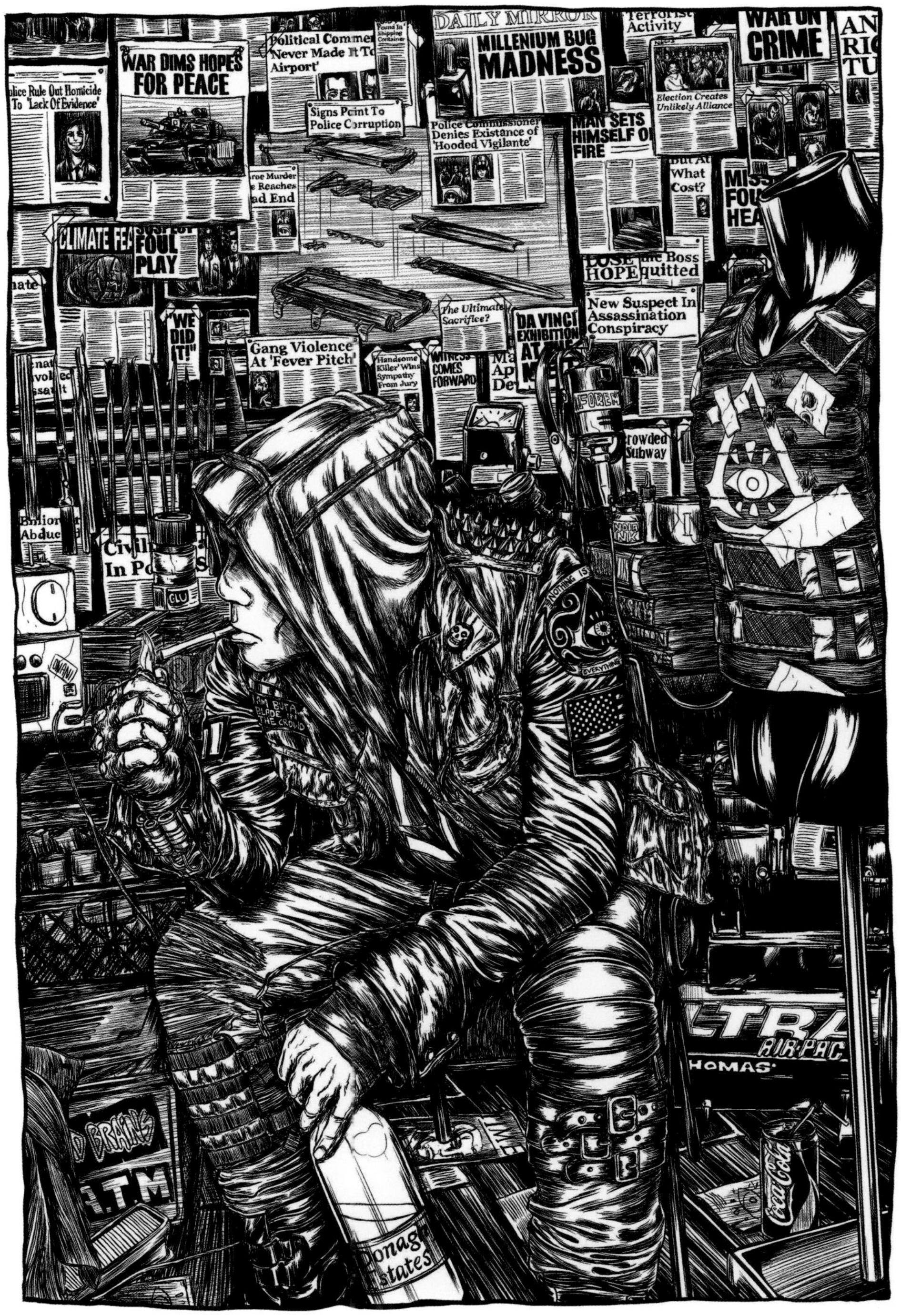

FREEDOM TO EXPERIMENT

As a bonus to 2011's comprehensive *Assassin's Creed Encyclopedia*, special edition purchasers were treated to a selection of additional artwork packaged as small card-stock posters. Numerous artists, including Craig Mullins, Gabz, and David Alvarez, were offered the chance to create their own new Assassin without any restrictions on time period, gender, ethnicity, or style. The results further illustrate the potential of the Assassin's Creed story conceit and set the imagination on fire with possibilities.

ABOVE: Artwork of a Mongolian Assassin (Karl Kerschl).
OPPOSITE: Illustration of a modern-day Assassin (James Jirat Patradoon).

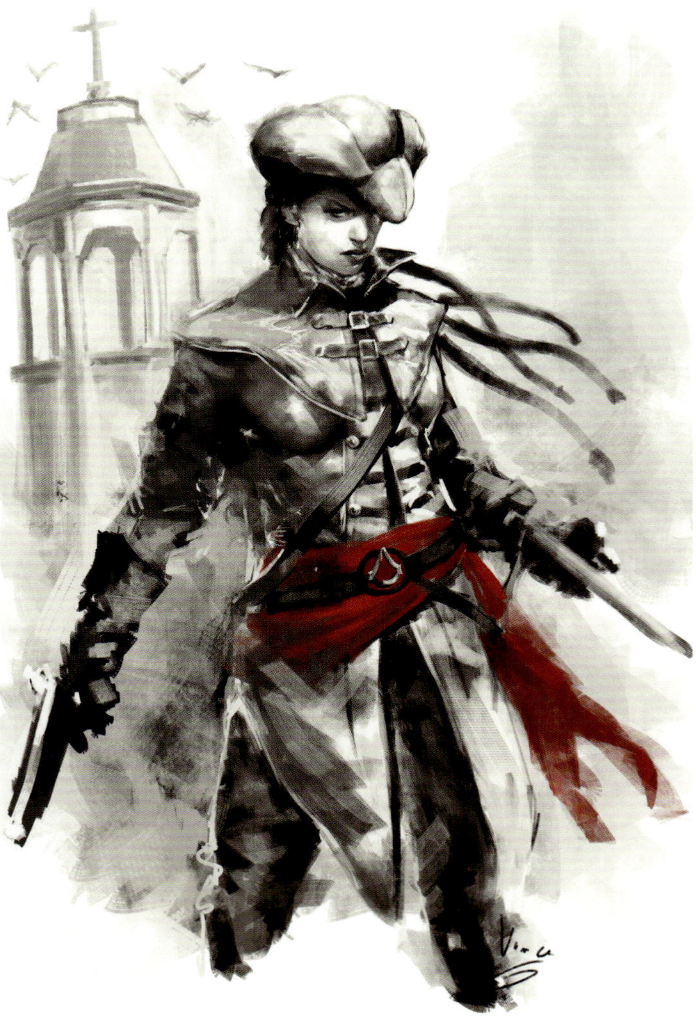

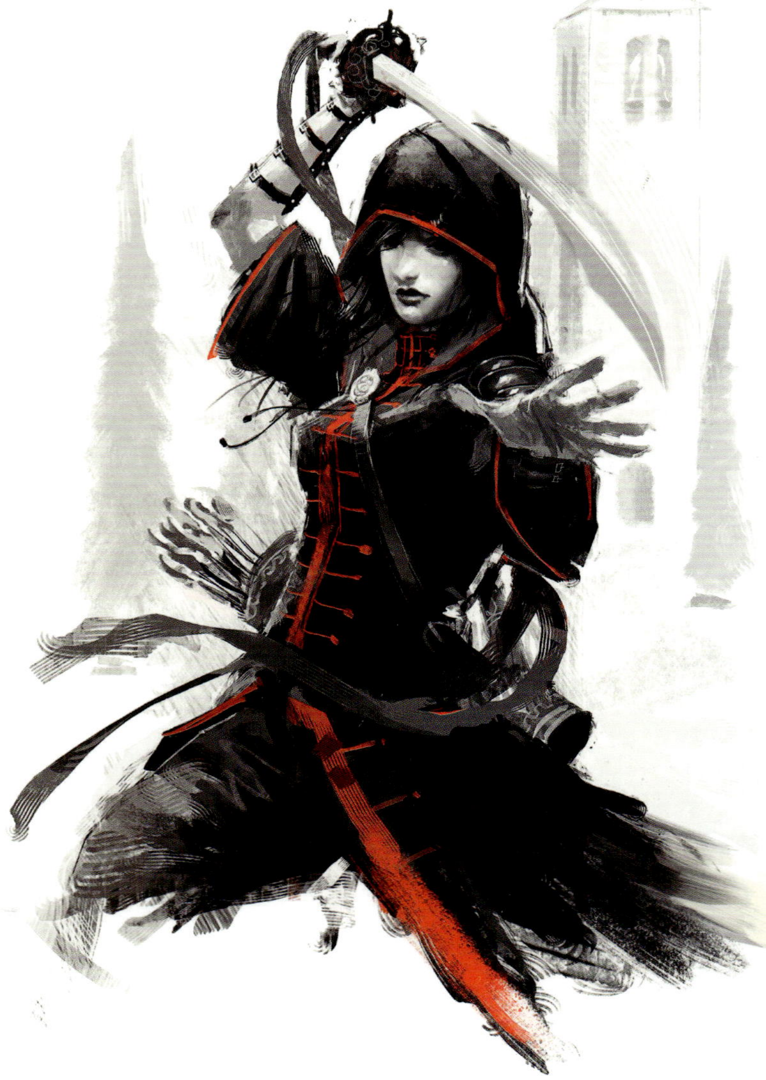

GRACING THE WALLS

In a continuing effort to meet fans of Assassin's Creed through whatever media they choose to enjoy the series, the Red Lineage print collection was born. These limited-edition, fine-art images are crafted by Ubisoft's character artists to showcase heroic figures from throughout the franchise history, but with a stylized approach that makes each image a suitable option for framing and display. Each artist was given the freedom to reimagine the characters within their own distinct artistic vision and help to further define the visual direction of the collection. With the Red Lineage collection, Ubi Workshop brought a unique project to life with a fine-art direction focused on a clean style and timeless quality.

THESE PAGES: Charcoal-styled art of Aveline, Shao Jun, and Arno (Vincent Gaigneux, Remko Troost).

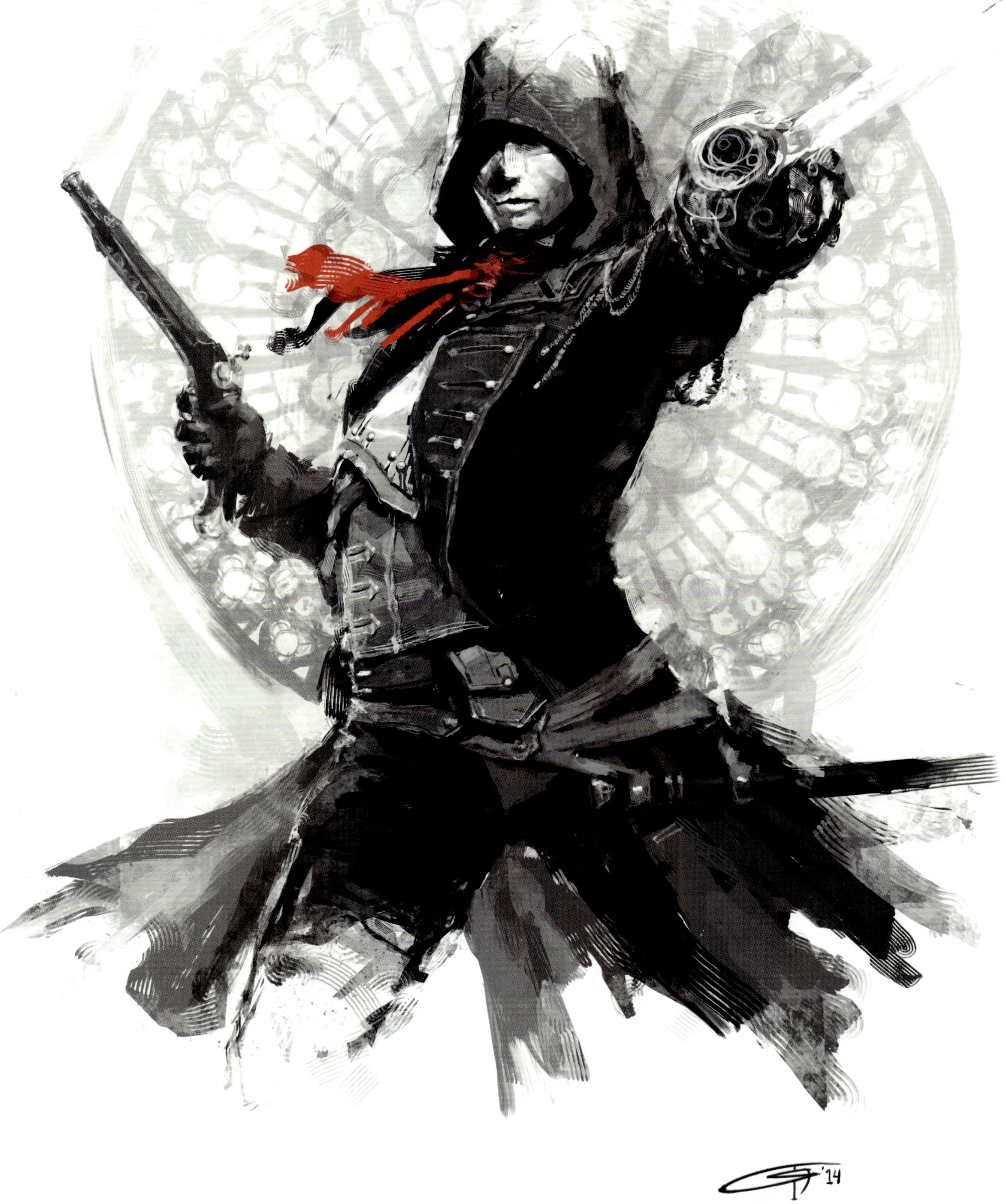

CONCLUSION

A LIFE OF ITS OWN

In its original incarnation, Assassin's Creed aimed to be a new variation on an established franchise, but nearly a decade of art creation and game development have taken it far beyond those original ambitions. As one of the most recognized brands in video games, the franchise has exceeded expectations and expanded into a media property of enormous magnitude.

However, its long-term legacy is likely to be less about its popularity and more about the ongoing enthusiasm of both its creators and fans to expand the franchise in new directions. Subsequent installments continue to introduce heroes and villains and chart their adventures through fascinating moments in history. Few media franchises have been able to change up such important elements while remaining true to their core themes. No matter where and when Assassin's Creed takes us, the same questions linger: Security or liberty? Freedom or control? Order or chaos? The themes resonate as modern-day touchstones but also apply to so many moments throughout history that it's hard to imagine Ubisoft running out of ideas.

The artists behind Assassin's Creed have helped to transport fans into the lives of individuals across the span of history and have given us thoughtfully realized characters and richly imagined settings time and again. The authenticity of their historical tableaus is a thrill, and fans eagerly wait to see how the same eternal conflict between Assassins and Templars will play out each time around. The grandeur of history, as filtered through the visuals of countless talented artists and game creators, makes one question more popular than any other for fans of Assassin's Creed: What comes next?

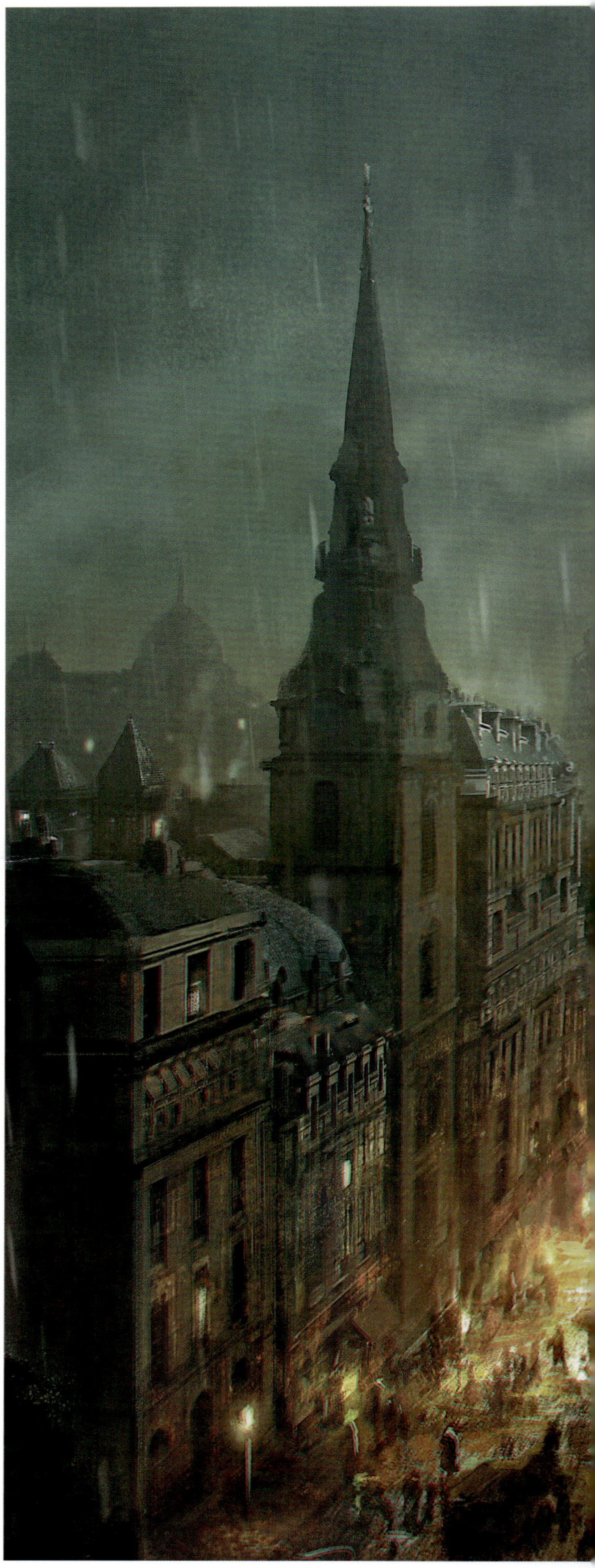

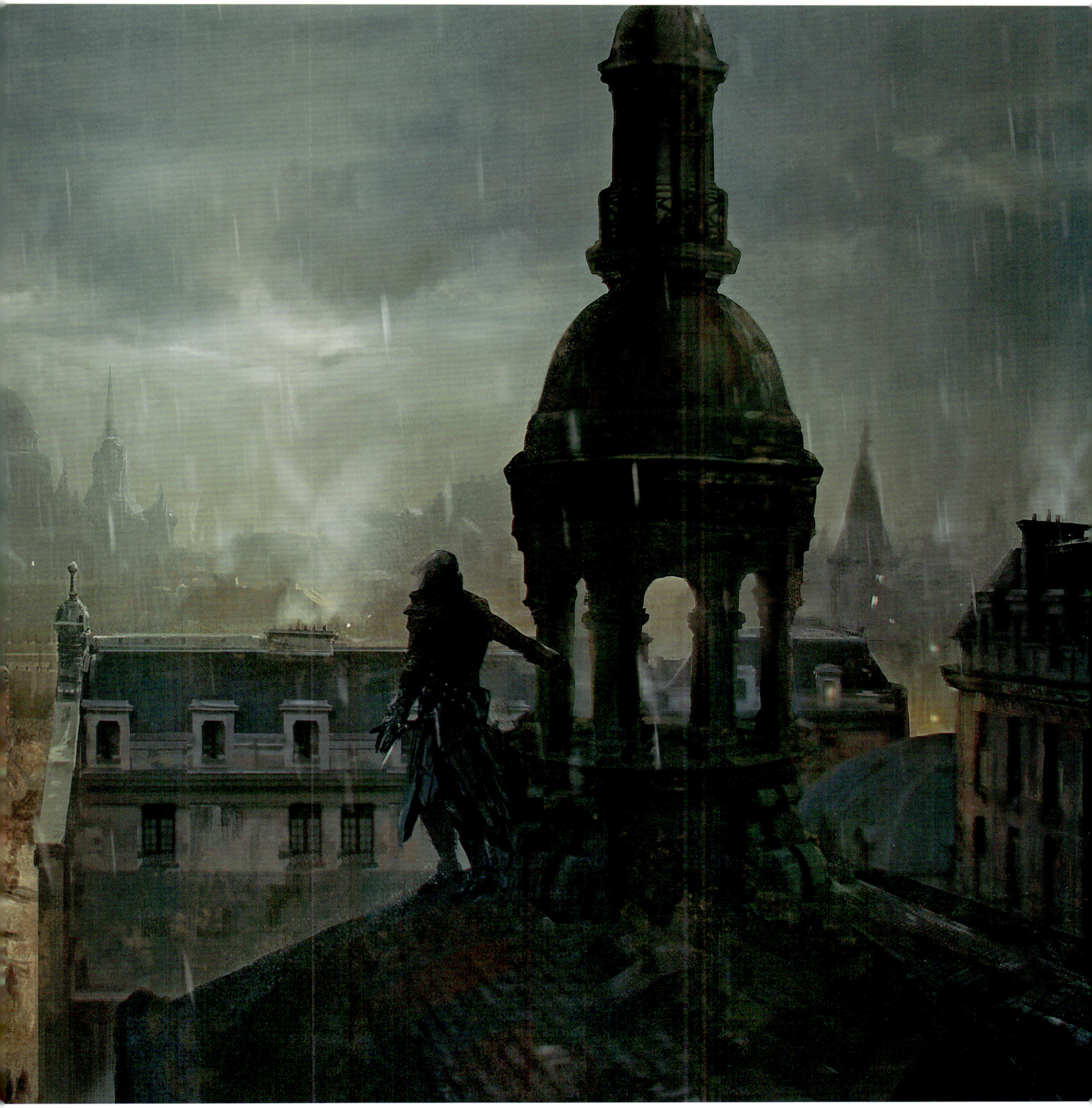

THESE PAGES: Jacob surveys the gaslit streets of London (Frédéric Rambaud).

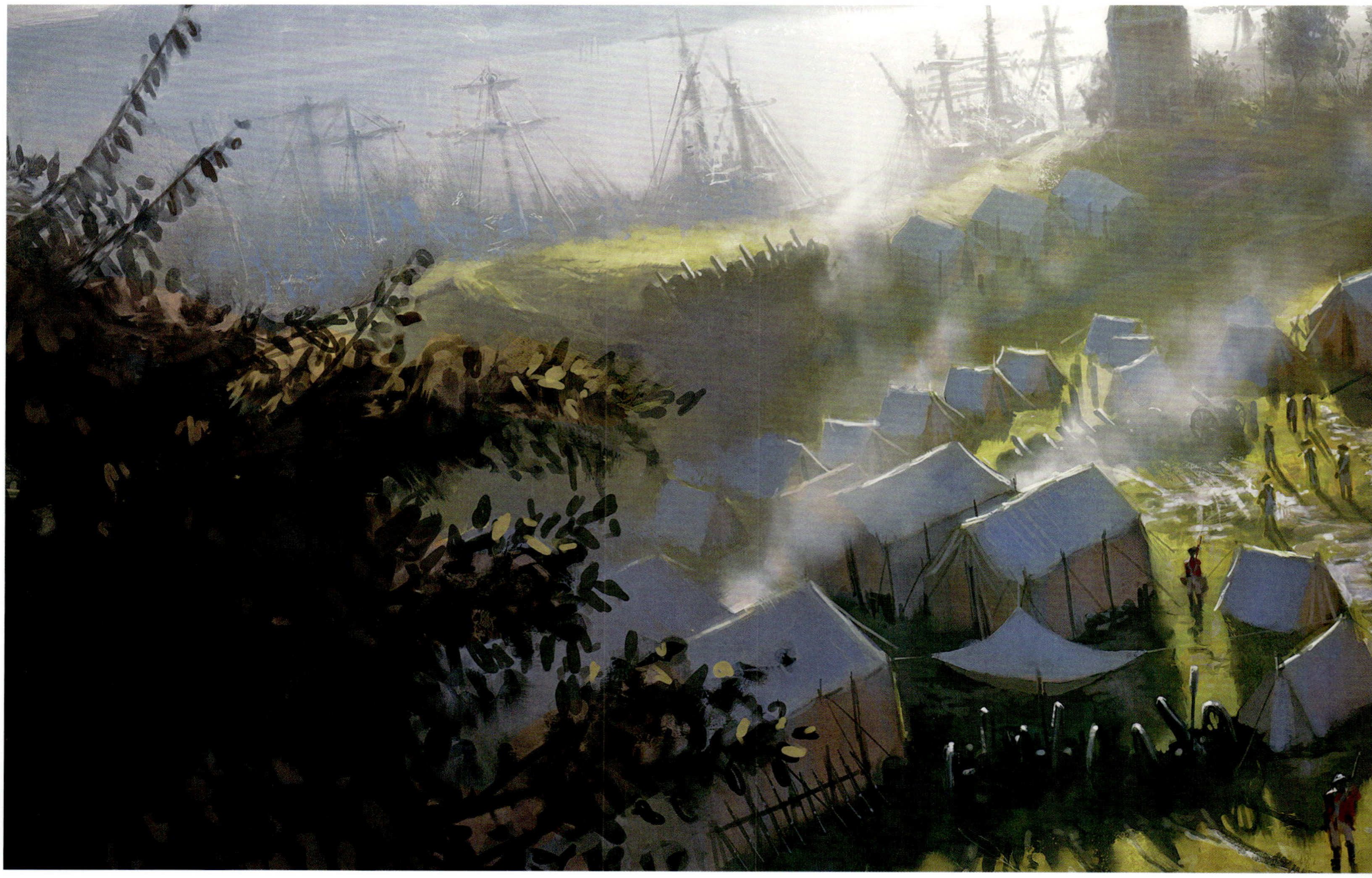

CREDITS

ASSASSIN'S CREED BRAND TEAM

Aymar Azaïzia
Anouk Bachman
Antoine Ceszynski
Richard Farrese
Jean Guesdon
Raphaël Lacoste

ART DIRECTORS

Eddie Bennun
Yannick Corboz
Thierry Dansereau
Olivier Donato
Nicolas Drolet
Felix Marlo Flor
Mohamed Gambouz
Mathieu Granjon
Alain Gurniki
Patrick Ingolsby
Frank Kitson
Raphaël Lacoste
Mufizal Mokhtar
The Chinh Ngo

PRESENTATION DIRECTION

Brent Ashe
Alexandre de Lamberterie
Mathieu Leduc
Daniel Lucchesi
Shadi Mallak
Laura de Young

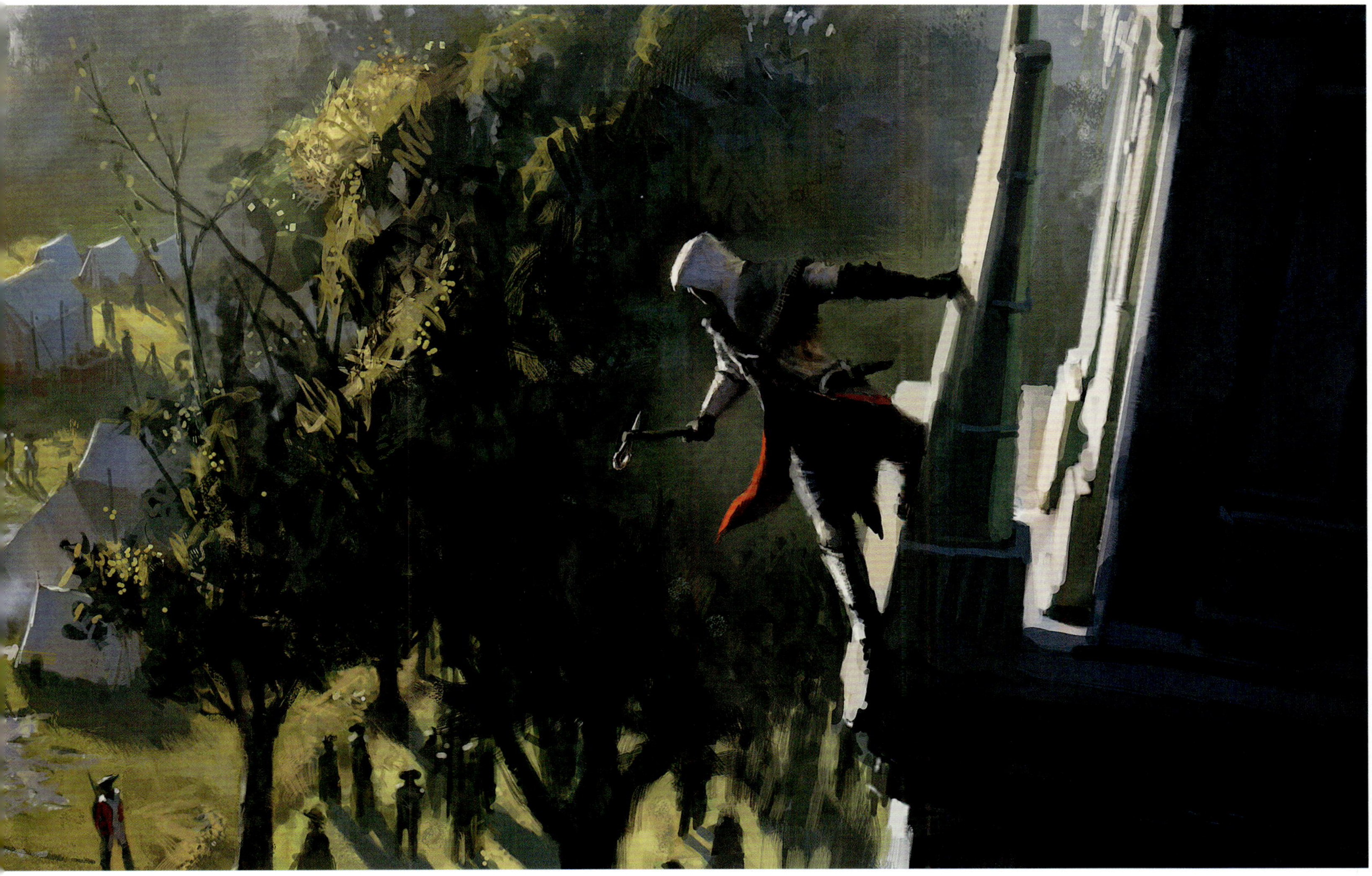

ARTISTS

Taissia Abdoulina
Fernando Acosta
David Alvarez
Daniel Atanasov
Gilles Beloeil
Eddie Bennun
Anaïs Bernabe
Pierre Bertin
John Bigorgne
Branko Bistrovic
Nicolas Bouvier
Nick Tan Chee
Sophie Codaire
Giani Cojan
Martin Deschambault
Patrick Desgreniers
Maxime Desmettre
Thierry Doizon
Olivier Donato
Nicolas Drolet
Encho Enchev
Nick Tan Chee Eng
Edvige Faini
Rémi Farjaud
Nicolas Ferrand
Vincent Gaigneux
Vincent Gauthier
Yuriy Georgiev
Melissa Golcberg
Johan Grenier
Grant Hillier
Diana Kalugina
Shamine King
Karl Kopinski
Konstantin Kostadinov
Ivan Koritarev
Raphaël Lacoste
Patrick Lambert
David Levy
Olivier Martin
Guillaume Menuel
Christophe Messier
Borislav Mitkov
Khai Nguyen
Tri Nguyen
Namwoo Noh
Félicien Nourry
Nicolas Oroc
Biser Parashkevov
Hugo Puzzuoli
Max Qin
Yu Li Qing
Frédéric Rambaud
Ludovic Ribardière
Jean-Charles Ripoll
Antoine Rol
Kobe Sek
Tony Zhou Shuo
Jeff Simpson
Caroline Soucy
Nikolay Stoyanov
Guang Yu Tan
Lixiong Tan
Yong Jin Teo
Remko Troost
Stéphane Turgeon
Jan Urschel
Jing-Cherng Wong
William Wu
Nacho Yagüe
Donglu Yu
Darek Zabrocki

UBISOFT MONTRÉAL - HELIX

Eve Berthelette
Christopher Dormoy
Fabien Troncal
Cyril Vergne

CLIMAX STUDIOS

Glenn Brace
Ben Blethyn
Saul Marchese
Kevin Martin
Michael Mowat
Neale Williams

STUDIO LOUNAK

Tyson Hesse
Karl Kerschl
Cameron Stewart
Nadine Thomas

UBISOFT NCSA PUBLISHING

Andrew Heitz
Caroline Lamache
Holly Rawlinson

AUTHOR'S ACKNOWLEDGMENTS

A book like this comes together only in small part through the work of the author. Even so, it has been a great honor to help chronicle and curate the history of a gaming series I've loved since before the first game released.

Thanks are most due to the incredible artists at Ubisoft, who not only have given shape to an entire universe of stories, but also contributed the works that grace these pages.

I also want to extend my appreciation to the broader team at Ubisoft, who opened their doors and granted access to so many members of their creative team. I particularly want to acknowledge Anouk Bachman for her tireless tracking down of artwork and her invaluable fact-checking as the manuscript progressed.

Insight Editions reached out and offered me the chance to take on this challenge, for which I'm immensely grateful. Thank you to Vanessa Lopez for ushering this book throughout the process, to Dustin Jones for his editorial insight, and to Katie DeSandro for shouldering the burden of so many words from our interview subjects.

My work on this project also would not have been possible without the support of my colleagues at *Game Informer*, especially my editors Andy McNamara and Andrew Reiner.

Thank you to all my friends and family, who unceasingly cheered me on through the most intense of deadlines. And finally, all my love and gratitude goes out to Jessica, for sharing in an adventure better than any fiction.

OPPOSITE: Altaïr seeking his target above the Templar army (Patrick Desgreniers).
PAGE 2-3: Raphaël Lacoste
PAGE 4: Martin Deschambault
PAGE 6-7: Martin Deschambault
PAGE 8-9: Martin Deschambault
PAGE 316-317: Gilles Beloeil
PAGE 319: Patrick Desgreniers
PAGE 320: Gilles Beloeil
BACK ENDPAPERS: Donglu Yu
FRONT ENDPAPERS: Dongu Yu

TITAN BOOKS

144 Southwark Street
London SE1 0UP
www.titanbooks.com
Find us on Facebook: www.facebook.com/TitanBooks
Follow us on Twitter: @TitanBooks

Published by Titan Books, London, in 2015.

Published by arrangement with Insight Editions, PO Box 3088, San Rafael, CA 94912, USA. www.insighteditions.com

A CIP catalogue record for this title is available from the British Library.
ISBN: 978-1-78329-882-2

INSIGHT EDITIONS
PUBLISHER: Raoul Goff
CO-PUBLISHER: Michael Madden
ACQUISITIONS MANAGER: Robbie Schmidt
ART DIRECTOR: Chrissy Kwasnik
DESIGNER: Malea Clark-Nicholson
EXECUTIVE EDITOR: Vanessa Lopez
PRODUCTION EDITOR: Rachel Anderson
EDITORIAL ASSISTANT: Katie DeSandro
PRODUCTION MANAGER: Jane Chinn

ROOTS of PEACE REPLANTED PAPER

Insight Editions, in association with Roots of Peace, will plant two trees for each tree used in the manufacturing of this book. Roots of Peace is an internationally renowned humanitarian organization dedicated to eradicating land mines worldwide and converting war-torn lands into productive farms and wildlife habitats. Roots of Peace will plant two million fruit and nut trees in Afghanistan and provide farmers there with the skills and support necessary for sustainable land use.

Manufactured in China by Insight Editions

10 9 8 7 6 5 4 3 2 1

SPECIAL THANKS

Marc-Alexis Côté, Clémence Deleuze, Aymeric Evennou, Andrien Gbinigie, Nicolas Guerin, James Nadiger, Susan Patrick, Xavier Penin, Sebastien Puel, Gregory Szriftgiser, the AC Community Development team, the Assassin's Creed Brand Team, the Assassin's Creed Marketing and PR teams, Ubisoft's Legal teams, Studio Lounak, UbiWorkshop. A big thank you to all the past, present, and future developers of the Assassin's Creed universe. And, most of all, our eternal gratitude to our fans, who never stop inspiring us. Thank you!

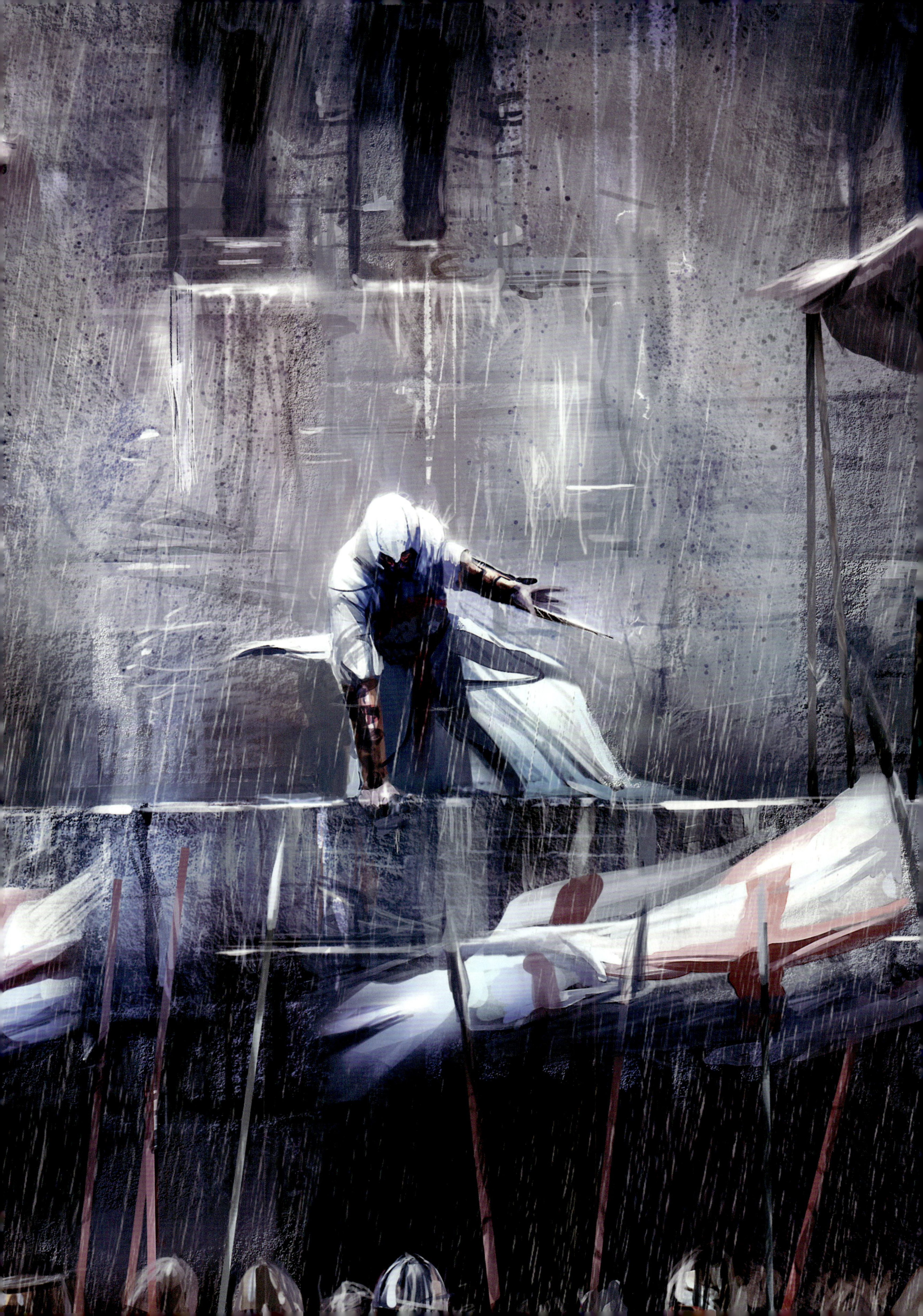

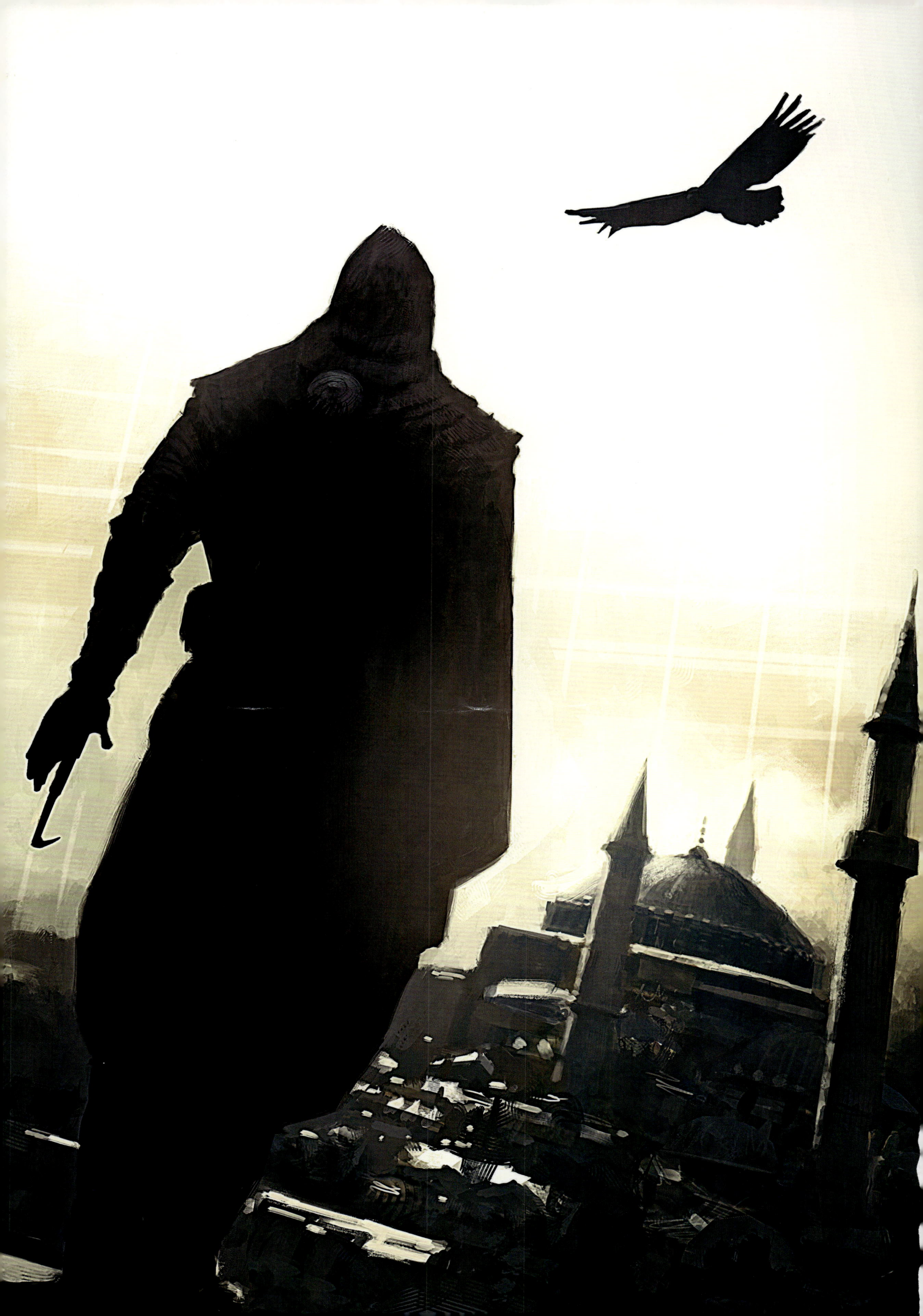

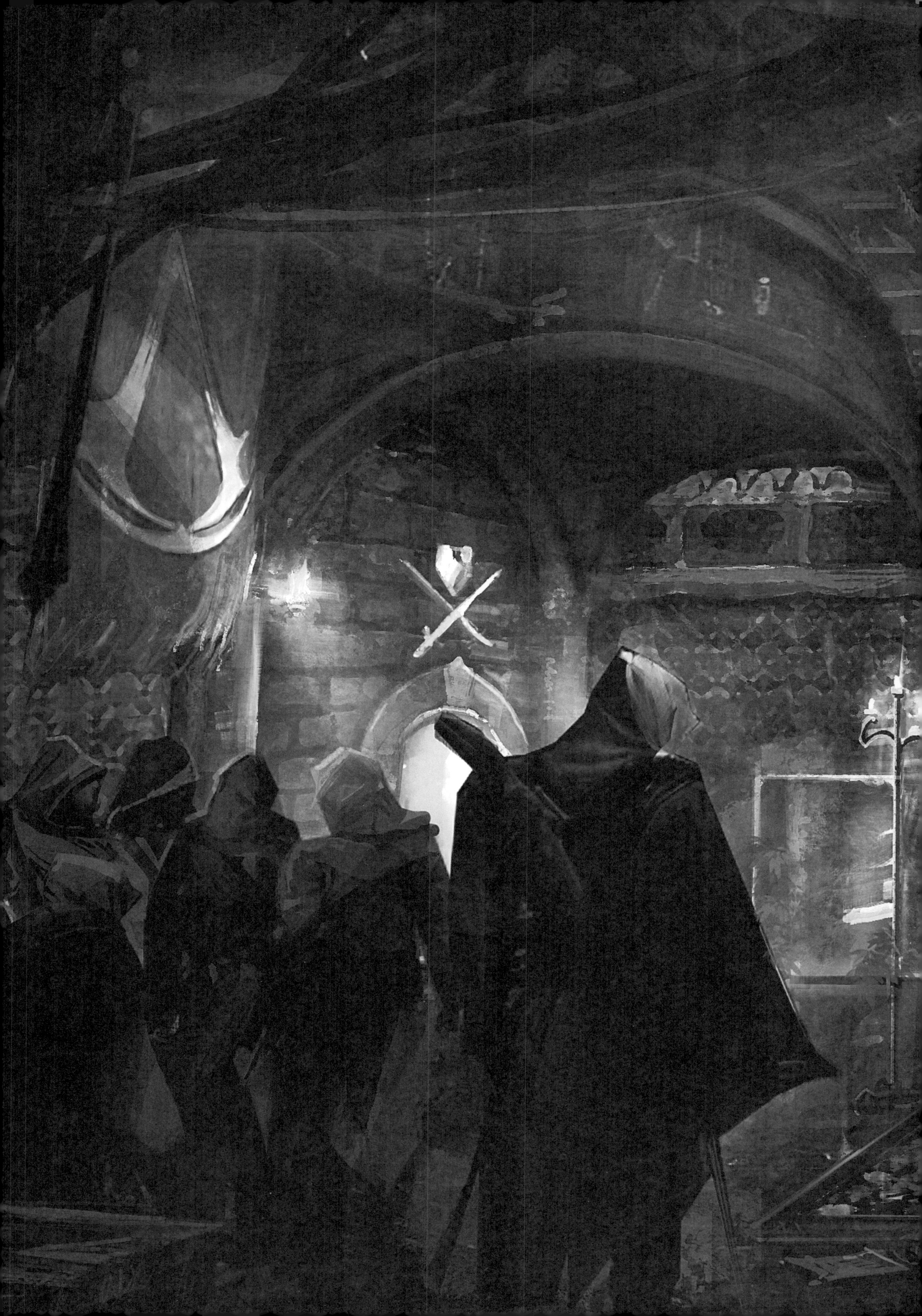